INTERNATIONAL COURTS
AND TRIBUNALS SERIES

General Editors

RUTH MACKENZIE
CESARE P. R. ROMANO
MIKAEL RASK MADSEN

Governance of International Courts and Tribunals

INTERNATIONAL COURTS AND TRIBUNALS SERIES

A distinctive feature of modern international law and society is the increased role played by international courts and tribunals. The International Courts and Tribunals Series is the dedicated home for scholarly works which address, in critical and analytical fashion, the legal and policy aspects of the functioning of international courts and tribunals. The series encourages both legal analysis of the institutional, substantive, and procedural aspects of international courts, and socio-legal studies that explore the issues these courts are called to address and how they are influenced by global developments. We publish both comparative works involving multiple courts and single-court studies.

Governance of International Courts and Tribunals

Institutions, Practices, and Norms

Edited by
SERGEY VASILIEV
Professor of International Law, Faculty of Law, Open University, The Netherlands

NIELS BLOKKER
Professor Emeritus of International Institutional Law, Faculty of Law, Leiden University, The Netherlands

with
ARMIN CUYVERS
Professor of European Law, Faculty of Law, Leiden University, The Netherlands

and
RICK LAWSON
Professor of European Human Rights Law, Faculty of Law, Leiden University, The Netherlands

OXFORD
UNIVERSITY PRESS

OXFORD
UNIVERSITY PRESS

Great Clarendon Street, Oxford, OX2 6DP,
United Kingdom

Oxford University Press is a department of the University of Oxford.
It furthers the University's objective of excellence in research, scholarship,
and education by publishing worldwide. Oxford is a registered trade mark of
Oxford University Press in the UK and in certain other countries.

Published in the United States of America by Oxford University Press
198 Madison Avenue, New York, NY 10016, United States of America.

British Library Cataloguing in Publication Data
Data available

Library of Congress Control Number: 2025949026

ISBN 978–0–19–892213–1

DOI: 10.1093/oso/9780198922131.001.0001

Printed and bound by
CPI Group (UK) Ltd., Croydon, CR0 4YY

The manufacturer's authorized representative in the EU for product safety is
Oxford University Press España S.A. of Parque Empresarial San Fernando de Henares,
Avenida de Castilla, 2 – 28830 Madrid (www.oup.es/en or product.safety@oup.com).
OUP España S.A. also acts as importer into Spain of products made by the manufacturer.

MIX
Paper | Supporting responsible forestry
FSC® C013604
FSC
www.fsc.org

Preface

Edited book projects invariably require tremendous and sustained collective effort, and they tend to take a long time to reach completion. This certainly applies to the present volume. We would like to take this opportunity to express our deep gratitude to the individuals and organizations without whose support this book would not have seen the light of day.

The inaugural conference of this project, originally entitled 'Governance of International Courts and Tribunals: Ensuring Judicial Independence and Accountability', took place at the Leiden Law School on 20–21 September 2019—what we now habitually refer to as pre-Corona and pre-war times. Since then, crises and disruptions beyond what we could have anticipated and removed from standard developments in international adjudication and institutional law have unfolded, impacting our lives and, indirectly, this project as well.

We are very grateful to the conference speakers and participants for their thoughtful and inspiring interventions. They gave an important impetus to this volume and informed our framing of the topic. These colleagues include former ICJ President and Judge Abdulqawi Ahmed Yusuf and former President of the Assembly of States Parties of the ICC and ICTY Judge O-Gon Kwon, who kindly delivered keynote addresses, which are included as Addenda in this book. We extend our gratitude to the former ICJ President and Judge Dame Rosalyn Higgins, Judge Liesbeth Lijnzaad (ITLOS), Judge Dean Spielmann (CJEU and formerly ECtHR), President Ekaterina Trendafilova (Kosovo Specialist Chambers), Ambassador Rolf Einar Fife (Norway), former Ambassador and ITLOS Judge Maria Teresa Infante Caffi (Chile), and Shehzad Charania (former Director and Deputy Head of the Attorney General's Office). We also thank our former employers, the Grotius Centre for International Legal Studies (Leiden University) and the Amsterdam Center for International Law (University of Amsterdam), for their financial and practical support in launching this project.

The process culminating in this book was intricate and unfolded over several additional stages. These included commissioning further chapters to address what we believed would otherwise be unaffordable gaps, developing the underlying ideas and research that informed individual contributions, engaging in multiple rounds of feedback and revision, and updating the chapters before the book could go to press. Our sincere thanks go to all the contributors for their unwavering commitment and patience throughout the lengthy editorial and production process. We are deeply grateful for their excellent and insightful chapters, which form the heart of this book. It has been a true pleasure to witness their contributions take shape and engage substantively with each of them.

We would not have managed without the unparalleled expertise, unflinching collegiality, and substantive involvement of our co-conspirators and dear friends Professors Rick Lawson and Armin Cuyvers, both of Leiden University. They not only co-organized the inaugural conference with us but also generously connected us with several contributors and offered valuable feedback on draft chapters.

We also wish to thank our former student assistants for their interest in the topic of international judicial governance and for their capable editorial support: Daniel Pakpahan, Mine Orer, Raphael Pierfederici, Vincenzo Elia, and Vera Figueira Lourenço (Leiden University), Jozefien Pommée, Nashab Parvez, and Ignacio Baeriswyl Uribe (University of Amsterdam), Luiza Martins (Federal University of Minas Gerais), and Jesse-Alexander Scheers (Open University of the Netherlands).

Last but not least, we express our gratitude to Robert Cavooris, Acquisitions Editor, and Paulina dos Santos Major, Project Editor, at Oxford University Press for their constant encouragement and kind support throughout this project.

Niels Blokker and Sergey Vasiliev
January 2026

Contents

PART VI: FUTURE OUTLOOK

PART VII: ADDENDA: KEYNOTE ADDRESSES

Detailed Contents

Abbreviations

AC	Appeals Chamber
ACABQ	Advisory Committee on Administrative and Budgetary Questions
ACC	Allied Control Council
ACDEG	African Charter on Democracy, Elections, and Governance
ACERWC	African Committee of Experts on the Rights and Welfare of the Child
ACJ	Advisory Committee of Jurists
ACN	Advisory Committee on Nominations of Judges (ICC)
ACtHPR	African Court on Human and Peoples' Rights
ACtJHR	African Court of Justice and Human Rights
AfCommHPR	African Commission on Human and Peoples' Rights
AGA	African Governance Architecture
ASP	Assembly of States Parties
AU	African Union
AUCIL	African Union Commission on International Law
CARICOM	Caribbean Community
CCNR	Central Commission for the Navigation of the Rhine
CEE	Central and Eastern Europe
CJEU	Court of Justice of the European Union
CM	Committee of Ministers (Council of Europe)
CoA	Court of Auditors
CoE	Council of Europe
COMESA	Common Market for Eastern and Southern Africa
CSO	civil society organization
DSB	Dispute Settlement Body
DSU	Dispute Settlement Understanding
EAC	East African Community
EACJ	East African Court of Justice
EAEU	Eurasian Economic Union
EALA	East African Legislative Assembly
ECCAS	Economic Community of Central African States
ECCC	Extraordinary Chambers in the Courts of Cambodia
ECHR	European Convention on Human Rights and Fundamental Freedoms
ECOSOCC	Economic, Social and Cultural Council
ECOWAS	Economic Community of West African States
ECtHR	European Court of Human Rights
EEA	European Economic Area
EFTA	European Free Trade Association
EU	European Union
GATT	General Agreement on Tariffs and Trade

GCEU	General Court of the European Union
HRC	Human Rights Committee
IACtHR	Inter-American Court of Human Rights
ICC	International Criminal Court
ICCPR	International Covenant on Civil and Political Rights (1966)
ICJ	International Court of Justice
ICT	international court and tribunal
ICTR	International Criminal Tribunal for Rwanda
ICTY	International Criminal Tribunal for the former Yugoslavia
IGAD	Intergovernmental Authority on Development
IIIC	International Independent Investigation Commission
ILC	International Law Commission
ILM	international legal materials
ILOAT	International Labour Organization's Administrative Tribunal
IMT	international military tribunal
IMTFE	international military tribunal for the Far East
IO	international organization
IOM	Independent Oversight Mechanism
IRMCT (or MICT)	United Nations International Residual Mechanism for Criminal Tribunals
ITLOS	International Tribunal for the Law of the Sea
JIU	Joint Inspection Unit
LoN	League of Nations
MOU	Memorandum of Understanding
NEA	Nuclear Energy Agency
NHRI	national human rights institution
OAS	Organization of American States
OAU	Organization of African Unity
OECS	Organisation of Eastern Caribbean States
OHADA Court	Court of the Organization for the Harmonization of Business Law in Africa
OIA	Office of Internal Audit
OIOS	Office of Internal Oversight Services
OLA	Office of Legal Affairs
OPCD	Office of Public Counsel for the Defence
OPCV	Office of Public Counsel for the Victims
OTP	Office of the Prosecutor
PACE	Parliamentary Assembly of the Council of Europe
PCA	Permanent Court of Arbitration
PCIJ	Permanent Court of International Justice
PDG	Principal Donors Group
PSC	Peace and Security Council
PTC	Pre-Trial Chamber
REC	regional economic community
SADC	Southern African Development Community
SCAP	Supreme Commander for the Allied Powers in the Far East
SCSL	Special Court for Sierra Leone

SPLOS	Meeting of the States Parties to the Convention of the Law of the Sea
STL	Special Tribunal for Lebanon
TC	Trial Chamber
TEU	Treaty on European Union
TFEU	Treaty on the Functioning of the European Union
UDHR	Universal Declaration of Human Rights
UN	United Nations
UNAKRT	United Nations Assistance to the Khmer Rouge Trials
UNCIO	United Nations Conference on International Organization
UNGA	United Nations General Assembly
UNIIICC	United Nations Independent International Investigation Commission
UNJSPF	United Nations Joint Staff Pension Fund
UNOIOS	United Nations Office of Internal Oversight Services
UNSC	United Nations Security Council
UNSG	United Nations Secretary-General
VCLT	Vienna Convention on the Law of Treaties
WTO	World Trade Organization

Contributors

Evelyn Anoya International justice expert; former Chief of Judicial Services at the Special Tribunal for Lebanon

Niels Blokker Professor Emeritus of International Institutional Law (Schermers Chair), Leiden University, Leiden, The Netherlands

Roeland Böcker Former Government Agent to the European Court of Human Rights and Permanent Representative to the Council of Europe

Peter Van den Bossche Chair Professor of International Economic Law, Xi'an Jiaotong University School of Law, Xi'an, People's Republic of China; former Chair and Member of the Appellate Body of the World Trade Organization, Geneva, Switzerland (2009–19); Professor Emeritus, University of Bern, Bern, Switzerland and Maastricht University, Maastricht, The Netherlands; former President of the Society of International Economic Law (SIEL) (2018–24)

Zsuzsanna Deen-Racsmány Independent researcher in international law; formerly Assistant Professor of Public International Law, Grotius Centre for International Legal Studies, Leiden University, Leiden, The Netherlands; PhD (Leiden University)

Silvia Fernández de Gurmendi Former President of the Assembly of States Parties of the International Criminal Court; former Judge and President of the International Criminal Court

Christian M De Vos Visiting Assistant Professor of Law, City University of New York School of Law, New York, USA; former Director of Research and Investigations at Physicians for Human Rights, New York, USA; former Senior Advocacy Officer, Open Society Justice Initiative, New York, USA; PhD (Leiden University)

Henri de Waele Professor of International and European Law, Radboud University, Nijmegen, The Netherlands; Visiting Professor, University of Antwerp, Antwerp, Belgium

Andrew Drzemczewski Former Head of the Legal Affairs and Human Rights Department, Parliamentary Assembly of the Council of Europe, Strasbourg, France (2005–16); Visiting Professor, Middlesex University School of Law, London, UK. The author was intricately involved in the Assembly's refinement of internal procedures which led to the setting-up of the Assembly's Committee on the Election of Judges to the ECtHR (AS/Cdh)

Serena Forlati Professor of International Law, University of Ferrara, Ferrara, Italy

Nicolas Guillou Judge, International Criminal Court; former Judge, Kosovo Specialist Chambers; former member of the Panel of Experts of the Independent Expert Review of the International Criminal Court and the Rome Statute System

Heikki Kanninen Judge and former Vice-President of the General Court of the European Union; former Judge of the European Union Civil Service Tribunal; former Judge of the Supreme Administrative Court of Finland

Yassir Khudayri Program Manager, Open Society Foundations, New York, USA

Huw Llewellyn Senior Global Fellow and Distinguished Visiting Scholar, Centre for International Law, National University of Singapore, Singapore; former Director, Codification Division, UN Office of Legal Affairs, New York, USA; PhD (Leiden University)

Adriana-Maria Manolescu Legal Officer, international judicial organization in The Hague, The Netherlands; former research assistant of the Independent Expert Review Committee of the ICC; former Case Manager on two defence teams before the ICC; PhD (Leiden University)

Dorine Nauleau Qualified Lawyer at the Paris Bar; LLM Public International Law (Leiden University, The Netherlands) and Master in International Law (University of Lille, Lille, France)

Hanneke Palm Coordinating Policy Officer at the Ministry of the Interior and Kingdom Relations and previously Justice Attaché at the Permanent Representation of the Kingdom of the Netherlands to the Council of Europe

Mariana Pena Senior Legal Counsel, Open Society Justice Initiative, New York, USA

Misha Ariana Plagis Assistant Professor of Public International Law, Grotius Centre for International Legal Studies, Leiden University, Leiden, The Netherlands

Karin Pluberg Human Rights Expert, Deutsche Gesellschaft für Internationale Zusammenarbeit (GIZ), Bonn and Eschborn, Germany

John Eudes Ruhangisa Associate Professor of Law, Tumaini University Makumira (TUMA), Makumira, Tanzania; Former Registrar of the East African Court of Justice; former Judge of the High Court in Tanzania

Christiaan Timmermans Former Judge of the EU Court of Justice, former member (2014–20) and former President (2018–20) of the 255 panel

Sergey Vasiliev Professor of International Law, Open University, Heerlen, The Netherlands

PART I
DEMARCATING AND MAPPING JUDICIAL GOVERNANCE

1
Introduction

Sergey Vasiliev and Niels Blokker

1.1 Prologue

Judicial institutions such as courts, tribunals, chambers, and panels of adjudicators—defined less by uniform labels than by their shared nature—have been a fixture of the international institutional landscape for over a century. Their establishment by states and international organizations for dispute settlement and resolution of legal questions reached its peak in the 1990s, often described as the 'golden era' of international adjudication. This was due not only to the rapid and seemingly unstoppable proliferation of international courts but also to the prestige and authority they commanded among states and civil society. In hindsight, this contrasts sharply with the mid-2020s, an era marked by open defiance of judicial authority and virulent politicized attacks on international courts. The conviction that these institutions can bring peace and stability to the world by addressing violations of international law still resonates strongly among international lawyers. Yet this belief—counterfactual to a degree—must increasingly contend with the realities of legal nihilism and mounting state disdain for the core institutions of international law.

International courts and tribunals have long fascinated scholars of international law, political science, and international relations. Few institutional creatures have been studied more extensively. Over the past three and a half decades, a vast body of literature has examined a wide range of issues arising from their operation: the role of courts in global governance through the peaceful settlement of disputes and the development of international law; the applicable legal frameworks and jurisprudence; their institutional character and organization; adjudicatory practices and procedure; and the systemic effects of cross-judicial communication on the coherence or fragmentation of international law. A full bibliography would fill a volume of its own. This book does not aim to add to it. In other words, this is *not* a book about international courts. Its purpose is to depart from that traditional focus, resisting the gravitational pull that judicialization continues to exert in international law. Instead, it shifts the spotlight to what has long remained at the periphery of adjudication. Hidden in plain sight and largely impenetrable for public scrutiny, this sphere is in fact central to the success—or failure—of international courts.

More specifically, this volume is concerned with the judicial governance of international courts and tribunals, typically exercised by (groups of) states, (organs of) international organizations, or dedicated political and executive bodies. These actors are referred to—and will be designated throughout this volume—as *in*ternational *ju*dicial *gov*ernance *ins*titutions (or, in short, *injugovins*).[1] As the peripheral sphere

[1] Using this term for the first time: Niels M Blokker, 'The Governance of International Courts and Tribunals: Organizing and Guaranteeing Independence and Accountability' in Andreas Føllesdal and Geir

Sergey Vasiliev and Niels Blokker, *Introduction* In: *Governance of International Courts and Tribunals*. Edited by: Sergey Vasiliev and Niels Blokker, Oxford University Press.
DOI: 10.1093/oso/9780198922131.003.0001

of international adjudication, judicial governance can safeguard—or subvert—the legal, institutional, financial, and political foundations on which international justice institutions depend. Despite the critical importance of the institutions, practices, and norms through which international judiciaries are governed, this domain of international institutional law and practice has until recently remained under-examined. The present book seeks to address this gap in a systematic manner and to serve as a stepping stone for future inquiries into the normative foundations and institutional forms of international judicial governance. It represents the first concerted effort to shed light on—and to map—this extensive legal and institutional field.

On a more personal note, diverse motivations have shaped the authors' engagement with the project, culminating in the present edited volume as one of its outcomes.[2] For the first author (Vasiliev), the primary impetus was academic curiosity, informed by unresolved questions arising from his earlier research into international (criminal) procedural law, institutional pluralism in international adjudication, and the legitimacy of international courts and tribunals. The cooperation struggles and crises of authority affecting international criminal tribunals—and, in particular, the challenges the International Criminal Court (ICC) began to face after its first decade of operation—prompted him to seek the underlying causes of these difficulties in their broader institutional framework. Already in the mid-2010s, he was struck by what he perceived as the somewhat desultory and underwhelming performance by the ICC's governance institution, the Assembly of States Parties—particularly its failure to provide strategic guidance to the Rome Statute system and to address the Court's manifold governance problems in a timely and effective manner. This impression became the main trigger for embarking on this journey.

For the second author (Blokker), there were two main drivers. On the one hand, during his service at the Dutch Ministry of Foreign Affairs (2000–13) he represented The Netherlands in several international judicial governance institutions, in particular the Assembly of States Parties of the ICC and during the ICC's 2010 Review Conference. It became clear to him that those governance institutions were scarcely analysed or even mentioned in existing academic research, in stark contrast to the considerable scholarly attention devoted to the courts and tribunals they oversee. On the other hand, the most relevant sub-field of international law within which such research could be conducted was the law of international organizations—Blokker's

Ulfstein (eds), *The Judicialization of International Law: A Mixed Blessing?* (OUP 2018); Niels M Blokker, 'Governance of the International Tribunal of the Law of the Sea: The Role of the Meeting of States Parties to the Law of the Sea Convention' in Angela del Vecchio and Roberto Virzo (eds), *Interpretations of the United Nations Convention on the Law of the Sea by International Courts and Tribunals* (Springer 2019). Adopting the terminology, among others: Sergey Vasiliev, 'Judicial Governance Entities as Power-Holders in International Criminal Justice: A Plea for a Socio-Legal Enquiry' in Morten Bergsmo and others (eds), *Power in International Criminal Justice* (Torkel Opsahl Academic E-Publisher 2020); Sergey Vasiliev, 'Governing International Justice: Whence the Uniform Principles?' in Rick Lawson and Ramses A Wessel (eds), *Unity in Diversity: Perspectives on the Law of International Organisations* (Brill Nijhoff 2025).

[2] The other, no less significant, results are in particular: Huw Llewellyn, *An Institutional Perspective on the United Nations Criminal Tribunals: Governance, Independence and Impartiality* (Brill Nijhoff 2021); Adriana-Maria Manolescu, *Judicial Independence and Accountability in the Financial Governance of International Courts: An Act of Balancing Powers* (Brill Nijhoff 2026); Kritika Sharma, *The Assembly of States Parties to the International Criminal Court: A Good Governance Approach* (Brill Nijhoff 2026).

area of specialization at Leiden University, where he held the Schermers Chair since 2003. Initially a part-time appointment, it became full-time in 2013, affording him more research time that could be dedicated to the project on the 'governance of international courts and tribunals'. With their mutually complementary backgrounds, and the impetus of sharing a workspace at Leiden University between 2016 and 2019, the authors' close collaboration on this project evolved organically. Two colleagues from Leiden Law School—Armin Cuyvers and Rick Lawson—joined them in organizing the inaugural international conference in September 2019, which laid the foundations for this edited volume.

The rest of this chapter is reserved for a brief presentation of the theme of international judicial governance, outlining the parameters of this field of international law and practice, as well as its contours as an emerging academic discipline (Section 1.2). It also sets out the book's approach and purposes (Section 1.3) and explains its organization and structure (Section 1.4). A more detailed conceptual framework is provided in the following two chapters by the authors.

1.2 Well-Trodden Yet Uncharted Terrain

1.2.1 From judicial to governance institutions

From only a handful of standing adjudicatory bodies prior to the onset of the 'golden era', the number of international courts has grown considerably over the past thirty years. Some non-permanent bodies—such as the UN ad hoc and special criminal tribunals—have since become defunct and been replaced by residual mechanisms. Today, the tally stands at roughly thirty institutions, excluding the nearly thirty additional administrative tribunals.[3]

During this period of intensive 'judicialization' of international affairs and the rapid proliferation of international judicial institutions, international adjudication has attracted sustained scholarly attention, generating a substantial body of work on its dynamics and systemic implications. Virtually every significant attempt to submit an international dispute to judicial resolution, and every notable judgment or decision of international courts and tribunals, has been dissected. Many dimensions of international adjudication—the courts' mandates and jurisdiction, applicable law, interpretative strategies and reasoning, institutional organization, and procedural practice—have been examined in minute detail. This scholarly fascination is understandable given the spectacular institutional growth, the plurality of judicial functions, and the broader legal and policy objectives attributed to international courts as paradigmatic rule-of-law institutions. Accordingly, a massive body of literature evaluates their role in the international system: assessing their contribution to the

[3] The total count is therefore at around sixty international courts and tribunals. Henry Schermers and Niels Blokker, *International Institutional Law* (7th edn, Brill Nijhoff 2025) 487 (noting that over twenty international courts were set up after 1990); Jason Morgan-Foster, 'International Administrative Tribunals and Cross-Fertilization: Evidence of a Nascent Common Jurisprudence?' (2024) 24(2) Chicago Journal of International Law 339, 341.

interpretation and development of international law; interrogating their legitimacy, both normatively and sociologically, across diverse constituencies; and analysing the challenges to their authority, as well as the judicial and institutional responses these challenges have elicited.

In contrast to international adjudication itself, the legal-institutional arrangements adopted by states and international organizations for the governance of international courts and tribunals have long remained without the attention they deserve. Although adjacent to the study of international adjudication, governance has largely remained an academic *terra incognita*. Paradoxically, given its centrality to the proper functioning of international courts and tribunals, coverage of this domain has been fragmentary and episodic. It has often been confined to discrete governance activities or to notorious 'problem cases' faced by particular courts—or classes of courts. Some works, for instance, address international judicial elections and the challenge of ensuring the quality of adjudicators,[4] as well as the financing of international courts and tribunals, along with the recurrent problem of budgetary shortfalls.[5] Others conceptualize international judicial authority, examining issues such as the enforcement of rulings, deficient state cooperation, and international judicial practice.[6] In addition, an extensive literature has developed on the politics of international adjudication, the legitimacy and effectiveness of international courts,[7] and the phenomena of state resistance and backlash. These studies lay bare the political context of international adjudication and, albeit tangentially and from varying perspectives, touch on the challenges of judicial governance.[8]

[4] eg Ruth MacKenzie and others, *Selecting International Judges: Principle, Process, and Politics* (OUP 2010); Ruth MacKenzie, 'The Selection of International Judges' in Cesare PR Romano, Karen J Alter, and Yuval Shany (eds), *The Oxford Handbook of International Adjudication* (OUP 2014); Manfred Elsig and Mark A Pollack, 'Agents, Trustees, and International Courts: The Politics of Judicial Appointment at the World Trade Organization' (2012) 20(2) European Journal of International Relations 391.

[5] eg Thordis Ingadóttir, 'The Financing of Internationalized Criminal Courts and Tribunals' in Cesare PR Romano, André Nollkaemper, and Jann K Kleffner (eds), *Internationalized Criminal Courts: Sierra Leone, East Timor, Kosovo, and Cambodia* (OUP 2004); Thordis Ingadóttir, 'The Financing of International Adjudication' in Romano and others (n 4); Giorgia Tortora, 'The Financing of the Special Tribunals for Sierra Leone, Cambodia and Lebanon' (2013) 13(1) International Criminal Law Review 93; Stuart Ford, 'How Much Money Does the ICC Need?' in Carsten Stahn (ed), *The Law and Practice of the International Criminal Court* (OUP 2015).

[6] eg Constanze Schulte, *Compliance with Decisions of the International Court of Justice* (OUP 2004); Karen J Alter, Laurence R Helfer, and Mikael Rask Madsen (eds), *International Court Authority* (OUP 2018); Olympia Bekou and Daley Birkett (eds), *Cooperation and the International Criminal Court: Perspectives from Theory and Practice* (Brill 2016); Jeffrey L Dunoff and Mark A Pollack, 'International Judicial Practices: Opening the "Black Box" of International Courts' (2018) 40 Michigan Journal of International Law 47.

[7] eg Karen J Alter, *The New Terrain of International Law: Courts, Politics, Rights* (Princeton University Press 2014); Yuval Shany, *Assessing the Effectiveness of International Courts* (OUP 2014); Nobuo Hayashi and Cecilia Bailliet (eds), *The Legitimacy of International Criminal Tribunals* (CUP 2017); Nienke Grossman and others (eds), *Legitimacy and International Courts* (CUP 2018).

[8] eg Karen Alter, James T Gathii, and Laurence R Helfer, 'Backlash against International Courts in West, East and Southern Africa: Causes and Consequences' (2016) 27(2) European Journal of International Law 293; Salvatore Caserta and Pola Cebulak, 'The Limits of International Adjudication: Authority and Resistance of Regional Economic Courts in Times of Crisis' (2018) 14 International Journal of Law in Context 275; Michael R Madsen, Pola Cebulak, and Micha Wiebusch, 'Backlash against International Courts: Explaining the Forms and Patterns of Resistance to International Courts' (2018) 14(2) International Journal of Law in Context 197–220; Henry Lovat, 'International Criminal Tribunal Backlash' in Kevin Jon Heller and others (eds), *Oxford Handbook on International Criminal Law* (OUP 2020); Courtney

Yet the core problems of governing international courts and tribunals—recurrent across the board and taking various forms and manifestations—have not previously been framed as challenges of judicial governance. Nor have they been addressed under this thematic umbrella or placed squarely within the institutional 'galaxies' in which international courts are embedded. Moreover, the few existing studies tend to focus on a single *injugovin*–court pair or on one specific function rather than examining the configuration and exercise of judicial governance functions across a representative set of jurisdictional regimes.[9] Works that address the symptoms and causes of the malaise afflicting international adjudication rarely consider the role of *injugovins* in channelling and alleviating—or exacerbating—state resistance and backlash against courts, or how such dynamics may translate into governance malpractices and abuses. Only very recently have the legal nature, organization, and workings of *injugovins* begun to attract sustained scholarly attention.[10] Yet studies adopting a judicial governance perspective on the operation and challenges of international judiciaries, and on the intricate relationships between international courts and their governance institutions, remain few and far between.

Neglect of judicial governance at the international level has often impeded the development of a holistic perspective on the common challenges and predicaments confronting international courts. Such 'judicial governance neglect' is certainly not an isolated phenomenon. It forms part of the broader 'institutional neglect' that has long characterized international relations. As Inis Claude observed long ago,

> one of the major tasks of twentieth-century statesmanship is to strike a balance between obsessive concern with institutional problems—which makes international organization an end in itself, and exclusive concentration upon substantive issues of current world politics—which neglects the building of an adequate institutional apparatus for international relations.[11]

This holds equally true for the twenty-first century. Although an impressive system of rules and organizations was created during and after the Second World War, its maintenance has often not been taken seriously. Attention has tended to focus on substantive issues to be addressed—such as sustainable development, criminal justice, human

Hillebrecht, *Saving the International Justice Regime: Beyond Backlash against International Courts* (CUP 2021). In addition, Jeffrey L Dunoff and Mark A Pollack, 'The Judicial Trilemma' (2017) 111(1) American Journal of International Law 225.

[9] The operation of some *injugovins*, such as the Assembly of States Parties of the ICC, has attracted more attention than others: eg Jonathan O'Donohue, 'The ICC and the ASP' in Stahn (n 5); Hannah Woolaver and Emma Palmer, 'Challenges to the Independence of the International Criminal Court from the Assembly of States Parties' (2017) 15(4) Journal of International Criminal Justice 641; Jennifer Trahan, 'The Assembly of States Parties' in Margaret deGuzman and Valerie Oosterveld (eds), *The Elgar Companion to the International Criminal Court* (Edward Elgar Publishing 2020); Ezequiel Jimenez Martinez, *Governing the International Criminal Court: The History and Practice of the Assembly of States Parties to the Rome Statute* (Brill 2025).

[10] Most studies to date have been authored by scholars affiliated with this project: eg sources listed in nn 1–2.

[11] Inis L Claude, *Swords into Plowshares: The Problems and Progress of International Organization* (4th edn, Random House 1971) 84.

rights, and international humanitarian law—while insufficient regard has been paid to sustaining an adequate institutional apparatus. The cost of this approach becomes most evident in harsh and uncertain times such as ours, when these rules and organizations are needed most and require the full support of states. Remedying this pervasive 'institutional neglect'—a fundamental weakness of the international legal order—remains a long-term undertaking.

This broader 'institutional neglect' has also manifested itself in the governance of international courts and tribunals, especially since the 1990s. It is evident both in practice and in academia. The experiences of *injugovins* and 'their' courts across different areas of international law and geographic regions have never been systematically juxtaposed or compared, even though many of the challenges they face are similar and call for comparable solutions, primarily in the realm of judicial governance. Common patterns or underlying causes have often remained obscured, with apparent failures typically (mis)attributed to international tribunals rather than linked to the (mis)performance of their *injugovins*. This misattribution produces cognitive distortions, which carry far-reaching policy implications and feed into populist and nationalist narratives.

The pervasive and diverse problems—for example, substandard quality of judicial decisions, institutional mismanagement, toxic work culture, disciplinary and financial accountability gaps, non-enforcement of judicial rulings, failure to secure political support, and political backlash and attacks against international courts—are regularly laid at the doorstep of the courts themselves. It is true that courts and their leadership must bear their share of responsibility for some of these failures. More often than not, however, such problems stem from malpractice and indecision in court governance—which we refer to elsewhere as 'misgovernance' or 'ungovernance'—by political and executive entities formally entrusted with oversight but unwilling or unable to exercise it competently. When responsibility is correctly attributed to the *injugovins* (and the states behind them), rather than displaced onto international courts as more dependent actors, the underlying problems can be identified more accurately and appropriate remedial measures pursued—rather than blame conveniently shifted to the courts alone while states are given a pass.

Conceptualizing the familiar political, institutional, and financial challenges confronting international courts and tribunals as deficiencies, gaps, and imbalances in judicial governance marks a shift in perspective from judicial bodies to the political and executive entities that govern them. The judicial governance dimension incorporates the prevailing framings of these problems—such as the 'law versus politics' dichotomy or the imperative of safeguarding judicial independence—but it necessarily goes beyond them. The very notion of judicial governance, as applied to international adjudicatory bodies, is a neologism that calls for systematic theorization in the distinctive context of the international legal order.

This governance framing is particularly promising for unpacking the power dynamics between international tribunals and the states involved in their governance, whether directly or indirectly through *injugovins*. It offers greater explanatory power and a deeper understanding of these dynamics, including the tensions and conflicts they generate, but also the solutions devised for their resolution. Such conflictual relationships may, on the one hand, keep courts in check, prompting them to operate accountably and to continuously improve their performance. On the other hand, they may erode the authority and effectiveness of international courts—dynamics that are external to the courts themselves and largely beyond their control.

The attribution of real or perceived failures to the proper actors—and the related question of accountability for those failures—has particular significance in today's political climate, marked by the global rise and, in some places, electoral success of far-right politicians and movements. These trends have deepened the ongoing crisis of multilateralism in international relations and accelerated the visible decline of the international rule of law. A number of powerful states and their allies not only abstain from multilateral institutions and avoid the compulsory jurisdiction of international courts but also actively undermine and attack courts they perceive as threatening their national interests. Against this backdrop, less powerful states feel less inhibited about withdrawing from international frameworks and undermining judicial mandates.

Even those states that continue to engage with international rule-of-law institutions and participate in the governance of international courts—including developed states and established liberal democracies—now appear more inclined to offer only selective or conditional support, allowing political considerations to seep into court governance. Many international courts and tribunals already operate under crippling budgetary constraints and extensive, at times counterproductive, reporting obligations. Increasingly, they are also subverted by non-cooperation from states legally obliged to cooperate, while being subjected to more subtle forms of sabotage and left unprotected from the virulent political attacks of non-party states.

Recent years have produced multiple examples of state manoeuvres that pose serious challenges to the authority and effectiveness of international adjudication and to the integrity of the international rule of law. Notable episodes include the continued blockage of appointments to the World Trade Organization's Appellate Body due to United States opposition; the budgetary chokehold that paralysed several tribunals—for instance, the Special Tribunal for Lebanon, which was forced to wind down its operations between 2021 and 2023; and the persistent non-enforcement of judicial decisions of the European Court of Human Rights, the International Court of Justice, and the ICC. The ICC, in particular, has been the target of repeated and serious interference by non-party states in recent years, including criminal proceedings against its principals, surveillance and espionage, and major cyberattacks. The most conspicuous instances of such interference and retaliation were the executive orders issued by the first and second Trump administrations in the United States in 2020 and 2025, respectively, and the coercive measures adopted thereunder against the ICC Prosecutors, Deputy Prosecutors, and several judges.[12]

Nowadays, the 'failures' of international courts quickly become ammunition for national-populist and autocratic leaders and their entourages who—driven by fears of accountability and domestic political fallout—seek to intimidate international civil servants and the courts' supporters by branding them as 'external enemies' or a 'fifth

[12] For discussion, see Sergey Vasiliev, 'Justitia and Leviathans: The Struggle for the International Rule of Law (inaugural lecture, Open University of the Netherlands, 13 June 2025) <www.ou.nl/documents/40554/10543295/25115_Oratieboekje_Sergey_Vasiliev.pdf#page=21>.

column', and even by taking retaliatory legislative and executive measures.[13] Both 'illiberal democrats' and autocrats deftly employ—often unfair and misdirected—critiques of international courts to discredit and ridicule them, destroy their authority, and press further assaults on their judicial independence. The legitimacy of these courts continues to be contested, both in terms of their legality and authority and with regard to their performance—reflected in allegations of insufficient quality of jurisprudence, unfairness, judicial activism or overreach, lack of accountability, inefficiency, and ineffectiveness.[14] Yet many of the critiques advanced by such political regimes and their leaders—even if partly relatable—undoubtedly serve ulterior motives and converge with overtly unlawful attacks on judicial authority and the fundamental principles of the rule of law.

The task of fashioning principled and effective policies, together with robust institutional and legal responses to politicized attacks, and of ensuring that international courts and tribunals are able to perform their mandates impartially, independently, and effectively, requires addressing the root causes of persisting problems—foremost among them those embedded in the sphere of judicial governance. *Injugovins*, scarcely researched to date, are too vital to the orderly, effective, and accountable functioning of international courts and tribunals to remain neglected. As Kosař has observed in the domestic context, judicial governance institutions matter.[15] The same holds true internationally. This book responds to the call for full recognition of the critical role *injugovins* play in safeguarding the independence, effectiveness, and accountability of international courts and tribunals. It places *injugovins* firmly at the centre of a wide-ranging research effort and represents the first attempt to remedy their prior neglect.

1.2.2 Legal-institutional (practice) field and scholarly discipline

International judicial governance has a longer lineage than it may at first appear: it has existed for as long as international courts and tribunals themselves. None of these

[13] In Putin's Russia, the provision of cooperation for the enforcement of decisions of international organizations to which Russia is not a party was criminalized by Federal Law No 157-FZ, adopted on 28 April 2023, which inserted a new Art 284.3 into the Criminal Code. The measure was aimed in particular at individuals who might assist the ICC in connection with its arrest warrant against Putin issued on 17 March 2023. Human Rights Watch, 'Russia: Law Targets International Criminal Court: New Move against Accountability for World's Most Serious Crimes' (5 May 2023) <www.hrw.org/news/2023/05/05/russia-law-targets-international-criminal-court>. On the draconian 'ICC Bill' advanced in Netanyahu's Israel: Itamar Mann, 'Criminalizing Knowledge: Israel's Legislative Attack on International Law Expertise' (*Verfassungsblog*, 21 February 2025) <https://verfassungsblog.de/criminalizing-knowledge>.

[14] John Bolton, 'Address to the Federalist Society on the International Criminal Court' (delivered 10 September 2018) <www.americanrhetoric.com/speeches/johnboltonfederalistsociety2018.htm>; Secretary of State, 'Secretary Michael R. Pompeo at a Press Availability with Secretary of Defense Mark Esper, Attorney General William Barr, and National Security Advisor Robert O'Brien' (11 June 2020) <https://2017-2021.state.gov/secretary-michael-r-pompeo-at-a-press-availability-with-secretary-of-defense-mark-esper-attorney-general-william-barr-and-national-security-advisor-robert-obrien>; Dmitry A Medvedev, 'Lost Illusions, or How the International Criminal Court Has Become a Legal Nonentity' (2025) 69(1) Pravovedenie 24.

[15] David Kosař, 'Beyond Judicial Councils: Forms, Rationales and Impact of Judicial Self-Governance in Europe' (2018) 19(7) German Law Journal 1567, 1577 ('authoritarian and populist political leaders care about the control of judicial self-governance bodies and thus we should care as well').

bodies emerged from, existed in, or disappeared into an institutional void. From the earliest and relatively rudimentary organizational forms to the most recent and comparatively sophisticated iterations, all have, in one way or another, been governed by their parent states and organizations: mandates defined, members appointed, budgets allocated, and premises provided. In this sense, the governance of international courts is as established a phenomenon as international adjudication itself.

Despite the accumulated experience of establishing, overseeing, refashioning, and terminating international judicial bodies—and the wealth of empirical data still awaiting discovery and analysis—there has been virtually no systematic accounting or critical assessment of these past experiments.[16] There has been little effort to distil lessons about which mechanisms and practices work, which do not, under what institutional conditions, and why. Nor has there been sufficient reflection on the specific legal constraints and normative standards that should guide the performance of international judicial governance. One reason may be that much of this governance consists of unspectacular bureaucratic and technical processes, unfolding behind closed doors and largely impenetrable—or uninteresting—to most external observers, including international lawyers. Another reason may be that each court and tribunal, or limited class thereof, operates within its own self-standing international legal-institutional 'galaxy', which does not necessarily interlock with others and therefore invariably requires tailor-made governance arrangements. This reality has reduced the immediate practical and policy relevance of any cross-systemic 'lessons learned'. As a result, the field of international judicial governance has persisted as a vast expanse of disparate episodes and disjointed experiences—overlaid, overshadowed, and gradually pushed into oblivion by more recent developments. This well-trodden yet still largely uncharted terrain must at last be reclaimed, rediscovered, and mapped.

The contours and outer limits of this field require preliminary clarification, with more detailed conceptual elaboration deferred to the following two chapters. As the reader will observe throughout this volume, the central notion of 'governance' is consistently employed in conjunction with the qualifiers 'international' and 'judicial'. This terminology serves to delimit our inquiry to those actors—international organizations, their constituent organs, or other institutions—entrusted with the functional responsibility of governing international judicial bodies, as opposed to the individual states represented within them. While states do participate in the governance of international courts and tribunals, they typically do so indirectly, through the powers and privileges associated with their membership in *injugovins*, regardless of the latter's legal status or institutional form.

At the same time, all international courts and tribunals are necessarily involved in their own governance through their presidents/presidencies and the heads of judicial divisions or chambers. A degree of judicial self-governance is, after all, an inevitable corollary of the principle of judicial independence as well as of considerations of judicial efficiency and expediency. In this sense, courts could even be seen as their own *injugovins*. This book, however, is primarily concerned with the external dimension of judicial governance: the institutions, practices, functions, and standards beyond

16 For discussion, see Niels Blokker, 'International Judicial Governance Institutions', in this volume.

the international courts themselves that constitute the objects of judicial governance. The fault lines and dynamics between (external) judicial governance and (internal) judicial self-governance form an essential aspect of the relationship between courts and their *injugovins*, and several chapters in this volume explore that interplay and the contestations it generates.

For the purposes of this book, international judicial governance is defined as the area of international (institutional) law and legal-institutional practice concerned with the establishment, oversight, and termination of international judicial bodies by external political and/or executive international institutions. This usage is deliberately limited to the legal dimensions of the governance of international courts and tribunals, with the recognition that judicial governance in the broader sense extends well beyond the legal discipline. In more expansive terms, it can be understood to encompass insights from other social sciences—such as political science and international relations, as well as from court administration and public management. Indeed, this is how the discipline of judicial governance is often framed in the domestic context, where political, executive, and expert oversight of judicial systems is a central focus.[17]

Accordingly, the field lends itself to a variety of other (inter-)disciplinary approaches and methodologies, including empirical research. The present project, however, is framed as a legal one rather than as a cross-over with political science, international relations, sociology, or other disciplines. Situated firmly within the domain of international institutional law, it focuses on the international legal and institutional frameworks of judicial governance, and is therefore deliberately modest in its disciplinary scope and methodological ambitions. Its intrinsic value, however, remains undiminished by that. First, given the relative under-development of the legal-institutional field, international lawyers and international justice experts still have considerable ground to cover and a wealth of empirical material to study and analyse in the years ahead. Second, this academic legal project is intended as a stepping stone for future multi- and interdisciplinary research on the governance of international courts and tribunals—research in which international institutional law will inevitably constitute a key component.

The material scope of international judicial governance, in terms of the activities it encompasses, is defined by the standard set of governance functions that *injugovins* are mandated—or assume the authority—to carry out in respect of the courts and tribunals they oversee. The enterprise of judicial governance spans the entire life cycle of international courts and tribunals and includes: (i) 'parenting'—that is, securing the legal and practical bases for bringing courts and tribunals into existence and sustaining their operation; (ii) exercising various forms of (management) oversight; and (iii) implementing institutional reforms as appropriate and terminating courts when their mandates are deemed no longer to serve their intended purposes. The standard functions constituting the core of governance performed by *injugovins* include:

(i) electing court principals (judges and, in the case of criminal tribunals, prosecutors);

[17] In more detail, see Sergey Vasiliev, 'What Is (International) Judicial Governance?', in this volume.

(ii) determining and adjusting courts' institutional structures and practical arrangements;
(iii) enacting and amending their legislative frameworks;
(iv) approving and allocating budgets and ensuring the availability of resources;
(v) providing administrative oversight, financial auditing, organizational review, and other requisite forms of institutional control and accountability;
(vi) ensuring the enforcement of judicial decisions; and
(vii) securing the necessary political support, operational assistance, and protection against politicized attacks on judicial independence.

The question of the disciplinary anchoring of this legal-practical field also calls for reflection. The law and practice of international judicial governance may be defined as a sub-discipline of international institutional law dedicated to the study of the legal and institutional arrangements established by states and international organizations to provide oversight of international courts and tribunals. This discipline has remained in an embryonic stage of development—and largely off the map of international legal scholarship—for far too long. It is high time to inaugurate it as a distinct and composite area of study, drawing theories, insights, and methods from international institutional law, the law and practice of international adjudication, and the specialist regimes of international law within which the respective judicial bodies operate, including human rights law, international trade and economic law, the law of the sea, and international criminal law. As the following chapter demonstrates, the discipline of judicial governance in domestic contexts is currently far more developed. In contrast to its international counterpart, it can boast a burgeoning body of academic literature—comprising full-length monographs, book chapters, and articles—as well as a specialized journal, research groups, and the other requisites of an established academic field.

The first significant steps in this direction have also been taken by international lawyers, which bodes well for the future. Yet much more remains to be done. The dialogue between national and international lawyers on judicial governance has begun, and it should be pursued at a deeper level.[18] There are different nuances in the governance of domestic and international judicial systems, reflecting the idiosyncrasies of their respective legal and institutional contexts.[19] However, the challenges and dilemmas arising in these adjacent fields are similar across the international–national divide. Consider, in particular, the interplay and tensions between safeguarding judicial independence and ensuring effective oversight with view to guaranteeing courts' accountable functioning, or the ever-present risks of illiberal capture of judicial governance institutions, which are bound to have deleterious consequences for judicial independence and the rule of law, whether at the international or domestic level. Although the parameters of the debate, the contours of the problems, and the potential solutions will inevitably differ between international and domestic judicial governance,

[18] Particularly notable is the rich 2018 special issue of the *German Law Journal*, edited by David Kosař, 'Judicial Self-Governance in Europe' (2018) 19(7) German Law Journal 1567–2188, which also includes several contributions on international courts.

[19] For discussion, see Sergey Vasiliev, 'What Is (International) Judicial Governance?', in this volume.

the need for dialogue is as self-evident as it is urgent—particularly in an era of widespread democratic and rule-of-law backsliding, both across multiple jurisdictions and globally. Domestic perspectives are of considerable interest to international lawyers working on issues of international court governance, and at least some of the lessons learned in that context may prove valuable for scholars of domestic judicial governance. There is ample scope for comparative and critical analysis, as well as for interdisciplinary collaboration in this domain—opportunities that, one hopes, will be fully pursued in the years ahead.

1.3 Objectives and Framing

This book places the theme of international judicial governance firmly on the map as both a distinct domain of international institutional law and practice and a field of scholarly inquiry. By developing a conceptual framework and critically reviewing governance arrangements across multiple international judicial systems, it invites deeper engagement with this crucial external dimension of international adjudication. The volume seeks to foster a fuller understanding of the forces shaping the operation of international judiciaries and to sharpen appreciation of the institutional and political constraints they face, as well as their multiple dependencies on governing institutions. The insights and perspectives presented in the following chapters lay the groundwork for future research into the governance of international courts—and potentially other international accountability institutions—and provide a foundation for more in-depth examination of aspects of judicial governance and *injugovins* not addressed here in sufficient detail.

The book aims to address this research gap in three principal ways. First, it advances existing knowledge of international judicial governance as a field of law and legal-institutional practice by elucidating the nature and organizational forms of *injugovins* and outlining governance schemes applicable across international adjudicatory regimes. Second, it clarifies the legal and regulatory frameworks through which international courts and tribunals are overseen by their governing bodies, with a focus on their powers and obligations, functions and working methods, and the legal and normative standards that constrain and guide their operation. Third, it examines and critically analyses the practical dynamics and challenges of exercising governance over international courts and tribunals. The coverage of judicial governance schemes paired with specific institutions and of individual governance functions is not intended to be exhaustive. The book's primary ambition is to demarcate this *terra incognita* as a subject worthy of systematic exploration, to highlight its key empirical and normative issues, and to lay the groundwork for future inquiry.

The project thus seeks to make a threefold contribution—theoretical, descriptive/empirical, and normative/critical. Its theoretical contribution lies in developing the building blocks of a conceptual framework for international judicial governance: its content and outer boundaries; the key distinctions and interplay between external and internal judicial (self-)governance; the notion and typology of *injugovins*; and the relationship between judicial independence and judicial accountability.

The descriptive/empirical contribution is embodied in the regime- and function-mapping exercise at the heart of the volume. It provides extensive and detailed accounts of the governance arrangements adopted for a representative set of historical and contemporary regimes across different areas of international law, together with a cross-regime survey and analysis of selected judicial governance functions. This material highlights the diversity of institutional arrangements for governing international courts and furnishes the system-specific empirical bases necessary for future comparative and critical evaluation.

As its normative/critical contribution, the volume takes stock of the salient practical challenges and normative dilemmas that arise in the context of international judicial governance. In particular, it examines conflicts, governance vacuums, and abuses of power that may disrupt the delicate relationship between *injugovins* and courts, or unsettle the balance between judicial independence, on the one hand, and effective oversight and accountability, on the other. Particular attention is given to the steps taken and measures adopted by *injugovins*, their constituent states, and the courts themselves to remedy known problems and respond to governance crises. Beyond clarifying the legal and regulatory standards that structure the relationship between *injugovins* and courts, this perspective also helps to identify sound governance practices and 'lessons learned' that may have broader applicability and be transposed to other contexts.

The analytical framing chosen for this project conceptualizes international judicial governance as a realm constituted by—and consolidating around—institutions, practices, and norms. At the centre of our inquiry lies a triad: (i) *injugovins* (and their subsidiary organs); (ii) the practices—activities and processes—through which *injugovins* discharge their responsibilities in governing international courts and tribunals; and (iii) the legal constraints and regulatory or normative standards, binding or otherwise and regardless of source, that de jure or de facto shape governance practices and relationships. The sequence of these three elements in the volume's title—institutions, practices, and norms—reflects the premise that an institutional focus on *injugovins* provides the most appropriate point of departure for this inquiry. Treating governance institutions as the entry point allows for deeper insights into both governance practices and standards—not only in the abstract, through legal regulations, protocols, and standard operating procedures, but also in empirical terms, as judicial governance unfolds in institutional life. The third element—norms—centres on but also extends beyond formal and binding legal principles that constrain the operation of *injugovins* (notably the principle of judicial independence) to encompass softer regulatory and normative parameters that (should) guide the discharge of *injugovins*' governance responsibilities.[20]

Identifying and articulating the content of governance practices and norms is not straightforward. It requires more than examining the often open-textured and inconclusive legal principles and frameworks governing *injugovins*' work. It must also take the form of an inductive exercise: deriving standards and established practices

[20] On the question of principles and standards in international judicial governance: Niels Blokker, 'International Judicial Governance Institutions', Section 3.5, in this volume; Vasiliev, 'Governing International Justice' (n 1).

from accumulated institutional experience. The ordering of institutions, practices, and norms reflects only the analytical approach adopted in this volume and does not imply a hierarchy of importance. Looking ahead, it is hoped that future research on the governance of international courts and tribunals—while further clarifying the empirical functioning of *injugovins*—will also engage more deeply with the legal and normative foundations of international judicial governance. It is precisely in this domain that international lawyers are uniquely positioned to make their most meaningful contribution.

1.4 Approach and Structure

The volume engages with its central theme on conceptual, descriptive, and normative levels, and this is reflected in its structure. Comprising seven parts, it moves (i) from an exploration of the definitional and conceptual issues of international judicial governance, (ii) to descriptive accounts of its institutions, practices, and norms across a range of regimes, together with a transversal survey of essential governance functions, (iii) to critical analyses of notable governance problems and the crisis-management strategies and institutional solutions employed in response, and finally (iv) to a forward-looking assessment of judicial governance as an area of law and practice inextricably intertwined with international adjudication.

Part I ('Demarcating and Mapping Judicial Governance') lays the conceptual and methodological groundwork for the project. It undertakes the preliminary definitional and taxonomic tasks and elaborates the 'judicial governance' framing—its qualifiers, scope, and outer limits—that underpins this book. In addition to the present chapter, it contains two substantive chapters by the editors. Together, these chapters delineate the field of international judicial governance, understood as the institutions, practices, and norms through which political and executive bodies, mandated by states, exercise external oversight over international courts and tribunals.

In deconstructing the central notion of (international) judicial governance, Chapter 2, by Vasiliev, situates this category in relation to other usages of 'governance'—for instance, within the terminologies of 'global governance' and 'good governance'—and distinguishes it from contiguous notions such as 'judicial self-governance' and 'court administration'.[21] Having highlighted the normative questions and tensions that define national judicial governance, the chapter reviews notable institutional models and considers whether lessons drawn from the domestic context can meaningfully inform the governance of international courts and tribunals, given their distinctive features and circumstances. By contrast, Blokker's Chapter 3 approaches international judicial governance on its terms and offers a 'topography'—an exploratory empirical overview—of *international* judicial governance institutions.[22] It highlights the key principles that inform the regulation and practice of the governance of international courts and tribunals, most notably judicial independence and accountability.

[21] Sergey Vasiliev, 'What Is (International) Judicial Governance?', in this volume.
[22] Niels Blokker, 'International Judicial Governance Institutions', in this volume.

Jointly, the two introductory chapters set the stage and establish the conceptual framework for the survey of specific judicial governance regimes in Parts II and III. The subsequent chapters in the volume proceed from a shared understanding of international judicial governance as articulated in Part I. At the same time, the editors did not aim to impose rigid taxonomic or structural parameters, but encouraged contributors to address the most salient aspects of judicial governance within specific regimes. Accordingly, many contributors develop their own normative insights and engage with broader questions of principle through critical analyses of the law and practice of governing particular courts or of performing specific governance functions.

Part II ('Historical Antecedents') reviews the governance schemes of early international tribunals. Although now defunct, these arrangements remain of more than antiquarian interest. First, they demonstrate the irreducible diversity of approaches devised by parent states and international organizations, as well as institutional building blocks that—though once consigned to the dustbin of institutional history—may re-emerge as usable variants in future experiments in tribunal design. Second, the historical antecedents highlight important continuities with present-day governance institutions: the embedding of tribunals within broader (quasi-)constitutional frameworks, the mechanisms and processes of governance employed, and the improvised solutions devised to meet practical challenges. With these continuities in view, Chapter 4, by Henri de Waele, focuses on the governance of the Permanent Court of International Justice (PCIJ), the predecessor to the International Court of Justice (ICJ).[23] Chapter 5, by Vasiliev, then examines the distinctive arrangements for the governance of the Nuremberg and Tokyo International Military Tribunals, which were embedded in the Allied occupation regimes of Germany and Japan.[24]

Part III ('Modern Regimes') continues the regime-specific approach by taking stock of the law and practice of international judicial governance within contemporary regimes. It comprises six chapters examining governance arrangements across three principal categories: generalist international courts (the ICJ); specialized regional courts in the fields of economic integration and human rights (the East African Court of Justice (EACJ), the Southern African Development Community Tribunal (SADC Tribunal), the African Court of Human and Peoples' Rights (ACtHPR), and the Court of Justice of the European Union (CJEU)); and international criminal courts and tribunals (including the UN ad hoc and special tribunals, such as the Special Tribunal for Lebanon). These chapters adopt a regime-driven approach to exploring the relationship between *injugovins* and the courts they govern, addressing salient issues and challenges, and analysing several governance functions for each *injugovin*–court tandem. Each contribution combines detailed description with critical normative analysis of the relevant institutions, practices, and norms. A deliberate effort has been made to avoid an exclusive focus on the most prominent and well-studied courts and to steer clear of Eurocentrism.

Chapter 6, by Serena Forlati, examines the governance institutions and practices relating to the ICJ, in particular the role of other principal organs of the UN in exercising

[23] Henri de Waele, 'Managing the Realization of "The Hope of Ages"', in this volume.

[24] Sergey Vasiliev, 'Governance of the International Military Tribunals at Nuremberg and Tokyo', in this volume.

oversight over the ICJ.[25] In Chapter 7, John Eudes Ruhangisa analyses the governance schemes of African regional integration courts, notably the EACJ and the SADC Tribunal.[26] Drawing on his experience as former EACJ Registrar, Ruhangisa highlights the tensions between governance and judicial independence and the challenges of safeguarding the latter in practice. This theme is further pursued in the contribution of Misha Ariana Plagis and Karin Pluberg (Chapter 8), which focuses on the African Union as the governance institution of the African Commission and the African Court on Human and Peoples' Rights.[27] Chapter 9, by Heikki Kanninen, judge and former Vice-President of the General Court of the European Union, surveys the position of the Court of Justice of the European Union within the EU's constitutional framework and the ways in which the judicial independence of its members is safeguarded as part of its governance scheme.[28]

The final two chapters of Part III turn to the governance frameworks of international criminal tribunals. Chapter 10, by Huw Llewellyn, offers a wide-ranging account of the schemes used to 'parent' and oversee UN criminal tribunals: the ad hoc tribunals for Yugoslavia and Rwanda (ICTY and ICTR) and their successor, the Residual Mechanism for International Criminal Tribunals (IRMCT/MICT), as well as the Extraordinary Chambers in the Courts of Cambodia (ECCC) and the Special Tribunal for Lebanon (STL).[29] Llewellyn also discusses the notions of parenthood, oversight, governance, and ownership for the purpose of his analysis before surveying the governance arrangements of these courts and examining the key tensions between external oversight and the principles of judicial independence and impartiality of criminal tribunals. Drawing on her extensive practical experience at the STL, Evelyn Anoya provides in Chapter 11 an in-depth analysis of its governance from an administrative perspective, highlighting the interplay between oversight and self-governance and the funding challenges that ultimately led to the tribunal's closure.[30]

Part IV ('Judicial Governance Functions') adopts a cross-cutting, function-centred approach. The chapters in this part provide an in-depth examination of the legal standards and practical operation of specific governance functions, either within a single court or across multiple tribunals. Particular attention is devoted to three functions: the election of judges, financial governance, and the enforcement of judicial rulings.

Chapter 12, by Andrew Drzemczewski, analyses the procedure for electing judges to the European Court of Human Rights (ECtHR) by the Parliamentary Assembly of the Council of Europe (CoE), focusing on the role of the Committee on the Election of Judges and the advisory panel established by the Committee of Ministers.[31] Chapter 13, by Christiaan Timmermans, turns to the EU and examines the procedure for the nomination of members of the Court of Justice and the General Court of the

[25] Serena Forlati, 'Governance of the International Court of Justice', in this volume.
[26] John Eudes Ruhangisa, 'Governance of Regional Integration Courts', in this volume.
[27] Misha Ariana Plagis and Karin Pluberg, 'Paper Lions?', in this volume.
[28] Heikki Kanninen, 'Governance of the Court of Justice of the European Union', in this volume.
[29] Huw Llewellyn, 'Governance of the United Nations Criminal Tribunals', in this volume.
[30] Evelyn Anoya, 'Governance of the Special Tribunal for Lebanon', in this volume.
[31] Andrew Drzemczewski, 'The Election of Judges onto the European Court of Human Rights', in this volume.

European Union, with particular emphasis on the mandate and functioning of the panel established under Article 255 of the Treaty on the Functioning of the European Union.[32]

Chapter 14, by Adriana-Maria Manolescu, examines the financing schemes of international courts and tribunals: which governance institutions exercise this function, how they do so, and how budgetary accountability is ensured in ways that remain compatible with judicial independence.[33] Drawing on extensive research into the financial oversight arrangements of seven permanent courts—the PCIJ, ICJ, the International Tribunal for the Law of Sea, the World Trade Organization's Appellate Body, the ICC, the Inter-American Court of Human Rights (IACtHR), and the CJEU—the chapter addresses the meaning of, and relationship between, the principles of judicial independence and accountability specifically in the context of the financial governance of international courts and tribunals.

The two subsequent chapters focus on the implementation of judicial rulings—a function for which international courts and tribunals, lacking their own enforcement capacities, are notoriously dependent on their *injugovins* and the states composing them or otherwise bound to cooperate. In Chapter 15, Dorine Nauleau conceptualizes enforcement as a distinct function of *injugovins* and underscores the importance of its unfailing performance for preserving the authority and effectiveness of courts before providing a comparative overview of the arrangements adopted for the ICJ, ICC, and ECtHR.[34] The final contribution of Part IV, Chapter 16 by Hanneke Palm and Roeland Böcker, offers a close analysis of the framework for enforcing ECtHR judgments, with particular attention to the supervisory role of the CoE Committee of Ministers and its recourse to infringement proceedings when member states refuse to comply.[35]

Continuing with a critical cross-cutting perspective, Part V ('Crises and Solutions') further problematizes the field of international judicial governance by focusing on *injugovins*' notorious failures to exercise their competences in governing 'their' courts and by reviewing the practices adopted to defuse governance crises. The thrust of this perspective lies in identifying problem cases—instances where *injugovins* abuse their powers or fail to exercise them properly and in a timely manner—and analysing their impact on courts, including compromises to judicial independence, accountability, effectiveness, or efficiency. Equally relevant are the sound governance practices, solutions, and strategies that can help to prevent or mitigate such outcomes.

This part opens with a chapter on the demise of the WTO Appellate Body as a consequence of the failure to appoint its members, written by its former chair Peter Van den Bossche.[36] Chapter 18, authored by Judge Silvia Fernández de Gurmendi—drawing on her experience as former ICC President and President of the Assembly of States Parties—sets out the features of the ICC's governance architecture and the

32 Christiaan Timmermans, 'The Procedure for Nominating Members of the EU Courts', in this volume.
33 Adriana-Maria Manolescu, 'Financial Governance of International Courts and Tribunals', in this volume.
34 Dorine Nauleau, 'The Enforcement of International Judicial Decisions', in this volume.
35 Hanneke Palm and Roeland Böcker, 'Implementation of Judgments of the European Court of Human Rights', in this volume.
36 Peter Van den Bossche, 'The Demise of the WTO Appellate Body', in this volume.

measures undertaken by its management oversight institution to address the Court's challenges.[37] The recurring issue of nominating and electing the best candidates for international judicial office, already highlighted in Part IV, takes centre stage in Chapter 19. Drawing on their experience of reviewing judicial election schemes across several international jurisdictions, Christian De Vos, Mariana Pena, and Yassir Khudayri underscore the importance of transparent, competitive, and merit-based appointment processes and the constructive role that independent advisory expert committees can play in achieving them.[38] Part V closes with Chapter 20 by Zsuzsanna Deen-Racsmány, which revisits the saga of MICT Judge Aydın Sefa Akay, arrested by Turkish authorities in 2016 despite his immunity as a UN judge.[39] Even more troubling, as Deen-Racsmány shows, the MICT's *injugovins*—the UN principal organs—failed to defend the tribunal's judicial independence.

Part VI ('Future Outlook') turns to the future of international judicial governance as a field of law and practice. It comprises two chapters. In Chapter 21, Nicolas Guillou and Adriana-Maria Manolescu present and analyse the so-called Three-Layered Governance Model (3LGM).[40] Devised originally as part of the Independent Expert Review of the International Criminal Court and the Rome Statute System, this model offers a framework for reconciling judicial independence and accountability in a coherent manner.[41] Under this model, each category of the court's activity determines the applicable lines of authority, the responsible overseeing actors, and the corresponding accountability instruments, thereby calibrating the appropriate balance between judicial independence and accountability. As such, the model's applicability may extend beyond the governance of the ICC alone and be adapted to shape the oversight arrangements of other international courts and tribunals. The concluding contribution by the editors (Chapter 22) distils the main takeaways from the preceding analyses, offers final reflections structured around seven dimensions, or dyads, of judicial governance, and outlines possible directions for future research.[42]

Finally, Part VII ('Addenda') contains two keynote addresses by distinguished practitioners deeply familiar with the governance of major international courts: former ICJ President and Judge Abdulqawi Ahmed Yusuf, and former ICTY Judge and former ASP President O-Gon Kwon.[43] Their addresses are reproduced as delivered at the 2019 inaugural Leiden conference of this project, subject only to minor formatting edits.

All weblinks included in this book were accessed in January 2026.

[37] Silvia Fernández de Gurmendi, 'Challenges to the Governance of the International Criminal Court', in this volume.

[38] Christian M De Vos, Mariana Pena, and Yassir Khudayri, 'Electing the Best?', in this volume.

[39] Zsuzsanna Deen-Racsmány, 'Deficient Protection of the Independence of International Judges by International Judicial Governance Institutions', in this volume.

[40] Nicolas Guillou and Adriana-Maria Manolescu, 'The Three-Layered Governance Model', in this volume.

[41] Independent Expert Review of the International Criminal Court and the Rome Statute System, Final Report, 30 September 2020, ICC-ASP/19/16 <https://asp.icc-cpi.int/iccdocs/asp_docs/ASP19/IER-Final-Report-ENG.pdf> paras 31–38.

[42] Niels Blokker and Sergey Vasiliev, 'Conclusion', in this volume.

[43] Abdulqawi Ahmed Yusuf, 'Keynote Address'; O-Gon Kwon, 'Keynote Address', in this volume.

2

What Is (International) Judicial Governance?

Sergey Vasiliev *

2.1 Introduction

In a book on international judicial governance as a field of international institutional law and practice, a range of preliminary questions arises concerning the meaning and scope of this central notion and its relationship to contiguous terms of art such as 'judicial self-governance' or 'self-government', 'court administration', and 'court management'. Some questions are descriptive or conceptual: what is meant by judicial governance, and what are its rationales? Which activities and actors fall within its ambit, and which processes or practices should be excluded? Others are normative: How should judicial governance arrangements be evaluated, and what criteria are appropriate for judging their adequacy? Put differently, how does one distinguish high-quality judicial governance from its opposite? The answers inevitably vary across legal orders. Many of the challenges and dilemmas of court governance are shared between international and domestic settings. Yet judicial governance at the international level raises issues of its own. How do the specific features of the international order in which international courts and tribunals (ICTs) operate shape the principles and arrangements through which they are governed?

The purpose of this exploratory chapter is neither to offer definitive answers nor to resolve the many quandaries in this field. Its aim, rather, is to delineate the contours of this area of law and practice and to unpack the core concept of judicial governance by drawing on the comparative judicial studies literature. In tandem with the following 'topography' of international judicial governance institutions (*injugovins*),[1] it sets the stage for the subsequent contributions, which examine judicial governance schemes and challenges in specific international legal-institutional contexts. Those chapters also engage with the categories of 'judicial independence', 'judicial accountability', and 'governance institutions', but primarily through the prism of individual court governance regimes and functions. Analysing their operationalization and related practical challenges provides the best vantage point for interrogating and refining these categories further. By contrast, the present chapter adopts a more conceptual and transversal approach, serving as a definitional prelude to the analyses that follow rather than a substitute for them.

First, the chapter delineates judicial governance both as a composite discipline and as a field encompassing the institutions, practices, and norms concerned with the external oversight and management of judicial bodies, with the aim of ensuring their

* The author thanks Niels Blokker for comments on an earlier draft.
[1] Niels Blokker, 'International Judicial Governance Institutions', in this volume.

Sergey Vasiliev, *What Is (International) Judicial Governance?* In: *Governance of International Courts and Tribunals*.
Edited by: Sergey Vasiliev and Niels Blokker, Oxford University Press. © Sergey Vasiliev 2026.
DOI: 10.1093/oso/9780198922131.003.0002

independent, orderly, and effective functioning (Section 2.2). Second, it undertakes a scoping exercise to map the normative and institutional issues of judicial governance arising at the domestic level, which may serve as a frame of reference for examining the governance of international courts. This includes an exploration of the key concepts and principles of judicial independence and accountability, an assessment of the relationship between external judicial governance and judicial self-governance, and a discussion of the principal institutional models (Section 2.3). Third, the chapter moves beyond domestic legal orders to consider how the transposition of adjudication and judicial governance into the international sphere reshapes its parameters, power relations, and normative constraints which provide the basis for judgements on the quality of judicial governance in that domain (Section 2.4).

2.2 Demarcating the Field

The term 'judicial governance', along with its variants such as 'judicial government' and 'court administration',[2] has been widely used in the domestic and comparative law literature on the organization and functioning of judicial systems. Fifteen years ago, Gar Yein Ng called for the recognition of 'judicial governance' as a dedicated subdiscipline: a multidisciplinary field that brings together law, political sciences, economics, public administration, and organizational management.[3] It is safe to say that this aspiration has since materialized. Over the past two decades, national judicial (self-)governance/government has attracted increasingly close scrutiny, giving rise to a surge of monographs and edited volumes, special journal issues, and countless articles on the subject.[4] There is now even at least one specialized journal devoted specifically to domestic court management and judicial governance.[5]

Scholarly and public interest in the governance of courts has been reinforced by a confluence of factors. Foremost among these are the controversies surrounding national court governance reforms and, in particular, the introduction of judicial councils—typically constitutionally entrenched bodies vested with far-reaching powers over judicial careers and court management. The establishment of judicial councils in Latin American and Central and Eastern Europe (CEE) countries was

[2] eg Doris Marie Provine, 'Judicial Government' (1988) 51 Law and Contemporary Problems 83.

[3] Gar Yein Ng, 'A Discipline of Judicial Governance?' (2011) 7(1) Utrecht Law Review 102, 104, and 115.

[4] Pablo Castillo-Ortiz, *Judicial Governance and Democracy in Europe* (Springer 2023) (examining empirically the relationship between judicial governance and democracy based on a dataset of forty-six European countries); Tim Bunjevac, *Judicial Self-Governance in the New Millenium: An Institutional and Policy Framework* (Springer 2021); Daniela Piana, *Judicial Accountabilities in New Europe: From Rule of Law to Quality of Justice* (Ashgate 2010); Carlo Guarnieri, 'Appointment and Career of Judges in Continental Europe: The Rise of Judicial Self-Government' (2004) 24(1–2) Legal Studies 169; David Kosař and Katarína Šipulová, 'Politics of Judicial Governance' in Mark Tushnet and Dimitry Kochenov (eds), *Research Handbook on the Politics of Constitutional Law* (Elgar Publishing 2023) 262–85; Katarína Šipulová and others, 'Judicial Self-Government Index: Towards Better Understanding the Role of Judges in Governing the Judiciary' (2023) 17 Regulation and Governance 22. An important special issue is David Kosař (ed), 'Judicial Self-Governance in Europe' (2018) 19(7) German Law Journal 1567–2188.

[5] Launched by the International Association for Court Administration, the *International Journal for Court Administration* (https://iacajournal.org/about) is an online journal that comes closest to a specialized periodical dedicated to this field.

driven by democratic and post-communist transformations and actively promoted by institutions such as the World Bank, the Council of Europe (CoE), and the European Union (EU). Yet in many states these reforms failed to produce the expected results, prompting scholars to critically reassess the role and performance of judicial councils and their impact on judicial independence, democracy, and the rule of law.[6] Other interrelated factors fuelling domestic debates include the opportunities and demands arising from technological innovation and digitization, the imperatives of advancing gender and racial equality within the judicial branch,[7] and the challenges posed by the global pandemic for the administration of justice and the protection of procedural rights.[8] The stakes in these developments are considerable. The positioning and autonomy of courts vis-à-vis the executive, legislatures, and other power brokers in domestic systems remain a live issue across the board. The question has become particularly acute against the backdrop of democratic and rule-of-law backsliding within the EU[9] and in its wider neighbourhood, notably in Turkey/Türkiye, Russia, and Israel. It is even more pressing today in light of the troubling erosion of the rule-of-law safeguards in the United States under the Trump 2.0 administration.

The existence of judicial governance as a sprawling and dynamic area of study and as a field of legal-institutional practice is no longer in doubt. Yet it continues to pose taxonomic challenges. The varied and inconsistent use of key terminology, coupled with unresolved overlaps with contiguous concepts, blurs both its content and its outer limits.[10] To address potential sources of confusion, some basic distinctions must be drawn at the outset. In one strand of literature, 'judicial governance' is taken to mean governance *by* and *through* courts—that is, the regulation of conduct or activities by courts as a form of global, transnational, or domestic governance in a broad sense.[11] This reading casts courts as agents exercising governance over other actors rather than as recipients of governance by external entities. While a legitimate perspective, this is not the sense in which the term will be used here. Nor does it align with the standard interpretation of judicial governance developed within the eponymous

[6] Nuno Garoupa and Tom Ginsburg, 'Guarding the Guardians: Judicial Councils and Judicial Independence' (2009a) 57 American Journal of Comparative Law 103; Nuno Garoupa and Tom Ginsburg, 'The Comparative Law and Economics of Judicial Councils' (2009b) 27(1) Berkeley Journal of International Law 53; Michal Bobek and David Kosař, 'Global Solutions, Local Damages: A Critical Study in Judicial Councils in Central and Eastern Europe' (2014) 15(7) German Law Journal 1257; David Kosař, 'Beyond Judicial Councils: Forms, Rationales and Impact of Judicial Self-Governance in Europe' (2018) 19(7) German Law Journal 1567, 1586.

[7] Garoupa and Ginsburg 2009a (n 6) 116–17; Kosař and Šipulová (n 4) 277–78.

[8] Guy Lurie, 'Ministerial Emergency Powers over Court Administration in the Israeli Judiciary' (2021) 12(2) International Journal for Court Administration 1; Kosař and Šipulová (n 4) 263.

[9] eg Laurent Pech and Kim Lane Scheppele, 'Illiberalism Within: Rule of Law Backsliding in the EU' (2017) 19 Cambridge Yearbook of European Legal Studies 3; Kriszta Kovács and Kim Lane Scheppele, 'The Fragility of an Independent Judiciary: Lessons from Hungary and Poland—And the European Union' (2018) 51(3) Communist and Post-Communist Studies 189–200; Robert Bottner and Hermann-Josef Blanke (eds), *The Rule of Law under Threat: Eroding Institutions and European Remedies* (Edward Elgar Publishing 2024).

[10] Yein (n 3) 102; Kosař and Šipulová (n 4) 265.

[11] Christopher A Whytock, 'Transnational Judicial Governance' (2012) 2(1) St John's Journal of International and Comparative Law 55; Christopher A Whytock, 'Litigation, Arbitration, and the Transnational Shadow of the Law' (2007–08) 18 Duke Journal of Comparative and International Law 449; Konrad Schiemann, 'Judicial Governance: A Judge's Perspective' (2006) Inter Alia 84.

scholarly discipline. This book instead frames (international) courts as recipients of governance and focuses specifically on the institutions, practices, and norms that together constitute judicial governance as a field of (international) institutional law.

Secondly, in the domestic context the terms 'judicial governance' and 'judicial self-governance/government' are often used interchangeably. This can be explained by the fluid boundaries between the external and internal dimensions of judicial governance and the push-and-pull among judiciaries, (semi-)external self-governance bodies, and institutions fully external to the judicial system. In many national jurisdictions, powers over judicial appointments and promotions have been transferred to judicial councils. Although frequently regarded as organs of judicial *self*-governance and occupying the intermediary position of buffers between courts and political branches, this categorization is not foolproof: judicial councils are institutionally separate from courts and thus properly external to them.[12] This book focuses on the governance of *international* courts, for which no equivalents to judicial councils exist. Here, the imperative of judicial independence is reinforced through stronger institutional autonomy and by placing the analogues of court services (known as 'registries') *within* the court structure. The distinction between judicial governance proper (the external dimension) and judicial *self*-governance (the internal dimension) is worth maintaining—and, indeed, drawn even more sharply—at the international level. Accordingly, in this chapter and throughout this volume, the term 'judicial governance' refers primarily to the *external* governance of courts by political or executive organs and not to (internal) judicial *self*-governance, unless specified otherwise. This does not negate the close and necessary interplay between the external and internal dimensions in the practice of international, and still more so national, judicial governance.[13]

Thirdly, 'judicial governance' is sometimes interpreted too narrowly, as domestic judicial studies scholars have also observed. It tends to be reduced to a single subset of governance activity: judicial personnel management, encompassing the selection, appointment, promotion, and disqualification of judges.[14] Yet court governance extends beyond judicial careers and disciplinary matters to include many other spheres of activity without which courts would be unable to function effectively and accountably: law-making on the organization of the judiciary, institutional oversight and review, budgetary allocation, financial auditing, and other management functions.[15] This book adopts the view that the field of judicial governance is broader than any one of these governance functions. On this understanding, it is 'an amalgamation of different activities required and studied in and out of courts by various actors', extending well beyond 'judicial administration', 'court management', or 'justice administration'.[16]

[12] cf Bobek and Kosař (n 6) 1266; Kosař and Šipulová (n 4) 262; Šipulová and others (n 4) 26. See Section 2.3.2.1.

[13] For discussion, see Sections 2.3.2.1 and 2.4.2.

[14] Kosař and Šipulová (n 4) 265.

[15] ibid ('a much broader field that concerns every single aspect of courts' functioning, including efficiency, transparency, ethical issues, and a more mundane day-to-day agenda of court administration, as well as … the relationship of the judiciary with the executive and the legislature.'); Castillo-Ortiz (n 4) 2 ('Judicial governance is about how to recruit judges, and by whom. It is about how and when to impose disciplinary sanctions on them. It is about how to administer, manage, and finance the judicial branch, and about how to ensure its independence and efficiency').

[16] Ng (n 3) 102 (defining 'judicial administration' as 'the way judges adjudicate and organise their hearings in the context of their court organisation'; 'court management' as 'organisation management of courts

Put differently, judicial governance may be defined as 'a structured model of social coordination which produces and implements a set of institutions, rules and practices which are collectively binding and which regulate how the judicial branch exercises its functions'.[17] As noted in Chapter 1, it is this broader conception—focusing on the institutions, practices, and norms that constitute the *external* judicial governance of international courts and tribunals—that is central to the present book.[18]

The task of demarcating 'judicial governance' more precisely—in terms of the activities and actors it encompasses—requires closer attention to its constituent elements: the basic characteristics of 'judicial', 'external', and 'governance'.[19] What does the qualifier 'judicial' mean, and what implications does it carry for the nature of an organ or activity and its relationship with the other departments of power? How does 'governance' differ from adjacent terms such as 'government' or 'administration'—and is the preference for the former term a substantive choice or merely a matter of terminological fashion? Addressing these elementary definitional questions is essential to clarify what the composite notion of 'judicial governance' covers and what it excludes. Only once clarity has been attained in this regard can the chapter turn to the further question of whether, and how, judicial governance is reconfigured when transposed to the international domain.[20]

2.3 Judicial Governance at the Domestic Level

2.3.1 Judicial versus non-judicial: independence, not insulation

What is meant by 'judicial', why are judicial functions standardly defined through independence, and how absolute is the magic spell of 'judicial independence'? No court—be it national or international—can exist in an institutional vacuum. To be able to fulfil their raison d'être, courts must be embedded in a broader organizational framework of a national government or another (supranational, international, or transitional) form of public administration. Courts are linked to one or more political and executive bodies tasked, on the one hand, with securing the practical bases for their operations and catering to their resource and organizational support needs and, on the other, with ensuring requisite forms of accountability (eg personal, disciplinary, managerial, and budgetary).[21] Judicial candidates need to be vetted, appointed or elected, receive further professional training, be subjected to professional ethics regimes, and be held to the respective standards. They must be provided with

in the context of a justice system'), and 'justice administration' as 'the whole gamut of organisations involved in the justice field ... [including] courts, prisons, fines collection, notaries, bailiffs, judicial training').

17 Šipulová and others (n 4) 26.

18 Sergey Vasiliev and Niels Blokker, 'Introduction', in this volume.

19 Section 2.3.

20 Section 2.4.

21 Accountability is 'a relationship between an actor and a forum in which the actor is obliged to explain and justify his conduct, the forum can pose questions and pass judgement, and the actor may face consequences': Francesco Contini and Richard Mohr, 'Reconciling Independence and Accountability in Judicial Systems' (2007) 3(2) Utrecht Law Review 26, 31 (citing M Bovens).

institutional and personal guarantees of independence such as adequate terms of service (tenure, remuneration, social security guarantees, and basic safety) and status (privileges and immunities). Law clerks and administrative support staff must be allocated to assist judges in their work. Adequate budgets, premises, materials, and logistical support should be placed at courts' disposal, without which their work would be rendered practically impossible. At the same time, accountability modalities such as reporting duties, oversight, disciplinary measures, and financial audits must be instituted to safeguard the judiciary's professionalism, integrity, and responsiveness to societal needs, and to prevent and act swiftly on misconduct, malpractice, or mismanagement.

Independent courts are necessarily dependent on all those externalities and attuned to the needs of society, and this is not paradoxical. Political dynamics and changing circumstances and demands produce shifts in the prevailing interpretations and configurations of the role and accountability of judges vis-à-vis the public. Nowhere do judiciaries work in blissful isolation from the other branches of government, and hence from politics.[22] This is for the better but also for the worse, as Zimmer put it:

> Over time, the larger political and institutional contexts and frameworks of government within which the judiciary operates run through erratic cycles of greater and lesser rationality, the consequences of which may threaten, undermine, ignore, or call for the repeal of declarations of judicial self-governance and independence on any number of legitimate, contrived, irrelevant, or sometimes spectacularly presumptive and histrionically elaborated grounds.[23]

Regardless, and particularly when faced with such oscillations, courts must remain independent both as judicial bodies and as the individuals composing them. This is not only the basic premise and key rationale of the democratic principle of the separation of powers,[24] but also the cornerstone guarantee of the rule of law.[25]

In domestic systems, the need to provide the judiciary with guarantees of individual independence, institutional autonomy, and adequate instrumentalities is taken for granted—in theory if not always in practice. It is widely accepted that the judicial branch should not be at the whim of the executive or legislature, which hold the purse strings and are equipped (and at times tempted) to pinch its lifelines. Courts must be

[22] Ng (n 3) 102–03 ('court activities are not merely in the sphere of judicial competence ... but they fit also within the responsibility of government, ergo politics').

[23] Markus B Zimmer, 'Judicial System Institutional Frameworks: An Overview of the Interplay between Self-Governance and Independence' (2011) 1 Utah Law Review 121, 137.

[24] James Crawford and Joe McIntyre, 'The Independence and Impartiality of the "International Judiciary"' in Shimon Shetreet and Christopher Forsyth (eds), *The Culture of Judicial Independence: Conceptual Foundations and Practical Challenges* (Brill 2012) 193 (the doctrine of the separation of power is a *means* of ensuring judicial independence—not a *cause*); Paul Mahoney, 'The International Judiciary: Independence and Accountability' (2008) 7 The Law and Practice of International Courts and Tribunals 313, 317.

[25] Judicial Group on Strengthening Judicial Integrity, 'Bangalore Principles of Judicial Conduct' (as revised at the Round Table Meeting of Chief Justices held at the Peace Palace, The Hague, 25–26 November 2002) Value 1 ('Judicial independence is a prerequisite to the rule of law and a fundamental guarantee of a fair trial'); Theodor Meron, 'Judicial Independence and Impartiality in International Criminal Tribunals' (2005) 99(2) *American* Journal of International Law 359, 359 ('Judicial independence is critical for the rule of law').

supported institutionally and budgetarily while being shielded from *improper* interference, even if disguised as measures to enhance accountability and effectiveness. By extension, they should possess sufficient room for manoeuvre in respect of the internal organization of adjudication and resource management at the level of courts and chambers (judicial *self*-governance).[26] Although there is no paradox between judicial *independence* and courts' irreducible *dependence* on justice ministries and parliaments, tensions pervade these relationships in practice. Demarcating judicial independence vis-à-vis the legitimate competences of other government branches is often contentious. Balancing it against judicial accountability is a delicate act, with margins for excesses and abuse either way.

The judicial versus non-judicial dichotomy is central to categorizing the organs and the decisions or activities judicial independence that covers, and it is also key to the present chapter's taxonomic task of determining what *judicial* governance is. The principle of judicial independence applies, firstly, to the components of an adjudicatory system—courts, tribunals, and, in certain cases, other (quasi-)judicial organs, whatever their label and specialization, that are designed to function as courts of law. Secondly, it extends to the exercise of such bodies' *adjudicatory* functions, ie substantive decision-making in individual cases, disputes, or advisory questions, whatever their subject-matter, brought before them for resolution in that judicial capacity. By contrast, with respect to their operation as institutions and the administrative aspects of their work, such bodies are not necessarily and universally entitled to the same absolute degree of independence. Judicial bodies are often 'appended' to executive, monitoring, and controlling organs performing organizational services, human resources management, and other forms of support. Courts bear financial and administrative accountability and are subject to oversight like any other public organization within a governmental structure. Yet any such management control and accountability measures must be designed and operationalized in full awareness of the *judicial* nature of the body and strictly in conformity with the separation of powers principle. They should never compromise judicial independence, which reigns supreme in matters within the intimate sphere of adjudication.

The bedrock principle of judicial organization, judicial independence is the DNA of the judicial function.[27] Ultimately, it is what distinguishes judging from *non-judicial* decision-making, which may also be carried out through the application of law to facts, albeit without the same guarantees of integrity associated with adjudication. Judicial independence is a complex and multi-layered phenomenon in which the individual/decisional and the institutional/structural dimensions are typically distinguished.[28]

[26] Šipulová and others (n 4) 26 (judicial self-governance 'captures the extent to which judges and courts participate in judicial governance'); John Bell, 'Sweden's Contribution to Governance of the Judiciary' (2007) 50 Scandinavian Studies in Law 83, 85 ('Cases cannot be resolved if there are too few judges, too few courtrooms, or too few support staff to enable the courts to function. As a result, the role of judges as resources managers can be critical for the character of justice.')

[27] Garoupa and Ginsburg 2009a (n 6) 105 ('inherent in the notion of judging'); Crawford and McIntyre (n 24) 212 ('necessary implication of the judicial function'); Mahoney (n 24) 316–17 ('indissociable from the very concept of justice').

[28] eg UNODC, 'Commentary on The Bangalore Principles of Judicial Conduct' (September 2007) 39 para 23 ('Judicial independence refers to both the individual and the institutional independence required for decision-making. Judicial independence is ... both a state of mind and a set of institutional and operational arrangements').

The former protects every judge's decision-making autonomy from *improper* external pressures such as political or private interests, whatever their source—litigants, other judges on the bench or higher up in the hierarchy, political parties, justice ministries, or other external actors. By contrast, the institutional dimension secures the autonomy of the judiciary as 'a coequal branch of government' from interference by the 'political' branches.[29] It enables individual independence through structural arrangements regarding how the judiciary is staffed, budgeted, organized, and overseen. These dimensions are interwoven and mutually reinforcing. Judges are not likely to be impervious to outside interference where their appointments and case allocations are patronage-driven and tainted by improper motives, where they do not benefit from security of tenure and adequate remuneration, or where their professional regulation and disciplinary oversight mechanisms are weak or unavailable.[30] Importantly, the interplay between decisional and structural aspects is not free from tensions either. If institutional independence is interpreted so that it closes the judiciary off to all accountability and oversight, it is bound to develop pathological symptoms that will eat away at the independence of individual judges.[31]

The principle of judicial independence is strongly rooted in domestic constitutional traditions, and key aspects of judicial status are often enshrined in constitutions.[32] It is a core requirement of the right to a fair and public hearing before an independent and impartial tribunal established by law. As such, it is set out in every international and regional human rights treaty, usually in tandem with the twin principle of judicial impartiality.[33] The latter refers to the absence of *inappropriate* biases or prejudices on the part of a judge; it does not require absolute impartiality but only guards against undue outside influences.[34]

[29] eg Anthony J Scirica, 'Judicial Governance and Judicial Independence' (2015) 90(3) New York University Law Review 779, 782.

[30] Commentary on The Bangalore Principles (n 28) 30 para 23: 'an individual judge may possess that state of mind, but if the court over which he or she presides is not independent of the other branches of government in what is essential to its functions, the judge cannot be said to be independent.'

[31] Bobek and Kosař (n 6) 1290 (cautioning against models which 'evince a strong favour for institutional independence of judges (or rather judicial leadership and the court presidents in particular), to the detriment of individual judicial independence and impartiality of judges').

[32] Zimmer (n 22) 122–24, 138 (noting, however, that few constitutions pay attention to the judiciary's institutional independence and the organizational framework giving it effect).

[33] Universal Declaration of Human Rights (adopted by UNGA 10 December 1948) UN Doc A/RES/217(III) Art 10 ('a fair and public hearing by an independent and impartial tribunal'); European Convention on Human Rights (opened for signature 4 November 1950, entered into force 3 September 1953) 213 UNTS 221 (ECHR) Art 6(1) ('a fair and public hearing within a reasonable time by an independent and impartial tribunal established by law'); International Covenant on Civil and Political Rights (opened for signature 16 December 1966, entered into force 23 March 1976) 999 UNTS 172, Art 14(1) ('a fair and public hearing by a competent, independent and impartial tribunal established by law'); American Convention on Human Rights (opened for signature 22 November 1969, entered into force 18 July 1987) 1144 UNTS 144 (ACHR) Art 8(1) ('the right to a hearing, with due guarantees and within a reasonable time, by a competent, independent, and impartial tribunal, previously established by law'); Charter of Fundamental Rights (18 December 2000, OJ 2000/C 3564/01) Art 47 ('a fair and public hearing within a reasonable time by an independent and impartial tribunal previously established by law'). Cf African Charter on Human and Peoples' Rights (adopted 27 June 1981, entered into force 21 October 1986) (1982) OAU Doc CAB/LEG/67/3 rev. 5, 21 ILM 58 (Banjul Charter) Art 7(1) ('the right to be tried within a reasonable time by an impartial court or tribunal').

[34] Crawford and McIntyre (n 24) 197.

Both tenets are functional and context-dependent rather than absolutist concepts because judicial independence and impartiality serve, and hence are subordinated to, the ultimate goal of ensuring the proper performance of the judicial function.[35] Within this duo, it is arguably judicial independence that is conceptually subordinate to impartiality—which otherwise cannot be demonstrably guaranteed—rather than the other way around.[36] Judicial impartiality certainly qualifies as a general principle of law.[37] But the same is said to be less clear, albeit not unequivocally, for judicial independence. This is because of divergent interpretations and the widespread practice of imposing limitations in domestic jurisdictions.[38] Be that as it may, judicial independence is typically couched as a secondary, instrumental principle, protected not for its own sake but as a means to guarantee the integrity and impartial character of judicial decisions.[39] Accordingly, the protections flowing from judicial independence are not absolute but subject to legitimate caveats, notably those related to the imperative of ensuring an *accountable* judiciary as another instrumental goal. Judicial independence and accountability are not a zero-sum game or opposite poles: they are mutually supportive, two sides of the same coin.[40] Domestic experience has amply shown that an excessive degree of institutional independence, when injected into an unprepared and unaccountable judiciary, gives rise to pathological symptoms and unseemly practices, including poor performance, corruption, and corporatism.[41]

The international human rights conventions do not elaborate in any detail on how the requirements of judicial independence bear on the competences of court-governing organs. Some guidance in this regard can be gleaned from the—often dialogical—jurisprudence of regional integration and human rights courts.[42] In the

[35] ibid 197–99.

[36] ibid 200, 202; Scirica (n 29) 781; John A Ferejohn and Larry D Kramer, 'Independent Judges, Dependent Judiciary: Institutionalizing Judicial Restraint' (2002) New York University Law Review 962, 965–76.

[37] Judgment, *Prosecutor* v *Furundžija*, IT-95-17/1-A, AC, ICTY, 21 July 2000, Declaration of Judge Shahabuddeen, para 256.

[38] André Nollkaemper, 'The Independence of the Domestic Judiciary in International Law' (2006) 17 Finnish Yearbook of International Law 261, 284 (qualifying judicial independence as a principle of general international law only tentatively considering the 'very imperfect application of this principle in practice' and that international law cannot ignore the many limitations thereon in domestic law).

[39] eg Contini and Mohr (n 21) 28; Pasquale Pasquino, 'Prolegomena to a Theory of Judicial Power' (2003) 2 The Law and Practice of International Courts and Tribunals 11, 25 ('an instrument to achieve the goal of *impartiality*'); Meron (n 25) 361 ('a dependent judge can hardly be impartial'); CoE, Consultative Council of European Judges, 'On Standards Concerning the Independence of the Judiciary and the Irremovability of Judges', Opinion No 1, 23 November 2001 ('CCJE Opinion No 1(2001)') para 11 (judicial independence is 'the guarantee of impartiality'); CoE, Consultative Council of European Judges, 'On the Principles and Rules Governing Judges' Professional Conduct, in Particular Ethics, Incompatible Behaviour and Impartiality', Opinion No 3, 19 November 2002 ('the pre-condition of the impartiality of the judge').

[40] As affirmed eg by Scirica (n 29) 781; Contini and Mohr (n 21) 28; Crawford and McIntyre (n 24) 199; Garoupa and Ginsburg 2009a (n 6) 131; Mahoney (n 24) 348.

[41] Bobek and Kosař (n 6) 1258 ('Making a post-totalitarian judiciary a self-administrative body before any genuine internal change and renewal has taken place may result—formally and constitutionally—in establishing institutionally independent judiciary without many individually independent judges in it'); Carlo Guarnieri, 'Judicial Independence in Europe: Threat or Resource for Democracy' (2013) 49 Journal of Representative Democracy 347–59, 353 (on Romania: this fostered 'a "supremacist" posture on the part of courts, in which the judiciary functions like a state within a state with little accountability') and 355.

[42] David Kosař and Lucas Lixinski, 'Domestic Judicial Design by International Human Rights Courts' (2015) 109(4) American Journal of International Law 713.

context of domestic rule-of-law backsliding over the past decade, the European Court of Human Rights (ECtHR) and the Court of Justice of the European Union (CJEU) have increasingly weighed in on issues of judicial organization in the member states. In particular, they have had to rule on the (non-)compliance of judicial governance arrangements with judicial independence and the requirement that tribunals be 'established by law'.[43] Moreover, numerous resolutions and opinions adopted by international and regional organizations, as well as recommendations by expert groups, contain soft-law restatements of the principles of judicial independence in connection with court administration and governance. What follows is an incomplete list:

- 1982 IBA Minimum Standards;[44]
- 1983 Montreal Declaration;[45]
- 1985 United Nations Basic Principles on the Independence of the Judiciary;[46]
- 1995 Beijing Statement;[47]
- 1998 European Charter on the statute for judges;[48]
- 1999 Universal Charter of the Judge;[49]
- 2002 Bangalore Principles of Judicial Conduct and 2010 Measures for the Effective Implementation;[50]
- 2005 Burgh House Principles on the guarantees of independence of the international judiciary;[51]

[43] ECHR art 6(1); EU Charter of Fundamental Rights art 47. Eg Case C-64/16 (*Associação Sindical dos Juízes Portugueses* v *Tribunal de Contas*) Judgment, GC, CJEU, 27 February 2018; *Denisov* v *Ukraine*, Judgment, App no 76639/11, GC, ECtHR, 25 September 2018; *Ramos Nunes de Carvalho e Sá* v *Portugal*, Judgment, Apps nos 55391/13 etc, GC, ECtHR, 6 November 2018; *Ástráðsson* v *Iceland*, Judgment, App no 26374/18, GC, ECtHR, 1 December 2020. Laurent Pech and Dimitry Kochenov, 'Respect for the Rule of Law in the Case Law of the European Court of Justice: A Casebook Overview of Key Judgments since the Portuguese Judges Case' (Sieps 2021:3) <https://sieps.se/media/wgzjhqje/sieps-2021_3-eng-web.pdf >; Iain Cameron, 'The European Court of Human Rights and Rule of Law Backsliding' (European Policy Analysis, Sieps March 2023:4epa) <https://sieps.se/media/dhwamjyv/2023_4epa.pdf>; Haukur Logi Karlsson, 'The Emergence of the Established "By Law" Criterion for Reviewing European Judicial Appointments' (2022) 23(8) German Law Journal 1051; Kosař and Šipulová (n 4) 264, 273.

[44] International Bar Association (IBA), 'Minimum Standards of Judicial Independence' (1982).

[45] Universal Declaration on the Independence of Justice (adopted at the First World Conference on the Independence of Justice, Montreal, 10 June 1983).

[46] Basic Principles on the Independence of the Judiciary (adopted at the Seventh United Nations Congress on the Prevention of Crime and the Treatment of Offenders held at Milan from 26 August to 6 September 1985; endorsed by UNGA resolutions 40/32 of 29 November 1985 and 40/146 of 13 December 1985).

[47] LAWASIA, 'Beijing Statement of Principles of the Independence of the Judiciary in the LAWASIA Region' (adopted 19 August 1995, amended 28 August 1997).

[48] European Association of Judges, 'European Charter on the statute of judges' (DAJ/DOC (98) 23, Strasbourg, 8–10 July 1998).

[49] International Association of Judges, 'The Universal Charter of the Judge' (adopted by the IAJ Central Council in Taiwan on 17 November 1999 and updated in Santiago de Chile on 14 November 2017).

[50] Bangalore Principles of Judicial Conduct (n 25) and 'Measures for the Effective Implementation of the Bangalore Principles of Judicial Conduct (The Implementation Measures)' (adopted on 21–22 January 2010) ('Bangalore Principles Implementation Measures').

[51] 'The Burgh House Principles on the Independence of the International Judiciary' (adopted by the ILA Study Group on the Practice and Procedure of International Courts and Tribunals, in association with the Project on International Courts and Tribunals) in Philippe Sands, Campbell McLachlan, and Ruth MacKenzie, 'The Burgh House Principles on the Independence of the International Judiciary' (2005) 4 The Law and Practice of International Courts and Tribunals 251 ('The Burgh House Principles').

- 2007 International Commission of Jurists' Practitioners' Guide;[52]
- 2008 Mount Scopus Principles;[53]
- 2010 Council of Europe Committee of Ministers' recommendations;[54]
- 2010 Magna Carta of Judges[55] and the Consultative Council of European Judges' opinions;[56]
- 2010 Venice Commission Report on Independence of Judges;[57]
- African Commission on Human and People's Rights Principles and Guidelines on the right to a fair trial;[58] and
- 2025 ELI-Mount Scopus European Standards.[59]

On the one hand, it is clear that there is no deficit of non-binding rules on organizing the judiciary's relationship with other branches, from which some general parameters of oversight over courts can be derived.[60] These progressive soft-law codifications overlap in some areas and can serve states and organizations as helpful frames of reference in reforming judicial systems and setting up their governance schemes. On the other hand, these recommendatory provisions have never consolidated into binding norms at the regional, let alone the global, level. More is not always better. The oversaturation of this sphere with non-enforceable standards of varying thematic emphases and degrees of authoritativeness may point to fragmentation and unsteady progress in this domain. It is still a long way before a compelling and uniform normative framework opposable to states can emerge.

2.3.2 External versus internal: functions and institutions

2.3.2.1 Two dimensions and self-governance

Another distinction that is key to defining 'judicial governance' for the purposes of this book is that between its external and internal dimensions. Judicial governance

[52] International Commission of Jurists, 'International Principles on the Independence and Accountability of Judges, Lawyers and Prosecutors, Practitioners Guide No 1' (2007).

[53] International Project of Judicial Independence of the International Association of Judicial Independence and World Peace, 'Mount Scopus International Standards of Judicial Independence' (approved in 2008, consolidated in 2015) ('Mt Scopus Standards').

[54] Council of Europe (CoE), Committee of Ministers, 'Judges: Independence, Efficiency and Responsibilities', Recommendation CM/Rec(2010)12 and explanatory memorandum (adopted 17 November 2010).

[55] CoE, Consultative Council of European Judges, 'Magna Carta of Judges (Fundamental Principles)' (2010).

[56] CCJE Opinion No 1(2001) (n 36); CCJE Opinion No 2 (2001) of the CCJE, 'On the Funding and Management of Courts with reference to the Efficiency of the Judiciary and to Article 6 of the European Convention on Human Rights' (CCJE Opinion No 2(2001)).

[57] European Commission for Democracy through Law, 'Report on the Independence of the Judicial System', Part I: The Independence of Judges (adopted 12–13 March 2010) ('Venice Commission Report on Independence of Judges').

[58] African Union, African Commission on Human and Peoples' Rights, 'Principles and Guidelines on the Right to a Fair Trial and Legal Assistance in Africa' (adopted 29 May 2003).

[59] European Law Institute, 'ELI-Mount Scopus European Standards of Judicial Independence' (approved by the ELI Council on 9 October 2024 and by the ELI Membership on 27 November 2024; published on 2 December 2024).

[60] For discussion, see Mahoney (n 24) 314–15.

at the domestic level is a decentralized—or rather, polycentric—enterprise involving a plethora of actors located within and outside the judiciary, and sometimes both, as they move between the two. The legal-institutional and political parameters of engagement between them, and the division of labour and competences, are contested and in constant flux.[61] The shifting balance of power among judiciaries, political branches, and intermediary bodies over the governance of courts affects the quality of judicial independence and their accountable and effective operation. Some governance tasks are performed within the courts themselves, while others are reserved to (semi-)external organs exercising regulatory, disciplinary, and oversight powers. There is an irreducible degree of interpenetration and personal overlap between the internal and external sides of judicial governance. In addition to the co-ordinational (as opposed to directional) character of governance,[62] it is notable that the same actors—chief justices, court presidents, and other top judicial officials—carry out governance responsibilities both 'on the inside' as managers of judicial organizations and 'on the outside' as court representatives and members of external governance bodies.[63]

Judicial *self*-governance is an omnipresent, yet confusingly elastic, notion in the domestic judicial studies literature. As an aspect of broader 'judicial governance', judicial *self*-governance is commonly understood as the degree to which judges participate in (external) judicial governance rather than as a binary distinction between judicial self- and non-self-governance.[64] Judicial *self*-governance bodies are typically defined as those comprising at least one judge and empowered to decide or advise on matters of court administration and judicial careers.[65] Scholars thus include a wide array of officials and organs under this heading: judicial councils, court presidents, praesidia, judicial academies and associations, appointment and promotion commissions, administrative tribunals, court services, and specialized departments in justice ministries.[66] Yet the breadth of such a definition raises difficulties, and there are nuances it neglects. Many of these bodies are *external* to the courts they govern, both institutionally and in terms of their composition. For example, judicial councils could rather be regarded as 'fourth-branch' institutions (guarantor or integrity branch) separate from the three classical branches of power.[67] The nexus between some 'judicial self-governance' organs and 'self-governed' courts is tenuous at best. They may feature little to no judicial membership or representation. For instance, judges sitting on those bodies do not necessarily represent the judicial corps. If anything can be summarily brought under judicial *self*-governance, whatever the degree of judicial influence, then

[61] Kosař (n 6) 1586.

[62] Section 2.3.3.

[63] Adam Blisa and David Kosař, 'Court Presidents: The Missing Piece in the Puzzle of Judicial Governance' (2018) 19(7) German Law Journal 2031; David Kosař and Samuel Spáč, 'Post-Communist Chief Justices in Slovakia: From Transmission Belts to Semi-Autonomous Actors' (2021) 13 Hague Journal of the Rule of Law 107.

[64] Kosař and Šipulová (n 4) 270 ('operat[ing] on a continuum rather than in the "either-or" fashion'); Kosař (n 6) 1572, 1594; Šipulová and others (n 4) 26.

[65] Kosař (n 6) 1586 (bodies 'with at least one judge whose primary function, entrenched in a legal norm, is to (a) decide about issues regarding court administration and/or the career of a judge, and/or (b) advise those who decide about such issues.')

[66] eg ibid 1571, 1581 (eg Germany), and 1587; Šipulová and others (n 4) 26.

[67] David Kosař, Katarína Šipulová, and Ondržej Kadlec, 'The Case for Judicial Councils as Fourth-Branch Institutions' (2024) 20 European Constitutional Law Review 82, 84.

the '*self-*' aspect becomes nominal and the broad notion of 'judicial self-governance' loses much of its descriptive value. A narrower approach is therefore preferable: reserving judicial *self-*governance for the internal dimension, while treating governance mechanisms *external* to the courts—even when judges are involved—as part of judicial governance proper.

The internal dimension of judicial governance refers to the sphere of self-organization and management within the court system that relates to its core business and falls under the managerial responsibility of judges. This is judicial *self-*governance in the narrow sense. Judicial independence requires that courts be granted sufficient autonomy to shield substantive decision-making from improper external influences and political interests. Within this framework, court presidents occupy apex positions, while presiding and senior judges oversee the day-to-day running of chambers with the support of staff. Most internal administrative matters connected with adjudication are handled within the system itself and, in some jurisdictions, with the assistance of dedicated and neutral court services. This arrangement is pragmatic: judges, clerks, and judicial administrators possess more first-hand knowledge of the routine functioning of courts than external bodies.[68] Elsewhere, notably in some CEE countries, court presidents also serve—sometimes prominently—on external governance bodies, a concentration of power that can be problematic.

The external dimension of judicial governance concerns the competences of organs situated outside the judiciary that exercise responsibilities in regulatory, institutional, human resources (ethical, disciplinary, and educational), and financial domains.[69] In domestic systems, this external sphere includes not only legislative bodies (parliaments) and executive organs (justice ministries) but also a range of dedicated oversight institutions: judicial councils, court services, appointment boards, and promotion committees. These are often labelled 'judicial *self-*governance bodies' because they operate in the judiciary's close orbit and, in some systems, judges participate—sometimes even dominate—in their work. Yet, as noted, these organs remain distinct from judicial organizations proper and therefore belong to the external dimension. The degree of judicial participation in governance varies considerably and is a recurring source of controversy. It is neither fixed nor absolute. In many states, judicial self-governance (in the broad sense of the term) has come under strain not only from authoritarian and populist governments[70] but also from legitimate critiques of self-referentiality, clientelism, and vulnerability to politicization.[71] Moreover, these dedicated governance organs do not exhaust the external dimension. Informal yet influential 'centres of gravity'—judicial academies, associations, and networks—can strengthen, undermine, or even partly displace official institutions, exerting

[68] Kosař and Šipulová (n 4) 268.

[69] Kosař (n 6) 1596–97; Šipulová and others (n 4) 26–27 (distinguishing eight dimensions of judicial governance: regulatory, personal, administrative, financial, educational, informational, digital, and ethical).

[70] Kosař (n 6) 1570 (on judicial reforms in Poland, Hungary, and Turkey: 'authoritarian and populist political leaders care about the control of judicial self-governance bodies').

[71] Kosař and Šipulová (n 4) 263 ('too much judicial self-governance may lead to self-replication, non-responsiveness and corporativism of judges') and 264 ('channels of politicisation of the judiciary never disappear completely').

significant impact on judicial independence and the rule of law.[72] The following section examines the main domestic models of (external) judicial governance.

2.3.2.2 Judicial governance models

In relation to domestic judicial governance institutions, the comparative literature discerns three principal contemporary models: (i) the Judicial Council; (ii) the Courts Service; and (iii) the Justice Ministry.[73] These models are ideal types rather than exact replicas of actual arrangements. Real-life schemes overlap, combine elements of different modes, and remain fluid as they evolve over time. Their idiosyncrasies invite further, at times inconsistent, classifications.[74] Alternative, if less representative, arrangements have also been identified. These include the socialist, hybrid, and *sui generis* models. The socialist model is no longer found in Europe but is still present in China, Cuba, Vietnam, North Korea, and some ex-USSR republics.[75] The hybrid schemes operate in a number of European and former socialist-camp countries.[76] The *sui generis* schemes are exemplified by the United States[77] and Israel.[78] These schemes do not capture the institutional pluralism of governance arrangements in Africa, the Middle East, and Asia, nor do they exhaust the spectrum of possibilities.

(i) The Judicial Council model entrusts decision-making over judicial careers (selection, appointment, promotions, discipline, and removal) and managerial powers (workload and complaints about courts' functioning) to independent colleges separate from both the courts and political functionaries in the executive and legislatures.[79]

[72] eg Guarnieri (n 41) 350 (reliance on judicial councils enhances the role of judicial associations in organising judges' participation in council elections); Kosař and Šipulová (n 4) 271 and 275–76 (judicial associations may politicize the judiciary and entrench patronage, gender segregation, and corruption); Kosař (n 6) 1579, 1592. On judicial associations (*correnti*) in Italy: Simone Benvenuti and Davide Paris, 'Judicial Self-Government in Italy: Merits, Limits and the Reality of an Export Model' (2018) 19(7) German Law Journal 1641, 1655; on France: Antoine Vauchez, 'The Strange Non-Death of Statism: Tracing the Ever Protracted Rise of Judicial Self-Government in France' (2018) 19(7) German Law Journal 1613.

[73] Bobek and Kosař (n 6) 1265–67; Castillo-Ortiz (n 4) 2–5 and 69–79; Kosař (n 6) 1585–86.

[74] For example, arrangements in England and Wales, Estonia, Finland, and Iceland are inconsistently classified as hybrid or otherwise.

[75] Under this model, powers over judicial careers and the court system are vested in the prosecutor-general, the supreme court, and court presidents, who remain under party control. Despite being defunct in Europe, the dominant supreme court and court presidents are the socialist model remnants surviving in post-communist European countries: Bobek and Kosař (n 6) 1266–68.

[76] eg Armenia, Azerbaijan, Cyprus, Hungary (after 2011), Kazakhstan, Luxembourg, Russia, Switzerland: Bobek and Kosař (n 6) 1266 and 1268 (on the 2011 transfer of power from the High Council for the Judiciary to the National Judicial-Office, rendering the Hungarian model hybrid). The Netherlands, too, has a judicial council as well as a courts service. Castillo-Ortiz (n 4) 6 (the hybrid model accounts for 17 per cent in his dataset of forty-six European jurisdictions).

[77] In the United States, state-level judges are elected, 'non-Article III' (magistrate, bankruptcy, administrative) federal judges are appointed for definite terms, and only 'Article III' federal judges at district and circuit courts and the Supreme Court, benefitting from elevated safeguards, are nominated by US President and appointed for life by the Senate: Bobek and Kosař (n 6) 1269. Disciplinary functions are exercised by the Judicial Conference and circuit judicial councils: Scirica (n 29) 784–87; Kosař and Šipulová (n 4) 271.

[78] In Israel, governance functions are entrusted to the Director of Courts who heads the Administration of Courts: Guy Lurie, Amnon Reichmann, and Yair Sagy, 'Agencification and the Administration of Courts in Israel' (2019) 14 Regulation and Governance 718, 720–21.

[79] Garoupa and Ginsburg 2009a (n 6) 119 (distinguishing housekeeping, appointment, and performance evaluation functions); Bobek and Kosař (n 6) 1266.

Besides judges, such bodies may also include political mandate-holders (eg heads of state *ex officio*), members of the legal professions, academics, and laypersons.[80] The rationale behind instituting councils is to insulate judicial appointment, promotion, and disciplinary decision-making from political interests and thereby enhance the independence (and, to a lesser degree, accountability) of the judicial system.[81] Reliance on this model has increased globally over the past four decades. In 1985, around 10 per cent of countries worldwide had judicial councils (or judicial appointment commissions) but by 2015 this number had grown to 60 per cent.[82] The model has swept across Latin America[83] and Europe.[84] In many countries, judicial councils were instituted as part of democratic transitions from dictatorial rule (eg in Spain and Portugal) and enshrined in constitutions in order to entrench judicial independence as an antidote to troubled historical legacies.[85]

The Judicial Council model presents a wide variation in specific arrangements. A further distinction is drawn between 'weak' councils with mere housekeeping functions akin to courts services and 'strong' ones that hold far-reaching powers over judicial careers.[86] The popularity of the model in Europe has been largely due to regional organizations' endorsement of its variant most closely resembling the arrangements in Italy.[87] The reception and reform of judicial councils in Central and Eastern European states proceeded in several waves: the 'transition' wave (1989–97)

[80] Judicial councils normally comprise multiple judges elected by their peers or, in some cases, by the parliament, to constitute the majority (Italy, Romania, and de facto Slovakia), the half (The Netherlands and de facto Slovakia), or the minority (eg France, Spain, and Portugal) of membership. Garoupa and Ginsburg 2009a (n 6) 120; Bobek and Kosař (n 6) 1268; Kosař (n 6) 1571, 1589; Castillo-Ortiz (n 4) 2–3; Guarnieri (n 4) 179–82; Guarnieri (n 41) 350.

[81] Nuno Garoupa and Tom Ginsburg, *Judicial Reputation* (Princeton University Press 2015) 103; Garnieri (n 4) 182–3; Guarnieri (n 41) 350; Bobek and Kosař (n 6) 1278–80; Šipulová and others (n 4) 22; Kosař and others (n 67) 82.

[82] Garoupa and Ginsburg (n 81) 101 and 138; Kosař and Šipulová (n 4) 262.

[83] In Latin America, supreme courts historically exercised appointment powers but were replaced by judicial council from late 1980s on: Castillo-Ortiz (n 4) 5; Andrea Pozas-Loyo and Julio Ríos-Figeroa, 'The Politics of Amendment Process: Supreme Court Influence in the Design of Judicial Councils' (2010) 89 Texas Law Review 1807, 1818–26; Garoupa and Ginsburg 2009a (n 6) 109; Garoupa and Ginsburg 2009b (n 6) 70–71 (on Brazil).

[84] eg Albania, Bosnia and Herzegovina, Bulgaria, Croatia, Estonia, France, Georgia, Greece, Hungary (before 2011), Italy, Kosovo Lithuania, Moldova, North Macedonia, Montenegro, Poland, Portugal, Romania, Serbia, Slovakia, Slovenia, Spain, Turkey, Ukraine: Castillo-Ortiz (n 4) 2–3, 6–7, 29, 61 (the model accounts for 50 per cent in the dataset of forty-six European states and is 'overrepresented' in countries with intermediate liberal democracy score; the fact that its adopters generally have a democracy of worse quality than, for example, countries with a courts service has more to do with historical trajectories, economic development, and other factors).

[85] For a comparative overview: Garoupa and Ginsburg 2009a (n 6) 106–17; ibid 121–24 (on constitutionalized vs. non-constitutionalized councils); Garoupa and Ginsburg 2009b (n 6) 67–82; Kosař (n 6) 1600.

[86] Castillo-Ortiz (n 4) 6–7. The Netherlands exemplifies the former model and Italy the latter. Elaine Mak, 'Judicial Self-Government in the Netherlands: Demarcating Autonomy' (2018) 19(7) German Law Journal 1801; Benvenuti and Paris (n 72).

[87] For a searing critique of the Euro-variant's undemocratic, opaque origins, as well as the CoE/EU role and domestic judicial elites' self-interest in its promotion: Bobek and Kosař (n 6) 1259–62, 1269–78; Bogdan Iancu, 'Government and Governance: The Constitutional Politics of Institutional Neutrality' in Bogdan Iancu and Elena Simina Tănăsescu (eds), *Governance and Constitutionalism: Law, Politics and Institutional Neutrality* (Routledge 2020) 27–28.

and the 'pre-accession' wave (1998–2006).[88] In that historical context, the model was exalted as 'best practice' in strengthening court systems and judicial independence in post-communist CEE countries that previously had ministerial or socialist models. The supranational promotion of the peculiar 'Euro-model'—'a *mélange* of judicial wishes'[89]—went so far as to render its adoption a soft, yet de facto binding, standard for EU accession. It was part of the 'pre-accession conditionality' in the lead-up to EU enlargements of 2004 (Czech Republic, Poland, Slovakia, Hungary, Slovenia, and the three Baltic states) and 2007 (Romania and Bulgaria).[90] The Czech Republic was the only CEE state to successfully resist the Commission's nudging.[91]

In its early adopters among countries with a more established tradition of judicial independence and *l'esprit de corps*, the model has fared fairly well, though not flawlessly.[92] However, in the new European democracies burdened with authoritarian justice baggage, this approach proved ill-suited and even counterproductive. Their senior judges had been socialized under illiberal values. The introduction of judge-dominated councils did not cure the judiciary of its maladies but made matters far worse.[93] A key problem with this governance reform was that it favoured judicial self-governance over accountability and failed to guard against *internal* threats to the judiciary's integrity. It enabled corporativism, nepotism, and the 'hijacking' of the system by non-representative groups of 'judicial bosses' (court presidents).[94] This is a cautionary tale about how an emphasis on *institutional* judicial independence—rather than on judicial ethics and *individual* independence—tends to undermine compliance with the principle in practice.[95] This problem only worsens over time because junior judges are selected and socialized within this perverse system.

[88] Piana (n 4) 162–65. Kosař (n 6) 1599–600 names also the third, illiberal populist, wave in Hungary and Poland.

[89] Bobek and Kosař identify the elements of the 'Euro-model' judicial council: constitutional status; judges are in the majority and elected by peers; concentration of real decision-making and not mere advisory powers over judicial careers; and chief justice of the highest court or a neutral head of state as a council chair: Bobek and Kosař (n 6) 1263, 1268, 1282.

[90] ibid 1261, 1275–76. Garoupa and Ginsburg (n 82) 137 and 139; Castillo-Ortiz (n 4) 35; Šipulová and others (n 4) 22 (the 'only game in town').

[91] Adam Blisa, Tereza Papoušková, and Marina Urbániková, 'Judicial Self-Government in Czechia: Europe's Black Sheep?' (2018) 19(7) German Law Journal 1951.

[92] Italy's *Consiglio Superiore della Magistratura*—the Euro-model's prototype—is viewed as successful although it was said to perpetuate judicial corporativism and accountability deficits: Garoupa and Ginsburg 2009a (n 6) 108; Garnieri (n 4) 176–77; Bobek and Kosař (n 6) 1270, 1283; Benvenuti and Paris (n 72); Iancu (n 87) 27.

[93] Bobek and Kosař (n 6) 1280 ('outright disastrous consequences') and 1283–88 ('sad example' of Slovak National Judicial Council); Šipulová and others (n 4) 22–23; Iancu (n 87) 27 ('de-coupling of the administration of justice as a whole and the judiciary as a caste from the expected mechanisms of democratic and social accountability').

[94] ibid 1264, 1271–72, 1288 ('"mafia-like" structure of intra-judicial oppression, run in the name of "judicial independence"'); Samuel Spáč, Katarína Šipulová, and Marina Urbániková, 'Capturing the Judiciary from Inside: The Story of Judicial Self-Governance in Slovakia' (2018) 19(7) German Law Journal 1741. In a similar vein, see Garoupa and Ginsburg 2009a (n 6) 110; Garoupa and Ginsburg 2009b (n 6) 63–64.

[95] Garoupa and Ginsburg 2009a (n 6) 130 ('little evidence in favor of the widespread assumption that councils increase quality or independence in the aggregate'); Kosař and Spáč (n 63) 11 (on the politicization of Slovak chief justices despite the existence of the judicial council); Castillo-Ortiz (n 4) 18 (powerful judicial councils may threaten individual judges' independence); Kosař (n 6) 1591; Šipulová and others (n 4) 23.

The Judicial Council scheme in itself does not preclude the politicization of the judiciary. Rather, it shifts leverage to other actors, which in turn may fall under direct political influence and become conduits of undue interference.[96] Much depends on the extent of power a judicial council wields and on its composition; in particular, who presides over it, how its members are elected or appointed, whether its judicial members are dominant vis-à-vis other colleagues, and whether rank-and-file judges, rather than only the top echelon, have a say.[97] 'Court-packing' by a captured and compromised governance organ can erode judicial independence and the rule of law in drastic ways. The Polish *Krajowa Rada Sądownictwa* (National Council of Judiciary), following its takeover by the PiS party in late 2017, is a highly notorious but not the only example.[98] As 'fourth-branch institutions' safeguarding the integrity of the judiciary, judicial councils are vulnerable to capture not only by the political branches but also by powerful actors within the judiciary, who may be intent on securing control over the system and promoting narrow corporate interests. Furthermore, even properly operating judicial councils do not completely extinguish external influences on the judiciary. Other branches may still hold the reins over the regulatory sphere, court budgets, court president appointments, and judicial careers.[99] Finally, research has also shown that judicial councils neither enhance the efficiency of court performance nor increase public confidence in the judiciary.[100]

(ii) The Courts Service model is found in a number of European jurisdictions.[101] It refers to the allocation of competences for judicial administration (control over caseloads, supervision of registry offices), management (court housing, human resources, training), and budgeting to dedicated and neutral administrative

[96] Garnieri (n 4) 184–85; Kosař (n 6) 1591 ('Power is just transferred to other hands and new channels of politicization of the judiciary are created'). Eg on Spain: Aida Torres Pérez, 'Judicial Self-Government and Judicial Independence: The Political Capture of the General Council of the Judiciary in Spain' (2018) 19(7) German Law Journal 1769.

[97] Judges may dominate a judicial council numerically or epistemically; that is, when non-judicial colleagues depend on them for information. Garoupa and Ginsburg 2009a (n 6) 125–26; Garoupa and Ginsburg 2009b (n 6) 65–66.

[98] The reform of the KRS, whose members were elected not by the judges but by the 3/5 parliamentary majority or, failing which, by a simple majority, and the degradation of judicial independence in Poland have been subject to extensive debate and litigation before the CJEU: eg *Joined Cases AK* v *Krajowa Rada Sądownictwa (C-585/18) and CP (C-624/18), DO (C-625/18)* v *Sąd Najwyższy*, Judgment of the Court, Grand Chamber, CJEU, 19 November 2019; *Case C-791/19*, Judgment of the Court, Grand Chamber, CJEU, 15 July 2021. Wojciech Sadurski, *Poland's Constitutional Breakdown* (OUP 2019); Wojciech Sadurski, 'Bad Response to a Tragic Choice: the Case of Polish Council of the Judiciary' (*Verfassungsblog*, 16 April 2018) <https://verfassungsblog.de/bad-response-to-a-tragic-choice-the-case-of-polish-council-of-the-judiciary>; Wojciech Sadurski, 'The Disciplinary Chamber May Go—but the Rotten System Will Stay' (*Verfassungsblog*, 11 August 2021) <https://verfassungsblog.de/the-disciplinary-chamber-may-go-but-the-rotten-system-will-stay>; Anna Śledzińska-Simon, 'The Rise and Fall of Judicial Self-Government in Poland: On Judicial Reform Reversing Democratic Transition' (2018) 19(7) German Law Journal 1839; Pech and Scheppele (n 9); Kovács and Scheppele (n 9).

[99] Kosař and Šipulová (n 4) 270.

[100] eg Marina Urbániková and Katarína Šipulová, 'Failed Expectations: Does the Establishment of Judicial Councils Enhance Confidence in Courts?' (2018) 19(7) German Law Journal 2105.

[101] eg Belgium, Denmark, Finland, Ireland, Iceland, Latvia, Malta, Netherlands, Norway, Sweden, and England and Wales (UK): Bobek and Kosař (n 6) 1266; Castillo-Ortiz (n 4) 6–7 ('far from residual', accounting for 24 per cent in his dataset of forty-six European jurisdictions and is conspicuously absent from the group of states with a low liberal democracy score).

organizations separate from courts.[102] This arrangement allows them to be distanced from direct political influence, even though the courts service remains subject to parliamentary authority.[103] Unlike judicial councils, their competences do not extend to judicial career decisions, which are reserved for special judicial appointment bodies, thus preserving judicial independence.[104] Court services' competences are limited to court support and housekeeping functions, exempting judges from onerous and distracting (and potentially corrupting) resource-management tasks.[105] This model ranks highly in terms of preserving judicial independence, though this may reflect its adoption in countries with an uninterrupted tradition of protecting it or by newly restored democracies that moved decisively to reinstate constitutional order after a period of illiberal rule.[106] The existence of independent judicial appointment commissions functioning outside the courts services is an even more important factor in securing judicial independence. Courts services themselves might be unable to preclude the erosion of this principle and the onset of rule-of-law backsliding should judicial appointment organs holding sway over judicial careers be captured and succumb to political interests.[107]

(iii) Under the Justice Ministry model, the judiciary is governed by the executive branch in key respects: judicial appointments, promotions, and dismissals, court management, and administrative matters.[108] This model has a respectable pedigree but is no longer as widespread in Europe.[109] The arrangement, whereby the judicial system is subjected to direct executive oversight or appointment and promotion powers exposes the judiciary to political influences and is often seen as suboptimal and dated.[110] This was why the Council of Europe and the EU favoured the transformation of judicial governance in the 'New Europe' away from the Justice Ministry and socialist models towards the Judicial Council model. Yet its operation in democratic rule-of-law states such as Germany—remarkably, as opposed

[102] Bobek and Kosař (n 6) 1266; Castillo-Ortiz (n 4) 3–4, 25. Judges can participate in the court services as board members, constituting the majority (eg England and Wales) or minority (eg Ireland): Bunjevac (n 4) 35–39. In Sweden, *Domstolsverket*, a public agency operating as a buffer between the Ministry of Justice and courts, was charged with overall management of courts, staffing, equipment, and efficiency monitoring; its board is composed of judges, politicians, and legal professionals: Bell (n 26) 96–97.

[103] eg in Denmark, the Court Administration Agency is accountable to the Parliament for the organization of the justice system, within the budget allocated by it: Bell (n 26) 87.

[104] Bobek and Kosař (n 6) 1266. In Norway a separate judicial appointment board, rather than a courts service, holds powers over judicial careers: Castillo-Ortiz (n 4) 22. On Ireland: Patrick O'Brien, 'Never Let a Crisis Go to Waste: Politics, Personality, and Judicial Self-Government in Ireland' (2018) 19(7) German Law Journal 1871.

[105] Castillo-Ortiz (n 4) 3.

[106] ibid 7, 25, 33, 37–38 (identifying a correlation between the courts service approach and a higher quality of democracy and economic prosperity).

[107] ibid 25–26.

[108] Bobek and Kosař (n 6) 1265; Castillo-Ortiz (n 4) 4.

[109] It is present in Austria, Belarus, Czechia, and Germany: Castillo-Ortiz (n 4) 6 (accounting for 9 per cent in his dataset of forty-six European jurisdictions). Belarus comes close to the socialist model as a 'perverse version of the classic Ministry of Justice model': Bobek and Kosař (n 6) 1267 fn 40–41.

[110] In Czechia, court presidents are formally appointed by the Justice Ministry and there is power-sharing: Castillo-Ortiz (n 4) 4; Bobek and Kosař (n 6) 1288; David Kosař, 'Politics of Judicial Independence and Judicial Accountability in Czechia: Bargaining in the Shadow of the Law between Court Presidents and the Ministry of Justice' (2017) 13 European Constitutional Law Review 96, 105.

to autocracies like Belarus—goes some way towards disproving the notion that the model is inherently detrimental to judicial independence. In Austria, Germany, and Czechia, the model accommodates significant degrees of judicial participation.[111] The risks of executive diktat over courts are reduced through the sparing use of de jure dismissal powers, avoidance of overly intrusive top-down decision-making, delegation of competences to court presidents, the secondment of judges to the ministry (as is the case with *Sektionschefs* in Austria), and the involvement of professional organizations in human resources issues.[112] In turn, the judiciary co-governing itself jointly with the ministry (eg through powerful court presidents in Czechia) poses dangers of its own. Informal arrangements between court presidents and ministers may result in accountability and transparency deficits. Under the ministerial model, like elsewhere, the health of the judiciary and the integrity of its governance system largely depend on the politico-institutional context in which they are embedded.[113]

This survey of domestic models showcases the complexity of judicial governance as a field of law and practice and leads to the following observations. First, the institutional arrangements associated with each scheme transcend country categorizations by geographic region, legal tradition, and democratic quality. It is an oversimplification to automatically associate any set of arrangements with higher or lower levels of judicial independence or rule-of-law compliance. Even though specific methods of setting up judicial governance have been assertively promoted by supranational institutions and donors, they have not been a panacea, as the tribulations of jurisdictions adopting judicial councils amply show.[114] Neither this nor any alternative model can be regarded as superior or inherently good or bad.

Second, there are no one-size-fits-all solutions or 'best practices' that will work in every setting. Their success or failure depends largely on the historical path dependencies and specific political, institutional, and societal circumstances in which judiciaries operate and are governed. Although there is a correlation between specific approaches and levels of judicial independence and quality, there is no basis for speaking of causation. The political, institutional-legal, and cultural context, along with the level of economic development, shapes how those models are operationalized in practice.

[111] Blisa and others (n 90); Fabian Wittreck, 'German Judicial Self-Government: Institutions and Constraints' (2018) 19(7) German Law Journal 1931; Kosař (n 6) 1574.

[112] Bobek and Kosař (n 6) 1265 and 1288 (this model is often mixed up with the Socialist model and criticized wrongly); Kosař (n 110) 106; Kosař (n 6) 1587, 1606; Kosař and Šipulová (n 4) 269–70. Castillo-Ortiz (n 4) 4 ('constraints on ministerial power over the judiciary... are often political, rather than strictly legal').

[113] Castillo-Ortiz (n 4) 7. Kosař (n 6) 1593 (the model may be 'a lesser evil' since it is 'the devil we know' and the minister's abuses of the judiciary are immediately visible and easier to mobilize against).

[114] Garoupa and Ginsburg (n 81) 139 (rejecting 'the simplistic view that importing or transplanting certain types of judicial council is likely to have a decisive impact on the quality of the judiciary') and 140 (judicial councils 'do not seem to provide universal solutions to the issues of finding the appropriate mix of judicial accountability and independence'); Kosař and Šipulová (n 4) 273–74 (supranational bodies rarely factor in the risk of judicial corruption and corporativism given the conflation of sectarian judicial interests with the general interest in the independent and rule-of-law-compliant judiciary).

Third, regardless of the model, judicial governance is not a one-way street. It is a polycentric undertaking with a network of multiple 'nodes' located within and outside the orbit of judicial systems. The 'ecosystem' in each jurisdiction is marked by complementarities, contestation, and mutual dependencies between the 'nodes' in asserting and exercising judicial governance competences or informal functions.

Fourth, the external and internal dimensions of judicial governance are not dichotomic but interlinked, akin to communicating vessels. Increased accountability demands and management excesses or inaction in the external sphere (judicial councils, appointment commissions, courts services, and justice ministries) are bound to affect the climate, shrink room for manoeuvre, and feed resistance from within the judicial (self-)governance sphere. In turn, dysfunction, abuses, and conflicts in the internal domain will gradually erode trust and trigger attempts to manage crises and tighten oversight of courts. Conversely, a smoothly operating judicial self-governance with competent management and effective internal checks and balances goes a long way towards securing the confidence of external governance bodies over time and in helping the judicial system gain greater institutional autonomy.[115]

2.3.3 Governance versus administration and government

The third element of the key concept in need of clarification is 'govern*ance*' as opposed to 'administration' and 'govern*ment*'. A buzzword in disciplines other than international law and international relations, 'governance' is as ubiquitous as it is fuzzy; it carries too many meanings for too many different audiences.[116] This may in part explain why it has been received in domestic and comparative judicial studies literature without much reflection on how it relates to the cognate terms of (judicial) 'government' and (court) 'administration'.

The term 'administration' is on occasion used interchangeably with the other two, particularly when referring to court administration. But it has a more down-to-earth ring that conveys a preoccupation with mundane and technical (rather than political or constitutional) aspects of running judicial organizations, the bulk of which normally falls within the purview of judicial (internal) self-governance or courts services' work. The judicial administration perspective is traditionally overshadowed by debates on streamlining procedures and working methods, resource-efficiency, and the imperatives of combating delays in judicial systems.[117] External governance bodies

[115] eg Zimmer (n 22) 138 ('Achieving an institutionally independent judicial system anticipates having in place an accountable self-governance framework built on effective internal control and enforcement mechanisms to ensure the confidence of the other branches and the trust of the people in its capacity to independently administer justice').

[116] David Levi-Faur, 'From "Big Government" to "Big Governance"?' in David Levi-Faur (ed), *The Oxford Handbook of Governance* (OUP 2012) 3; Bogdan Iancu and Elena Simina Tănăsescu, 'Introduction' in Bogdan Iancu and Elena Simina Tănăsescu, *Governance and Constitutionalism: Law, Politics and Institutional Neutrality* (Routledge 2020) 3.

[117] eg Mark W Cannon, 'Judicial Administration: Why Should We Care?' (1974) Arizona State Law Journal 521.

may at times grow preoccupied with inefficiencies of court administration, especially when those defects affect overall judicial performance and public satisfaction with, or confidence in, the judiciary. But the judicial governance perspective is immeasurably broader than administration alone; it encompasses, but cannot be reduced to, efficiency concerns.

The distinction between 'governance' and 'government' is less straightforward and self-explanatory. The choice between them is seldom addressed in judicial governance scholarship. Exceptionally, Kosař justified his slight preference for the term 'judicial self-govern*ance*' rather than 'govern*ment*' by referring to the fact that the former is better suited to studying judiciaries *beyond* the state and reflects more closely the changing context in, and the new processes by, which judiciaries are governed.[118] Guidance on what 'governance' stands for generally can be sourced from public management and political theory. Even then, experts in those disciplines readily acknowledge the sheer complexity and varied usages of this concept. Without pursuing the ambition to examine 'governance' in all of its conceptual richness (or vacuity), a brief incursion into non-legal literature can help shore up one's definitional choices.

Both 'governance' and 'government' are derived from the Greek word *kybernan* (and Latin *gubernare*), which means 'steering a boat' or 'being at the helm'.[119] Over time, the meanings of 'governance' and 'government' diverged; the difference is subtle but significant.[120] As a result, the terms should no longer be used interchangeably.[121] According to one account, the concept of 'governance' was coined by Harlan Cleveland in the 1970s.[122] He predicted that 'organizations that get things done will no longer be hierarchical pyramids with most of the real control at the top ... [and] will be systems—interlaced webs of tension in which control is loose, power diffused, and centers of decision plural', whereby decision-making would become 'an increasingly intricate process of multilateral brokerage' and 'more collegial, consensual, and consultative'.[123]

Distinguished from government along the axes of structures, processes, mechanisms, and strategies,[124] governance is defined as a system of rule or regulation in the context of the 'displacement of nation-state, normative constitutionalism by standards and benchmarks (treaties, soft law, indicators) deriving from a dense, multilayered

[118] Kosař (n 6) 1571 n 21.

[119] Levi-Faur (n 116) 5. In Mandarin Chinese, 'governance' is signified by the word *Zhili*, a combination of *Zhi* (putting something under control) and *Li* (regulate or put something in order): ibid 15; B Guy Peters, 'Governance as Political Theory' in David Levi-Faur (ed), *The Oxford Handbook of Governance* (OUP 2012) 20.

[120] Anita Bagai, 'Understanding Governance in the Twenty-First Century' in Shivani Singh (ed), *Governance: Issues and Challenges* (SAGE Publications 2016) 10.

[121] Levi-Faur (n 116) 10 ('governance is not government. It may be considered as more than government or an alternative to government, but it is not synonymous with it').

[122] H George Frederickson, 'Whatever Happened to Public Administration? Governance, Governance Everywhere' in Ewan Ferlie, Lawrence E Lynn Jr, and Christopher Pollitt (eds), *The Oxford Handbook of Public Management* (OUP 2007) 282–304 (attributing the first use of the term 'governance' to Cleveland's turn of speech, 'What the people want is less government and more governance'). Tracing the notion back to yet another source (Oliver Willianson) and presenting a different trajectory based on social sciences literature citations since the late 1970s: Levi-Faur (n 116) 5–6.

[123] Harlan Cleveland, *The Future Executive: A Guide for Tomorrow's Managers* (Harper and Row, 1972) 13.

[124] Levi-Faur (n 116) 8–10.

network of interactions'.[125] Governance can successfully operate beyond and without government.[126] Governance fills the voids left by the absence of govern*ment*, particularly at the global level where one government, ie *the* government, is lacking and multiple states must cooperate with each other and other actors.[127]

The two notions overlap in that both refer to a system of rule and enforcement backed by public authority directly or indirectly. Yet, governance decentres state institutions, dilutes the coercive aspects of authority in favour of multilateral coordination, and moves away from formal decision-making structures towards non-governmental mechanisms and networks, public–private partnerships, and more horizontal and informal decision-making processes.[128] The expansion of 'governance' to stakeholders, mechanisms, and actors beyond state institutions entails a blurring of boundaries between public and private sectors, as well as between the state and civil society.[129] Thus, governance is conceived in terms of the coordination of activities and networks among public authorities, private actors, and the civic sector, who jointly contribute to 'policy-making and public service delivery in solving public problems'.[130]

Their modalities are also different. The interdependence of different actors in policy-making and service delivery necessitates interaction, negotiation, and trust as principal governance methods, as opposed to the wielding of unilateral power and top-down command. While the exercise of formal competences defines 'government', power and hierarchy are present in, yet not as central to, 'governance'. Governance is a 'softer order', replacing 'stagnating bureaucracies and centralized state controls with softer and collaborative forms of policy-making'.[131] As Bagai explains, 'while the government rules and controls, governance means orchestrating and managing', with the power being shared, not wielded, and the authority being performed with the consent and cooperation of those subjected to it.[132] Last but not least, 'governance' comes with a connotation of flexibility, dynamism, and amenability to change, whereas 'government' presents a more rigid conservationist paradigm. It is usual for scholars to define

[125] Iancu and Simina Tănăsescu (n 116) 3 (this leads to 'agencification'—the proliferation of neutral regulatory and monitoring agencies—and the 'reassessment of inherited structures of justification, notably the separation of powers and representations about democratic accountability and legitimacy').

[126] Tanja Börzel and Thomas Risse, 'Governance without a State: Can It Work?' (2010) 4 Regulation and Governance 113.

[127] 'Global governance is generally defined as an instance of governance in the absence of government. There is no government at the global level.' John G Ruggie, 'Foreword' in Thomas G Weiss and Ramesh Thakur, *Global Governance and the UN: An Unfinished Journey* (Indiana University Press 2010) xv. I thank Niels Blokker for bringing this source to my attention.

[128] Bagai (n 120) 11.

[129] Huanming Wang and Bing Ran, 'Network Governance and Collaborative Governance: A Thematic Analysis on their Similarities, Differences, and Entanglements' (2023) 25(6) Public Management Review 1187, 1189.

[130] Ibid (with further references). In a similar vein, Levi-Faur (n 116) 5 ('The departure point is a particular division of tasks and responsibilities in the role of civil society, business, and government in supplying or exerting governance').

[131] Levi-Faur (n 116) 7.

[132] Bagai (n 120) 10 and 11 ('To rule would mean to be the sole authority, which implies that the government may rely on force to obtain compliance [whereas] governance, or orchestrating, would mean that that everyone (formal/informal organizations) has a part to play in moving the society forward ... To control would be to direct action and decision-making on each part of the system ... Governance, thus, chooses management over control because this kind of system permits room for outside influences and subjects decisions to evaluations of the entire society').

'governance' through change, as the system for coordinating, orchestrating, and managing societal, political, and economic shifts in and across global, transnational, and local settings.[133] To Rhodes, it is 'a change in the meaning of government, referring to *new* processes of governing; or *changed* conditions of ordered rule; or *new* methods by which society is governed'.[134]

Considering these characteristics of 'governance', its use in connection with institutions, processes, and norms for operating and steering judicial systems—indeed, for *governing* them if one were allowed to use the very term being defined, despite circularity—makes sense. It clearly presents a superior alternative to 'government'. In no jurisdiction, whatever the model or the legal order, is judicial governance performed in a plainly hierarchical and unilateral manner. Courts are everywhere governed through a complex constellation of institutions, actors, and processes, formal as well as informal whereby power-sharing, coordination, and collaborative standard-setting are the prevalent methods. These are not limited to state institutions and formal lines of authority but include actors both within and outside the judiciary. Court principals, justice executives, collegial expert and monitoring bodies, and professional associations partake in judicial governance and exercise delegated and informal competences. Governance can exist and deliver beyond the framework of state government. The term 'government', by contrast, betrays its inadequacy the very moment the governance of international courts is brought up. These creatures operate in a strange context, where a single government holding sway over them is absent altogether.

2.4 Judicial Governance at the International Level

2.4.1 Courts in a strange context

International justice is the result of the extrapolation of adjudication as a distinct form of legal governance from the domestic to the international level. It is a patchwork of separate judicial institutions rather than an integrated 'judicial system' in the traditional sense. Established collectively by (communities of) states, whether directly or via international organizations, ICTs are mandated to decide cases within and across multiple areas of international law, ranging from border disputes and the law of the sea to trade and investment, human rights complaints, individual criminal responsibility, and more. ICTs perform adjudicatory functions of dispute-settlement, fact-finding, and norm-advancement in ways comparable to domestic courts.[135] Their *modi operandi* are properly judicial. International judges decide cases by applying law to facts

[133] Levi-Faur (n 116) 7–8 ('science of shiftology').

[134] RAW Rhodes, 'Waves of Governance' in David Levi-Faur (ed), *The Oxford Handbook of Governance* (OUP 2012) 30 ('the changing boundaries between public, private, and voluntary sectors, and ... the changing role of the state').

[135] The literature on purposes and functions of international adjudication is too voluminous to list here. Yuval Shany, 'No Longer a Weaker Department of Power' (2009) 20(1) European Journal of International Law 73; José E Alvarez, 'What Are International Judges for? The Main Functions of International Adjudication' in Cesare PR Romano and others (eds), *The Oxford Handbook of International Adjudication* (OUP 2012) 158 and other chapters; David D Caron, 'Towards a Political Theory of International Courts and Tribunals' (2006) 24(2) Berkeley Journal of International Law 401.

established to the requisite standard. They (are meant to) do so impartially and free from improper external influences or interference, in accordance with fair process.[136] If a body works like a court and decides like a court, it *is* a court. By their very nature and functions, ICTs *are* courts of law, not mere simulacra or copycats of national courts.[137]

Like their domestic counterparts, ICTs are—at any rate must be—entitled to judicial independence and be governed competently: they do not inhabit an institutional neverland. For the smooth and accountable performance of their mandates, they depend on 'parent' and 'oversight' bodies, ie international judicial governance institutions (*injugovins*).[138] But ICTs' legal-institutional environments differ in consequential ways from the habitats in which domestic judiciaries are embedded. Different gravitational forces and even laws of gravity are at work. The parameters of judicial governance require recalibration when transposed to the international level. As discussed previously, national judiciaries are integrated within the constitutional architecture of the state, as a branch autonomous from, and coequal with, the other departments of government. The classic notion of the separation of powers stems from the recognition that courts' independence must be protected from the legislative and executive powers. The devil is in the details of the implications of this principle. But its essence is uncontested, and it heavily informs judicial governance reforms and their critiques. By contrast, ICTs are 'free particles' suspended in the international order's 'universe' or pulled into the 'institutional galaxies' of international and regional organizations: the UN, CoE, EU, African Union, ECOWAS, and so on.

Acting directly or indirectly via international organizations, states establish and confer jurisdiction on ICTs, govern them, and wind down their activities. There is no single government to which these courts belong or on which they depend, but instead plural collectives of states that establish them and/or sit in their *injugovins*. The inter-state frameworks and the broader international order ICTs are nested in, are poorly comparable with domestic systems. The international system features no apex sovereign or super-state. Except for the imperfect analogy of the UN Security Council, there is no supreme authority to arbitrate power disputes, dictate the means of settling conflicts, resolve competence-related and jurisdictional overlaps, or enforce international law.[139] Despite the temptation to dub the UN Charter the constitution of the

[136] Crawford and McIntyre (n 24) 190, 194; Ruth Mackenzie and Philippe Sands, 'International Courts and Tribunals and the Independence of the International Judge' (2003) 44(1) Harvard International Law Journal 271, 275–76; Fabien Gélinas, 'The Independence of International Arbitrators and Judges: Tampered with or Well Tempered?' (2011) 24(1) New York International Law Review 1.

[137] *Legal Consequences for States of the Continued Presence of South Africa in Namibia (South West Africa) notwithstanding Security Council Resolution 276 (1970)*, Advisory Opinion of 21 June 1971, [1971] ICJ Reports 16, 23 para 29 ('in that capacity, [ICJ] acts only on the basis of the law, independently of all outside influence or interventions whatsoever, in the exercise of the judicial function entrusted to it alone by the Charter and by its Statute. A court functioning as a court of law can act in no other way').

[138] On 'parenthood' and 'oversight' in relation to 'governance', see Huw Llewellyn, 'Governance of the United Nations Criminal Tribunals', Section 10.2.3, in this volume; on *injugovins*, see Niels Blokker, 'International Judicial Governance Institutions', in this volume and Niels Blokker, 'The Governance of International Courts and Tribunals: Organizing and Guaranteeing Independence and Accountability' in Andreas Føllesdal and Geir Ulfstein (eds), *The Judicialization of International Law: A Mixed Blessing?* (OUP 2018) 27.

[139] Crawford and McIntyre (n 24) 190.

international community, the present international order is not particularly receptive to the constitutional paradigm.[140] As the ICJ and the ICTY Appeals Chamber held in unison, the separation of powers is applicable neither to the international legal order writ large nor within its organizations such as the UN.[141] The same can be said for regional organizations.[142]

2.4.2 Recalibrating judicial independence and (self-)governance

Despite the strangeness of the international order, the rationales for safeguarding international courts' independence—including, and especially, in the judicial governance sphere—by no means disappear. On the contrary, in setting up ICTs, consenting to their jurisdiction, and bringing cases to them for resolution, states and organizations trust, as a basic premise, that they will operate as courts of law. Litigants expect them to decide on the basis of a careful consideration of relevant facts and applicable law, reaching conclusions impartially and free from improper external influences.[143] Failing that, what reason would there be to create, fund, and maintain those institutions—let alone call them 'courts' or 'tribunals'—and insist on compliance with their decisions? The act of establishing an international court comes with the judicial function 'lock, stock, and barrel'. There are no reasons to depart from the cornerstone notion that ICTs *must* decide cases in accordance with the standards of independence and impartiality that international law itself sets for national courts.[144]

But judicial independence is a context-dependent and relational concept. Its content requires readjustment at the international level. The distinct features of that context include, first, the irrelevance of the *trias politica* doctrine and the lack of a sovereign authority responsible for, among other things, protecting international judicial independence. Second, cases within ICT dockets are routinely interlaced with highly charged matters of international politics, incomparably more so than is the case with much domestic adjudication. Their mandates lend themselves more easily to politicization, and their independent and impartial performance comes under

[140] eg Bardo Fassbender, *The United Nations Charter as the Constitution of the International Community* (Brill 2009); Nico Krisch, *Beyond Constitutionalism: The Pluralist Structure of Postnational Law* (OUP 2012).

[141] *Military and Paramilitary Activities in and against Nicaragua (Nicaragua v United States of America)*, Jurisdiction and admissibility, Judgment of 26 November 1984, [1984] ICJ Reports 392, 433 para 92 ('municipal-law concepts of separation of powers . . . are not applicable to the relations among international institutions for the settlement of disputes'); Decision on the Defence Motion for Interlocutory Appeal on Jurisdiction, *Prosecutor* v *Tadić*, IT-94-1, AC, ICTY, 2 October 1995, para 43 ('the legislative, executive and judicial division of powers which is largely followed in most municipal systems does not apply to the international setting nor, more specifically, to the setting of an international organization such as the United Nations. Among the principal organs of the United Nations the divisions between judicial, executive and legislative functions are not clear cut').

[142] Kosař (n 6) 1596 (on the lack of 'classical tripartite separation of powers' at the CoE and 'a peculiar separation of powers' in the EU).

[143] Kenneth J Keith, 'Challenges to the Independence of the International Judiciary: Reflections on the International Court of Justice' (2017) 30 Leiden Journal of International Law 137, 140; Crawford and McIntyre (n 24) 212–13; Meron (n 25) 359.

[144] Crawford and McIntyre (n 24) 191; Mahoney (n 24) 315.

intense scrutiny.[145] Third, ICT jurisdiction invariably rests on state consent, which can be given and withdrawn, while their institutional support structures remain fairly underdeveloped. ICTs are fully reliant on states for engagement, evidentiary and enforcement cooperation, and every conceivable form of assistance—including, but not limited to, funding.[146] The financial side of international justice, in particular, entails a highly 'uncomfortable position of dependency' vis-à-vis states and parent organizations.[147] They are supposed to fund and staff ICTs adequately to enable them to perform their mandates effectively.[148] But what if those parent and oversight entities decide that a court's mandate is no longer needed or has become too costly, and that it should therefore be scaled back or that the court should disappear altogether?

These features combine to burden, if not handicap, international courts with incommensurably heavier dependencies than any domestic court in an (ideal) stable liberal democracy. They expose these 'giants without arms and legs'[149] to heightened risks of interference and pressure from (groups of) states and their government branches, non-governmental organizations and interest groups, and powerful individuals. If anything, these vulnerabilities call for stronger, not weaker, protections of judicial independence.[150] Without a resolute reinforcement of the principle, ICTs become easy prey for unscrupulous political operators in states that neglect the rule of law or lack a strong tradition of respecting judicial independence. The independence of international judges ought to ascend to an overarching, quasi-constitutional principle pervading the international legal order. It is questionable whether it has already attained that status, given that its regulation in general international law remains insufficiently robust.[151] The principle is laid down expressly in the instruments governing adjudication within the individual regimes of international and regional organizations. The twenty-year-old Burgh House Principles are the only (soft-law) restatement tailored specifically to safeguard the independence of international judiciaries.[152] That said, significant overlaps in the regime-specific articulations of underlying requirements

[145] Crawford and McIntyre (n 24) 206; Mahoney (n 24) 317–18; Meron (n 25) 361.

[146] On UN criminal tribunals, see Huw Llewellyn, 'Governance of the United Nations Criminal Tribunals', Section 10.2.1, in this volume.

[147] Mahoney (n 24) 318, 335–36 (on ICTs' 'economic fragility' and 'budgetary starvation' as dangers to judicial independence). For comprehensive analyses: Adriana-Maria Manolescu, 'Financial Governance of International Courts and Tribunals', in this volume and Adriana-Maria Manolescu, *Judicial Independence and Accountability in the Financial Governance of International Courts: An Act of Balancing Powers* (Brill Nijhoff 2026).

[148] The Burgh House Principles (n 51) para 6 ('States parties and international organisations shall provide adequate resources, including facilities and levels of staffing, to enable courts and the judges to perform their functions effectively').

[149] Cassese described the ICTY thus due to its dependence on state cooperation but the sobriquet applies to all international courts in relation to a wide range of matters. Antonio Cassese, 'On Current Trends towards Criminal Prosecution and Punishment of Breaches of International Humanitarian Law' (1998) 9 European Journal of International Law 1, 13 ('The ICTY remains very much like a giant without arms and legs—it needs artificial limbs to walk and work. And these artificial limbs are state authorities. If the cooperation of states is not forthcoming, the ICTY cannot fulfil its functions. It has no means at its disposal to force states to cooperate with it').

[150] Mahoney (n 24) 318, 346; Crawford and McIntyre (n 24) 206.

[151] Mahoney (n 24) 317 (paradoxical reticence of international organizations in affirming guarantees of international judicial independence), 346 ('amorphous state of affairs').

[152] The Burgh House Principles (n 51).

allow one to speak of an emergent cross-cutting normative framework of *international* judicial independence.

The principle finds reflection in ICT statutes, taking the form of provisions: (i) guaranteeing that the institutions themselves and individual judges are independent; (ii) establishing requirements for judicial qualifications, elections, professional ethics, and conditions for removal; (iii) setting the duration of tenure and conditions of service (eg remuneration); and (iv) regulating courts and judges' privileges and immunities.[153] On top of that, courts and tribunals exercising criminal jurisdiction over individuals must be independent as a corollary of the right of the accused to a fair trial before a competent, independent, and impartial tribunal established by law.[154] The right, as contained in human rights treaties, is directed at states rather than international organizations and courts, which are not parties thereto. However, the right to a fair trial forms part of customary international law and hence is binding on international courts exercising public authority over individuals.[155] Judicial independence is owed to the beneficiaries of the right to a fair trial in proceedings before international courts and thus is also opposable to organizations and collectives of states that set up and govern those courts.

Furthermore, the institutional judicial independence of ICTs is reinforced via their self-enclosed institutional architecture. It gives effect to a clearer division between the *internal* and the *external* dimensions of judicial governance than is observed at the domestic level.[156] As a result of the non-applicability of the classical separation of powers doctrine, many ICTs enjoy a higher degree of self-governance when it comes to the core domain of adjudication, case-management, conduct of proceedings, and internal administration.[157] In some courts, this autonomy extends to the legislative competence to adopt rules of procedure, besides lower-tier sources such as regulations and practice guidelines, although in others states retain the regulatory power over the rules of procedure as well.[158] This also includes judicial powers to elect *primi inter pares*—the important figures of court presidents and vice-presidents—and to elect and appoint the registrar.[159] The availability of neutral offices headed by registrars, responsible for non-judicial aspects of court administration and services under the court president's authority, points to an elevated degree of institutional autonomy.[160]

153 Niels Blokker, 'International Judicial Governance Institutions', in this volume; Crawford and McIntyre (n 24) 209–10. Eg ICJ Statute arts 2, 13(1). 19; ICC Statute preamble para 9, arts 36(3)(a) and (9)(a), 40(1), 48(2); ITLOS Statute arts 2–3, 5(1), 10, 18(5).

154 Sources in n 33; eg Report of the Secretary-General pursuant to paragraph 5 of Security Council resolution 955 (1994) of 13 February 1995, UN Doc S/1995/134, para 106; ICC Statute art 67; MICT Statute art 19.

155 Huw Llewellyn, 'Governance of the United Nations Criminal Tribunals', Section 10.5.1, in this volume.

156 Section 2.3.2.1.

157 On the ECtHR and CJEU: Kosař (n 6) 1575, 1596 ('far more autonomy in court administration' and 'regulatory self-governance', ie 'organization of sessions and deliberations, setting up sections and chambers, and determining case allocation' and procedure).

158 eg ICJ Statute art 30(1); ITLOS Statute art 16; ECHR art 26(d); ICTY Statute art 15; TFEU art 253(6). Cf ICC Statute art 51.

159 eg ICJ Statute art 21; ECHR art 25; TFEU art 253(3) and (5); ICC Statute arts 38(1) and 43(4). On the role of ICTY President: Meron (n 25) 363–65.

160 eg ICC Statute art 43(1)–(3).

The registries' placement within the court's structure and not within secretariats-general or other parent organization's organs is another indication.[161] The allocation of judges into chambers and panels, appointment of presiding judges, and distribution of caseload are also matters within judicial self-governance. Unlike what is at times suggested, although other actors may participate in the nomination and vetting of judicial candidates,[162] the function of judicial elections rests with the states parties.[163] This is hardly a compelling example of *self*-governance: the role entrusted to screening bodies composed of justice experts and former international judges is important for ensuring the quality of judges but still fairly limited.[164]

The prerogative of judicial independence vested in international courts and their judges, and the right of parties to justice administered in an independent and impartial manner, give rise to the corresponding duty to respect and protect judicial independence. This duty is opposable to states as contracting parties to the respective agreements as well as to international organizations and their organs which establish ICTs and under whose auspices they operate.[165] This holds equally for any *injugovins*: states may not shirk their obligations by creating bodies exempt from those same obligations. Just as judicial independence inheres in the international judicial function, respect for it inheres in the function of international judicial *governance*. Absent clearly defined and specific parameters of judicial independence in that context, ICT–*injugovin* relationships are fraught with risks of compromising that principle and *injugovins* overstepping the limits it imposes. This happens, for example, when an *injugovin*, driven by political expediency and economic efficiency considerations, adopts an interventionist approach and encroaches upon matters within judicial self-governance. One precedent that generated much anxiety at the time was the UN Security Council setting the timeline for the completion of mandates by the UN ad hoc tribunals, although the deadlines were repeatedly adjusted and the judicial process was permitted to run its course.[166] Another, more extreme situation of disregard for the integrity of the judicial function was the abrupt closure of the Special

[161] Mahoney (n 24) 334–35.

[162] eg ICJ Statute art 4. See Andrew Drzemczewski, 'The Election of Judges onto the European Court of Human Rights', Christiaan Timmermans, 'The Procedure for Nominating Members of the EU Courts', and Christian M De Vos and others, 'Electing the Best?', in this volume.

[163] Cf Kosař (n 6) 1572, 1575, regarding the 255 Panel and the Advisory Panel of Experts verifying qualifications of CJEU and ECtHR judicial candidates respectively, as judicial self-governance bodies even though they do not feature incumbent judges of these courts and the judges are elected by the common accord of the EU member state governments and by the PACE, respectively (TFEU art 253; ECHR art 22). It is not decisive that those panels include former ECtHR and CJEU judges, or that court presidents have a say in the panel composition.

[164] Başak Çalı and Stewart Cunningham, 'Judicial Self Government and the Sui Generis Case of the European Court of Human Rights' (2008) 19(7) German Law Journal 1977, 1978(characterizing the ECtHR self-governance as 'strong post-election and weaker pre-election'). In detail on the role of such panels, see Andrew Drzemczewski, 'The Election of Judges onto the European Court of Human Rights', Christiaan Timmermans, 'The Procedure for Nominating Members of the EU Courts', and Christian M De Vos and others, 'Electing the Best?', in this volume.

[165] The Burgh House Principles (n 51) preamble and para 1.2 ('Where a court is established as an organ or under the auspices of an international organisation, the court and judges shall exercise their judicial functions free from interference from other organs or authorities of that organisation').

[166] Huw Llewellyn, 'Governance of UN the United Nations Criminal Tribunals', Section 10.7.5, in this volume.

Tribunal for Lebanon in 2023 due to the unwillingness of major donor states sitting in its management committee to keep funding the tribunal.[167]

2.4.3 Functions and institutions

The specificities of international adjudication and the unique context entail reliance on judicial governance models that are *sui generis*, rather than mere replicas of national approaches. The domestic experiences of (re)designing court governance schemes and conceptualization of judicial independence, accountability, and integrity underpinning them certainly informed the solutions adopted at the international level as a major source of inspiration as well as cautionary tales. Registries operating *within* international courts are comparable to courts services that support some national judiciaries *externally*.[168] However limited, parallels can also be drawn between, on the one hand, the advisory committees and expert panels charged with screening international judicial candidates (the CoE Advisory Panel of Experts for the ECtHR, the '255 Panel' for the CJEU, or the Advisory Committee on Nominations for the ICC),[169] and, on the other hand, the appointment board and 'weak' judicial councils.[170] While tempting, broad and unnuanced comparisons between domestic and international judicial governance schemes come with epistemological risks. A reasonable degree of caution is in order when drawing on domestic know-how for the purpose of extrapolating insights and lessons to the international sphere. The institutional templates for governing domestic courts and their constitutional backdrops are too different to make them directly usable for international courts, and vice versa.[171]

The legal-institutional arrangements adopted for the governance of ICTs vary by individual court or group of courts established in a similar fashion. As will be outlined in the following chapter, the main (ideal) types of *injugovins* are distinguished depending on their character as organs of an international organization, standalone treaty bodies, or a loose gathering of states.[172] The *injugovins*, in turn, invariably establish subsidiary or second-tier governance bodies to which specific functions or aspects thereof are entrusted. An additional 'managerial' sub-type, incorporated in the so-called management or steering committees, can arguably be identified, composed of states especially interested in the operation of the ICT. These often have only a scant treaty and are rooted mostly in informal arrangements.[173] The degree and

[167] Evelyn Anoya, 'Governance of the Special Tribunal for Lebanon', in this volume.
[168] Section 2.3.2.2.
[169] Andrew Drzemczewski, 'The Election of Judges onto the European Court of Human Rights' and Christiaan Timmermans, 'The Procedure for Nominating Members of the EU Courts', in this volume; Brian McGarry and Josef Ostřanský, 'Before the Law: Assessing the Process and Impact of Judicial Screening Bodies' in Freya Baetens (ed), *Legitimacy of Unseen Actors in International Adjudication* (OUP 2019) 189–214.
[170] Section 2.3.2.2.
[171] Kosař (n 6) 1777–78.
[172] Niels Blokker, 'International Judicial Governance Institutions', Section 3.4.2, in this volume.
[173] Huw Llewellyn, 'Governance of the United Nations Criminal Tribunals', Section 10.4, in this volume; Sergey Vasiliev, 'Judicial Governance Entities as Power-Holders in International Criminal Justice: A Plea for a Socio-Legal Enquiry' in Morten Bergsmo and others (eds), *Power in International Criminal Justice* (Torkel Opsahl Academic E-Publisher 2020) 538. Eg SCSL Agreement art 7; STL Agreement art 6.

forms of institutionalization of judicial governance vary by regime. Specific modalities are often developed improvisationally in response to perceived needs and take full shape only after an ICT goes into operation and faces legal and practical challenges. Like in domestic contexts, actual governance schemes of international courts often combine elements of different models.[174]

While individual states participate in court governance, they do so mostly *not* directly as such but by virtue of their membership in *injugovins*, whatever their legal status and organizational form, and under the terms governing their operation. States therefore should not be equated with *injugovins*. As mediators of a plurality of states and subject to their own regulatory instruments, procedures, and practices, most *injugovins* are more than a sum of their parts: they acquire agency and dynamics of their own, distinct from those of individual states participating in them. There is greater scope for individual states to get involved directly in judicial governance processes and leave their mark on decision-making in the case of ICTs overseen by smaller institutions. The management or steering committees composed of major donor states that governed the voluntarily funded UN criminal tribunals (Special Court for Sierra Leone, Special Tribunal for Lebanon, and the Extraordinary Chambers in the Courts of Cambodia) offer an example of this approach.[175] Given that it was anchored in a particular funding scheme, it is not as widespread. The majority of *injugovins* have a thicker institutional veil.

There is thus no single institutional blueprint to serve as a generally representative snapshot of international judicial governance. It can best be described in terms of the functions it encompasses, ie recurrent activities that *injugovins* must carry out when discharging their responsibilities in governing 'their' courts. The primary functions are equivalent and recognizable across multiple regimes: the adoption and amendment of legislation, the election of principals (judges and, for criminal courts, chief prosecutors), the adoption of court budgets and the provision of funds, and management oversight. *Injugovins* also perform implicit, spin-off competences enabling them to perform their primary duties and provide for follow-up measures. These include putting in place accountability measures (financial audit, investigations into alleged misconduct, and comprehensive or thematic expert reviews of performance and working methods), ensuring organizational and logistical support, dealing with non-cooperation by states, and protecting courts against political backlash and external threats to their independence. Moreover, the 'primordial' functions of formally establishing and kickstarting ('birthing' and 'parenting') ICTs, as well as closing them down when the time comes—the act that strains the anthropomorphic 'parenting' metaphor—are quintessential acts of judicial governance. Even if the parent organization or organ is not intensively involved in the day-to-day oversight, it has nonetheless devised the judicial mandate, laid down the legal framework, and bears responsibilities vis-à-vis the ICT it 'birthed'.

[174] On AU judicial governance, see Misha Ariana Plagis and Karin Pluberg, 'Paper Lions?', Section 8.4.3, in this volume.

[175] Huw Llewellyn, 'Governance of the United Nations Criminal Tribunals'000000, in this volume. In more detail: Huw Llewellyn, *An Institutional Perspective on the United Nations Criminal Tribunals: Governance, Independence and Impartiality* (Brill Nijhoff 2021) 175–92.

Like domestic court governance, international judicial governance cannot be a top-down exercise: this is, as discussed, not what *governance* is about.[176] It is a polyphonic and coordinate, rather than strictly and exclusively hierarchical, undertaking involving manifold actors both within and outside the court governed. It comprises ICT principals and officials, 'parent' international organizations and organs with relevant competences, and *injugovins*. It also involves individual states acting through Foreign and Justice Ministry officials in capitals, diplomatic staff at the UN, in host states and in the countries where ICTs operate. On the inside, the principals—the presidency, registrars, and, for criminal tribunals, chief prosecutors—and their support staff play key roles in the court's *self*-governance by ensuring the smooth operation of their respective offices and the judicial organization as a whole. Moreover, the principals and assigned staff members represent ICTs externally by carrying out regular reporting obligations and by engaging with states parties and their officials at *injugovins*, thereby contributing to *external* judicial governance in consequential ways. Yet, they are not the central actors in international judicial governance properly so called; the *injugovins* are.

On the outside, a range of *injugovins* deliver governance for the benefit of 'their' ICTs. In some cases, there will be one dedicated, typically treaty-based, *injugovin*—an oversight but not a parent body—exercising the full palette of governance functions for the court. This is a rare scheme, exemplified notably by the Assembly of States Parties for the ICC and the Meeting of States Parties to UNCLOS for the International Tribunal for the Law of the Sea.[177] These *injugovins* adopt court budgets, elect principals, and discharge other key responsibilities. By contrast, where an ICT is an organ of, or associated with, a larger (typically parent) international organization, distinct functions are often exercised jointly by, or distributed between, the other organs of the same organization and are subsumed within their regular competences. The function of electing judges of the ICJ and UN ad hoc criminal tribunals is/was exercised jointly by the UN Security Council and General Assembly, with these courts also being financed from the UN budget approved by the Assembly.[178] For the ECtHR, the Committee of Ministers of the Council of Europe supervises the enforcement of final judgments and approves the CoE general budget, of which the Court's budget forms a part.[179]

There is no one-size-fits-all model. Different schemes are agreed by parent states and organizations. Similar schemes evolve organically and may grow apart depending on the context and past experiences. Each scheme presents its own advantages and

[176] Section 2.3.3.

[177] On the ASP, see Silvia Fernández de Gurmendi, 'Challenges to the Governance of the International Criminal Court', in this volume; Niels M Blokker, 'Governance of the International Tribunal of the Law of the Sea: The Role of the Meeting of States Parties to the Law of the Sea Convention' in Angela del Vecchio and Roberto Virzo (eds), *Interpretations of the United Nations Convention on the Law of the Sea by International Courts and Tribunals* (Springer 2019).

[178] ICJ Statute arts 4(1) and 17(1). For the UN ad hoc tribunals, the UN Secretary-General played a key coordinating role in the election process: ICTY Statute art 13*bis*; ICTR Statute art 12*bis*; MICT Statute art 10.

[179] Dorine Nauleau, 'The Enforcement of International Judicial Decisions' and Hanneke Palm and Roeland Böcker, 'Implementation of Judgments of the European Court of Human Rights', in this volume. ECHR arts 46(2) and 50.

risks. On the one hand, the existence of a dedicated *injugovin* makes it likely that specific needs of the judicial organization will be catered to rather than lost in the bowels of the parent organization's bureaucracy. On the other hand, the distribution of distinct functions among different organs in the same organization prevents the concentration of all power over the court in the same institutional hands and puts multiple overseers in a position to keep each other in check. If the domestic experience is anything to go by (with all due caution), a healthy degree of diffusion of governance authority is a safer model.[180] Even if it does not rule out governance abuses completely, it can at least mitigate the negative impact on judicial independence and enable timely intervention and remedial measures.

Likewise, an *injugovin*'s institutional form, size, and degree of formality can be a factor in risk-benefit analyses. Organs of an international organization or treaty bodies operating as bureaucratized structures and/or diplomatic gatherings carry out agreed competences rooted in elaborate rules of procedure, sub-laws, and institutional practices. Leaner bodies of the executive-committee type benefit from more informal arrangements and working methods. Large plenary meetings of states parties that are run according to formal rules and diplomatic protocols, such as the ICC's ASP, are on average more sluggish in their decision-making and in their responses to urgent challenges. Managerial *injugovins* not representative of the full membership of the parent organization have smaller gears and shorter lines of communication. They win in speed and efficiency but are less transparent and accountable. If captured by political agendas unconcerned with the proper administration of justice, such bodies can trample on judicial independence and inflict damage without facing timely and decisive pushback.

2.4.4 Towards judicial governance standards

The questions of more robust regulation of international judicial governance and ensuring better, more effective, and accountable *injugovins*—for the sake of stronger international justice—loom large and are the proverbial elephant in the room.[181] This final section must flag the issue of normative standards which (should) apply to judicial governance institutions at the international level. Such standards will include, first, hard legal constraints binding on *injugovins* as bottom-line requirements they must meet and, second, good practices and rules of thumb going beyond minimum requirements which can help to optimize and deliver the highest-quality judicial governance in specific settings.

The principle of judicial independence, intrinsic to the international judicial function, undoubtedly constitutes a hard legal standard which validly constrains *injugovins*' competences and working modalities. This is regardless of whether this principle is

[180] cf Kosař (n 6) 1591 ('the diffusion of powers in the area of judicial governance among different bodies perhaps even with a different composition, might be a better solution than the creation of the strong judicial council, which concentrates virtually all powers into one institution, because the former solution is more resistant to capture').

[181] In similar terms, see Niels Blokker, 'International Judicial Governance Institutions', Section 3.5, in this volume.

uniformly understood, adequately codified in regime-specific instruments, and effectively enforceable or subject to any form of accountability for offending *injugovins*—it is not (yet). But, as noted, the principle requires more robust codification when it comes to international courts, while the accountability of *injugovins* for crossing the 'red line' and interfering with court's independence remains underdeveloped, normatively and institutionally. Still, this is without prejudice to the binding character of the principle of judicial independence, which governing bodies are obligated both to respect (the negative obligation not to breach it) and to protect (the positive obligation to actively safeguard and enforce it) whenever discharging their responsibilities vis-à-vis ICTs under their patronage.

Another set of legal constraints which are (or should be) opposable to *injugovins* flows from the fundamental principle of the rule of law.[182] This is admittedly an elastic 'catch-all' assortment of principles. But certain core elements—such as legal certainty, avoidance of arbitrariness, supremacy of the law, fair and equal application of the law, compliance with international human rights, and procedural and legal transparency—are relevant and applicable to international organizations and their organs.[183] As legal requirements, they are also valid in the sphere of international judicial governance and binding upon organs exercising international public authority vis-à-vis international courts.[184]

It bears noting that judicial independence and the rule of law are only minimum requirements *injugovins* must comply with as a matter of legal obligations. They do not in and of themselves guarantee 'good' international judicial governance. Rather, these are the non-binding rules of thumb, 'lessons learnt', and 'best practices', which can be gleaned from past institutional experience of success and failure, that could help *injugovins* notch up the quality of judicial governance. Moreover, the guiding parameters of 'good governance' articulated in the fields of international development and organizational management potentially constitute a meaningful frame of reference for *injugovins*.[185] 'Good governance' checklists subsume legal constraints but also go beyond them to include other criteria: eg impartiality, the rule of law, transparency, accountability, participation, inclusivity, and combating corruption;[186] representation,

[182] Niels Blokker, 'International Judicial Governance Institutions', Section 3.5, in this volume; Sergey Vasiliev, 'Governing International Justice: Whence the Uniform Principles?' in Rick Lawson and Ramses A Wessel (eds), *Unity in Diversity: Perspectives on the Law of International Organisations* (Brill Nijhoff 2025) 290–92.

[183] eg Report of the UN Secretary-General, 'The rule of law and transitional justice in conflict and post-conflict societies', UN Doc S/2004/616 (2004) para 6 ('a principle of governance in which all persons, institutions and entities … are accountable to laws that are publicly promulgated, equally enforced and independently adjudicated, and which are consistent with international human rights norms and standards. It requires, as well, measures to ensure adherence to the principles of supremacy of law, equality before the law, accountability to the law, fairness in the application of the law, separation of powers, participation in decision-making, legal certainty, avoidance of arbitrariness and procedural and legal transparency'); TEU art 2.

[184] *Tadić* (n 141) para 42 ('This does not mean … that … an international criminal court could be set up at the mere whim of a group of governments. Such a court ought to be rooted in the rule of law').

[185] eg Huw Llewellyn, 'Governance of the United Nations Criminal Tribunals', Section 10.2.3, in this volume; Kritika Sharma, *The Assembly of States Parties to the International Criminal Court: A Good Governance Approach* (Brill Nijhoff 2026), who uses the 'good governance' framework as the analytical tool in assessing the institutional design and performance of the ICC's Assembly of States Parties.

[186] UN Human Rights Council resolution, 'The role of good governance in the promotion and protection of human rights', UN Doc A/HRC/RES/51/5 (2022) para 13.

responsiveness, effectiveness and efficiency, ethical conduct, human rights, sound financial management;[187] and consensus.[188] These parameters can be used to critically evaluate and improve the quality of judicial governance and *injugovins*' performance. But, where they are not also matched by legal obligations, they are only recommendatory. Without further contextualization, they are also too open-ended and inconclusive to offer tangible guidance or justify strong preferences for certain solutions over competing options.

Well-calibrated institutional designs and effective checks and balances are essential to ensuring high-quality judicial governance. But it is the attitude, agency, and conduct of the governing institutions in discharging their 'duties of care' towards ICTs that are even more decisive. There are many things that can go wrong—and disastrously so—leading to crises and major setbacks for ICTs. Since the vocabulary to refer to international judicial governance inadequacies and instances of 'bad governance', or judicial governance malpractice, is currently lacking, the following tentative terminology is proposed here: '*mis*governance' and '*un*governance'. Whether an *injugovin* can reasonably be blamed for either is a contextual determination and can only be gauged on a case-by-case basis.

In those cases where *injugovins* gravely or systematically overstep statutory competences, or allow their governance powers to be abused by individual members (states) without reining them in, it is possible to speak of what I propose to call judicial *mis*governance. This is what is done to a court when an *injugovin* exercises its functions improperly or systematically fails to exercise them in a timely and appropriate fashion, thereby seriously compromising the court's independence, effectiveness, or other core aspects of its work. There are multiple cases on the record that can potentially qualify as such, with some being tackled in this book.[189] Milder forms of 'bad governance' characterized by inertia and indecision on the part of an *injugovin* due to underlying (political) disagreements on the objectives or methods of governance can by contrast be termed *un*governance.[190] Ungovernance is not a total lack of governance or inactivity by governance bodies but rather governance through procrastination whereby an *injugovin* remains anaemic in the face of known problems that

[187] Committee of Ministers (CoE), 'Strategy for Innovation and Good Governance at Local Level' (2008) <https://rm.coe.int/1680746f16> (listing twelve 'European Principles of Good Democratic Governance').

[188] UN Economic and Social Commission for Asia and the Pacific, 'What Is Good Governance?' (10 July 2009) <https://hdl.handle.net/20.500.12870/3794>.

[189] eg John Eudes Ruhangisa, 'Governance of Regional Integration Courts', in this volume (on the backlash against the SADC Tribunal following its *Campbell* judgment against Zimbabwe and on the abuses of governance power by the summit of heads of state in respect of the EACJ); Peter Van den Bossche 'The Demise of the WTO Appellate Body', in this volume (on the failure to appoint WTO AB members leading to a paralysis of the dispute-settlement mechanism); and Zsuzsanna Deen-Racsmány, 'Deficient Protection of the Independence of International Judges by International Judicial Governance Institutions', in this volume (on the UN organs' failure to protect judicial independence in the case of the MICT judge from Turkey arrested and detained by Turkish authorities).

[190] The term has been used for different purposes yet in a compatible sense in constitutional theory scholarship: Deval Desai and Andrew Lang, 'Introduction; Global Un-governance' (2020) 11(3) Transnational Legal Theory 219; Christine Bell, '"It's Law Jim, But Not as We Know It": The Public Law Techniques of Ungovernance' (2020) 11(3) Transnational Legal Theory 300, 300 (a 'mode of governance' in which 'the complexity of the institutional form mirrors and acts as a container for the complexity of the disagreement underlying the attempt to govern, rather than reflecting a political agreement as to the project of government').

are within its power and capacity to address.[191] This encumbers the court's operation without reaching the levels of disruption associated with *mis*governance and poses risks of dysfunction that strain the *injugovin*–ICT relationship and may erupt in the public domain. Constant postponement, decision-avoidance, burying pressing issues in sub-committees' paperwork, passing the buck, and looking the other way are characteristic of judicial ungovernance and can typically be observed in large *injugovins* operating as multilateral inter-state forums. The debacle with the indexation of ICC judicial salaries, leading embarrassingly to a case brought by the judges against their Court before the ILO Administrative Tribunal in 2020, serves as one example.[192] The issue was finally addressed when, following the recommendation of a specially appointed panel, the ASP reformed the system of remuneration for ICC judges, aligning it with the UN Under-Secretary-General package level.[193]

2.5 Conclusion

International judicial governance is not a new phenomenon. It is coeval with the project of international justice itself: every international court or tribunal, from the earliest specimens to the latest hybrid experiments, has had to be governed by states or international organizations in order to exist and perform their judicial functions. But the governance of international courts has long remained in obscurity, being the reserved domain of court officials and civil servants, ministry officials in capitals, and international justice experts. By contrast, the scholarship on domestic court governance as part of comparative judicial studies has had a two-decade head-start. It presents a rich repository of conceptual thinking, comparative data, critical debates, and cautionary tales on how judiciaries should be designed, governed, and optimized to ensure that courts perform their functions independently and impartially while remaining answerable to society. It has addressed complementarities and tensions between these core principles of judicial organization, the institutional and individual aspects of judicial independence, and the relationship between external oversight and self-governance of courts. The insights from domestic experiences into how various forms of judicial governance give effect to the separation of powers and the rule-of-law principles, prevent the capture of the judiciary by political actors, and contribute to the resilience of democracy and human rights, are revealing. In some respects, this experience could serve as a frame of reference for international judicial governance.

This chapter has primarily served the exploratory and taxonomic tasks of defining and mapping the legal and institutional field of (international) judicial governance, as well as attaining clarity on select conceptual and normative issues. Secondly, it has endeavoured to catch up with domestic judicial governance debates and to identify insights and lessons potentially transferable to the sphere of governance of international

[191] For specific examples from the African regional courts' governance, see John Eudes Ruhangisa, 'Governance of Regional Integration Courts', Section 7.3.4, in this volume.

[192] *H and others* v *ICC*, Judgment no 4354, 131st session, ILOAT, 7 December 2020.

[193] ICC-ASP, 'Resolution on the remuneration of judges of the ICC' (ICC-ASP/19/Res.3, 16 December 2020). Manolescu (n 147) 264–66.

courts. The hope is that bridging this nascent discipline with its more established domestic counterpart could nudge its further development. Comparative judicial governance scholars and international justice experts have much to discuss. Many themes and challenges are common and familiar to both groups. Institutional differences and wildly divergent legal contexts in which domestic and international courts operate and are governed also set limits on the possible cross-fertilization of insights, given the risk of falling into the trap of false analogies.

International judicial governance is defined broadly as the field of international institutional law and practice that concerns the operation of, and coordination among, institutions and actors in the exercise of their competences and roles in governing ICTs, with a view to ensuring their independent, impartial, accountable, and effective performance. It is a system of legal norms and practices regulating how the international institutions overseeing and managing international adjudicatory organs must enable them to carry out their judicial mandates in accordance with these requirements. Similarly to domestic court governance, and in contrast to the contiguous yet incommensurable notion of 'government', international judicial *governance* is a collective and polycentric enterprise. It implies power-sharing, delegation, and coordination between the 'nodes' of the multi-actor network situated both within and outside courts themselves. Governance is not—and should not be—a blunt wielding of vertical power and turf wars over competences and influence. In the international context, judicial *self*-governance should be interpreted narrowly due to a starker division between the internal and external dimensions of court governance and because judicial participation in external governance bodies is negligible as compared to domestic settings. Accordingly, this chapter clarifies that international judicial *self*-governance is exercised within the *internal* sphere of the core business and internal administration of ICTs. The category of international judicial governance is reserved exclusively for external governance, ie the competences and functions of *external* judicial governance bodies.

This chapter has surveyed the meaning of, and the interplay between, the core tenets of judicial independence and accountability in connection with main judicial governance models and the dilemmas and challenges arising in both the national and international context. This review reveals that judicial independence is integral to the judicial function, which is common to both national and international courts, and that, accordingly, the duty to respect and protect judicial independence is integral to the function of judicial governance, whether domestically or internationally. Judicial independence is not protected for its own sake; it is both qualified and reinforced by the imperative of judicial accountability. The experiences related to national judicial councils teach a poignant lesson in this respect: judicial *self*-governance, particularly when taking the form of court leadership's predominance within external court governance bodies, has a dark side.[194] Strong institutional autonomy without sufficient emphasis on judicial ethics, individual independence, and accountability, is a recipe for producing an insulated, corporatist, and self-serving judicial caste in which rank-and-file and senior judges alike may forfeit individual independence. The public trust

[194] Bobek and Kosař (n 6) 1290; Kosař (n 6) 1591 (against the 'rosy view of judicial self-governance').

in the judiciary and its legitimacy, which are required for higher levels of institutional independence, must be earned. The requisite integrity of the judicial corps cannot be achieved without robust professional ethics regimes and accountability mechanisms: independence and accountability are closely interlinked.

In addition, this chapter has outlined why the situation of international judges is different from that of their domestic peers, and how their institutional-constitutional embedment in the international legal order or within the frameworks of multilateral organizations reformats the arrangements for court governance. Operating beyond states and vested with mandates untethered from a single sovereign in order to safeguard judicial independence, ICTs deal with politically charged dockets and face formidable institutional and practical challenges. They are stared down by a plurality of Leviathans with stakes in their cases in a system where the separation of powers offers them no protection. Even more than in domestic contexts, transferring governance powers to dedicated *injugovins* does not extinguish the risk of undue influences, political pressures, or capture. International courts are constantly walking a tightrope as they carry out their functions, in a manner befitting courts of law. The standards of institutional judicial independence for international judiciaries exist at the level of individual treaty and statutory regimes, but they are neither uniform across the board nor robustly regulated in general international law.

Finally, the different types of *injugovins* in use are no match for domestic models. Each offers advantages but also carries risks of its own. Much like at the domestic level, there is no single superior fit for every context. Unitary *injugovins* facilitate concerted attention to judicial governance matters but may be unwieldy and inefficient. International organizations are over-bureaucratic and distracted by other priorities, potentially leading their organs to lose sight of ICTs' nature and needs as *judicial* institutions. But they may also be less threatening to judicial independence due to the diffusion of authority. This chapter proposes a tentative categorization of defects and breaches of trust in governing courts depending on the *injugovin*'s conduct: *mis*governance as a serious or systemic abuse of governance mandates and *un*governance as a dereliction of governance duties affecting the court's functioning. Qualifying the *injugovin*'s behaviour as *mis-* or *un*governance is a context-dependent determination. The chapters in this book provide detailed accounts of troubling incidents and debacles in international judicial governance practice that might warrant such assessments. To retool the 'Anna Karenina principle' for international judicial governance, 'All happy judicial governance regimes are alike; each unhappy one is unhappy in its own way.'

3

International Judicial Governance Institutions

Topography, Typology, and Guiding Principles

Niels Blokker[*]

3.1 Introduction

This chapter aims to provide an inventory of the existing international judicial governance institutions (*injugovins*), as defined in Chapter 1 of this book. This overview is mostly descriptive and comparative. It is partly a topography as it describes ('-graphia') the place ('topos') where key decisions are made for the governance of international courts and tribunals, regarding, in particular, the election of judges, the adoption of budgets, and the enforcement of judgments. In addition, it provides a typology of *injugovins* and briefly discusses the guiding principles of their work.

The subject-matter of this book requires, at the outset, a topography, an inventory of the governance institutions that are analysed in more detail in subsequent chapters. While such an inventory would no longer be necessary in a research project on international courts and tribunals (most of which have been studied extensively),[1] this is different for their governance institutions. In practice, the governance schemes have often been developed *after* the international courts and tribunals were created, rather than before.[2] In a similar vein, governance issues have long been neglected in academic writings about international judicial institutions. The dearth of research in this field is inversely proportional to the abundance of raw material and the urgency

* I would like to thank my former students Whitny Kapa and Yiannis Milionis for their research assistance, and my colleagues Armin Cuyvers and Sergey Vasiliev for their comments on a draft of this chapter.

[1] Cesare PR Romano, Karen J Alter, and Yuval Shany (eds), *The Oxford Handbook of International Adjudication* (OUP 2014); Karen J Alter, *The New Terrain of International Law: Courts, Politics, Rights* (Princeton University Press 2014).

[2] Huw Llewellyn, 'Governance of the United Nations Criminal Tribunals', in this volume, demonstrates that oversight mechanisms for UN criminal tribunals were mostly developed in practice, in an ad hoc way, *after* the creation of these tribunals. The failure to notice (not to use the word 'oversight' in a different meaning) the need for an adequate governance mechanism is striking. Two other examples are the governance of the International Tribunal of the Law of the Sea (ITLOS) and the International Criminal Court (ICC). On the former: Niels M Blokker, 'Governance of the International Tribunal of the Law of the Sea: The Role of the Meeting of States Parties to the Law of the Sea Convention' in Angela del Vecchio and Roberto Virzo (eds), *Interpretations of the United Nations Convention of the Law of the Sea by International Courts and Tribunals* (Springer 2019) 82–91. On the latter: Adriaan Bos, 'Assembly of States Parties' in Antonio Cassese, Paola Gaeta, and John RWD Jones (eds), *The Rome Statute of the International Criminal Court: A Commentary* (OUP 2002) 300 ('only at the very end of the discussions in the PrepCom was serious attention given to the establishment of an Assembly of States Parties').

Niels Blokker, *International Judicial Governance Institutions* In: *Governance of International Courts and Tribunals*.
Edited by: Sergey Vasiliev and Niels Blokker, Oxford University Press. © Niels Blokker 2026.
DOI: 10.1093/oso/9780198922131.003.0003

of governance problems.[3] A large amount of 'raw material' on the governance of international courts and tribunals is available to be researched. To some extent, it is true what the Russian composer Nikolaj Medtner has observed: 'We create nothing, everything is already there. We only discover.'[4] In addition, Einstein's aphorism comes to mind: 'Die Welt vor uns, ein geöffnetes Buch. Wenn wir es nur lesen können.'[5]

Therefore, as a modest but necessary first step, this raw research material must be 'discovered', collected, and presented before it can be analysed. Section 3.2 will further explain the scope of this chapter. Section 3.3 will provide a topography of *injugovins*. It will distinguish between different governance functions: the election of judges, the adoption of the budget, and the enforcement of judgments. Next, based on this overview, Section 3.4 will propose a typology of *injugovins*. Subsequently, the guiding principles for their work—the independence and accountability of international courts and tribunals—will briefly be discussed in Section 3.5. Section 3.6 will offer some conclusions.

3.2 Scope of Inquiry

The topography that follows covers the governance institutions of all currently existing international courts and tribunals and of some that are now dormant or have ceased to exist but were created since 1990. The governance legacy of the courts no longer in operation may also be relevant for our understanding of the evolution of governance of international courts and tribunals during the last three decades. Before presenting this topography, a few considerations and explanations should be provided.

This chapter only deals with the *external* governance of international courts and tribunals. To a considerable degree, these courts and tribunals also govern themselves, ie are subject to *internal* governance. They make their own rules and decisions concerning their internal organization and functioning. For example, they adopt internal rules of procedure and elect their presidents and vice-presidents; they also make internal decisions on judges' dismissal or disqualification. Internal governance is fundamentally different from external governance. The latter involves decisions—often of crucial importance—that international courts and tribunals cannot make themselves and for which they need to rely on those who govern them. Immediately, this brings into play some fundamental requirements, particularly the duty to respect the independence of courts and tribunals.

Each international court or tribunal has its own *injugovin*. Many have more than one. For example, the UN General Assembly and the UN Security Council perform governance functions for the International Court of Justice (ICJ). The ICJ budget is part of the UN budget, which the General Assembly adopts.[6] The Security Council

[3] For further information, see Sergey Vasiliev and Niels Blokker, 'Introduction', in this volume.

[4] This quotation is taken from the explanatory introduction to a CD with recordings of songs composed by Medtner (1880–1951): Medtner, *Incantation—Complete Songs* (Vol 1, 2020), performed by Ekaterina Levental and Frank Peters.

[5] Jürgen Neffe, *Einstein: Eine Biographie* (Rowohlt Taschenbuch 2005) 169('The world before us, an open book. If only we were able to read it.' Translated by the author).

[6] Charter of the United Nations (opened for signature 26 June 1945, entered into force 24 October 1945) 1 UNTS 16 (UN Charter) Art 17(1)1.

may play a role in the enforcement of ICJ judgments.[7] The members of the Court are elected jointly by the General Assembly and the Security Council.[8] This example of the judicial governance roles of the General Assembly and the Security Council also illustrates that the work of *injugovins* may only be a small part of their activities. In other cases, this judicial governance role is in the hands of a dedicated organ. An example of such an *injugovin* whose activities exclusively concern an international court or tribunal, is the Assembly of States Parties (ASP) of the International Criminal Court (ICC).[9]

Since many international courts and tribunals do not have one single *injugovin* (dedicated or not), an inventory of *injugovins* cannot, for each court and tribunal, simply mention one institution that performs all necessary governance functions. Rather, it should indicate the specific governance institution that is responsible for specific governance functions. Key governance functions are the election of judges, the adoption of the budget, and the enforcement of judgments. Several contributions to this book discuss these functions in more detail. The purpose of the inventory below is to map the specific governance institutions that are responsible for each of these main functions.

There are different ways to categorize the relevant raw governance research material. A distinction could be made between *injugovins* of universal and regional (and even sub-regional) courts and tribunals. *Injugovins* may also be classified according to the jurisdiction *ratione materiae* of 'their' courts and tribunals, from the general (ICJ) to the specific (eg the International Tribunal for the Law of the Sea (ITLOS) and the ICC). However, for the purpose of this inventory, it is best to keep the relevant governance material as raw as possible, without 'putting it into boxes' at the outset, and to present the *injugovins* in the chronological order in which their courts and tribunals were established. Column 1 of Table 3.1 at the start of Section 3.3 therefore contains a chronologically ordered list of international courts and tribunals. Almost two-thirds of the thirty-four courts and tribunals mentioned in Table 3.1 have been established since 1990. Two of the twelve courts and tribunals created before 1990 are universal: the ICJ and the ITLOS. The other ten are regional. Six are European (the European Court of Human Rights, the Court of Justice of the European Union, the OECD Nuclear Energy Agency Tribunal, the Chamber of Appeal of the Rhine Commission, the Benelux Court, and the European Tribunal on State Immunity). Three are in the Americas (the Eastern Caribbean Supreme Court, the Inter-American Court of Human Rights, and the Andean Court), and one is in the Arab region (the Judicial Tribunal of the Organization of Arab Petroleum Exporting Countries (OAPEC Tribunal)). Therefore, before 1990, no regional courts or tribunals existed in Africa, Asia, Australia, and Oceania, although these parts of the world have the majority of all states and almost 80 per cent of the

[7] ibid Art 94(2).

[8] Statute of the International Court of Justice (opened for signature 26 June 1945, entered into force 24 October 1945) 33 UNTS 993 (ICJ Statute) Art 4.1.

[9] Rome Statute of the International Criminal Court (opened for signature 17 July 1998, entered into force 1 July 2002) 2187 UNTS 3 (ICC Statute) Art 112.

Table 3.1 *Injugovins* for key governance functions

International court/ tribunal	Functions of *injugovins*		
	Election of judges	**Adoption of budget**	**Enforcement of judgments**
1. ICJ (1945)	UNGA and UNSC	UNGA	UNSC
2. ECtHR (1950)	PACE (CoE)	Committee of Ministers	Committee of Ministers
3. CJEU (1951)	Member States' Governments (MSt Governments)	EU Council and European Parliament	European Commission; CJEU; domestic
4. OECD Nuclear Energy Agency Tribunal (1957)	OECD Council	OECD Council	Steering Committee
5. Rhine Chamber of Appeal (1963)	Central Commission for the Navigation of the Rhine	Central Commission for the Navigation of the Rhine	domestic
6. Benelux Court (1965)	Benelux Committee of Ministers	Benelux Committee of Ministers	domestic
7. Eastern Caribbean Supreme Court (1967)	Judicial and Legal Services Commission	MSt Governments	domestic
8. Inter-American Court of Human Rights (1969)	States Parties (StP) to the Convention	OAS GA	OAS GA and StP
9. Europ. Trib. for State Immunity (1972)	PACE (CoE)	CoE Committee of Ministers	CoE Committee of Ministers
10. OAPEC Judicial Tribunal (1981)	OAPEC Council	OAPEC Council	domestic
11. ITLOS (1982)	Meeting of StP to the UNCLOS (SPLOS)	SPLOS	domestic
12. Andean Community Court of Justice (1984)	MSt Governments	Andean Commission	domestic
13. Central American Court of Justice (1991)	Supreme Courts of MSt	MSt Governments	domestic
14. EFTA Court (1992)	MSt Governments	MSt Governments	EFTA Surveillance Authority
15. Economic Court of the CIS (1992)	StP (same procedure as for judges of higher national courts)	Council of Heads of Govs	unknown
16. SADC Tribunal (1992)	Council	Council	Summit; domestic
17. ICTY (1993)	UNGA and UNSC	UNGA	ICTY; MSt
18. ECOWAS Court (1993)	Authority	Council of Ministers	domestic
19. OHADA Court (1993)	Council of Ministers	Council of Ministers	domestic
20. COMESA Court (1993)	Council of Ministers	Council of Ministers	domestic

Continued

Table 3.1 Continued

International court/ tribunal	Functions of *injugovins*		
	Election of judges	**Adoption of budget**	**Enforcement of judgments**
21. CEMAC Court (1994)	Conference of Heads of States	Conference of Heads of States	Conference of Heads of States
22. ICTR (1994)	UNGA and UNSC	UNGA	ICTR; MSt
23. WTO Appellate Body (1994)	WTO Dispute Settlement Body (DSB)	General Council	DSB
24. Afr. Ct on Human and Peoples' Rights (1998)	AU Assembly	AU Assembly	AU Assembly
25. ICC (1998)	ICC Assembly of States Parties (ASP)	ASP	ICC; ASP; MSt
26. East African Community Court (1999)	East African Community Summit	East African Community Assembly	MSt
27. Court of the Eurasian Economic Community (2000)	Interparliamentary Assembly	Inter-State Council	Inter-State Council
28. Caribbean Court of Justice (2001)	Judicial and Legal Services Commission and MSt	Trust Fund	domestic
29. SCSL (2002)	SGUN and Government of Sierra Leone	Management Committee	SCSL; MSt (Sierra Leone)
30. MERCOSUR Perm. Rev. Trib. (2002)	MERCOSUR MSt	MERCOSUR MSt	-
31. STL (2007)	SGUN and Government of Lebanon	Management Committee	STL; MSt (Lebanon)
32. Residual SCSL	SGUN and Government of Sierra Leone	Oversight Committee	Residual SCSL; MSt
33. International Residual Mechanism for Criminal Tribunals (IRMCT) (2010)	UNGA and UNSC	UNGA	IRMCT; MSt
34. Court of the Eurasian Economic Union (2014)	Supreme Council	Supreme Council	-

world population). Since 1990, this situation has changed dramatically. Out of the twenty-two newly created courts and tribunals, two are universal (WTO Appellate Body and ICC) and the others are regional, now also including courts and tribunals in Africa and Eurasia.

Regarding the scope of their jurisdiction *ratione materiae*, only the ICJ has general jurisdiction, covering the entire field of international law. Many regional integration and human rights courts and tribunals also cover broad subject-matters, but they only operate in a particular region. Moreover, even though they may be open-minded in terms of taking general international law into account, their primary orientation remains more specific (ie regional integration and/or human rights).[10] Some other courts and tribunals operate in more specific areas of international law, such as the law of the sea (ITLOS) and criminal law (ICC and ad hoc or special criminal tribunals). Finally, a few courts and tribunals have been set up for highly specific purposes. One example is the Chamber of Appeal of the Central Commission for the Navigation of the Rhine (discussed in Section 3.2.1). Governance of international administrative tribunals created to deal with complaints of staff of international organizations, is excluded from the analysis in this chapter.[11]

There is great diversity among the thirty-four international courts and tribunals this chapter covers. Two of them are yet to consider any cases: the OECD Nuclear Energy Agency Tribunal and the European Tribunal on State Immunity. Others have hundreds or even thousands of cases each year. As a result, the following inventory features institutions that govern grossly unequal courts. At the same time, there is unity within diversity. All these courts have in common that they need independent judges and an adequate budget; enforcing judgments is also a common challenge.

Most of the courts and tribunals mentioned in Table 3.1 in Section 3.3 have been researched rather extensively. Moreover, since this chapter deals with *injugovins* rather than 'their' courts and tribunals, there is no need to provide a brief analysis of each of those courts and tribunals. However, an exception is made for a few of them, either because they are barely or not at all covered by the available literature, or because their mandate deviates from that of the others (or both). This is true for the Chamber of Appeal of the Central Commission for the Navigation of the Rhine, the Caribbean Court of Justice, the Eastern Caribbean Supreme Court, and the Court of the Eurasian Economic Union. The following brief discussion of these four courts also illustrates that the generic term 'international courts and tribunals' covers a wide variety of judicial bodies. It remains to be seen whether that is also the case for their *injugovins*.

[10] John Eudes Ruhangisa, 'Governance of Regional Integration Courts', in this volume.

[11] Before 1980, only two such tribunals existed: the ILO Administrative Tribunal and the UN Administrative Tribunal. Since then, many organizations have established their own administrative tribunals. For an overview, see Chris de Cooker, 'Proliferation of International Administrative Tribunals', (2022) 12 Asian Journal of International Law 232–47. The governance of these tribunals has hardly been analysed.

3.2.1 Chamber of Appeal of the Central Commission for the Navigation of the Rhine

The Central Commission for the Navigation of the Rhine (CCNR or Central Commission), which was established by the Vienna Congress in 1815, is widely regarded as the first international organization. The 1868 Mannheim Convention introduced legal remedies for infringements of the police rules on navigation (criminal procedure) or in the event of a dispute concerning damage caused during navigation on the Rhine (civil cases). Each member state was required to designate the courts of first instance competent to deal with such disputes.

For appeals from these 'Rhine River Court' judgments, parties can either follow the normal appeal procedures under the national legal system concerned or directly address the CCNR. As the Central Commission is not composed of judges but rather of representatives from the member states, this appeal procedure could originally not be regarded as a judicial procedure. However, this changed when the 1963 Strasbourg Convention established the Chamber of Appeal as an independent judicial body of the CCNR.[12] The Chamber of Appeal is composed of one judge and one deputy judge proposed by each member state and appointed by the CCNR for a period of six years.[13] The judges are required to have received legal education or to have experience in Rhine navigation.[14] They are fully independent, free from any instruction, and may not sit in a case in which they have previously been involved in another capacity.[15] The 1963 Strasbourg Convention entered into force in 1967. The Chamber of Appeal delivered its first judgment on 23 June 1970. Since then, it has issued hundreds of judgments.[16] The plenary meeting of the Central Commission, composed of representatives of the governments of the five member states (Belgium, France, Germany, The Netherlands, and Switzerland), is the *injugovin* of the Chamber of Appeal of the CCNR. It appoints the judges of the Chamber of Appeal and adopts the CCNR budget which includes the costs of the Chamber of Appeal.

[12] In more detail: Willem E Haak and Bonifacius C de Savornin Lohman, *Procederen in Rijnvaartzaken* (Sdu Uitgevers 2008) 10–11 and 63–90. As the Dutch government indicated in its Explanatory Memorandum to the Draft Law of Approval of the Strasbourg Convention (Kamerstukken II, Zitting 1965–66, 8364, nr 3, 3): 'Hiermede wordt beoogd, de onafhankelijkheid van de Centrale Commissie bij de uitoefening van haar rechtsprekende taak te waarborgen' (translation by the author: the Chamber of Appeal is created to guarantee the independence of the Central Commission in the performance of its judicial function).

[13] Revised Convention on the Navigation of the Rhine (opened for signature 17 October 1868, entered into force 1 July 1869, as amended by the 1963 Strasbourg Convention) (Revised Convention) Art 45*bis* states 'qui seront proposées'. This proposal is binding: Haak and de Savornin Lohman (n 12) 21.

[14] Revised Convention (n 13) Art 45*bis*: 'qui doivent avoir une formation juridique ou une expérience de la navigation du Rhin'.

[15] ibid: 'Les membres de la Chambre des Appels exercent leurs fonctions en pleine indépendance et ne sont liés par aucune instruction. Ils ne peuvent siéger dans une affaire dont ils ont déjà eu à connaître en une autre qualité.'

[16] Haak and de Savornin Lohman (n 12) 87. For further information on the Chamber of Appeal, see <https://ccr-zkr.org/12060200-en.html> (with references to literature). At the end of September 2024, the Chamber of Appeal had delivered 794 judgments (published by the Institute for German and International Transport Law of the University of Mannheim, <http://iwt-law.uni-mannheim.de>).

3.2.2 International courts in the Caribbean

Two other less well-known international courts are the regional courts in the Caribbean: the Caribbean Court of Justice and the Eastern Caribbean Supreme Court. The latter is the older of the two. It is currently one of the so-called Institutions of the Organisation of Eastern Caribbean States (OECS, established in 1981), but it antedates this organization, which was created in 1967 as the West Indies Associated States Supreme Court.[17] Subsequently renamed as the Eastern Caribbean Supreme Court, it is the supreme court for six OECS member states (Antigua and Barbuda, Dominica, Grenada, St Kitts-Nevis, St Lucia, and St Vincent and the Grenadines) and three associate OECS member states (the British Overseas Territories Anguilla, the British Virgin Islands, and Montserrat), with a total population of some 660,000. One of the special features of this Court is how its judges are elected, which resembles the procedure for the election of judges of the Caribbean Court of Justice.

The Caribbean Court of Justice was established in 2001.[18] Unlike the Eastern Caribbean Supreme Court, it postdates the organization to which it is related, the Caribbean Community (CARICOM) which was created in 1973. CARICOM currently has fifteen member states (Antigua and Barbuda, Bahamas, Barbados, Belize, Dominica, Grenada, Guyana, Haiti, Jamaica, Montserrat, St Kitts-Nevis, St Lucia, St Vincent and the Grenadines, Suriname, and Trinidad and Tobago) and five associated members (Anguilla, Bermuda, British Virgin Islands, Cayman Islands, and Turks and Caicos Islands), with a total population of some 18.5 million. The Caribbean Court of Justice is formally not an organ of the Caribbean Community, although it is closely connected to it.[19] At present, twelve of the fifteen member states are parties to the Court's constituent instrument (Bahamas, Haiti, and Montserrat have not yet joined). The Caribbean Court of Justice has two distinct functions. Under its 'original jurisdiction', it is an international court with exclusive jurisdiction to interpret and apply the CARICOM constitution (the 2001 Revised Treaty of Chaguaramas). Under its 'appellate jurisdiction', the Court is the final court of appeal for civil and criminal matters for those Caribbean countries that have accepted this role (currently Barbados, Belize, Dominica, and Guyana).[20] As to the governance of the Court, two characteristics deserve special attention: the election of the judges and the financing of the Court. These characteristics are discussed next.

The CCJ judges are not elected by a policy-making organ of CARICOM or by the state parties to the Court's constituent instrument, but by a separate institution instead: the Regional Judicial and Legal Services Commission, which was also created by the 2001 Agreement Establishing the Caribbean Court of Justice. The

[17] By UK legislation, the West Indies Associated States Supreme Order No 223 (1967). At the time, the participating countries were not yet independent.

[18] By the Agreement Establishing the Caribbean Court of Justice (opened for signature 14 February 2000, entered into force 23 July 2003) (CCJ Agreement). The Court was inaugurated on 16 April 2005.

[19] The CCJ Agreement is open to member states of the Caribbean Community as well as to 'any other Caribbean country which is invited by the Conference to become a Party to this Agreement' (CCJ Agreement (n 18) Art II).

[20] CCJ Annual Report 2020–21 <https://ccj.org/wp-content/uploads/2022/02/CCJ-Annual-Report-2020_2021.pdf> 5.

Commission is not composed of representatives of the governments of the state parties to this agreement. Its members are the President of the Court (chairman of the Commission), two persons nominated jointly by the Organization of the Commonwealth Caribbean Bar Association and the Organization of Eastern Caribbean States Bar Association, one chairman of the Judicial Services Commission of a Contracting Party (selected in rotation in the English alphabetical order for a period of three years), the Chairman of a Public Service Commission of a Contracting Party (selected in rotation in the reverse English alphabetical order for a period of three years), two persons from civil society nominated jointly by the Secretary-General of the Community and the Director General of the OECS for a period of three years following consultations with regional non-governmental organizations, two distinguished jurists nominated jointly by the Dean of the Faculty of Law of the University of the West Indies, the Deans of the Faculties of Law of any of the Contracting Parties and the Chairman of the Council of Legal Education, and two persons nominated jointly by the Bar or Law Associations of the Contracting Parties.[21] The President of the Court, who by virtue of his office is also the Chair of the Commission, is appointed by a three-quarters majority vote of the parties to the 2001 Agreement on the recommendation of the Commission.[22]

The way in which the Caribbean Court of Justice is financed is unique.[23] A loan of US $100 million was raised on the international market by the Caribbean Development Bank and repaid by the participating states. This loan was put in a Trust Fund. A Board of Trustees is responsible for investing these assets and paying the Court's expenses. This exceptional way of financing was chosen to protect the independence of the Court, more specifically to deal with concerns that the judges could have been subject to informal pressure if they had been paid by their governments.[24]

3.2.3 The Court of the Eurasian Economic Union

The Court of the Eurasian Economic Union (EAEU Court) is yet another example of a less well-known international court.[25] This Court is one of the organs of the Eurasian

21 CCJ Agreement (n 18) Art V.1.

22 ibid Art IV.6.

23 ibid Art XXVIII; Revised Agreement Establishing the Caribbean Court of Justice Trust Fund (opened for signature 12 January 2004, entered into force 27 January 2004); Protocol to the Agreement Establishing the Caribbean Court of Justice Relating to the Tenure of Judges, Rules of the Court, Financial Arrangements and Withdrawal from Agreement as well as the Relationship between Provisions on the Original Jurisdiction of the Caribbean Court of Justice and the Constitutions of the States Parties (opened for signature 17 February 2005, entered into force 6 March 2006) Art IV. The Regional Judicial and Legal Services Commission is also financed from this Trust Fund.

24 CCJ Trust Fund (CCJ) <https://ccj.org/about-the-ccj/ccj-trust-fund>.

25 There is only limited literature in English on this Court, eg Ekaterina Diyachenko and Kirill Entin, 'The Court of the Eurasian Economic Union: Challenges and Perspectives' (2017) 5(2) Russian Law Journal 53; Tatiana Neshataeva and Pavel Myslivskiy, 'Court of the Eurasian Economic Union: The Beginning' (2019) 7(3) Russian Law Journal 134; Elena Babkina, 'The Court of the Eurasian Economic Union' in Alexander Trunk, Azar Aliyev, and Marina Trunk-Fedorova (eds), *Law of International Trade in the Region of the Caucasus, Central Asia and Russia* (Brill Nijhoff 2022) 336–50.

Economic Union (EAEU).[26] It replaced the Court of the EAEU's predecessor, the Eurasian Economic Community (EAEC). The EAEU Court is not a legal successor of the EAEC Court but was created as an entirely new institution,[27] with a more limited jurisdiction than its predecessor.[28] The Court is based in Minsk (Belarus). The EAEU currently has five member states: Armenia, Belarus, Kazakhstan, Kyrgyzstan, and the Russian Federation. Annex 2 of the constituent instrument of the EAEU contains the Statute of the Court. The Court is composed of two judges from each member state, appointed for a term of nine years.[29] Judges are appointed by the EAEU Supreme Council (the 'supreme body of the EAEU' composed of the heads of state of the member states),[30] upon nomination by the member states.[31] The judges may be discharged from their duties by the Supreme Council. This raises questions about their independence. The Statute of the Court lists eleven grounds for such a discharge that do not exist in other international courts and tribunals; for example, 'conduct of activity incompatible with the duties of a judge' and 'entry into force of judgment of guilt against the judge or court decision on application of compulsory medical measures to him/her'.[32] If judgments of the Court are not implemented, the EAEU Supreme Council may adopt the necessary measures.[33] The Court's expenses are covered by the budget of the EAEU, which is adopted by the Supreme Council.[34] As is evident from the above brief overview, the Supreme Council of the Eurasian Economic Union is the *injugovin* of this Court.

3.3 A Topography of *Injugovins* for Key Governance Functions

This section will provide a topography of the institutions that perform key governance functions for the thirty-four international courts and tribunals covered by this chapter. These institutions are listed in Table 3.1. The first column lists the thirty-four international courts and tribunals covered in the chronological order of their establishment. The second, third, and fourth columns list the *injugovins* that elect the judges,

[26] Treaty on the Eurasian Economic Union (opened for signature on 29 May 2014, entered into force 1 January 2015) 3049 UNTS 4, Arts 8.1 and19. For the website of the Court, see <http://courteurasian.org> (texts in Russian).

[27] This decision may have been prompted 'not only by the intent to substantially review the competence and operation of the Court through drafting a new Statute and Rules of Procedure but also by the desire of some of the Member States to appoint new judges and to get more control over their appointment and dismissal': Diyachenko and Entin (n 25) 54.

[28] For example, it does not have the power to give preliminary rulings at the request of national courts, although it should be noted that in practice, hardly any preliminary rulings were requested from the EAEC Court: Diyachenko and Entin (n 25) 60–62.

[29] Statute of the Court of the Eurasian Economic Union (Annex 2 to the Treaty on the Eurasian Economic Union (n 26)) Art II paras 7–8.

[30] Treaty on the Eurasian Economic Union (n 26) Art 10.

[31] Statute of the EAEU Court (n 29) Art II para 10.

[32] ibid Art II para 12. The quoted parts are taken from the English translation of the Court's Statute <www.wto.org/english/thewto_e/acc_e/kaz_e/WTACCKAZ85_LEG_1.pdf>.

[33] ibid Art VII para 114.

[34] Treaty on the Eurasian Economic Union (n 26) Arts 12(2)–(6) and 20(1).

adopt the budget, and are involved in the enforcement of judgments. Sections 3.3.1 through 3.3.3 discuss the different institutions for these three governance functions.

3.3.1 Election of judges of international courts and tribunals

The election of judges is a core function of *injugovins*.[35] International courts and tribunals cannot settle disputes and deliver justice, as defined in their statutes or other constituent instruments, without well-qualified and independent judges.[36] While this is also true for national courts, it is even more so at the international level, where sovereign and sometimes very powerful states rule and where courts are not embedded in a solid legal order and tradition. In such a context, where the rule of power may be stronger than the rule of law, judges of high authority and reputation are needed even more than at the national level. This is reflected in the legal provisions encapsulating the qualifications for these positions.[37]

Two stages must be distinguished in the process of electing international judges: the nomination of candidates and the final election. The constituent instruments of international courts and tribunals contain specific rules governing each stage. While these rules share some common characteristics, there are also considerable differences. Some of these differences may be explained by the fact that several courts have judges from each of the participating states (eg Court of Justice of the EU (CJEU), European Court of Human Rights (ECtHR), EAEU Court), while others have judges from only a limited number of states parties (eg ICJ, Inter-American Court of Human Rights (IACtHR), World Trade Organization Appellate Body (WTO AB), and ICC). In the case of the former, there is an obligation to elect judges from each participating state; in the case of the latter, candidates often need to campaign, and the *injugovins* involved must choose between nominees from different states parties. Notably, not all (sub-)regional courts are composed of judges from all member states. Examples are the OECD Nuclear Energy Agency Tribunal, the IACtHR, the OAPEC Judicial Tribunal, the Court of the Organization for the Harmonization of Business Law in Africa (OHADA Court), the ECOWAS Court, and the Caribbean Court of Justice.

With regard to the two above-mentioned stages, the governments of the relevant states often play a dominant role, especially during the final election. However, already in 1920, when the Permanent Court of International Justice (PCIJ) was created, the awareness existed that it was in the common interest that nominations should be made at some distance from governments, by the national groups of the Permanent

[35] Andrew Drzemczewski, 'The Election of Judges onto the European Court of Human Rights', Christiaan Timmermans, 'The Procedure for Nominating Members of the EU Courts', and Christian M De Vos and others, 'Electing the Best?', in this volume, are devoted to specific topics related to this function.

[36] In 2011, the Institut de Droit International adopted a Resolution on the Position of the International Judge. According to the first paragraph of this resolution, 'the quality of international courts and tribunals depends first of all on the intellectual and moral character of the judges' (Session de Rhodes, 6 RES EN FINAL, 9 September 2011).

[37] For instance, judges of several international courts and tribunals must possess the qualifications required in their countries for appointment to the highest judicial offices (eg ICJ, CJEU, Andean Court of Justice, ECOWAS Court of Justice, ICC, and the EAEU Court).

Court of Arbitration (PCA).[38] Hence, the nomination task was given to experts who were deemed more qualified to assess the extent to which candidates met the requirements of the Statute. The final choice was still to be made by organs composed of government representatives, but at least there were some guarantees that this choice concerned qualified candidates (and not, to put it bluntly, less independent 'friends of the governments', whether qualified or less so). At present, there is considerable variation in the way candidates are nominated. The nomination procedure involving the national groups of the PCA is currently used not only for the ICJ but also as one of the two nomination procedures for ICC judges.[39] For other international courts, nominations are in most cases made by the governments of the relevant states. Often, they *must* (eg ECtHR and the Andean Court of Justice) or *may* (eg IACtHR, ITLOS, and ECOWAS Court) present more than one candidate, which gives the electing organ the advantage of choice. In recent years, the nomination of candidate judges for some international courts has become less of a (near-)exclusive prerogative of the governments concerned due to increased screening by external bodies (eg ECtHR, CJEU, and ICC).[40]

Once nominations have been completed, final election decisions must be made. In Table 3.1, the second column shows the institutions that elect the judges of the respective international courts and tribunals. It is sometimes observed that judges of international courts and tribunals are generally elected by organs composed of representatives of the governments of the participating states.[41] However, Table 3.1 shows that there is room for nuance here. While in most cases (twenty-four out of the thirty-four courts) international judges are indeed elected by organs composed of representatives of governments, in the other ten cases judges are elected in fundamentally different ways. These include the election of judges by:

- a parliamentary organ (three courts: ECtHR, ETSI, and EECC);
- the UN Secretary-General (UNSG) and the government of the state concerned (eg SCSL and STL);
- a commission of experts, the 'judicial and legal services commission' (two Caribbean courts);
- the supreme courts of the participating states (Central American Court of Justice);
- the states parties, in the same way they elect judges of their higher economic and commercial courts (CIS Court).

Therefore, the election of international judges is not the exclusive domain of bodies composed of representatives of governments; there is a variety in the types of *injugovins* responsible for such elections. Additionally, in at least one out of the twenty-four cases where international judges are elected by bodies composed of

[38] Further on the governance of the PCIJ, see Henri de Waele, 'Managing the Realization of "The Hope of Ages"', in this volume. This is still the procedure today for nominations of ICJ judges: ICJ Statute (n 8) Arts 4–6.

[39] ICC Statute (n 9) Art 36(4)a.

[40] For further information on this, see Andrew Drzemczewski, 'The Election of Judges onto the European Court of Human Rights', Christiaan Timmermans, 'The Procedure for Nominating Members of the EU Courts', and Christian M De Vos and others, 'Electing the Best?', in this volume.

[41] eg Ruth MacKenzie, 'The Selection of International Judges' in Romano and others (n 1) 738.

representatives of governments (the EU), expert advice is offered on the candidates before election decisions are made. The so-called 255 Panel gives its 'opinion on candidates' suitability to perform the duties of Judge and Advocate-General of the Court of Justice and the General Court before the governments of the Member States make the appointments'.[42] Between March 2010 and October 2019, 20.8 per cent of the first-term opinions of the Panel were unfavourable.[43] According to Timmermans, even though the Panel opinions are not binding, they have always been followed, even if they were unfavourable.[44] Thus, it is not entirely left to politics (the governments of the EU member states) when it comes to making the necessary election decisions.

Finally, it should be noted that nineteen out of the twenty-four *injugovins* composed of government representatives are proper organs. In the remaining five cases (CJEU, IACtHR, Andean Court, EFTA Court, and Mercosur PRT) the election decisions are made by dedicated ad hoc gatherings, convened for the single purpose of the elections.

3.3.2 Adoption of the budgets of international courts and tribunals

Apart from the election of judges, another core function of *injugovins* is the adoption of the budget. In most cases, the budget is adopted for a period of one year; in a few cases, this is two years.[45] It is obvious that international courts and tribunals require an adequate budget that enables them to perform their functions. At the same time, it is also self-evident that the views of international courts on what is 'adequate' may differ from those of politicians who ultimately decide on these budgets. This is also true for national courts. However, this difference may be even greater at the international level. Here, states with different legal systems, traditions, levels of prosperity, and diverging views on the necessary degree of courts' autonomy must find common ground and agree on the finances of their international courts and tribunals. This is not always easy, as was illustrated in 2007–08, when the ICJ and the UN General Assembly clashed about the remuneration of the judges and the principle of equality of all judges,[46] and in June 2021, when the Special Tribunal for Lebanon had to cancel the commencement of the trial in the (second) *Ayyash* case after the Registrar had indicated that the Tribunal no longer had the necessary funds to perform its mandate.[47]

The *injugovins* that adopt the budgets of international courts and tribunals are often the same as the ones that elect their judges: these are the organs composed of

[42] Consolidated Version of the Treaty on the Functioning of the European Union (opened for signature 13 December 2007, entered into force 1 December 2009) 2008 OJ (C 115) 47 (TFEU) Art 255.

[43] Christiaan Timmermans, 'The Procedure for Nominating Members of the EU Courts', in this volume.

[44] ibid.

[45] Independent Expert Review of the International Criminal Court and the Rome Statute System, Final Report, 30 September 2020, ICC-ASP/19/16 <https://asp.icc-cpi.int/iccdocs/asp_docs/ASP19/IER-Final-Report-ENG.pdf> (IER Report) paras 347–48.

[46] For further on this, see Niels M Blokker, 'The Governance of International Courts and Tribunals: Organizing and Guaranteeing Independence and Accountability' in Andreas Føllesdal and Geir Ulfstein (eds), *The Judicialization of International Law: A Mixed Blessing?* (OUP 2018).

[47] For further details on this, see Huw Llewellyn, 'Governance of the United Nations Criminal Tribunals' and Evelyn Anoya, 'Governance of the Special Tribunal for Lebanon', in this volume.

representatives of governments. However, while judges are sometimes elected in other ways as well, this is hardly the case when it comes to the adoption of the budget.

The budgets of almost all of the thirty-four international courts and tribunals covered in this chapter are adopted by plenary policy-making organs, composed of representatives of the governments of the member states. Some of these are organs of the same organization of which the relevant court or tribunal forms part (eg UN General Assembly, the CCNR, the Andean Commission, Assembly of the African Union, the Supreme Council of the Eurasian Economic Union, and the WTO General Council). Others are separate treaty bodies (eg Meeting of the States Parties to the Convention of the Law of the Sea (SPLOS) and ICC ASP). Still others are ad hoc gatherings of the participating states (eg with respect to the Eastern Caribbean Supreme Court, the Central American Court, and the EFTA Court). Exceptionally, the budget of the CJEU (which forms part of the annual budget of the EU) is adopted by the European Parliament and the Council, and it is for the President of the European Parliament to 'declare that the budget [of the EU] has been definitively adopted'.[48] Only in two other cases—the ECOWAS Court and the East African Community Court—do parliamentary organs (the ECOWAS Parliament and the East African Assembly, respectively) play a role in the decision-making about the budget of the organization (including the budget of these courts). This exceptional role of international parliaments may be explained by the more supranational nature of the regional organizations concerned, in which decisions are increasingly taken outside of the spheres of control of national parliaments. The resulting 'democratic deficit' is repaired by giving budgetary (and legislative) powers to a parliamentary organ of the organization. A final exception to the practice that the budgets of almost all international courts and tribunals are adopted by plenary policy-making organs is the Caribbean Court of Justice, which is fully financed by income from a Trust Fund (Section 3.2.2).

3.3.3 Enforcement of judgments of international courts and tribunals

A third key function of governance institutions of international courts and tribunals is the enforcement of judgments.[49] Themis holds both a scale and a sword. As Pascal observed in the seventeenth century: 'La justice sans la force est impuissante' ('justice without might is powerless').[50] This is true for national courts, but even more so for their counterparts at the international level. The international legal order traditionally lacks enforcement mechanisms similar to those existing at the national level.[51] Only

[48] TFEU (n 42) Art 314.9.

[49] For further details on this, see Dorine Nauleau, 'The Enforcement of International Judicial Decisions' and Hanneke Palm and Roeland Böcker, 'Implementation of Judgments of the European Court of Human Rights', in this volume.

[50] Blaise Pascal, *Pensées* (2008) 124 (original edition published posthumously in 1669; Pascal died in 1662). This is only the first half of Pascal's proposition. The other half is: 'la force sans la justice est tyrannique' ('might without justice is tyrannical').

[51] Already in 1969, Reisman observed: 'Most frequently the real problem is not in arriving at an answer in law, but in *enforcing* an answer in law.' WM Reisman, 'The Enforcement of International Judgments' (1969) 63 American Journal of International Law 1.

in a limited number of cases are states willing to submit themselves to the jurisdiction of international courts and tribunals and their binding judgments. Their willingness to also accept *the enforcement* of such judgments is even more limited, as is evident from the overview of the international courts and tribunals in this chapter.

Almost all of the statutes or other legal instruments governing international courts and tribunals explicitly state that judgments are binding and must be complied with. However, what should happen in cases of non-compliance? What if one of the disputing parties claims that the other party or parties did not implement a judgment? The answers to this question vary. For instance, in the case of the EAEU Court, enforcement is explicitly left to the disputing parties (and therefore left to power politics).[52] In other cases, a variety of soft or more stringent instruments and measures exist to improve compliance with judgments.[53] In several cases, *injugovins* play a role in this regard, although this is sometimes more evident on paper rather than in practice.

A closer look at the thirty-four international courts and tribunals covered by this chapter shows that, in some cases, a party claiming that a judgment is not implemented may resort to the same court again, but only with a new claim this time: that of non-compliance with a judgment of the court.[54] If the court concludes that its judgment is not implemented, this may create additional pressure on the non-complying party. The next question, then, is whether there are any other instruments to be used to ensure compliance.

Another important implementation instrument can be found in the domestic legal order of states parties. Existing *national* rules, procedures, and institutions for the enforcement of judgments of national courts (indicated in Table 3.1 as 'domestic') may sometimes be used to enforce judgments of international courts and tribunals as well. For example, decisions of the Seabed Disputes Chamber of ITLOS 'shall be enforceable in the territories of the States Parties in the same manner as judgments or orders of the highest court of the State Party in whose territory the enforcement is sought'.[55] Similarly, the judgments of the OAPEC Tribunal

> shall be considered final, binding and res judicata upon the parties and shall be enforceable per se in the territories of the members. The party concerned shall present the judgment to the local authority responsible for execution, and the competent local authorities shall, after verifying that the document forwarded is official, execute the judgment.[56]

[52] Statute of the EAEU Court (n 29) Art VII para 103: 'Disputing parties shall independently determine the form and manner of the enforcement of the Court decision.'

[53] On the role of the Committee of Ministers (CoE), see Hanneke Palm and Roeland Böcker, 'Implementation of Judgments of the European Court of Human Rights', in this volume.

[54] eg ECtHR (European Convention on Human Rights (opened for signature 4 November 1950, entered into force 3 September 1953) 213 UNTS 221 (ECHR) Art 46); SADC Tribunal (Protocol on Tribunal in the Southern African Development Community (opened for signature 18 August 2014) (Protocol on SADC Tribunal) Art 32(4)).

[55] Statute of the International Tribunal of the Law of the Sea (opened for signature 10 December 1982, entered into force 16 November 1994) 1833 UNTS 561 (ITLOS Statute) Art 39.

[56] Agreement of the Organization of Arab Petroleum Exporting Countries (entered into force 9 January 1968) (OAPEC Agreement) Art 24.

Other examples are the Chamber of Appeal of the Rhine Commission,[57] the Andean Court,[58] the Central American Court,[59] the Southern African Development Community (SADC) Tribunal,[60] and the OHADA Court.[61] Some instruments specifically provide that the execution of decisions involving financial penalties, compensatory damages etc is done in accordance with the relevant rules of the relevant state (ie rules of civil procedure, rules governing the execution of judgments against the state etc).[62] In all these cases, national rules, procedures, and institutions perform a dual executive function: one within national legal systems and another within the international legal order.[63] There is something paradoxical in performing the latter executive function. National rules, procedures, and institutions (including courts) are both friends and foes of international courts and tribunals when it comes to the enforcement of their judgments. On the one hand, they are an ideal ally: positioned within national legal systems, they may provide the international Themis with a much-needed sword. On the other hand, positioned within national legal systems, they may also be reluctant to use this sword, having their first and foremost executive function at the domestic level and a natural loyalty towards the relevant national authorities.[64] How this paradox plays out in practice depends on many variables, such as the independent position of national courts within their domestic legal order, the specific international court and case at hand, and, more generally, a more open or more closed tradition of interacting with the international legal order. There is a dearth of research in this field.[65]

Judgments of international criminal courts and tribunals are executed by states.[66] But these courts and tribunals themselves supervise the enforcement of a sentence

[57] Haak and de Savornin Lohman (n 12) 75.

[58] Treaty Creating the Court of Justice of the Cartagena Agreement, Arts 27 and 5.

[59] Convention on the Statute of the Central American Court of Justice (opened for signature 10 December 1992, entered into force 2 February 1994) 1821 UNTS 292 (Statute of the Central American Court) Art 39 (judgments of the Court will be executed as if they were a judgment of a national court of the respective state).

[60] Protocol on SADC Tribunal (n 54) Art 32(1).

[61] Treaty on the Harmonization of the Business Law in Africa (opened for signature 31 March 1965, entered into force 1 January 1974) (OHADA Treaty) Art 20.

[62] Benelux Court (Treaty Concerning the Establishment and Statute of a Benelux Court of Justice (opened for signature 10 December 1992, entered into force 2 February 1994) 924 UNTS 42 (Statute of the Benelux Court) Art 11(5bis); IACtHR (American Convention on Human Rights (opened for signature 22 November 1969, entered into force 18 July 1987) 1144 UNTS 144 (ACHR) Art 68(2); COMESA Court (Treaty Establishing the Common Market for Eastern and Southern Africa (opened for signature 5 November 1993, entered into force 8 December 1994) 2314 UNTS 265 (COMESA Treaty) Art 40; East African Court (Treaty for the Establishment of the East African Community (opened for signature 30 November 1999, entered into force 7 July 2000) 2144 UNTS 255, Art 44).

[63] This is an example of what Scelle called *dédoublement fonctionnel*. Antonio Cassese, 'Remarks on Scelle's Theory of Role Splitting (*dédoublement fonctionnel*) in International Law' (1990) 1 European Journal of International Law 210.

[64] Alexandra Valeria Huneeus, 'Compliance with Judgments and Decisions' in Romano and others (n 1) 449.

[65] André Nollkaemper, *National Courts and the International Rule of Law* (OUP 2011); André Nollkaemper, 'Conversations among Courts: Domestic and International Adjudicators' in Romano, Alter, and Shany (n 1) 523–49; Yvonne Dutton, *Rules, Politics, and the International Criminal Court* (Routledge 2013); Courtney Hillebrecht, *Domestic Politics and International Human Rights Tribunals: The Problem of Compliance* (CUP 2014).

[66] eg ICC Statute (n 9) Art 103 (the Statute refers to 'the State of enforcement').

of imprisonment by states. For example, in the case of the International Criminal Tribunal for the former Yugoslavia (ICTY),

> Imprisonment shall be served in a State designated by the International Tribunal from a list of States which have indicated to the Security Council their willingness to accept convicted persons. Such imprisonment shall be in accordance with the applicable law of the State concerned, subject to the supervision of the International Tribunal.[67]

Likewise, in the case of the ICC, '[t]he enforcement of a sentence of imprisonment shall be subject to the supervision of the Court'.[68]

Finally, in eleven out of the thirty-four cases, policy-making organs (often the supreme organ of the organization of which the relevant court forms part) play a specific role in the enforcement of judgments and decisions. In some of these cases, it is for one of the states concerned to raise an issue of non-compliance before the relevant organ: the UN Security Council (ICJ),[69] and the Inter-State Council, at the level of heads of state (Eurasian Economic Community Court).[70] With regard to the ICC, the Rome Statute empowers the Court to refer cases of non-cooperation by states to the ASP and, in the context of a referral of the situation by the UN Security Council, to the Council.[71] The Rome Statute does not specify what measures the ASP or the Security Council could take. In other cases, it is standard procedure for the policy-making organ concerned to supervise the execution of court judgments: the Committee of Ministers of the Council of Europe (ECtHR),[72] the European Commission (CJEU),[73] the WTO Dispute Settlement Body (WTO Appellate Body),[74] the AU Assembly (the African Court on Human and Peoples' Rights (ACtHPR)),[75] and to some extent the OAS General Assembly (IACtHR).[76] Sometimes it is at the full discretion of

[67] Statute of the International Tribunal for Prosecution of Persons Responsible for Serious Violations of International Humanitarian Law Committed in the Territory of the Former Yugoslavia, UNSC Res 827 (25 May 1993) UN Doc S/Res/827, Annex (ICTY Statute) Art 27. The Statutes of the Rwanda Tribunal, the Special Court for Sierra Leone, the Special Tribunal for Lebanon, and the International Residual Mechanism for Criminal Tribunals have a similar provision.

[68] ICC Statute (n 9) Art 106(1).

[69] UN Charter (n 8) Art 94(2).

[70] Statute of the EAEU Court (n 29) Art 20(2).

[71] ICC Statute (n 9) Arts 87(5) and (7) and 112(2)(f). The statutes of the ad hoc criminal tribunals do not have a similar provision.

[72] ECHR (n 54) Art 46.2.

[73] TFEU (n 42) Art 260.

[74] Marrakesh Agreement Establishing the World Trade Organization (opened for signature 15 April 1994, entered into force 1 January 1995), Annex 2 (WTO Dispute Settlement Understanding) Art 21(6).

[75] The Protocol establishing this Court, adopted in 1998, provides that the Council of Ministers of the OAU shall monitor the execution of judgments on behalf of the Assembly. The African Union succeeded the OAU in 2002; this task is now performed by the African Union's Assembly.

[76] American Convention on Human Rights (signed at San José on 22 November 1969, entered into force on 18 July 1978) OAS Treaty Series No 36, 1144 UNTS 123 (ACHR) Art 65. This provision lays down an obligation for the Court rather than a power of the Assembly to systematically supervise the implementation of judgments ('To each regular session of the General Assembly of the Organization of American States the Court shall submit, for the Assembly's consideration, a report on its work during the previous year. It shall specify, in particular, the cases in which a state has not complied with its judgments, making any pertinent recommendations').

the policy-making organ to decide what measures are to be taken in cases of non-compliance: 'recommendations' or 'measures' (UN Security Council);[77] 'measures' (Council of Europe Committee of Ministers);[78] 'appropriate action' (SADC Summit);[79] with regard to the OECD Nuclear Energy Agency Tribunal, the Steering Committee 'shall take whatever steps are needed to execute the decision of the Tribunal'.[80] Alternatively, specific sanctions are mentioned. In the EU, the European Commission 'shall specify the amount of the lump sum or penalty payment' to be paid by the member state that has not complied with a CJEU judgment; it is then up to the Court to impose such a lump sum or penalty payment.[81] Another example is the Andean Court (restriction or suspension of advantages of the Cartagena Agreement in relation to the non-complying party).[82] With respect to the WTO Appellate Body, the WTO Dispute Settlement Body may adopt sanctions; for example, it may authorize suspension of the application to the member state concerned of concessions or other obligations under the covered agreements.[83]

The EU has the most advanced system for the enforcement of judgments of the CJEU. To some extent, this system resembles the enforcement rules for judgments of the ECtHR. However, in the EU, it is for the European Commission (not for an organ composed of representatives of governments) to supervise the implementation of judgments. In addition, the Court may impose a lump sum or penalty payment on the state concerned at the end of the procedure.[84] This is not a mere theoretical possibility, and the amount of money to be paid may be considerable. For example, in October 2021 the Court ordered Poland to pay the Commission a periodic penalty payment of one million euros per day, because Poland did not comply with its obligations under an order of the Court of 14 July 2021 (it had not suspended the application of the provisions of national legislation relating, in particular, to the areas of jurisdiction of the Disciplinary Chamber of the Polish Supreme Court).[85]

It may be concluded that judgments of international courts and tribunals are often enforced in a decentralized way, by using rules, mechanisms, and institutions for the enforcement of judgments of national courts. At the international level, *injugovins* only play a limited role in the enforcement of judgments of 'their' courts and tribunals.

[77] UN Charter (n 6) Art 94(2).
[78] ECHR (n 54) Art 46(5).
[79] Protocol on SADC Tribunal (n 54) Art 32(4) and (5).
[80] Convention on the Establishment of a Security Control in the Field of Nuclear Energy (opened for signature 20 December 1957, entered into force 22 July 1959) 2952 UNTS 267, Art. 13.b. The Steering Committee is the highest decision-making body of the Nuclear Energy Agency (NEA). It is composed of senior officials from national atomic energy authorities and associated ministries: NEA Steering Committee for Nuclear Energy (30 October 2020) <www.oecd-nea.org/jcms/pl_47909/nea-steering-committee-for-nuclear-energy-meeting>.
[81] TFEU (n 42) Art 260.
[82] Treaty of Creation of the Court of Justice of the Cartagena Agreement (n 62) Art 27.
[83] WTO Dispute Settlement Understanding (n 75) Art 22(2).
[84] TFEU (n 42) Art 260.
[85] CJEU press release no 192/21, 'Order of the Vice-President of the Court in Case C-204/21 R, *Commission v. Poland*' (27 October 2021) <https://curia.europa.eu/juris/document/document.jsf?text=&docid=248261&pageIndex=0&doclang=EN&mode=lst&dir=&occ=first&part=1&cid=16075240>.

3.4 Some Observations and a Typology

3.4.1 Some observations

If we review the topography in Section 3.3, several observations may be made. First, the governance of the thirty-four international courts and tribunals covered here is mostly partial, not integral. For each court or tribunal, the three governance functions under review are in most cases not carried out by one and the same body. It is the exception rather than the rule that there is one single *injugovin* for a court or tribunal. Examples of such exceptions are the ICC ASP and the EAEU Supreme Council. It is difficult to assess whether this has any implications. Is it better to unite all governance functions for a particular international court or tribunal within one institution, so that it can have a *vue d'ensemble*? Or is it better, for example, to have budget decisions adopted by governmental organs while placing some elements of the procedure for electing judges outside the control of governments? Answers to such questions may be different in different parts of the world and may also depend on whether one takes the perspective of a court or that of a government.

Second, it is rare for an international court or tribunal to have one *dedicated injugovin*. The example of the ICC ASP is exceptional. The exclusive raison d'être of the ASP is the ICC. For another universal court, the ICJ, this is completely different. The agendas of the General Assembly and the Security Council of the UN are filled with many topics; the ICJ represents only a very small part of their activities. Again, it is difficult to assess whether this has any implications. When ICJ President Higgins addressed the Security Council in 2006, she stated: 'The Security Council, faced with the massive problems in its agenda, might be forgiven for wondering whether judgments by a Court with no enforcement powers of its own—indeed, the Charter provides that the enforcement of Court judgments lies ultimately with the Security Council—will, in fact, be complied with.'[86] Do states consider the Security Council as a body that should fully focus on questions of war and peace rather than on compliance with judgments of the World Court?

Third, there may be different factors that influence or determine the governance arrangements for an international court or tribunal: its jurisdiction *ratione materiae*, the region of the world where it is based, the time of its creation, the availability of an obvious organizational context within which it can be embedded, political or personal preferences of the countries and their representatives involved in designing the governance arrangements, and other factors. Jurisdiction *ratione materiae* plays a role, as is clear from the fact that international criminal tribunals and the ICC themselves supervise the execution of judgments. Some European courts have supranational governance characteristics (eg the election of judges of the ECtHR by a parliamentary body, the role of the European Commission in supervising the implementation of judgments of the CJEU), while governance of Eastern European courts is largely intergovernmental. The governance characteristics of the Eastern Caribbean Supreme Court can partly be explained by the (late colonial) time of its creation. In many cases,

[86] UN Security Council, 5474th Meeting, 22 June 2006, UN Doc S/PV.5474, p 7.

international courts and tribunals are part of a larger international organization, making it obvious that governance functions are carried out by other, policy-making, organs of the same organization. A case-by-case analysis is required to see what factors have played a key role in shaping the governance design of an international court or tribunal.

Fourth, the governance of international courts and tribunals is not the exclusive domain of bodies composed of representatives of governments. More specifically, the election of judges as well as the enforcement of judgments are partly carried out in other ways. Only with regard to the adoption of budgets, bodies composed of representatives of governments almost always take the key decisions (the main exception being the cases in which parliamentary organs also play a role).

Fifth, the third governance function mentioned above—the enforcement of judgments—is rather underdeveloped compared to the election of judges and the adoption of the budget. This is unsurprising, as the enforcement of international law generally and the enforcement of judgments of international courts and tribunals in particular, is an area in which states are reluctant to relinquish control. However, even in this area, the demands of compliance may prevail over holding on to sovereign control, as is demonstrated by the possibility in the EU to impose lump sums and penalty payments on non-complying states.

3.4.2 A typology

The states participating in the creation of an international court or tribunal organize their judicial governance cooperation in different ways. Leaving aside the cases in which governance functions are performed by domestic institutions (particularly in the field of enforcement), the existing governance structures for international courts and tribunals follow one of the three following models:

- The *injugovin* is an organ of an international organization. It is embedded within the larger international organization of which 'its' court or tribunal is also part. This is the case for the large majority of *injugovins*. Examples are the General Assembly and the Security Council of the UN (eg ICJ, ICTY, ICTR), the WTO Dispute Settlement Body (WTO AB), the Committee of Ministers and the Parliamentary Assembly of the Council of Europe (ECtHR), the Andean Commission (Andean Court), the Assembly of the African Union (ACtHPR), the East African Legislative Assembly (East African Court), the Eurasian Supreme Council (EAEU Court), and the governance institutions of a number of courts of other regional organizations. This is to some extent the prototype of an *injugovin*. The other two models came later and are less common.
- The *injugovin* is a treaty organ.[87] As such, it is self-standing and not part of an international organization; it normally lacks its own international legal

[87] On treaty organs, see Geir Ulfstein, 'Reflections on Institutional Design Especially Treaty Bodies' in Jan Klabbers and Åsa Wallendahl (eds), *Research Handbook on the Law of International Organizations* (Edward Elgar Publishing 2011) 431–47; Geir Ulfstein, 'Treaty Bodies and Regimes' in Duncan B Hollis (ed), *The Oxford Guide to Treaties* (OUP 2012) 428–47; Gloria Fernández Arribas, 'Rethinking

personality. This type of *injugovin* is rare. The two only examples are the ASP (ICC) and SPLOS (ITLOS). *Injugovins* that are treaty organs may have their own secretariat (as is the case for the ASP), or they may rely on a 'host organization' that provides secretariat functions (SPLOS, which is supported by the UN Secretariat).[88]

- In other cases, the cooperation between the states concerned is organized within a loose gathering of relevant states, not created as an organ of an international organization or a treaty organ. For example, the judges of some international courts and tribunals are appointed by the states parties to the constituent instruments establishing these courts and tribunals: the judges of the CJEU are appointed 'by common accord of the governments of the member states',[89] and the judges of the IACtHR 'shall be elected by the states parties to the Convention, at the OAS General Assembly'.[90] Other examples are the gatherings of states that adopt the budget of the Central American Court,[91] and the budget of the Caribbean Court of Justice.[92] This third model, meetings of states parties, is also used for the UN human rights treaty bodies.[93]

These three models show that international judicial governance is structured in diverging ways, covering the whole gamut of institutionalized international cooperation: from almost pure ad hoc meetings having hardly any pre-established rules to fully fledged international organs that are almost always organs of an international organization (of which in most cases the relevant international court or tribunal

International Institutionalisation through Treaty Organs' (2020) 17 International Organizations Law Review 457.

[88] The Secretariat of the ASP—which is not mentioned in the Rome Statute—was created by ASP Res ICC/ASP/2/Res.3. On the administrative functions of the UN Secretariat for SPLOS: United Nations Convention on the Law of the Sea (opened for signature 10 December 1982, entered into force 16 November 1994) 1833 UNTS 397, Art 319.2(e); UNGA Res 37/66, UN Doc A/RES/37/66, 3 December 1982; UNGA Res 49/28 UN Doc A/RES/49/28, 19 December 1994; UNGA Res 52/26 UN Doc A/RES/52/26, 2 March 1998.

[89] Treaty on European Union (opened for signature 29 July 1992, entered into force 1 November 1993) 1992 OJ (C 191) 1 (TEU) Art 19(2).

[90] Statute of the Inter-American Court of Human Rights (opened for signature 31 October 1979, entered into force 1 January 1980) Art 6(1).

[91] Statute of the Central American Court of Justice (n 59) Art 41.

[92] CCJ Agreement (n 18) Art XXVIII(1).

[93] While UN human rights treaty bodies cannot be qualified as courts or tribunals, the governance issues discussed in this chapter apply equally to them. Robin R Churchill and Geir Ulfstein, 'Autonomous Institutional Arrangements in Multilateral Environmental Agreements: A Little-Noticed Phenomenon in International Law', (2000) 94 American Journal of International Law 623, 655–56. In 2009, the authoritative Dublin Statement on the Process of Strengthening of the United Nations Human Rights Treaty Body System recommended, inter alia, that 'States; acting multilaterally, consider such reform issues as the enhancement of the role and the potential of meetings of States parties to the various treaties, enhancement of the manner in which the reports of treaty bodies are received by the relevant political organs of the United Nations and the creation of an adequate financing basis for the treaty body system. States should also consider means to improve procedures for the nomination and the election of members of the treaty bodies, whereby the independence and expertise of elected members is fully assured.' The Dublin Statement on the Process of Strengthening of the United Nations Human Rights Treaty Body System (Office of the High Commissioner of Human Rights, 19 November 2009) <www2.ohchr.org/english/bodies/HRTD/docs/DublinStatement.pdf>.

is also an organ). International courts and tribunals sometimes have one single *injugovin*, belonging to one of the three models mentioned above (for instance, the ASP for the ICC). In other cases, they have two or more *injugovins*, either belonging to one model or to more. For example, while the *injugovins* of the CJEU (Council, European Parliament, and Commission) belong to the first model mentioned above, the judges of this Court are not appointed by one of the institutions of the Union, but 'by common accord of the governments of the member states' (the third model mentioned previously).[94] Another example is provided by the ECtHR. While its *injugovins* (the Committee of Ministers and the Parliamentary Assembly of the Council of Europe) fit in model one, several key governance declarations concerning this Court were in fact adopted by ad hoc conferences of the states parties (model three) that took place in Interlaken (2010), Izmir (2011), and Brighton (2012), not by the Committee of Ministers.[95]

The above-mentioned three models by which states establishing an international court or tribunal organize their judicial governance cooperation raise the questions to what extent and how international judicial governance institutions are more than the sum of their members. This is hardly (if at all) the case in the third model (a loose gathering of relevant states), since this gathering lacks an organic nature. This is different for the other two models (organs of international organizations and treaty organs). By definition, these are living organisms, with an existence and a practice of their own, having the capacity to develop the necessary *esprit de corps*. They are created by treaties, which may lay down legal boundaries which restrict the sovereign discretion of the participating states and within which these institutions must operate. Such legal boundaries are mostly of a procedural nature: the decision-making and other procedural rules of the governance institution concerned must be respected. For example, member states of the UN are not free to nominate candidate judges of the ICJ in any way they want; the ICJ Statute has detailed rules on the nomination of such candidates. For reasons related to the independence of judges, nominations are made not by governments of the member states but by national groups of the PCA. Elections are conducted by the General Assembly and the Security Council. UN member states are not free to elect members of the ICJ in any way they want. They must do so in their capacity as members of the General Assembly and the Security Council and by

94 TEU (n 90) Art 19(2). The difference between the first and the third model has implications for the jurisdiction of the CJEU. The Court shall review the legality of legislative acts and of acts of, inter alia, the Council, the Commission, the European Parliament, and the European Council intended to produce legal effects vis-à-vis third parties: TFEU (n 42) Art 263). It does not have jurisdiction to do so with respect to decisions taken by meetings of representatives of the governments of the member states. For this main reason, the Court dismissed in June 2021 the appeal by former Advocate-General Sharpston of the Court (she was not allowed to complete her term of office following Brexit). By this appeal, Sharpston sought to have set aside an earlier order of the General Court by which it rejected her application seeking partial annulment of the Declaration by the Conference of the Representatives of the Governments of the Member States on the consequences of the withdrawal of the UK from the EU for Advocates General of the Court. For further on this, see Kieran Bradley, 'Appointment and Dis-Appointment at the CJEU: Part II—The *Sharpston* Litigation' (2022) 21 The Law and Practice of International Courts and Tribunals 178; Dimitry V Kochenov and Graham Butler, 'Independence of the Court of Justice of the European Union: Unchecked Member States power after the Sharpston Affair' (2022) 27 European Law Journal 262.

95 For the text of the Interlaken, Izmir, and Brighton Declarations, see Reform of the Court (European Court of Human Rights) <www.echr.coe.int/Pages/home.aspx?p=basictexts/reform&c>.

following specific procedural rules laid down in the ICJ Statute, applicable since 1945 and reflecting the international community's requirements for selecting the judges of the World Court. These rules for nominating and electing the members of the ICJ have also inspired the rules for nominating and electing the judges of the ICC.

For these reasons, *injugovins* are more than the sums of their members if they are organs of international organizations or treaty organs. Does this matter? It will never be possible to demonstrate convincingly that such *injugovins* elect better judges and adopt more adequate budgets for 'their' international courts or tribunals than any ad hoc gatherings of representatives of state parties. There is no alternative history that would allow such a comparison. However, there are good reasons for arguing that it is preferable not to make governance decisions that are so vital for the successful functioning of international courts and tribunals in an ad hoc, improvised, or haphazard way, but instead to follow a more organized model, based on predetermined procedures, following past practice where applicable. In short: this should be done more in accordance with the rule of law. If this is done, if the relevant decision-making is not only power-based but rule-based as well, there is also more room for decision-making to be guided by two key governance principles: the independence and accountability of international courts and tribunals.

3.5 Guiding Governance Principles: Independence and Accountability of International Courts and Tribunals

The three above-mentioned key functions for the governance of international courts and tribunals (the election of well-qualified judges, the adoption of an adequate budget, and the enforcement of judgments) can only be performed properly if two overarching principles are respected: the principles of independence and accountability of international courts and tribunals. These principles are well established at the domestic level for national courts and tribunals. The requirement that courts and their judges are independent is generally recognized.[96] The requirement that courts are accountable is generally recognized as well, even though it is more abstract and not well covered in (international) legal instruments. While the principles of independence and accountability are also important for national courts and tribunals, they are even more important in the international society, where sovereign and sometimes very powerful states rule and where courts are not embedded in a strong legal order. In such a context, in which the rule of power may be stronger than the rule of law, courts and tribunals cannot perform their functions if they are not fully independent and if they are not also fully perceived as such. Nor can they perform their functions if they are not or not sufficiently accountable, first of all to the states that have established them but also to the wider public.

The principle of independence is usually explicitly mentioned in the statutes and other legal instruments of international courts and tribunals. A distinction should be

[96] eg Universal Declaration of Human Rights (adopted by UNGA 10 December 1948) UN Doc A/RES/217(III) Art 10; International Covenant on Civil and Political Rights (opened for signature 16 December 1966, entered into force 23 March 1976) 999 UNTS 172, Art 14(1).

made between the independence of international courts and tribunals as organs,[97] and the independence of their judges.[98] Usually, these statutes and other legal instruments contain a variety of provisions to ensure the independence of courts and tribunals and their judges. Examples are provisions on the privileges and immunities of the court and the judges, the inviolability of the premises of the court, the qualifications of the judges, the prohibition to dismiss judges (unless the other judges conclude that one of them no longer fulfils the required conditions).[99]

However, practice demonstrates that these provisions are not always observed. In May 2016, the US blocked the reappointment of one of the WTO AB members, Seung Wha Chang (South Korea). The US was of the opinion that 'his service did not reflect the role assigned to the Appellate Body' and mentioned that it was concerned about 'the manner in which Mr. Chang conducted oral hearings' and about 'the Appellate Body's adjudicative approach'.[100] Subsequently, the US also blocked the appointment of new Appellate Body members, and when the terms of office of the sitting members came to an end, the Body could no longer operate. In a meeting of the Dispute Settlement Body (the *injugovin* of the Appellate Body) many members criticized the US and stated that the independence and impartiality of the Appellate Body were at stake. Some stated that 'the United States' statement of opposition based on previous Appellate Body decisions could create a dangerous precedent for other reappointment proceedings and affect an Appellate Body member's decision-making during their first term', while the other six members of the Appellate Body wrote a letter in support of their colleague to all members of the WTO emphasizing his 'integrity, independence and impartiality'.[101] Therefore, within the *injugovin* concerned there was the necessary resistance to the US. Here, a 'flaw in the system' was the rule that decisions must be taken by consensus, without a fallback option of deciding by (qualified) majority vote if no consensus can be achieved.

Another example is the arrest and detention of the Turkish Judge Akay of the International Residual Mechanism for Criminal Tribunals in September 2016 in

[97] eg ICC Statute (n 9) Preamble, para 9 ('independent permanent International Criminal Court'); Revised Treaty of Economic Community of West African States (ECOWAS) (opened for signature 24 July 1993, entered into force 23 August 1995) 2373 UNTS 233 Art 15.3 ('The Court of Justice shall carry out the functions assigned to it independently of the Member States and the institutions of the Community').

[98] eg ICC Statute (n 9) Art 40.1 ('The judges shall be independent in the performance of their functions'); see Revised Convention (n 13) Art 45*bis* ('Les membres de la Chambre des Appels exercent leurs fonctions en pleine indépendance et ne sont liés par aucune instruction'). While independent, judges can only perform their functions adequately if, in doing so, they act as members of a collegiate body and thereby respect the independence of the other judges. ICJ Statute (n 8) Art 2 ('The Court shall be composed of *a body of* independent judges' (italics added)). IER Report (n 45) para 455.

[99] Only in the case of the EAEU Court, judges may be dismissed by its *injugovin*, the EAEU Supreme Council, for a variety of reasons to be interpreted by the Supreme Council (see Section 3.2). The founding fathers of this Union and of its Court therefore did not want to establish a truly independent court.

[100] See WTO members debate appointment/reappointment of Appellate Body members (WTO, 23 May 2016) <www.wto.org/english/news_e/news16_e/dsb_23may16_e.htm> at 2.

[101] ibid 3. Not much later, all the former, living members of the Appellate Body also sent a letter in support of Chang to the Chairman of the Dispute Settlement Body. In this letter, they warned that '[u]ndermining the impartial independence of the Appellate Body now would not only call into question for the first time the integrity of the Appellate Body; it would also put the very future of the entire WTO trading system at risk'. They also suggested to abolish the system of reappointments, and instead to have a single, longer term for the members of the Appellate Body (quotations taken from Blokker (n 46) 38). For detail on this crisis, see Peter Van den Bossche, 'The Demise of the WTO Appellate Body', in this volume.

Turkey. He was convicted in June 2017 on a single charge of being a member of a terrorist organization and was sentenced to seven and a half years' imprisonment.[102] All of this violated the immunity of Judge Akay, and the Mechanism was unable to fully perform its functions without him. Despite all necessary attempts by President Meron of the Mechanism, its *injugovins* (the UN Secretariat, the General Assembly, and the Security Council) failed to take action against Turkey.[103]

These two cases are different: in the former, the US took action not only against a member of the Appellate Body but also against this organ as a whole; in the latter, Turkey's actions were only directed against Judge Akay (even though they also affected the operation of the entire Mechanism). However, both examples are similar in demonstrating that a single powerful, assertive state may obstruct the functioning of international courts and tribunals by not fully accepting and respecting the independence of their judges. Notwithstanding widespread criticism of these obstructions, the *injugovins* concerned could not hold the states concerned to account and make them comply with their obligations. If the states concerned are unwilling, and the relevant *injugovins* are unable, the limits are reached of what can be done to guarantee the independence of international courts and tribunals.

The principle that judges and their international courts and tribunals are independent is generally recognized as a key principle. At the same time, 'independent' does not mean 'unaccountable'. With independence comes responsibility. The principle of independence is closely connected to the principle of accountability. International courts and tribunals need to be accountable about their performance. There must be an external authority, an institution to which they are answerable, where they explain their work, and how they perform their functions effectively and efficiently. The principle of independence does not shield international courts and tribunals from any outside interference. In this context, it may be useful to distinguish between the judicial functions of courts and the way in which they are organized and managed. The principle of independence applies in particular to the former, the principle of accountability in particular to the latter. Such a distinction is easier made in theory than applied in practice;[104] it is true neither that there should be no accountability at all for the exercise of judicial functions nor that courts and tribunals should not enjoy a sufficient amount of independence in organizing and managing their work. Nevertheless, this distinction may still provide some guidance in defining the spheres of responsibilities of international courts or tribunals and their *injugovins*.

One specific instrument by which international courts and tribunals can implement the principle of accountability is the budget, more specifically the draft budget that is

[102] Statement of the Mechanism on Conviction of Judge Aydın Sefa Akay by Turkish Criminal Court of First Instance (*IRMCT*, 15 June 2017) <www.unmict.org/en/news/statement-mechanism-conviction-judge-aydin-sefa-akay-turkish-criminal-court-first-instance>.

[103] The *Akay* case is discussed in detail in Zsuzsanna Deen-Racsmány, 'Deficient Protection of the Independence of International Judges by International Judicial Governance Institutions', in this volume.

[104] As was illustrated in 2015, when the President, the Prosecutor, and the Registrar of the ICC wrote an exceptional joint letter to the President of the ASP, in which they expressed 'great concern that a number of issues have been proposed for discussion at the Assembly which relate to matters falling clearly within the judicial and prosecutorial competence of the Court', and urged the ASP 'to ensure that the Court's judicial and prosecutorial independence is not undermined, or perceived to be undermined, by proceedings of the Assembly' (quoted in Blokker (n 46)).

prepared by the court or tribunal and needs to be adopted by the relevant *injugovin*. By carefully explaining the proposed budget to the states parties, the court or tribunal should demonstrate why it needs the finances that should enable them to perform the mandate that states parties defined when creating the court or tribunal. However, no matter how well explained and justified, the budget proposal cannot be considered as a non-negotiable offer. The principle of independence does not entail blank cheques. At the same time, having established an international court or tribunal entails certain obligations, including financial obligations. In each specific case, the court or tribunal and its *injugovin* need to balance the principles of accountability and independence when adopting the budget. A minimum of trust between the two parties is always indispensable to bring budget discussions to a satisfactory end.[105]

Another accountability instrument for international courts and tribunals is the annual report, in which they can both summarize their judicial activities and explain the effectiveness and efficiency of their internal organization. The statutes and other rules of only a limited number of the thirty-four international courts and tribunals covered in this chapter explicitly lay down an obligation to prepare an annual report. Examples are ITLOS, the SADC Tribunal, the ad hoc criminal tribunals (but not the ICC), the ACtHPR, and the EAEU Court. However, many of the other international courts and tribunals have initiated on their own accord a practice to publish such reports. The CJEU publishes an annual report that is divided into two parts: one covering its judicial activity and the other being a management report.[106] The ICJ itself took the initiative of submitting annual reports to the UN General Assembly in 1968, following the much-criticized 1966 judgments in the Southwest Africa cases.[107] The ICC has done so at its own initiative from the beginning. In practice, the General Assembly and the ASP normally 'take note' of these annual reports—a neutral term recognizing the independence of these courts.[108] There is usually no discussion on substance. In practice, an important function of these annual reports is that they create a reason for the President of the Court to be present in the relevant meeting of the *injugovin*.[109] In

[105] IER Report (n 45) para 330 ('The budget process is one instance where it is apparent that the trust relation between the Court and the ASP (including its subsidiary bodies) can and should be improved. On the one hand, some States Parties believe that the Court could and should be able to deliver more with the resources it has available. On the other hand, there seems to be a perception within some quarters of the Court that States Parties are using the budget process to interfere with the Court's cases').

[106] Annual Report 2020 Judicial Activity (Court of Justice of the European Union, February 2021) <https://curia.europa.eu/jcms/upload/docs/application/pdf/2021-04/ra_jud_2020_en.pdf>.

[107] Shabtai Rosenne, *The Law and Practice of the International Court 1920–2005, Vol. I* (4th edn, Martinus Nijhoff Publishers 2006), 111–12. Rosenne explains that the Court 'had become "conscious of the need for closer co-operation with the other organs of the United Nations". It was a public relations exercise, not a political or organizational requirement'. Salo Engel, 'Annual Reports of the International Court of Justice to the General Assembly' (1970) 44 British Yearbook of International Law 193, 198–99.

[108] eg UNGA Decision 67/510, UN Doc A/67/49 (Vol II), 1 November 2012; more recently, UNGA Decision 76/510, UN Doc A/76/49 (Vol II), 28 October 2021. ASP Official Records, 2nd session, ICC-ASP/2/10, 6 (para 22); ASP Official Records, 20th session, Vol I, ICC-ASP/20/20, 8 (para 24). By contrast, the UN General Assembly 'welcomes' the report prepared by the ICC in the context of the UN–ICC relationship agreement (eg UNGA Res 75/3, UN Doc A/RES/75/3, 4 November 2020, para 1).

[109] In his address to the UN General Assembly on 5 November 2015, ICJ President Ronny Abraham referred both to the modest resources of the ICJ and to the endeavours by the Court to use these resources efficiently: 'la Cour entend s'efforcer d'utiliser de façon optimale les ressources modestes qui sont mises à sa disposition'. Discours de S Exc M Ronny Abraham, Président de la Cour Internationale de Justice, à

this way, it offers a framework for informal consultations, a key ingredient for building and maintaining the necessary trust in the relationship of international courts and tribunals with their *injugovins*.

The statutes and other rules of international courts and tribunals are often not only silent on an obligation to report, but also more generally on the accountability functions of governance institutions. An exception is Article 112(2)(b) of the ICC Statute, according to which the ASP shall 'provide management oversight to the Presidency, the Prosecutor and the Registrar regarding the administration of the Court'. Referring to this obligation, the ASP has created a Study Group on Governance in 2010, to facilitate 'a structured dialogue between States Parties and the Court with a view to strengthening the institutional framework of the Rome Statute system and enhancing the efficiency and the effectiveness of the Court while fully preserving its judicial independence'. While this Study Group has made a number of recommendations, it was also reported in 2020, that '[t]here is widespread distrust of the ASP within all Organs of the Court' and that the Study Group is an instrument of the ASP to micromanage the operation of the Court.[110]

3.6 Concluding Observations: Towards Better *Injugovins* for Better International Courts and Tribunals

This chapter has offered a topography and a typology of *injugovins*. It has also briefly discussed the key governance principles of independence and accountability that guide their work. Above all, it is a plea to take the governance of international courts and tribunals more seriously, both in academic research and in practice. Half a century ago, Inis Claude wrote:

> one of the major tasks of twentieth-century statesmanship is to strike a balance between obsessive concern with institutional problems—which makes international organization an end in itself, and exclusive concentration upon substantive issues of current world politics—which neglects the building of an adequate institutional apparatus for international relations.[111]

More than fifty years later, it is clear that 'the building of an adequate institutional apparatus for international relations' has been far from neglected as far as the 'judicialization' of international relations is concerned. The growth in the number of international courts and tribunals since the 1990s is without precedent. However,

l'Occasion de la Soixante-Dixième Session de l'Assemblée Générale des Nations Unies (ICJ, 5 November 2015) <www.icj-cij.org/public/files/press-releases/0/000-20151105-PRE-01-00-BI.pdf>10.

110 IER Report (n 45) para 948 (referring to the Study Group and The Hague and New York Working Groups, 'which make frequent and time-consuming requests for more information on [the Court's] programs and management decisions. The Experts heard from certain staff that the requests for reporting leave little time for them to work on their regular tasks, as opposed to reporting on them').

111 Inis L Claude Jr, *Swords into Plowshares: The Problems and Progress of International Organization* (4th edn, Random House 1971) 84.

what *has* to some extent been neglected is 'the building of an adequate institutional apparatus' for the *governance* of all these courts and tribunals. When new international courts and tribunals were created, their governance was sometimes treated like a Cinderella.

The first aim of this chapter was to provide a topography of these somewhat neglected governance institutions, the *injugovins* of thirty-four international courts and tribunals. Table 3.1 in Section 3.3 provided an overview of these *injugovins*. Each international court and tribunal is unique, and there is great diversity among them. The jurisdiction and the broader role and activities of the Chamber of Appeal of the CCNR have little in common with the jurisdiction, role, and activities of the ICJ, the Andean Court, the East African Court, and the EAEU Court. However, all these unique international courts and tribunals are similar as far as their external governance is concerned. They all need good judges and adequate budgets, and they all face the challenge of enforcing their judgments. Therefore, they all need well-built governance institutions.

The topography of *injugovins* in this chapter has demonstrated a significant variation in the governance arrangements for international courts and tribunals. Although the governments of participating states are indeed omnipresent and play a pivotal role, in several cases governance functions are performed by institutions outside their control. At an early stage, it has been recognized that there is merit in limiting the exclusive role of governments in the nomination and election of judges. At present, there are nomination committees composed of independent experts; their influence is significant, as is demonstrated in other chapters of this book.[112] Exceptionally, judges are elected by an international parliamentary organ, such as the Parliamentary Assembly of the Council of Europe and the Interparliamentary Assembly of the EAEC. In some cases, international parliamentary organs play an important role in adopting the budget of international courts and tribunals. Finally, the governments' role is limited in enforcing judgments—precisely where it could be more robust. In several cases, this is left to the existing rules, mechanisms, and institutions available within the domestic legal orders of the state parties. Traditionally, at the international level, only some weak instruments exist; states have long been reluctant to accept inroads into their sovereignty in this field. However, more recently, the financial EU sanctions ('specified' by the European Commission and imposed by the CJEU in cases of non-compliance with judgments of the Court) have shown that there may be justifications for overcoming such reluctance.

This chapter has also provided a typology of *injugovins* (Section 3.4). This typology demonstrates that organs of an international organization (of which the relevant court or tribunal is also part) are the prototype *injugovin*. Another type of *injugovins*, treaty organs, exists only in two—important—cases, the ASP of the ICC and SPLOS in the case of the ITLOS. A third type of *injugovin* is the ad hoc gathering of the participating states. It was suggested that this third type is less suitable for performing the necessary governance functions. It is preferable to use a more organized model and to perform these functions based on predetermined rules and procedures, following past practice

[112] Andrew Drzemczewski, 'The Election of Judges onto the European Court of Human Rights' and Christiaan Timmermans, 'The Procedure for Nominating Members of the EU Courts', in this volume.

where applicable. Organs of international organizations and treaty organs provide better guarantees that the relevant decision-making is not only power-based but also rule-based.

A reference to rule-based decision-making raises the question of what rules apply to the exercise of governance functions. These rules are specific for each *injugovin*. It was outside the scope of this chapter to examine such rules in detail to see to what extent a body of 'good governance' rules has evolved in this field. However, it was argued that decision-making on the governance of international courts and tribunals must be guided by two key principles: independence and accountability. It is generally agreed that these principles are not only essential for the governance of national courts and tribunals but also—and even more—at the international level.

The topography and the typology mapped in this chapter demonstrate the existing variety of *injugovins*. But this is only the beginning. Much of the law and practice of *injugovins* is available for further research. The governance of international courts and tribunals should also be taken more seriously in practice when a new court or tribunal is created. It is telling that while only scant attention was paid to governance questions when the ICC was created, two decades later, a true governance crisis impeded this court's proper functioning and resulted in a 348-page report prepared by a body of nine authoritative experts, with no fewer than 384 recommendations.[113] There can be no well-functioning international courts and tribunals, no international justice without well-built *injugovins*.

[113] IER Report (n 45).

PART II
HISTORICAL ANTECEDENTS

4

Managing the Realization of 'The Hope of Ages'

Governance of the Permanent Court of International Justice

Henri de Waele

4.1 Introduction

At the time of its establishment, the Permanent Court of International Justice (PCIJ) could rightly be labelled as the most sophisticated judicial body internationally. It constituted the first standing court ever bestowed with a potentially global competence.[1] While studies on its creation and practical functioning have mushroomed in the last couple of decades, seemingly no focused and sustained attention has been paid so far to the concomitant judicial governance dimension. Thus, the current chapter neatly fills a lacuna in the existing scholarship, and complements the other contributions to this volume looking at modern tribunals that may by and large be regarded as successors to the PCIJ.[2]

Even at its historical nadir in the late 1930s and early 1940s, the Court was considered a tremendous asset, having produced a heritage worth preserving and nurturing.[3] Witnessing the genesis of the institution in 1920, the American scholar James Brown Scott remarked with satisfaction that '[t]he hope of ... ages is in the process of realization'.[4] As is known, proposals to found a permanent court of justice had already been tabled at the Hague Conferences of 1899 and 1907, but the idea only managed to fully gain traction after the First World War. Over a period of barely twenty years, the PCIJ came to accommodate the work of thirty judges, four deputy judges, twenty-three judges ad hoc, and two registrars in sixty-five proceedings leading to thirty-two judgments, thirty-seven advisory opinions, and one hundred and thirty-seven orders.[5]

[1] Ole Spiermann, *International Legal Argument in the Permanent Court of International Justice: The Rise of the International Judiciary* (CUP 2005) 13; Philippe Sands and Pierre Klein, *Bowett's Law of International Institutions* (6th edn, Sweet & Maxwell 2009) 357.

[2] The latter goes most obviously for the PCIJ's direct heir, the International Court of Justice (ICJ), discussed by Serena Forlati in Chapter 6. Unavoidably, there are various parallels to be drawn with the ICJ, as the present chapter will detail.

[3] eg Manley Hudson, *International Tribunals: Past and Future* (Carnegie Endowment/Brookings Institution 1944) 238; Stephen Schwebel, 'Reflections on the Role of the International Court of Justice' (1986) 61 Washington Law Review 1061, 1063.

[4] James Brown Scott, 'A Permanent Court of International Justice' (1920) 15 American Journal of International Law 52, 55.

[5] Spiermann (n 1) 395.

Henri de Waele, *Managing the Realization of 'The Hope of Ages'* In: *Governance of International Courts and Tribunals*. Edited by: Sergey Vasiliev and Niels Blokker, Oxford University Press. © Henri de Waele 2026.
DOI: 10.1093/oso/9780198922131.003.0004

Of course, all of this did not materialize spontaneously without internal debate, strife, or friction. As remarked by the first President of the Court, Bernard Loder, the task of the judges was honourable but difficult.[6] The same went for the PCIJ as a whole: being the first of its kind, confronted with a range of sanguine yet cagey interlocutors, it had to try to carve out its own space with caution. The vast expanse of public international law—to some a shockingly open-ended legal system—posed myriad substantive challenges; yet such was the broader political context within which a viable course had to be plotted. For the plurality of sovereign states, the international plane was something rather more residual, a complementary layer to the primary domestic legal continuum. Experiments had been undertaken before on that higher plane with other specialized bodies being put in place, limited to the sphere of arbitration. The creation of the League of Nations (LoN) marked a new beginning, but few dared to guess how long that era might last. The effective management of the PCIJ, just as how well its eventual output was received and implemented, would serve as a litmus test for any subsequent endeavours of creating international courts.

The present chapter aims to unpack this 'managerial side' of the Court, reviewing a series of salient issues concerning the PCIJ's governance. The study commences with a brief sketch of the Court's institutional surroundings, highlighting the run-up to its launch and background ideas underpinning its design, and explaining its relation to the League as such (Section 4.2). Hereafter, we investigate the Court's principal governance architecture, discussing the bodies entrusted with powers to oversee, steer, or modify the PCIJ's workings, how these competences could theoretically be exercised, and how they actually were (Section 4.3). Next, a closer scrutiny is undertaken of the judicial selection and appointment process, portraying the official modus operandi, followed by an appraisal of its merits after taking stock of the real-life dynamics (Section 4.4). Attention is then paid to the financial control and supervision aspects of governance, dissecting the general setup for administering the PCIJ's expenditure, including the arrangement of the judges' emoluments regime (Section 4.5). We round off with a series of concluding remarks that underscore the lessons that may be learnt from the PCIJ's pioneering experience, part of which have been taken to heart, while others have been less well heeded in subsequent international judicial institution-building initiatives (Section 4.6).

4.2 Establishment and Institutional Context

In spite of the great optimism about and lofty ideals of internationalism at the start of the twentieth century, the attempts to install adjudication as a stable fixture in international law failed to attract sufficient support during the 1899 and 1907 Hague Peace Conferences. In the late nineteenth century, blueprints had sprung from such venerable associations as the Institut de droit international, the International Law Association, and the Inter-Parliamentary Union—to no avail. On the rebound, in the immediate aftermath of the First World War, countless initiatives were launched once

[6] PCIJ Rep Series D, No 2 (1922) 330.

again for a world organization and a world court, no doubt spurred on by President Wilson's celebrated Fourteen Points manifesto.[7] Still, the initial plans for the construction of a LoN that were contemplated at the Paris Peace Conference (1919) did not bother to mention a judiciary. Apparently, Wilson himself believed a council of delegates should take centre stage, with potential arbitral or judicial procedures only serving as modes of appeal. Nevertheless, in the second plenary of the Conference, a commission was mandated to not only draw up a draft constitution for the League but equally research the feasibility of a court of justice.[8] Thanks to the positive efforts of this commission, Article 14 of the LoN Covenant came to state the following:

> The Council shall formulate and submit to the Members of the League for adoption plans for the establishment of a Permanent Court of International Justice. The Court shall be competent to hear and determine any dispute of an international character which the parties submit to it. The Court may also give an advisory opinion upon any dispute or question referred to it by the Council or by the Assembly.

In 1920, the Council mandated an Advisory Committee of Jurists (ACJ) to prepare a draft Statute. The result was approved by the Assembly in a resolution of 13 December 1920, instructing the Council to forward it to the members of the League.[9] The Statute entered into force on 20 August 1921, when a majority of them had ratified the annexed Signature Protocol.

The adjective 'permanent' was employed deliberately, meaning to mark a break with the past, as well as a stark contrast with the manifold ad hoc alternatives for dispute settlement. In reality, it morphed into an awkward reason for bemusement due to the close resemblance to the Permanent Court of Arbitration (PCA) that precisely lacked the envisaged stability. Moreover, the similar names caused the two to be regularly confused with each other in the popular press.[10]

The PCIJ was perceived by many, and appreciated generally, as an integral part of the LoN framework.[11] In an early memo to President Wilson, his advisor Colonel House referred to it as 'a necessary part of the machinery' that 'might well prove the strongest part of it'.[12] In the same vein, the ACJ had opined that '[t]he new Court, being the judicial organ of the League of Nations, can only be created within this League', emphasizing that '[a]s it is to be a component part of the League, it must originate from an organisation within the League, and not from a body outside it'.[13] Tellingly,

[7] Point XIV reading: 'A general association of nations must be formed under specific covenants for the purpose of affording mutual guarantees of political independence and territorial integrity to great and small states alike.'

[8] Arthur Eyffinger, *The World Court, Volume I: The Constitution (1870–1920)* (Wolf Legal Publishers 2022) 103.

[9] League of Nations, *Records of the First Assembly: Plenary Meetings* (1920) 468. On the activities and accomplishments of the ACJ, consult especially P Sean Morris (ed), *Transforming the Politics of International Law: The Advisory Committee of Jurists and the Formation of the World Court in the League of Nations* (Routledge 2021).

[10] Eyffinger (n 8) 109.

[11] Manley Hudson, *The Permanent Court of International Justice 1920–1942* (Macmillan 1943) 310.

[12] David Hunter Miller, *The Drafting of the Covenant* (GP Putnam's Sons 1928) vol I, 13.

[13] Procès-Verbaux of the Proceedings of the Advisory Committee of Jurists (1920) 704.

the French version of the Protocol of Signature referred to 'La Cour permanente de Justice internationale de la Société des Nations'—yet these last five words were not reproduced in the English equivalent.[14] However, as pointed out by Judge Yusuf in his contribution to the present collection, the PCIJ did not constitute the principal judicial organ of the organization, contrary to the position of today's International Court of Justice (ICJ) within the framework of the United Nations (UN).[15] Despite there being strong ties in practice, as indicated in the sections below, the PCIJ Statute was formally disconnected from the Covenant, and the members of the League were not automatically parties thereto. One circumstance attesting to the separation of the LoN and the PCIJ is the fact that over time, no fewer than four judges from the USA sat on the Court's bench, while their native country steadfastly refused to join the organization. Indeed, the PCIJ was open to states seeking to join from across the globe, without the requirement of membership of the League. There is no consensus in legal doctrine on how the interrelation between the League and the Court can best be described.[16] From Article 1 of the Statute, it does become clear that the PCIJ was intended to serve in addition to the PCA and supplementary arbitration tribunals that countries would be minded to set up. Perhaps the most plausible middle way is offered by Manley Hudson's view that the Court ought to be seen as 'an institution closely associated with the League'.[17]

4.3 Principal Governance Architecture

4.3.1 The groundwork

Although the Court was meant to have a distinct role of its own, the Great Powers of the day (France, the United Kingdom, Italy, and Japan) ensured they could directly or indirectly keep tabs on what went on in The Hague. Prefiguring the model adhered to in the UN Charter with regard to the ICJ, they based the governance of the Court on a polycentric structure, which assigns administrative functions (pertaining e.g. to the internal organization, staffing, and budgetary matters) to several different organs. It is possible to interpret this choice of architecture as motivated by the wish to secure judicial independence, since the ensuing checks and balances could strengthen the Court's autonomy: after all, the outsourcing of duties and prerogatives to multiple actors entails that the decision-making cannot be dominated by one of them.[18] Simultaneously, the deployment of a plurality of oversight bodies may place a double or even triple lock on the manoeuvring space of the Court.

We saw above how the ACJ exerted a supreme influence on the contents of the Statute, and therewith on the basic design of the Court, thus engaging in a form

[14] PCIJ Rep Series D, No 1 (1926) 5.

[15] Keynote address by Abdulqawi Ahmed Yusuf, 'The Governance of the International Court of Justice' (Addendum 1), in this volume, para 12.

[16] Malcolm Shaw, *Rosenne's Law and Practice of the International Court 1920–2015* (5th edn, Brill Nijhoff 2016) 100–1.

[17] Hudson (n 3) 144.

[18] Yusuf (n 15) para 28.

of proto-governance.[19] Ultimately, the trio of the Council, the Assembly, and the Secretary-General of the LoN were made the principal institutions possessing the *suprema potestas* to take all quintessential administrative decisions vis-à-vis the PCIJ. This could strike one as odd in light of the fact that the Statute, as said, was not linked to the Covenant. Nevertheless, it resulted in some extra distance between the overseer and the overseen, reinforcing the external quality of the supervision, which is arguably a good thing—albeit that the contemporary approach in the UN, which features a close(r) nexus between the documents and the respective institutions, should not necessarily be considered more problematic. The key competences of the aforementioned League organs related to the election of the judges (Articles 4–14 of the Statute), decision-making in relation to the Court's financial management (Articles 32–33 of the Statute), and the approval of modifications to the Statute prior to ratification by its parties.[20] Conversely, the PCIJ was the master of its own Rules, with the Council and Assembly being relegated to an advisory capacity on the issue of proposed revisions.[21]

The architects of the League thought it of paramount importance for the political and judicial branches not to trespass on each other's turf, in the classic spirit of *séparation des pouvoirs*. In keeping with that ideal, the Council and the Assembly rarely relented whenever the PCIJ's composition was at stake, yet accorded the Court complete independence as regards the substance of its judgments.[22] The same went to a considerable degree for the Court's running of its own administration, giving the registrar a free hand to craft the preferred schemes. The League organs interfered neither with the staff regulations nor with the Instructions for the Registry.[23] The successive registrars did an excellent job maintaining communication with the organs of the League, the individual Great Powers, and the wider public.[24]

However, the cruciality of installing an authoritative external body to guarantee due execution of the PCIJ judgments was well understood. Like in today's UN, the Council was meant to carry out this task ex Article 13(4) of the Covenant. Remarkably, it had little business on this front, since during the lifespan of the Court every single judicial pronouncement was complied with.[25]

[19] In the periphery, note besides the role of the Carnegie Foundation, a charity (established in 1905) that had welcomed the Court to the Peace Palace (officially opened in 1913), and concerned itself with the infrastructural exigencies of the PCIJ and the PCA. It is meticulously researched in Jens Wegener, 'Creating an "International Mind"? The Carnegie Endowment for International Peace in Europe, 1911–1940' (PhD thesis EUI, 2015).

[20] In essence, this took the form of a de facto developed convention, for which Art 14 of the Covenant served as a dubious foundation.

[21] This document was made up of two chapters which addressed the PCIJ's constitution and internal workings (Arts 1–31) and its procedure (Arts 32–75). Rules of Court, adopted by the Court on 24 March 1922 <www.icj-cij.org/public/files/permanent-court-of-international-justice/serie_D/D_01.pdf>.

[22] Eyffinger (n 8) 347.

[23] Hudson (n 11) 301.

[24] For an elaboration of the sterling performance by Åke Hammerskjöld (from 1922 to 1936) and López Oliván (from 1936 to 1946), see Arthur Eyffinger, *The World Court, Volume II: The Permanent Court of International Justice (1921–1946)* (Eleven Legal Publishing 2024) 56–67.

[25] Christian Tams, 'Peace through International Adjudication: The Permanent Court of International Justice and the Post-War Order' in Michel Erpelding, Burkhard Hess, and Hélène Ruiz-Fabri (eds), *Peace through Law: The Versailles Peace Treaty and Dispute Settlement after World War I* (Nomos 2018) 217, 230.

4.3.2 Operationalization

Two short case-studies neatly demonstrate how the legal groundwork of the PCIJ was operationalized. The premier occasion where the Council and the Assembly had to engage in their governance roles related to the assessment of the outcome of the ACJ's deliberations. As flagged above, this Advisory Committee had actually been vested with delegated authority from the Council. The draft PCIJ Statute it compiled by the end of 1920 met with objections from that same Council, primarily on the proposed jurisdiction, prompting the insertion of the infamous 'optional clause', to the dismay of certain Assembly members.[26] Agreement was nevertheless procured fairly swiftly, enabling an effectuation of the Statute by 1921, upon the parties' ratification.

A subsequent, more complicated dossier worthy of highlighting concerns the procedure for the Statute's revision, and the protracted attempt to do so in the late 1920s. This saga illustrates how cumbersome the interplay between the main organs did occasionally turn out to be—in no small measure due to the (unexpected) participation of secondary actors. The Statute amendment process fell squarely outside the province of judicial self-government, demanding the initiative and wholesale cooperation of both the Council and the Assembly. At the first plenary of the latter, the Great Powers made it known that they envisaged a gradual extension of the PCIJ's jurisdiction, but for almost a decade no follow-up action was taken. On 7 September 1928, the French delegation to the Ninth Assembly put forward a draft resolution aimed at amending the Statute, co-signed by twenty other countries. It drew attention to the urgency of modifications against the background of a steadily increasing case-load and requested the Council to submit such proposals as could prove necessary to the Assembly's next ordinary session. Pushing its own envelope, the Assembly dared to go quite far in outlining a specific route:

> In order to enable it to formulate the proposals to be submitted by it to the Assembly in accordance with the above resolution, it would seem that the Council might with advantage appoint a small Committee of Jurists to make a preliminary study of the subject. Having regard to the terms of the Assembly's decision, the Committee should have wide terms of reference; namely, to report what amendments appear desirable in the various provisions of the Court's Statute. The Committee would, of course, be competent to examine such suggestions as may reach it during its work from authoritative sources. Further, it would fall to the Committee to ascertain the opinion of the Permanent Court of International Justice in respect of the working of the Court.[27]

In truth, the issue of the fora that needed to be involved in discussing the changes was more opaque than these words convey: beyond the Assembly and the Council, a credible interest lay also with the countries that had originally signed the Signature Protocol of 1920, no less than with the then members of the LoN.[28] The proposed

[26] League of Nations, *Records of the First Assembly: Plenary Meetings* (1920) 445–49.
[27] League of Nations, *Records of the Ninth Assembly: Plenary Meetings* (1929) 171.
[28] Eyffinger (n 24) 185.

revisions committee was constituted nonetheless, reporting back to the Council in mid-1929.[29] The Council hereafter forwarded the propositions to the League members, the associated countries mentioned in the annex to the Covenant, and the US government as a separate signatory, calling for a conference of states parties to the Statute to be convened in September that year. At its conclusion, the conference entrusted its general findings to rapporteurs that were to appear before the LoN's Tenth Assembly. The latter adopted a resolution expressing its satisfaction with the input:

> The Assembly adopts the amendments to the Statute of the Permanent Court of International Justice and the draft Protocol which the Conference convened by the Council of the League of Nations has drawn up after consideration of the report of the Committee of Jurists, which met in March 1929 at Geneva and which included among its members a jurist of the United States of America.[30]

The Assembly moreover expressed the hope that the draft Protocol drawn up by the conference would receive as many signatures as possible, and that all the governments concerned would do their utmost to secure the entry into force of the Statute amendments. Disappointment lurked around the corner, for a phenomenal delay ensued, and it was only at the Sixteenth Assembly in 1936 that the completion of the ratification trajectory could be announced. The Council effectuated the final implementation of the revision on 1 April the same year, authorizing the Secretary-General to declare it operational, 'unless, contrary to all expectations, objections should be notified'—anticipating possible resistance from other interlocutors, but none materialized.[31]

Remarkably, insightful as the picture of these back-and-forths may be, the upshot of the whole story is rather underwhelming. The core of the Statute remained intact; a mere sixteen of the sixty-four articles were altered and four new provisions copied in. Somewhat more significantly, the number of judges was increased to fifteen (by abolition of the post of deputy judges), and henceforth the PCIJ would be permanently in session instead of sitting for designated intermittent periods.[32]

As noted above, the Council and Assembly merely held an advisory capacity as regards proposed modifications to the Court's Rules. Such revisions were introduced on the PCIJ's own motion in 1926–27. During the lengthy wait for the changes to the Statute to enter into force, in June 1930 it was proposed in the Council to let the Court provisionally adjust this document in line with the forthcoming changes. The Assembly saw fit to give its blessing to the move by resolution of 25 September 1930.[33] The PCIJ was not coerced but surely goaded in going ahead with this, culminating in a short reform process the next year.[34]

[29] League of Nations, *Official Journal*, Vol 10 (1929) 1113.

[30] League of Nations, *Records of the Tenth Assembly: Plenary Meetings* (1929) 434.

[31] League of Nations, *Official Journal*, Vol 17 (1936) 118.

[32] The increase of the PCIJ's members to fifteen was pre-emptively carried out in 1930 by mutual agreement of the Council and the Assembly, pending the ratification of the Protocol.

[33] PCIJ Rep Series D, No 2 (1922), Add 2; PCIJ Rep Series E, No 7 (1929–30) 339–43.

[34] Coincidentally, the second cohort of judges took their office by January 1931, three of whom had served on the aforementioned revisions committee, in all likelihood fortifying the internal support. After a series of meetings, it was decided to amend eighteen articles of the Court's Rules and beef up the total number from seventy-five to eighty-six, entering into force in February 1931.

4.4 Judicial Selection and Appointments

4.4.1 Points of departure

At the Hague Conference of 1907, the intention to establish an international court of arbitral justice foundered due to vehement disagreement on the methods for the selection of the judges. The major difficulty had lain in the reconciliation of the demand of the Great Powers for permanent representation, on the one hand, and the principle of equality for smaller nations, on the other.[35] In the contemporaneous proposal for an International Prize Court, some limited progress was made, but its Statute never entered into force.[36]

In the so-called Root–Phillimore plan, hatched within the ACJ, eleven judges and four deputy judges were foreseen for the PCIJ. This was meant as a provisional formula, a cautious step towards the gradual implementation of a court of fifteen judges once its jurisdiction had been extended. For the moment, it was believed that eleven judges could ensure adequate representation, with nine making up the quorum. The true genius of the plan resided in entrusting the League's two political institutions with the election process, guaranteeing a reasonable respect for the idea of equality via the Assembly, as well as for the position of the Great Powers that dominated the Council.[37] To limit the influence of individual states and the prior diplomatic horse-trading that was otherwise likely to take place, on the initiative of the chairman of the committee, the 'national groups' represented at the PCA would choose the candidates. The Council and the Assembly could then proceed with the elections in simultaneous but separate sessions. About a week of discussions ensued. Despite the floating of alternative propositions, including one for a tribunal counting no fewer than twenty-five members, the plan was put to the vote, adopted by the ACJ as a whole, and embraced by the PCIJ's founders.[38] The outcome has been hailed by commentators as its single most significant novelty, additionally showcasing the polycentricity that characterizes the Court's governance.[39] It was integrally maintained for the ICJ in 1946, while the four deputy judge posts were upgraded to a full seat through the Statute revision of 1936.

Article 5 of the PCIJ Statute brought in the Secretary-General, making clear that he/she would care to send out the invitations to the national groups to come up with nominations.[40] Prospective addressees were to be the 'members of the Court of

[35] Hudson (n 11) 241.

[36] According to Arts 14 and 15 of Convention (XII) relative to the Creation of an International Prize Court (The Hague, 18 October 1907), the entity was to consist of fifteen members, with a possibility for them to be replaced by deputy judges in case of the former being absent or prevented from sitting. The members appointed by eight contracting parties—namely, Austria-Hungary, France, Germany, Great Britain, Italy, Japan, the USA, and Russia—were always to be summoned to sit. On the other hand, the judges and deputy judges appointed by the other contracting parties would be convoked on the basis of rotation.

[37] Procès-Verbaux of the Proceedings of the Advisory Committee of Jurists (1920) 108–09.

[38] Procès-Verbaux of the Proceedings of the Advisory Committee of Jurists (1920) 163–77.

[39] Yusuf (n 15) para 21; Ole Spiermann, 'Historical Introduction' in Andreas Zimmerman, Karin Oellers-Frahm, Christian Tomuschat, and Christian J Tams (eds), *The Statute of the International Court of Justice: A Commentary* (2nd edn, OUP 2012) 42.

[40] Each national group was to nominate four candidates, no more than two of their own nationality, with the number of nominees not exceeding double the seats to be filled.

Arbitration belonging to the states mentioned in the annex to the Covenant, or to the states which join the League subsequently'.[41] The same provision enjoined that the invitation of the Secretary-General be sent out 'at least three months' before the election. The nominations were to be made 'within a given time', as also fixed by the Secretary-General. In accordance with Article 7 of the Statute, upon receipt of the nominations, the Secretary-General was to prepare a list of the eligible nominees in alphabetical order and submit it to the Assembly and Council.[42] Identical to the present-day UN system, the latter are then to organize their elections, the ground rule being that a successful candidate will need to have garnered an absolute majority of the votes cast.[43] The President of the Assembly announced the results of the voting in both bodies. Consonant with Article 11, if thereafter one or more seats remained to be filled, a second and, if needed, a third meeting had to be convened. Equally familiarly from a present-day perspective, this could possibly flow over into the 'joint conference' under Article 12 becoming a tie-breaker—and should even this body fail to cut the knot, the PCIJ members appointed already were to choose from the candidates brought before the Assembly or the Council.[44]

4.4.2 Real-life dynamics

The original Statute neglected to specify an exact moment for electing the judges. After the 1936 modification, it did stipulate that the Council was to determine the date for a by-election at the first session after the occurrence of a vacancy. In reality, the Secretary-General sent out invitations for states to come up with nominations much earlier than the prescribed three months before the election. While not required formally, the Secretary-General always asked the Council's permission before doing so.[45] Since 1930, the Secretary-General made a habit of drawing the attention of the national groups to a recommendation from the conference of signatories to the Statute, endorsed by the Assembly, with regard to the candidates' legal experience, linguistic skills, and the appending of a short résumé.[46]

Regardless of the fact that the Statute did not contain any instructions on the matter, ordinarily the election sessions of the Council and the Assembly coincided. At the same time, both bodies made sure that the results of the process in one did not become known in the other. Article 21 of the Assembly's Rules of Procedure dictated that

[41] The discrepancy between the members of the PCA—all signatories to the Hague Conventions of 1899 and 1907—and the members of the LoN was resolved by allowing the latter category to compose an ad hoc national group.

[42] Mind that the joint conference laid down in Art 12 of the Statute was competent to unanimously agree on a person fulfilling the required conditions, even when not included in the list of the secretary-general.

[43] PCIJ Statute Art 10. The familiar point of departure in Art 9 is that the electors were supposed to 'bear in mind that not only should all the persons appointed as members of the Court possess the qualifications required, but the whole body also should represent the main forms of civilization and the principal legal systems of the world'. This was never verified, nor were potential trespasses ever penalized (in 1939, the Egyptian government demanded that the Court 'include a jurist representing Islamic civilization and Moslem [*sic*] law': League of Nations, Document A.30 (1939) V).

[44] In the event of an equality of votes amongst the judges, the eldest judge shall have a casting vote.

[45] Hudson (n 11) 243.

[46] League of Nations (n 30) 119–21.

'all decisions relating to individual shall be taken by secret ballot'. Nonetheless, the voting in the Assembly always took place in public, whereas the Council preferred to go about it behind closed doors.[47]

Although logic leads one to assume that the first elections could only be staged when the Statute had officially entered into force, the Council deigned to authorize the Secretary-General to initiate a nomination trajectory on 25 February 1921, when only Sweden had deposited its instrument of ratification.[48] In keeping with that authorization, on 2 June 1921, the members of the national groups were requested to come up with nominations by 15 August, provided elections could be held at the next Assembly. On 5 September, the list was held to be closed upon the receipt of eighty-nine candidates proposed by thirty-four national groups.[49]

Remarkably, the procedure to be observed caused trepidation in the Assembly, which was in all likelihood sparked by the lack of precedent and the amount of discretion available to tailor the approach. Shortly before the election was to commence in this forum, its president thought it useful to offer an elaboration, proclaiming that Rule 21 of the Assembly would be applied to restrict the voting on every consecutive ballot to the unsuccessful candidates who obtained the greatest number of votes on previous ballots, the number of such candidates being not more than twice the number of positions remaining to be filled.[50] When nine candidates immediately received an absolute majority of the votes cast, the Assembly decided not to apply Rule 21 to exclude any candidate in later ballots. The second ballot yielded another successful candidate, the third and fourth did not, but at the fifth ballot the list of eleven was completed. The names overlapped almost fully with the results in the Council, where six ballots were necessary, with only two exceptions—deviating nominations that were subsequently endorsed by the Assembly in a sixth ballot. For the election of the deputy judges, four ballots in the Assembly yielded three nominees that figured too on the shortlist of the Council. The position of the fourth deputy judge turned out to be extremely contentious. When the Council and Assembly repeatedly failed to reach consensus on an identical nominee, this culminated in a joint conference, producing the desired final candidate on 16 September 1921.[51]

Over the course of time, the election processes began to progress ever more smoothly. The death of a PCIJ member in 1923 created a vacancy which was promptly filled by unanimous agreement between the Council and the Assembly at the first ballots.[52] The same happened after the resignation of a judge in 1928, the death of two further PCIJ members in 1929, another resignation in 1930, and a passing away in 1935.[53]

[47] In application of Art 10 of the Council's rules of procedure: 'All decisions concerning persons shall be taken at a private meeting. On the demand of any member of the Council, the voting shall be by secret ballot.'

[48] League of Nations, *Minutes of the Council: 12th Session*, Vol 18 (1921), 115–16.

[49] PCIJ Rep Series E, No 1 (1922–25) 28–45.

[50] League of Nations, *Records of the Second Assembly: Plenary Meetings* (1921) 222–23.

[51] ibid 273–93.

[52] League of Nations, *Records of the Fourth Assembly: Plenary Meetings* (1923) 22–23.

[53] League of Nations (n 27) 72; League of Nations (n 30) 153. The resignation of a judge in 1928 happened to cause an upset, since neither the Statute nor the Rules had catered to that possibility. The Council nevertheless provisionally accepted it, subject to the Assembly's approval, which was procured four months later.

The general election of 1930 was held at the session of the Assembly and the Council which immediately preceded the expiration of the nine-year term of the sitting cohort of judges. In March, the Secretary-General sent out a call for nominations to the national groups. Sixty nominees were put forward. Meanwhile, in September, the Council circulated a proposal that the PCIJ's membership should be increased to fifteen, even when the revised Statute had not yet been signed off on. The Assembly quickly gave its consent, raising the total number of potential electees, with the deputy judges that were to be appointed that year destined for redundancy once the modified Protocol would have entered into force.[54] Fourteen candidates received an absolute majority at the first ballots in both organs. Choosing the fifteenth judge, as well as the deputy judges, led to a much heavier tussle, requiring no fewer than seventeen ballots. The procedure was, however, completed in a single day, and the convening of a joint conference averted.

In 1936, elections pursuant to three interim vacancies posed problems due to the withdrawal of Brazil, Germany, and Japan from the LoN, countries that were actually still parties to the Statute and the Signature Protocol. The Council showed itself open to them casting a vote in the Assembly, as condoned by the latter in a resolution adopted in October, declaring as follows:

1. If a State which is not a Member of the League but is a party to the Statute of the Court notifies the Secretary-General of its desire to participate in the election of members of the Court, such State shall *ipso facto* be admitted to vote in the Assembly;
2. At any election of members of the Court which may take place before January 1, 1940, Germany, Brazil and Japan, being States which are not Member of the League but are parties to the Statute of the Court, if they notify their desire to do so to the Secretary-General, shall, as a provisional measure and without prejudging any question of principle, also be admitted to vote in the Council;
3. The Secretary-General is instructed to take the necessary measures to allow States which, though parties to the Statute of the Court, are not Members of the League of Nations to participate in the elections.[55]

Germany eventually declined to take part, but Brazil and Japan did participate, with two vacancies being filled at the first ballot and the third at the second. In 1938, these two countries again participated in the election of a new PCIJ member in lieu of a deceased predecessor.

The Assembly was scheduled to meet in September 1939 for its twentieth ordinary session to elect the third regular cohort of judges for a nine-year term. Because of the outbreak of hostilities, the planned session was adjourned to December, where it was decided to regard the election as 'postponed to another session'.[56] This triggered the

[54] League of Nations, *Records of the Eleventh Assembly: Plenary Meetings* (1930) 131.
[55] League of Nations, *Records of the Seventeenth Assembly: Plenary Meetings* (1936) 105.
[56] League of Nations, *Records of the Twentieth Assembly: Plenary Meetings* (1939) 6.

clause contained in Article 13 of the Statute, stipulating that the judges 'shall continue to discharge their duties until their places have been filled'.[57]

4.4.3 Appraisal

Overall, the interplay between the Council and the Assembly in this sphere of court governance appears to have been largely harmonious. The overt and latent desire for representation, harboured especially by the Great Powers, strained the implementation of the provision in Article 2 of the Statute that judges would be 'elected regardless of their nationality'—a motley crew of PCIJ members, chosen in an open and random manner, was not seriously imaginable. The Assembly apparently took the same view, hammering out the needed common accord with pleasant speed. The upshot was that in the general elections of 1921 and 1930, each of the states with a permanent seat on the Council saw their candidate prevail for a position at the PCIJ—a convention we have equally been able to witness, at least until fairly recently, at its successor institution, the ICJ.[58] In other words, the double lock, with an ancillary role for the Secretary-General, did not produce hindrance or stagnation. Incidentally, the clever 'joint conference' solution succeeded in securing the intended results.

No less recognizable for contemporary observers is the second sentence of Article 10 of the Statute, which determined that 'In the event of more than one national of the same Member of the League being elected by the votes of both the Assembly and the Council, the eldest of these only shall be considered as elected.' This could have led to an infelicitous outcome when, as a result of a previous election, a national of a LoN member was already represented on the PCIJ—since the cited rule seems to express the basic principle that no state ought to ever have two nationals on the Court. In the envisaged system of governance, it is logical to assume that the Council and the Assembly would then have had to resolve such conundrums, which thankfully never materialized. In the same vein, no Court member ever had to be dismissed, a situation which undoubtedly would have provoked additional difficulties.

The task of proposing nominees was conveniently outsourced to national groups, creating an invaluable nexus with the PCA and avoiding an undue influence from either the governments of League states or the LoN's dominant governance institutions.[59] Naturally, this setup benefitted the independence of the (members of the) governed court. It may be objected that the degree of transparency associated with this arrangement was (and is) far from ideal, or that it did not give sufficient assurances with regard to the quality of the candidates to allow for the competent governance

[57] In November, the Court itself had taken a decision that on the occasion of Art 13 becoming operative, all members would continue to discharge themselves of their duties until they were replaced (League of Nations, Document C.402–M.306 (1939), V).

[58] During the lifespan of the League, the importance of the convention did wane as a consequence of the gradual enlargement of the Council, diluting the Great Powers' dominance, and, by the end of the 1930s, by the departure of Italy, Germany, and Japan.

[59] Albeit that in various cases, a national group's nomination was conveyed to the secretary-general via the relevant ministry of foreign affairs, or even directly relayed by the latter.

institutions to focus on other interests in composing the bench.[60] Yet, on the whole, not least compared to the troubles that might otherwise have been, there was plenty to commend the chosen modus operandi for.

4.5 Financial Supervision and Administration

As the PCIJ was initially expected to constitute a League organ, understandably the LoN's budget was supposed to cover all the related expenditure. In this vein, Article 33 of the Court's Statute determined that the expenses of the Court shall be borne by the LoN in such a manner as shall be decided by the Assembly upon the proposal of the Council.

When this plan did not come through, the idea to create a separate method of financing did not gain much traction, since by that time multiple agencies had been set up for collecting and disbursing the League's funds. Consequently, the running costs of the Court were paid for out of the general budget; that is, also by countries who refused to accede to the Statute. Conversely, the Statute did not contain any provision on the contributions to be made to cover the PCIJ's operating costs by the states party to the Protocol of Signature. That leads to the somewhat startling conclusion that the non-League parties to the Signature Protocol were not under any official burden-sharing obligation as regards the Court, although there remained a moral duty, to an extent demonstrated by the occurrence of voluntary payments.[61] Moreover, Article 35(3) of the Statute posited that if a non-member of the League appeared as a party to a dispute, a contribution could still be demanded when such a state was not yet chipping in voluntarily. However, this left the exact amount unclear, and practice varied.[62]

Article 33 of the PCIJ Statute confers a mandate upon the Assembly, proceeding from the Council's initiative, to determine the further specifics, as it did right from the start when determining the Court's budgetary items to be financed from the League's first budget in 1920. The Assembly decided to set aside a percentage of the contributions of the League members, determined annually, for the purpose of financing the Court—an approach maintained during its entire lifespan. The League's working capital and guarantee fund were made available for covering any extra unforeseen costs.[63] A few years later, the Assembly approved of a suggestion by the PCIJ's President to henceforth table its own budget for adoption.[64] In 1924, the LoN Covenant was amended to remove the Council's general right of initiative in this domain.[65] With

[60] Manley Hudson, 'The Election of Members of the Permanent Court of International Justice' (1930) 24 American Journal of International Law 718.

[61] Eyffinger (n 24) 68.

[62] In the *Lotus* case, Turkey was, eg, asked to pay 5,000 Dutch florins (the PCIJ's preferred currency), whereas Germany was taxed at 35,000 in the *German Interest in Polish Upper Silesia* case. Consult the correspondence reproduced respectively in PCIJ Rep Series C, No 13-II (1927) 459, and PCIJ Rep Series C, No 11-III (1926) 1293.

[63] League of Nations (n 9) 707.

[64] League of Nations, *Official Journal*, Vol 17 (1936) 1013.

[65] Article 6(5) of the Statute came to read: 'The expenses of the League shall be borne by the members of the League in the proportion decided by the Assembly.'

Article 33 of the Statute kept unaltered, though, the Council did retain a say in what would be allocated to the Court.

The PCIJ was responsible for the proper administration of its own expenditure within the confines of the Financial Regulations approved by the Assembly in 1923.[66] The Court's Registrar was to frame estimates and, upon approval by the President or by the full Court, convey these to the League's Secretary-General.[67] The annual budget was then scrutinized and approved in accordance with the League's procedures, and the Court's accounts were likewise audited four times a year. It was thereby monitored by a trio of LoN organs, viz the Supervisory Commission, the Fourth Committee of the Assembly, and the Assembly's plenum.[68]

Article 32 of the Court's Statute provided that the judges should receive an 'annual indemnity', determined by the Assembly on the proposal of the Council, supplemented by a 'grant for the actual performance of their duties'.[69] In December 1920, the Council opted for an inverse route, requesting the Assembly's Third Committee to make a proposal.[70] The latter forum convened twice to make up its mind, settling for a basic judicial salary of 15,000 Dutch florins, next to a *per diem* allowance of 100 more, duly approved by the Assembly.[71] The 1929 Committee of Jurists revised the scheme, wishing to see the judges abandon any side-jobs, introducing a basic salary of 45,000 Dutch florins without allowances. The protracted delay in the Statute's entering into force, described above, induced the Assembly to fix an interim scale with a basic salary of 35,000, coupled with a *per diem* of fifty Dutch florins. In 1939, the Council requested the Supervisory Commission to take yet another look, but the matter was abruptly put on hold pursuant to the decision to postpone the general election of judges.[72]

Overall, the PCIJ's financial arrangements may be labelled as relatively accomplished, with little noticeable friction visible on this front between the Court's central governance institutions. The PCIJ therefore never had to fear running out of funds—nor did it ever do so for much of its existence, its effective yearly expenditure oscillating from about 700,000 to 1,200,000 Dutch florins. The crisis era of the 1940s saw the work of the Council, Assembly, and Secretary-General grind to a halt, placing the Court in severe penury. It might have recovered from that predicament only at the moment when it was about to be dissolved.

[66] League of Nations, *Records of the Third Assembly: Plenary Meetings* II (1923) 207. Eventually, these Regulations were internalized via the Instructions for the Registry, PCIJ Rep Series E, No 14 (1937–38) 33.

[67] Instructions for the Registry, Art 31. For a detailed account of the 'micro-electronics', see, eg, PCIJ Rep Series E, No 8 (1931–32) 333–36.

[68] The Supervisory Committee informed the Fourth Committee, which in turn reported to the plenary Assembly (Eyffinger (n 24) 69). In these proceedings, the Registrar represented the Court, being the only official competent to incur liabilities in its name, obtaining prior approval from the president or the full bench where necessary (Instructions for the Registry, Art 36).

[69] It called for special regulations on the members' pensions, laid down by the Assembly on the proposal of the Council in 1924, expanded in 1936 with rules on the administration of the Court's pension fund. On the basis of the same provision, the remuneration of the Registrar was settled in a similar way. Hudson (n 11) 320–22.

[70] League of Nations, *Minutes of the Council: 11th Session* (1920) 27, 136.

[71] League of Nations (n 9) 747. The Third Committee's motion was carried to let the salaries be exempted from taxation or offer adequate compensation for taxes levied.

[72] League of Nations (n 30) 113; League of Nations (n 54) 132–33; League of Nations, *Official Journal*, Vol 20 (1939) 272.

4.6 Concluding Remarks

Instead of being in the process of realization, Brown Scott's 'hope of ages' could have ended up a wholly anodyne franchise, not living up to its promise due to construction errors or faulty implementation. Thankfully, the founding fathers of the PCIJ assembled in the ACJ possessed the Midas touch. It was in the context of the Permanent Court that the world experienced the rise of the international judiciary, and both as an institution and a project of international justice, it has deservedly been hailed a success.[73] It was also in the context of the Permanent Court that the world had its first experiences (*pace* the PCA) with the management of a genuine international judiciary, sowing the seeds for future endeavours.

As has recently been pointed out, distinct features from the PCIJ architecture have been emulated in various quarters—observable, for instance, in the requirement of geographical diversity on the bench, the possibility to appoint ad hoc judges, and the staggered judicial terms of nine years, if one compares respectively the Appellate Body of the World Trade Organization, the Inter-American Court of Human Rights, and the European Court of Human Rights.[74] The supervision structures do differ, depending not least on the tasks of the institution established and on the objectives of the overarching organization, which results in granting more or less autonomy and enabling more or less external scrutiny. The system for electing the PCIJ's judges, with the unprecedented majoritarian method, formed a veritable breakthrough in light of the deadlocks that had frustrated previous attempts to realize a court with a similarly broad jurisdiction. A modern rendition of this approach may be how selection and appointment proceeds at the International Tribunal for the Law of the Sea.[75] Possibly exceeding the wildest dreams of its architects, the framework functioned quite efficiently. Apart from the incidental tensions noted above, particularly surrounding the amendment of the Statute, grave clashes between the Council and the Assembly could be averted.

Moving into the post-Second World War era, the most fundamental transformation has obviously been the full absorption of the Court into the UN cadre, with the concomitant conferral of the status of official (and the UN's principal judicial) organ.[76] The coupling of the ICJ Statute with the Charter forced every UN member to become a party to the Statute, albeit that this far from insured a country's actual participation in litigation. In spite of the new organic link, the sponsors of the UN did understand the importance of letting the ICJ carry out its substantive mission independently.[77] The UN Security Council and the General Assembly were thus endowed

[73] Spiermann (n 1) 401.

[74] Brian McGarry, 'Legacy of the Statute of the Permanent Court of International Justice, 100 Years Onwards' (*EJILTalk!*, 30 December 2020) <www.ejiltalk.org/legacy-of-the-statute-of-the-permanent-court-of-international-justice-100-years-onward>.

[75] Where nominees are appointed judge if they obtain the largest number of votes and a two-thirds majority of the states parties present and voting (so long as a majority of the states parties is present at that meeting). United Nations Convention on the Law of the Sea (opened for signature 10 December 1982, entered into force 16 November 1994) 1833 UNTS 397, Annex VI, Art 5.

[76] As is known, the PCIJ as such was disbanded but materially replaced by the ICJ. In that spirit, at Dumbarton Oaks, it was decided to keep the numbering of articles in the Statute as it was.

[77] Shaw (n 16) 103.

with much the same competences as their predecessors, inter alia in the election of judges and the enforcement of judgments. As regards the finances, the sole revolutionary proposal of the Washington Committee of Jurists (1945), embraced by the UN's founders, was to delete the words 'on the proposal of the Council' from Article 33 of the Statute, handing the General Assembly exclusive rights of control.[78] By amalgamating UN membership and being party to the ICJ Statute, a happy solution was found to the quandary of outsiders (not) paying for the institution highlighted above in respect of the PCIJ. Articles 24–36 of the present-day Instructions for the Registry detail the internal financial administration. On the request of the ICJ, its accounts may be scrutinized by the Board of Auditors appointed by the General Assembly, alongside the Joint Inspection Unit and Office of Internal Oversight Services, offering important safeguards for its accountability.[79] The foregoing shows how the erstwhile means of oversight have been improved upon, reflecting further 'lessons learnt' from the PCIJ.

Darker sides to this history ought not be overlooked, of course; and indeed, the fact that the Court repeatedly sought to amend its Statute and Rules evinces that its legal framework resembled a less than perfect template.[80] Nonetheless, for a pioneering institution, its performance deserves due credit, and no less so the diligent conduct of its overseers. With the PCIJ's creation, judicial governance issues appeared on the international agenda, becoming solidly entrenched upon the wondrous multiplication of tribunals in the second half of the twentieth century. The volume containing the current chapter handsomely testifies to that development.

[78] UNCIO Vol XIII (1945) 163; UNCIO Vol XIV (1945) 837.

[79] Yusuf (n 15) para 42.

[80] Eyffinger (n 24) 702. Cf also, generally, Christian J Tams and Malgosia Fitzmaurice (eds), *Legacies of the Permanent Court of International Justice* (Brill Nijhoff 2013); Henri de Waele and Christian J Tams (eds), *Realising the Hope of Ages? Novel Perspectives on the Permanent Court of International Justice* (Nomos 2025).

5
Governance of the International Military Tribunals at Nuremberg and Tokyo

Sergey Vasiliev[*]

5.1 Introduction

The International Military Tribunal for the prosecution and punishment of the major war criminals of the European Axis countries at Nuremberg (IMT, or the Nuremberg Tribunal) and the International Military Tribunal for the Far East (IMTFE, or the Tokyo Tribunal) were the first-ever international tribunals to exercise criminal jurisdiction over individuals. Set up in the aftermath of the Second World War, they were mandated to try 'major war criminals'—the former leaders of defeated Nazi Germany and Japan, respectively—for crimes against peace, war crimes, and crimes against humanity.[1] The denomination 'military' reveals their umbilical connection to the military occupation authorities in postwar Germany and Japan. The IMTs were short-lived institutions and completed only one multi-accused trial each.[2] However, both proved of momentous and lasting importance: they jump-started international criminal justice as an ideological and institutional project.

A massive body of literature has been produced on the IMT and, to a lesser extent, on the IMTFE, including trial participants' memoirs, observers' accounts, and works in legal and popular history, some of which are fairly recent and based on newly available archival materials.[3] This literature covers in a comprehensive manner the

* The author is grateful to Niels Blokker for his comments on a draft of this chapter.

1 Charter of the International Military Tribunal (London, 8 August 1945) 82 UNTS 280 (IMT Charter) arts 1 and 6; Charter of the International Military Tribunal for the Far East (26 April 1946, Tokyo) in Neil Boister and Robert Cryer (eds), *Documents on the Tokyo International Military Tribunal: Charter, Indictment and Judgments* (OUP 2008) 7–11 (IMTFE Charter) arts 1 and 5.

2 The IMT's life-span was over a year, whereas the IMTFE was in operation for over two and a half years. At Nuremberg, the indictment was filed on 18 October 1945, the trial against twenty-two defendants commenced on 20 November 1945, and the judgment was rendered on 1 October 1946. In Tokyo, the indictment was filed on 29 April 1946; the trial against twenty-eight defendants ran for two and a half years until the delivery of the judgment (3 May 1946 to 12 November 1948). The IMT was followed by the trials held by each of the four Allied powers within their zones of occupation. The IMTFE was initially supposed to hold several trials but was dissolved upon completing the first trial due to US's releasing over forty 'Class A' suspects, who were meant to be tried later.

3 Major full-length works and anthologies on the IMT include: Robert E Conot, *Justice at Nuremberg* (Caroll and Graf Publishers 1983); Whitney R Harris, *Tyranny on Trial: Evidence at Nuremberg* (Barnes & Noble 1954); Telford Taylor, *The Anatomy of the Nuremberg Trials* (Little, Brown and Company 1992); Ann Tusa and John Tusa, *The Nuremberg Trial* (BBC Books 1983); Guénaël Mettraux (ed), *Perspectives on the Nuremberg Trial* (OUP 2008); Francine Hirsch, *Soviet Judgment at Nuremberg: A New History of the International Military Tribunal after World War II* (OUP 2020). On the IMTFE: Richard H Minear, *Victors' Justice: The Tokyo War Crimes Trial* (Princeton University Press 1971); Yuma Totani, *The Tokyo War Crimes Trial: The Pursuit of Justice in the Wake of World War II* (Harvard University Press 2008);

Sergey Vasiliev, *Governance of the International Military Tribunals at Nuremberg and Tokyo* In: *Governance of International Courts and Tribunals*. Edited by: Sergey Vasiliev and Niels Blokker, Oxford University Press. © Sergey Vasiliev 2026.
DOI: 10.1093/oso/9780198922131.003.0005

historical and political background to the establishment of the IMTs, the development and application of their legal frameworks, the conduct of proceedings, the innovations and blind spots in their judgments, and their contributions to international criminal law. Paradoxically, the information on the IMT governance schemes has remained notably scarce. Any analyses of their management oversight, financing, and justice administration arrangements are few and far between. Apart from the constitutional 'acts of creation' and issues related to the start-up phase, little is known about the organizational and practical approaches adopted to enable and oversee their operations. Where institutional matters have been addressed, they have not been considered through a judicial governance prism. Indeed, the governance of the historic tribunals has been largely eclipsed by other, more prominent aspects of their legacy.

The purpose of the chapter is to address this blind spot and examine the significance of these institutional precedents for the broader field of international judicial governance. In recovering the IMT and IMTFE governance arrangements from obscurity, the chapter brings to light their distinctive features and the unique challenges they posed for safeguarding judicial independence and ensuring effective judicial operations. First, the chapter elaborates on the constitutional methods used to establish the IMTs, their divergent governance designs, and the structure and competences of their respective *injugovins* (Section 5.2). The subsequent sections examine the performance of specific governance functions with respect to the tribunals, including the appointment of judges, prosecutors, and other key staff (Section 5.3); the provision of financing and practical assistance (Section 5.4); and post-trial responsibilities such as the review and enforcement of penalties (Section 5.5). Section 5.6 offers conclusions and a general assessment of the IMT and IMTFE governance models.

5.2 Constitutional and Governance Architecture

The Nuremberg Tribunal was established by an (initially quadripartite) agreement between the UK, France, the United States, and the USSR, to which the IMT Charter was annexed.[4] These instruments, particularly the Charter, required tough and protracted negotiations at the London conference held between 26 June and 8 August 1945) before their adoption, due to persistent disagreement between the Allied Powers' representatives on the appropriate rules of criminal procedure and liability concepts such as conspiracy, among others.[5] Following its adoption, the IMT

Neil Boister and Robert Cryer, *The Tokyo International Military Tribunal: A Reappraisal* (OUP 2008); Yuki Tanaka, Tim McCormack, and Gerry Simpson (eds), *Beyond Victor's Justice? The Tokyo War Crimes Trial Revisited* (Brill Nijhoff 2010); Mei Ju-ao, *The Tokyo Trial and War Crimes in Asia* (Palgrave Macmillan 2018); David Cohen and Yuma Totani, *The Tokyo War Crimes Tribunal: Law, History, and Jurisprudence* (CUP 2019); Gary J Bass, *Judgment at Tokyo: World War II on Trial and the Making of Modern Asia* (Alfred A Knopf 2023).

[4] Agreement for the prosecution and punishment of the major war criminals of the European Axis (signed on 8 August 1945 in London) 82 UNTS 279 (IMT Agreement).

[5] For the full documentary record, see *Report of Robert H Jackson, United States Representative to the International Conference on Military Trials, London 1945* (US Department of State Division of Publications 1949); in addition: Conot (n 3) 18–24; Tusa and Tusa (n 3) 74–90.

Agreement was adhered to by nineteen other nations by notice given to the UK government.[6] The Agreement states that it was concluded by the parties 'acting in the interests of all the United Nations and by their representatives duly authorised', but the IMT was not linked to the UN Organization, whose Charter had already been signed but had not yet entered into force.[7]

The IMT Agreement was notably reticent regarding judicial governance arrangements. It mentioned the main *injugovin*, the Allied Control Council (ACC) for Germany, only in passing, envisaging the establishment of the Tribunal 'after consultation' with the Council.[8] The Council was set up towards the end of the Potsdam Conference (17 July to 2 August 1945) as the joint organ of the Commanders-in-Chief in accordance with the 1944 Agreement on Control Machinery.[9] The Allied Powers conferred on the ACC the 'supreme authority in matters affecting Germany as a whole'.[10] It is clear, however, that the decision to institute the IMT rested fully with the parent states. Consultation with the Council on this matter was meant merely to flesh out practical modalities and details, not to obtain its principled consent. Like the IMT, the ACC was, after all, both the creature and the tool of the Allied Powers' joint occupation of Germany.

The Control Council gathered for its first meeting on 30 July 1945 and operated until the spring of 1948.[11] It consisted of the four Commanders-in-Chief at the helm and was the first of the four tiers of the Allied Control Authority—the 'sum total of the quadripartite Allied administration'.[12] The second tier, in turn, was the Commanders' deputies, who formed the Coordinating Committee; the third was represented by the ten Directorates responsible for specific areas of military government; and the fourth was the Secretariat and other subsidiary organs of Allied control. Decision-making in all echelons of the quadripartite Allied Control Authority had to be unanimous, which

[6] IMT Agreement art 5. Australia, Belgium, Czechoslovakia, Denmark, Ethiopia, Greece, Haiti, Honduras, India, Luxembourg, Netherlands, New Zealand, Norway, Panama, Paraguay, Poland, Uruguay, Venezuela, and Yugoslavia became parties to the London Agreement.

[7] Charter of the United Nations (signed at the conclusion of the United Nations Conference on International Organization on 26 June 1945 in San Francisco, entered into force on 24 October 1945).

[8] IMT Agreement art 1.

[9] Agreement on Control Machinery for Germany (adopted by the European Advisory Commission; signed at London on 14 November 1944, and amended by a further agreement signed at London, 1 May 1945) in *Treaties and Other International Acts Series* 3070; *United States Treaties and Other International Agreements*, vol 5, part 2, 2062.

[10] Control Council Proclamation No 1 'Establishing Control Council' (done at Berlin, 30 August 1945) in *Enactments and Approved Papers of the Control Council and Coordinating Committee, Allied Control Authority, Germany, 1945, vol. I* (Legal Division, Office of Military Government for Germany, US) 44, art II.

[11] The ACC held no meetings after March 1948 and was effectively dissolved towards the end of that month due to the breakdown of the partnership between the Soviet and the other three Allied Power representatives. The Soviets opposed French, UK, and US trilateral discussions on future plans for Germany. On 20 March 1948, the Soviet representative, Marshal Vasily Sokolovsky, accused the US and UK of destroying the quadripartite machinery, announcing that the ACC was no longer an operational organ of government before withdrawing from the meeting. 'Allied Control Council for Germany' (1948) 2(2) International Organization 389, 390.

[12] 'The Political Adviser for Germany (Murphy) to the Secretary of State, 740.00119 Control (Germany)/1-647, Berlin, January 6, 1947' (Document 321) in *Foreign Relations of the United States, 1947, Council of Foreign Ministers; Germany and Austria, Vol II* <https://history.state.gov/historicaldocuments/frus1947v02/d321> 832–33.

caused enormous difficulties and inefficiencies: 'a moribund organism incapable of withstanding the virus of Allied dissension'.[13]

The IMT governance architecture combined thinly institutionalized governance performed by the ACC with direct governance by the Allied Powers separately. The Tribunal's constitutional framework envisaged that some functions—notably the appointment of judges, alternates, and members of the prosecution—were to be carried out by each of the four Powers. Other aspects of governance lay within the mandate of the ACC as the supreme authority in Germany. The Charter only referenced its role in designating the venue in Berlin where the members of the Tribunal and Chief Prosecutors were to convene for the first meeting,[14] as well as its functions in the execution of sentences.[15] As the scarce regulation attests, its governance scheme had not been fully shaped by the time the IMT started operations in September 1945. The Council and the Allied Powers had to improvise along the way.

The ACC's governance of the IMT constituted a tiny fraction of its activities.[16] There was no dedicated unitary organ charged with such responsibilities. Within the ACC, decision-making on most issues of principle rested with the Coordinating Committee. It was *de facto* the highest-level executive organ, consisting of delegates holding the rank of General or equivalent.[17] The Committee was charged with preparing and carrying out the decisions of the Council, exercising authority over the Allied *Kommandatura* in Berlin,[18] and coordinating the work of the Directorates. The specialized Directorates—Legal, Political, Finance, and Internal Affairs and Communications—handled matters relating to the IMT within their areas of competence.[19] For example, the Legal Directorate was charged with 'developing measures

[13] ibid 845–46 ('That the present quadripartite administration of Germany has been a failure from the US standpoint is almost universally acknowledged').

[14] IMT Charter art 22. The venue of the IMT trial became Courtroom 600 of the Palace of Justice at Nuremberg in the US zone of occupation which was chosen because the building was undamaged in war and could accommodate the proceedings. The Soviet representative at the London Conference, and future IMT judge, Iona Nikitchenko agreed to this arrangement as it allowed the Soviets to 'have the prestige of hosting the tribunal without the burden of providing the logistical support for the trials': Hirsch (n 3) 73.

[15] IMT Charter arts 28–29. Section 5.5.

[16] Agreement on Control Machinery (n 9) art 3 ('(i) to ensure appropriate uniformity of action by the Commanders-in-Chief in their respective zones of occupation; (ii) to initiate plans and reach agreed decisions on the chief military, political, economic and other questions affecting Germany as a whole, on the basis of instructions received by each Commander-in-Chief from his Government; (iii) to control the German central administration, which will operate under the direction of the Control Council and will be responsible to it for ensuring compliance with its demands; (iv) to direct the administration of 'Greater Berlin' through appropriate organs').

[17] 'The Political Adviser for Germany (Murphy) to the Secretary of State' (n 12) 834 ('the higher level working organ which resolves or attempts to resolve the problems of quadripartite administration and is in effective charge of the everyday operation of the machinery in Berlin').

[18] A portmanteau of the German *Kommando* and Russian *комендатура*, *Kommandatura* was the first quadripartite organ to sit in Berlin from July 1945 on. Headed by four Commandants of the US, UK, French, and USSR troops garrisoning the city, it was charged with overall direction and control function, performing 'in miniature what the Control Council was originally intended to do for the whole of Germany': ibid 841–42.

[19] Agreement on Control Machinery (n 9) art 6(a) provided for twelve Divisions. But the Council consisted of ten Directorates, most with numerous (sub-)committees and 'working parties' (Combined Services; Transport; Economic; Finance; Reparations, Deliveries and Restitution; Internal Affairs and Communications; Legal; Manpower; Prisoner of War and Displaced Persons; German External Property): ibid 835–39.

and procedures, and recommending them for Control Council action' with regard to the Council's functions pursuant to the London Agreement and with '[a]cting for the Control Council as directed by it in the execution of such measures and procedures approved by the Control Council'.[20] The Allied Control Authority also ordered it to hold at its disposal the record of all proceedings upon the delivery of the sentences for the purpose of processing petitions for clemency, along with the indictments, judgment, and the relevant parts of the trial record and evidence.[21]

The Coordinating Committee and specialized Directorates issued directives on a broad range of operational and outreach issues raised by the Nuremberg Tribunal's work. Here is a sample of their IMT-related tasks: (i) arranging for payment of defence counsel's fees and costs in connection with the trial;[22] (ii) deciding on the representation of political parties at Nuremberg;[23] (iii) sending of representatives of educational institutions to the trial;[24] and (iv) the maintenance of the official record of the proceedings, admission, and procedure in relation to petitions for clemency by persons condemned to death, as well as matters concerning the execution of sentences.[25]

Last but not least, the secretarial duties of keeping central files, providing interpretation and translating services, and preparing documents for all echelons of the Allied Control Authority, were performed by the quadripartite Allied Secretariat composed of the staff appointed by each of Allied Power.[26] The Secretariat's Liaison and Protocol Section dealt with foreign missions, while the Administrative Section operated the building the US put at the Allied Control Authority's disposal in its sector.

[20] Control Council Directive No 9 'Developing Measures and Procedures Regarding Major War Criminals of European Axis', 30 August 1945, in *Enactments and Approved Papers, vol I* (n 10) 45.

[21] Control Council Directive No 35 'Sentences of the International Military Tribunal' (done at Berlin on the 7th day of September, 1946, CORC/P(46)284-Final, paras 1–2) in *Enactments and Approved Papers of the Control Council and Coordinating Committee, Allied Control Authority, Germany, 1945, vol IV* (Legal Division, Office of Military Government for Germany, US) 89.

[22] 'Payment of Defending Counsel's fees and Costs in Connection with War Criminals' Trial', Coordinating Committee, CORC/P(46)99, DFIN/P(46)39 Revise (approved at Berlin, 18 March 1946) in *Enactments and Approved Papers of the Control Council and Coordinating Committee, Allied Control Authority, Germany, 1945, vol III* (Legal Division, Office of Military Government for Germany, US) 21. In detail: see Section 5.4.

[23] 'Representation of German Political Parties at Nuremberg', Memorandum from the Political Directorate to the Coordinating Committee, Allied Control Authority' CORC/P(45)205 (approved at Berlin, 21 December 1945) in *Enactments and Approved Papers, vol I* (n 10) 316 (conceding to a request by leaders of four political parties in Berlin to receive representation at the Nuremberg trial and recommending that it be allowed and 'extended to the representatives of Democratic political parties which have been authorized in all four zones of occupation in Germany', '[w]ith a view to associating the German Democratic political parties with the trial and to assist in bringing home to the German people the guilt of its former Nazi leaders').

[24] 'Dispatch of the Representatives of the Educational Committee of the City of Berlin to the Trials in Nuremberg', Coordinating Committee, CORC/P(46)81 (BK/ACC(46)15) (approved at Berlin, 12 March 1946) in *Enactments and Approved Papers, vol III* (n 22) 14 (inquiring whether the Allied Control Authority would agree in principle to the educators' visit to Nuremberg 'to witness a part of the Nuremberg trials with a view to Anti-Nazi education', as proposed by the Education Committee of the Allied *Kommandatura* of Berlin); 'Sending of Representatives of Educational Institutions to the Nuremberg Trials (Note by Allied Secretariat)' in ibid 78 (reporting the Internal Affairs and Communications Directorate's decision 'to request the Coordinating Committee to approve the sending of two representative of educational institutions per week from each zone of occupation to the Nuremberg trials').

[25] Control Council Directive No 35 (n 21) paras 2–5. Section 5.5.

[26] 'The Political Adviser for Germany (Murphy) to the Secretary of State' (n 12) 839 (they were the personnel of assigning states, not international public servants).

Like any other Allied control organ, the Secretariat was subject to the unanimity rule. Its US branch grew larger than the other three national components and numbered forty-five military and civilian staffers in 1947.[27] The Allied Secretariat was a conduit between the Council structures, on the one hand, and the IMT Secretariat and prosecution and defence counsel, on the other.

Although the IMTFE design was loosely modelled on the IMT's, their constitutional and governance architecture diverged significantly. This was a result of the different balance of power in the Pacific theatre, particularly the reduced European and Soviet interest in being actively involved in the postwar settlement in the Far East.[28] The Tokyo Tribunal came into being by fiat of the Supreme Commander for the Allied Powers in the Far East (SCAP), General Douglas MacArthur, who had been appointed to that role by US President Truman and acted on orders from the US Joint Chiefs of Staff. The direct legal basis for establishing the Tokyo Tribunal was the SCAP Special Proclamation.[29] The Proclamation was, however, adopted under the authority conferred on the SCAP jointly by the US, Great Britain, USSR, and China to issue all necessary orders for the effectuation of Japan's terms of surrender.[30] One term articulated in the Potsdam Declaration, which was signed by the US, UK, and China (and adhered to later by the USSR), was 'stern justice shall be meted out to all war criminals'.[31]

The IMTFE sat permanently in the former headquarters of the Ministry of War and Imperial Japanese Army General Staff Office in Ichigaya, Tokyo.[32] The Tokyo Tribunal was, in essence, an American-driven project. The US, as the 'Biggest of the Eleven', played a leading role in launching it and exercised a nearly-total control over every key aspect of its operations.[33] However, the IMTFE was international in legal character because the SCAP exercised authority delegated by all Allied Powers.[34] The US dominance came only with a nominal degree of Allied influence. Exerted through the supreme organ of joint Allied policy, the Far Eastern Commission in Washington,

[27] ibid.

[28] Neil Boister and Robert Cryer, 'Introduction' in Boister and Cryer (n 1) xxxix ('the only communist nation in the Allied camp at that time (the USSR) had little to say on Japan, having only entered the Pacific war under dubious circumstances two weeks prior to the Japanese surrender' (footnote omitted)); Totani (n 3) 26–28.

[29] Special Proclamation—Establishment of an International Military Tribunal for the Far East (Supreme Commander for the Allied Powers, signed on 19 January 1946 in Tokyo) arts 1–2 in Boister and Cryer (n 1) 5–6.

[30] ibid preambular paras 4–6; Instrument of Surrender (signed on 2 September 1945 at Tokyo Bay) in Boister and Cryer (n 1) 3–4.

[31] The Potsdam Declaration (Proclamation Defining Terms for Japanese Surrender) (26 July 1945) para 10 in Boister and Cryer (n 1) 1–2. Mei (n 3) 7.

[32] For a detailed first-hand description, see Mei (n 3) 46–53.

[33] In his unfinished manuscript, Judge Mei Ju-ao, the Chinese member, shared his candid and highly uncomplimentary thoughts on the US 'arrogance and dominance' over the Tribunal and the methods by which the SCAP exercised it: Mei (n 3) 8 fn9 ('he arrogated to himself all the power, acting as an emperor for the *Tenno*') and 10 fn10 (the SCAP placed entry restrictions on the Soviet seventy-strong team, regarded as too large; only twenty persons were allowed and the arrival of the Soviet member was therefore delayed).

[34] The US Supreme Court found as much in *Hirota* v *MacArthur, General of the Army, and others*, 338 US 197 (20 December 1948) 198 ('The military tribunal set up in Japan by General MacArthur as the agent of the Allied Powers is not a tribunal of the United States and the courts of the United States have no power or authority to review, affirm, set aside, or annul the judgments and sentences imposed by it on these petitioners, all of whom are residents and citizens of Japan').

and the Allied Council for Japan sitting in Tokyo, such influence bore on the framing of the final version of the IMTFE Charter.

The initial Charter was drafted by the team of SCAP legal advisors led by Joseph Keenan, who in due course became the chief prosecutor of the Tribunal.[35] General MacArthur approved the Charter on the same day as the Proclamation. In contrast to the process that led to the Nuremberg Charter, the enactment of the IMTFE Charter was not preceded by an intergovernmental conference. This allowed the US to forgo cumbersome negotiations with the other Allies and avoid some of the disputes that had dominated the London conference in the start-up phase (only to see them resurface later at trial).[36] The Allied members represented in the Far Eastern Commission were consulted on the IMTFE Charter only after it was adopted.

However, this consultation was not in vain and led to a significant amendment.[37] All Commission members—not only the signatories of the Instrument of Surrender, as originally envisaged—obtained the right to nominate justices and associate counsel.[38] This enabled India and the Philippines (neither of which were sovereign states prior to 1945) to have their judges on the Tokyo bench.[39] In addition, the Far Eastern Commission established that the diplomatic representatives of the members of the Allied Council for Japan had to be consulted before the SCAP's review of the Tribunal's sentences. This agreement was not reflected in the Charter and remained confidential for a while. It was later formalized in a new policy issued in the name of the Commission and handed down to the SCAP by the US government.[40]

Save for the episodic involvement by the Far Eastern Commission and the Allied Council, the SCAP remained the IMTFE's parent and governance organ, concentrating extensive powers over it. This design choice reflected the US policy of controlling the court unilaterally and prioritizing institutional cohesion, which was impossible to achieve with the quadripartite arrangements at Nuremberg.[41] Under the SCAP's undivided authority, his General Headquarters operated as the Tokyo Tribunal's principal *injugovin*, encompassing not only the Commander himself but also an elaborate organizational structure of departments backed by significant resource capacity. The SCAP's statutory competences related to the IMTFE covered the appointment of key staff (Judges, General Secretary, and Chief of Counsel) and the execution and review of sentences, but the Headquarters' influence went much

[35] Mei (n 3) 139. A close associate and friend of General MacArthur, Joseph B Keenan (US) came to combine the functions of SCAP legal advisor, head of the International Prosecution Section, and the IMTFE chief of counsel (the post to which he was appointed by US President Harry S Truman).

[36] Totani (n 3) 24–25. One grand debate was the concept of criminal conspiracy: Minear (n 3) 20 and 39–42.

[37] SCAP General Order no 20 of 26 April 1946 (amending the IMTFE Charter); Boister and Cryer (n 1) xxxvii.

[38] Mei (n 3) 39, 53 (IMTFE and Commission membership was to be aligned); Minear (n 3) 20–21, 75–76; Totani (n 3) 28.

[39] Pakistan, Burma, and Ceylon lacked the membership of the Far Eastern Commission and were excluded; Indonesia and Vietnam were still struggling for their independence and were not represented: Mei (n 3) 53–54.

[40] 'The Secretary General of the Far Eastern Commission (Johnson) to the Secretary of State' (4 April 1946) in *Foreign Relations of the United States: Diplomatic Papers, vol 8* (US Department of State 1946) 425; Solis Horwitz, 'The Tokyo Trial' (1950) 28 International Conciliation 475, 482; Totani (n 3) 28.

[41] Totani (n 3) 29.

deeper at every level.[42] The SCAP was responsible for apprehending suspects, investigating crimes, and initiating trials. The arrests of 118 persons listed by the US War Department were carried out—and most of them released after the selection of twenty-eight defendants for the first and only trial—under SCAP's authority.[43]

5.3 Appointment and Status of Principals and Key Staff

At the IMT, the primary signatories of the London Agreement retained the full extent of appointment powers, and the ACC had no role therein. The 'Big Four' directly appointed the principals: the members of the Tribunal, alternates, and chief prosecutors. Each Power assigned one member of the Tribunal and one alternate, resulting in an eight-strong bench.[44] The early proposal to open this pool to representatives of other states that adhered to the Charter did not survive until the London conference.[45] Under the Charter, IMT judges were specifically considered representatives of parent states.[46] The signatories had the power to replace judges or alternates they had appointed for reasons of health or for other good reasons, subject to the limitation that 'no replacement may take place during a Trial, other than by alternate'.[47] The Allied Powers also appointed their chief prosecutors 'for the investigation of the charges against and the prosecution of major war criminals'.[48]

The IMT Charter neither set requirements regarding judges or chief prosecutors' qualifications nor contained guarantees of institutional or individual independence. Article 3 prohibited challenges to the Tribunal or requests for disqualification of its members and alternates from the parties. The degree of actual judicial independence was questionable and varied by member. Thus, the Soviet members of the Tribunal were firmly believed by their brethren to have received instructions from Moscow on every consequential matter—not least the indictment, verdicts, and sentences.[49] This is amply corroborated by Francine Hirsch's findings from Soviet archival sources: the

[42] Sections 5.3 and 5.5. For instance, the SCAP was involved in selecting defendants; the decision not to put the Japanese Emperor on the list was also his: Minear (n 3) 101–17.

[43] Mei (n 3) 40–41; Yuma Totani, 'The Case against the Accused' in Tanaka and others (n 3) 148–49 (with reference to 'Appendix "D": Draft Joint Chiefs of Staff Directive on the Identification, Apprehension and Trial of Persons Suspected of War Crimes' in 'Report by the State–War–Navy Coordinating Subcommittee for the Far East, 12 September 1945' in *Foreign Relations of the United States: Diplomatic Papers, vol* 6 (US Department of State 1945) 932–6).

[44] IMT Charter art 2.

[45] cf Memorandum to President Roosevelt from the Secretaries of State and War and the Attorney General, 22 January 1945 ('The court might consist of seven members, one each to be appointed by The British Commonwealth, the United States, the Soviet Union and France, and three to be appointed by agreement among the other United Nations who become parties to the proposed procedure') and American Draft of Definitive Proposal, Presented to Foreign Ministers at San Francisco, April 1945, para 15 ('Each International Military Tribunal shall consist of four members and four alternates').

[46] IMT Charter art 3 ('*its* member of the Tribunal') and 4(b) ('the *representative* of that Signatory'). Emphasis added.

[47] IMT Charter art 3.

[48] IMT Charter art 14 (chapeau).

[49] Francis Biddle, *In Brief Authority* (Doubleday & Co 1962) 466 ('the Russians . . . wrote, in accordance with their instructions, that all of the defendants should have been found guilty') and 472 ('little distinction was drawn between by the Soviet members between prosecution and court. They were but complementary arms of the state, with the same common goal.).

regularity and nature of communication between Soviet officials at the IMT and the leadership—via the governmental commission headed by the notorious Andrei Vyshinsky—left no room whatsoever for judicial or prosecutorial independence, even in the most formal sense.[50] Moreover, the American member later described the bench as a whole in terms more akin to a court-martial than a regular court.[51]

Formally, IMT members and alternates played a different role in the proceedings. Nevertheless, all eight actively participated in the Tribunal's work and deliberations, enjoying equality as members of a collegial court. From early on, judges insisted on a protocol ensuring equal treatment regardless of their status as members or alternates. US Judge Biddle recounted a telling incident in his memoir. During the first visit by the judges to the Nuremberg courtroom, his alternate, Judge Parker, got 'visibly angry' about the fact that alternates had been allocated 'seats that were smaller and lower, not mean and hard, but less exalted' than those reserved for members and raised what he saw as inappropriate inequality and the alternates' lower status.[52] The judges shared his concern and requested that the army replace 'the lesser thrones' with 'greater seats, so that, examining only the chairs, a spectator could not distinguish between a member and alternate'.[53]

The IMT Charter directed members (not alternates) to agree amongst themselves on the selection of the President from their number before the main trial, or to elect one by a vote of no less than three members.[54] Aside from the national sensitivities involved, this issue was consequential from both the judicial self-governance perspective and from the fact that the President's vote was decisive in cases where votes were evenly divided (except that convictions and sentences could only be imposed by a majority).[55] Over the Soviet member's objections, the judges decided that the presidency would not rotate and would be held by one of them throughout the trial.[56] No vote to elect the President ultimately proved necessary because the members reached an agreement. Proposed by the French member Donnedieu de Vabres, Lord Geoffrey Lawrence was the only candidate standing after the American member Biddle, who had been proposed by the Soviet Judge Nikitchenko, withdrew in favour of Justice

[50] Soviet prosecutors and judges kept Moscow closely informed of developments both before and during the trial, and they received detailed instructions from the leadership regarding the steps to be taken. This communication extended to the content of ostensibly private judicial deliberations and included directives on the positions the Soviet member was expected to adopt concerning individual convictions and sentences. Hirsch (n 3) 103 ('Everyone knew that Rudenko and Nikitchenko were acting under direct orders from Moscow'), 270 (on Biddle's speculation that the two were 'in cahoots' on the issue of disallowing the defence to call witnesses to refute the Katyn massacre charge, while both 'were of course ... taking instructions from Vyshinsky'); 374, 377–79 (despite security measures, Judge Nikitchenko kept Soviet leaders abreast of the *confidential* judicial deliberations on the verdicts and secretly transmitted draft parts of the judgment to Moscow; the Vyshinsky Commission then issued detailed instructions— personally reviewed by Molotov and Stalin—on the verdicts and sentences, as well as on how the judge was to attempt to persuade his colleagues).

[51] Biddle (n 49) 480 ('although the Tribunal was far more judicial than most courts-martial, we were not judges of the court in the strict sense, but members of a tribunal appointed by the heads of state' as Commanders-in-Chief of the armed forces').

[52] ibid 373–74.

[53] ibid.

[54] IMT Charter art 4(b).

[55] IMT Charter art 4(c).

[56] This decision was reached on 11 October 1945: Hirsch (n 3) 99.

Lawrence.[57] This early judicial consensus helped strengthen the collegial and cooperative character of the bench. This was put to the test soon enough, when the Western judges accommodated the Soviets' request to grant the prosecution an extension for filing the indictment.[58]

Likewise, the IMT chief prosecutors from the 'Big Four' were equal and operated in a horizontal quadripartite structure. They formed, and acted jointly as, a coordinating organ—the Committee for the Investigation and Prosecution of Major War Criminals. Each chief prosecutor had unqualified autonomy in developing work plans and managing staff within their teams, determining the final designation of persons to be tried, and preparing their parts of the indictment, accompanying documents, and their respective cases.[59] The Committee also had functions beyond investigation and prosecution, notably drawing up and recommending to the Tribunal, for its approval, draft rules of procedure.[60] The Committee decided by majority on most matters and appointed a chairman—a rotational post carrying no decisive vote.[61]

The IMT Charter omits the issue of the Secretariat or registry entirely. All official documentation had to be produced, and all proceedings conducted, in English, French, Russian, and German.[62] That these gargantuan secretarial and interpretation tasks would have to be performed under such daunting circumstances was an afterthought. The scale of the paperwork the Tribunal generated was staggering, given the volume of evidence and submissions, multiplied by the multilingual character of the proceedings. The quadripartite IMT Secretariat (not to be confused with the Allied Secretariat) was set up within the Tribunal to receive and process submissions, but it was badly underpowered in the pre-trial stage. So much so that, according to Judge Biddle's recollections of what he encountered upon arrival in Nuremberg, the work had ground to a halt and the Secretariat was in disarray: the four secretaries appointed

[57] No one suggested the French or Soviet members for president, but the Soviet Judge was allowed to preside over the first meeting of judges to be held at the permanent seat of the Tribunal in Berlin and accepted the presidency of Justice Lawrence. Justice Biddle explained his decision to decline the presidency—a decision urged also by Robert Jackson—on the grounds of the need to ensure the international character of the proceedings, given that the trial was to be held at Nuremberg in the US zone of occupation, the US army had arrested most defendants, and most of the evidence had been gathered and would be presented by the Americans. Biddle (n 49) 383–85 ('If any international flavour was to be preserved it was essential that an American must not preside, and it would seem that the best choice would be Lord Lawrence'); Hirsch (n 3) 99 ('Jackson had convinced Biddle to support Lawrence lest the Americans, who were playing host and supplying the majority of the defendants, be seen as completely running the show').

[58] Biddle (n 49) 386–89 (on the bench's response to the delayed filing of the Soviet indictment and collegiality shown towards Judge Nikitchenko by granting a three-day extension). As Hirsch recounts, this delay resulted from Soviet stalling tactics: Judge Nikitchenko and Prosecutor Rudenko—so much for their 'independence'—awaited the Kremlin's directives concerning revisions to the indictment, the most sensitive of which concerned the fabricated charge related to the Katyn massacre and the German-Soviet Non-Aggression Pact (along with the explosive matter of the secret protocol thereto): Hirsch (n 3) 101–06.

[59] IMT Charter art 14.

[60] The rules of procedure were adopted by the IMT judges, who could accept, with or without amendments, or to reject the rules recommended by the prosecutors' Committee: IMT Charter arts 14(e) and 13; IMT Rules of Procedure, 29 October 1945.

[61] On issues of prosecutorial strategy, namely the designation of defendants for trial and the selection of specific charges against them, deference was to be shown to the chief prosecutor making the proposal: IMT Charter art 14.

[62] IMT Charter art 25 (moreover, '[s]o much of the record and of the proceedings may also be translated into the language of any country in which the Tribunal is sitting, as the Tribunal considers desirable in the interests of justice and public opinion'. Fortunately for the IMT, this provision remained a dead letter).

by the Allied Powers were inexperienced in operating under the conditions of occupation and 'unable to handle the flood of applications and submissions that were pouring in'.[63] In his view, the chaos could only be reined in by putting in charge 'an army officer with full backing from the top'; precisely for that purpose, he sought (and obtained) assistance from General Dwight Eisenhower, who seconded no less than a Brigadier General to make the necessary arrangements for the Secretariat's US section.[64]

By contrast, US authorities in Japan were able to secure a more unitary approach to the IMTFE's structure, although they still had to live with multilateral membership. The imperative of centralized command necessitated different design choices in the Tribunal's organization. The original Charter set the number of justices at between five and nine, but the revised version provided for a composition of between six and eleven judges.[65] Unlike at Nuremberg, no alternates were envisaged. The SCAP was the sole appointing authority, although he had to choose from the list of nominated candidates and was in fact bound by it. The governments of the nine nations which countersigned the Instrument of Surrender (Australia, Canada, China, France, the Netherlands, New Zealand, the UK, the US, and the USSR), as well as India and the Commonwealth of the Philippines, nominated their judicial candidates. Theoretically, the SCAP could select fewer justices than the allowed maximum. But given the understanding that all Far Eastern Commission countries would be represented on the bench, eleven members were appointed, essentially ratifying the Allies' selection.

The IMTFE Charter set no judicial qualification requirements; by chance, the only judge with expertise in international law was the member from India. Unlike the IMT Charter, the Tokyo Charter did not contain a prohibition on challenges to the Tribunal or its members.[66] The IMTFE had to deal with (and dismiss) defence requests to disqualify Judges Webb, Jaranilla, and Cramer. The justices represented and were accountable directly to their governments rather than to any Allied authority.[67] With hindsight, this posed risks to judicial independence: no protection other than the judge's own conscience stood between him and his government if it sought to exercise undue influence. The government of the Netherlands, displeased with Judge Bert Röling's intention to issue a dissenting opinion, attempted to prevent him from doing so and backed down only after he threatened to resign.[68] By contrast with modern

[63] Biddle (n 52) 396.

[64] ibid 397–98 ('I explained to him the lack of any organization in the secretary's office, the enormously increasing flow of work, the confusion. We must have a general officer to take charge. "When do you want him?" "At once." … Brigadier General William D. Mitchell reported promptly, and in his efficient and tactful hands order gradually shaped itself out of chaos, and a vast load of detail was removed from the Tribunal's back').

[65] IMTFE Charter art 2.

[66] Cf IMT Charter art 3. For discussion, see Mei (n 3) 54–56.

[67] Mei (n 3) 57 ('Theoretically, those judges were international, but they represented their home country, as recognized by the national flags displayed behind the bench and displayed on the cars they drove'); Totani (n 3) 29.

[68] Bert VA Röling and Antonio Cassese (eds), *The Tokyo Trial and Beyond: Reflections of a Peacemonger* (Polity Press 1993) 61; Robert Cryer, 'Röling in Tokyo: A Dignified Dissenter' (2010) 8(4) Journal of International Criminal Justice 1109, 1125; L Van Poelgeest, *Nederland en het Tribunaal van Tokio: Volkenrechtelijke polemiek en internationale politiek rond de berechting en gratiëring van de Japanse oorlogsmisdadigers* (Gouda Quint BV 1989) 82–95.

customary practice, the SCAP had the power to appoint the Tribunal President—the judges were not allowed this standard privilege.[69] Justice William Webb (Australia) was appointed President. The imposed presidency did not serve the Tribunal well. As a *primus inter pares*, Webb did not seem to command full authority with the brethren and was probably not the best candidate for the job, leading to diminished collegiality on the bench.[70]

The SCAP designated the chief prosecutor (Chief of Counsel), who was charged with the investigation and prosecution of charges, as well as with providing legal assistance to the SCAP.[71] The other ten states appointed associate counsel 'to assist the Chief of Counsel'.[72] Therefore, the Charter imposed a hierarchy within the International Prosecution Section by placing ten (non-US) associate prosecutors under the authority of one (US) chief prosecutor. This ensured a more unified—and US-exclusive—leadership compared to the horizontal prosecution structure at Nuremberg, where each of the four chief prosecutors from the 'Big Four' led a separate team responsible for its portion of the case.[73] On the other side of the aisle, the accused had the right to select their defence counsel, yet 'subject to disapproval of such counsel at any time by the Tribunal', while the Tribunal itself had the power to designate counsel should the accused be unrepresented.[74] Each defendant at the Tokyo Tribunal benefited from the assistance of US counsel in addition to representation by Japanese counsel. US advocates were recruited directly from the US or employed by the SCAP. Their role was advisory and secondary, namely assisting their Japanese counterparts with the Tribunal's common-law procedure, which was unfamiliar to most of them.[75]

Finally, the Secretariat—composed of assistant secretaries, clerks, interpreters, and other personnel as deemed necessary—was organized and directed by the General Secretary, who was appointed by the SCAP rather than by the judges.[76] The General Secretary was a staffer of the General Headquarters and operated in coordination with the President but under SCAP authority.[77] Acting as the IMTFE's registry, the Secretariat was responsible for processing documents addressed to the court, maintaining its records (including the transcript of the proceeding, exhibits and documents), and providing clerical support to the bench, among other duties.[78] With

[69] IMTFE Charter art 3(a).

[70] In detail on the bench dynamics: Mei (n 3) 62–67 (at 64 conveying his concern about 'the President's morality and integrity'), 68–69 ('attitude and words were explicit, sometimes rash and impatient, which often elicited resistance and conflicts within the Tribunal', 'rude to defence counsel'); (Minear (n 3) 83–86 (President Webb bore himself with arrogance and was rude towards parties and witnesses).

[71] IMTFE Charter art 8(a).

[72] IMTFE Charter art 8(b).

[73] Totani (n 3) 29; Mei (n 3) 84–86 (on Keenan's 'strong sectionalism', efforts 'to frame the prosecution work ... into an American-led play', leading to irritation among associate counsel from other states, as well as 'his domineering and arrogant attitude ... before the Tribunal') and 139 ('dictatorial system').

[74] IMTFE Charter 9(d).

[75] Mei (n 3) 96.

[76] IMTFE Charter art 3(b).

[77] Mei (n 3) 99.

[78] IMTFE Charter art 13(e).

regard to all administrative matters, expenses, personnel issues, and archiving, the Tribunal was therefore fully dependent on the SCAP.[79]

5.4 Financing and Practical Support

As the Nuremberg IMT's *injugovin*, the ACC administered its budgetary matters. In accordance with the Charter, the IMT's expenses were to be charged by the signatories of the Agreement against the funds allotted for the maintenance of the Control Council.[80] There was no further specification of how the budget was to be determined, approved, and allocated, or how specific expenditures would be handled: the IMT was, after all, a fleeting ad hoc affair. Within the Council, the Finance Directorate dealt with matters of ACC financial administration, and that responsibility extended to the budgetary governance of the Tribunal. Given its unprecedented character, the financial aspects of its operation as a judicial institution—and a criminal court at that—were uncharted territory. Creative—or, less charitably, clumsy—solutions had to be improvised on the spot to address pressing budgetary needs.

A prime example is the payment of defence counsel fees. This issue was emblematic of the financial limbo of the IMT as a whole and incidentally provided a vehicle for covering the Tribunal's general costs. Defendants had the right to represent themselves or to be assisted by counsel.[81] The IMT appointed lawyers to represent defendants but had been provided no funds to pay for their work. It was not until November 1945 that the Council made a decision on the compensation of counsel fees and costs.[82] But it is not self-evident how this came about. It turned out that already in the preceding weeks the IMT judges had requested the Allied Control Authority to urgently allocate a budget for the defence, yet no meaningful response was forthcoming. This meant that German counsel might have to depart and the trial would have to be postponed, which could not be afforded.[83] For help with this matter as well, Judge Biddle turned to General Eisenhower, which led to a remarkable exchange:

> If they were not paid they would go home—even Germans must live—and the trial would be postponed, perhaps indefinitely. We had applied to the Control Authority, who 'had it under consideration'... but you know what that means, general; we must have the money now, at once. 'How much?' We planned, I told him, to recompense them at the rate of $300 or $400 a month, out of which they would have to pay their assistants, stenographers, and traveling expenses. He seemed to think this a modest request, and again rang a bell. To the officer who answered, General Eisenhower said, 'Print enough money to keep Judge Biddle going.' And that was that.[84]

[79] Mei (n 3) 100 ('as to administration and personnel, the Tokyo Tribunal was not independent; it was a subsidiary of the GHQ'; 'neither independent nor "international"').
[80] IMT Charter art 30.
[81] IMT Charter art 16(d).
[82] 'Payment of Defending Counsel's Fees and Costs in Connection with War Criminals' Trial', paras 1–2, in *Enactments and Approved Papers, vol III* (n 22) 21.
[83] Biddle (n 52) 397.
[84] ibid 397–98.

Within the Council, the proposal was introduced by the US member of the Finance Directorate and subsequently endorsed by the Coordinating Committee.[85] The pilot scheme for counsel payments was expanded into the framework applicable to the 'costs of Tribunal and of the present trial' in its entirety.[86] The French, British, and Soviet authorities on the Council authorized US members to pay advances through the Reichsbank at Nuremberg to a designated IMT representative, who controlled the disbursement of funds with a view to covering specific expenses. Such advances were to be separately accounted for and repaid. Total costs were shared by the Zones 'in any manner approved by the Council', and advances were repaid 'in any manner deemed appropriate by each Zone'.[87] Besides that, the Finance Directorate was charged with certain responsibilities under Directive No 35 concerning sentences. In particular, it carried out parts of the sentences providing for the payment of fines by the defendants, confiscation of their property, the disposal of such fines or confiscated property. and the delivery to the Council of any stolen property in the possession or control of any of the defendants of which by the IMT ordered forfeiture.[88]

Unlike the IMT Charter, the SCAP Proclamation and the Tokyo Charter omitted the question of finances altogether. The IMTFE's functioning under SCAP authority and US dominance over its governance predetermined more straightforward funding arrangements. Given the unwieldy decision-making process in the Allied Council Authority in Germany, the US was eager to dispense with the need to seek consensus with other Allied states and 'save the day' with ad hoc schemes invented from scratch. The IMTFE did not operate a budget of its own and was not allocated funds to shoulder major costs such as salaries. It was only allocated limited funds to make direct payments of administrative expenses, the largest items being summonses (witness travel and accommodation) and printing paper costs.[89] Such expenses were paid by the SCAP and later incorporated in the 'occupation fee' the US was eventually to charge to the Japanese government.[90] The costs related to equipment purchases, building maintenance, refurbishment of the courtroom, and so on were borne by the US side as an integral part of SCAP accounts. This arrangement worked smoothly overall, albeit not without embarrassing hiccups. Judge Mei recalled that judges had to go on strike and suspend the trial for one week during the exceptionally hot summer of 1946 as a last resort to compel the SCAP to provide for air conditioning.[91]

85 'Payment of Defending Counsel's Fees and Costs in Connection with War Criminals' Trial' (n 82) paras 3–4.

86 ibid (adding the revision generalizing the financial solution for counsel to the IMT costs). Cf 'Proposal for the payment of defending counsel's fees and costs in connection with war criminals' trials', Coordinating Committee, Financial Directorate, CORC/P(45)158, 22 November 1945, paras 3–4, in *Enactments and Approved Papers, vol I* (n 10) 203.

87 'Payment of Defending Counsel's Fees and Costs in Connection with War Criminals' Trial' (n 82) paras 3–4.

88 Control Council Directive no 35 (n 21) para 6.

89 For detail, see Mei (n 3) 113. For witnesses residing in Japan, the cost was much lower than for the overseas witnesses, whose plane or steamer tickets, accommodation, and board had to be paid for, over and above payment of US$1 per day as pocket money. The amount of printing paper used was 'staggering' (reportedly 3–5 tons a day), leading to a 'huge expenditure': ibid 114.

90 Critical of this solution as lacking transparency and accountability: ibid 114 ('As for the total amount of the "occupation fee" and how it was spent, [it] was a mystery because the Americans always regarded the [General Headquarters] as their own "housework," the financial issues of the GHQ were never open').

91 ibid 46 (the judges' strike was 'scorned by the public').

The largest article of expenditure—the costs related to the appointment of staff and defence counsel fees—was borne by the US, the other ten Allies, and Japan. The salaries of the judges, associate counsel, and staff from the Allied nations were paid separately by the sending countries, while the salaries of US staff—including judicial, prosecutorial, secretarial, provost marshals, and security staff—were budgeted as part of the army expenses of the SCAP General Headquarters.[92] The Tribunal did not have to pay these large staffing costs, nor other major personnel-related expenses such as accommodation, transportation, board, and vacation trips for the judges. These expenses were deducted from the 'Japanese indemnity' to the countries that had appointed the respective members.[93]

Unlike at the IMT, there were no unanticipated stumbling blocks with the payment of IMTFE defence counsel fees and costs. Japanese counsel were reimbursed by the Japanese government, while US defence lawyers who assisted them were reimbursed from SCAP accounts.[94] All Japanese staff, including translators and interpreters, and other workers (cleaners, drivers, cooks, etc), who were employed by the IMTFE, were regarded as personnel 'expropriated' from the Japanese government by General Headquarters and paid for by Japan.[95] It is fair to say that, although Japan did not appoint any judicial, prosecutorial, or other staff to the Tribunal, it was made into its major financier through direct expenses, indemnities to Allied Powers, and the occupation fee due to the United States.

5.5 Enforcement and Review

The IMT Charter granted the ACC express competence in the area of the execution of sentences. First, it stipulated that any stolen property which the Nuremberg Tribunal could alienate from convicted persons, over and above the imposed penalty, was to be handed over to the ACC.[96] Second, it provided that, in the case of a finding of guilt, sentences were to be carried out in accordance with ACC orders, and the Council was authorized 'at any time [to] reduce or otherwise alter the sentences' but 'not increase severity thereof'.[97] The Control Council was also required to report to the Committee of Chief Prosecutors the discovery of fresh evidence that could potentially serve as the basis for new charges against a convicted and sentenced defendant, for appropriate action in the interests of justice.[98]

The enforcement and review function became an important line of work for the ACC.[99] While the Council normally held meetings at least every ten days, it now had

[92] ibid 112.

[93] ibid 75–76 and 113 (critical of the SCAP's generosity about judges' weekend and vacation tours and the staff's luxurious lifestyle, the costs of which were deducted from Japan's indemnity towards their countries).

[94] ibid 96, 112–13. Noting the staggering number of defence counsel (over one hundred Japanese and twenty American): ibid 92.

[95] ibid 113.

[96] IMT Charter art 28.

[97] IMT Charter art 29.

[98] IMT Charter art 30.

[99] 'Report by the Coordinating Committee on Matters of Procedure in Connection with the Consideration of the Sentences of the International Military Tribunal by the Control Council and the Execution of the Condemned Men', Note by the Allied Secretariat, CONL/P(46)65, in *Enactments and*

to convene more frequently for extraordinary sessions to consider pleas for clemency from the persons convicted by the Tribunal.[100] In the exercise of its Article 29 authority, the ACC issued Directive No 35 on the execution of death sentences, the service of sentences of imprisonment, and detention pending the execution, while assigning those tasks to a quadripartite commission of military commanders appointed by each Zone commander and the Allied *Kommandatura* of Berlin.[101]

The Directive provided that, to be receivable, petitions for clemency by persons condemned to death by the IMT were to be addressed to the Council and lodged with the IMT Secretariat within four days of the passing the sentences.[102] Executions had to be carried out on the fifteenth day after pronouncement of sentences in open court, unless the Tribunal or the ACC ordered otherwise.[103] Petitions for clemency were filed on behalf of fifteen defendants and four organizations that had been declared criminal, with some pleading for a substantive review of the judgment—a request at odds with the parameters of review under the Charter.[104] The Control Council dealt with those petitions at its meeting of 10 October 1946 and denied all of them.[105] The executions of those sentenced to death took place during the night of 15–16 October 1946.[106] The IMT convicts sentenced to terms of imprisonment served their penalties in Spandau prison in Berlin in full, except for the three unconditional paroles granted on grounds of poor health.[107]

The Tokyo Tribunal was not granted any enforcement competences in the post-judgment phase. When its work was done, the IMTFE was dissolved and General MacArthur reigned supreme. In its final provision, the IMTFE Charter stipulated that he would receive the record of the trial 'for his action thereon', implying the issuance of orders for the execution of the sentences.[108] The SCAP held the power under Article 17 at any time to reduce or otherwise alter the sentence, except when this would

Approved Papers vol IV (n 21) 107–08; Report of the Quadripartite Commission for the Execution of the Major War Criminals, Coordinating Committee Minutes (Meeting of 29 October 1946), CORC/M(46)57, 31 October 1946, in *Enactments and Approved Papers of the Control Council and Coordinating Committee, Allied Control Authority, Germany, 1945, vol V* (Legal Division, Office of Military Government for Germany, US) 97.

[100] 'The Political Adviser for Germany (Murphy) to the Secretary of State' (n 12) 833.

[101] Control Council Directive No 35 (n 21) paras 3–5.

[102] ibid para 2. The sentences of all the defendants were passed on 1 October 1946 and the four-day term expired on 5 October 1946.

[103] ibid para 3.

[104] The individual defendants were Bormann, Frick, Rosenberg, Streicher, Raeder, Göring, Funk, Dönitz, Keitel, Von Neurath, Jodl, Seyss-Inquart, Von Ribbentrop, Hess, and Sauckel; the four criminal organizations were the SS, SD, Gestapo, and the Leadership Corps of the Nazi Party. Raeder requested that as 'an act of mercy' he be shot rather than imprisoned for life, which the ACC denied as it could only decrease the sentence. No petitions came from Kaltenbrunner and Speer. Counsel for Shirach (unsuccessfully) reserved the right to petition at a later date. Harris (n 3) 482–84.

[105] ibid 485.

[106] ibid 485–87.

[107] Von Neurath, who was sentenced to fifteen years, was released in 1954; Raeder and Funk, both sentenced to life imprisonment, left Spandau in 1955 and 1957, respectively. John Mendelsohn, 'War Crimes Trials and Clemency in Germany and Japan' in Robert Wolfe (ed), *Americans as Proconsuls: United States Military Government in Germany and Japan, 1944–1952* (Southern Illinois University Press 1984) 228 fn2 and 258–59.

[108] IMTFE Charter art 17.

increase its severity. As noted in Section 5.2, this provision was complemented by the policy urged upon the SCAP by the Far Eastern Commission in early 1946, requiring him to consult the diplomatic representatives of states sitting in the Allied Council for Japan *before* exercising the review of Tribunal penalties.[109] This arrangement was kept 'top secret' in the early stages of the trial and, as Minear argued, exacerbated its political undertones: the administrative review of judicially determined sentences was suddenly preceded by diplomatic consultations.[110]

The defendants convicted by the Tokyo Tribunal were given ten days to plead for clemency, which they did through a consolidated defence appeal to the SCAP—to no avail. The SCAP obtained the views of every participating state in the Allied Council at its 24 November 1948 session on whether the sentences imposed by the Tribunal were to be altered or left intact. Although the SCAP's obligation to review sentences mirrored the competence of the ACC in Germany with respect to IMT penalties, it was apparently far from his favourite task.[111] The requests for clemency and for the commutation of death penalties to life imprisonment came from the representatives of countries where death penalty had been abolished and whose judges had issued dissenting opinions (India, France, and the Netherlands). The SCAP decided, however, that all sentences as pronounced must remain unchanged, ordering the Commanding General of the Eighth Army to execute them.[112] The capital punishments were carried out on 23 December 1948.

Since Article 17 of the IMTFE Charter provided for a continuing power of review ('at any time'), the SCAP continued dealing with the predicament of imprisoned convicts despite his professed repulsion for the task. On 7 March 1950, he issued a circular instituting a parole board empowered to authorize the commutation of sentences by two-thirds for good behaviour and to order parole after fifteen years for those serving life sentences.[113] Only one convict—Shigemitsu Mamoru—benefited from this clemency procedure under the SCAP mandate.[114] The Allied Occupation of Japan ended in 1952, and until April 1958 Japanese authorities handled IMTFE convicts' requests for parole. By the end of 1958, however, every one of the remaining ten—out of the initial

[109] Horwitz (n 40) 482; Minear (n 3) 21, 33.

[110] Minear (n 3) 160–61.

[111] General MacArthur in his own words: 'No duty I have ever been called upon to perform in a long public service replete with many bitter, lonely and forlorn assignments and responsibilities is so utterly repugnant to me as that of reviewing the sentences of the Japanese war criminal defendants adjudged by the International Military Tribunal for the Far East.' 'Review of Judgments of the IMTFE by the SCAP' in Boister and Cryer (n 1) 70.

[112] ibid ('I can find nothing of technical commission or omission in the incidents of the trial itself of sufficient import to warrant my intervention in the judgements which have been rendered. No human decision is infallible but I can conceive of no judicial process where greater safeguard was made to evolve justice ... If we cannot trust such processes and such men we can trust nothing'); Minear (n 3) 165–66.

[113] Boister and Cryer (n 3) 264–65, referencing Circular No 5 of 7 March 1950 per archival document 'Parole of Japanese War Criminals', New Zealand External Affairs, 9 June 1950, File no EA 106/3/22, Part 11.

[114] Shigemitsu Mamoru, the former foreign minister in the Tojo Hideki's cabinet (since 1943), signed the Japanese surrender (jointly with Umezu Yoshijiro) and had served four years and seven months of his seven-year sentence from arraignment by the time he was released on 21 November 1950 as part of the SCAP clemency programme. Four years later, he again became foreign minister and deputy prime minister (1954–56), and even negotiated the release of all his former fellow prisoners sentenced by the IMTFE. Minear (n 3) 172–75; Bass (n 3) 632–33.

nineteen—imprisoned 'Class A' convicts was set free unconditionally from Tokyo's Sugamo Prison: release conditions were lifted and sentences effectively terminated.[115]

5.6 Conclusion

The IMT and IMTFE governance models can be dismissed as defunct and irrevocably archaic: no more than a historical curiosity for contemporary scholars of international institutional law. Such an assessment would not be entirely off-target. The unprecedented character of these historic courts and the unique context in which they operated predetermined ad hoc schemes that were not replicated in subsequent international tribunal-building experiments.[116]

Their skeletal and largely improvised governance arrangements were underpinned by contemporaneous, and therefore embryonic, conceptions of *international* judicial independence and accountability. Both IMTs were neither part of nor associated with any international organization; the United Nations was only just being created when the Nuremberg Tribunal commenced its work. They were, in essence, ad hoc military tribunals—a species of international courts-martial and (joint) occupation courts with broader international participation.[117] Connected closely to the occupation authorities in postwar Germany and Japan, these courts were firmly entrenched in the Allied Control Authority and the headquarters of Supreme Commander of the Allied Powers, respectively, and were affected accordingly by the positions taken within those *injugovins* and the prevailing power dynamics. Naturally, their governance arrangements were of no precedential value for the UN criminal tribunals that came nearly half a century later.[118] This is also part of the reason for the relative lack of interest in how IMTs were run.

Nevertheless, the IMT and IMTFE governance schemes deserve closer attention not only from legal historians but also from international law scholars and judicial institution architects because their schemes occupy a landmark place on the spectrum of legal-institutional options. Although understudied to date, their *injugovins*' experience may prove particularly relevant for international or domestic courts set up under military occupation and/or in post-conflict settings. The IMTs' governance was characterized by a thin bureaucratic buffer that was barely more than a sum of the states constituting it and took the form of lean, multitasking structures. These institutions were charged with tribunal governance among other, often more urgent, tasks and routinely had to play by ear. They served facilitatory and administrative purposes and did not dispense with the need for direct involvement by the 'Big Four' at Nuremberg

115 Mendelsohn (n 107) 257–58.

116 The closest—albeit still rather remote—analogue is perhaps the US-backed Iraqi Special Tribunal (later renamed the Iraqi High Tribunal), which tried Saddam Hussein and other members of the Ba'ath Party for international crimes under Iraqi law. Although it was established by the Iraqi Governing Council, itself appointed by US authorities, the tribunal was, by its legal character, a national court—not an international one rooted in an occupation regime. The general assessment of the administration of justice by that institution remains predominantly unfavourable.

117 On the IMT: Biddle (n 49) 480 ('an ad hoc military tribunal, in substance a court-martial').

118 On the governance of the UN criminal tribunals, see Huw Llewellyn, 'Governance of the United Nations Criminal Tribunals', in this volume.

and the US (and, to a lesser degree, the other ten Allies) in Tokyo. The *injugovins*' role as intermediaries was heavily qualified by the presence of parent states, which appointed key personnel and intervened whenever challenges called for the Gordian-knot solutions.

Despite the truism of the IMTFE being modelled on the IMT, the governance modalities were nonetheless distinct, as the Allies' degrees of investment in the two institutions were not the same. The Nuremberg governance scheme was premised on a quadripartite approach which not only guaranteed but also necessitated the 'Big Four' equal status and participation in judicial governance. This led to more coordinate and 'democratic', but also to more contentious and less agile unanimous decision-making on the manifold issues arising in connection with IMT governance. The same egalitarian logic was reflected in the quadripartite IMT structure, including the appointment of co-equal principals in every organ. Judges, prosecutors, and members of the Secretariat were assigned by, and represented, each of the Allied Powers. They were not appointed jointly by states or by the Council, which played no role at all.

By contrast, the Tokyo IMT governance was concentrated in the hands of the SCAP, albeit acting under the Allied authority. The national principle for the appointment of key staff held in Tokyo but was interlaced with the more vertical organization of the governance architecture. US dominance over the IMTFE was qualified only minimally by the involvement of other ten states sitting in the Far Eastern Commission and the Allied Council for Japan. The same pyramidal logic shaped the internal structure of the IMTFE, which was appreciably more hierarchical than that of the IMT. The President was appointed by the SCAP, not elected by judicial peers, and the US Chief of Counsel heading the International Prosecution Section was 'more equal' than the associate counsel and their teams drawn from the other ten Allies.

The division of competences, judicial or administrative, between the IMT and IMTFE organs and their governing institutions was not clear-cut—even as a matter of law, let alone in practice.[119] The Tribunals' constituent instruments provided no express guarantees of institutional and individual judicial independence, much less prosecutorial independence. All of their principals were thought of, and regarded themselves, as representatives of the appointing states. Unsurprisingly, the *injugovins*' and states' meddling in judicial matters was not ruled out. Nor were the IMT and IMTFE governing institutions expected or empowered to impede and counter attempts by the appointing states to exert undue influence on 'their' judges. Indeed, instances of such attempts are on the record for both tribunals. These aspects of IMTs' governance legacies serve as cautionary tales of lasting relevance to modern architects of military justice institutions and occupation courts—international or domestic—even more so than to regular courts and civilian justice institutions under the auspices of international transitional administrations.

That said, it is only fair to be mindful of the special context in which the historic IMTs were embedded and to beware of ahistorical criticisms holding them to the more advanced contemporary standards of good judicial governance. Moreover, this

[119] eg Control Council Directive No 35 (n 21) para 7 ('In case the sentence of the Tribunal is in disagreement with any provisions of this Directive, the sentence shall prevail, *unless otherwise directed by the Control Council*').

same feature (or was it a 'bug'?)— their embeddedness in occupation regimes—was the key factor in their relative institutional success. It may help explain why, by contrast, most contemporary courts, rooted in cardinally different forms of international authority, struggle hopelessly with enforcement challenges whenever their pursuit of international justice is misaligned with the interests of major powers. This, in turn, recalls the perennial and ever-relevant Schwarzenbergerian question of the very possibility of international criminal law.[120]

[120] Georg Schwarzenberger, 'The Problem of an International Criminal Law' (1950) 3(1) Current Legal Problems 263.

PART III
MODERN REGIMES

6
Governance of the International Court of Justice

Serena Forlati

6.1 Introduction

The International Court of Justice (ICJ, the Court) was established in 1945 as the 'principal judicial organ' of the United Nations (UN).[1] This status marks a difference with its predecessor, the Permanent Court of International Justice (PCIJ) which—despite the strong institutional ties to the League of Nations—was not formally an organ of the League.[2] All Members of the Organization 'are *ipso facto* parties to the Statute of the International Court of Justice',[3] which forms an 'integral part of' the UN Charter.[4] It is therefore hardly surprising that the UN 'machinery' plays a critical role in shaping the Court's work and operability.[5]

Indeed, the formal and informal ties between the ICJ and other UN organs are prominent as regards the exercise of the Court's judicial function: for example, the Court provides assistance to the UN's main political bodies through its advisory opinions under Article 96 of the UN Charter;[6] it relies (or should be able to rely) on the Security Council to ensure the enforcement of its judgments under Article 94;[7] it interacts with the General Assembly and the Secretariat at a number of levels;[8] and it engages in a 'symbiotic relationship' with the International Law Commission (ILC) in the clarification and development of international law.[9] More generally, it was noted that '[t]he integration of the ICJ into the UN framework ... has implications

[1] Statute of the International Court of Justice (adopted on 26 June 1945, entered into force on 24 October 1945) (ICJ Statute) Art 1; Charter of the United Nations (opened for signature 26 June 1945, entered into force 24 October 1945) 1 UNTS 16 (UN Charter) Arts 7 and 92. On the process that led to the establishment of the Court and the negotiations at San Francisco, see Malcolm N Shaw, *Rosenne's Law and Practice of the International Court 1920–2015* (Brill 2016) 49ff.

[2] Henri de Waele, 'Managing the Realization of "The Hope of Ages"', in this volume.

[3] UN Charter (n 1) Art 93.

[4] ibid Art 92.

[5] Tom Ginsburg, 'The Institutional Context of the International Court of Justice' in Carlos Espósito and Kate Parlett (eds), *The Cambridge Companion to the International Court of Justice* (CUP 2023) 87.

[6] On the role of the ICJ's advisory function: Kolb, *The International Court of Justice* (Hart 2013) 1019ff.

[7] On the lack of effectiveness of this mechanism: Christian Tams, 'Article 94 UN Charter' in Andreas Zimmermann and Christian J Tams (eds), *The Statute of the International Court of Justice* (3rd edn, OUP 2019) 263.

[8] Shaw (n 1) 149; further, Section 6.3.

[9] James Crawford, 'The International Court of Justice and the Law of State Responsibility' in Christian J Tams and James Sloan (eds), *The Development of International Law by the International Court of Justice* (OUP 2013) 71 at 73; Ginsburg (n 5) 91.

Serena Forlati, *Governance of the International Court of Justice* In: *Governance of International Courts and Tribunals*.
Edited by: Sergey Vasiliev and Niels Blokker, Oxford University Press. © Serena Forlati 2026.
DOI: 10.1093/oso/9780198922131.003.0006

for the jurisprudence of the Court. In particular, when carrying out its judicial functions ... the ICJ must remain guided by the purposes and principles of the UN Charter'.[10]

Nonetheless, the Court's constituency is not limited to the United Nations and its membership: indeed, according to Article 93 of the UN Charter, the ratification of the Court's Statute is open to states which are not members of the UN 'on conditions to be determined in each case by the General Assembly upon the recommendation of the Security Council'.[11] Moreover, the ICJ may be open to states not parties to the Statute either when they fulfil the conditions stipulated by Security Council resolution 9(1946)[12]—an option that is currently of limited practical relevance since the UN has reached almost universal membership[13]—or under 'the special provisions contained in treaties in force' as stipulated by Article 35(2) of the ICJ Statute. The Court's case law basically deprived this stipulation of any actual impact,[14] thus emphasizing its own link to the Organization of which it is an organ.

This notwithstanding, the Court does 'speak to' non-state actors beyond the United Nations—including specialized agencies and individuals.[15] Moreover, its singular ability to shape the development of the international legal system, as the only international court of general jurisdiction, also contributes to its special status beyond the UN institutional architecture—to the point that the present Court, as the PCIJ before it, views itself as an 'organ of international law'.[16]

On a different level, the independence of the ICJ is not only a corollary of the principle of equality among UN principal organs.[17] It is also a key feature of adjudication at the international and the domestic level[18]—even more considering that the Court is often asked to decide on the legal aspects of heavily politically charged disputes among sovereign states.

[10] Simon Chesterman and Karin Oellers-Frahm, 'Article 92' in Zimmermann and Tams (n 7) 212.

[11] ICJ Statute (n 1) Art 35(2).

[12] UNSC Res 9(1946) (15 October 1946) UN Doc S/RES/9, 'Admission of States not parties to the Statute of the Court'. The resolution requires non-party states to submit declarations of acceptance of the Court's jurisdiction, and an undertaking 'to comply with the ... decisions of the Court and to accept all the obligations of a Member of the United Nations under Article 94 of the Charter'.

[13] cf however declarations under resolution 9(1946) submitted by Palestine of 4 July 2018 and 31 May 2024 <https://icj-cij.org/states-not-parties>.

[14] ICJ, *Legality of Use of Force (Serbia and Montenegro v Belgium)*, Preliminary Objections, Judgment of 15 December 2004, *ICJ Reports 2004*, 324 para 114.

[15] For the list of specialized agencies entitled to seek advisory opinions from the Court: ICJ, 'Report of the International Court of Justice, 1 August 2022 to 31 July 2023', *General Assembly Official Records Seventy-eighth Session, Supplement No 4*, 14. For a discussion of the idea that individuals may be parties to disputes that the Court is called upon to decide in the framework of advisory proceedings: *Judgments of the Administrative Tribunal of the ILO upon complaints made against the UNESCO*, Advisory Opinion, 23 October 1956 [1956] ICJ Rep 77, 84–85.

[16] ICJ, *Corfu Channel (United Kingdom v Albania)*, Judgment of 9 April 1948, *ICJ Reports 1948*, 35. Cf PCIJ, *Certain German Interests in Polish Upper Silesia*, Judgment of 25 May 1926, *Series A*, No 7, 19.

[17] Keynote by Judge Abdulqawi Ahmed Yusuf, Judge and former President of the ICJ, addendum in this book, para 17.

[18] eg Gilbert Guillaume, 'Some Thoughts on Independence of International Judges' (2003) 2 Law and Practice of International Courts and Tribunals 163. Further references may be found in Serena Forlati, 'Due Process and Protection of the Parties' Rights' in Joanna Gomula, Stephan Wittich, and Markus Stemeseder (eds), *Research Handbook on International Procedural Law* (Edward Elgar Publishing 2024) 380–85.

It is thus no surprise that the 'tension between the Court's role as a main organ of the United Nations and its need for judicial independence'[19] is widely acknowledged and leads to a number of specificities. These peculiarities are reflected not only in the Court's exercise of its judicial function but also in the complex and 'polycentric' framework that regulates its governance[20]—spanning from the sophisticated rules concerning the composition of the ICJ down to apparently more trivial aspects such as the choice of the Court's seat[21] or the organization of support activities.

Many such issues are regulated by the UN Charter or by the Court's Statute—that is, by an international treaty concluded by states. Even beyond that, the governance of the ICJ is a clear example of the 'paradoxical' role that states play vis-à-vis international courts, which are 'independent from states but at the same time fully depend on them for their effective functioning'.[22] Indeed, individual states and political bodies such as the UN General Assembly (which now includes all states parties to the Statute)[23] and the Security Council play a key role in this regard. At the same time, however, a number of other actors shape the Court's governance, including not only other UN organs but also civil society at different levels, and—last but certainly not least—the Court itself, which enjoys a wide measure of organizational and administrative autonomy. This chapter will discuss how these different players interact in regulating the functioning of the Court and ensuring its independence and efficiency by looking at a few salient aspects: notably, the appointment of members of the Court (Section 6.2); the organization of the Registry (Section 6.3); the budget, accountability for the use of resources, and external support for the Court's activities, including by the host state (Section 6.4); the privileges and immunities of Judges and Staff (Section 6.5);[24] the procedure for amending the Statute (Section 6.6). Concluding remarks will follow in Section 6.7.

[19] Robert Jennings, Rosalyn Higgins, and Peter Tomka, 'General Introduction' in Zimmermann and Tams (n 7) 5.

[20] Keynote by Judge Yusuf (n 17) para 19. On governance institutions as the set of decision-makers that enable international courts to 'carry out their judicial tasks independently': Niels M Blokker, 'The Governance of International Courts and Tribunals: Organizing and Guaranteeing Independence and Accountability' in Andreas Føllesdal and Geir Ulfstein (eds), *The Judicialization of International Law: A Mixed Blessing?* (OUP 2018); also Niels Blokker, 'International Judicial Governance Institutions', in this volume.

[21] The choice of The Hague, under Art 22 of the ICJ Statute, not only emphasizes the continuity with the PCIJ but also visually symbolizes the Court's independence vis-à-vis the other principal organs of the UN: Jennings, Higgins, and Tomka (n 19) 5. Generally on the transition to the new Statute, see Manley O Hudson, 'The Twenty Fourth Year of the World Court' (1946) 40 American Journal of International Law 14; Hersch Lauterpacht, 'The Revision of the Statute of the International Court of Justice: With an Introduction by Sir Elihu Lauterpacht' (2002) 1 Law and Practice of International Courts and Tribunals 55; Geoffrey Marston, 'The London Committee and the statute of the International Court of Justice' in Vaughan Lowe and Malgosia Fitzmaurice (eds), *Fifty Years of the International Court of Justice* (CUP 1996) 40; Shaw (n 1) 49ff.

[22] Blokker, 'The Governance' (n 20) 33.

[23] All states that, in the past, were parties to the ICJ Statute but not members of the United Nations have gradually acquired membership status.

[24] On the relevance of these elements to the impartiality of international courts, Kenneth Keith, 'Challenges to the Independence of the International Judiciary: Reflections on the International Court of Justice' (2017) 30 Leiden Journal of International Law 137, 139, and 141ff.

6.2 The Appointment of Members of the Court

The complexity of the Court's governance is apparent when looking at the rules concerning the election of the fifteen members of the Court,[25] which remain close to those of the PCIJ.[26] Substantive constraints concerning the qualification of individual judges and the overall composition of the Court are laid out in Articles 2,[27] 3,[28] and 9[29] of the Statute, and are aimed at ensuring, on the one hand, the technical competence and personal independence of judges; and, on the other hand, the ability of the ICJ to truly act as a 'World Court'. The relationship between these two requirements is complex.[30] Practice confirms that their reading can shift over time. Thus, the implicit assumption that permanent members of the UN Security Council would be 'entitled' to see a judge of their own nationality elected as a member of the Court have recently been dispelled,[31] whereas considerations of gender balance, which are not set forth in the ICJ Statute or the other governing instruments,[32] have become increasingly relevant

[25] A further layer of complexity, which will not be discussed here, relates to the variable composition of the bench in any given instance, depending on choices made by the parties (notably, as regards the appointment of judges ad hoc under Art 31 of the ICJ Statute or the request to submit a case to a Chamber under Art 26). In other cases, similar choices are entrusted to the President, the interested Judges or the full Court (eg when assessing the existence of special reasons for which a Member of the Court should not sit in a case, under Art 24, the setting up of Chambers under Art 29 or the appointment of Assessors under Art 30 of the Rules of Court). For further references, see Serena Forlati, *The International Court of Justice: An Arbitral Tribunal or a Judicial Body?* (Springer 2014) 31ff.

[26] Notably, an attempt to delete Art 9 in the transition between the PCIJ and the ICJ was not successful: Keith (n 24) 144 fn 26. On the choice to keep the number of Judges at fifteen: François Alabrune, 'Le nombre et le choix des juges: Le regard des États' in Jean-Marc Thouvenin and Jessica Joly-Hébert (eds), *La Cour internationale de Justice à 75 Ans* (Pedone 2023) 15–16.

[27] ICJ Statute (n 1) Art 2 stipulates: 'The Court shall be composed of a body of independent judges, elected regardless of their nationality from among persons of high moral character, who possess the qualifications required in their respective countries for appointment to the highest judicial offices, or are jurisconsults of recognized competence in international law'. Cf 'The Burgh House Principles on The Independence of The International Judiciary', adopted in 2004 by the Study Group of the International Law Association on the Practice and Procedure of International Courts and Tribunals, in association with the Project on International Courts and Tribunals, reprinted in (2005) 4 Law and Practice of International Courts and Tribunals 247–60, with an Introductory Note by Philippe Sands, Campbell McLachlan, Ruth Mackenzie) Principle 2.1.

[28] According to ICJ Statute (n 1) Art 3(1), 'The Court shall consist of fifteen members, no two of whom may be nationals of the same state'. Para 2 regulates cases of multiple nationality.

[29] This provision sets forth: 'At every election, the electors shall bear in mind not only that the persons to be elected should individually possess the qualifications required, but also that in the body as a whole the representation of the main forms of civilization and of the principal legal systems of the world should be assured'. Georges Abi-Saab, 'The International Court as a World Court' in Lowe and Fitzmaurice (n 21) 3.

[30] On the complex relationship between competence and geographical representation: Keith (n 24) 144.

[31] On the 2017 elections, which for the first time led to a Court without a sitting Member of British nationality, Security Council, 'Press Release: Security Council, General Assembly, Elect Four Judges to International Court of Justice' (9 November 2017) <www.un.org/press/en/2017/sc13063.doc.htm>. Dapo Akande, 'ICJ Elections 2017: UN General Assembly and Security Council Elect Four Judges to the ICJ but Fail to Agree on a Fifth, Yet Again!' (*EJIL: Talk!*, 11 November 2017) <www.ejiltalk.org/icj-elections-2017-un-general-assembly-and-security-council-elect-four-judges-to-the-icj-but-fail-to-agree-on-a-fifth-yet-again-trivia-question>. In 2023, the candidate of Russian nationality, Judge and former Vice-President Gevorgian, did not secure re-election, while a candidate of Romanian nationality, Bogdan-Lucian Aurescu, was elected together with Judges Sarah Hull Cleveland (United States); Juan Manuel Gómez Robledo Verduzco (Mexico); and Dire Tladi (South Africa). 'Five Judges Elected to United Nations' Top Court' (*UN News*, 9 November 2023) <https://news.un.org/en/story/2023/11/1143417>.

[32] cf Rome Statute of the International Criminal Court (opened for signature 17 July 1998, entered into force 1 July 2002) Art 36(8)(a)(iii).

to the election procedure, possibly also in light of evolving 'external' legal standards.[33] How these and other considerations actually influence the election process depends on the interplay between the different actors involved in its various stages.

The initial phase of nominating candidates is not formally in the hands of states. According to Article 4(1), it is mainly for the national groups in the Permanent Court of Arbitration (PCA) to form the list of nominees,[34] with the opportunity for states which are parties to the Statute but not members of the PCA to also contribute to the process.[35] This choice, which was originally made as regards the appointment of members of the PCIJ, was aimed at 'diluting' the role of states and favouring the candidates' qualification, with other requirements also having similar aims: eg the encouragement to nominate individuals that are not of the relevant state's nationality under Article 5(2)[36] and the recommendation 'to consult its highest court of justice, its legal faculties and schools of law, and its national academies and national sections of international academies devoted to the study of law' under Article 6. While this provision is not mandatory, and it is implemented unevenly depending on the national groups,[37] it is interesting to note the formal involvement of academia, and therefore civil society, in the nomination process. This cannot detract from the fact that the nomination process retains a highly political component, also given that the members of the national groups are appointed by their respective Governments and thus often close to them.[38]

Moreover, the (mostly informal) negotiations at the UN level leading to actual success in the election depend on a number of factors besides the personal qualifications of candidates and regional representation.[39] The election as such is entrusted to the two main UN political organs, the Security Council and the General Assembly, which shall proceed independently of one another to elect the members of the Court.[40] An

[33] On the relevance to this process of Art 8 CEDAW, Liesbeth Lijnzaad, 'The Smurfette Principle: Reflections about Gender and the Nomination of Women to the International Bench' in Freya Baetens (ed), *Identity and Diversity on the International Bench: Who Is the Judge?* (OUP 2020) 36.

[34] ICJ Statute (n 1) Art 4(3) and General Assembly Resolution 264 (III) of 8 October 1948 states that are parties to the Statute but not members of the United Nations participate 'on an equal footing with the Members of the United Nations' to the nomination and election process. No State currently falls under the scope of this provision.

[35] ICJ Statute (n 1) Art 4(2). On the ratio between PCA national groups and ad hoc national groups in recent years, see Patricia Georget, 'Article 4' in Zimmermann and Tams (n 7) 323ff.

[36] ICJ Statute (n 1) Art 5(2): 'No group may nominate more than four persons, not more than two of whom shall be of their own nationality.'

[37] Patricia Georget, 'Article 6' in Zimmermann and Tams (n 7) 343.

[38] Gilbert Guillaume, 'Report on "The Position of the International Judge"' (2011) 74 Yearbook of the International Law Institute (Rhodes Session) 12–13, noting that the National Groups 'jouissent d'une réelle indépendance, mais demeurent bien entendu conscients du fait que les décisions finales au moment des votes à New York dépendent des Etats. Aussi demeurent-ils en contact d'une manière ou d'une autre avec les ministères des affaires étrangères.'

[39] Rosalyn Higgins and others, *Oppenheim's International Law: United Nations* (OUP 2017) 1140, pointing out that a 'minority of member states of the Security Council and the General Assembly will not bargain politically about Court candidates. Other states will do so, taking into account other placings in the UN to which they are seeking to have candidates elected.' See further Shaw (n 1) 391ff and, for a recent analysis, Mario JA Oyarzábal, 'Les tractations électorales sont-elles évitables?' in Thouvenin and Joly-Hébert (n 26) 57.

[40] ICJ Statute (n 1) Art 8. The Institut de Droit International encouraged lack of communication between the two bodies during the election process so as to preserve their mutual independence: Resolution on 'The Composition of the International Court of Justice', Sienna Session, 24 April 1952, para 2 in (1952-II) 44 Annuaire de l'Institut de Droit International 474–75.

absolute majority of both bodies is required, and it is often not easy for candidates to reach this threshold. Divergences have sometimes been settled in favour of the candidate supported by the Security Council, but more often in favour of the one preferred by the General Assembly.[41]

The involvement of the Security Council in the election has led to several criticisms and reform proposals.[42] Some commentators, however, highlight that it enhances the legitimacy of the Court.[43] It is also noteworthy that deliberations within the Security Council 'shall be taken without any distinction between permanent and non-permanent members'.[44] This important balancing factor did not prevent the Permanent Members of the Security Council from almost constantly seeing judges of their own nationality on the ICJ bench. Still, the last two elections have confirmed that traditions are not unmodifiable, and the current legal framework does allow for change and adaptation to new social requirements also in other respects.[45]

The mechanisms envisaged by Article 12 of the ICJ Statute for cases where the Security Council and the General Assembly do not agree on the election of one or more candidates—namely, the possibility to refer the issue to a joint conference and, ultimately, to entrust the deliberation to the members of the Court who have already been elected—are another important governance element of the election process. Resort to the joint conference is understood to be an option, and not a mandatory step.[46] UN Member States have been reluctant to trigger the mechanism, which was used once as regards the PCIJ but remains untested within the UN so far, and could lead to significant delays in the election of judges.[47] Nor was the possibility that the appointment of judges be left to the elected members of the Court ever explored in practice, and significant doubts remain as to the interpretation of the relevant provision of the Charter.[48] However, these options are an important safeguard against the possible risks of frustration of the electoral process by individual states unhappy with

[41] Georget, 'Article 4' (n 35) 329.

[42] ibid 330.

[43] Alabrune (n 26).

[44] ICJ Statute (n 1) Art 10.

[45] For further on this, see Alabrune (n 26); Georget (n 37) 329.

[46] See United Nations Office of Legal Affairs, Internal Memorandum on the ICJ Election Procedure (1984) *UN Juridical Yearbook* 173–75, para 14. Cf Bardo Fassbender, 'Article 12' in Zimmermann and Tams (n 7) 404.

[47] For the analysis of the UK House of Common's Foreign Affairs Committee on the 2017 election and the stalemate between the Security Council (which had consistently supported the re-election of Judge Greenwood over five rounds of votes) and the General Assembly (which had supported the re-election of Judge Bhandari): Foreign Affairs Committee (27 February 2018) para 11, <https://publications.parliament.uk/pa/cm201719/cmselect/cmfaff/860/86004.htm>. For further on this and other examples, see Georget (n 37); Fassbender, 'Article 12' (n 46) 406–07.

[48] ibid 406, as to whether Art 12(3) of the UN Charter requires all members of the Court or only those who were successful in a specific election to 'to fill the vacant seats by selection from among those candidates who have obtained votes either in the General Assembly or in the Security Council'. The former option seems preferable as it is better suited to enhance the legitimacy of the election.

the Court's work—as in the recent occurrences concerning, for instance, the SADC Tribunal[49] or the WTO Appellate Body.[50]

6.3 The Registry and the Organization of the Court's Work

Efficient support staff who is, as much as possible, free from external control is a key element for appropriate governance of international judicial institutions. The Court's regulatory instruments reflect this need. Differently from the other UN principal organs, the Court has its own administrative body, the Registry, and a wide measure of organizational and administrative autonomy.

The UN Secretariat does interact with the Court at several levels; for instance, the Secretary-General is involved in the election process under Articles 5 and 7 of the Statute, receives the Court's proposals as regards the budget and notification of judges' dismissals under Article 18(2). The Secretary-General also interacts with the Court in the framework of its judicial activity, eg as regards notifications of new contentious cases under Article 40(3) of the Statute; by transmitting requests for advisory opinions; or by managing the Secretary-General's Trust Fund to Assist States in the Settlement of Disputes through the ICJ that was established in 1989 in consultation with the Court's President. However, the Secretary-General has no authority over the Court.

This organization, which is typical of international courts[51] and heightens the independence of the ICJ,[52] finds its legal basis in Article 21(2) of the Statute which states: 'The Court shall appoint its Registrar and may provide for the appointment of such other officers as may be necessary'. The Rules of Court set forth the modalities of appointment (an election by secret ballot) and the term of office (seven years).[53] This long term of office was never modified notwithstanding suggestions to this effect.[54] Nor were the rules concerning dismissal[55] and the election of the Deputy Registrar, which are the same as for the Registrar.[56] The remaining staff members are usually

[49] The SADC member states brought about the demise of the SADC Tribunal also by refraining to reappoint or replace judges whose terms of office had expired. SADC, Communiqué, Extraordinary Summit, Heads of State and Government of the Southern Africa Development Community, Windhoek (20 May 2011); Laurie Nathan, 'The Disbanding of the SADC Tribunal: A Cautionary Tale' (2013) 35 Human Rights Quarterly 870, 878; John Eudes Ruhangisa, 'Governance of Regional Integration Courts', in this volume.

[50] The United States was in a position to unilaterally dismantle the WTO Appellate Body due to the rule of consensus that governed its electoral process: eg Peter Van den Bossche, 'The Demise of the WTO Appellate Body', in this volume.

[51] Cf, however, the criticism in ibid, as regards the 'hold' of the WTO Secretary-General on the WTO Appellate Body's Secretariat.

[52] Jennings, Higgins, and Tomka (n 19) 5.

[53] ICJ Rules of Court (adopted on 14 April 1978, entered into force on 1 July 1978) Art 22(1).

[54] Report of the Joint Inspection Unit, 'Review of Management and Administration in the Registry of the International Court of Justice', UN Doc JIU/REP/2000/8, iv. More recently, amendments to Art 22(2) of the Rules of Court adopted in 2019 established a more transparent selection procedure, stipulating that the 'Court shall give public notice of a vacancy or impending vacancy either forthwith upon the vacancy arising, or, where the vacancy will arise on the expiration of the term of office of the Registrar' at least six months in advance.

[55] ICJ Rules of Court (n 53) Art 29.

[56] ibid Art 23.

appointed 'by the Court on proposals submitted by the Registrar'.[57] Although they are now subject to conditions of office that reflect the United Nations staff regulations and are included in the UN staff dispute settlement system, this step was taken upon request of the staff.[58] These measures should be seen at enhancing transparency and institutional accountability, rather than as a threat to the independence of the Court.

Moreover, the Court enjoys complete autonomy in organizing its work (including as regards its management). It is for the Court to elect its President and Vice-President,[59] to set up committees, and to adopt governing instruments such as its Rules of Court,[60] practice directions, the resolution concerning the internal judicial practice of the Court,[61] and decisions regulating the external activities of its members,[62] which should guide the Registrar too.[63] The Court also 'prescribe[s] the organization of the Registry' upon proposal of the Registrar,[64] and approves the Instructions for the Registry and the Staff Regulations drafted by the Registrar.[65] More generally, the Court is responsible for the efficient management of the resources that states put at its disposal through the UN budget or otherwise: the task of ensuring appropriate management lies with the Registrar,[66] under the supervision of the ICJ President,[67] but also of other members of the Court.[68] The Registrar, in turn, 'is responsible for all departments of the Registry. The staff are under his authority, and he alone is authorized to direct the work of the Registry, of which he is the Head'.[69] The Staff Regulations for the Registry clearly set forth that in 'the performance of their duties staff members ... shall neither seek nor accept instructions from any Government or from any other source external to the Court'.[70]

The Court's and the Registry's autonomy does not mean that there are no forms of accountability for its exercise. The ICJ is mainly accountable to the General Assembly as regards the use of financial resources; moreover, both the General Assembly and other oversight bodies review other aspects of the Court's organization, having to

[57] ibid Art 25(1). Staff members in the General Service and short-term staff are appointed directly by the Registrar, under Art 25 of the Rules of Court and Art 5(2) of the Staff Regulations.

[58] Keynote by Judge Yusuf (n 17) para 44; Jennings, Higgins, and Tomka (n 19) 6; further Higgins and others (n 39) 1185.

[59] ICJ Statute (n 1) Art 21(1).

[60] ibid Art 30(1).

[61] The Resolution currently in force was adopted on 12 April 1976.

[62] 'Compilation of decisions adopted by the Court concerning the external activities of its Members' in *Yearbook of the International Court of Justice 2020–2021*, 165.

[63] ibid 165 (sub (C)(5)).

[64] ICJ Rules of Court (n 53) Art 28(2).

[65] ibid Art 28(3) and (4).

[66] ibid Art 26(j): 'The Registrar shall ... be responsible for all administrative work and in particular for the accounts and financial administration in accordance with the financial procedures of the United Nations.'

[67] Report of the Joint Inspection Unit (n 54) 3 para 20.

[68] ibid paras 21–22 ('For a judge serving as President, a significant part of his/her time must be spent on supervision of the administration of the Court ... Nevertheless, it is noteworthy that the judges, even when not serving as President, do become involved in management of the Court, inter alia, through the numerous deliberations of the full Court on budgetary and administrative matters and their participation in the work of different standing or ad hoc committees').

[69] Instructions for the Registry (as drawn up by the Registrar and approved by the Court on 20 March 2012) Art 1.

[70] ICJ, Staff Regulation for the Registry (16 June 2023) Art 2(1).

do with human resources and the overall management of its activities. This aspect, which has occasioned 'regular—albeit occasional—tensions between the UN and the Court',[71] is discussed in the next section.

6.4 Budget, Accountability, and External Support

The provision for appropriate budget is another key practical condition enabling the Court to perform its activities. In this area, the Court is dependent on, and accountable to, the United Nations General Assembly. Indeed, under Article 33 of the Statute, it is for the General Assembly to decide on its expenses, which are borne by the UN budget.[72] Thus, member states contribute to the Court's expenses 'as apportioned by the General Assembly' under Article 17(2) of the UN Charter.

In practice, a budget proposal is drafted by the Registrar[73] and approved, first, by the Budgetary and Administrative Committee and, subsequently, by the full Court. It is then transmitted to the UN Secretary-General, who forwards it to the Advisory Committee on Administrative and Budgetary Questions (ACABQ). After a thorough analysis, the Court's budget is submitted to the Fifth Committee of the General Assembly and lastly adopted by the plenary.[74]

As was noted, Article 33 of the ICJ Statute implies that there is an obligation by the General Assembly to provide the Court with a budget.[75] Sincere cooperation between UN organs also requires that the General Assembly provides a budget that is adequate to fulfil the Court's functions appropriately. According to the Court, moreover, the General Assembly may not renege expenses that were already undertaken:

> the function of approving the budget does not mean that the General Assembly has an absolute power to approve or disapprove the expenditure proposed to it; for some part of that expenditure arises out of obligations already incurred by the Organization, and to this extent the General Assembly has no alternative but to honour these engagements.[76]

[71] Higgins and others (n 39) 1189 for a critical appraisal of this relationship.

[72] The budgetary system of the Court largely reflects the one of the PCIJ: Shaw (n 1) 447–48. States parties to the Statute but not members of the UN would also contribute an amount fixed by the General Assembly in consultation with them (ICJ, Report of the International Court of Justice—1 August 1999 to 31 July 2000, para 337), while other states to which the Court is open pay a contribution to the expenses that the Court fixes (ICJ Statute (n 1) Art 35(3)).

[73] Instructions for the Registry (as drawn up by the Registrar and approved by the Court on 20 March 2012) Art 24.

[74] ICJ Report 2022–23 (n 15) paras 240–41 and, for a more detailed description, Shaw (n 1) 449 ff; Carlos Espósito, 'Article 32' in Zimmermann and Tams (n 7) 618–38. Income generated by the Court (such as sums originating from staff assessment, sales of publications, or bank interest) are recorded as United Nations income: ICJ, 'Report of the International Court of Justice: 1 August 2015 to 31 July 2016', *General Assembly Official Records Seventy-first Session Supplement No 4*, para 309.

[75] Keynote by Judge Yusuf (n 17) para 30. Shaw (n 1) 475 ff.

[76] ICJ, *Effects of awards of compensation made by the United Nations Administrative Tribunal*, [1954] ICJ Rep 59. Cf also ICJ, *Certain expenses of the United Nations (Art 17, paragraph 2, of the Charter, Advisory Opinion of 20 July 1962)*, [1962] ICJ Rep 151 at 169.

Be that as it may, the budget covers the remuneration of judges, which is thus under the control of the General Assembly.[77] However, Article 32 of the Statute regulates some key aspects, stipulating that members of the Court 'shall receive an annual salary',[78] with a special allowance envisaged for the President and the Vice-President,[79] and the provision for pensions upon retirement.[80] Compensation for each day of work of ad hoc judges is also envisaged.[81] Salaries, allowances, and other emoluments are fixed by the General Assembly; adjustments are usually decided with the involvement of the Secretary-General and the ACABQ, and in consultation with the Court.[82]

According to Article 32(5) of the ICJ Statute, salaries, allowances, and compensation may not be decreased during the term of office; the Court strongly advocated an interpretation of this rule in light of the principle of equality among judges, which is expressed also in Article 31(6) of the Statute. In light of this, the General Assembly eventually accepted that judges' emoluments could not, in fact, be decreased,[83] aligning itself to a position that the Court had made formally known to it through a letter of President Higgins.[84]

More generally, the Court is conscious of the implications that financial deliberations may have on its work; hence the practice of explaining in detail the judicial activities of the Court alongside its budgetary requirements and the use of the resources allocated to it through its yearly report to the General Assembly. Moreover, the Court's President regularly delivers speeches presenting the Court's activities to the General Assembly and to its 6th Committee. Thus, for instance, when discussing the decision to appoint experts assisting the Court in 2016, the President specifically mentioned a corresponding request for financial support to remunerate them, seeking the 'understanding and support of the Assembly in this respect'[85] as 'the expert opinion in question has indeed been deemed by the Court, in the sovereign exercise of its responsibilities under the Statute, to be essential for the sound administration of justice in the present instance' and 'the additional cost of this operation ... cannot be absorbed by the Court's current budget, which has been reduced by 10% in comparison with the appropriations for the biennium 2014–2015'.[86] Similarly, a significant raise was sought in the late 1990s in connection to an increase of the Court's caseload. It was eventually granted, thus providing, inter alia, the resources for legal assistants to the President and the Members of the Court.[87] The General Assembly is often sensitive

[77] The main component of the Court's expenditure relates to the Registry, with support activities as a third line of cost. ICJ Report 2015–16 (n 74) 54–55.

[78] ibid paras 1 and 6 (the salary of the Registrar).

[79] ibid paras 2–3.

[80] ibid para 7.

[81] ibid para 4. This is a significant component of the Court's 'unforeseen expenditure': Shaw (n 1) 455.

[82] ibid 459ff.

[83] Keynote by Judge Yusuf (n 17) para 37ff.

[84] Letter dated 3 April 2007 from the President of the International Court of Justice to the President of the General Assembly, UN Doc A/61/837, 10 April 2007.

[85] Speech by HE Mr Ronny Abraham, President of the International Court of Justice, on the Occasion of the Seventy-First Session of the United Nations General Assembly, 27 October 2016, 7.

[86] ibid.

[87] On the role of legal assistants, see Mamadou Hébié, 'Des hombres furtives au Palais de la Paix? Coup de projecteur sur les assistants juridiques des Membres de la Cour internationale de Justice' in Thouvenin and Joly-Hébert (n 26) 73–98.

to the Court's requests: the Court's budget in 2023 amounted to US$29,110,900, and its request for 2024 was US$29,783,100.[88] At the same time, in her last speech to the General Assembly, President Donoghue explained that 'the Court is currently experiencing one of the most dynamic periods of its history—a trend that shows no sign of slowing',[89] adding further:

> the resources allocated to the Court and the size of our very lean and dedicated Registry do not come close to matching the significant increase in the Court's docket in recent years. The workload ahead of the Court in the coming years will likely call for appropriate adjustments of the Court's budgetary resources to ensure that it can continue to fulfil its mandate under the United Nations Charter.[90]

This hope may not necessarily be fulfilled: while the ICJ's budget requests for 2024 were accepted by the General Assembly,[91] and 2025 saw a significant increase[92] previous years also witnessed reductions.[93] Criticism of the ICJ's case law had occasional repercussions on the budget,[94] but cuts were more frequently linked to the need to curb expenditure of the UN in general rather than targeting the Court. Regrettably, displeasure with particular pronouncements recently led a state (rather than the General Assembly) to pass legislation withholding funds specifically from the ICJ.[95] Should this attitude become widespread, it could certainly hamper the Court's ability to perform its tasks efficiently. Still, the almost universal membership of the United Nations allows for some leeway in counterbalancing non-performance of obligations under Article 17 of the UN Charter even by the UN's largest donor.

[88] ICJ Report 2022–23 (n 15) 55. The Court's request was accepted (with the addition of recosts): see General Assembly Resolution 78/254 of 22 December 2023, 'Proposed Budget 2024', 67. By way of comparison, the first budget of the Court, in 1946, was of US$ 617,250 (Shaw (n 1)); in 2000, it amounted to approximately US$10 million (Report of the Joint Inspection Unit (n 54) iv). The current budget remains low as compared to other international courts: the Assembly of State Parties to the Statute of the International Criminal Court apportioned €187,084,300 for 2024 (Resolution ICC-ASP/22/Res.4 Adopted at the 10th plenary meeting, on 14 December 2023, by consensus).

[89] 'Speech by HE Judge Joan E Donoghue, President of the International Court of Justice, on the Occasion of the Seventy-Eighth Session of the United Nations General Assembly', 26 October 2023, 10.

[90] ibid. For the observation that 'the ICJ is by far the most inexpensive court', see Jennings, Higgins, and Tomka (n 19) 87.

[91] Text in n 76.

[92] 'Report of the International Court of Justice 1 August 2024–31 July 2025', *General Assembly Official Records – Eightieth Session Supplement No. 4*, 57; 'Speech by HE Judge Iwasawa Yuji, President of the International Court of Justice, on the Occasion of the Eightieth Session of the United Nations General Assembly', 30 October 2025. The budget was not cut for 2026 notwithstanding the current financial crisis of the United Nations: see 'Revised estimates relating to the proposed programme budget for 2026 and the support account for peacekeeping operations for the 2025/26 period Report of the Secretary-General', UN doc A/80/400, 4 September 2025, para 54.

[93] On the cuts of the biennium 2014–15: speech by President Abraham (n 85) 7. For a critical appraisal of the budget system, see Shaw (n 1) 513ff.

[94] Shaw (n 1) 455 fn 1, on the General Assembly's reaction to the 1966 Judgments in *South West Africa*.

[95] United States House of Representatives, 'Bill Making appropriations for the Department of State, foreign operations, and related programs for the fiscal year ending September 30, 2025, and for other purposes' (3 June 2024), stipulating that 'the funds appropriated or otherwise made available by this Act and prior Acts making appropriations for the Department of State, foreign operations, and related programs may be made available for a contribution, grant, or other payment to the International Court of Justice, notwithstanding any other provision of law'; the Bill was explained (inter alia) as a measure of support to Israel.

Once the UN budget is approved, the Secretary-General makes the necessary appropriations.[96] Control over the use of the Court's financial resources is entrusted to the Registrar. While enjoying judicial and administrative autonomy, the Court is subject to review by the UN's external oversight bodies: the Joint Inspection Unit (JIU), the Board of Auditors, and the Office of Internal Oversight Services (OIOS), to the extent mandated by the UN General Assembly, to which it is ultimately accountable. It is noteworthy that, while the Court's organization and activities usually come under review together with those of other UN organs, according to the JIU it was the Court itself that suggested a more intense scrutiny over the Registry in the late 1990s, as a way to help address a widespread 'malaise' within the institution.[97]

Like with other UN bodies, the Court's work is also supported by civil society: an example of this is the fact that the Court's seat, the Peace Palace in The Hague, is put at the Court's disposal by the Carnegie Foundation on the basis of an agreement approved by the UN General Assembly.[98] The ICJ thereby undertook to pay yearly instalments for the use of the Peace Palace and to contribute to refunding loans granted by the Government of the Netherlands. The latter still funds the activities of the Carnegie Foundation in The Netherlands[99] and takes responsibility for some aspects of the upkeeping of the Court's seat.[100] A more recent and different example of collaboration is the Judicial Fellowship Programme, which is sponsored by universities worldwide (as well as by an UN Trust Fund). While aimed at 'enabling students ... to familiarize themselves with the work of the Court and develop their skills in the field of the peaceful settlement of international disputes through the law',[101] the Programme is also instrumental in facilitating appropriate support for the judges have and hence in enhancing the Court's efficiency.[102]

More generally, as President Schwebel noted in his speech to the UN General Assembly of 26 October 1999, 'The financial resources of the Court cannot be divorced from those of the Organization that provides them. The financial fabric of the United Nations must be repaired, most fundamentally by renewed performance of the treaty obligations of Members of the United Nations to pay their assessments, as determined by this General Assembly in the exercise of the authority deliberately and expressly entrusted to it by the terms of the Charter' (UN doc A/54/PV.39, 4–5).

[96] Shaw (n 1) 453.

[97] Report of the Joint Inspection Unit (n 54) 1, para 6, and 6, paras 38–39. Compare, however, Higgins and others (n 39) 1185.

[98] UN General Assembly Resolution on Agreement between the United Nations and the Carnegie Foundation concerning the use of the premises of the Peace Palace at The Hague, and concerning the repayment of loans (11 December 1946) and Annex A thereto. For 2023, the United Nations paid the Carnegie Foundation 1,662,631 euros (ICJ Report 2022–23 (n 15) para 50).

[99] 'Carnegie Foundation' <www.vredespaleis.nl/carnegie/carnegie-foundation/?lang=en>. On the complex process that eventually allowed Andrew Carnegie to fund the construction of the Peace Palace: Tanja Aalberts and Sofia Stolk, 'Building (of) the International Community: A History of the Peace Palace through Transnational Gifts and Local Bureaucracy' (2022) 10 London Review of International Law 169.

[100] On the plans for removal of asbestos and their implementation, see 'Speech by HE Iwasawa Yuji' (n 92) 13.

[101] 'Terms of reference of the trust fund for the Judicial Fellowship Programme of the International Court of Justice', Annex to UN General Assembly Resolution 74/129, 'Trust fund for the Judicial Fellowship Programme of the International Court of Justice' UN Doc A/RES/74/129 (14 December 2020) para 4.

[102] On the appointment and tasks of judicial fellows: Hébié (n 87) 78, 80.

6.5 Privileges and Immunities

The privileges and immunities enjoyed by international courts are also crucial to their effective independence.[103] While in this regard courts are mostly not different from other international organizations, some specificities may derive from the judicial nature of their functions.[104] In the case of the ICJ, Article 105 of the UN Charter has only partial relevance because of the specific stipulation of Article 19 of the ICJ Statute which provides that 'The members of the Court, when engaged on the business of the Court, shall enjoy diplomatic privileges and immunities.' This provision, which reflects the corresponding text of the PCIJ Statute,[105] has a limited personal scope, insofar as it applies only to members of the Court and arguably to judges ad hoc (in light of the provision of Article 31(6) of the ICJ Statute to the effect that judges ad hoc 'shall take part in the decision on terms of complete equality with their colleagues').[106] The protection envisaged by Article 19 of the Statute appears to cover the whole period of office of judges, including as regards activities performed outside The Hague (such as transit to and from the Court or on-site visits), as well as activities performed after the term of office has formally ceased, to 'finish any cases which they may have begun.'[107] Differently, Article 105 of the Charter provides a basis for safeguarding the Court's Registrar and other Court officials.

These provisions are complemented by a series of arrangements regulating the status of ICJ judges and personnel, which are an apt exemplification of the multiplicity of actors involved in the Court's governance.[108] The General Assembly played a key role in setting up these arrangements, that are distinct from the Convention on the Privileges and Immunities of the UN of 13 February 1946.[109] It is noteworthy that, before deliberating on measures aimed at ensuring that the ICJ had the 'privileges, immunities and facilities necessary for the exercise of its functions and the fulfilment of its purposes, in the country of its seat and elsewhere', the General Assembly formally sought the Court's recommendations.[110] This emphasizes respect for the Court's autonomy and independence. In following up on the General Assembly's invitation, President Guerrero identified Articles 19 and 42 of the Statute as

[103] Blokker (n 20) 38.

[104] David D Caron, 'International Tribunals and the Role of the Host Country' in David D Caron and John R Crook (eds), *The Iran-United States Claims Tribunal: Its Contribution to the Process of International Claims Resolution* (Transnational Publishers 2000) 27–36.

[105] On the drafting history: David Anderson and Samuel Wordsworth, 'Article 19' in Zimmermann and Tams (n 7) 465. Differently, the PCIJ Statute included no equivalent to what is now Art 42(3), stipulating that the 'agents, counsel, and advocates of parties before the Court shall enjoy the privileges and immunities necessary to the independent exercise of their duties.' This provision is also crucial in safeguarding equality of arms and the overall fairness of judicial proceedings. Moreover, Art 32(8) of the Statute provides that the 'salaries, allowances and compensation' received by judges 'shall be free of all taxation.'

[106] Anderson and Wordsworth (n 105) 470.

[107] ICJ Statute (n 1) Art 13(3). For this broad, functional interpretation of Art 19: Anderson and Wordsworth (n 105) 469ff.

[108] On the contents of the relevant legal regime: ibid.

[109] Convention on the Privileges and Immunities of the United Nations (adopted by the UN General Assembly on 13 February 1946, entered into force on 17 September 1946) 1 UNTS 15.

[110] Resolution 22(C)I of 13 February 1946, 'Privileges and Immunities of the International Court of Justice.'

> [t]he Assembly's reason for dealing separately with the case of the International Court of Justice and for asking it to formulate proposals .... Another reason was, doubtless, that the Court is an organism whose members, with their small staff, perform duties of a special character and whose requirements are consequently different from those of the other organs of the United Nations.[111]

This excerpt is part of the agreement by exchange of letters which the Court negotiated directly with its host state, the Kingdom of The Netherlands, as regards 'the general principles that should govern the matter',[112] granting diplomatic status to judges, the Registry staff, and family members.[113] The General Assembly approved the agreement in its resolution 90(I) of 11 December 1946, which also includes some recommendations as to the treatment of judges, the Registrar, and other Court officials, assessors, agents, counsel, advocates, witnesses, experts and persons performing missions by order of the Court in places other than The Netherlands. While these 'recommendations' are not formally binding,[114] member states are bound by Article 105 of the Charter, Articles 19 and 42 of the Statute, and the 1946 Convention, which is currently in force for 162 states. This instrument remains applicable to the Court alongside the exchange of letters with The Netherlands and could come into play insofar as it offered additional protections[115] or in relation to states other than the host state. Vis-à-vis states which are not parties to the 1946 Convention, the Court would also be able to rely on any relevant customary rules. Indeed, state practice since 1946 reflects respect for the recommendations of the General Assembly, possibly crystallizing customary international law. Privileges and immunities are in any case conferred in the interests of the Court and the United Nations Organization,[116] and can be waived.[117]

[111] Letter from the President of the International Court of Justice to the Minister for Foreign Affairs of The Netherlands, 26 June 1946 <www.icj-cij.org/other-texts/letter-from-the-president> and Letter from the Minister for Foreign Affairs of the Netherlands to the President of the International Court of Justice, 26 June 1946 <www.icj-cij.org/other-texts/letter-from-the-minister>.

[112] Letter from the President of the ICJ (n 111).

[113] ibid, Annex, sections I and III. Specifically, Judges and staff 'who are of Netherlands nationality, are not answerable to the local jurisdiction for acts performed by them in their official capacity and within the limits of their duties' and are exempt from direct taxation (section II). Section V complements Art 42 of the ICJ Statute, as it affords assessors, agents, counsel and advocates 'such privileges, immunities and facilities for residence and travel as may be required for the independent exercise of their functions', while also safeguarding witnesses and experts. A later agreement on the order of precedence between Judges and Members of the Diplomatic Corps in The Netherlands is reflected in the Letter from the Minister for Foreign Affairs of The Netherlands Luns to the President of the International Court of Justice 26 February 1971 <www.icj-cij.org/other-texts>; on the difficulties in adjusting the agreement to the presence of new international courts in The Hague: Higgins and others (n 39) 1192–93.

[114] cf Anderson and Wordsworth (n 105), who question this conclusion.

[115] *Yearbook of the International Court of Justice 2021–2022*, 93.

[116] ICJ Statute (n 1) Art 19; Staff Regulations for the Registry (n 70) Art 4.

[117] Letter from the President of the ICJ (n 111) para IV.

6.6 Amendment Proceedings

Amendment proceedings are an important aspect of institutional governance and are worth discussing even if the ICJ Statute has so far never been modified.[118] According to its Article 69,

> Amendments to the present Statute shall be effected by the same procedure as is provided by the Charter of the United Nations for amendments to that Charter, subject however to any provisions which the General Assembly upon recommendation of the Security Council may adopt concerning the participation of states which are parties to the present Statute but are not Members of the United Nations.

States which are parties to the Statute but not members of the United Nations participate on an equal footing with member states in the amendment process: in 1969, the UN General Assembly decided that such states 'may participate in the General Assembly in regard to amendments to the Statute in the same manner as the Members of the United Nations',[119] and that any amendments 'shall come into force for all States which are parties to the Statute' after adoption and ratification 'by two-thirds of the States which are parties to the Statute'.

The procedure laid out in Article 108 of the Charter requires amendments to be 'adopted by a vote of two thirds of the members of the General Assembly and ratified ... by two thirds of the Members of the United Nations, including all the permanent members of the Security Council', and the one envisaged for 'alterations' by Article 109 is equally cumbersome. States have been reluctant to engage in such exercises notwithstanding proposals to this effect,[120] due to the risk of eventually failing. As Robert Kolb observes, furthermore, the rules of the Statute were on the whole well-tested owing to the experience of the PCIJ, and 'the States Parties to the Statute attach great value to legal certainty about questions relating to the Court. They are apprehensive that one amendment may lead to another, in the end opening up a kind of Pandora's box'.[121]

The Court seems to share the same caution, as it never availed itself of its prerogative to propose amendments to the Statute under Article 70 thereof. This provision is nonetheless worth noting as it confirms that states parties to the Statute formally entrust the Court with a role also in this key aspect of its governance; a role that is actually enhanced by the perceived political unfeasibility of amending the Statute and by the impossibility for states to denounce it without withdrawing from the UN as such.[122]

[118] Differently, the Statute of the PCIJ was amended through a Protocol which entered into force in 1936: Henri de Waele, 'Managing the Realization of "The Hope of Ages"', in this volume.

[119] UN General Assembly resolution 2520(XXIV) (4 December 1969) UN Doc A/RES/2520(XXIV), 'Participation of States which are Parties to the Statute of the International Court of Justice, but are not Members of the United Nations, in the Procedure for Effecting Amendments to the Statute', letter a).

[120] Shaw (n 1) 96ff.

[121] Kolb (n 6) 87.

[122] ibid.

Moreover, the Court deems itself to be the only institution entrusted with the authoritative interpretation of its Statute[123] and has at times done so liberally, relying on 'common sense' rather than on its express stipulations.[124] Indeed, even without any change in the Statute, the ICJ can adjust its working methods and procedure by changing the Rules of Court and the other governing instruments, as well as through the evolution of its case law—thus adapting to new needs emerging from the evolution of the docket and of the international legal system. While most of these changes affect the judicial activity of the Court, some do touch upon the Court's governance: apt examples in this respect are its determinations aimed at avoiding risks to appearance of impartiality and of conflict of interests, such as those encompassed in Practice Directions VII and VIII and in its determinations of 2018 and 2020 on the external activities of its members.[125]

6.7 Conclusions

Appropriate governance of international courts enables them to pursue their tasks enjoying actual and not only formal independence, with a suitable degree of efficiency and accountability. In the case of the ICJ, the well-honed, polycentric governance system envisaged by its Statute allows the Court to fulfil its role as an organ of the UN and of international law appropriately. Moreover, the institutional link to the UN is an important element adding to the Court's stability, whereas the UN political organs are respectful of the Court's independence and organizational autonomy.

The Court's own role in its governance is also prominent. The Statute gives the ICJ some competences that are not typical for international courts (such as the residual role in the election of its own members or the power to propose amendments under Article 69). Moreover, the perceived political impossibility of amending that instrument enhances the Court's role in shaping at least specific aspects of its organization. The Court uses its prerogatives in order to jealously guard its independence and the appropriate exercise of its judicial function. The Court's authoritativeness in exercising such function further underpins its governance system.

This does not mean that the system is flawless. For instance, the election mechanism has heavy political connotations (as is almost inevitable for international courts). The deliberations on the Court's budget sometimes look more at the need to curb the UN's expenses than at providing the Court with the means to fulfil its very specific

[123] cf in this regard, 'Conditions of service and compensation for officials other than Secretariat officials: members of the International Court of Justice and judges and ad litem judges of the International Tribunal for the Former Yugoslavia and the International Criminal Tribunal for Rwanda: Report of the Secretary-General', UN Doc A/62/538, 8 November 2007, para 39: 'The International Court of Justice is deeply concerned about the implications that resolution 61/262 might have for the integrity of the Statute and the Rules of Court. The Court does not dispute that the provisions of its Statute attribute certain functions to the General Assembly, such as the provisions governing the election of judges or budgetary matters, which can be interpreted by the General Assembly. However, the Court considers that matters relating to the proper administration of justice require it alone authoritatively to interpret the Statute.'

[124] Jennings, Higgins, and Tomka (n 19) 87.

[125] 'Compilation of decisions adopted by the Court' (n 62).

functions. The withholding of funding specifically due to the ICJ by individual states is an extremely worrying precedent that will hopefully not be repeated. Still, differently from other contexts, backlash against the ICJ is usually shaped in terms of reducing or cancelling acceptance of the Court's jurisdiction—eg by withdrawing or modifying unilateral declarations under Article 36(2) ICJ Statute. This phenomenon is, of course, regrettable, but it does give the Court the chance to recover the trust of its main 'clients' in time (as happened, for instance, after the crisis connected to the *South West Africa* judgments) and to continue fulfilling its role vis-à-vis the 'willing' parties. In the long run, this may turn out to be less disruptive than developments such as the slow 'asphyxiation by lack of appointments' that befell the WTO Appellate Body. Thus, the lack of compulsory jurisdiction, which is usually perceived a shortcoming of the Statute, may paradoxically act as a safeguard against direct attacks on the Court's governance.

7

Governance of Regional Integration Courts—EACJ and SADC Tribunal

Perspectives from Africa

John Eudes Ruhangisa

7.1 Introduction

The concept of 'governance' forms a central theme of discussion in the modern world, particularly among individuals and institutions charged with organizational tasks. It refers to the process of decision-making and the process by which decisions are implemented or not implemented.[1] Accordingly, a governance process can be graded as either good or bad. It is good governance if it embraces and facilitates development, whereas bad governance is usually characterized as the kind that prevents it. Additionally, to qualify as good governance, the process must be participatory, consensus-orientated, accountable, transparent, responsive, effective, efficient, equitable, and inclusive, and one that follows the rule of law.

Consequently, governance is considered to be good if it is free from abuse and corruption, pays due respect to the rule of law, facilitates organized and informed participation of the public in public affairs, is subject to fair legal frameworks that are enforced impartially, protects and promotes human rights, and has an independent judiciary and impartial law-enforcing institutions. These characteristics of good governance provide benchmarks for the above-stated elements, or lack thereof, in a system of governance.[2] Regional integration courts or tribunals are creatures of the treaties that establish their respective regional communities.[3] They are judicial arms of the organizations, designed to settle the disputes that may arise out of cooperation.[4] Consequently, regional courts, like other institutions of these communities established by treaties, are subjects of governance by their respective governance institutions as provided under the treaties. The governance institutions being referred to are the highest bodies that perform governance functions and have the final say over the

[1] United Nations Economic and Social Commission for Asia and the Pacific (ESCAP), 'What Is Good Governance?' 10 July 2009 <www.unescap.org/sites/default/files/good-governance.pdf>.

[2] Beatrice Birungi Kiraso, 'Opening Address by the Deputy Secretary General of the East African Community' in Sam Tindifa (ed), *Public Accountability and Good Governance in East Africa* (Fountain Publishers 2009) 48–49.

[3] eg Treaty for the Establishment of the East African Community (opened for signature 30 November 1999, entered into force 7 July 2000) ('EAC Treaty') Art 9(1)(e); Treaty of the Southern African Development Community (opened for signature 17 August 1992, entered into force 30 September 1993) Art 16, and Protocol on Tribunal in the Southern African Development Community (2000) Art 2.

[4] EAC Treaty (n 3) Art 23(1) and SADC Treaty (n 3) Art 16(1).

John Eudes Ruhangisa, *Governance of Regional Integration Courts—EACJ and SADC Tribunal* In: *Governance of International Courts and Tribunals*. Edited by: Sergey Vasiliev and Niels Blokker, Oxford University Press. © John Eudes Ruhangisa 2026. DOI: 10.1093/oso/9780198922131.003.0007

rest of the institutions/organs within the structural framework of the regional economic communities. In the case of East African Community (EAC), these bodies are the Summit of Heads of State and the Council of Ministers. In the case of the Southern African Development Community (SADC), it is the Troika of the Summit.[5] Since regional integration courts are international courts, their respective governance institutions are also known as international judicial governance institutions.

This chapter aims to fill a gap in the existing literature on African regional courts' governance by launching an enquiry on the manner in which the characteristics of good governance are embraced or excluded by the relevant governance actors when running the affairs of courts or tribunals. The analysis will focus primarily on the governance of the judicial institutions of the EAC and SADC, ie the East African Court of Justice (EACJ) and SADC Tribunal respectively. These can be seen as case-studies that are fairly representative of the rest of the regional communities in Africa due to the similarities of their constitutive treaties and operations. This chapter first examines the nature of regional integration courts to the extent necessary to appreciate the arrangements and challenges of governance of such courts (Section 7.2). It then proceeds to analyse the common features of the EACJ and SADC Tribunal's governance schemes, referring to the key elements of governance such as appointment and removal of judges, the financing of these courts, and enforcement of their judgments (Section 7.3). Lastly, the chapter outlines the principal challenges and concerns arising in connection with the governance of regional integration courts (Section 7.4), followed by concluding remarks (Section 7.5).

7.2 Understanding African Regional Courts

7.2.1 Definition of regional courts

In order to have an understanding of the term 'regional (integration) courts', it is important that we first appreciate the meaning of the word 'courts'. There have been attempts by various scholars to define it depending on the (legal, judicial, social, or relational) context in which it is to be used. For the purposes of this chapter, I prefer the definition by William Hughes and co-authors of a court as 'a permanently organized body, with independent judicial powers defined by law, meeting at a time and place fixed by law for the judicial public administration of justice'.[6] Simply put, a court, also called court of law, is a person or body of persons having legally recognized judicial authority to hear and resolve disputes in civil and criminal cases.

Ordinarily, the term 'regional court' shoots from two words 'region' and 'court', respectively describing a particular area of the world and a place where legal cases are heard or, in other words, a place for settlement of dispute and administration of justice. Against this background, and drawing inspiration from international law, the

[5] SADC Treaty (n 3) Art 9A(2).

[6] William J Hughes and others, *Federal Practice, Jurisdiction and Procedure, Civil and Criminal, with Forms* (West Publishing 1931) 8, quoted in Bryan A Garner (ed), *Black's Law Dictionary* (8th edn, Thomson West 2004) 378.

term 'regional court' refers to a judicial organ of a particular cooperation framework involving two or more sovereign states that agree to work closely together as a team to achieve peace, stability, wealth, and economic development. This teamwork in such organizations is regularly referred to as integration process whereby neighbouring states that form a particular region enter into an agreement in order to upgrade co-operation through common institutions and rules.

Therefore, regional integration courts, just like other courts, are judicial institutions in a regional integration structure responsible for the resolution of disputes arising out of the agreed cooperation in a particular region. The term 'regional court' presupposes the existence of a definite region pursuing integration that a court is created to serve and assist through settlement of disputes. The idea to put regional courts in place originates from the fact that any active relationship is bound to generate disagreements and disputes. For that reason, partners in a particular regional cooperation regime establish in advance a judicial institution that constitutes a neutral arbiter to address mischiefs whenever variances arise between the organs of the regional organizations, member states, or their citizens. Such judicial institutions are entrusted with interpretation of community law and solving differences between member states and cases involving individuals' and communities' fundamental rights, as well as disputes between citizens of the member states. For the purposes of this chapter, the terms 'regional courts' and 'regional integration courts' can be deemed interchangeable.

7.2.2 Regional integration courts in Africa

On the African continent, regional integration courts are exemplified by the East African Court of Justice (EACJ),[7] the Economic Community of West African States (ECOWAS) Court of Justice,[8] the SADC Tribunal,[9] the Common Market for Eastern and Southern Africa (COMESA) Court of Justice,[10] and the African Court on Human and Peoples' Rights in the African Union (AU).[11]

Regional integration courts in Africa can be placed within the ongoing debate amongst legal scholars on what is frequently being referred to as the 'proliferation of international courts'.[12] Creation of these courts in Africa follows a movement of

[7] EAC Treaty (n 3) Art 9(1)(e).

[8] Revised Treaty of the Economic Community of West African States (opened for signature 24 July 1993, entered into force 23 August 1995) Art 6.

[9] SADC Treaty (n 3) Art 9(1)(g).

[10] Treaty Establishing the Common Market for Eastern and Southern Africa (opened for signature 5 November 1993, entered into force 8 December 1994) ('COMESA Treaty') Art 7(1)(c).

[11] eg Misha Ariana Plagis and Karin Pluberg, 'Paper Lions?', in this volume.

[12] For a detailed discussion on the topic: John E Ruhangisa, 'The East African Court of Justice' in Rok Ajulu (ed), *The Making of a Region: The Revival of the East African Community* (Institute for Global Dialogue 2005); Karin Oellers-Frahm, 'Multiplication of International Courts and Tribunals and Conflicting Jurisdiction: Problems and Possible Solutions' (2001) 5 Max Planck Yearbook of United Nations Law 67; Benedict Kingsbury, 'Foreword: Is the Proliferation of International Courts and Tribunals a Systematic Problem?' (1999) 31 NYU Journal of International Law and Politics 679; Nikolaos Lavranos, 'Regulating Competing Jurisdictions among International Courts and Tribunals' (2008) 68 Heidelberg Journal of International Law 575; Fausto Pocar, 'The Proliferation of International Criminal Courts and

regional integration that started soon after decolonization in the early 1960s with the establishment of regional economic communities (RECs).[13] RECs, as the name suggests, aim primarily at fostering economic cooperation and development among the contracting member states. To spot the momentousness and commitment to regional cooperation, member states undertake to respect the regional courts' decisions and the laws specifically enacted to govern the cooperation and to be bound by the said laws which are normally formulated to define and provide for the scope of cooperation. The member states' undertaking is made with the awareness of the governance role they give to themselves in relation to the regional courts as judicial institutions of the communities they are created to serve.

African countries under the auspices of the AU, like the rest of the world, have not been left behind in embracing regional integration. In the mind of the AU's architects, particularly at the time of its inauguration in 2002, RECs were to act as building blocks towards realization of the United States of Africa. The entire move was seen as a rational response to the difficulties faced by a continent with many small national markets and landlocked countries. Consequently, African governments have, through treaties, established a high number of regional integration arrangements,[14] several of which have significant membership overlap.[15]

Today African countries embrace regional integration as an important module of their development strategies predominantly driven by the economic cogent of overpowering the constraint of trifling and fractioned economies working in isolation. As a result, a number of RECs in Africa included in their respective constitutive documents an article establishing regional courts among the institutions designed to spearhead the integration process.[16] However, the member states to the RECs subsequently made sure to maintain the governance role over the said regional courts. This is a common characteristic of all treaties establishing RECs in Africa which decided to include judicial institutions among the organs mandated to spearhead their integration agenda. It is therefore not a surprise when these RECs exhibit similar reactions to the decisions and orders of the regional courts.

That said, during the early 1980s, Africa experienced a somewhat unusual situation where its leaders had a change of heart as to whether to entrust the resolution of their conflicts to a third body outside their countries. Instead, there has been a growing inclination of African states to entrust the settlement of their disputes to the International Court of Justice, the principal judicial organ of the United Nations.[17] It

Tribunals: A Necessity in the Current International Community' (2002) 2 Journal of International Criminal Justice 304.

[13] Lucyline N Murungi and Jacqui Gallinetti, 'The Role of Sub-Regional Courts in the African Human Rights System' (2010) 7 SUR—International Journal on Human Rights 119, 120.

[14] Besides the already mentioned ECOWAS, EAC, COMESA, and SADC, such RECs include the Intergovernmental Authority on Development (IGAD) and the Economic Community of Central African States (ECCAS).

[15] Trudi Hartzenberg, 'Regional Integration in Africa' (2011) Staff Working Paper ERSD-2011-14, 2–6 <www.wto.org/english/res_e/reser_e/ersd201114_e.pdf>.

[16] eg EAC Treaty (n 3) Art 9(1)(e); Revised ECOWAS Treaty (n 8) Art 6; SADC Treaty (n 3) Art 9(1)(g); COMESA Treaty (n 11) Art 7(1)(c).

[17] For a detailed discussion, see Fatsah Ouguergouz, *The African Charter on Human and Peoples' Rights: A Comprehensive Agenda for Human Dignity and Sustainable Democracy in Africa* (Martinus

was against this tendency that RECs in Africa embraced the idea of setting up judicial organs of their own to champion the integration process, leading to the establishment of regional courts.

7.2.3 Mandate of regional integration courts

The regional international courts are international courts proper since their respective jurisdictions extend beyond one specific state but cover all states constituting a particular REC. Regional integration courts, being treaty creatures, have their mandate spelt out in the respective treaties and constituent instruments. There is commonality among them in terms of mandate. All agree on the interpretation of their respective treaties as the main function of these courts.[18] Taking the EACJ as an example, it was created by the Treaty for the Establishment of the East African Community ('EAC Treaty'), and its main mandate as enshrined in Article 23(1) is to 'ensure the adherence to law in the interpretation and application of and compliance with [the] Treaty'. Likewise, the SADC Tribunal set up under the Treaty of the Southern African Development Community ('SADC Treaty') makes no exception in terms of its mandate. This institution was established to ensure that there is proper interpretation of the provisions of the SADC Treaty and subsidiary instruments and adherence thereto.[19] Included in the treaties establishing regional integration courts are principles of good governance, including the adherence to the rule of law, transparency, human rights, social justice, gender equality, democracy, and accountability.[20] Inevitably, member states' actions relating to the stated areas call for regional integration courts' interpretation. For that reason, member states have found themselves being regular respondents in court cases required to answer complaints filed against them by aggrieved persons.

Although the protection and promotion of human rights is a cross-cutting objective of many RECs, there is glaring hesitation by the 'partner states'—which is how member states of EAC are called—to directly confer human rights jurisdiction to their regional courts and articulate the same in the treaties.[21] The EAC Treaty, after conferring human rights jurisdiction on the EACJ, went on to suspend its operationalization to a 'suitable' subsequent date to be determined by the Council of Ministers, and established that a protocol will have to be concluded to that effect.[22]

Nijhoff 2021) 688–96; Rosalyn Higgins, 'The International Court of Justice and Africa' in Emile Yakpo and Tahar Boumedra (eds), *Liber Amicorum Judge Mohammed Bedjaoui* (Kluwer Law International 1999) 343–69.

[18] SADC Treaty (n 3) Art 6; EAC Treaty (n 3) Art 27(1); COMESA Treaty (n 11) Art 23(1); Revised ECOWAS Treaty (n 8) Art 15(3) and Protocol A/P.1/7/91 relating to the ECOWAS Court of Justice (as amended by Supplementary Protocol A/SP.1/01/05) Art 9(1).

[19] SADC Treaty (n 3) Art 16(1).

[20] eg EAC Treaty (n 3) Art 6(d).

[21] eg SADC Treaty (n 3) which, instead of directly bestowing human rights jurisdiction upon the court, simply recognizes it in Art 4(b) as one of the principles governing the affairs of the cooperation.

[22] EAC Treaty (n 3) Art 27(2).

This raises the question as to why partner states embrace indecisiveness when it comes to conferring human rights jurisdiction to the regional courts. There would be several possible answers but the one that immediately comes to mind is suspicion. Ordinarily, the principal violators of human rights are states, and complaints or court cases for infringements of human rights are usually filed against states. For that reason, partner states are not enthusiastic to create institutions that will check their powers and question their actions. Even where courts are established, albeit with restricted mandate, still states would like to control them under disguise of governance and accountability. If courts are rarely popular with state leadership, especially in fragile and weak democracies, then regional integration courts are in an even tougher situation because they are established at the supranational level to adjudicate disputes involving sovereign states and their citizens. Debating or evaluating the independence and effectiveness of regional courts in our environment is therefore not a futile exercise. It is through such debates that regional integration takes the required shape while regional courts assume their appropriate roles. To do otherwise is to leave the integration process solely in the hands of the politicians, and this may not be healthy for the process.

Regional integration courts, therefore, play a crucial role in the process towards integration of the (sub-)region in which they are established as mechanisms to adjudicate on the interpretation of the treaty and/or to settle disputes among the parties. This role can be effectively realized through these courts' effective and efficient execution of their mandate as arbiters in dispute-resolution, thereby contributing to confidence-building in the respective region. Invariably, by playing their roles effectively the regional courts are expected to enhance the observance and upholding of human rights through good governance and strengthening democratic institutions in their regions. All these aspirations and objectives must be reflected in the ways regional integration courts conduct their activities.

The operations of some regional courts are ad hoc.[23] This means the judges in such situation are not required to permanently reside at the seat of the court. Instead, they only convene to conduct the business of the court as and when the need to do so arises. Arguably, this arrangement might have drawn inspiration from the idea that during their infancy regional courts need time to lay their feet on the ground as the litigants might not be expected to immediately file cases enough to justify full-time presence of the judges at the seat of the court. However, the seemingly genuine intention could be the subject of abuse by partner states making it difficult for the court to convene when there are cases filed against them. A clear example is the situation experienced by the EACJ whose judges have been meeting on an ad hoc basis for the past twenty-three years despite the fact that the number of cases has tremendously increased, even leading to a backlog.[24]

[23] eg EAC Treaty (n 3) Art 140(4) categorically provides that until such time as the Council determines that the Court is fully operational, a judge appointed shall serve on an ad hoc basis. Likewise, Protocol on SADC Tribunal (n 3) Art 6(2) and (3) vests the power to determine full-time status of the Tribunal in the Council of Ministers and states that the Tribunal shall sit when required to consider a case submitted to it and that members shall not be appointed on full-time basis. The COMESA Treaty (n 11) is silent about the full-time or ad hoc nature of the services of the judges, but practice shows that judges convene only when there is business for them to carry out.

[24] As of 6 February 2024, there were 214 References, 2 Claims and 38 Interlocutory Applications in the First Instance Division of EACJ. In the Appellate Division there were five Appeals and four Applications in

The EACJ has on several occasions appealed to the Summit of Heads of State and the Council of Ministers as governance institutions to change this scheme, yet without meaningful results. The main reason behind the hesitation to make the judges full-time is the cost aspect which partner states claim to be very high. This is a lightweight argument as they know that justice has never been cheap. We cannot rule out lack of motivation on the part of governance institutions to let the judges work on full-time basis as partner states are common and regular respondents in the cases being filed in the court. Arguably, letting the judges be present full-time at the Court, the partner states think, would amount to authorizing their own maim.[25]

7.3 Governance of Regional Integration Courts in Africa: Common Features

7.3.1 Participation

Reference to participation in the governance of any court is different from the democratic context of the term in which case people are essentially required to participate in the decision-making processes of the court as jurors and as parties to the case or their legal representatives. The *internal* administration of the courts as judicial institutions is the responsibility of the judges usually assisted by the registrar and other staff of the court who are employed to perform specific roles.

The governance of regional international courts in Africa makes no exception to these well-known traditions, although, as noted, member states play a major role in their functioning and *external* governance through governance institutions created by them and constituted of their representatives. Member states perform such governance functions in relation to regional courts and tribunals in different ways including recruitment of the judges and non-judicial staff of the courts, making policies that bind the courts as well, and determining their budget. Commenting on this eye-catching state of affairs, Blokker observed: 'These governance institutions elect the judges of international courts and tribunals, adopt their budgets, supervise the

the Court Registries pending hearing. The President of the EACJ through the Registrar has unsuccessfully brought this fact to the attention of the Council of Ministers as a ground for his request that the Judges of First Instance Chamber, that generates business for the Appellate Chamber, be present full-time at the seat of the court.

[25] In November 2019, after losing almost all cases filed against it in the African Court on Human and Peoples' Rights, the United Republic of Tanzania rescinded its decision to grant direct access to individuals and NGOs to the African Court. Since Tanzania's situation in the East African Court of Justice was no better than or different from that in the African Court on Human and Peoples Rights, underground campaign was started by Tanzania to clip the wings of the EACJ jurisdiction by amending the Treaty through introduction of a requirement for exhaustion of local remedies before one can take a matter to the EACJ for adjudication. The process to amend the treaty is ongoing. For a detailed discussion on this, see Salome Mushi, 'Tanzania's Withdrawal of the Declaration on Individuals' and NGOs' Direct Access to the African Court on Human and Peoples' Rights: A Critical Analysis', dissertation submitted to the Faculty of Law in partial fulfilment of the requirements for the award of the degree of Master of Laws (LLM) in International Law with International Relations (Tumaini University Makumira, Tanzania, 2021) 3–5, 70–76.

implementation of judgments and take other decisions that are of fundamental importance for the way in which international courts and tribunals can carry out their judicial tasks independently.'[26]

In the case of the EACJ, judges are appointed by the Summit from among persons recommended by the partner states,[27] whereas the Registrar of the Court and other staff are appointed by the Council of Ministers.[28] The situation in the SADC Tribunal with regard to the appointment of judges is the same,[29] except for the recruitment of the Registrar and other staff of the court who are appointed by the Tribunal itself.[30]

Likewise, the judges of the COMESA Court of Justice are appointed by the head of states or governments of member states ('the Authority')[31] from among persons who are impartial and independent and fulfil the conditions required for the holding of high judicial office in their respective countries of domicile or who are jurists of recognized competence.[32] Member states propose the names of the judges to the Authority for appointment, provided that no two or more judges shall at any time be nationals of the same member state. The Authority is the supreme Policy Organ of the Common Market responsible for the general policy and direction and control of the performance of the executive functions of the Common Market and the achievement of its aims and objectives.[33] The directions and decisions of the Authority are binding on the member states and on all other organs of the Common Market other than the Court of Justice only if it is in the exercise of its judicial function.[34] This raises a fundamental question over this unusual micro-management of the regional court on who gets to decide what is judicial and what is not. The Treaty Establishing the Common Market for Eastern and Southern Africa (COMESA Treaty) does not provide any assistance on this matter. It is clear that the Treaty confers to the Authority's governance powers over the COMESA Court of Justice. Similar powers are given to the Council of Ministers over the COMESA Court of Justice.[35] Just like in the situation with the EACJ and SADC Tribunal, the budget of the COMESA Court of Justice is considered and approved by the Council of Ministers.[36]

It is these kinds of interferences and micro-management by representatives of member states that raise concern over the independence of African regional integration courts and tribunals in executing their mandates.

[26] Niels Blokker, 'The Governance of International Courts and Tribunals: Organizing and Guaranteeing Independence and Accountability' in Andreas Føllesdal and Geir Ulfstein (eds), *The Judicialization of International Law: A Mixed Blessing?* (OUP 2018) 27.
[27] EAC Treaty (n 3) Art 24(1).
[28] ibid Art 45.
[29] SADC Treaty (n 3) Art 16(3); Protocol on SADC Tribunal (n 3) Arts 4 and 6.
[30] Protocol on SADC Tribunal (n 3) Art 12.
[31] COMESA Treaty (n 11) Arts 3, 7, and 8.
[32] ibid Arts 20(1) and 20(2).
[33] ibid Art 8(2).
[34] ibid Art 8(3).
[35] ibid Art 9(2)(c).
[36] ibid Art 9(2)(f).

7.3.2 Rule of law

Good governance calls for fair legal frameworks that are enforced fairly and without bias. Generally, such legal frameworks should seek to provide full protection of human rights, particularly those of minorities and the disadvantaged. Unbiased enforcement of laws presupposes the existence of an independent judiciary. Being judicial organs of RECs, regional integration courts, like any other court, should emulate this important precept in the administration of justice. It is against this background that the first important activity to be undertaken by regional courts after swearing in the judges is to formulate the rules of the court that provide for procedures to govern litigation and other judicial proceedings in that particular court.[37] Ordinarily, the process to make the rules of the courts is a participatory one in the sense that regional courts strive to incorporate the views of their stakeholders in the rules by taking into account their comments. Such stakeholders include civil society under the umbrella organizations, business community, lawyers, judges and magistrates of national courts, members of academia, politicians, and other persons with a stake in the court's performance of its judicial function.

By formulating the rules of procedure, regional courts provide binding guidelines, certainty, and predictability as they handle disputes and shy away from whimsical and arbitrary decisions. This raises the fundamental question whether their governance institutions observe the rule of law principles when exercising their governance powers over regional courts. To answer this question, a critical survey of how these institutions have performed their governance mandates over regional courts has to be made.

The rule of law entails a process or mechanism that supports the equality of all citizens before the law and prevents the arbitrary use of power. It is a doctrine that seeks to protect the weak against oppression by tyrants and ruthless autocrats. We will return to it in Section 7.4 when examining the reactions of the heads of state to the decisions of the EACJ and SADC Tribunal.

7.3.3 Transparency

Transparency means intelligibility or simplicity of the decisions taken by the court, as well as that enforcement of decisions is done in a manner that follows established rules and regulations. This principle also represents the understanding that important information must be freely available and directly reachable by those who will be affected

[37] eg East African Court of Justice Rules of Procedure 2019 (adopted 15 February 2019, entered into force 23 July 2019) <www.eacj.org/?page_id=3842>. This is the updated version of the rules that revoked the EACJ Rules of Procedure 2013 and other previous amendments to the rules. See also African Court on Human and Peoples' Rights Rules of Court (adopted 1 September 2020, entered into force 25 September 2020) <https://www.african-court.org/wpafc/wp-content/uploads/2021/04/Rules-Final-Revised-adopted-Rules-eng-April-2021.pdf>; COMESA Court of Justice Rules of Procedure 2016 (adopted 15 October 2016, entered into force 15 October 2016) <https://comesacourt.org/wp-content/uploads/2018/10/RULES-of-the-Court_final.pdf>.

by such decisions and their enforcement. It further requires that sufficient information is provided in a timely manner and in easily understandable forms and media.

The African regional integration courts' activities of a judicial nature are transparent as they are conducted with utmost openness to the public. Hearing of cases is conducted in open court where members of the public are free to attend. There is no similar openness when the heads of state exercise their governance power over regional courts. One example is the procedure leading to the appointment of judges of regional courts. There is no transparency in the process. The procedure is opaque, and offers room for arbitrary exercise of powers by the heads of state as appointing authority.

In the case of the EACJ there is not much to guide the appointing authority in appointing the judges. The EAC Treaty prescribes the qualifications, the number, and the domain from which a judge may be selected, leaving the rest to the partner states to decide:

> Judges of the Court shall be appointed by the Summit from among persons recommended by the Partner States who are of proven integrity, impartiality and independence and who fulfill the conditions required in their own countries for the holding of such high judicial office, or who are jurists of recognized competence, in their respective Partner States.[38]

The EAC Treaty does not provide a uniform and detailed procedure to be followed by the partner states before presenting the names of judges to the Summit for appointment. It is not clear which partner state institutions should take responsibility or consult with anyone to get the judicial candidate's name for presentation to the Summit for appointment. As a result, each partner state is free to decide on a suitable procedure, especially one that goes well with those in power and may include handpicking of a person. This is compounded by the fact that what is normally put forward is not a list of names for the Summit to select from but only one name.

The lack of transparency in the appointment of judges is a fertile ground for arbitrary exercise of power by whoever makes the nomination and a potential source of incompetence and erosion of the independence of the judge as a person and that of the court as an institution. These worries are exacerbated by the fact that partner states do not present more candidates to the Summit than the number of judges to be appointed. In real terms, the Summit is therefore given no option but to appoint the sole candidate(s) presented by partner states to fill the judicial vacancy in the EACJ.

The obscure atmosphere surrounding the appointment of EACJ judges has led to an embarrassing situation where the said appointment was challenged in the same court. In the case of *East Africa Law Society* v *The Attorney General of the United Republic of Tanzania and another*,[39] the applicant challenged the appointment of Lady Justice Sauda Mjasiri as a judge of the EACJ Appellate Division on the ground that the appointment contravened Article 24 of the EAC Treaty. At the time of her appointment

[38] EAC Treaty (n 3) Art 24(1).

[39] *East Africa Law Society v Attorney General of United Republic of Tanzania and Another* (Ref No 1 of 2019) [2020] EACJ, 25 November 2020.

as a judge to the EACJ, Lady Justice Sauda Mjasiri had formally retired from the Court of Appeal of Tanzania upon attaining the mandatory retirement age and was therefore not qualified to hold a judicial office in Tanzania by virtue of her age. According to the applicant, a retired judge could not be legally appointed a judge to the EACJ for she no longer qualified to be appointed judge in her country, which is a necessary condition under Article 24 of the Treaty. This objectionable action by Tanzania was attributed to the opaque process leading to the nomination, which fell short of the principles of transparency, accountability, and good governance. It was further argued that in effect the impugned process amounted to denying other qualified citizens of Tanzania from competing for the job.[40]

The EACJ First Instance Division held that the process of nominating persons to be appointed as judges, beyond the qualifications set out in Article 24 of the Treaty, are reserved to the sovereignty of the individual partner state.[41] Further, the court took the view that partner states are collectively at liberty to put in place a uniform process if they wish, but absence of one does not necessarily amount to a Treaty violation.[42] In total, the first instance Division held that the process of nominating and appointing Hon Lady Justice Mjasiri to the Appellate Division did not contravene the provisions of articles 6(d), 7(1), and 24(1) of the Treaty. Aggrieved by the decision of the First Instance Division, the applicant sought recourse to the appellate instance. The matter was finally settled by the Appellate Division on 31 August 2022 when it dismissed the appeal on the ground that the Summit used the second limb of Article 24 of the Treaty which is the alternative to those conditions that required such appointed person to be of proven integrity, impartiality, and independence and to fulfil the conditions required in their own countries for the holding of such high judicial office.[43] According to the Appellate Division, Lady Justice Mjasiri was appointed by the Summit to the Appellate Division because she happened to be a jurist of recognized competence in a partner state that nominated her much as she was no longer fulfilling the conditions required in her own country for the holding of such high judicial office.[44]

The concern over the opaqueness of the appointment procedure for EACJ judges was also exhibited by another case, *Male H Mabirizi K Kiwanuka* v *Attorney General of the Republic of Uganda and Secretary General of the East African Community*.[45] In that case, the applicant challenged the renomination for appointment of Lady Justice Monica Kalyegira Mugenyi to the Summit of Heads of State by the Government of Uganda as violating articles 6(d), 7(2), 24(1), and 25(1) of the Treaty. Lady Justice Monica Kalyegira Mugenyi had earlier served her full term of seven years in the EACJ First Instance Division and then retired. However, after one year she was renominated by her country for appointment to serve in the EACJ Appellate Division. The reappointment was challenged on the ground that the judge had been appointed earlier

[40] ibid paras 10–12.
[41] ibid para 50.
[42] ibid para 51.
[43] *East Africa Law Society v The Attorney General of the United Republic of Tanzania & Another* (Appeal No 2 of 2021) [2021] EACJ, 31 August 2022.
[44] ibid paras 66–69.
[45] *Male H Mabirizi K Kiwanuka v The Attorney General of the Republic of Uganda & Secretary General of the East African Community* (Ref No 48 of 2021) [2021] EACJ, 8 December 2021.

on and had already served in the EACJ and was therefore ineligible for reappointment to serve the court for a second time.

Arguably, had there been more transparency in the process leading to her reappointment, all concerns would have been addressed before she was even nominated. This raises the following important questions that require further attention in scholarship, namely: why has the process for appointment of EACJ judges been non-transparent despite the demands for transparency? Who benefits from the non-transparent procedure for the judges' appointment? Is this practice good for the independence of the judge herself and that of the court as an institution?

7.3.4 Responsiveness

Good governance requires that the court, as an institution, and all its processes serve all stakeholders and are completed within a reasonable timeframe. The administration of justice should be done in a timely manner for justice delayed is justice denied.

To embrace the element of responsiveness, the EACJ formulated its Rules of Procedure, which address the temporal aspect in the administration of justice. In formulating the rules governing litigation in the Court, due regard was paid to the provisions of the Treaty, the international character of the Court itself, the need to make the rules user-friendly, and the need to avoid problems facing litigation in national courts including unnecessary adjournments,[46] delays with pronouncing judgment after the hearing has been concluded,[47] *ex parte* orders and hearings,[48] and delays on account of summoning witnesses.[49]

Sessions and sittings of the Court are conducted at its temporary premises in Arusha for the time being until the Summit determines the permanent seat of the Court. However, if the Court considers it desirable, it can conduct its activities at a place other than the seat of the Court and, if such activities involve hearing of a case, the Court will direct the parties accordingly.[50]

Invariably, the responsiveness of the Summit of Heads of State and the Council of Ministers as governance institutions of the EACJ has been unimpressive. It has been about twenty-four years since the EACJ was launched on 30 November 2001, but the Summit of Heads of State and the Council of Ministers have still not been able to resolve the issues of the permanent seat of the Court and the ad hoc nature of the services of judges—despite repeated demands from the Court.

The operations of the EACJ during the transition period are ad hoc.[51] As noted, this means that judges are not required to reside permanently in Arusha where the temporary seat of the Court is located, but only convene at the Court when necessary to perform their functions.[52] This includes carrying out activities like holding in-house

46 EACJ Rules (n 37) Rule 76.
47 ibid Rule 79.
48 ibid Rules 52(3), 84(2), and (3).
49 ibid Rules 66(1) and 67(1).
50 ibid Rule 9.
51 EAC Treaty (n 3) Art 140(4).
52 Section 7.2.3. Arusha is still regarded as the temporary seat of the Court for to date the Summit has not determined the permanent seat of the Court as required under EAC Treaty Art 47.

administrative meetings as well as eventual hearing of cases. This position will continue until such time as the Council of Ministers determines that the Court can be fully operational, even though the Court faces an increasing backlog of cases. How long will it take for the Court to pass the transitional period envisaged by Article 140(4) of the Treaty? Since the Treaty does not provide the timeline within which to act and everything has been left to the Council of Ministers to decide, there is a possibility that the transition period will become permanent. However, the Council of Ministers has already approved full-time presence of only the President of the Court and the Principal Judge for ease of preliminary judicial and administrative interventions. Whatever justification may be given, the inaction by the Summit and the Council of Ministers as the EACJ's governance institutions adversely affects the efficient performance of the Court in executing its mandate under the Treaty. In addition, since 2005 the Summit of EAC Heads of State and the Council of Ministers have offered a deaf ear to the demands by various stakeholders, including the business community, civil society, and members of the bar and human rights defenders, that the presently deferred appellate and human rights jurisdiction of the Court,[53] be operationalized as soon as possible. According to Article 27(2) of the EAC Treaty, operationalization of the human rights jurisdiction will be determined by the Council of Ministers at a suitable subsequent date, equally to be determined by the Council of Ministers. Attempts to get the human rights jurisdiction of the Court operationalized have met resistance despite popular demands and judicial pronouncements.[54]

In this context, the actual substantive jurisdiction of the EACJ, and possibly that of other regional courts in Africa, depends on the member states' executives who are given power by the treaties to go beyond normal governance. In this regard, a comparison can be drawn with the European Union (EU) where, upon realizing that the court was overwhelmed by cases, the EU first created a specialist court to deal with employment matters and later even doubled the size of the General Court, instead of making it harder for the Court of Justice of the EU.[55] This is in sharp contrast with the punitive reasons that militated for the creation of two divisions (First Instance Division and Appellate Division) in the EACJ following its decision in the *Anyang' Nyong'o* case,[56] as well as the closure of the SADC Tribunal following its decision in the *Campbell* case.[57]

The EACJ, however, has not shied away from attending to human rights cases simply because the Council of Ministers failed to operationalize its human rights jurisdiction. Almost all cases that the Court has heard under Article 6(d) of the EAC Treaty had a bearing on human rights. Indeed, there is a thin line between human rights and good governance, democracy, the rule of law, accountability, transparency,

[53] EAC Treaty (n 3) Art 27(2).

[54] eg *Hon Sitenda Sebalu v The Secretary General of East African Community and 3 Ors* (Ref No 1 of 2010) [2011] EACJ, 30 June 2011, reported in BJ Mwimali and others, *The East Africa Court of Justice Law Digest: 2005–2011* (East African Law Society 2011) 110.

[55] Heikki Kanninen, 'Governance of the Court of Justice of the European Union', in this volume.

[56] *Prof Peter Anyang' Nyong'o and 10 Ors v Attorney General of Kenya and 2 Ors (with Abdurahin Haitha Abdi and 11 Ors intervening)* (Ref No 1 of 2006) [2007] EACJ, 6 February 2007, reported in Mwimali and others (n 54) 173.

[57] *Mike Campbell and Ors v Republic of Zimbabwe*, SADC (T) No 2/2007, 11 October 2007.

social justice, equal opportunities, and gender equality, as well as the recognition, promotion, and protection of human and peoples' rights in accordance with the provisions of the African Charter on Human and Peoples' Rights. These are the fundamental and operational principles of the EAC Treaty that the Court can interpret even without having to wait for operationalization of its human rights jurisdiction by the Council of Ministers.[58] This is only possible, however, where a court has jurisdiction over such substantive matters and is bold enough to use judicial means of interpretation to get around limits on its jurisdiction, with all its attendant consequences, including bracing itself for a possible clash with the executive organs.

For instance, the SADC Tribunal suffered such consequences at the hands of its governance institution, the Summit of Heads of State and Government, in relation to demands by the people to make the operations of the Tribunal full-time. Further, when the SADC Tribunal decided in the *Campbell* case that Zimbabwe government had discriminated against white farmers on the basis of race and had violated the SADC Treaty by passing a discriminatory legislation on land,[59] Zimbabwe determined not to comply with it. Arrogantly, Robert Mugabe (then President of Zimbabwe) referred to the Tribunal's judgment as 'an exercise in futility'.[60] The President of the Tribunal wrote a report to the Summit of Heads of State and Government informing them of the unpleasant status of implementation of the Tribunal's decision by the government of Zimbabwe, but no action was taken.[61] The only remarkable response of the Summit to the Tribunal President's report was when it launched the conspicuous campaign against the Tribunal. This led to the demise of the Tribunal after its mandate had been changed, thereby obviously leaning towards Zimbabwe's defiance. Arguably, the whole reaction by the Summit erases the cherished distinctive line of interaction, imaginary perhaps, between the Summit's formal governance powers over the Tribunal and the substantive judicial activity, which is supposed to be the exclusive mandate of the Tribunal.

This raises a fundamental question as to where the Summit got the power to curtail the competence of the SADC Tribunal. The Tribunal is the creature of the Treaty/Protocol and the Treaty is the agreement establishing SADC and the amendments thereto. Since the Treaty was adopted by SADC member states and they can amend it at will,[62] it goes without saying that the member states can take away what they had earlier given to the Tribunal in the form of jurisdiction, provided there is consensus among themselves.[63]

[58] For the decision of the EACJ in its first case on human rights-related issues: *James Katabazi and 21 Ors v the Secretary General of the East African Community and the Attorney General of the Republic of Uganda* (Ref No 1 of 2007) [2007] EACJ, 20 November 2007, reported in Mwimali and others (n 54) 29.

[59] *Campbell* (n 57).

[60] Blokker (n 26) 28.

[61] It is a legal requirement under SADC Treaty Arts 32(4) and 32(5) for the President of the Tribunal to report to the Summit of Heads of State and Government where a member state has failed to comply with a decision of the Tribunal.

[62] SADC Treaty (n 3) Art 36.

[63] Protocol on SADC Tribunal (n 3) Art 14 ('The Tribunal shall have jurisdiction over all disputes and all applications referred to it in accordance with the Treaty and this Protocol which relate to: ... (c) All matters specifically provided for in any other agreements that States may conclude among themselves or within the community and which confer jurisdiction on the Tribunal').

7.3.5 Consensus

There are multiple actors and constituencies in any given society that a court is established to serve. For regional courts, good governance requires mediation of the different interests in the region to reach a broad consensus in society on what is in the best interest of the whole community and how this can be achieved. Regional courts, like national courts, do so through judicial pronouncements arising from the matters that are presented to them. In their decisions, regional courts should not fall short of broad and long-term perspective on what is needed for sustainable human development and how to achieve its goals. This is only possible if they understand the historical, cultural, and social contexts of a given society or community. Regional courts in Africa attempt to demonstrate these qualities in their decisions by contextualizing both the descriptive and prescriptive import of the integration agenda as stated in the preambles and the articles to the treaties.

Decisions of regional courts are consensus-orientated, meaning that in the spirit of collegiality judges reach informed agreement in the form of a majority on issues that are presented for determination.[64] However, where agreement cannot be reached, the treaties allow a judge disagreeing with the majority to write a dissenting opinion.[65] The COMESA Treaty is silent on the question whether a disagreeing judge is allowed to write a dissenting opinion but it directs the court to deliver only one judgment in every reference reached by majority verdict.[66] If only one judgment is allowed and that is the one reached by the majority, then indirectly the second judgment which in this case should be the one reached by the minority is not allowed.

Unlike the situation obtaining in the regional courts' decision-making processes, in all governance institutions within the particular RECs, decisions are reached by consensus.[67] This approach to decision-making is preferred by politicians to that of regional courts as it seeks to preserve state sovereignty, which is a syndrome that has haunted international law. Further, it attempts to protect the economically weak and therefore vulnerable states from being weighed down by the economically better-placed states. Such attempts may have provided a rather deceptive feel-good therapy to the perceived underprivileged member states, yet have not been practised without consequences for the integration agenda. Very little progress, often at a snail's pace, is made under this arrangement especially when the number of member states grows, making it difficult to have a meeting of minds. In early stages of EAC integration, when partner states were only three,[68] it was easy to make decisions by consensus. However, after the Community enlarged to include Burundi and Rwanda, it became

[64] EAC Treaty (n 3) Art 35(2); Protocol on SADC Tribunal (n 3) Art 24(2).

[65] eg EAC Treaty (n 3) Article 35(2). It was on the authority of this provision that two judges of the Appellate Division in the case of *Manariyo Desire* wrote a dissenting opinion against the majority decision on the meaning of a phrase 'resident in a Partner State' as per EAC Treaty Art 30(1) for purposes of filing cases before the EACJ. *Manariyo Desire v Attorney General of Burundi* (Appeal No 1 of 2017) [2018] EACJ, 28 November 2018 (Judges ad hoc Ringera and Kiryabwire, Dissenting Opinion) paras 6–45.

[66] COMESA Treaty (n 11) Art 31(2).

[67] eg ibid Art 8(7); EAC Treaty (n 3) Art 12(3); SADC Treaty (n 3) Art 19.

[68] The Republics of Kenya, Uganda, and the United Republic of Tanzania as the founding members of EAC.

more difficult, and worsened with the joining of South Sudan and later the Democratic Republic of the Congo.

To get out of this quagmire, the Council of Ministers at one time, and for the first time in its history, had to file a request for advisory opinion,[69] seeking the EACJ's opinion on the meaning and application of the principles of consensus and variable geometry. Some of the partner states wanted to make progress by invoking the principle of variable geometry and leave behind those states which were dragging their feet so that the latter could catch up with the former when they would be ready. The idea was objected to by other partner states on the ground that the Treaty requires the decisions to be by consensus. Stemming from the above, the Council of Ministers directed the Secretariat to seek an advisory opinion of the EACJ under Article 36 of the EAC Treaty on the application of the principle of variable geometry vis-à-vis the requirement for consensus in decision-making by the institutions of the Community.

The Court held that there was no possibility for the principle of variable geometry to conflict with the requirement for consensus in decision-making as variable geometry should be resorted to as an exception not as the rule.[70] Further, the court opined that consensus does not in any way mean unanimity.[71] This could be confusing and therefore open up for debate what the Court actually meant.

7.3.6 Equity and inclusiveness

Simply put, equity means the quality of being fair and impartial. In performing its function, a regional court is expected to enhance a society's well-being by doing justice according to the law, specifically being free from bias or favouritism. Regional courts, like domestic courts or any other court worth the name, are under obligation to rely on the law and avoid partisanship if they are to be relevant to the community they serve. Indeed, regional courts in Africa have dutifully fulfilled this obligation and sometimes suffered the consequences, especially when the decisions were not to the governance institutions' liking.[72]

In any community, a society's well-being depends on its ability to guarantee that all its members feel that they have a stake in it and are not excluded regardless of their status in the community. This requires that all groups, but particularly the most vulnerable, have opportunities to improve or maintain their well-being. Regional courts have attempted to achieve this through the quality of the judgments they write and their rules of procedure that allow free and easy access to the court by people from all walks of life irrespective of their status.[73] International judicial institutions have drawn inspiration from the fact that in order to assist the community achieve its objectives, the court should be accessible and independent, capable of rendering timely

[69] Advisory Opinion (Application No 1 of 2008) [2009] EACJ, 24 April 2009.

[70] ibid 34.

[71] ibid 37–39.

[72] This is attested, for example, by the reaction of the Summits of Heads of State of EAC and SADC respectively to the decisions of the courts in *Anyang' Nyong'o* and *Campbell* cases. See Section 7.4.

[73] For example, the EACJ can be engaged by both natural and legal persons and no fees are payable at the time of filing a case.

justice, and have good working relationship with its stakeholders. Above all, courts should make themselves known to the people they were created to serve. These are the basic strategies that the African regional courts have adopted from the start.

However, member states, and the governance institutions of African regional courts, do not always fully embrace the spirit of dispensing meaningful—equitable and inclusive—justice. This manifests itself especially when member states attempt to give to themselves unusual discretion not to comply with court orders that are unfavourable to them through treaties. Whereas the regional court's decision is binding on all the parties and has to be unquestionably executed by national courts as their own decision, this is not the case where member states decide not to comply with the order of the court.[74] Enforcement of court orders against member states depends on the goodwill of a particular partner state and its undertaking under the treaty to abide by the principles of good governance.[75] The EAC Treaty makes no provision for sanctions or actions to be taken against partner states that fail to implement or comply with EACJ orders. As a result, many court orders remain unimplemented, thereby undermining the Court itself and effectively perpetuating impunity on the part of partner states. The study conducted in 2019 by the East African Law Society on the status of implementation of the decisions of the EACJ revealed that only 47 per cent of the cases decided that required implementation had been implemented by EAC partner states.[76] Attainment of a 100 per cent rate of compliance with the court's decisions has been one of the key challenges the court is grappling with given its lack of enforcement mechanisms and reliance on the goodwill of the partner states.[77]

The SADC Tribunal equally faced a challenge with regard to the implementation of its decisions. Taking the *Campbell* case, for example, instead of implementing the court's decision, Zimbabwe lobbied the other SADC member states to suspend the Tribunal's power to hear complaints filed by individuals against states. Finally, the Tribunal was in essence disbanded. Likewise, the African Court on Human and Peoples' Rights has experienced similar challenges relating to the implementation of its decisions by member states.[78] Instead of implementing the court's decisions, some member states decided to withdraw their signatures to the declaration that allowed their citizens and NGOs to file cases with the Court directly.[79] All withdrawing states offered vague and unsubstantiated rationales for their decisions, but their actions followed their dissatisfaction with the outcomes of particular cases against them. Such responses represent an attack on the independence of the Court and potentially undermine its integrity.

[74] EAC Treaty (n 3) Art 44.

[75] ibid Art 7(2).

[76] Hanningtone Amol and David Sigano, 'Report: The Study of the Status of Implementation of the Decisions of the East African Court of Justice and Level of Understanding of the Court Among Key Actors' (2019) East African Law Society-Raoul Wallenberg Institute Regional Africa Programme, 24.

[77] ibid 42.

[78] Misha Ariana Plagis and Karin Pluberg, 'Paper Lions?', in this volume.

[79] These member states include the Republic of Rwanda, the United Republic of Tanzania, the Republic of Benin, and the Republic of Côte d'Ivoire.

7.3.7 Accountability

Accountability is a key requirement of good governance. Regional courts should operate from the premise that not only governmental institutions but also the private sector and civil society organizations must be accountable to the public and to their institutional stakeholders. Who is accountable to whom varies depending on whether decisions or actions taken are internal or external to an organization or institution. In general, an institution should be accountable to those who will be affected by its decisions or actions. Accountability cannot be enforced without transparency and adherence to the rule of law. Lack of accountability of the judicial governance institutions potentially exposes regional courts to the risk of being controlled by the executives thereby corroding the principle of independence of the judiciary.

Just like heads of other regional courts, the President of the EACJ does not directly answer to the Summits of Heads of State on matters that are related to their work as judges. However, the structures of the Communities they serve, and the reality on the ground, negate this perception. Every time the Council of Ministers and the Summit of Heads of State meet, the EACJ presents a written report on the performance of its duties. The report of the Court to the Council of Ministers and the Summit of Heads of States includes the number of cases filed with the registry, cases heard, and cases decided, among other things.[80] Likewise, even before its demise, the SADC Tribunal was required under the Protocol to submit to the Council of Ministers and subsequently to the Summit of Heads of State and Government, a report for guidance and appropriate actions on the member states' failure to implement the Tribunal's orders.[81] It is uncommon within the justice systems to let the executive decide on the orders of the court and make parallel orders. Ordinarily, orders and decisions of the court must be respected at all times. To allow any practice to the contrary undermines the court itself and effectively erodes public confidence in its ability to dispense justice.

The summits of heads of state in African RECs are not accountable to anyone. They have no obligation to report, explain, or be answerable to anybody. They are supreme institutions of their Communities that enjoy finality in the decisions they make, and for that reason they cannot be legally questioned within the structural frameworks of their RECs.[82] They constitute the authority that is responsible for the general direction and control of their communities and are mandated to take all measures to ensure progressive development and the realization of their objectives.[83] This includes oversight over the functioning of community institutions such as respective regional courts.

It was due to such a lack of accountability that the EAC Summit of Heads of State could arbitrarily decide to punish EACJ judges by amending Article 26 of the EAC Treaty and expanding the list of reasons for removing a judge from office by including

[80] Finance matters and court budget such as reallocation of its funds or request for additional funds, if required, form part of the court report to the policy organs (Council of Ministers as a governance institution) for its consideration.

[81] Protocol on SADC Tribunal (n 3) Art 63.

[82] This is how the Authority of Heads of State and Government of ECOWAS is described in Revised ECOWAS Treaty (n 8) Art 7(1).

[83] ibid Arts 7(2) and 7(3).

'all possible reasons'.[84] It thereby targeted individual EACJ judges from Kenya who were not on good terms with their government back home. These judges had been suspended on political grounds in Kenya where they also served as judges and were subject of enquiry. Yet, for more than a year no enquiry had taken place, and the government of Kenya felt defeated when the same judges continued to serve in the EACJ. It was not clear why the government of Kenya did not have courage to initiate the disciplinary action under the EAC Treaty against those EACJ judges but was insisting on the automatic application of their suspension in EACJ since they were suspended back in Kenya. The answer for this was later deduced when the hearing in Kenya commenced and led to their vindication. One judge was cleared and gazetted accordingly before the hearing commenced and the second judge was cleared by the committee that conducted the enquiry.

For ease of reference and quick understanding of the argument above, it is worth reproducing Article 28 of the EAC Treaty on the removal of judges from office that was amended specifically to target the EACJ judges from Kenya, with the relevant amendments in italics:

1. *A Judge shall not be removed from office except by the Summit–*
   (a) *for misconduct or for inability to perform the functions of his or her office due to infirmity of mind or body;*
   Provided that a Judge shall only be removed from office under this subparagraph if the question of his or her removal from office has been referred to an ad hoc independent tribunal appointed for this purpose by the Summit and the tribunal has recommended that the Judge be removed from office for misconduct or inability to perform the functions of his or her office; or
   (b) *in the case of a Judge who also holds judicial office or other public office in a Partner State–*
      (i) *is removed from that office for misconduct or due to inability to perform the functions of the office for any reason; or*
      (ii) *resigns from that office following allegation of misconduct or of inability to perform the functions of the office for any reason;*
   (c) *if the Judge is adjudged bankrupt under any law in force in a Partner State; or*
   (d) *if the Judge is convicted of an offence involving dishonesty or fraud or moral turpitude under any law in force in a Partner State.*
2. *Where–*
   (a) *the question of removing a Judge has been referred to a tribunal under paragraph 1(a) or*
   (b) *a Judge is subject to investigation by a tribunal or other relevant authority of a Partner State with a view to his or her removal from an office referred to in paragraph 1(b); or*

[84] See East African Community (Heads of State), '8th Summit of the East African Community Heads of State Joint Communiqué' (Arusha 30 November 2006), Legal Notice No EAC/11/2007, 23 <https://gazettes.africa/archive/eac/2007/eac-gazette-dated-2007-12-30-no-4.pdf>.

(c) *a Judge is charged with an offence referred to in paragraph 1(d) under any law in force in a Partner State,*
the Summit may, subject to paragraph 2B, suspend the Judge from the exercise of the functions of his or her office

2A. *Where a Judge is suspended under paragraph 2, his or her respective Partner State shall recommend a person qualified in terms of Article 24 to the Summit for appointment as a temporary Judge for the duration of such suspension.*

2B. *The suspension of a Judge under paragraph 2 may, at any time, be revoked by the Summit and shall, in any case, cease to have effect if–*
(a) *the tribunal appointed under paragraph 1(a) recommends to the Summit that the Judge should not be removed from office; or*
(b) *a tribunal or other relevant authority of a Partner State recommends that the Judge should not be removed from an office referred to in paragraph 1(b); or*
(c) *the Judge is acquitted of an offence referred to in paragraph 1(d) by a court of competent jurisdiction in a Partner State.*

3. The tribunal appointed under *paragraph 1(a)* of this Article shall consist of three eminent Judges drawn from within the Commonwealth of Nations.
4. *At any time when the President of the Appellate Division, or the Principal Judge of the First Instance Division of the Court is for any reason unable to perform the functions of his or her office, those functions shall be performed by the Vice-President or the Deputy Principal Judge, as the case may be.*
5. The procedure for filling vacancies in the Court shall be prescribed in rules of the Court.
6. *If a Judge is directly or indirectly interested in a case before the Court, and if he or she considers that the nature of his or her interest is such that it would be prejudicial for him or her to take part in that case, such a Judge shall, if in the First Instance Division, make a report to the Principal Judge, or, if in the Appellate Division, make a report to the President, and if the President or Principal Judge considers the Judge's interest in the case prejudicial, the President or Principal Judge, as the case may be, shall make a report to the Chairperson of the Summit, and the Summit shall appoint a temporary Judge to act for that case only in place of the substantive Judge.*
7. If the President *or Principal Judge* of the Court is directly or indirectly interested in a case before the Court he or she shall, if he or she considers that the nature of his or her interest is such that it would be prejudicial for him or her to take part in that case, make a report to the Chairperson of the Summit and the Summit shall appoint a temporary President *or Principal Judge* of the Court to act as President *or Principal Judge* of the Court for that case only in place of the substantive President *or Principal Judge* of the Court.[85]

This amendment was a retaliation measure of the Summit of Heads of State that sought to intimidate the judges following the Court's ruling against the government of Kenya in *Anyang' Nyong'o* case.

[85] EAC Treaty (n 3) Art 26.

We can note a similar reaction by the SADC Summit of Heads of State and Government to the SADC Tribunal's ruling against the government of Zimbabwe in the *Campbell* case. Without consulting the citizens of SADC member states, the Summit went ahead and changed the mandate of the Tribunal by confining it to mere interpretation of the SADC Treaty and settlement of disputes between member states only.

It is my strong view that if these highest organs with governance powers over the EACJ and SADC Tribunal had been accountable to any institutions other than themselves, they would not have reacted to the regional courts' discharge of their mandate the way they did. Accountability is a very important tenet of good governance. Through it, the effectiveness of public bodies such as the Summits can be evaluated, their proper performance can be ensured, and their responsiveness to the community ascertained. Lack of accountability means absence of the above-stated advantages. The summits of heads of state in African RECs decide on matters affecting the regional courts and tribunals without allowing them to participate in the respective decision-making processes. They also develop various laws or policies affecting the courts and tribunals without providing space for being held responsible for any of their policies or programmes.

7.4 Some Concerns on the Governance of Regional Courts in Africa

When reference is made to governance, our minds are immediately directed to the 'management of affairs' of the institution.[86] Governance of regional courts therefore refers to the management of the affairs of regional courts and the extent to which courts can allow member states' involvement in running their affairs. Although regional courts are creatures of the treaties and therefore 'property' of the partner states, they must maintain independence and accountability in the management of their affairs. They have distinct organizational structures, but implementation of their projects and activities depends on the budgets usually determined by the executive and legislative organs whose powers are checked by the court.[87] The constitutive treaties that establish the different regional courts state categorically that the courts are independent organs of the community and that they receive no directions from any institution while exercising their judicial function.[88]

Regional courts in Africa do not have funding arrangements of their own. All depend on the subscription that each partner state contributes towards the budget of a particular community and are therefore accountable to the states that fund them. Since regional courts, just like any other institution of a REC, survive on the funding

[86] Mbembe Binda, 'Good Governance and Foreign Direct Investment: A Legal Contribution to a Balanced Economic Development in the East African Community' PhD Thesis (Utrecht University, 2015) 59 <https://dspace.library.uu.nl/handle/1874/318087>.

[87] eg, according to EAC Treaty (n 3) Arts 14(3)(e) and 133, the budget of the Community including that of the Court is determined by the Council of Ministers and approved by the East African Legislative Assembly.

[88] eg EAC Treaty (n 3) Art 14(3)(c).

by the member states, the possibility of such states attempting to influence their decisions cannot be ruled out. Arguably, member states are tempted to invoke the old English adage that 'he who pays the piper calls the tune'. They would like to be the ones to determine the tunes of justice to their favour. This may sound fictitious and imaginary had it not been for the incident that happened in 2016 during Law Day Celebrations in Dar es Salaam when the then President of the United Republic of Tanzania, while addressing the judges, lawyers, and other stakeholders, promised the judiciary to have its budget raised if the judges decided all pending tax-related cases swiftly and favourably to the government. His speech was aired live by national television and radios. This gives an impression of the attitude and the thinking of the governance institutions of the regional courts.

Further, the policy organs of the RECs, the executive arms for that matter, are responsible for the appointment of judges and officers of the regional courts. At the same time the structures of the regional courts under the treaties raise questions as to their independence. It is the executive arm of the cooperation that appoints the judges, sometimes with no concrete guidelines, thereby creating the possibilities for the executives to appoint as judges the persons who suit the interests of the appointing authorities and not the broader interest of the community.[89] Further, the budget of the court is normally determined by the executives. Although normally the court prepares its budget proposals, it submits the same to the executive for consideration and determination.[90]

The recruitment of court staff has to be sanctioned by the executive arm of the cooperation, although the treaty gives power to the court to employ its staff other than the judges and the registrar.[91] It is this kind of apparent misnomers that suggest the existence of circumstances which may result in the erosion of court's independence in the performance of its duties. The executive arm is a regular customer of the court as respondent and at the same time the financier of its activities. This concern is not a mere fantasy but real and well-founded, as the decision of the EACJ in *Anyang' Nyong'o*,[92] and the drama that followed soon after delivery of the ruling on that matter, may confirm.

The EAC Treaty provides that the national assembly of each partner state *shall* elect, not from among its members, nine members of the East African Legislative Assembly (EALA) in accordance with such procedure as it may determine.[93] It states further that the elected members shall as much as feasible be representative of specified groups, and sets out the qualifications for election.[94] Instead of *electing*, as directed by the Treaty, the National Assembly of the Republic of Kenya simply remitted to the EALA a list of nominees presented to the House by the House Business Committee, as members of EALA elected by the National Assembly of Kenya. Aggrieved by this, the Applicants filed a reference with the EACJ seeking an interpretation and application

89 EAC Treaty (n 3) Art 24(1), on the procedure for appointing judges of the EACJ; ECOWAS Protocol A/P.1/7/91 (n 18) Art 3, on the appointment of judges of the ECOWAS Court of Justice.

90 EAC Treaty (n 3) Arts 14(3)(e) and 132.

91 ibid Art 45(2).

92 *Anyang' Nyong'o* case (n 56).

93 EAC Treaty (n 3) Art 50(1).

94 Specified groups include the various political parties represented in the national assembly, shades of opinion, gender, and other special interest groups in the partner states.

of the EAC Treaty regarding the validity of the nomination and election of the Kenya's nine representatives to EALA. They contended that Kenya's National Assembly did not undertake an election within the meaning of Article 50 of the EAC Treaty. They also successfully filed an application for an interim injunction to prevent the said nine persons from being sworn in as members of EALA until the reference was determined. The partner states, especially the Republic of Kenya, were not amused by the court's intervention when it issued an injunctive order.

In their Joint Communiqué of the 8th Summit, being a reaction to the Court's ruling and temporary injunction against the Government of Kenya in the *Anyang' Nyong'o* application, the EAC Heads of State directed 'that the procedure for the removal of Judges from office provided in the Treaty be reviewed with a view to including all possible reasons for removal other than those provided in the Treaty' and that 'a special Summit be convened very soon to consider and to pronounce itself on the proposed amendments of the Treaty in this regard'.

Soon after the Summit directive, the Treaty was surreptitiously amended and amendments ratified by the legislatures in the partner states, hence becoming operational. It appears from the reaction by the executives that the judges, by deciding the case the way they did, committed an act that would have led to the invocation of the newly amended Article 26 of the EAC Treaty with a view to suspending or removing them from office. However, since such act was not covered by the Treaty, an amendment to the Treaty had to be effected so that should there be similar occurrence or a repeat of such an act by the judges in the future, the suggested punitive measures can be taken. This is nothing but an unfortunate backlash by the EAC Heads of State against the EACJ judges because of their impartiality and independence in dispensing justice. Although the court remained unshaken as an independent and impartial body, the whole saga evidences that the Court has experienced and survived apparent intimidation from the executive while discharging its noble duty as the temple of justice.

It was an affront to the rule-of-law doctrine when the heads of state decided to use their governance power over the EACJ to exhibit tyranny and ruthlessness just like any dictator would have done. Respect for the rule of law includes respecting the decisions of courts as the only institutions charged with settling disputes upon hearing both sides because no one should be above the law.

Indeed, the EAC Treaty amendments put the security of tenure for EACJ Judges seriously at risk. However, this unfortunate reaction of the Summit did not deter the judges from acting impartially and independently as it transpired in the main suit and in subsequent decisions of the Court.[95] Despite the retaliation by the Summit in response to the ruling on the interlocutory order, the Court went on to hear the main suit and decided that the National Assembly of Kenya did not undertake an election within the meaning of Article 50 of the EAC Treaty. It ordered the National Assembly of Kenya to carry out the election according to the Treaty.

The SADC Tribunal also faced a serious backlash from the heads of state when it decided against the interests of the government of Zimbabwe in the *Campbell* case.[96]

[95] *Anyang' Nyong'o* case (n 56) 173.
[96] *Campbell* case (n 57).

In its judgment, the SADC Tribunal had to determine whether Zimbabwe's controversial programme of land redistribution for resettlement purposes was compatible with the SADC Treaty. The Tribunal provided one of the few avenues of redress for farmers deprived of their property without compensation. It held that the land reform programme breached the treaty on the grounds that the property owners had been denied access to the domestic courts, that the applicants had been victims of racial discrimination, and that the state had failed to pay compensation for the lands compulsorily acquired. The reaction by the heads of state was catastrophic to the extent of virtually disbanding the Tribunal by reconstituting it afresh as a court dealing with interstate disputes only.[97] The judges and registrar were retired or could not have their contracts renewed.

The spirit of these decisions of the EACJ and the SADC Tribunal was to provide guidance on governance issues that faced the respective communities. This is the courts' mandate under their constituent treaties, but the executives took offence and went on to use their governance powers over the courts to punish them.

It is not uncommon to see the executive attempting to interfere with the regional courts' operations through micro-management of their affairs by withholding funding when required and in part of human resources. Taking the EACJ as an example, there were no court sessions from May 2019 to December 2019 largely due to lack of funds. Later on, when the Ad Hoc Human Resources Committee established by the Council of Ministers made a job analysis in the organs and institutions of the Community, it proposed a reduction of staff including EACJ staff as a measure to cut the running costs. The Court like the EAC Secretariat assisted by the civil society had to stand up in arms opposing this recommendation as these institutions were understaffed and the Committee had exceeded its mandate.[98]

The situation with respect to underfunding of the EACJ has not changed as of March 2024, as the Court Registrar was reported lamenting for the backlog of cases being experienced by the court because of lack of funds to enable it conduct an extraordinary session of the court. The court wanted to have one additional session in the year to address the backlog challenge. But this was not possible without making a formal request to the Council of Ministers every time the needed to have such extraordinary court session arose. The Registrar expressed discomfort about going back to the Council of Ministers to plead for funds in order for the Court to discharge its mandate. This frustration can be found in the Deputy Registrar's statement during interview with a journalist Jackson Mutinda when she said:

> we have made a request to the Council of Ministers for an extraordinary session of the court—to have one additional session in the year. So we are moving from four sessions to five in the hope that will reduce the case backlog. *We want the Council to formalise this: it had recommended this as a one-off but a one-off is not going to resolve a backlog.*[99]

[97] For a detailed account on the episodically disbanded SADC Tribunal: Blokker (n 26) 3–4.

[98] *East African Law Society v The Secretary General of the East African Community*, Reference No 1 of 2020.

[99] Christine Mutimula-Wekesa, 'Our Judges Are Overwhelmed and Our Budget Is Inadequate' (*The East African News Paper*, 23–29 March 2024) 22 <www.theeastafrican.co.ke> (emphasis added).

7.5 Conclusion

This chapter made a twofold argument. First, RECs establish regional courts to enforce their integration agenda which is sustained by a common legal framework that all member states agree to apply uniformly. Second, the effectiveness of regional courts depends on factors that are both internal and external to them. Internal factors include experience, competences, and skills, as well as integrity and impartiality of individual judges, while external factors include political support and the rate of enforcement of their decisions.

According to the EAC Treaty, the responsibility to implement a judgment of the Court lies with the concerned partner state or the Council, and every partner state is required by the Treaty to take, without delay, the measures required to implement a judgment of the Court.[100] Judgments and other decisions of the EACJ shall be executed according to the rules of civil procedure in force in the partner state in which the execution is due to take place.[101]

This shows that the EACJ, like other regional or international courts, has no mechanism of its own to implement or enforce its decisions. Enforcement of decisions against the executive therefore depends solely on the goodwill and discretion of the member states. This is not good as it undermines the courts. The treaties should provide for penalties and sanctions which may be imposed when partner states defy regional courts' orders instead of perpetuating impunity that undermines their judicial authority.

For law to have a meaningful role in enhancing the regional integration agenda, there must furthermore exist, as a precondition, a general culture among the member states of respect for the rule of law, including internal and supranational law, an independent and active judiciary whose decisions are respected and enforced by the member states, and a level of understanding by the citizenry of the importance of justice. If all these conditions are met, it is my conviction that the law and in turn regional courts will play a significant role in spearheading the integration agenda.

I am not pessimistic, but I am afraid that the fate of the SADC Tribunal may have a contagious spill-over effect. It started being felt at the EACJ soon after delivery of its ruling in *Anyang' Nyong'o*. The Court faced apparent intimidation by the EAC Summit of Heads of State and was accordingly punished by amending the Treaty, threatening the independence of the Court and the security of tenure of its Judges.[102] Thereafter, the world came to witness yet another unfortunate reaction by the SADC Summit of Heads of State and Government abolishing the Tribunal and reconstituting it afresh in a rather mutilated manner simply because it decided against the wish and interests of one member state, namely Zimbabwe. Important questions that a reader may wish to ask herself in this scenario are whether the regional courts belong to the summits of heads of state (the governance institutions) or to the people in the region, and how long this lamentable state of affairs shall be allowed to continue.

[100] EAC Treaty (n 3) Art 38(3).
[101] ibid Art 44.
[102] ibid Art 26.

While some common features have been eminently observed, regional courts' design, internal functioning, and procedures may relatively vary. It is my strong view that judicial governance denotes the courts' efforts to infuse accountability in the functioning of governmental institutions and the growth and development of human rights jurisprudence. Whichever approach is chosen by governance institutions of regional courts in Africa, it is important to keep asking the above questions. Courts' integrity and independence must be safeguarded to maintain their institutional status in the democratic and constitutional system, rather than simply allowing them to become another government statistic.

8

Paper Lions? The Governance of Africa's (Quasi-)Judicial Human Rights Institutions

*Misha Ariana Plagis and Karin Pluberg**

8.1 Introduction

State resistance and backlash against Africa's international courts is a well-publicized phenomenon.[1] The African Court on Human and Peoples' Rights (ACtHPR, or (African) Court) is no exception.[2] Some institutions have survived these battles better than others. For example, the Economic Community of West African States (ECOWAS) Court of Justice found its position strengthened after The Gambia's attempted backlash, while the Southern African Development Community (SADC) Tribunal saw its jurisdiction significantly reduced by the reprisals led by Zimbabwe.[3] The backlash against and resistance to Africa's Regional Economic Community (REC) courts have related almost exclusively to the human rights mandates of these courts, which are often not their primary mandates.[4] The African Court—which has an explicit human rights mandate emanating from the African Charter on Human and Peoples' Rights (Banjul Charter)[5] and the Protocol to the African Charter on Human and Peoples' Rights on the Establishment of an African Court on Human and Peoples' Rights (the Court Protocol)[6]—has been facing its biggest existential crisis

* The chapter reflects legal and institutional developments up to November 2021, with two notable additions: Tunisia's withdrawal of its special declaration, and Angola's ratification of the Malabo Protocol.

[1] Karen J Alter, James Thuo Gathii, and Laurence R Helfer, 'Backlash against International Courts in West, East and Southern Africa: Causes and Consequences' (2016) 27 European Journal of International Law 293.

[2] Nicole De Silva and Misha Plagis, 'A Court in Crisis: African States' Increasing Resistance to Africa's Human Rights Court' (*Opinio Juris*, 19 May 2020) <https://opiniojuris.org/2020/05/19/a-court-in-crisis-african-states-increasing-resistance-to-africas-human-rights-court>; Tom Gerald Daly and Micha Wiebusch, 'The African Court on Human and Peoples' Rights: Mapping Resistance against a Young Court' (2018) 14 International Journal of Law in Context 294.

[3] Alter, Gathii, and Helfer (n 1). See also John Eudes Ruhangisa, 'Governance of Regional Integration Courts', in this volume.

[4] One notable exception is the ECOWAS Court of Justice. James Thuo Gathii, 'Saving the Serengeti: Africa's New International Judicial Environmentalism' (2016) 16 Chicago Journal of International Law 390.

[5] African Charter on Human and Peoples' Rights (adopted 27 June 1981, entered into force 21 October 1986) (1982) OAU Doc CAB/LEG/67/3 rev. 5, 21 ILM 58.

[6] Protocol to the African Charter on Human and Peoples' Rights (adopted 10 June 1998, entered into force 25 January 2004) (1998) OAU Doc LEG/MIN/AFCHPR/Prot (1) Rev 2, Compendium.

Misha Ariana Plagis and Karin Pluberg, *Paper Lions? The Governance of Africa's (Quasi-)Judicial Human Rights Institutions*
In: *Governance of International Courts and Tribunals*. Edited by: Sergey Vasiliev and Niels Blokker, Oxford University Press.
 DOI: 10.1093/oso/9780198922131.003.0008

since it started operating in 2006.[7] Three states withdrew their special declarations under Article 34(6) of the Court Protocol, which provides individuals and NGOs direct access to the Court, within just a few months of each other.[8] Tanzania—the ACtHPR's host state and most frequent respondent in the cases it decides—, Benin, and Côte d'Ivoire declared their withdrawals in November 2019, March 2020, and April 2020 respectively. Rwanda had previously announced withdrawal of its Article 34(6) declaration in March 2016, and Tunisia subsequently withdrew its declaration in March 2025, making a total of five states parties to have withdrawn their special declarations to date.[9] This leaves only eight states[10] that accept direct access for individual and NGO complaints to the ACtHPR out of a potential fifty-five states that are members of the African Union (AU).[11]

These withdrawals of special declarations by states raise important questions about the future of the human rights system in Africa, and in particular the future of the (quasi-)judicial institutions that exercise jurisdiction over human rights issues. It also raises other questions, such as how the governance relationship between the AU and its (quasi-)judicial institutions is organized. What changes are taking place in terms of how these institutions are governed, and what does this mean for their ability to remain independent, and operate effectively in challenging political settings? This chapter addresses these questions from the perspective of the AU's two human rights (quasi-)judicial bodies: the ACtHPR and the African Commission on Human and Peoples' Rights (ACommHPR, or Commission).

Most of the analyses of the state resistance experienced by the Court have focused predominantly on what is happening at the level of the individual state party and on its responses to the Court's jurisdiction.[12] However, the AU and its other member states have been deafeningly silent on these developments. This silence does not imply that there is indifference or one uniform attitude towards the AU's (quasi-)judicial

[7] For an analysis of the causes of this crisis, see Sègnonna Horace Adjolohoun, 'A Crisis of Design and Judicial Practice? Curbing State Disengagement from the African Court on Human and Peoples' Rights' (2020) 20 African Human Rights Law Journal 1.

[8] De Silva and Plagis (n 2).

[9] For a full overview, see ACtHPR, 'Declarations Entered by Member States' <https://www.african-court.org/wpafc/declarations/>.

[10] ibid. After the withdrawals, there were six remaining states: Burkina Faso, Ghana, Malawi, Mali, The Gambia, and Tunisia. In late 2021, two further states submitted special declarations—Niger and Guinea-Bissau—bringing the total back up to eight states with special declarations in place.

[11] Fifty-four AU member states are party to the Banjul Charter. A full list of signatures and ratifications of the Banjul Charter is available at AU, 'List of Countries Which Have Signed, Ratified/Acceded to the African Charter on Human and People's Rights' (15 June 2017) <https://au.int/sites/default/files/treaties/36390-sl-african_charter_on_human_and_peoples_rights_2.pdf>.

[12] De Silva and Plagis (n 2); Apollin Koagne Zouapet, '"Victim of Its Commitment … You, Passerby, a Tear to the Proclaimed Virtue": Should the Epitaph of the African Court on Human and Peoples' Rights Be Prepared?' (*EJIL:Talk!*, 5 May 2020) <www.ejiltalk.org/victim-of-its-commitment-you-passerby-a-tear-to-the-proclaimed-virtue-should-the-epitaph-of-the-african-court-on-human-and-peoples-rights-be-prepared>; Tetevi Davi and Ezéchiel Amani, 'Another One Bites the Dust: Côte d'Ivoire to End Individual and NGO Access to the African Court' (*EJIL:Talk!*, 19 May 2020) <www.ejiltalk.org/another-one-bites-the-dust-cote-divoire-to-end-individual-and-ngo-access-to-the-african-court>; Oliver Windridge, 'Under Attack? Under the Radar? Under-Appreciated? All of the Above? A Time of Reckoning for the African Court on Human and Peoples' Rights' (*Opinio Juris*, 7 May 2020) <https://opiniojuris.org/2020/05/07/under-attack-under-the-radar-under-appreciated-all-of-the-above-a-time-of-reckoning-for-the-african-court-on-human-and-peoples-rights>.

institutions. As this chapter will demonstrate, the extent of their respective competences and especially the governance context amongst these institutions, the AU, and its member states is anything but static. The AU has to come to terms with the weaknesses and complexities of its governance structures. For example, over twenty treaties and declarations related to human rights and governance have been adopted in the past decade,[13] which collectively make up what is referred to as the AU's 'Shared Values Instruments' (SVI).[14] The African Governance Architecture (AGA)[15] was created to enhance coordination and synergies between the various AU organs, including the Court and the Commission, that are mandated to interpret and ensure compliance with these SVIs. However, the AGA is just one part of the broader governance structures at the AU level, raising challenges with regard to ensuring the independence and accountability of its courts and quasi-judicial organs.

Therefore, this chapter attempts to fill a gap in terms of understanding the complex layers of relationships between the Court and Commission, these two (quasi-)judicial institutions and the AU, and the various structures within the AU that deal with their governance. The focus is on how the structures developed by the AU impact the independence and accountability of these human rights (quasi-)judicial institutions. In essence, this chapter asks whether the independence and accountability of the ACtHPR and ACommHPR are assured through the governance mechanisms of the AU under which they operate, or whether these (quasi-)judicial institutions are muzzled by the governance framework that regulates their actions, rendering them 'paper lions', tamed by the political realities on the continent.

The chapter starts by providing an overview of the mandate and functions of the AU's two (quasi-)judicial institutions, followed by an introduction to the AU governance architecture (Section 8.2). It then goes on to discuss four core areas related to the independence and accountability of the Court and Commission, and how this affects their functioning in practice (Section 8.3). Finally, the last section looks towards the future with two important moves for reform (Section 8.4), before concluding.

8.2 AU's Human Rights Architecture

8.2.1 AU as an *injugovin*

Almost twenty years into the political integration of Africa—initially under the Organisation of African Unity (OAU), which was succeeded by the AU in 2002—the first African human rights quasi-judicial institution was created: the ACommHPR. In

[13] Governance here is used in the sense of domestic governance, not governance in the sense of how international courts are governed as used elsewhere in this chapter. For the latter, see chapters in Part I of this book, as well as Niels Blokker, 'The Governance of International Courts and Tribunals: Organizing and Guaranteeing Independence and Accountability' in Andreas Føllesdal and Geir Ulfstein (eds), *The Judicialization of International Law: A Mixed Blessing?* (OUP 2018).

[14] For a full list: African Union, *The African Governance Report: Promoting African Union Shared Values*, 2019, 27–28 <https://au.int/sites/default/files/documents/36843-doc-aga_report_-_english_-_online.pdf>.

[15] AGA Platform <https://au.int/aga/about>.

the years that followed, the ACtHPR was established as a judicial institution to complement the mandate of the ACommHPR. In addition, the AU has been in the process of creating the African Court of Justice and Human Rights (ACtJHR) through merging the ACtHPR and the Court of Justice of the African Union (ACJ), which has a mandate to rule on disputes over the interpretation of AU treaties.[16] The yet-to-be-established ACtJHR would also be endowed with criminal jurisdiction over international and transnational crimes if and when the much-discussed Malabo Protocol comes into force.[17]

Like other *injugovins*,[18] the AU wields power over its (quasi-)judicial institutions through its governance regime. However, an important distinction needs to be made in the African context, where varying forms of resistance to regional (quasi-)judicial institutions have taken place on account of cases relating to human rights, the rule of law, and democracy.[19] On the one hand, there are states taking individual action to undermine the authority or operation of these institutions. Examples include such efforts by The Gambia concerning the ECOWAS Court of Justice,[20] as well as special declaration withdrawals by Tanzania, Benin, and Côte d'Ivoire in the case of the African Court.[21] On the other hand, actions of this nature can be undertaken by states as part of the organ that governs those institutions (the *injugovin*). One example is how Zimbabwe leveraged the power of the SADC Summit of Heads of State and Government to help it do its bidding in narrowing the jurisdiction of the SADC Tribunal.[22] Within the context of the AU, states can also act through the AU organs. The latter is demonstrated by the reforms of the AU Executive Council, led by Egypt, regarding the procedures of the Commission following the acceptance (and subsequent withdrawal) of the observer status of a South African NGO, the Coalition of

[16] Protocol on the Statute of the African Court of Justice and Human Rights (adopted 1 July 2008, not yet in force) Assembly/AU/Dec.196(XI), reprinted in Olufemi Elias, 'Introductory Note to the Protocol on the Statute of the African Court of Justice and Human Rights' [2009] 48 ILM 334.

[17] Protocol on Amendments to the Protocol on the Statute of the African Court of Justice and Human Rights (adopted 27 June 2014, not yet in force) (2014) AU Doc Assembly/AU/Dec.529 (XXIII) (Malabo Protocol) <https://au.int/sites/default/files/treaties/36396-treaty-0035_-_protocol_on_the_statute_of_the_african_court_of_justice_and_human_rights_e.pdf>. For an overview of the changes, see Amnesty International, 'The State of African Regional Human Rights Bodies and Mechanisms 2018–2019' (AFR 01/1155/2019, 21 October 2019) 16–17. For discussions on the Malabo Protocol, see Charles C Jalloh, Kamari M Clarke, and Vincent O Nmehielle (eds), *The African Court of Justice and Human and Peoples' Rights in Context Development and Challenges* (CUP 2019).

[18] Blokker (n 13).

[19] Alter, Gathii, and Helfer (n 1); Mikael Rask Madsen, Pola Cebulak and Micha Wiebusch, 'Backlash against International Courts: Explaining the Forms and Patterns of Resistance to International Courts' (2018) 14 International Journal of Law in Context 197; Daly and Wiebusch (n 2).

[20] Alter, Gathii, and Helfer (n 1) 296–300.

[21] De Silva and Plagis (n 2).

[22] ibid 306–14. See also Erika de Wet, 'The Rise and Fall of the Tribunal of the Southern African Development Community: Implications for Dispute Settlement in Southern Africa' (2013) ICSID Review 1; Apollin Koagne Zouapet and Misha Ariana Plagis, 'Braamfontein Encroaching? An Internationalist Reading of the South African Constitutional Court Judgment on the SADC Tribunal' (2019) 35 South African Journal on Human Rights 378; Erika de Wet, 'The Controversial Role of Litigation in the Struggle to Revive Individual Access to the Tribunal of the Southern African Development Community' (2020) International Organizations Law Review 1; and John Eudes Ruhangisa, 'Governance of Regional Integration Courts', in this volume.

African Lesbians.[23] The focus in this chapter is on the second scenario, namely where the *injugovin* plays a central role in carrying out resistance to (quasi-)judicial bodies, rather than emphasizing the behaviour of individual states.

The role of the *injugovin* is not only significant because it has direct power to influence the functioning of the relevant court or tribunal, but also because the actions of the *injugovin* are a demonstration of a wider (political) willingness to either protect or weaken the independence and accountability of these institutions.[24] The *injugovin*, therefore, reflects and responds to the dynamics that are present within the group of states parties that together form the *injugovins*—although those states 'do not act as individual states, but within a collective body that is functioning on the basis of predetermined rules and established practices'.[25] The focus on the *injugovin* is important as it requires consensus-building among state parties constituting it. This also comes with certain risks, as it narrows the space for open dissent by other states parties. In the context of the AU, this often leaves it up to civil society and other stakeholders to contest the resistance or backlash against a specific (quasi-)judicial institution. Therefore, in the context of increasing resistance to the ACommHPR and the ACtHPR, we move beyond the focus on the actions and reactions of individual states. Instead, we look at the AU as the *injugovin* of these two institutions, and the significant role the AU plays in ensuring (or not) their success.

8.2.2 The Court and Commission

The Court and Commission are interlinked via Article 45(1)(c) of the Banjul Charter, which describes the mandate of the ACommHPR as including the cooperation 'with other African and international institutions concerned with the promotion and protection of human and peoples' rights'. The ACommHPR is the longest standing of the AU's three human rights bodies, established in 1987 following the entry into force of the Banjul Charter in 1986. In between the Commission and the Court, the African Committee of Experts on the Rights and Welfare of the Child (ACERWC) was also established in 2001, following the entry into force of the African Charter on the Rights and Welfare of the Child (ACRWC) in 1999.[26] The ACtHPR followed with the first judges sworn in in 2006 after the minimum number of required ratifications of the Protocol was reached in 2004. Each of the AU's human rights bodies has a slightly different mandate, but the three were designed to work in a complementary manner.[27]

[23] Japhet Biegon, 'The Rise and Rise of Political Backlash: African Union Executive Council's Decision to Review the Mandate and Working Methods of the African Commission' (*EJIL:Talk!*, 2 August 2018) <www.ejiltalk.org/the-rise-and-rise-of-political-backlash-african-union-executive-councils-decision-to-review-the-mandate-and-working-methods-of-the-african-commission>.

[24] The situation is not always dire. A good example of where the resisting state did not succeed in building broader consensus was in the case of the resistance to the ECOWAS Court of Justice by The Gambia. Alter, Gathii, and Helfer (n 1) 299.

[25] Blokker (n 13) 37.

[26] African Charter on the Rights and Welfare of the Child (ACWRC) (adopted 11 July 1990, entered into force 29 November 1999) (1990) OAU Doc CAB/LEG/24.9/49.

[27] Protocol establishing the Court (n 6) Art 2.

Nevertheless, in practice, the Court and Commission do not always achieve this intended complementarity, as will be discussed in this chapter.[28]

The tasks of the ACommHPR are three-fold: the promotion, protection, and interpretation of the Banjul Charter.[29] The promotion mandate refers primarily to advocacy and outreach to governments and stakeholders about the Banjul Charter. Activities that fall under this mandate comprise sensitization missions, public mobilization, and information dissemination, as well as providing guidelines, resolutions, and general comments on human rights.[30] The fact-finding missions and reports on the human rights situations in AU member states, which fall under the Commission's promotion mandate, have become one of its most effective tools. These reports have proven to be both accurate and independent, and are, therefore, often used in the political sphere and by civil society actors. For example, it is common practice for development partners to rely on these reports. In some cases, the ACommHPR undertakes fact-finding missions upon request of the AU, investigates potential human rights violations, and makes recommendations.[31] This 'AU referral' strengthens the position of the Commission during the missions and makes it more challenging for the respective member state to oppose the mission.[32] More generally, the efficacy of ACommHPR's state reports is due to their timely releases,[33] and the fact that issuance of the reports is not subject to domestic legal proceedings in the way communications are, which require the exhaustion of domestic remedies.

The protection mandate relates to the ACommHPR's function as a quasi-judicial body. It includes the Commission's ability to receive complaints through its communication procedure, friendly settlement of disputes, state-reporting procedure (including consideration of NGOs' shadow reports), urgent appeals, as well as referring complaints to the Court. The latter is of utmost importance in communications where the application stems from a member state that has not submitted a special declaration under Article 34(6) of the Court Protocol. Finally, the Commission is mandated to interpret the provisions of the Banjul Charter upon request by a state party, organs of the

[28] Although the ACERWC could arguably be considered a quasi-judicial institution based on its mandate (ACRWC (n 26) Art 42), it is not included here due to the disconnect between its mandate and the mandates of the ACtHPR and ACommHPR. This could change in the future. For example, the request to accept the ACERWC as an applicant to the African Court has been submitted to the AU in 2018. This request was initially rejected by the AU Specialized Technical Committee due to formalities, but is currently under review once again. It would allow the ACERWC to file cases on behalf of children, putting it on par with the status of the ACommHPR as a potential applicant before the ACtHPR.

[29] Banjul Charter (n 5) Arts 45(1)–(3).

[30] The main aim of this function is to sensitize the population and disseminate information on human and peoples' rights in Africa: ACHPR, 'History' <https://achpr.au.int/en/about/history>.

[31] This was the case in Burundi after the elections in 2015, where the Peace and Security Council of the AU had requested a mission report and recommendations from the ACommHPR on the post-electoral situation. Peace and Security Council of the African Union, 'Communiqué of the 565th meeting of the PSC on the situation in Burundi', Communiqué IV, PSC/PR/COMM.(DLI), 28 December 2015.

[32] Yet the acting government in Burundi did not allow the ACommHPR to undertake a second mission in 2018.

[33] In the case of Burundi, the elections took place in April 2015, the ACommHPR mission took place in December 2015, and the report was released in May 2016. See ACommHPR, 'Report of the Delegation of the African Commission on Human and Peoples' Rights on Its Fact-Finding Mission to Burundi, 7–13 December 2015' (ACommHPR, 17 May 2016) <https://achpr.au.int/sites/default/files/files/2025-03/achpr-report-fact-finding-burundieng.pdf>.

AU, or individuals. To date, a handful of NGOs have approached the ACommHPR for interpretation of various articles of the Charter or offered their support in doing so.[34]

The ACtHPR has jurisdiction over 'all cases and disputes submitted to it concerning the interpretation and application of the Banjul Charter, the [Court] Protocol and any other relevant Human Rights instrument ratified by the States concerned'.[35] It has two types of jurisdiction: contentious and advisory.[36] The Court may receive cases filed by the ACommHPR, states party to the Protocol, or African intergovernmental organizations.[37] NGOs with observer status before the ACommHPR and individuals can also institute cases directly before the Court, as long as the state against which they are complaining has ratified the Banjul Charter and the Court Protocol, as well as deposited an Article 34(6) special declaration recognizing the jurisdiction of the Court to accept cases directly from individuals and NGOs.[38]

8.2.3 The AU governance architecture

Blokker highlights three areas worthy of consideration when it comes to *injugovins*: (1) they comprise representatives of states; (2) they are organized into three different structural models; and (3) they 'are more than the sum of their members' or, in other words, legal restrictions are placed on the freedom of states to take action independently.[39] There is a lot of commonalities between the various *injugovins*, as they perform similar functions. They also face similar challenges concerning financial contributions to courts and tribunals, electing capable judges, deciding on the procedures for nominating judges, and the need for *injugovins* 'to function as responsible frameworks to which international courts and tribunals can be accountable'.[40] According to Blokker, there are three models in terms of the structures of *injugovins*. They can be an organ of an international organization, a treaty organ, or a cooperation between states.[41] A mix of these three models is also possible.[42]

In the case of the AU, while the governance of the Court and Commission might initially appear to fall squarely into the model of *injugovins* that describes judicial governance by an organ of an international organization, the AU system is perhaps

[34] eg the Centre for Human Rights (CHR) of the University of Pretoria was part of a task group to develop General Comments on article 14(1)(d) and (e) of the Protocol to the African Charter on Human and Peoples' Rights on the Rights of Women in Africa (adopted 1 July 2003, entered into force 25 November 2005) AU Assembly/AU/Dec.14(II) (Maputo Protocol) <https://archives.au.int/bitstream/handle/123456789/2057/General%20comment%20on%20Article%2014_E.pdf?sequence=1&isAllowed=y>. CHR News & Events (19 October 2012) <www.chr.up.ac.za/news-archive/2012/1609-african-commission-on-human-and-peoples-rights-adopts-first-general-comment-clarifying-article-14-1-d-and-e-of-the-african-women-s-protocol>.

[35] Protocol establishing the Court (n 6) Art 3(1). For a discussion on the breadth of the jurisdiction of the Court: Adamantia Rachovitsa, 'On New "Judicial Animals": The Curious Case of an African Court with Material Jurisdiction of a Global Scope' (2019) 19 Human Rights Law Review 255.

[36] Protocol establishing the Court (n 6) Arts 4 and 5.

[37] ibid Art 5(1).

[38] ibid Art 5(3).

[39] Blokker (n 13) 35.

[40] ibid 36.

[41] ibid 34.

[42] ibid 35.

best characterized as mixed. This is because the AU, as an international organization, is the primary overarching body under which the Court and Commission function. However, some of the processes that determine their effective functioning, notably the appointment of judges and commissioners, includes direct involvement of member states.[43] On the one hand, with the election of judges to the Court, the nominations are done by states party to the Court Protocol,[44] with a maximum of three candidates allowed per state.[45] On the other hand, the actual election of judges is done by the Executive Council,[46] and their appointment is pronounced by the AU Assembly,[47] both of which are organs of the AU.[48] Although the nominations of candidates is restricted to states party to the Court Protocol, the election of judges by the Executive Council is open to all fifty-five member states of the AU. Another interesting point to note is that the candidates proposed by states parties do not need all to be nationals of the states nominating them.[49]

It is also important to emphasize the distinct context of the Court and Commission vis-à-vis their counterparts in other regions. In Europe, the ECtHR is the human rights court of the Council of Europe—and often seen as the European counterpart to the African Court—while the Court of Justice of the European Union is an organ of the European Union (EU), mandated to decide disputes over the interpretation of EU integration treaties.[50] In Africa, human rights and regional integration are not dealt with by two separate international organizations, since both these themes are housed within the auspices of the AU. Furthermore, the AU has opened the door for the creation of the ACtJHR, once the Protocol on the Statute of the ACtJHR as well as subsequent protocols enter into force.[51] The ACtJHR will consist of three chambers: one for general matters related to the interpretation of AU treaties, one for human rights, and one for criminal matters.[52] Therefore, the AU system is more akin to the system of the Organization of American States (OAS), which also brings human rights together with other issues, such as trade and regional integration within the sphere of one international organization.

In the case of Africa, the *injugovin* of the Court and Commission is the AU and its relevant organs and departments. Formally the AU Assembly holds most of the power, but in reality, the AU Executive Council and the AU Commission also play

43 For a detailed overview of the election process of Court judges: International Justice Resource Centre, 'AfCHPR: Composition & Election Process' (15 July 2020) <https://ijrcenter.org/wp-content/uploads/2020/07/AfCHPR-mini-guide-final.pdf>.

44 Protocol establishing the Court (n 6) Art 13; for the Commission: Banjul Charter (n 5) Art 33.

45 Protocol establishing the Court (n 6) Art 12; for the Commission: Banjul Charter (n 5) Art 34.

46 For the composition of the Executive Council (either Ministers of Foreign Affairs, or equivalent): Constitutive Act of the African Union (adopted 11 July 2000, entered into force 26 May 2001) OAU Doc CAB/LEG/23.15, Art 10.

47 Protocol establishing the Court (n 6) Art 14. African Union Commission and New Zealand Ministry of Foreign Affairs and Trade/Manatū Aorere, 'A Guide for Those Working with and within the African Union: African Union Handbook 2019' (2019) 6th edition, 127.

48 For the Commission: Banjul Charter (n 5) Art 34.

49 Of the three candidates a state may propose, at least two must be nationals. See Protocol establishing the Court (n 6) Art 12.

50 Heikki Kanninen, 'Governance of the Court of Justice of the European Union', in this volume.

51 Protocol on the Statute of the ACtJHR (n 16). This replaces the 2003 Protocol establishing the African Court of Justice, and the 1998 Protocol establishing the current Court (n 6).

52 The latter is subject to the entering into force of the Malabo Protocol (n 17).

pivotal roles in the functioning of the Court and Commission. The structures governing the institutions focusing on human rights are not harmonized. The Court and Commission fall under the AU Commission's Department of Political Affairs (DPA), while the ACERWC is placed under the Department of Social Affairs (DSA). The July 2021 changes could also affect the focus on human rights, with the DPA being merged with the Department of Peace and Security to form the Department of Political Affairs, Peace and Security (PAPS).

More generally, the AU has a number of, sometimes overlapping, layers of organs and departments that are responsible for a variety of functions. One of the newcomers to this complex structure is the AGA Platform. It was established in 2010 in an effort to accelerate the implementation of various treaties, protocols, policies, and declarations in the field of human rights and governance.[53] While the 'governance' in AGA is directed at governance in terms of the domestic settings (in the sense of 'ensuring standards of good governance and the rule of law') in AU member states, the existence of AGA itself also creates an 'overall political institutional framework' for its participating organs.[54] It provides a structure linking the 13 AU institutions[55] that engage with the themes of the AU's Shared Values Instruments—including the rule of law, human rights, and democracy—and was placed under the DPA (now PAPS) with its own Secretariat.[56]

The position of AGA, as well as the Court and Commission, in the AU organigram changed in 2021. The DPA was replaced by the PAPS, placing all three under this new department. The move was part of the AU reforms aimed at more integrated approaches to dealing with security and governance issues on the continent, especially between the AGA (originally under the DPA) and the African Peace and Security Architecture (APSA) (originally under the Department for Peace and Security (DPS)).[57]

The aim of the AU Commission when establishing AGA was to create a platform for dialogue between the various stakeholders with similar mandates to harmonize efforts, deepen synergies, and share capacities, in addition to translating the objectives of the legal and policy pronouncements in the AU SVI.[58]

[53] 'AGA Platform' <https://au.int/aga/about>.

[54] African Governance Architecture and Platform Secretariat, Department of Political Affairs, African Union Commission, 'The African Governance Architecture (AGA) and Platform—Framework Document' (2017) 4–5 and 10 <www.scribd.com/document/244925257/The-African-Governance-Architecture-AGA-and-Platform-Notebook>.

[55] ibid 17. These include the African Court, African Commission, African Peer Review Mechanism (APRM), African Union Commission on International Law (AUCIL), AU Advisory Board on Corruption (AUABC), Pan-African Parliament (PAP), Specialised Technical Committees (STCs), Economic, Social and Cultural Council (ECOSOCC), Permanent Representatives Committee (PRC), Regional Economic Communities (RECs, i.e. EAC, SADC, ECOWAS), New Partnership for Africa's Development (NEPAD), ACERWC, and PSC. These are the formal founding members; however, they meet in a variety of constellations.

[56] African Union Commission (n 47) 100.

[57] For more collaboration: AU Press Release, 'AU Reforms Present a Unique Opportunity for Greater Synergy in Addressing Inter-Related Issues of Security and Governance in Africa' (*African Union*, 17 June 2021) <https://au.int/en/pressreleases/20210617/au-reforms-present-unique-opportunity-greater-synergy-addressing-inter>.

[58] The AU SVI 'are built around common principles and values that impose a sense of collective responsibility by AU Member States'. African Governance Architecture and Platform Secretariat (n 54) 10.

While the content of the AU SVIs that underpin AGA are directed at states, the AGA Platform serves as the coordinating arm for monitoring and reporting the implementation status of the SVI for platform members. In other words, the AGA structure is not just a collection of norms and standards for member states to apply in their national systems, it also provides an institutional 'umbrella' mechanism for AU and REC human rights institutions to coordinate, and support the relationships between continental, regional, and national levels and institutions to help ensure that they better fulfil their mandates.[59] One important function of the AGA, especially for the Court and Commission, is its role in fostering the 'effective implementation of AU organs decisions', which creates a structure they can turn to for support for the harmonized implementation of their decisions.[60] The AGA also provides a platform for interaction and active engagement between the various organs, including the Court and Commission, to 'facilitate information flows, knowledge exchanges, dialogue, synergies, and joint action between the various African governance actors, and monitor compliance and implementation'.[61]

The governance mandate of the AGA Platform is significant for two reasons. First, it places (quasi-)judicial institutions, social, and political organs under the same umbrella.[62] In addition, the AGA itself is placed under the DPA (now PAPS), while not all AGA Platform members are part of the DPA themselves. For example, the ACERWC, African Union Commission on International Law (AUCIL), Economic, Social and Cultural Council (ECOSOCC), and the Peace and Security Council (PSC) all fall under the scope of the DSA, which is a distinct department to the DPA, without any established hierarchy between the two. The merger of the DPA and DPS into the PAPS has not resolved this issue. This creates potential challenges for the respective organs as with different departments come different policies and priorities, which might not always be aligned with the dynamics of the AGA, on the one hand, and the PAPS, on the other. Therefore, the intended, and much-needed, harmonization of the AU governance institutions through a joint AGA Platform has resulted in a rather complicated construct, and the reforms have not alleviated the issue.

Second, the difference in departments and their structures is also significant because of the symbolic and practical implications of having (quasi-)judicial institutions *under* a political department. In fact, the AU places certain groups—for example, women's rights, as well as children's rights and the ACERWC—under the less contentious label of social affairs,[63] while human rights more generally are classified as being of a political nature, hence the Court and Commission falling under the DPA (now PAPS). Having (quasi-)*judicial* institutions under a *political* department (DPA/PAPS) brings into contention their independence, at least at face value.

[59] ibid 11.

[60] ibid 10 and 16.

[61] African Governance Architecture and Platform Secretariat (n 54) 16.

[62] African Union Commission (n 47) 100. While the African Union Commission lists the (quasi-)judicial organs and RECs as separate, it is somewhat misleading as they also explicitly fall under the DPA through the AGA.

[63] Maputo Protocol (n 34). The Maputo Protocol does not have its own enforcement mechanism, and is implemented, monitored, and interpreted by the ACommHPR and ACtHPR: ibid Arts 26 and 27.

As a result, the Court and Commission find themselves as part of a multi-layered and complex system of governance organs that influence different parts of their operations. The creation of the AGA Platform has led to additional reporting structures, and the need to manage the (lack of) strategic alignments between the Court and Commission's own departments (DPA/PAPS and DSA) and activities planned by the AGA Platform. In a worst-case scenario, this could result in considerable discrepancies and discord regarding the effectiveness of the respective organs. Therefore, although the AGA Platform offers additional avenues of cooperation for the human rights institutions, the reality of enhanced complementarity created by the AGA between the Court and the Commission does not necessarily translate into practice.

8.3 Independence and Accountability

The fact that '*[i]njugovins* wield enormous power over the tribunals'[64] is illustrated well by the case of the AU and its (quasi-)judicial institutions. However, when it comes to 'regulatory, human-resources, management oversight, co-operation enforcement, as well as budgetary and financial audit functions',[65] their relationship has proven problematic not only because of the stances taken by the AU and/or its member states, but also because of the *lack* of a clear stance when issues arise in practice. Examples include challenges related to the institutional design of the Court,[66] and the non-implementation of Court and Commission decisions. While historically much attention has been paid to the (lack of) protection of rights in the Banjul Charter,[67] emphasis should also be placed on how the institutional designs of the Court and Commission impact their functioning in practice and their relationship with different AU organs, and what the role of those AU organs as the *injugovin(s)* should be. For example, the ACommHPR faces many significant challenges in its day-to-day operation. Those that relate specifically to the *injugovin* include the AU's supervisory role in the implementation of decisions, under-staffing and lack of resources, the absence of AU Executive Council and AU Assembly oversight, and a general lack of clarity and guidance on the relationship between the various human rights institutions and AU organs.

In terms of independence and accountability of the (quasi-)judicial institutions, the AU Commission has taken the stance that the independence of the ACommHPR is merely 'functional in nature and [does] not [amount to] independence from the same organs that created the body'.[68] Nevertheless, in academic literature, independence

[64] Sergey Vasiliev, 'Judicial Governance Entities as Power-Holders in International Criminal Justice: A Plea for a Socio-Legal Enquiry' in Morten Bergsmo and others (eds), *Power in International Criminal Justice: Towards a Sociology of International Justice* (TOAEP 2020) 483.

[65] ibid.

[66] On systemic issues with the Court's design, eg Adjolohoun (n 7).

[67] eg Loveness Mapuva, 'Negating the Promotion of Human Rights Through "Claw-Back" Clauses in the African Charter on Human and People's Rights' (2016) 51 International Affairs and Global Strategy 1.

[68] African Union, 'Decision on the Report on the Joint Retreat of The Permanent Representatives' Committee (PRC) and the African Commission on Human and Peoples' Rights (ACHPR)' AU Doc EX.CL/Dec.1015(XXVIII) para 5. See also Biegon (n 23).

is defined as the independence of the organ itself, as well as that of its representatives.[69] As a result, attention needs to be paid to the position of commissioners and judges, as well as to the independence of the institutions themselves, and whether they have the 'proper status, privileges, and immunities'.[70] Accountability concerns the external authority over the court or tribunal, ie to whom the institution is answerable and through which line of reporting.[71] Accountability instruments can include the annual reports of the institutions, establishing budgets, or diplomatic briefings.[72] This section follows the conceptual framework set out by Blokker, and applies and adapts it to the main themes that affect the independence and accountability of the Court and Commission in theory and in practice.

8.3.1 Execution of decisions

Both the Court and the Commission can monitor and report the progress related to the implementation of their decisions, and the Banjul Charter in general, to organs of the AU.[73] Thus far, the AU has remained rather passive in taking up action from those monitoring reports. The current state of affairs indicates that the AU contents itself with receiving and adopting reports, but without following up when clear patterns of non-implementation of decisions occur.

The ACtHPR's execution mandate is not robust.[74] The Court sends its annual reports to the AU Executive Council,[75] where they are presented and adopted. In those reports, the Court indicates which of the member states have not yet, or not fully, implemented its decisions. Generally, the Court suffers from a low implementation rate, even in cases where the state does not contest its authority. One of the more encouraging examples of implementation stems from the case of *Lohe Issa Konate and others* v *Burkina Faso*.[76] However, in many other instances, decisions have remained unimplemented.[77] In 2018, there was an attempt to weaken this mechanism for reporting non-compliance. More specifically, the AU Executive Council requested the

[69] Blokker (n 13) 37.
[70] ibid 38.
[71] ibid.
[72] ibid 39.
[73] Banjul Charter (n 5) Arts 54 and 59.
[74] The Protocol leaves the execution of judgments up to the individual state: Protocol establishing the Court (n 6) Art 30.
[75] ibid Art 31.
[76] *Lohe Issa Konate* v *Burkina Faso* (Judgment on Reparations), App No 004/2013, AfCtHPR, 3 June 2016. In April 2018, the State transmitted a report detailing the measures taken to comply with the Judgment. The report indicated all amendments ordered to be undertaken with regard to the decriminalization of defamation were done through the promulgation of Law Number 057-2015/CNT of 4 September 2015, *Portant Régime Juridique de la Presse écrite au Burkina Faso* and Law Number 058-2015/CNT of 4 September 2015, *Portant Regime Juridique de la Presse en Ligne au Burkina Faso*. African Court of Human and Peoples' Rights, 'Activity Report of the African Court on Human and Peoples' Rights (AfCHPR)' AU Doc (2018) EX.CL/1126 AU Executive Council 13–18.
[77] For an overview of case implementation: eg AU Executive Council, 'Activity Report of the African Court on Human and Peoples' Rights (AfCHPR) 1 January–31 December 2018' (Addis Ababa, 7–8 February 2019) AU Doc EX.CL/1126 (XXXIV) 8–55.

Court to no longer mention those states that fail to implement decisions of the Court by name. However, the Court did not comply with this request as it continues to mention in its reports those states that are unwilling or unable to implement its decisions, since it is empowered to do in accordance with Article 31 of the Court Protocol. This (partially) failed attempt by the AU Executive Council to provide a proverbial invisibility cloak to non-compliant states is indicative of the fact that the AU human rights system is still driven by the underlying agendas of individual states. In practice, however, the AU Executive Council has also been partially successful: Although the Court continues to name states in its annual reports, only the AU Executive Council can initiate sanctions.[78] Nonetheless, the Court has proposed a 'Draft Framework for Reporting & Monitoring Execution of Judgments and other Decisions of the African Court on Human and Peoples' Rights'.[79] It envisages setting up a monitoring unit at the Court itself,[80] mandated to enter into dialogue with states when they do not comply, and eventually offer support in implementing decisions.[81]

The Commission finds itself in a similar position. Udombana described the situation back in 2006 as follows: '[the Achilles heel of the Commission] lies in the reality that African leaders always exhibit a spirit of furious indifference to the Commission's findings and recommendations'.[82] The ACommHPR decisions are non-binding, and it can only publish its reports after the AU's Executive Council and the Assembly provide authorization.[83] The Commission's Rules of Procedure (RoP) and the Banjul Charter do not foresee mechanisms to ensure the implementation of ACommHPR decisions. While the Commission disposes of a fairly strong mechanism under the 2010 RoP to ensure that states comply with its decisions,[84] it has never been used in practice.[85] Nonetheless, the newly adopted 2020 RoP contain a similar mechanism to move the issue of compliance to the political arena of the AU. The 2020 RoP provide for reporting of non-compliance in any given case referenced in the Commission's activity reports,[86] and/or the 'refer[ral] of the matter to the attention of the competent policy organs of the AU'.[87] This relationship with the AU's other organs and

[78] Constitutive Act of the AU (n 46) Art 23(2).

[79] AU Executive Council (n 77) Annex 1.

[80] For an overview: Rachel Murray, 'Implementation of the Judgments of the African Court on Human and Peoples' Rights' (*The ACtHPR Monitor*, 6 August 2019) < www.acthprmonitor.org/implementation-of-the-judgments-of-the-african-court-on-human-and-peoples-rights>.

[81] African Court on Human and Peoples' Rights, 'African Court on Human and Peoples' Rights Strategic Plan 2021–2025: Deepening Trust in the African Court by Enhancing Its Efficiency and Effectiveness' (Arusha, 7 June 2021) <www.african-court.org/wpafc/wp-content/uploads/2021/06/ACtHPR-Strategic-Plan-2021-2025-Deepening-Trust-in-The-African-Court.pdf>.

[82] Nsogurua J Udombana, 'The African Commission on Human and Peoples' Rights and the Development of Fair Trial Norms in Africa' (2006) 6 African Human Rights Law Journal 298, 330.

[83] Banjul Charter (n 5) Art 59.

[84] Rules of Procedure of the African Commission on Human and Peoples' Rights (2010) Rule 112(8).

[85] This was pointed out by Dr Japeth Bigeon from Amnesty International during the Centre for Human Rights webinar. Dr Japeth Bigeon, 'Civil Society Reflections on the Rules of Procedure of the ACHPR' (Centre for Human Rights webinar, 13 August 2020) <www.chr.up.ac.za/news-archive/2020/2209-invitation-webinar-on-civil-society-reflections-on-the-rules-of-procedure-2020-of-the-african-commission-on-human-and-peoples-rights>.

[86] Rules of Procedure of the African Commission on Human and Peoples' Rights (2020) Rule 125(9).

[87] ibid Rule 125(8).

institutions is further regulated in Rule 138,[88] which allows the Commission to 'request those organs to take the necessary measures for the implementation of its decisions'. The implementation of the Commission's decisions is further hampered by, for example, the Commission's restrictive interpretation of Article 59 of the Banjul Charter on confidentiality and implementation.[89] Although the implementation of the protection mandate is problematic, the situation is worse for its promotional mandate. There are no procedures foreseen in the Banjul Charter or the RoP for the implementation of recommendations to the states parties as part of the Commission's promotional mandate, which undercuts its effectiveness. In addition, past incidents of interference have placed further pressure on the Commission's ability to grant observer status,[90] which is a crucial issue for NGOs and for the independence of the Commission.

More generally, depending on the legal system of the member states, the implementation of Court or Commission decisions sometimes calls for domestic legal and judicial reforms.[91] However, the 'practices of member states [regarding their human rights pledges] are a jumble of inconsistencies'.[92] This issue is compounded by the fact that the AU legal system does not require the transposition of AU law into the domestic legal systems of its member states. As a result, the AU can continue to adopt documents, such as those found in the SVI, promoting human rights and good governance without its member states having to effect legal changes. Overall, while there have been some successes,[93] the fact remains that without the AU Executive Council taking decisive steps towards pressuring member states to implement decisions of the Court or the Commission and therefore enhancing mechanisms of accountability, the Court and Commission's work will remain relatively ineffective for the individual applicants that rely on them.

[88] Erroneously mentioned as Rule 137 in RoP 2020 (n 86) Rule 125(8).

[89] For a critique of this interpretation by the Commission: Rachel Murray, 'Confidentiality and the Implementation of the Decisions of the African Commission on Human and Peoples' Rights' (2019) 19 African Human Rights Law Journal 1.

[90] On the Coalition of African Lesbians (CAL) incident: Biegon (n 23).

[91] eg *Consolidated Matter of Tanganyika Law Society, Legal and Human Rights Centre and Reverend Christopher R. Mtikila* v *Tanzania*, App Nos 009 and 011/2011, AfCtHPR, 14 June 2013, para 126(3) on electoral laws; *Association pour le Progrès et la Défense des droits des femmes Maliennes (APDF) and the Institute for Human Rights and Development in Africa (IHRDA)* v *Mali*, App No 046/2016, AfCtHPR, 10 May 2018, para 135(x), on provisions regarding the inheritance rights of girls and women in the National Code of Persons and the Family; and *Actions Pour la Protection des Droits de l'Homme (APDH)* v *Côte d'Ivoire*, App No 001/2014, AfCtHPR, Judgment 18 November 2016, para 153(7), regarding the composition of the National Electoral Commission.

[92] Udombana (n 82) 332.

[93] For example, the implementation of the *Beneficiaries of Late Norbert Zongo, Abdoulaye Nikiema Alias Ablasse, Ernest Zongo and Blaise Ilboudo & the Burkinabè Movement on Human and Peoples' Rights* v *Burkina Faso*, Judgment on Reparations, App No 13/2011, ACtHPR, 5 June 2015; Murray (n 89). On the contribution of African states to shaping and broadening the protection of international human rights law: Frans Viljoen, 'Africa's Contribution to the Development of International Human Rights and Humanitarian Law' in Eunice N Sahle (ed), *Human Rights in Africa: Contemporary Debates and Struggles* (Palgrave Macmillan 2019).

8.3.2 Allocation of budget and staffing

The Amnesty International report on 'The State of African Regional Human Rights Bodies and Mechanisms 2018–2019' pointed to many of the systemic funding and capacity issues the Court and Commission face.[94] These issues are not specific to these institutions alone within the AU. The AU as a whole is facing problems related to funding.[95] For one, the Court and Commission often depend on 'donors and development partners to fill gaps in their operation costs'.[96] From a practical perspective, some international partners[97] distinguish between the on- and off-budget support they provide to the Court and Commission. Off-budget refers to funding coming from partners to implement certain activities not included in the institution's annual budget, which gives it more flexibility. On-budget refers to the funding received from these partners that is included in the annual budget of the institution, which requires a higher level of pre-planning and approval. However, the latter could also eventually lead to budget reductions in terms of the AU's contributions due to these alternative funding streams.

In the AU context, both the Court and the Commission receive off-budget contributions. This is not only a question of practical budgetary policy, but also an ideological issue. To the extent that AU political organs engage on the topic, it is often related to the alleged need to 'shield the mechanisms from perceived external interference on account of donor funding and support'.[98] This led the AU Assembly to state in a 2016 declaration that the AU Commission should 'ensure the independence and integrity of AU organs with [a] human rights mandate by providing adequate financing[,] and shielding them from undue external influence'.[99] From the perspective of the institutions carrying out their mandates to the fullest extent, on- and off-budget contributions are of great importance.[100] For example, the Court's budget from the AU only covers salaries and sessions, but not missions and other outreach activities and operations. Therefore, off-budget contributions that help the Court 'popularize' its mandate, which the AU endows it with, become essential.

For the Commission, the current situation results in activities related to the Commission's promotion mandate being exclusively funded by international partners.[101] Although this external funding is viewed as contentious, it provides the

[94] Amnesty International (n 17).

[95] Philomena Apiko and Luckystar Miyandazi, 'Discussion Paper No. 258: Self-Financing the African Union: One Levy, Multiple Reforms' (ECDPM, 2019) 3–4, <https://ecdpm.org/application/files/8816/5968/9392/Self-Financing-African-Union-Levy-Reforms-ECDPM-Discussion-Paper-258.pdf>.

[96] Amnesty International (n 17) 43.

[97] Such as *Deutsche Gesellschaft für Internationale Zusammenarbeit* (GIZ), the EU, the United Nations (UN), USAID, and others.

[98] Amnesty International (n 17) 43.

[99] African Union Assembly, 'Declaration by the Assembly on the Theme of Year 2016' (Addis Ababa, 17–18 July 2016) AU Doc Assembly/AU/Decl.1(XXVII)Rev 1, para 7.

[100] Apiko and Miyandazi (n 95) 5.

[101] Sabrina Lauer, *Die Implementierung Menschenrechtlicher Verträge in Afrika: Eine Analyse Der Zentralen Implementierungsorgane Und -Mechanismen Des Afrikanischen Regionalsystems* (Nomos 2018) 63.

Commission's Secretariat with a wide scope of discretion on how to spend donor funds.[102] Overall, there are also inconsistencies around the budget cycles, compounded by the lack of harmonization in terms of the release of funds, as well as fragmented funding from donors, all of which impose burdens on the effective cashflow management and programme implementation of the Commission.[103]

This leaves the (quasi-)judicial institutions in a difficult position. The AU is working towards sustainable financing from its member states, and moving away from foreign contributions. The current bifurcation of the running costs of the Court and Commission between contributions from the AU and donors has, therefore, resulted in pushes for reform, such as the so-called Kagame reforms.[104] These reforms should, in theory, address the problem of irregular contributions from member states to the AU, and, by extension, the issues related to the operational costs of the Court and Commission.[105]

On- and off-budget contributions are not the only challenge, in fact, as the budgets of the Court and Commission have been a contentious issue more generally. While the budget of the Court has grown relatively consistently since 2013 to approximately US$ 13,9 million in 2019,[106] the budget of the Commission has fluctuated. For example, the Commission faced a significant budget decrease in 2014, and a slight decrease in 2017. The budget set for the Commission in 2019 was US$ 7 million,[107] significantly less than that of the Court. To understand why this dynamic is problematic, it is worth reflecting on the number of cases and communications dealt with by each institution in a year. For example, in 2019 the cases pending before the ACtHPR amounted to 177 applications and one request for an advisory opinion,[108] whereas the ACommHPR had 238 pending cases.[109]

This distribution of the workload and budget is also problematic from the perspective of the number of staff working at each institution. With approximately one hundred staff members (excluding the judges), the Court is twice the size of the Commission, which should have approximately fifty staff members.[110] The Commission has also suffered from staffing issues. Amnesty International highlighted the issue of staffing shortages, and suggested they were due to the Commission not being in charge of

[102] The AU, as per its regulations, does not allocate any budget to the promotion mandate of the ACommHPR.

[103] For a discussion on budget: Lauer (n 101) 63.

[104] See Section 8.4.1.

[105] In 2015, only 25 per cent of the AU's annual budget was covered by member states' contributions: Lauer (n 101) 63. Out of this group, five states—Egypt, South Africa, Morocco, Algeria, and Nigeria—were found to contribute the most (48 per cent). The second tier of twelve countries was found to have contributed 37 per cent, and the third tier of thirty-seven countries only 15 per cent.

[106] Amnesty International (n 17) 44. The budget decreased slightly in 2014, but to a far lesser extent than the budget of the ACommHPR in the same year. AU Executive Council, 'Activity Report of the African Court on Human and Peoples' Rights (AfCHPR)' (Addis Ababa, 6–7 February 2020) AU Doc EX.CL/1204(XXXVI) 10.

[107] Amnesty International (n 17) 44.

[108] AU Executive Council (n 106) 4.

[109] ACommHPR, '47th Activity Report of the African Commission on Human and Peoples' Rights' (2019) para 27.

[110] These data were current as of August 2020 and are based on the personal/informal correspondence between Karin Pluberg and the institution representatives.

its recruitment processes.[111] Instead, the recruitment process is done in collaboration with the AU Commission, in accordance with the AU's rules and regulations.[112] This has resulted in repeated requests by the ACommHPR that it be given full autonomy over its recruitment processes, without success.[113] Although the Commission's approved organizational structure now allows for forty-six staff members (compared to the thirteen approved under the 2003 structure), there were still twenty-five unfilled positions at the end of 2017.[114]

Aside from the actual staffing shortage, other organizational choices have created further issues for the Commission. For example, the Secretariat opted to combine both the promotion and the protection mandates of the Commission in its legal unit. This has caused further capacity issues.[115] Civil society and development partners have long called for the Commission to establish a specific litigation unit.[116] However, the legal unit is still tasked with multiple other activities mainly related to the promotion mandate (eg sensitization visits, preparing sessions, and summit meetings). This is especially problematic for two reasons. First, it has contributed to the high backlog of pending complaints. Second, communications referred to the Court by the Commission are represented by the Commission, not the original applicants. This places a high burden on the Commission, and can only be an effective process if the required staff are appointed, and have the time to engage the Court. When combined, these staffing issues have led to a large backlog of communications at the Commission,[117] which is also connected to its low response rate, as well as fewer or delayed referrals of communications to the ACtHPR.

8.3.3 Election of commissioners and judges

Judges and commissioners 'must be "independent" and "impartial"'.[118] In the ACommHPR's extensive body of decisions on the right to a fair trial, the independence of the judiciary (at the domestic level) has featured prominently.[119] However, the independence of commissioners, and of the Commission itself, was hotly contested during the drafting process of the Banjul Charter.[120] According to Viljoen, the draft provision that made an appointment as a commissioner incompatible with

[111] Amnesty International (n 17) 46.

[112] ibid.

[113] ibid; eg ACommHPR (n 109) para 65.

[114] Amnesty International (n 17) 45–46; also ACommHPR (n 109) para 51, where the staff situation is referred to as not having improved.

[115] Katja Schemmann, 'Strengthening the African Governance Architecture (AGA): Area of Activity African Commission on Human and Peoples' Rights: Capacity Assessment of the Secretariat of the African Commission on Human and Peoples' Rights and Recommendations for Organisational Development' (2015) 8 (on file with authors).

[116] ibid 18; also Vincent O Orlu Nmehielle, *The African Human Rights System: Its Laws, Practice, and Institutions* (Kluwer Law International 2001) 183.

[117] There are 238 communications pending before the Commission: ACommHPR (n 109) para 27.

[118] Ruth Mackenzie and Philippe Sands, 'International Courts and Tribunals and the Independence of the International Judge' (2003) 44 Harvard International Law Journal 271, 275.

[119] For an overview of the Commission's stance: Udombana (n 82) 326–29.

[120] Viljoen (n 93) 324.

'membership of a Government or the Diplomatic Corps' was the only provision 'deleted in its entirety' between the Dakar and Banjul Meetings.[121] As a result, several commissioners have indeed also been members of the government or diplomatic corps of their home countries.[122] This trend is similar to that in respect of judges at the Court. Since the procedures for both institutions are similar, this section looks predominantly at the rules and procedures around the nomination, terms of office, and qualifications of judges at the Court, and the role of states in those processes.

In the case of the eleven judges of the ACtHPR, member states may nominate up to three candidates, of which at least two must be nationals of that state.[123] The nominees are then elected by secret ballot at the AU level. Elected judges serve a six-year term, which is renewable only once.[124] The election of judges should take into consideration the AU requirements of diversity in terms of the geographic region, legal tradition, language, and gender equality.[125] Articles 17(2) and 22 of the Court Protocol help protect the independence and impartiality of the Court by specifying that a judge cannot sit on a case to which their country is a party. Judges also enjoy immunity and independence in accordance with international law.[126] In terms of qualifications, Article 11 of the Court Protocol requires that candidates be a national of a member state of the AU, and that they be 'from among jurists of [a] high moral character and of recognised practical, judicial or academic competence and experience in the field of human and peoples' rights'. However, in reality, the requirement of 'competence in human rights law' is not always met. During the selection process, it does not appear that particular weight is always given to the need for candidates to be an expert in human rights law—rather than another field of law (ie criminal or commercial law)—or to have worked in the legal profession (ie practitioner or academic) by either the states nor the AU Commission.[127] Hence, questions can be raised about the prior experience of several judges at the Court.[128]

When it comes to ensuring the independence and impartiality of judges, there are a number of areas of concern. For example, aside from the Court's President, who is appointed on a full-time basis, the other judges are only appointed on a part-time basis. Therefore, in addition to their role as a judge at the Court, judges keep their other functions in their respective countries (eg as judges, academics, attorneys, ministers, etc). As a result, the judges are never truly disconnected from their national system and most of them are likely to continue working in their national systems throughout their tenure at the Court.[129] This has also resulted in a plethora of administrative issues for many of those sitting on the bench related to conflicting agendas and deadlines. To complicate matters further, this situation also results in judges receiving salaries from both the AU and their national governments, further blurring the lines

[121] ibid.
[122] ibid.
[123] Protocol establishing the Court (n 6) Art 12(1).
[124] ibid Art 15.
[125] ibid Arts 12 and 14(3).
[126] ibid Art 17.
[127] Frans Viljoen, *International Human Rights Law in Africa* (2nd edn, OUP 2012) 423–24.
[128] ibid.
[129] Rules of Court (2021) Rule 5(2) changed this dynamic by restricting the other roles judges may have while sitting on the Court.

and compromising their independence and accountability in relation to their work at the Court.

One major cause for concern about the Court's accountability as a whole is the blend between administrative and judicial duties of the judges. In the early days of the Court, judges were engaged in a wide array of activities, including administrative tasks. However, as the docket of the Court expanded, and as it only sits four times a year, these duties were overburdening the judges and contributed to delays in the delivery of decisions. Although the Strategic Plan 2021–2025 addresses delays in decision-making and the Court's efficiency,[130] it remains to be seen how this issue will be dealt with in practice to ensure the accountability of the Court towards the individuals and peoples it serves.

8.3.4 Independence and complementarity

In theory, the Court and Commission work in unison based on complementarity. They ensure that the Banjul Charter, its protocol on women's rights, and the African Charter on Democracy, Elections, and Governance (ACDEG) and other instruments are promoted, respected, and implemented in a harmonized manner across the continent. While complementarity exists on paper, it faces several challenges in practice.

The politically and legally complex relationship between the ACommHPR and the ACtHPR constitutes a key challenge to the smooth functioning of the AU human rights system. Although the Court and Commission have an official relationship regulated by the Banjul Charter and the Court Protocol, the foundations of the relationship between the ACommHPR and ACtHPR are rather different to those that used to underlie the relationship between the (now defunct) Commission and the Court in the European human rights system.[131]

One of the most important elements of this relationship is the ability of the Commission to refer communications to the Court. To date, this has only happened three times.[132] Although the exact reasons for the lack of referrals from the Commission to the Court are unclear, there is one known point of contention: the problem of *res judicata* and *de novo* consideration of referred applications.[133] Essentially, this is about when and how the Commission may seize the Court. Under the 2010 version of the Commission's RoP, the ACommHPR could transfer complaints to the ACtHPR if: (1) the state did not comply with the recommendations of the Commission; (2) the state did not comply with provisional measures indicated by the

[130] African Court (n 81).

[131] Rachel Murray, 'A Comparison between the African and European Courts of Human Rights' (2002) 2 African Human Rights Law Journal 195, 196–97.

[132] ACtHPR, 'Statistics' <www.african-court.org/cpmt/statistic>.

[133] A *de novo* review, in the context of the complementarity between the AU human rights institutions, means that the ACtHPR considers every legal question afresh without being bound by any interpretation or decision taken by the ACommHPR on the same legal question. Linked to that is the principle of *res judicata*, which refers to a case in which there has been a final judgment and is no longer subject to appeal. If the admissibility of a communication has been decided by the ACommHPR, this rule would dictate that the ACtHPR would not provide a contradicting decision.

Commission; (3) the communication before the Commission constituted a serious or massive violation of human rights; or (4) the Commission deemed it necessary, at any stage of a proceeding.[134] Under the revised 2020 RoP, the Commission has effectively narrowed down the situations when communications can be transferred to one: 'The Commission may, before deciding on the admissibility of a Communication ... decide that the Communication should be referred to the Court, *provided that the respondent State has ratified the African Court Protocol*.'[135] While this solves the *res judicata/ de novo* issue—as the Commission can now only transfer cases before deciding on admissibility—it raises a new point of contention: should it be up to the Commission to decide the Court's jurisdiction? The main issue with the inclusion of the latter part of the requirement—namely, that the state must have ratified the Court Protocol—is that it effectively provides an interpretation of Article 5 of the Court Protocol, on the jurisdiction of the Court, by the Commission. As the Registrar of the Court pointed out, this should be an area for the Court to decide, not the Commission.[136]

This lack of harmonization on the complementarity between the Court and Commission is especially important due to the above-mentioned withdrawals by several states of their special declarations providing direct access to the Court to individuals and NGOs under Articles 5(3) and 34(6) of the Court Protocol.[137] On the one hand, the Commission holds a strong protection mandate as the first-response institution for applicants: all states that have ratified the Banjul Charter give the ACommHPR jurisdiction to hear individual complaints. On the other hand, the Court suffers from the vast majority of AU member states failing to deposit a special declaration under Article 34(6) of the Court Protocol.[138] The argument here is not to bypass the Article 34(6) system, as this could potentially subject the ACommHPR to political pressure and even resistance or backlash by states. However, the ACommHPR's significant discretionary power in determining whether and when to refer cases to the ACtHPR needs to be recognized, especially given the relative accessibility of the Commission in comparison to the Court. Although this could be seen as an opportunity for the Commission, due to its significant backlog of communications, it also creates challenges as the Commission has limited financial resources to represent cases before the Court. This is because when applications are transferred from the ACommHPR to the ACtHPR, the Commission becomes the applicant in the proceedings before the Court.[139]

[134] RoP (2010) Rule 118.

[135] RoP (2020) Rule 130 (emphasis added).

[136] Such was the argument made by Dr Robert Eno, Registrar of the ACtHPR, during a webinar organized by the Centre for Human Rights, University of Pretoria: Robert Eno, 'Civil Society Reflection on the Rules of Procedure 2020 of the African Commission on Human and Peoples' Rights' (Centre of Human Rights webinar, 13 August 2020) <www.chr.up.ac.za/news-archive/2020/2209-invitation-webinar-on-civil-society-reflections-on-the-rules-of-procedure-2020-of-the-african-commission-on-human-and-peoples-rights>.

[137] De Silva and Plagis (n 2).

[138] Following the recent withdrawals, only six of fifty-five member states of the AU remain having deposited a special declaration under Protocol establishing the Court (n 6) Art 34(6): ACtHPR, 'Declarations Entered by Member States' (n 9).

[139] RoP (2010) Rule 120, now RoP (2020) Rule 132.

The timing of the changes that took place, in terms of the special declaration withdrawals and the changes to the RoP of the Commission, further put a spotlight on the complementarity tensions. For example, the subtle shift in language between the 2010 and 2020 versions of the Commission's RoP is notable. Under the 2010 version, the ACommHPR 'shall consult with the Court before the modification of any of its Rules relating to their relationship'.[140] However, under the 2020 version, the ACommHPR shall only consult the Court on amendments 'as appropriate',[141] therefore no longer requiring the input of the Court. This change came just months after the special declaration withdrawals.

As a result, the relationship between the Court and Commission remains complex. Aside from the more technical and legal arrangements between the Court and the Commission, the practice of the two institutions does not appear to be sufficiently aligned. This reveals an underlying weakness of the AU human rights system: the downside of having overlapping mandates paired with the absence of accountability mechanism leaves too much discretion to the leadership and institutional agendas of particular institutions. This discounts opportunities to work as a united front on human rights issues, and leaves applicants wanting in terms of their access to justice—whether at the Commission or the Court.

8.4 Looking to the Future

The governance of the African human rights system is not static. As the AU continues to adopt new frameworks that place human rights at the centre of its policy areas—such as with the Africa Agenda 2063 and the Shared Values Instruments—it has also developed new structures, such as the AGA, and adopted reforms on how Africa's human rights (quasi-)judicial institutions will be governed in the future. In this section, two reforms in progress are examined: first, the Kagame reforms, and second, the new protocols expanding the jurisdiction of the Court.

8.4.1 The Kagame reforms

A more efficient bureaucracy, thorough implementation of decisions, and adequate funding from within the AU were among the most pressing issues at the 27th Ordinary Session of the AU Assembly of Heads of State in July 2016. During this session, it was 'determined that there was an urgent need to accelerate the ongoing reform of the African Union'.[142] The President of Rwanda, Paul Kagame, was tasked with proposing a new set of reforms and submitted his report to the AU in January 2017—the

[140] RoP (2010) Rule 115(4).
[141] RoP (2020) Rule 129(4).
[142] AU, 'Summary of the 27th AU Summit Decisions: Tax Imports to Finance AU; Establish Protocol to Issue African Passports to Citizens; and Extend Mandate of Chairperson and Commission' (Press Release, 25 July 2016) <https://au.int/en/pressreleases/20160725/summary-27th-au-summit-decisions-tax-imports-finance-au-establish-protocol>.

so-called Kagame Report.[143] It comprises nineteen (later expanded to twenty-one)[144] recommendations across six reform areas.[145]

One recommendation from the Kagame Report explicitly deals with the judicial and legislative organs of the AU—the proposed ACtJHR and the Pan-African Parliament in particular—and the need to review and clarify their overlapping mandates. However, the Report did not go beyond posing questions, and offered no answers or solutions to the problems identified.[146] One proposed concrete reform was to create an agency that would operate as an umbrella institution with a single secretariat and place most of the human rights institutions within its mandate (ie ACommHPR, ACERWC, but also the AU Advisory Board on Corruption), while the ACtHPR would remain outside of that structure. This proposal was, however, not further elaborated upon. It is also revealing that the Kagame reforms did not raise the issue of the ACtHPR not being afforded an independent position as a judicial institution within the AU, and would leave the Court embedded in the DPA (which now falls under the PAPS).

Nonetheless, four areas of the reform were relevant for changes to the governance setting of the AU human rights (quasi-)judicial bodies. First, the proposal for a department merger, which involves the institutional setup of the AU Commission, effectively constituted the decision to cut the number of AU Commissioners from eight to six by 2021 and to combine the DPS and the DPA under a single commissioner (the PAPS). According to the Kagame Report, a leaner commission should make for more effective decision-making and implementation, and it is a natural fit for the two departments to be combined.[147] This reform took place in 2021. However, its exact effects and implications on the operation of the AGA are not yet clear,[148] especially for those AGA members that were traditionally placed under departments other than the DPA. In other words, this change has not helped resolve the 'lack of institutional clarity [that] lays a burden on an AU institutional architecture that is often short on resources and that struggles to coordinate effectively between different organs'.[149]

[143] Paul Kagame, 'The Imperative to Strenghten Our Union: Report on the Proposed Recommendations for the Institutional Reform of the African Union' (AU Assembly, 29 January 2017) AU Doc Assembly/AU/Dec.606(XXVII) 5.

[144] As presented in a subsequent report: Paul Kagame, 'Report on the Implementation of the Decision on the Institutional Reform of the African Union' (AU Assembly, July 2017) AU Doc Assembly/AU/Dec/635(XXVIII).

[145] The six reform areas are: 'focusing on fewer priority areas, ensuring a clear division of labour between AU structures, making the AU Commission more effective and efficient, improving decision-making and implementation following AU summits; strengthening the current sanctions mechanism; addressing management and recruitment issues; and implementing the Kigali Financing Decision (the so-called "Kaberuka Plan" ...)'. Yarik Turianskyi and Steven Gruzd, 'The "Kagame Reforms" of the AU: Will They Stick?' (South African Institute of International Affairs, Occasional Paper 299, 2019) 2 and 4.

[146] eg: '[s]hould the PAP have legislative powers and if so in what areas? ... What is impeding the merger of the Court of Justice and African Court [on] Human [and Peoples'] Rights?': Kagame (n 143) 9.

[147] Turianskyi and Gruzd (n 145) 10.

[148] For a discussion on the potential outcomes on the AGA structures, see Martin Roncerary, Lidet Tadesse Shiferaw, and Ueli Staeger, 'Discussion Paper No. 303: Merging Peace and Politics—Drivers, Dilemmas and Options for the AU's New Governance Setup' (ECDPM, June 2021), <https://ecdpm.org/application/files/6216/5546/8571/Merging-Peace-Politics-Drivers-Dilemmas-Options-AU-New-Governance-Setup-ECDPM-Discussion-Paper-303-2021.pdf>.

[149] ibid 9.

The second proposal was to limit the participation of external parties at the summits of the AU, and to allow their participation only in exceptional circumstances and only for a specific purpose. This might stem from the perception that the presence of external parties, such as development partner representatives, could detract from the AU's focus and decision-making at summits. The overly broad definition of the term 'external parties' might, however, mainly affect continental or local civil society organizations and prevent them from attending AU summits. The accreditation process for civil society organizations to the AU summits has always been opaque, and accreditations have been difficult to obtain.[150] Hence, the implementation of this recommendation could legalize and entrench this exclusion going forward.[151] This would be problematic as civil society participation in summits helps ensure greater transparency around the meetings, as well as to establish additional linkages between African leaders and their citizens. Civil society also plays a vital role in monitoring the implementation of Court and Commission decisions, for example by submitting shadow reports and presenting the findings.

Third, as already mentioned, the AU's programmatic budget relies mainly on external funding,[152] and the operational budget, which is covered with member states' contributions for the most part, suffers from delays in payment.[153] Therefore, the proposal—which is based on the so-called Kigali Financing Decision developed by Rwandan economist Donald Kaberuka—is to fund the AU through a 0.2 per cent levy on all eligible exports of member states with a penalty mechanism for non-compliance.[154] External funding and external partner engagement remain possible, but should not exceed certain levels in particular categories.[155] While the idea is solid in theory, a number of concerns were raised regarding its practical implementation. There are administrative challenges due to certain products being excluded from the proposed levies and the need to adjust national tax systems. There are also conflicts between the proposal and certain constitutional provisions in many member states.[156] The levy proposal could also raise conflicts with World Trade Organization obligations of AU member states.[157]

[150] The situation deteriorated under the AU Commission leadership of Dr Nkosazana Dlamini-Zuma (October 2012 to January 2017), 'when civil society was prevented from attending mid-year summits'. Turianskyi and Gruzd (n 145) 11.

[151] ibid.

[152] The Kagame Report notes that AU programmes are 97 per cent funded by donors, while member states are failing to pay their dues in full despite having committed to do so. Kagame (n 143) 13.

[153] ibid. By December 2016, only twenty-four of fifty-four (then) member states had paid their full contributions for that financial year. An additional fourteen states had 'paid more than half their contribution and 15 [had] not made any payment'.

[154] ibid 14.

[155] AU member states shall finance 100 per cent of the operating budget, 75 per cent of the programme budget, and 25 per cent of the peace support operations budget: ibid. An AU Summit decision from February 2019 adopted a new scale of assessment for the Financing Decision by 'reducing the dependence on the five or six biggest states from 60% to 45% for programmes and operations'. Turianskyi and Gruzd (n 145) 18.

[156] One example is South Africa, where 'all revenue collected by the state should be deposited into the National Revenue Fund'. ibid 17.

[157] ibid.

Lastly, there are concerns about compliance and transparency in implementing the proposed reform. For example, the AU has historically been reluctant to 'name and shame' states that do not pay their annual fees, with their financial contributions not always being disclosed.[158] Member states do not always prioritize financial support to the AU if this is not directly beneficial for them, with some rather preferring to support, both financially and politically, the REC body to which they belong.[159] This, in turn, might further deepen the gap between continental and regional initiatives, and hamper political support for a harmonized coordination between the two levels.

8.4.2 The African Court of Justice and Human Rights

The ACtJHR will, once the minimum required number of fifteen ratifications has been reached,[160] replace the ACtHPR. The history of the AU's apex court begins in 1998 with the adoption of the Court Protocol that established the ACtHPR, which entered into force in 2004. The Protocol of the Court of Justice of the African Union came in 2003,[161] which created a court to deal with competences of the AU and violations of obligations by member states. Both of these protocols are meant to be replaced by the Protocol on the Statute of the African Court of Justice and Human Rights, which will merge the two courts once it enters into force.[162] This original amendment to the Protocol Establishing the African Court of the AU was to create the ACtJHR with two chambers, one for general (AU) affairs and one for human rights cases.[163] The (potential) jurisdiction of the ACtJHR was further expanded in 2014 by adding a third chamber that would deal with international and transnational criminal law.[164] These changes would be passed with the adoption of the much-debated Protocol on the Amendments to the Protocol on the Statute of the African Court of Justice and Human Rights, commonly referred to as the Malabo Protocol.[165] However, the Malabo Protocol only has fifteen signatures, and only one ratification, out of the fifteen ratifications required for it to come into force.[166]

158 Turianskyi and Gruzd (n 145) 15–16. However, there is evidence of the AU publishing information by member state in terms of the implementation of the levy. Third Specialised Technical Committee on Finance, Monetary Affairs, Economic Planning and Integration, Experts Meeting, 'Status and Progress Report on Financing of the Union: Financing the Union—Towards the financial autonomy of the African Union, Draft Status Report, Version Two', AU Doc ECO/STC/MAEPI(III)/EXP/5, 28 December 2018.

159 ibid. One relevant example is South Africa and SADC.

160 Protocol on the Statute of the ACtJHR (n 16) Art 9(1).

161 Protocol of the Court of Justice of the African Union (adopted 11 July 2003, entered into force 11 February 2009) reprinted in (2005) 13 African Journal of International and Comparative Law 115.

162 Protocol on the Statute of the ACtJHR (n 16). To come into force, it requires fifteen ratifications. As of December 2023 the number of ratifications stands at eight. AU, 'Status List' <https://au.int/sites/default/files/treaties/36396-sl-PROTOCOL%20ON%20THE%20STATUTE%20OF%20THE%20AFRICAN%20COURT%20OF%20JUSTICE%20AND%20HUMAN%20RIGHTS.pdf>.

163 Elias (n 16) 334; Protocol on the Statute of the ACtJHR (n 16) Art 19.

164 Malabo Protocol (n 17) Art 3(1).

165 Jalloh, Clarke, and Nmehielle (n 17).

166 On 31 May 2024, the Republic of Angola became the first AU member state to ratify the Malabo Protocol. For prior status: AU, 'Status List' <https://au.int/sites/default/files/treaties/36398-sl-PROTOCOL%20ON%20AMENDMENTS%20TO%20THE%20PROTOCOL%20ON%20THE%20STATUTE%20OF%20THE%20AFRICAN%20COURT%20OF%20JUSTICE%20AND%20HUMAN%20RIGHTS.pdf>.

Irrespective of the debates on the jurisdiction of the ACtJHR, in terms of the governance of the new Court, the Protocol on the Statute of the ACtJHR adopts a slightly different language on independence than the current Court Protocol. Article 12(3) specifies that '[i]n performance of the judicial functions and duties, the [ACtJHR] and its Judges shall not be subject to the direction or control of any person or body'.[167] Therefore, it addresses not only the independence of the judges, but also that of the institution as a whole. The Malabo Protocol leaves this provision unchanged.[168] However, it makes significant changes to the list of organs of the ACtJHR, as it adds an Office of the Prosecutor and a Defence Office.[169]

The Protocol on the Statute of the ACtJHR (and the Malabo Protocol) also explicitly recognize the complementarity between the ACtJHR and the Commission *and* the ACERWC.[170] However, it replicates the gatekeeping mechanism familiar from the Court's Protocol, which requires member states to submit a 'declaration accepting the competence of the Court to receive cases under Article 30(f)' from individuals and NGOs.[171]

The language on the enforcement of future ACtJHR judgments has been strengthened when compared to the current Court Protocol. Article 46 of the Protocol on the Statute of the ACtJHR elaborates on the binding force and execution of judgments: 'Where a party has failed to comply with a judgment, the Court shall refer the matter to the Assembly, which shall decide upon measures to be taken to give effect to that judgment'.[172] It also allows the Assembly to 'impose sanctions' if judgments are not complied with.[173]

While these proposals might appear appealing to a certain extent on paper, as with the existing system, it remains to be seen how these will take effect in practice. The *injugovins* do not always lend the support they were intended to in the case of the Court and Commission. It would, therefore, be prudent to take these developments with a grain of salt until the practice of the AU, its organs, and its member states demonstrates otherwise.

8.5 Conclusion

There are many considerations that inform the determination of whether the governance of Africa's human rights (quasi-)judicial institutions allows them to have real power, or whether they are simply powerful in theory and tamed in practice—effectively rendering them 'paper lions'.

The ability of the Commission and the Court to decide on human rights matters in the AU, while also having the political and economic support required to fulfil their mandates, remains a difficult issue. On the one hand, there are serious concerns about the way the AU has structured the governance of these (quasi-)judicial human rights institutions.

[167] Protocol on the Statute ACtJHR (n 16) Annex.
[168] Malabo Protocol (n 17) Annex.
[169] ibid Art 2 and Arts 22A–C, Annex.
[170] Protocol on the Statute ACtJHR (n 16) Art 27, Annex (unchanged by Malabo Protocol).
[171] ibid Arts 8 and 30(f), Annex (unchanged by Malabo Protocol).
[172] ibid Art 46(4), Annex (unchanged by Malabo Protocol).
[173] ibid Art 46(5), Annex (unchanged by Malabo Protocol).

The policy and practice of the AU Assembly and AU Commission do not always support the independence and accountability of the Commission and Court. Initiatives such as the AGA, and replacing the DPA with the PAPS, do not necessarily provide for clearer structures or more efficient rules that elucidate how the (quasi-)judicial institutions should work together. In addition, the available mechanisms to ensure the execution and enforcement of judgments and decisions are relatively weak, and there is often a lack of political will to pressure non-compliant states by the AU organs charged with those powers, such as the AU Commission. The precarity of adequate financing and staffing also persists. Recent developments around the Court's jurisdiction have further highlighted the lack of complementarity in practice between the Court and Commission. Combined with the voluntary jurisdiction of the Court, this poses a threat to the overall functioning of the AU human rights system. In particular, it endangers the ability of the Court to hear cases brought directly to it by individuals and NGOs in a timely manner in the future.

On the other hand, there are attempts to change the status quo. The creation of the AGA was an attempt at effecting the necessary changes, although new challenges and inconsistencies also arose as a result. Replacing the DPA with the PAPS ushers in a new era, despite the potential of this reform remaining unclear. The proposed Kagame reforms take on a number of challenges related to the governance of the AU's (quasi-)judicial institutions, yet fail to deal with the known bottlenecks. Some areas will be strengthened in theory, such as the enforcement of judgments, due to the shift to the ACtJHR and the changes in its protocols. However, others are unchanged, such as voluntary jurisdiction for direct access to the future ACtJHR for individuals and NGOs. It is uncertain whether these reforms are being implemented, and if so, how they will operate in practice.

As the AU continues to refine its approach to governing its human rights (quasi-)judicial institutions, it will be important to observe how much power the Court and Commission will be given to ensure that human rights are respected and protected on the continent. In some respects, the Court and Commission were in fact designed to be hamstrung in certain areas. Therefore, claiming they are 'paper lions' would be something of a misnomer as they were never intended to be powerful in the first place. In other respects, the actual operation of the (quasi-)judicial institutions, and how they interact with each other, is indicative that it is not only the AU governance framework that limits their powers, but the lack of cooperation on the part of the institutions themselves has also impeded their envisioned complementarity and effectiveness.

The AU human rights system has been around for more than thirty years, and yet it still has teething problems. As with the Kagame reforms, the main bottleneck for the implementation is the self-interest of member states. With regional heavyweights refraining from subjecting themselves to the Court's jurisdiction, and the AU Commission being viewed as a vehicle to carry out the decisions and wishes of member states, rather than being an independent actor, the future is not particularly bright. Nonetheless, the member states of the AU did adopt the Banjul Charter, and all the subsequent treaties and protocols over the years, which established a broad infrastructure to protect human rights in the AU. Only time will tell whether the organizational culture of the AU will change to ensure that these institutions not only exist but that the AU bodies as their *injugovins* can also properly support their mandates and ensure that they are effective, both on paper and in practice.

9
Governance of the Court of Justice of the European Union

Heikki Kanninen[*]

9.1 The Court of Justice of the European Union: More Than an International Court

Since the early days of European integration, the Court of Justice of the European Union (CJEU) has highlighted the special nature of European Union (EU) law in respect of both its member states' legal orders and international law. The crux is that national and international law do not determine the nature of EU law. As the CJEU held in the landmark judgment of *Costa* v *ENEL*, Community law (now EU law) constitutes 'the law stemming from the [EEC] treaty, an independent source of law'.[1] The place of EU law in national legal systems, the CJEU concluded in the equally memorable *Van Gend* & *Loos* judgment, is not for each member state to determine. It is a matter of EU law.[2] This independence is often described as the autonomy of EU legal order.[3] To be sure, the EU is a product of international treaties concluded between sovereign states—currently the Treaty on European Union (TEU), the Treaty on the Functioning of the European Union (TFEU), and the Euratom Treaty. But these treaties and the amendments thereto, as interpreted by the CJEU, not only make up the core of EU primary law but have also established a new and special legal order.

The special features of EU law are not limited to the particular status of the EU legal order vis-à-vis national legal orders and public international law. The EU as an organization of its members states differs in many additional respects from other intergovernmental organizations. The EU, as embodied in its institutions, possesses its own legislature and executive branch, as well as an independent judiciary. The Union also has its own budget. EU institutions have the power to adopt acts that are binding on member states and individuals. These acts are of a legislative, regulatory, or individual nature. This rather complex and sophisticated constitutional framework, where the EU is at the same time autonomous from, and interlinked with, the member states, has required the establishment of innovative judicial and non-judicial control systems in which the CJEU plays a key role.

[*] All views expressed are personal. I am grateful to Sven Frisch, former *référendaire* at the General Court of the European Union, for his valuable comments on a previous draft.

[1] Case C-6/64 *Costa v ENEL* [1964] ECR 01141, ECLI:EU:C:1964:66, 594.

[2] Case C-26/62 *Van Gend en Loos/Administratie der Belastingen* [1963] ECR 00003, ECLI:EU:C:1962:42, 10–12.

[3] In the case law, see, eg, Case C-791/19 *Commission v Poland (Régime disciplinaire des juges)* [2021] ECLI:EU:C:2021:596, para 165.

Heikki Kanninen, *Governance of the Court of Justice of the European Union* In: *Governance of International Courts and Tribunals*. Edited by: Sergey Vasiliev and Niels Blokker, Oxford University Press. © Heikki Kanninen 2026.
DOI: 10.1093/oso/9780198922131.003.0009

The CJEU has jurisdiction over actions against acts by EU institutions and bodies, infringement proceedings against member states and preliminary references from national courts. In the first category of actions, which can be initiated by members states, EU institutions, and natural or legal persons, the CJEU is a kind of administrative or constitutional court.[4] Its role is to ensure that EU institutions and bodies comply with EU law. Infringement proceedings, on the other hand, resemble litigation between states before international courts.[5] But they differ from traditional inter-state litigation in one key respect: they do not generally involve two member states that oppose one another, but a member state and the Commission, which initiates the proceedings. By contrast, actions initiated by a member state against another member state are very rare,[6] highlighting a strong reliance on the supranational control mechanism.

The preliminary reference procedure, where a national court may and under some circumstances is legally obligated to request a ruling from the CJEU, is a sophisticated complement to the infringement procedure and the cornerstone of the framework designed to ensure the consistent national application of EU law.[7] It has helped secure the primary role of the national courts in this framework while conferring on the CJEU the ultimate power to decide on the interpretation and validity of EU law. As EU law is integrated in the national legal orders (without fully blending with them), national authorities and courts apply, implement, and enforce it. National courts exercise their general jurisdiction under EU law ('*juge de droit commun du droit de l'Union*'). As such, it is primarily up to the national legal system to provide legal remedies to ensure compliance with EU law and secure effective legal protection in the member states. Conversely, the role of the CJEU in that respect is that of a specialized EU law court. That role is secondary but ultimately decisive in that the mechanism of preliminary rulings and the infringement procedure give it the final say as to the validity[8] and interpretation[9] of EU law.

The respective roles of the CJEU and of national courts appear clearly from Article 19(1) of the TEU, which provides that '[the CJEU] shall ensure that in the interpretation and application of the Treaties the law is observed' and that 'Member States shall provide remedies sufficient to ensure effective legal protection in the fields covered by Union law'. Article 47 of the Charter of Fundamental Rights of the European Union also codifies the right to an effective remedy and to a fair trial on the EU and national level in matters of EU law.

The CJEU accordingly does not fit easily into the neat categories of traditional legal analysis and has multiple facets. It is not a national court, although it contributes substantially to proceedings before national courts through the preliminary reference procedure. Yet it is not a traditional international court either. As EU law is distinct

[4] Treaty on the Functioning of the European Union (consolidated version) OJ L 326/47–326/390 (TFEU) Art 263.

[5] ibid Arts 258–60.

[6] For a recent example, see Case C-557/18 *Slovenia/Croatia* [2020] ECLI:EU:C:2020:65.

[7] TFEU (n 4) Art 267. A reform of the preliminary reference procedure in 2024 transferred jurisdiction over preliminary reference cases in selected areas from the Court of Justice to the General Court.

[8] Case 314/85 *Foto-Frost* [1987] EU:C:1987:452, paras 17–18.

[9] Opinion of Advocate General Hogan in Case C-497/20 *Randstad Italia* [2021] ECLI:EU:C:2021:725, para 92.

from public international law and shares many of the features of national legal orders,[10] it is more proper to define the CJEU as the domestic court of the EU.[11] That does not mean that one could ignore the many features of the CJEU that are similar to those of international courts.[12] It is therefore appropriate and useful to include the CJEU in a study on the governance of international courts.

That said, it bears emphasizing that the CJEU is not technically speaking a court of justice either. It is a court system or court organization that makes up the judiciary of the EU. Article 19(1) of the TEU provides that the CJEU includes the Court of Justice, the General Court, and specialized courts.

The minimum number of courts within the CJEU is set at two (the Court of Justice and the General Court), while the establishment of specialized courts depends on a decision by the European Parliament and the Council acting in accordance with the ordinary legislative procedure.[13] To date, only one specialized court has ever been established, namely the Civil Service Tribunal in 2005. However, this Tribunal was short-lived, since it was dissolved just eleven years later, in 2016. That happened despite that Tribunal's success in carrying out its judicial activities, as a collateral consequence of the 2016–19 reform of the General Court, which doubled the number of judges at the General Court. It is very rare that an international treaty creates not only one court of justice but two or more of them.[14] This shows, once again, the specificities of the EU judicial system.

On the one hand, the judicial relations between the two existing EU courts resemble those between courts in the member states that constitute different levels of the national court system. With the exception of preliminary reference cases, the decisions of the General Court may be appealed to the Court of Justice. Appeals to the Court of Justice are limited to points of law. An initial admission mechanism (leave to appeal) applies to appeals where the dispute has already been examined by an appeal body before the General Court.[15] In such cases, the examination of an appeal is subject to the Court of Justice's authorization. On the other hand, the administrative relations between the Court of Justice and the General Court are particular and worth examining in the context of the present study of the governance of the CJEU.

[10] Allan Rosas and Lorna Armati, *EU Constitutional Law: An Introduction* (3rd edn, Hart Publishing 2018) 14–17.

[11] The establishment of the European Free Trade Association (EFTA) Court by the European Economic Area (EEA) Agreement was modelled on the CJEU and they are often referred to as 'sister courts'. However, the nature of the EFTA Court is not completely identical to that of the CJEU due to differences in their jurisdiction and in the characteristics of EU law and EEA law.

[12] On the definition of international courts and tribunals, see, eg, Tobias Lock, *The European Court of Justice and International Courts* (OUP 2015) 5–7 and 74–77.

[13] TFEU (n 4) Art 257.

[14] One example is the internal justice system in the United Nations for staff cases where the UN Appeals Tribunal reviews appeals, notably against judgments rendered by the UN Dispute Tribunal.

[15] Decisions taken in trademark matters by the European Union Intellectual Property Office and also cases in which a decision has been taken by other EU bodies and agencies such as the European Chemicals Agency are subject to the admission mechanism. In such cases, the action before the General Court is brought against a decision of an independent board of appeal of the offices and agencies that has already examined the legality of the original decision. The admission mechanism also applies to disputes relating to the performance of contracts containing an arbitration clause, within the meaning of Art 272 TFEU (see Statute of the Court of Justice of the European Union (TFEU Protocol No 3) OJ L, 2024/2019, 12.8.2024 ('CJEU Statute') Art 58a).

9.2 The CJEU in the EU Institutional Framework

The CJEU is one of seven institutions that make up the EU's institutional framework.[16] Under Article 13(2) of the TEU, 'each institution shall act within the limits of the powers conferred on it in the Treaties, and in conformity with the procedures, conditions and objectives set out in them'. According to the case law, 'that provision reflects the principle of institutional balance, characteristic of the institutional structure of the EU, a principle which requires that each of the institutions must exercise its powers with due regard for the powers of the other institutions'.[17] From a separation-of-power perspective, that principle enshrines the CJEU's independence and judicial monopoly at the EU level.

The CJEU's judicial independence is all the stronger because the EU legal system lacks a ministry of justice or an independent authority (judicial council) in charge of managing the courts. That said, the purpose of the CJEU's independence is to protect judicial action from external influence, not to exclude any relationship with other institutions or public actors. In carrying out its non-judicial activities, the CJEU has to operate within the institutional framework defined in the TEU and TFEU. Since the other institutions as well as the member states can be parties to the judicial proceedings before the CJEU, the nature and intensity of the relations between the CJEU and these institutional stakeholders play a crucial role in defining the parameters of the independence and the (financial) governance of the CJEU. These issues are examined in Sections 9.4 and 9.5. Sections 9.6 and 9.7 focus on the internal governance of the CJEU, including the relationship between the two EU Courts. Case allocation in collegial courts is a complex question which concerns both court administration and judicial procedure. The rules and practices in the two EU Courts are discussed in Section 9.8. Finally, the Court of Justice's case law regarding the independence and impartiality of courts is presented in Section 9.9. Before considering these issues, it is useful to outline the way in which the CJEU participates in the establishment of the provisions governing it (Section 9.3).

9.3 Establishing the Rules Governing the EU Courts

A court of justice is not a legislature. But that does not exclude its participation in the preparation and even in the adoption of the rules governing its functioning. This is closely linked to the question of the extent to which a court should have the power to organize its own internal operations. If the legislative or executive branches subject a court's internal organization to very detailed and rigid rules and thereby restrict its ability to govern itself, questions may arise as to that court's independence. On the other hand, it follows from the separation of powers that at least the main organizational and procedural rules are to be enacted by the legislative branch.

[16] The other six are the European Parliament, the European Council, the Council, the European Commission, the European Central Bank, and the Court of Auditors.

[17] See Case C-409/13 *Council v Commission* [2015] ECLI:EU:C:2015:217, para 64 and case law cited therein.

These considerations mainly apply to nation states that have a classic constitutional structure consisting of three separate branches. They may not so readily apply to international organizations, which are not always structured in the same way. In any case, a close involvement of other entities, especially of the states, in the internal organization of an international court would weaken that court's judicial independence.

However, the EU constitutional system has features that make it easier to compare to nation states than traditional intergovernmental organizations. Notably, these features include, in addition to the jurisdiction of the CJEU, the power to legislate (the European Parliament and the Council) and a strong executive (the Commission and the Council). Even if the respective functions of these institutions do not completely follow the classic principle of separation of powers, that principle is relevant in the EU context as already explained in the previous section.

The general judicial and organizational rules of the CJEU are laid down in the Treaties (in particular, the TFEU), the Statute of the Court of Justice of the European Union, and the two EU courts' respective Rules of Procedure. The Treaties contain all the essential provisions relating to the foundations of the judicial system. Their amendment requires the unanimous approval of the twenty-seven member states. This is beneficial in that it helps secure the system's stability. But it can turn out to be inconvenient as it makes it more difficult to enact necessary reforms.

The establishment and removal of specialized courts does not require amending the Treaties. An act of the European Parliament and of the Council in accordance with the ordinary legislative procedure suffices.[18] This means that the continuity of the functioning of a specialized court is not as secure as that of the Court of Justice and of the General Court. The unexpected and sudden dissolution of the Civil Service Tribunal in 2016 is a clear illustration of that vulnerability, especially as there was no prior analysis of its impacts on the adjudication of staff matters. As noted above, the abolition of the Civil Service Tribunal was a collateral consequence of the decision to double the number of the judges of the General Court.[19] The difficulties faced in appointing judges to the Civil Service Tribunal was also a contributing factor.

The Statute of the CJEU, which is a protocol to the TFEU, can be amended more easily than the Treaties, namely by an act of the European Parliament and of the Council, in accordance with the ordinary legislative procedure.[20] Such an act may be taken at the request of the Court of Justice and after consulting the Commission or on a proposal from the Commission and after consulting the Court of Justice.[21] However, this easier method of revision does not concern chapter 1 of the Statute of the CJEU, which governs the status of judges and advocates general, and Article 64 which concerns the rules governing the language arrangements at the CJEU.[22] The Statute's

[18] The ordinary legislative procedure is specified in TFEU (n 4) Art 294.

[19] Heikki Kanninen, 'The Future of the General Court within the Court of Justice of the European Union' in Koen Lenaerts and others (eds), *An Ever-Changing Union? Perspectives on the Future of EU Law in Honour of Allan Rosas* (Hart 2019) 127.

[20] Second sentence of TFEU (n 4) Art 281.

[21] In practice, it is the CJEU that has so far taken the initiative.

[22] The modification of the CJEU Statute (n 15) ch 1 and Art 64 requires the same procedure as the amendment of the TFEU.

remaining provisions essentially lay down the CJEU's basic internal organization and essential procedural provisions.

Article 19(2) of the TEU links the number of judges of the Court of Justice to the number of member states, which means that the Court of Justice consists of one judge per member state.[23] By contrast, the Treaties do not specify exactly how many Advocates General assist the Court of Justice. According to Article 252 of the TFEU, eight Advocates General do so. But, at the request of the Court of Justice, that number may be increased by a unanimous decision of the Council.[24]

Similarly, the Treaties only set the minimum number of judges of the General Court. Under Article 19(2) of the TEU, the General Court has at least one judge per member state. Article 254 of the TFEU provides that the number of judges shall be determined by the Statute of the CJEU. Article 48 of the Statute of the CJEU further specifies that the General Court shall consist of two judges per member state. That provision is among those that are subject to amendment according to the ordinary legislative procedure. There is accordingly no ceiling on the number of judges that may be added to the General Court, even without the unanimous agreement of the member states. This could risk leaving the door open to influencing the proper functioning of the General Court by expanding its composition.

The Rules of Procedure of the two EU courts contain the detailed provisions necessary for applying and, where required, supplementing the Statute of the CJEU.[25] Those provisions touch upon matters of internal organization and judicial procedure. In the legal orders of many member states, they would fall within the scope of statutory law. It is therefore not surprising that Articles 253 and 254 of the TFEU only empower the EU Courts to establish their own rules of procedure subject to the Council's approval. The Rules of Procedure of the General Court also requires the agreement of the Court of Justice. Conversely, neither of the two EU courts' Rules of Procedure can be modified without the respective court's consent.[26]

The CJEU's strong influence over its organizational and procedural rules is key to securing its independence. At the same time, this points to the unusual degree of self-regulation and active legislative and regulatory roles of the CJEU in an institutional environment where there is no organ equivalent to a ministry of justice or a judicial council.[27]

[23] The number of judges of the Court of Justice has constantly increased following the addition of new members to the EU until Brexit brought about the first decrease.

[24] TFEU (n 4) Art 252 does not mention the possibility of decreasing the number of the Advocates General back to the minimum of eight. Brexit caused the (somewhat delayed) departure of the Advocate General designated from the United Kingdom. This departure did not happen without some legal turbulence: see, eg, Case C-684/20 P *Sharpston v Council and Conférence des Représentants des Gouvernements des États membres* [2021] ECLI:EU:C:2021:486. The total number of Advocates General has remained the same even after Brexit (eleven).

[25] CJEU Statute (n 15) Art 63.

[26] A modification of the Rules of Procedure may of course become necessary in order to comply with an amendment of EU Treaties or the CJEU Statute.

[27] The lack of an external judicial council can be seen as strengthening the autonomy of the CJEU. On the other hand, the creation of such a body could contribute to defending the independence of the EU courts, eg against improper interference by external actors. It could also have a balancing role in some areas of the common administration of the EU courts.

9.4 The Independence of the Members of the CJEU

The rules governing the appointment, removal, and disciplining of judges rank among the key elements that determine the level of independence of a judiciary.[28] While removals and discipline are typically handled by the courts themselves or by other independent bodies, appointments can hardly be completely internal to the judiciary.

9.4.1 Appointment of CJEU members

The appointment of members to the Court of Justice or to the General Court and the possible renewal of their six-year term are in the hands of the member states. Article 19(2) of the TEU and Articles 253 and 254 of the TFEU provide that the members of the two EU courts are to be appointed by common accord of the governments of the member states. In practice, each government of the member states proposes the candidate for the position to be filled by a person from that member state. EU law does not establish specific rules for how governments make the national selection. It depends on national law or practice and varies significantly between member states.[29]

However, the Treaties lay down some requirements for prospective appointees. According to Article 19(2) of the TEU, the members of the CJEU are chosen amongst persons whose independence is beyond doubt and who satisfy the conditions set out in Articles 253 and 254 of the TFEU. Under those provisions, appointees to the Court of Justice must possess the ability required for appointment to the highest judicial offices or be jurisconsults of recognized competence. Appointees to the General Court must possess the qualifications required for appointment to high judicial office. The Treaty of Lisbon has strengthened the monitoring of compliance with these conditions by setting up the panel provided for in Article 255 of the TFEU, which gives 'an opinion on candidates' suitability to perform the duties' of members of the Court of Justice and the General Court.[30] This panel's members are appointed by the Council.[31]

The establishment of the Article 255 panel has proved to be a major improvement in the appointment procedure. It has already on several occasions issued negative opinions on a candidate proposed by a government.[32] The member states have always followed those opinions, even where the appointing member state governments may

[28] eg European Commission for Democracy through Law (Venice Commission) 'Compilation of Venice Commission Opinions and Reports Concerning Courts and Judges' (Strasbourg, 11 December 2019) CDL-PI(2019)008.

[29] For a critical perspective on such arrangements in the context of regional integration courts in Africa, see John Eudes Ruhangisa, 'Governance of Regional Integration Courts', in this volume. See also Case C-119/23, *Valančius* [2024] ECLI:EU:C:2024:653.

[30] An opinion of the panel is also required for candidates for renewal of a term of office.

[31] On the '255 Panel': Christiaan Timmermans, 'The Procedure for Nominating Members of the EU Courts', in this volume.

[32] Between its inception in 2010 and the year 2022, the panel has issued negative opinions in around 11 per cent of all cases and in about 21 per cent of cases involving candidates for a first term of office; see Panel provided for by Article 255 of the Treaty on the Functioning of the European Union ('255 Panel'), 'Seventh Activity Report of the panel provided for by Article 255 of the Treaty on the Functioning of the European Union' (October 2022) <https://curia.europa.eu/jcms/upload/docs/application/pdf/2022-07/2022.2597-qcar22002enn_002.pdf>.

not have welcomed them. No government has really tried to block the appointments of other governments in retaliation to an unfavourable opinion concerning its own candidate.

Still, the current system is imperfect. A government can show its dissatisfaction by refusing to propose a candidate or by dragging its feet, though delays are sometimes due to internal difficulties relating to deciding on a suitable candidate. Such situations are detrimental to the proper functioning of the EU Courts and highlight the vulnerability of the current system. Ultimately, a refusal to propose candidates could paralyze the proper functioning of the CJEU.

It is remarkable that the drafters of the Statute of the CJEU anticipated the problems resulting from delays in the appointment of a new member. Article 5 of the Statute of the CJEU provides that a 'judge shall continue to hold office until his successor takes up his duties'. However, this provision has not always been applied strictly since 2011. This new practice has on several occasions brought about a situation where the composition of the Court of Justice or of the General Court was incomplete. In fact, the combination of the large number of judges, their relatively short (though renewable) term of office, and the difficulties encountered at member state level to appoint them in due time has caused the General Court to not be fully staffed between 2016 and 2026.

The provision of Article 5 of the Statute of the CJEU has, however, not lost its relevance, especially when a member state has failed to propose a candidate in due time. In this case, the member in office has been able to continue to sit on the EU Courts, sometimes for several years.

Many of the problems related to the appointment of members of the CJEU could be avoided or mitigated if the term of the members were longer than six years. In the current system, in both EU courts, the term of half of the members expires at the same time every three years. This short three-year cycle complicates the proper administration of justice, especially the planning of the handling of the cases. In fact, there is only one 'normal' year every three years. After each partial renewal, the first year requires expending resources on integrating the new members. In the last year of the three-year cycle, the planning of the cases has to take into account the situation of the departing members (including the potential departure of the members whose eventual reappointment has not yet been confirmed).

The stability of the composition of the two EU Courts is largely in the hands of the governments of the member states. It appears that the need to ensure that stability is generally taken into account when considering the reappointment of the judges and advocates general.

9.4.2 Disciplinary regime of CJEU members

The members of the EU courts cannot be removed, save in exceptional circumstances and only by a decision of the Court of Justice. The security of tenure of the members is enshrined in Article 6 of the CJEU Statute, which states that a member may be deprived of his office only if he no longer fulfils the requisite conditions or meet the obligations arising from his office. The decision to deprive a member of his office requires the unanimous opinion of the judges and advocates general of the Court of Justice other than the member in question, who does not take part in the deliberation.

Unlike many national judges, the members of the CJEU are not subject to an external body's disciplinary or ethics control, at least with regard to their judicial functions. However, the CJEU and its members are not completely excluded from the administrative and financial control exercised by: (i) the Court of Auditors; (ii) the European Parliament in the context of the observations presented during the budgetary discharge (Article 319 of the TFEU); and (iii) the European Anti-Fraud Office (OLAF).[33] In addition, the European Ombudsman is empowered to conduct inquiries and receive complaints concerning maladministration in the activities of the Union institutions. However, Article 228 of the TFEU excludes the CJEU from the competence of the European Ombudsman insofar as the CJEU is acting in its judicial role.

The only disciplinary measures that may be imposed on members of the CJEU are listed in Article 6 of the CJEU Statute. These are the removal from office or the deprivation of their rights to a pension or other benefits. But the CJEU has taken the disciplinary control of its members into its own hands. The establishment of a code of conduct for members and former members of the CJEU in 2007, replaced by a new code first in 2017 and later in 2021,[34] was a major step forward in terms of safeguarding the standards of judicial ethics. The President of the Court of Justice is entrusted with ensuring the proper application of the Code and is assisted in carrying out that task by a three-member Consultative Committee that may in individual cases make its opinion known to the (former) member concerned.[35] If a member or a former member of the General Court is concerned, three members of that Court take part in the deliberation of the Committee.

9.5 The Financing of the CJEU

Justice is a public service the funding of which cannot depend on fees paid by the parties to proceedings. Public financing is an important element that guarantees free access to independent and impartial justice. This requires that the financing be sufficient and stable over time. The rules and practices governing the financing of courts also have an impact on their independence. Attention can notably be paid to the question of which authorities participate in this procedure and what weight the courts have in this context.[36]

[33] The Commission Decision 1999/352/EC, ECSC, Euratom of 28 April 1999 establishing the European Anti-fraud Office (OLAF) [1999] OJ L136/20.

[34] Code of Conduct for Members and former Members of the Court of Justice of the European [2021] OJ C397/1.

[35] The opinion is not, in a strict sense, disciplinary in nature. The Consultative Committee is common to the two EU courts but the General Court has also its own Ethics Committee, the main task of which is to advise the Court's members on deontological issues.

[36] On financial governance of international courts: Adriana-Maria Manolescu, 'Financial Governance of International Courts and Tribunals', in this volume.

The CJEU's functioning is funded through the EU's annual budget. The handling of a case is free of charge for the parties, which means that the CJEU does not get any revenue from its activities. The CJEU does not have any special status in the EU's budget or in the budgetary procedure. The CJEU's budget is part of the general budget, like the budget of other EU institutions.

All items of revenue and expenditure of the EU are included in estimates to be drawn up for each financial year and shown in the budget.[37] Article 311 of the TFEU states that the EU provides itself with the means necessary to attain its objectives and carry through its policies. This means that there is a legal obligation to give the CJEU the necessary resources to carry out its tasks. This obligation leaves some room for interpretation as to which of the CJEU's expenditures should be accepted in the budget.

The European Parliament and the Council together constitute the budgetary authority. They have joint powers over all budget expenditure. The Commission's role is to prepare the budget. Each year, before 1 July, the CJEU draws up estimates of its expenditure for the following financial year (which corresponds to the calendar year). These estimates are communicated to the Commission, which consolidates the different institutions' estimates in a draft budget. The Commission's numbers may differ from those put forward by the various institutions. The Commission forwards the draft budget to the Council and Parliament by 1 September at the latest.[38] The Commission may modify the draft budget at a later stage to take account of new developments. The Council then adopts its position on the draft budget and forwards it to the European Parliament by 1 October at the latest.[39] The Council must inform the European Parliament in full of the reasons that have led it to adopt that position. The European Parliament may then either approve the Council's position or decline to take a decision, in which case the budget is deemed finally adopted. The European Parliament can also adopt amendments by a majority vote, in which case the amended draft is forwarded back to the Council and to the Commission. A conciliation procedure is then initiated whereby the representatives of the Council and the Parliament have the task of reaching an agreement on a joint text. If the Conciliation Committee agrees on a joint text and the European Parliament and the Council approve it or fail to take a decision, the draft budget is approved. If there is no agreement within the Conciliation Committee, or if either branch of the budgetary authority rejects the joint text, the Commission shall submit a new draft budget. At every stage of the budgetary procedure, the representatives of the CJEU have the opportunity to be heard before the Commission, the Council, and the Parliament. This is particularly important if the CJEU's estimates are not fully accepted.

The annual budget is drafted and adopted taking into account the multiannual financial framework, the object of which is to ensure that the EU's expenditure develops in an orderly manner and within the limits of its own resources.[40] This financial framework is adopted by the Council with the consent of the European Parliament. It is established for a period of at least five years and currently covers seven years.

[37] TFEU (n 4) Art 310(1).
[38] ibid Art 314(2).
[39] ibid Art 314(3).
[40] The CJEU's annual budget for 2025 was 542 million euros.

The implementation of the EU budget by the CJEU (and other institutions) is subject to different external controls. One of them is the discharge procedure. The discharge is a European Parliament decision that reflects its conclusions on the way the CJEU has carried out its task of implementing the EU budget. When taking its decision on the discharge, the European Parliament also adopts a resolution, which contains its comments in respect of the implementation of the budget. These comments may require changes to the procedures and practices, or call for improvements in the functioning of the CJEU. The European Parliament has shown particular interest in the ethics and integrity of the members of the CJEU. In this context, it has raised questions related, for example, to the financial interests and the external activities of the members, the use of official cars and drivers, and post-term employment. It has also called for greater transparency and for the publication of some information on the CJEU's members.[41] As to the CJEU's judicial activities, the Parliament's observations have remained of a very general nature.[42]

The Court of Auditors, which carries out the EU's audit, has an important role in the discharge procedure.[43] It assists the European Parliament and the Council in the context of their powers of control over the implementation of the budget. The Court of Auditors carries out audits, draws up an annual report, may submit observations in the form of special reports on specific questions, and may deliver opinions at the request of an institution. The Court of Auditors issued a special report No 14/2017 on the Examination of performance in the management of cases at the Court of Justice of the European Union, published in September 2017.[44]

As mentioned, the external control carried out by the European Parliament and the Court of Auditors exceeds strict financial aspects and covers questions related to management even in court cases and deontological issues as well. On the other hand, this control and the propositions expressed in this context can in no way affect the individual decision-making or how the two EU Courts arrange their internal judicial organization and procedure in the limits fixed in the legal norms.

Finally, in the context of monitoring the 2016-2019 reform of the EU's judicial structure, consisting notably in the doubling the number of General Court judges and the dissolution of the Civil Service Tribunal, the European Parliament and the Council required that a report be drawn up by the end of 2020 on the functioning of the General Court. In particular, that report had to focus on the efficiency of the General Court, the necessity and effectiveness of the increase in the number of judges, the use and effectiveness of resources, and the further establishment of specialized

[41] eg European Parliament resolution of 29 April 2021 with observations forming an integral part of the decision on discharge in respect of the implementation of the general budget of the European Union for the financial year 2019, Section IV—Court of Justice of the European Union (2020/2143(DEC)), points 17–28. See also CJEU 'Annual Activity Report for the Financial Year 2020 (Annual Management Report)' (Luxembourg, 2021) 51–53.

[42] eg the resolution mentioned in the previous footnote, points 50–57.

[43] TFEU (n 4) Art 319.

[44] Court of Auditors (EU), 'Special Report No 14/2017: Performance Review of Case Management at the Court of Justice of the European Union' (26 September 2017) <www.eca.europa.eu/en/Pages/DocItem.aspx?did=42128>.

chambers and/or other structural changes. The task of preparing this report was given to the Court of Justice, which had to use an external consultant. The external advisers used by the Court of Justice were two judges from national supreme courts. The report is thus a product of the judiciary itself.[45] Later, the Council adopted its conclusions on that report.[46]

9.6 The CJEU's Administrative Organization

It is important to distinguish the CJEU's judicial organization from its administrative organization. The former is closely linked to the judicial procedure. Administrative activities relate to questions such as human resources and personnel administration, budget and financial affairs, buildings and security, information technology, communications, and library services. These services all support the CJEU's judicial activities. Like other courts, the CJEU has special staff to handle such administrative matters. However, since these matters may indirectly affect judicial activities, it is important that the CJEU's members participate to some extent in the decision-making process in that area.[47] To that effect, the plenary or another collegial organ of the CJEU usually takes the most important administrative decisions. In addition, the President of the CJEU is the head of the CJEU's administration.

The autonomy of a court in administrative matters may be limited by the powers of a ministry of justice and, especially, by an independent organ for court administration. This does not apply to the CJEU, which enjoys particularly broad autonomy in administrative matters. In many other respects as well, the CJEU has special features that make the comparison with national courts or even international courts difficult. First, the CJEU's administration is very large: it comprises about 2,250 people. Second, even if the CJEU has only one working language (French), a total of twenty-four languages can be used in judicial proceedings. This explains why nearly 1,000 people work for the CJEU's language services (translation and interpretation). Third, as is detailed in Section 9.7, the CJEU's administration is shaped by the existence of two (or possibly more) courts within one and the same institution. On the one hand, part of the CJEU administration is shared between the two EU Courts. On the other hand, each of these two courts has its own administration.

[45] CJEU, 'Report Provided for under Article 3(1) of Regulation 2015/2422' (21 December 2020) <https://curia.europa.eu/jcms/upload/docs/application/pdf/2020-12/tra-doc-en-div-t-0000-2020-202009736-05_02.pdf>.

[46] Council conclusions on the report of the Court of Justice on the functioning of the General Court of the European Union (adopted on 22 June 2021), Annex, Outcome of Proceedings (10790/21, Brussels, 13 July 2021) <https://data.consilium.europa.eu/doc/document/ST-10790-2021-INIT/en/pdf>.

[47] CoE, Committee of Ministers, 'Judges: Independence, Efficiency and Responsibilities', Recommendation CM/Rec(2010)12 and explanatory memorandum (adopted 17 November 2010) para 41: 'Judges should be encouraged to be involved in courts' administration.'

9.7 One Institution—Two (or More) Courts: Multilevel Administration

Initially, when the European Communities were created, there was only one court within the Community legal order. At the time, one could not yet speak of a court system. The establishment of the General Court in 1989 (originally named the Court of First Instance of the European Communities) brought about a major change in that respect. The administrative relationship between the courts of the CJEU has evolved as the EU judicial system underwent reforms.

In the first years, the Court of First Instance of the European Communities was 'attached' to the Court of Justice. This meant that the Court of First Instance was organizationally and administratively dependent on the Court of Justice. The Treaty of Nice in 2003 ended this formal 'attachment' to the Court of Justice. However, that did not bring about a full separation from the Court of Justice since both EU courts remained part of one and the same institution.[48]

The 'cohabitation' between the Court of Justice and the General Court is governed in particular by Article 52 of the Statute of the CJEU. The use of common resources requires intelligent cooperation and coordination. It is indeed inevitable that the interests or priorities of the two courts may diverge on some issues. That can sometimes give rise to complicated trade-offs.

Article 52 of the CJEU Statute provides that the presidents of the two courts determine, by common accord, the conditions under which officials and other servants render services to the General Court.[49] Certain officials, concretely the staff working in the cabinets of the judges of the General Court or in the registry of the General Court, are placed under the authority of the General Court. However, this mechanism must be seen in a broader context. To a large extent, administrative, budgetary, legislative, regulatory, and disciplinary matters belong to the General Meeting of the Court of Justice which comprises all members of the Court of Justice. On the other hand, the General Meeting has delegated part of its competence to an Administrative Committee, composed of members of the two courts.[50] In the management of common resources, the President and the Registrar of the Court of Justice also have important powers.

In recent developments on the governance of the CJEU, the General Court has been increasingly involved in the process of preparing and making administrative decisions that affect the entire institution. This takes place not only within the Administrative Committee, but also within other joint committees or in the framework of the cooperation between the respective committees of the two courts.

[48] The Civil Service Tribunal, during its lifetime 2005–16, was similarly 'attached' to the General Court. If a new specialized tribunal were to be created, it would be attached to the General Court as well. In this respect, the TFEU formally distinguishes the relationship between the Court of Justice and the General Court from the relationship between the General Court and a specialized tribunal.

[49] CJEU Statute (n 15) Annex I Art 46 contained provisions similar to CJEU Statute Art 52. That article stated that the Civil Service Tribunal 'shall be supported by the departments of the Court of Justice and of the General Court'.

[50] The Administrative Committee is composed of eight members of the Court of Justice and four members of the General Court. The Registrars of both EU Courts take part in its meetings.

The expansion of the General Court as a result of the doubling of the number of its judges increased the number of administrative and organizational issues that require resolution. The General Court therefore has a heavier workload and more weight than before within the CJEU. The proper functioning of a court also depends on its administrative management. The 'cohabitation' of two EU Courts within the same institution, through the sharing of resources, certainly brings positive synergies. However, the adaptation of the current administrative structure to the changing legal architecture has been slow and may need further reassessment.

The result of this 'cohabitation' is that the administrative organization of the CJEU, the Court of Justice and the General Court consists of: (i) the common administrative services; (ii) joint organs (Administrative Committee and some other joint bodies); (iii) organs of the Court of Justice (General Meeting, President, Vice-President, Registrar, and committees), whose tasks extend to matters concerning the whole institution; and, finally, (iv) the General Court's own administrative organs (Plenary, Administrative Council, President, Vice-president, Registrar, and committees).

The General Court's autonomy in administrative matters covers mainly decision-making in staff matters concerning the judges' collaborators (legal secretaries and assistants) and the Registry. In budgetary matters, the General Court submits its own proposal on its legal staff and Registry to the Administrative Committee, which examines the proposal together with the proposal of the whole institution. The proposal is then adopted by the General Meeting of the Court of Justice and sent to the Commission.

9.8 Case Allocation—Between Court Administration and Judicial Procedure

The efficiency of a collegial court depends heavily on how cases are assigned to judges. This includes the choice of the judge-rapporteur; that is, the judge with whom the main responsibility for preparing the case lies. But case allocation is not only a question of the proper use of human resources in an organization. It is also closely related to the independence of judges. This consideration speaks for objectivity and stability in case allocation, whereas efficiency may plead for greater flexibility. It is therefore not surprising that there are many international documents that address this issue.[51] The main takeaway is that case allocation should be an internal court matter free from the interference of external bodies and that cases should be allocated either on a random basis or following objective criteria pre-established by the court itself.

At the General Court, case allocation is subject to detailed internal rules, which are published in the *Official Journal of the European Union*.[52] According to those

51 eg Recommendation CM/Rec(2010)12 (n 47) para 24, and CoE, 'Council of Europe Plan of Action on Strengthening Judicial Independence and Impartiality' (CM(2016)36 final, 13 April 2016) Action 2.1.

52 Notice on Criteria for the assignment of cases to Chambers [2025] OJ C 5487, 13.10.2025. The following notices can also be mentioned: Formation of Chambers and assignment of Judges to Chambers [2025] OJ C 5485, 13.10.2025, Composition of the Grand Chamber and of the Intermediate Chamber [2025] OJ C 5486, 13.10.2025, and Designation of a Judge to replace a Judge who is prevented from acting [2025] OJ C 5488, 13.10.2025.

rules, there is a degree of specialization between the ten Chambers of the General Court: civil service cases are dealt with by three chambers and intellectual property cases by the seven remaining chambers. Two of these seven chambers are also responsible for preliminary reference cases. The other cases are allocated to all ten chambers in turn, following two separate rotas. However, the President of the General Court may derogate from the rotas to take account of a connection between cases or with a view to ensuring an even spread of the workload. This gives an otherwise rather mechanical system some flexibility.

As a general rule, the panel of judges to whom the case is allocated should deal with the case until the final judgment. However, for various reasons, a judge may have to be replaced. Except in situations where a judge has to withdraw because of bias or due to another cause preventing him or her from hearing the case, such replacements are a rather sensitive question. In its *Strack* v *Commission* judgment of 2 October 2014, the Court of Justice stated that 'the reassignment of a case, in the interest of the good administration of justice, with a view to ensuring an even spread of the workload, pursues the objective of processing cases within a reasonable time, in accordance with the second paragraph of Article 47 of the Charter'.[53]

In line with that judgment, Article 27(3) of the Rules of Procedure of the General Court now provides that, in the interest of the proper administration of justice, the President of the General Court may designate another judge-rapporteur. Before taking that decision, which has to be reasoned, the President hears the former and new judge-rapporteurs and the presidents of the chambers concerned. Their consent is not a condition for the case to be reassigned. However, there are two important limits: the reassignment cannot be taken after the judge-rapporteur has presented his or her preliminary report to the panel and reassignments must remain exceptional.

The first assignment and the reassignment of cases at the Court of Justice are not regulated as precisely as at the General Court. The composition of the chambers of the Court of Justice is published in the *Official Journal of the European Union*. Article 15 of the Rules of Procedure of the Court of Justice provides that the President of that court designates a judge to act as rapporteur in a case. According to Article 16 of the same rules, the First Advocate General shall assign each case to an advocate general.

9.9 National Courts and the CJEU: Towards EU Standards for Court Governance?

Both national courts and the two EU Courts interpret and apply EU law and therefore operate within the same legal order. They do not form a common hierarchical organization with one single court at the top but there is a strong link between them. The preliminary reference procedure is the cornerstone in the relationship between the Court of Justice and national courts.[54]

Even if the national courts and the EU Court do not belong to the same court organization, the legal remedies enshrined in the Treaties and national remedies constitute

[53] Case C-127/13 P *Strack v Commission* [2014] ECLI:EU:C:2014:2250, para 52.
[54] Section 9.1.

a comprehensive system of legal protection. In this respect, the EU Courts and the national courts form an integrated legal system in the fields of EU law. Within this sophisticated judicial architecture, the organization of national courts and national judicial procedures largely remain a matter of national law. EU law only establishes minimum standards when national courts apply material EU law.[55] In some specific areas, EU legislation goes further and imposes detailed rules for national legal remedies (eg in public procurement). However, it is still accurate to speak of the procedural autonomy of member states. The autonomy of member states in judicial matters is perhaps strongest as regards the governance and administration of national courts. However, some recent judgments of the Court of Justice show that not only procedural features but also structural aspects of court administration can come under the scrutiny of the EU Courts.

The first case that warrants attention concerns the EU courts themselves but may have wider implications. In its judgment of 26 March 2020 in *Simpson* v *Council and HG* v *Council*, the Court of Justice held that a court may examine, on appeal and of its own motion, whether there is a defect in the legality of the appointment of a judge who heard the case at first instance.[56] The Court of Justice then held that an irregularity committed during the appointment of judges within the judicial system concerned entails an infringement of the first sentence of the second paragraph of Article 47 of the Charter. This is so particularly when that irregularity is of such a kind and of such gravity as to create a real risk that other branches of government, in particular the executive, could exercise undue discretion undermining the integrity of the outcome of the appointment process and, in turn, this could give rise to a reasonable doubt in the minds of individuals as to the independence and the impartiality of the judge or judges concerned. That, the Court of Justice specified, is the case when what is at issue are fundamental rules forming an integral part of the establishment and functioning of that judicial system.[57]

Applying these principles to the case at hand, the Court of Justice ruled that there had been an irregularity in the procedure of the appointment of one judge to the EU Civil Service Tribunal. However, the Court of Justice took the view that this formal error did not in and of itself justify the setting aside of a judicial decision adopted by the panel of judges to which the judge in question was assigned at first instance. According to the Court of Justice, the error was not, in the circumstances of the case, sufficiently serious and liable to infringe the appellants' right to a tribunal established by law, as guaranteed by Article 47 of the Charter.[58]

The Court of Justice has also issued several judgments where it took a position on national measures concerning judges. These judgments[59] have concerned the reduction of the salaries of the judges in a member state,[60] the disciplinary regime applicable

[55] Treaty on the European Union (consolidated version) OJ C 202 7.6.2016, 13, Art 19 and TFEU (n 4) Art 47.
[56] Joined Cases C-542/18 RX-II, C-543/18 RX-II *Réexamen Simpson v Council* [2020] ECLI:EU:C:2020:232.
[57] ibid para 76.
[58] ibid paras 81 and 82.
[59] Based on the case-law as of the end the year 2023.
[60] Case C-64/16 *Associação Sindical dos Juízes Portugueses* [2018] ECLI:EU:C:2018:117.

to judges,[61] the independence of the disciplinary chamber of a supreme court,[62] the independence of ordinary courts,[63] the independence of a supreme court,[64] the procedure for the appointment to a position as a judge to a supreme court,[65] the independence of the members of the judiciary of a member state,[66] the personal liability of judges in the event of judicial error,[67] the principles of the irremovability of judges and judicial independence,[68] the liability of judges who do not comply with a decision of the Constitutional Court,[69] compliance with the EU law requirement concerning an independent and impartial tribunal previously established by law,[70] and the promotion of judges.[71]

9.10 Concluding Remarks

The special features of EU law, which place it somewhere between national law and international law, also mean that the CJEU is a 'special court'. Indeed, to a certain extent, it is difficult to compare it not only to national courts but also to international courts. That is why it is sometimes called the domestic court of the member states of the EU. Furthermore, the CJEU is not itself a court of justice but a court system or court organization currently composed of two courts.

Despite these particularities, the two EU Courts themselves are courts of justice like any other in that they must meet the universal requirements of an independent and impartial tribunal. The governance of the EU Courts must comply with these requirements both as to the relationships between them and with the other Union institutions and the member states.

The CJEU has an important role in establishing the organizational and procedural provisions governing the functioning of the two EU Courts. In this area, it acts as a quasi-legislator. Although it cannot decide on its own on the modification of rules, it has a right of initiative and its agreement thereto is often decisive. As for disciplinary

[61] *Commission v Poland* (n 3); Case C-817/21 *Inspecţia Judiciară* [2023] ECLI:EU:C:2023:391.

[62] Joined cases C-585/18, C-624/18, and C-625/18 *A K (Independence of the Disciplinary Chamber of the Supreme Court)* [2019] ECLI:EU:2019:982; Case C-615/20 and C-671/20 *YP and Others (Lifting of a judge's immunity and his or her suspension from duties)* [2023] ECLI:EU:C:2023:562.

[63] Case C-192/18 *Commission v Poland (Independence of ordinary courts)* [2019] ECLI:EU:C:2019:924.

[64] Case C-619/18 *Commission v Poland (Independence of the Supreme Court)* [2019] ECLI:EU:C:2019:531.

[65] Case C-824/18 *A B and Others (Appointment of judges to the Supreme Court—Action)* [2021] ECLI:EU:C:2021:153; Case C-748/19 to C-754/19 *Prokuratura Rejonowa w Mińsku Mazowieckim and Others* [2021] ECLI:EU:C:2021:931.

[66] Case C-896/19 *Repubblika* [2021] ECLI:EU:C:2021:311 and joined cases C-748/19 to C-754/19 *Prokuratura Rejonowa w Mińsku Mazowieckim* [2021] ECLI:EU:C:2021:931.

[67] Cases C-83/19, C-127/19, C-195/19, C-291/19, C-355/19 and C-397/19 *Asociaţia 'Forumul Judecătorilor Din România'* [2021], ECLI:EU:C:2021:393; and Cases C-357/19, C-379/19, C-547/19, C-811/19 and C-840/19 *Euro Box Promotion and Others* [2021] EU:C:2021:1034.

[68] Case C-487/19 *W. Ż. (Chamber of Extraordinary Control and Public Affairs of the Supreme Court—Appointment)* [2021] ECLI:EU:C:2021:798.

[69] Case C-430/21 *RS (Effect of the decisions of a constitutional court)* [2022] ECLI:EU:C:2022:99.

[70] Case C-204/21 *Commission v Poland (Independence and private life of judges)* [2023] ECLI:EU:C:2023:442.

[71] Case C-216/21 *Asociaţia 'Forumul Judecătorilor din România'* [2023] ECLI:EU:C:2023:628.

monitoring and sanctions and, in general, ethical issues concerning judges and advocates general, they remain in the hands of the CJEU, without there being any external control body to provide oversight. These features strengthen the autonomy of the CJEU. On the other hand, the CJEU is no different from most other courts as regards its financing and the appointment of its members. These matters fall within the purview of external organs; that is, other EU institutions and member states.

The CJEU's size and the fact that it is composed of at least two courts make its internal governance and administration a complex matter. A common administration for two courts offers the benefit of saving resources and enabling institutional synergies. On the other hand, two courts cannot have an entirely common administration without endangering the independence of each of them. This has turned out to be the most difficult aspect of the governance of the CJEU. The problems in 'cohabitation' between the Court of Justice and the General Court have sometimes been significant. A fresh understanding of the administrative functioning of the CJEU that takes into account the bigger size of the institution and the evolving role of the General Court in the judicial architecture of the EU has therefore become necessary.

Finally, the Court of Justice's recent case law on the independence and impartiality of courts is a timely reminder of the importance of having due regard to these fundamental features of the rule of law. Article 19(1) of the TEU and Article 47 of the Charter have proved to be powerful tools in the Court of Justice's hands when it comes to securing basic standards for the governance of courts.

10
Governance of the United Nations Criminal Tribunals

*Huw Llewellyn**

10.1 Introduction: An Institutional Perspective

This chapter examines the governance of the five United Nations (UN) criminal tribunals: the International Criminal Tribunal for the Former Yugoslavia (ICTY), the International Criminal Tribunal for Rwanda (ICTR), the Special Court for Sierra Leone (SCSL), the Extraordinary Chambers in the Courts of Cambodia (ECCC), and the Special Tribunal for Lebanon (STL).[1] It is also concerned with the governance of the residual bodies that have been established by the UN to continue the essential functions of the ICTY, the ICTR, and the SCSL, which have closed. Establishment of each of the criminal tribunals was mandated by a principal organ of the UN—the Security Council in the case of the ICTY, the ICTR, the SCSL, and the STL. In the case of the ECCC, the General Assembly mandated the conclusion of the Agreement between the UN and the Royal Government of Cambodia which set the conditions for the UN's participation in the ECCC.

The ICTY and the ICTR were set up against a background of long-term efforts to create an international criminal court which came to fruition in the wake of the Second World War with the establishment of the Nuremberg[2] and Tokyo[3] international military tribunals by the Allies to try the defeated political and military leaders of Germany and Japan. Criticized as victors' justice, those post-war tribunals were succeeded by efforts within the newly-established UN to create a truly international criminal jurisdiction. These were unsuccessful during the Cold War years,[4]

* The views expressed in this chapter are personal to the author and do not necessarily represent the views of the United Nations. The chapter is based on the author's PhD dissertation, submitted to the Grotius Centre for International Legal Studies at Leiden University, and defended in September 2019.

[1] The term 'UN criminal tribunals' is preferred to 'UN international criminal tribunals' because the ECCC was established as a national court of Cambodia, not as an international tribunal.

[2] Agreement for the Prosecution and Punishment of Major War Criminals of the European Axis (8 August 1945) 82 UNTS 280. The Charter of the Nuremberg International Military Tribunal was annexed to this Agreement: Annex to the Agreement for the Prosecution and Punishment of Major War Criminals of the European Axis (8 August 1945) 82 UNTS 284.

[3] Special Proclamation by the Supreme Commander for the Allied Powers at Tokyo, 19 January 1946, TIAS No 1589, 4 Bevans 20. On the governance of the historic IMTs: Sergey Vasiliev, 'Governance of the International Military Tribunals at Nuremberg and Tokyo', in this volume.

[4] In 1948, the UN General Assembly requested the International Law Commission to study the possibility of establishing such a body as a 'Criminal Chamber of the International Court of Justice' UNGA Res 260 B (III) (9 December 1948) UN Doc A/810 (1948) 177. The International Law Commission concluded that the establishment of an international judicial organ would be desirable and possible, but not as a Chamber of the International Court of Justice. *Yearbook of the International Law Commission* vol II (1950)

Huw Llewellyn, *Governance of the United Nations Criminal Tribunals* In: *Governance of International Courts and Tribunals*. Edited by: Sergey Vasiliev and Niels Blokker, Oxford University Press. © Huw Llewellyn 2026.
DOI: 10.1093/oso/9780198922131.003.0010

but successful in 1993 when the Security Council, released from its Cold War paralysis, established the ICTY,[5] and the following year, the ICTR.[6] These two tribunals were established as subsidiary organs of the Security Council, and thus, within the UN Organization, financed from UN assessed contributions.[7]

These innovative actions by the Security Council began the era of UN engagement in the prosecution of international crimes, and demonstrated that international criminal tribunals could be made to function. This paved the way for the negotiation and establishment in 1998 of the International Criminal Court (ICC)[8] through a multilateral treaty concluded among states outside the UN Organization. Shortly afterwards, the SCSL (2002),[9] the ECCC (2003)[10] and the STL (2007)[11] were established through negotiation and partnership between the UN Secretary-General, acting through the UN Office of Legal Affairs (OLA) on behalf of the UN Organization, and the states concerned. Unlike the entirely international courts such as the ICTY and the ICTR, these three tribunals were established outside the UN, on varying legal bases. They were equipped with a mix of national and international judges, and were meant to apply both national and international law. The progression away from tribunals established directly by UN organs, within the UN Organization, to tribunals mandated by UN organs for establishment outside the UN Organization, reflected the developing wish of the UN member states to find cheaper and more rapid forms of pursuing justice for international crimes.

As temporary tribunals with finite mandates, each of the UN criminal tribunals has an establishing and terminating body (the 'parent' body) and a body charged with overseeing its functioning, responsible for its external financial and administrative management, and shepherding it to carry out and complete its mandate in the most

document A/1316, paras 128–45. Consideration of the issue by the General Assembly and by a committee established by the Assembly for this purpose led to the drafting of a statute in the early 1950s, but successive decisions thereafter effectively shelved further consideration of the matter until 1989. See *Work of the International Law Commission* (8th edn, UN 2012), Vol 1, 89–92.

[5] The ICTY was established by UNSC Res 808 (22 February 1993) UN Doc S/RES/808 and UNSC Res 827 (25 May 1993) UN Doc S/RES/827, which approved the 1993 report of the Secretary-General: Report of the Secretary-General Pursuant to Paragraph 2 of Security Council Resolution 808 (1993) (3 May 1993) UN Doc S/25704 ('UNSG report on the ICTY') and annex containing the ICTY Statute.

[6] The ICTR was established by UNSC Res 955 (8 November 1994) UN Doc S/RES/955.

[7] 'UN assessed contributions' refers to compulsory financial contributions by UN member states, as determined by the General Assembly in accordance with Art 17 of the UN Charter.

[8] Established outside the UN Organization by the Rome Statute of the International Criminal Court (adopted 17 July 1998, entered into force on 1 July 2002) 2187 UNTS 90 ('Rome Statute').

[9] Agreement between the United Nations and the Government of Sierra Leone on the Establishment of a Special Court for Sierra Leone, with annexed Statute (signed 16 January 2002, entered into force 12 April 2002) 2178 UNTS 137.

[10] Although 2003 is given as the relevant date here, the ECCC was in fact first established by the Law on the Establishment of the Extraordinary Chambers in the Courts of Cambodia, 10 August 2001, which is Cambodian national legislation. This was subsequently amended by the Law to Amend the 2001 Law on the Establishment of the Extraordinary Chambers in the Courts of Cambodia, 27 October 2004. Both pieces of Cambodian national legislation are set out on the ECCC website <https://www.eccc.gov.kh/en/about/legal-framework>. 2003 is the year given in the text because the Agreement between the UN and the Government of Cambodia concerning the Prosecution under Cambodian Law of Crimes Committed during the Period of Democratic Kampuchea was signed on 6 June 2003, 2329 UNTS 117.

[11] UNSC Res 1757 (30 May 2007) UN Doc S/RES/1757, with annexed draft Agreement and draft Statute.

efficient and cost-effective manner possible (the 'oversight' body). The parent and oversight bodies of the UN criminal tribunals are the international judicial governance institutions ('*injugovins*') that are the subject of this book. Experience shows that establishing and overseeing international criminal tribunals is an expensive and long-term undertaking. The parent and oversight bodies have a natural interest in trying to control their cost and duration. There is an inherent tension between these needs and the imperative that the tribunals, as judicial bodies, function independently and impartially.

This chapter assesses the legal rules, principles, and political checks and balances that regulate this tension in the tribunals' parent and oversight relationships. It does so by taking an institutional perspective, as it identifies the institutional forms in which the tribunals and their oversight bodies have been established, and the legal rules and principles relating to authority and control that flow from these institutional forms and relationships. Section 10.2 describes the unique context within which the UN criminal tribunals operate and discusses a number of concepts that are essential to understanding how the relationships between the UN criminal tribunals and their parent and oversight bodies function, including parenthood, oversight, and the lifecycle through which each of these temporary judicial institutions passes. Section 10.3 examines the varying institutional forms in which the UN criminal tribunals were established, and the effect that these variations have on the nature of the parental and oversight relationships and the legal rules and principles that govern them. Section 10.4 describes the establishment of the UN criminal tribunals' oversight bodies, in particular the transition from oversight of subsidiary judicial organs by the Security Council taking place within the UN Organization, to oversight of the voluntarily funded tribunals by small dedicated 'management committees' of the most interested states, taking place outside the UN Organization.

Section 10.5 examines the requirement under international law that courts and tribunals function independently and impartially, and assesses the applicability of this requirement to the UN criminal tribunals as a rule of customary international law, as a general principle of law, and through the operation of the tribunals' constituent instruments. Section 10.6 examines the relevant legal rules relating to authority and control that arise from the tribunals' institutional architecture, ie rules contained in their constituent instruments, and the principles of international institutional law inherent in the various forms in which the UN criminal tribunals were established. Section 10.7 describes examples of tensions that have arisen in the governance of each of the UN criminal tribunals during the various stages of their lifecycles. Section 10.8 makes concluding remarks.

10.2 Context and Essential Concepts

Before embarking on a tribunal-by-tribunal institutional assessment, it is helpful to describe the unique context in which the UN criminal tribunals (indeed, all international tribunals) operate, and to set out some concepts that are foundational to understanding how the tribunals and their parent and oversight relationships function.

10.2.1 Unique context

The constitutional and institutional setting in which the UN criminal tribunals function is entirely different to that in which national courts function. Indeed, this is the case for all international tribunals. National courts form part of an integrated judicial system and are 'so deeply woven into the social fabric that their continued existence is not seriously threatened'.[12] They operate within an established constitutional setting and enjoy extensive support networks of existing national law-enforcement and criminal justice institutions that provide access to crime sites, ensure the availability and participation of witnesses, execute arrest warrants and enforce prison sentences.

By contrast, the UN criminal tribunals were created individually and temporarily on the basis of ad hoc legal instruments negotiated and concluded for this purpose. Each tribunal is a singular entity, not part of a system of courts with a network of supporting criminal justice institutions, and each sits in a direct bilateral relationship with the state(s) and/or UN organ that created it and which oversee it. The lack of a support network of law-enforcement and criminal justice institutions means that the tribunals depend on third parties, usually states and international organizations, for these and other acts of cooperation. The tribunals thus have a greater legal, political, financial, and practical dependence on third parties for the carrying out of their functions.

Furthermore, the UN criminal tribunals bring the judicial, investigative, prosecutorial, defence, and administration functions together in one institution. In national systems, each of these aspects of the criminal justice process is separately constituted, in particular with the judicial and prosecutorial functions being distinct and supported by their own administrations. The creation of the UN criminal tribunals as single entities causes competing interests within each tribunal, requiring an internal structure of separate organs to maintain the critical separation and independence of these functions. Internal tribunal leadership and coordination are required to manage the resulting complex relationships and to harmonize and coordinate the activities of the separate organs. Leadership within the tribunal rests primarily with the President, who is the *de facto* head of the institution, supported by the Prosecutor and the Registrar.

10.2.2 The life cycle and the residual phase

Each of the five UN criminal tribunals has a natural life cycle of establishment (as a matter of law), commencement and functioning (in practice), completion of the case-load, and closure. They were established at what are sometimes referred to in the literature as 'Nuremberg moments'[13]—moments in time when there is a sufficient confluence of political and financial will among UN member states to embark on the

[12] David Caron, 'Towards a Political Theory of International Courts and Tribunals' (2006) 24 Berkeley Journal of International Law 401, 410.

[13] Laura Bingham, 'Strategy or Process? Closing the International Criminal Tribunals for the Former Yugoslavia and Rwanda' (2006) 24(2) Berkeley Journal of International Law 687, 691.

lengthy and expensive business of initiating and sustaining international or internationalized criminal tribunals.

Nuremberg moments pass. The voluntary-funding basis of the SCSL, the ECCC, and the STL arose out of growing concerns in the late 1990s about the slow pace of proceedings and high costs of the ICTY and the ICTR, which gave rise to a search for a faster and cheaper model of UN criminal tribunal. These concerns shifted the focus of international attention to the need for 'completion' of the cases before these tribunals, leading ICTY President Jorda in 2000 to initiate discussion within the tribunal to identify a timeframe for fulfilling its work,[14] and resulting in 'completion strategies' in 2003 and 2004 for the ICTY, the ICTR, and the SCSL to hasten this result.[15]

The temporary nature of the UN criminal tribunals, and the consequent need for the parent and oversight bodies at some point to determine when they should close, has been described as the 'paradox'[16] inherent in independent yet terminable tribunals. As thoughts turned to completion and eventual closure of the UN criminal tribunals, there was a growing recognition from around 2005 that certain essential continuing functions ('residual functions') would need to subsist after the tribunals were closed down. Prosecutions and trials of serious international crimes inevitably generate a number of long-term functions that do not end with the closure of the institution, such as the continuing need to maintain a trial capacity in the event that any fugitives are subsequently apprehended, to protect witnesses who may be under threat, and to review judgments where new evidence comes to light.

These developments resulted in 2010 in the establishment of the International Residual Mechanism for Criminal Tribunals ('Residual Mechanism') to carry out the residual functions of the ICTY and the ICTR, and the Residual Special Court for Sierra Leone ('Residual SCSL') to carry out the residual functions of the SCSL. The SCSL closed at the end of 2013, the ICTR closed at the end of 2015, and the ICTY closed at the end of 2017. The STL closed at the end of 2023 following the suspension of ongoing judicial proceedings in June 2022 for lack of funding. Following the completion of all judicial proceedings, the ECCC entered a 3-year residual phase on 1 January 2023. The Residual SCSL and the Residual Mechanism remain in operation.

10.2.3 Parenthood, oversight, and governance

Parenthood and oversight of individual tribunals have no equivalents in national criminal jurisdictions. 'Parent' or 'parents' are terms used in this chapter to refer to the entity or entities that undertake the legal act that creates the tribunal and maintain

[14] ICTY press release, 'Statement by Judge Claude Jorda, President of the International Criminal Tribunal for the Former Yugoslavia' (CC/P.I.S./466-E, The Hague, 27 January 2000) <www.icty.org/sid/7905>.

[15] UNSC Res 1503 (28 August 2003) UN Doc S/RES/1503 and UNSC Res 1534 (26 March 2004) UN Doc S/RES/1534 set out the completion strategies for the ICTY and the ICTR. The first version of the SCSL Completion Strategy was presented to the SCSL Management Committee on 6 October 2004. See Third Annual Report of the President of the Special Court for Sierra Leone, January 2016 to December 2016, 27 <www.rscsl.org/Documents/AnRpt3.pdf>.

[16] Bingham (n 13) 691.

it in existence. 'Oversight' consists of a range of functions related to the external budgetary and administrative management of the tribunals, but as we will see later in this chapter, it has also in practice straddled the boundary with judicial management, including the tribunals' case schedules and the overall timeline within which they should complete their mandates, raising tensions between oversight and the tribunals' independent functioning. Oversight is essentially a bilateral and one-directional term—it is what the oversight body does to the tribunal. The word is not comprehensive enough to take in any of the broader cooperative relationships necessary for the tribunal's functioning, nor is it ideal to describe the notion that the oversight body-tribunal relationship is a two-way cooperative partnership.

'Governance' is a broader concept that has a long history in political science and public management.[17] The term has given rise to a considerable literature in those fields and many definitions.[18] These definitions tend to be subject area specific, and a general definition has proved elusive. Dictionary definitions of 'governance' begin to provide some content for a concept that is difficult to pin down, for example: 'the way that organisations or countries are managed at the highest level, and the systems for doing this'.[19] Governance has been described as relating to 'the processes of interaction and decision-making among the actors involved in a collective problem'[20] and involving 'the process of decision-making and the process by which decisions are implemented'.[21]

Governance in the context of the UN criminal tribunals could thus be understood to encompass the broad range of actions that the parent and oversight bodies need to undertake in partnership with the tribunals aimed at ensuring that the tribunals receive the legal, political and financial support and cooperation from a broad range of actors that they need in order to function effectively. Perceptions of any organization's governance are important because they impact its authority and effectiveness, but this is particularly the case where the organization is a judicial institution due to the imperative that it be, and be seen to be, independent in its judicial functions. The characteristics of authoritative, well-governed institutions that tend to support their credibility and effectiveness include 'transparency', 'accountability', and 'participation', all of which feed into perceptions of an organization's legal and political authority.[22] These qualities are widely seen as a motivation for compliance and cooperation with

[17] eg Ali Farazmand, 'Governance in the Age of Globalization: Challenges and Opportunities for South and South-East Asia' (2013) 13(4) Public Organization Review 349–63.

[18] See an overview in Mohammed Asaduzzaman, 'Governance Theories and Models', *Global Encyclopedia of Public Administration, Public Policy and Governance* (Springer International Publishing 2017) 1–13.

[19] Cambridge English Dictionary, online version <https://dictionary.cambridge.org/dictionary/english/governance>.

[20] Marc Hufty, 'Investigating Policy Processes: The Governance Analytical Framework' in Urs Wiesmann and Hans Hurni (eds), *Research for Sustainable Development: Foundations, Experiences, and Perspectives* (Geographica Bernensia 2011) 403.

[21] UN Economic and Social Commission for Asia and the Pacific, 'What Is Good Governance?' (10 July 2009) 1–3 <www.unescap.org/sites/default/files/good-governance.pdf>.

[22] eg Rüdiger Wolfrum, 'Legitimacy in International Law', *Max Planck Encyclopedia of Public International Law* (OUP 2015) <http://opil.ouplaw.com/view/10.1093/law:epil/9780199231690/law-9780199231690-e1960>; Markus Krajewski, 'International Organisations or Institutions, Democratic Legitimacy', *Max Planck Encyclopedia of Public International Law* (OUP 2015) <http://opil.ouplaw.com/view/10.1093/law:epil/9780199231690/law-9780199231690-e495?rskey=0krplA&result=2&prd=OPIL>;

decisions and requests because they instil a sense of obligation rooted in acceptance that such decisions and requests are procedurally and normatively appropriate.[23] The addressees tend to comply, even in the absence of a legal obligation or an effective enforcement capability on the part of the organization.

Transparency concerns the openness and inclusiveness of decision-making processes within an organization and their visibility to the outside world.[24] Informal decision-making among a few of the more powerful members would tend to undermine transparency and the effective participation of all members, thereby weakening the 'democratic legitimacy' of the way that the organization functions.[25] Accountability involves an obligation to report, explain, and justify conduct, so that information can be monitored, questions can be posed, and depending on the form of accountability, consequences may ensue.[26] Participation refers primarily to the ability of citizens to participate in political processes at the national level that affect them.[27] Direct participation of citizens in international organizations is not ordinarily feasible, but can be pursued through participation, for example, by civil society organizations or parliamentary societies. The UN criminal tribunals have found it necessary to bridge this participation gap through 'outreach' efforts to engage and inform the populations affected by the atrocities over which they have jurisdiction. These efforts have been considered vital in establishing the relevance of the tribunals' work in pursuing justice for victims, and in post-conflict reconciliation efforts.

10.2.4 Ownership

'Ownership', in the author's experience, describes well what is needed from the parent and oversight bodies for a successful partnership with the tribunal. It complements the wide notion of governance discussed above in that it describes the political and financial commitment and willingness necessary on the part of the parent and oversight bodies. This is not only to forge a strong bond of partnership with the tribunal itself but also to use that partnership to develop good and productive relationships across the spectrum of actors from whom the tribunal needs cooperation. The cooperative relationships needed are often less based on legal obligations than they are on political goodwill. The actions of the parent and oversight bodies to promote knowledge of, and enhance confidence in, the work of the tribunals can therefore be vital.

and Jacob Katz Cogan, Ian Hurd, and Ian Johnstone (eds), *The Oxford Handbook of International Organizations* (OUP 2017) ch 52–55.

[23] Dominik Zaum, 'Legitimacy' in Katz Cogan, Hurd, and Johnstone (n 22) 1110–11.
[24] Krajewski (n 22) paras 21–23.
[25] ibid.
[26] Allen Buchanan and Robert Keohane, 'The Legitimacy of Global Governance Institutions', Memo prepared for a Conference on the Normative and Empirical Evaluation of Global Governance, Princeton University, 16–18 February 2006 <www.princeton.edu/~pcglobal/conferences/normative/papers/Session1_Buchanan_Keohane.pdf>.
[27] Klaus Dingwerth and Patrizia Nanz, 'Participation' in Katz Cogan, Hurd, and Johnstone (n 22) 1126.

10.2.5 Political checks and balances

The wider cooperative relationships that the UN criminal tribunals rely on are often not based on legal instruments. As will be illustrated below, this is also the case for the relationships between the voluntarily funded UN criminal tribunals (the SCSL, the ECCC, and the STL) and their oversight bodies. Even where the parental and oversight relationships are based on legal instruments, namely, the UN Charter for the ICTY and the ICTR, the decisions of the state representatives carrying out oversight functions in the relevant Security Council and General Assembly meetings are not determined or motivated by a 'judge over their shoulder'. The legal rules and principles applicable as between these UN principal organs and the judicial subsidiary organs of the Council are not enforceable in any judicial forum.

In practice, there are checks and balances of a political nature at work among the UN member states that influence decision-making. A number of international lawyers and political theorists have addressed the question of why, in the absence of enforceable legal obligations, states behave as they do, taking as the starting point the proposition that 'almost all nations observe almost all principles of international law and almost all their obligations almost all the time'.[28] Koh, for example, describes multiple complex interactions of a political and legal nature that play out among governments and others (including national courts, civil society, and academics) to bring about compliance with international law.[29] Johnstone describes the iterative process and 'the power of deliberation', particularly within international organizations. The discourse exerts pressure on states because they have an interest in maintaining a reputation for good faith compliance with the law.[30] Franck relies on similar principles in arguing that the key to compliance by states is the 'fairness' and 'legitimacy' of the international rules to be applied, which are indicated by considerations of both substance and process.[31] Wood, in the context of states' compliance with Security Council resolutions, and taking a practitioner's perspective, referred to the discursive process and inter-state interactions as 'checks and balances within the system'.[32] He considers these to include discussion among the lawyers of UN member states in New York and those in capitals, and the 'ultimate check', the potential disregard of the Council's decisions by states where they do not regard them as carrying sufficient authority or respect among UN member states. In Wood's view, it is these 'checks and balances' that place limits on the Council's actions, not the 'judge over your shoulder'.[33]

[28] Louis Henkin, *How Nations Behave* (2nd edn, Columbia University Press 1979) 47.

[29] Harold Koh, 'The 1994 Roscoe Pound Lecture, Transnational Legal Process' (1996) 75 Nebraska Law Review 181 and Harold Koh, 'Why Do Nations Obey International law?' (1997) 106 Yale Law Journal 2599; Alec Stone Sweet, *Governing with Judges, Constitutional Politics in Europe* (OUP 2000) 1 and 12–20 (describing the process of 'judicialization' when courts exercise authority over the interactions and frictions described by Koh).

[30] Ian Johnstone, *The Power of Deliberation, International Law, Politics and Organisations* (OUP 2011). See also Abram Chayes and Antonia Handler Chayes, *The New Sovereignty: Compliance with International Regulatory Agreements* (CUP 1995) 25.

[31] Thomas M Franck, *Fairness in International Law and Institutions* (Clarendon Press 1995) 30–46.

[32] Michael Wood, 'The Security Council's Powers and Their Limits', 2006 Lauterpacht Lectures, Second Lecture, 8 November 2006 (transcript on file with the author).

[33] ibid 17–21.

10.3 The Institutional Forms of the UN Criminal Tribunals

The institutional forms in which the UN criminal tribunals were established determine the nature of their oversight arrangements and the legal principles applicable that regulate the oversight relationships.

10.3.1 The ICTY and the ICTR

The status of the ICTY and ICTR as subsidiary organs of the Security Council was not expressly stated in the constituent resolutions, but set out in the Secretary-General's 1993 report that underpinned the establishment of the ICTY, endorsed in its entirety by the Council. The report stated that the Council would be establishing:

> as an enforcement measure under Chapter VII, a subsidiary organ within the terms of Article 29 of the Charter, but one of a judicial nature. This organ would, of course, have to perform its functions independently of political considerations; it would not be subject to the authority or control of the Security Council with regard to the performance of its judicial functions.[34]

The 1993 report thus identified the need for the independent functioning of the tribunals, and by implication also the possibility of authority and control over non-judicial matters by the parent organ, but did not tackle these issues in any detail, nor attempt to identify any legal rules or principles applicable in this parent–subsidiary relationship. The Council's establishment of the ICTR in the following year was not on the basis of a preceding Secretary-General's report, but negotiated directly by the Council members. The institutional architecture was, however, identical to that of the ICTY. In a subsequent report, the Secretary-General stated that the ICTR was: 'dependent in administrative and financial matters on various United Nations organs; as a judicial body, however, it is independent of any one particular State or group of States, including its parent body, the Security Council'.[35] The Residual Mechanism for the ICTY and the ICTR was established in December 2010 by Security Council resolution 1966 (2010)[36] as a subsidiary organ of the Council, like the ICTY and ICTR before it. This is again not explicitly stated in the resolution, but it is the only plausible conclusion to draw from the Mechanism's establishment by the Council under Chapter VII in the same manner as the two ad hoc tribunals. The Mechanism was established as a single subsidiary organ with two branches: one in Arusha to carry out the residual functions of the ICTR, and one in The Hague to carry out the residual

[34] UNSG report on the ICTY (n 5) paras 74–78.

[35] Report of the Secretary-General pursuant to paragraph 5 of Security Council resolution 955 (13 February 1995) UN Doc S/1995/134, para 8.

[36] UNSC Res 1966 (22 December 2010) UN Doc S/RES/1966.

functions of the ICTY. It commenced functioning while the ICTY and ICTR were still conducting trials and appeals.[37]

10.3.2 The voluntarily funded UN criminal tribunals

The establishment of UN criminal tribunals directly by the Security Council as subsidiary organs within the UN Organization was not repeated after 1994. Widespread concern among states about the cost and slow pace of work of the ICTY and ICTR[38] led the UN to move to new institutional models of tribunal, intended to be cheaper, faster, and funded primarily by voluntary contributions by states. This development gave rise to the three very different kinds of the institutional architecture described below.

10.3.2.1 The establishment of the SCSL and the Residual SCSL as treaty-based international organizations

The SCSL had its origin in a request by the Government of Sierra Leone in 2000 for the assistance of the Security Council in establishing a 'strong and credible court that will meet the objectives of bringing justice and ensuring lasting peace' in Sierra Leone.[39] The negotiations with the Government were mandated by the Security Council[40] and conducted by OLA on behalf of the Secretary-General. The Security Council, through its recently established Informal Working Group on International Tribunals,[41] played an active role, commenting on the Secretary-General's report to the Council and submitting revisions to, and ultimately approving, the draft constituent instrument.[42] The SCSL was thus established by a 2002 treaty between the UN and the Government of Sierra Leone to which the SCSL Statute was annexed.[43]

Although the SCSL is often referred to as a hybrid tribunal, this term is misleading in so far as its institutional nature was concerned because it neither formed part of the UN Organization nor of the domestic court structure of Sierra Leone.[44] The SCSL

[37] Brigitte Benoit Landale and Huw Llewellyn, 'The International Residual Mechanism for Criminal Tribunals: The Beginning of the End for the ICTY and the ICTR' (2011) 8(2) International Organisations Law Review 349.

[38] eg Ralph Zacklin, 'The Failings of Ad Hoc International Tribunals' (2004) 2 Journal of International Criminal Justice 541, 542; Dominic Raab, 'Evaluating the ICTY and Its Completion Strategy: Efforts to Achieve Accountability for War Crimes and their Tribunals' (2005) 3(1) Journal of International Criminal Justice 82–102.

[39] Letter dated 12 June 2000 from the President of Sierra Leone to the President of the Security Council, annexed to the letter dated 9 August 2000 from the Permanent Representative of Sierra Leone to the President of the Security Council, UN Doc S/2000/786.

[40] UNSC Res 1315 (14 August 2000) UN Doc S/RES/1315.

[41] The Working Group is an informal meeting of the legal officers of the fifteen Security Council members, not a formal subsidiary body of the Council, which is why there is no founding decision of the Council.

[42] Report of the Secretary-General on the Establishment of a Special Court for Sierra Leone (4 October 2000) UN Doc S/2000/915; and a series of letters exchanged between the Secretary-General and the President of the Security Council dated 12 January 2001, UN Doc S/2001/40; 31 January 2001, S/2001/95; 12 July 2001, UN Doc S/2001/693; 23 July 2001, UN Doc S/2001/722; and 6 March 2002, UN Doc S/2002/246/Corr.3.

[43] SCSL Agreement (n 10) and SCSL Statute (n 9).

[44] The Sierra Leone Parliament passed the Special Court Agreement (2000) (Ratification) Act 2002 to give effect to the powers and competences of the Special Court in the national legal system.

was established by a treaty, as a free-standing tribunal, with juridical capacity to enter into agreements with states for the exercise of its functions.[45] Although described by the Secretary-General as a 'treaty-based *sui generis* court' of mixed composition and jurisdiction, the subsequent case law of the SCSL clarified that the SCSL was an international tribunal and an international organization in its own right:[46] '[t]he Special Court is established by treaty and has the characteristics associated with classical international organisations (including legal personality; the capacity to enter into agreements with other international persons governed by international law; privileges and immunities; and an autonomous will distinct from that of its members)'.[47]

The Residual SCSL was established to carry out the residual functions of the SCSL in 2012 by the Residual SCSL Agreement, which is a bilateral treaty between the UN and the Government of Sierra Leone.[48] The Residual SCSL was, like the SCSL, established as an international organization in its own right.

10.3.2.2 The establishment of the ECCC as a national court of Cambodia

The ECCC was established to prosecute the shocking and wide-scale crimes committed during the period of the Khmer Rouge regime, which held power in Cambodia from April 1975 to January 1979. Estimates of the numbers who died during that period range from 1.7 to 2.2 million.[49] In June 1997, the Co-Prime Ministers of Cambodia wrote to the Secretary-General to request assistance in establishing a tribunal to prosecute those most responsible for those atrocities.[50] The Security Council was unable to react to the request. China, which had had close ties with Democratic Kampuchea, was considered likely to veto any resolution mandating negotiations to establish a tribunal.[51] The General Assembly accordingly took the lead through its Third (Human Rights) Committee,[52] asking the Secretary-General to examine the Cambodian request.[53]

The negotiations revealed a fundamental difference of approach between the UN and the Government of Cambodia, representing what the Secretary-General regarded as two visions of justice: on the one hand, an independent tribunal meeting international standards of independence and impartiality guaranteed through an international majority in judicial decision-making and, on the other hand, what the

[45] SCSL Agreement (n 10) Art 11(d).

[46] Decision on Preliminary Motion on Lack of Jurisdiction Materiae: Illegal Delegation of Powers by the United Nations, *Prosecutor* v *Moinina Fofana*, SCSL-2004-14-AR72(E), AC, SCSL, 25 May 2004.

[47] Decision on Immunity from Jurisdiction, *Prosecutor* v *Charles Ghankay Taylor*, SCSL-2003-01-AR72(E), AC, SCSL, 31 May 2004, para 41.

[48] Agreement between the United Nations and the Government of Sierra Leone on the Establishment of a Residual Special Court for Sierra Leone, and its annexed Statute (adopted 29 July 2010 and 11 August 2010, entered into force 2 October 2012) 2871 UNTS 333.

[49] See the website of the ECCC at <https://www.eccc.gov.kh/en/about>.

[50] Letter from the First and Second Prime Ministers of Cambodia to the Secretary-General (21 June 1997) UN Docs A/51/930 and S/1997/488.

[51] Daphna Shraga, 'The Second Generation UN-Based tribunals: A Diversity of Mixed Jurisdictions' in Cesare Romano, André Nollkaemper, and Jann Kleffner (eds), *Internationalised Criminal Courts* (OUP 2004) 15–38. Shraga was a Principal Legal Officer in the Office of the UN Legal Counsel at the relevant time.

[52] Lindsey Raub, 'Positioning Hybrid Tribunals in International Criminal Justice' (2009) 41 New York University Journal of International Law and Politics 1045; Shraga (n 51) 17–19.

[53] UNGA Res 52/135 (27 February 1998) UN Doc A/RES/52/135.

UN officials involved at the time saw as an institution subjected to the risk of a politically controlled judicial process.[54] The Cambodian Government achieved something of a fait accompli in the negotiations through the adoption of the Cambodian 'ECCC Law', which established the ECCC as a national court in 2001, while the negotiations with the UN Legal Counsel were ongoing.[55] The Secretary-General made clear that the tribunal as envisaged by the Government 'would not guarantee the independence, impartiality, and objectivity that a court established with the support of the United Nations must have'.[56]

In concluding the negotiations, the Secretary-General and the UN Legal Counsel remained unconvinced that the draft Agreement with Cambodia would ensure an independent and impartial process given the 'precarious state of the judiciary in Cambodia'.[57] Nevertheless, the General Assembly in its resolution 57/228B of 13 May 2003 approved the draft Agreement.[58] With serious misgivings on the part of the UN Secretary-General and the Legal Counsel, therefore the treaty between the UN and the Government of Cambodia ('ECCC Agreement') was signed on 6 June 2003.[59]

The ECCC was thus established as a national court of Cambodia under domestic legislation in 2001,[60] which was subsequently amended in 2004 following the conclusion of the ECCC Agreement between the UN and the Government of Cambodia in 2003. Its legal basis is therefore in domestic law, and as stated in the preamble to the ECCC Agreement, the ECCC sits 'within the existing court structure of Cambodia'.[61] The ECCC Agreement did not establish the ECCC, but 'provides, *inter alia*, the legal basis and the principles and modalities' for the cooperation between the UN and the Government of Cambodia.[62] In accordance with the terms of the ECCC Agreement, the ECCC has a UN component embedded within it. This component is known as UN Assistance to the Khmer Rouge Trials (UNAKRT), comprising UN judges,

[54] Shraga (n 51) 18.

[55] Law on the Establishment of the Extraordinary Chambers in the Courts of Cambodia for the Prosecution of Crimes Committed during the Period of Democratic Kampuchea (originally promulgated on 10 August 2001 and amended on 27 October 2004) <https://www.eccc.gov.kh/en/about/legal-framework>.

[56] Report of the Secretary-General on the Khmer Rouge Trials (31 March 2003) UN Doc A/57/69; Shraga (n 51) and Craig Etcheson, 'The Politics of Genocide Justice in Cambodia' in Romano and others (n 51) 181, recount that there is little history of independent and impartial justice in Cambodia—the courts have traditionally been a place to assert the authority of the state, with little or no recognition of the rights of individuals. Amnesty International and Human Rights Watch were strongly critical of the ECCC Law, and supported the Secretary-General's withdrawal from the negotiations. See Amnesty International, 'Cambodia: Amnesty International's preliminary views and concerns about the draft agreement for the establishment of a Khmer Rouge special tribunal' (19 November 2002) AI Index: ASA 23/010/2002 <www.amnesty.org/download/Documents/104000/asa230032003en.pdfs>; Human Rights Watch, 'Cambodia: Khmer Rouge Tribunal Must Meet International Standards' (20 December 2002) <www.hrw.org/news/2002/12/19/cambodia-khmer-rouge-tribunal-must-meet-international-standards>.

[57] Report of the Secretary-General on the Khmer Rouge Trials (n 56) para 79.

[58] UNGA Res 228 B (22 May 2003) UN Doc A/RES/57/228B.

[59] ECCC Agreement (n 10).

[60] The Law on the Establishment of the Extraordinary Chambers in the Courts of Cambodia (10 August 2001) subsequently amended by the Law to Amend the 2001 law on the Establishment of the Extraordinary Chambers in the Courts of Cambodia (27 October 2004) <https://www.eccc.gov.kh/en/about/legal-framework>.

[61] ECCC Agreement (n 10) fourth preambular paragraph.

[62] ibid Art 1.

prosecutors, and administrative staff. UNAKRT forms part of the UN Secretariat,[63] which is a principal organ of the UN.[64]

This dual component structure arguably positions the ECCC, in institutional terms, at the boundary between national and international tribunals. The ECCC Pre-Trial Chamber found in Case 001 that the ECCC 'holds indicia of an international court applying international law' and 'for all practical and legal purposes ... is, and operates as, an independent entity within the Cambodian court structure'.[65] The Trial Chamber determined in the same case that the ECCC is 'a separately constituted, independent and internationalised court'.[66] At an early stage in Case 002, the Co-Investigating Judges determined that the ECCC constituted an 'autonomous legal regime' for the purpose of application of certain forms of criminal liability under customary international law.[67]

10.3.2.3 The establishment of the STL by the Security Council

The STL's mandate was to prosecute those responsible for carrying out the attack of 14 February 2005 in Beirut that killed twenty-two people, including the former Lebanese Prime Minister, Rafiq Hariri, and possibly also related attacks.[68] The STL was the only one of the UN criminal tribunals to focus on the crime of terrorism and a single attack, or series of connected attacks, occurring in peacetime, not in a situation of armed conflict. As in the case of the ECCC, its institutional form and parentage were not straightforward.

Following a visit by a UN Fact-finding Commission to Beirut in March 2005,[69] the Security Council acted under Chapter VII of the UN Charter in its resolution 1595 (2005)[70] to establish the UN Independent International Investigation Commission (UNIIIC), based in Lebanon, to assist the Lebanese authorities in investigating the Hariri bombing. On 13 December 2005, following a series of other killings and bombings in Lebanon, the Prime Minister wrote to the Secretary-General to request the UN to establish 'a tribunal of international character' to try all those responsible for the attack of 14 February 2005 and other attacks.[71] In response, the Security Council requested a report from the UN Legal Counsel,[72] on the basis of which, the Council

[63] UNAKRT website available at <www.unakrt-online.org>.
[64] UN Charter Art 7.
[65] Decision on Appeal against Provisional Detention Order of Kaing Guek Eav, alias 'Duch', *Kaing Guek Eav*, Case file 001/18-07-2007-ECCC-OCIJ (PTC01), PTC, ECCC, 3 December 2007, para 19.
[66] Decision on Request for Release, *Kaing Guek Eav*, 001/18-07-2007-ECCC/TC, TC, ECCC, 15 June 2009, para 10.
[67] Decision on the Appeals Against the Co-Investigating Judges' Order on Joint Criminal Enterprise, *Nuon Chea and others*, 002/19-09-2007-ECCC/OCIJ (PTC38), PTC, ECCC, 20 May 2010, para 48.
[68] UNSC Res 1757 (2007) (n 11). For a discussion, see also Evelyn Anoya, 'Governance of the Special Tribunal for Lebanon', in this volume.
[69] Report of the Commission of Inquiry into the Circumstances, Causes and Consequences of the 14 February Beirut Bombing (24 March 2005) UN Doc S/2005/203, which was prepared pursuant to the UNSC Presidential Statement (15 February 2005) S/PRST/2005/4.
[70] UNSC Res 1595 (7 April 2005) UN Doc S/RES/1595.
[71] Letter from the Prime Minister of Lebanon to the Secretary-General (13 December 2005) UN Doc S/2005/783. See also Nadim Shehadi and Elizabeth Wilmshurst, 'The Special Tribunal for Lebanon: The UN on Trial?' (Chatham House, Middle East International Law Briefing Paper, 1 July 2007) 4. <www.chathamhouse.org/sites/default/files/public/Research/Middle%20East/bp0707lebanon.pdf>.
[72] Report of the Secretary-General pursuant to paragraph 6 of resolution 1644 (2005) (21 March 2006) UN Doc S/2006/176.

decided unanimously to request the Secretary-General to negotiate an agreement with the Government of Lebanon.[73] The UN Legal Counsel conducted the negotiations, reaching a consensus with the Lebanese authorities on the draft Agreement and draft Statute in November 2006 to establish the tribunal.[74]

In Lebanon, the question of a tribunal led to a constitutional crisis.[75] The speaker of the Lebanese Parliament considered himself unable to call a session of Parliament to ratify the draft Agreement, which could not therefore enter into force in accordance with its terms. The Prime Minister, supported by a petition of seventy members of Parliament, wrote to the Secretary-General to ask that the Security Council nevertheless bring the STL into effect.[76] France, the United Kingdom, the United States, Belgium, Italy, and Slovakia presented a draft resolution to the Council in May 2007. Two weeks later, following negotiations among Council members, the Security Council adopted resolution 1757 (2007) under Chapter VII of the UN Charter.[77] Resolution 1757 (2007) was drafted to bring 'the provisions of' the draft STL Agreement and draft STL Statute, annexed to the resolution, into effect under Chapter VII of the UN Charter.[78] As explained by the sponsors of resolution 1757 (2007), paragraph 1 of the resolution had been consciously drafted not to bring the draft Agreement as such into effect, but to bring its 'provisions' into effect under Chapter VII. In other words, the intention of the drafters was that the Council would give mandatory force under Chapter VII to the words contained in the draft documents, not bring the Agreement as such into force as a treaty between the UN and Lebanon.[79]

The STL Appeals Chamber later determined in a 2012 decision that '[t]he Tribunal is purely a creature of a Security Council resolution' and that resolution 1757 (2007) was the sole legal basis of the STL's establishment. The Agreement that had been negotiated with the Government of Lebanon was not the legal basis of the STL.[80] The Chapter VII legal basis raises the question whether the STL was therefore a Council subsidiary organ like the ICTY and ICTR. The STL has been regarded in all respects as a free-standing international tribunal outside the UN Organization, similar to the SCSL. The practice of the Security Council, the General Assembly, member states, and the UN Secretariat since the adoption of resolution 1757 (2007) attests to this effect. In particular, the STL did not report to the Council,[81] its financing did not come

[73] UNSC Res 1664 (29 March 2006) UN Doc S/RES/1664.

[74] Report of the Secretary-General on the establishment of a special tribunal for Lebanon (15 November 2006) UN Doc S/2006/893.

[75] Shehadi and Wilmshurst (n 71) 6.

[76] Letter of 14 May 2007 from the Prime Minister of Lebanon to the Secretary-General, annexed to the letter of 15 May 2007 from the Secretary-General to the President of the Security Council (2007) UN Doc S/2007/281.

[77] UNSC Res 1757 (2007) (n 11).

[78] ibid para 1.

[79] UNSC Verbatim Record of the 5685th meeting (30 May 2007) UN Doc S/PV.5685, in particular the statement of the Permanent Representative of France.

[80] Decision on the Defence Appeals against the Trial Chamber's Decision on the Defence Challenges to the Jurisdiction and Legality of the Tribunal, *Prosecutor* v *Ayyash and others*, STL-11-01, AC, STL, 24 October 2012, paras 46 and 53.

[81] In accordance with Art 10(2) STL Agreement annexed to UNSC Res 1757 (2007) (n 73), the President of the STL reports annually to the 'parties', the Secretary-General, and the Government of Lebanon.

from UN assessed contributions,[82] its staff were not UN staff members,[83] the tribunal was accepted into the UN Joint Staff Pension Fund on the basis of being an international organization,[84] and budgetary and administrative decision-making lay not in the hands of the Fifth Committee of the General Assembly, but with the Management Committee of the STL.[85] Furthermore, under Article 7 of the draft STL Agreement, the STL had the juridical capacity to enter into treaties with states within the sphere of its competence.

All of these factors point towards the STL being regarded in the practice of the UN and its member states as an international organization in its own right, not a subsidiary organ of the Council.

10.4 Establishment of the Oversight Bodies

Oversight of the UN criminal tribunals was not a pre-formed and fully developed concept at the time of the establishment of the ICTY and the ICTR in 1993 and 1994 respectively. Their constituent resolutions and Statutes set up periodic reporting obligations by the presidents of the tribunals to the Security Council and to the General Assembly, but did not specify what was to be reported on exactly, or what these UN principal organs were to do with this information when received. Apart from the budgetary and administrative aspects of the running of the tribunals, for which there was already a well-established General Assembly process of consideration,[86] no guidance was given on the nature and content of the oversight role of the Council and the Assembly, nor indeed was the word 'oversight' used in the constituent instruments.

The search by UN member states for a cheaper and more rapid form of UN engagement in the prosecution of international crimes had a profound effect on the oversight of the subsequent UN criminal tribunals. The oversight bodies of the SCSL, the ECCC, and the STL were established as small entities, each comprising a handful of representatives of the most directly interested states, meeting informally, as frequently as necessary, and at short notice. These oversight bodies go by differing names, but are referred to generically in this chapter as 'management committees'. Time and experience have shown that the matters reported on by the UN criminal tribunals, which form the basis of their dialogue with the oversight bodies, can be roughly grouped into the following categories: administrative and budgetary matters; progress on investigatory, prosecutorial, and judicial activities; activities of the Registry, including defence support, and the activities of the Defence Office in the STL; diplomatic relations, including fundraising where appropriate; outreach and public affairs; capacity-building and legacy issues; and completion and residual issues (later in the life of the tribunal).

82 ibid Art 5.

83 Evelyn Anoya, 'Governance of the Special Tribunal for Lebanon', in this volume.

84 ibid.

85 The Management Committee is mentioned in the STL Agreement annexed to UNSC Res 1757 (2007) (n 11) Art 6.

86 Consideration takes place in the Fifth Committee of the General Assembly, one of the main committees established in Rule 98 of the Rules of Procedure of the General Assembly (18 September 2016) UN Doc A/520/Rev.

10.4.1 Oversight bodies of the ICTY, the ICTR, and the Residual Mechanism

The Security Council established the oversight framework of the ICTY and the ICTR through their constituent resolutions and Statutes. It did so, however, only briefly and obliquely. The ICTY Statute[87] and the ICTR Statute[88] establish the annual reporting obligation of the Presidents of the two tribunals to the Security Council and to the General Assembly. The Statutes also establish the tribunals' funding scheme.[89] As subsidiary organs forming part of the UN, these two tribunals are financed from UN assessed contributions which, in accordance with Article 17 of the UN Charter, fall to the General Assembly to determine. The Council and the Assembly were thus established as the oversight bodies, but no details were given in the constituent resolutions and Statutes regarding the specific functions that they were to carry out. In particular, the General Assembly had two roles—as the recipient of an annual report from the presidents of the two tribunals, and as the UN organ responsible for their administrative and budgetary aspects.

The budgetary and administrative oversight authority of the General Assembly under Article 17 is exclusive of the Council and other UN organs, and its functions are exercised through its Fifth Committee.[90] The Committee consists of the budgetary and administrative experts of all 193 UN member states' Permanent Missions in New York. It receives advice and recommendations on the carrying out of its role from the Advisory Committee on Administrative and Budgetary Questions (ACABQ), consisting of twenty-one independent experts elected by the General Assembly on a three-yearly basis.[91]

The role of the Security Council and the General Assembly in relation to non-budgetary and administrative aspects of the ad hoc tribunals' oversight, on the other hand, was an unknown quantity in 1993 and 1994. The constituent resolutions and Statutes triggered the obligation to provide annual reports to both organs without a stated vision of what role each organ would play in this regard. Nor was there any pre-existing practice to draw on. Indeed, it was only in 1998 that the Council began to engage actively in scrutiny of the information that it was receiving from the tribunals. Until that point, the Council undertook only its parental functions associated with the appointment of the judges and the Prosecutor. From 1998 onward, the Council began to engage in particular in the timelines for the completion of the investigative, prosecutorial, and judicial functions of the ad hoc tribunals. Similarly, the plenary of the General Assembly did not react to the annual reports of the two tribunals in their early years of existence. It was not until 1997 that these reports began to be debated

[87] Statute of the ICTY (n 5) Art 34.
[88] Statute of the ICTR (n 6) Art 32.
[89] ICTY Statute (n 5) Art 32; ICTR Statute (n 6) Art 30.
[90] UNGA Rules of Procedure of the General Assembly, as amended up to September 2007(2008) UN Doc A/520/Rev 17, Rule 98.
[91] The functions and responsibilities of ACABQ, as well as its composition, are governed by the provisions of UNGA Res 14 (I) (13 February 1946) and UNGA Res 32/103 (14 December 1977), and Rules 155 to 157 of the Rules of Procedure of the General Assembly (n 93). The membership has recently been expanded to twenty-one; see UNGA Res 74/267 (14 January 2020) UN Doc A/RES/74/267.

in annual meetings of the Assembly, usually held in October during the main General Assembly session, with the presidents attending to make presentations.[92]

The oversight function for the ad hoc tribunals was thus split between the two principal organs of the UN. The form of non-financial oversight so created for the ICTY and ICTR in the establishing resolutions and Statutes was periodic in nature, being based on annual reports from the presidents, unspecific as to its substantive content, and non-dedicated, being entrusted to UN organs with considerable other responsibilities. The establishment of the Security Council's Informal Working Group on International Tribunals in 2000 improved this situation to some extent.[93] It was attended by the legal experts of the fifteen Council members, and met informally and as frequently as necessary to discuss any tribunals issues arising. A lawyer from the UN Office of the Legal Counsel attended all Working Group meetings to advise and support the members, and to act as a channel of communication and liaison with the offices of the senior officials of the tribunals. The meetings of the Security Council and the General Assembly, in their capacity as the oversight bodies, took place in public, and their decisions were a matter of public record.[94] The ICTY and ICTR oversight relationships took place within the legal framework of the internal rules of the UN Organization.

The Security Council, through resolution 1966 (2010) and its annexed Statute, established essentially the same oversight arrangements and financing for the Residual Mechanism as it had for the ICTY and ICTR, and it did so equally briefly and obliquely.[95]

10.4.2 The SCSL Management Committee and the Residual SCSL Oversight Committee

Consideration of the oversight arrangements for the SCSL took place in the period from 2000 to 2002, in parallel with the establishment and commencement of the SCSL. This period was the height of the international community's concern about the costs and perceived slow pace of the proceedings before the ICTY and the ICTR, when the Security Council was focused on the development of their completion strategies. The proposal to establish a 'management or oversight committee' for the SCSL was first made by the President of the Security Council in December 2000,[96] four

[92] ICTY press release, 'The President of The International Tribunal addresses The United Nations' General Assembly' (CC/PIO/255-E, The Hague, 4 November 1997) <www.icty.org/en/press/president-international-tribunal-addresses-united-nations-general-assembly>.

[93] On the Working Group, see n 41.

[94] The Council's Informal Working Group meets in private to discuss tribunals matters, but the fruits of its labour come to the Council for adoption. Not all Fifth Committee meetings take place in public—there are a certain number of private informal meetings with tribunals' officials, and the ACABQ does not meet in public. Nevertheless, the budget submissions of the ad hoc tribunals, and the ultimate decisions thereon by the General Assembly, are all matters of public record.

[95] UNSC Res 1966 (n 36) Arts 30 and 32.

[96] Letter from the President of the Security Council addressed to the Secretary-General (22 December 2000) UN Doc S/2000/1234. Such exchanges of letters between the President of the Security Council and the Secretary-General are relatively common. The President of the Council sends the letter after consulting the members of the Council and receiving their approval for the terms of his proposed reply. In other words, consensus, or at least lack of opposition, is required among the Council members.

months after the Council had adopted resolution 1315 (2000) mandating the negotiation of the SCSL Agreement. The reason underlying the proposal was to address the Secretary-General's opposition to an international criminal tribunal functioning on the basis of voluntary contributions, which he considered not to be viable.[97]

The UN Legal Counsel discussed the proposal for a committee with a broad group of thirty or so states interested in the SCSL ('the SCSL group of interested states'),[98] which included many potential donors to the tribunal.[99] It took until August 2001, one year after the adoption of resolution 1315 (2000), for the terms of reference for the SCSL Management Committee to be finalized.[100] The terms of reference were not incorporated into an agreement or any other legal instrument, but were sent as a unilateral letter from the Permanent Representative of Canada (Canada would later chair the SCSL Management Committee) to the UN Legal Counsel.[101] The letter stated that agreement had been reached among the member states of the SCSL group of interested states. It did not ask for a reply or confirmation of agreement, but rather requested that the text be brought to the attention of the Secretary-General 'for his information'. The terms of reference clearly did not amount to a treaty between the members of the SCSL group of interested states, the UN, and the Government of Sierra Leone. The terms of reference were not published—it requires a concerted effort to find them attached as an appendix to the Secretary-General's letter to the President of the Security Council in March 2002.[102] They stated expressly that the SCSL Management Committee was to be an informal arrangement and limited it to an assisting and advisory role in relation to the non-judicial aspects of the SCSL's functioning, as originally envisaged by the President of the Security Council. The terms of reference stated that the Committee would report regularly to a broader more representative group—the SCSL group of interested states. Article 7 of the SCSL Agreement, which was under negotiation with the Government of Sierra Leone at the time, referred to 'the understanding of the Parties that interested States will establish a management committee to assist the Secretary-General'.[103] In November 2001, the SCSL group of interested states selected the following Management Committee members: Canada, Lesotho, the Netherlands, Nigeria, the UK, and the US. Lesotho and Nigeria were selected as African states to provide regional support. Canada, the Netherlands, the

[97] Report of the Secretary-General on the establishment of a Special Court for Sierra Leone (4 October 2000) UN Doc S/2000/915.

[98] The existence and original size of this group of interested states is referred to in the First annual report of the President of the Special Court for Sierra Leone, 2 December 2002 to 1 December 2003, 29 <www.rscsl.org/Documents/AnRpt1.pdf>.

[99] Giorgia Tortora, 'The Financing of the Special Tribunals for Sierra Leone, Cambodia and Lebanon' (2013) 13 International Criminal Law Review 93, 104–06.

[100] For a detailed account of the negotiations, see Phakiso Mochochoko and Giorgia Tortora, 'The Management Committee for the Special Court for Sierra Leone' in Romano and others (n 51) 141–56.

[101] Letter dated 21 August 2001 from the Permanent Representative of Canada to the United Nations in New York to the UN Legal Counsel, on file with the author.

[102] Letter dated 8 March 2002 from the Secretary-General to the President of the Security Council, Report of the Planning Mission on the Establishment of the Special Court for Sierra Leone (8 March 2002) UN Doc S/2002/246.

[103] SCSL Agreement (n 9) Art 7.

UK, and the US became the major donors, providing approximately 75 per cent of the tribunal's financing over its lifetime.[104]

Subsequent events demonstrated that the role of the SCSL Management Committee and its status vis-a-vis the Secretary-General and the tribunal were anything but advisory. The major donors opposed the establishment of the SCSL within the financial, administrative and staff regulatory system of the UN, which they considered would replicate the excessive costs and inefficiencies of the ad hoc tribunals.[105] The SCSL functions under the Financial Rules approved by the SCSL Management Committee. The SCSL Registrar, although a UN staff member, was made responsible to the Management Committee for the financial administration of the SCSL.[106] The Committee took further decisions regarding the salary and benefits packages of the judges, Prosecutor and staff, considered and approved the budget, and approved the SCSL Staff Rules.[107]

The new form of oversight that emerged from these SCSL negotiations therefore combined, in effect, the oversight roles played by the Security Council and the General Assembly for the ad hoc tribunals into one dedicated oversight body that could meet as frequently as necessary. As the annual reports of the SCSL President demonstrate, the Committee could call at any time for information and dialogue with the Registrar, the Prosecutor and other senior officials of the tribunal, and the SCSL's liaison officer in New York.[108] Through the vehicle of the Management Committee, those states most closely interested and invested in the success of the SCSL, were directly and continuously connected with it, informed of its progress, and in a strong position to determine its efficiency and cost-effectiveness. The major donors, by this means, established their strong ownership of the Court.

This new form of oversight arrangement, however, lacked a legal basis, clarity, transparency, and accountability to any broader, more representative group of UN member states.[109] The UN and the Government of Sierra Leone, as the parents of the SCSL and the parties to the SCSL Agreement, were the parties responsible for ensuring the tribunal's independent and impartial functioning in accordance with the Agreement and the Statute. Through the financing and oversight arrangements, however, they did not have effective control over the means to fulfil these obligations—in particular, in respect of the funding of the tribunal and decision-making authority over its budgetary and administrative management. Conversely, the Management Committee and its members had control over these matters, but no corresponding obligations under the SCSL Agreement, to which they were not party. As a consequence, they had no legal obligations under the SCSL's constituent instruments regarding the independent and impartial functioning of the SCSL.

104 See the account in Tortora (n 99) 102, 104–06. In practice, Lesotho and Nigeria were not frequent attenders of Management Committee meetings.

105 ibid.

106 ibid 105.

107 SCSL, Staff Rules of the Special Court for Sierra Leone (21 March 2002) referred to in the later version of the Staff Rules of 2 February 2005 <www.rscsl.org/Documents/SCSL_Staff_Rules.pdf>.

108 See the full collection of the annual reports of the SCSL President on the website of the Residual SCSL at <https://rscsl.org/the-scsl/scsl-annual-reports/>.

109 In the author's experience, no briefings to the SCSL group of interested states took place during the period from 2004 to the tribunal's closure at the end of 2013.

The Residual SCSL Agreement and Statute also deal briefly with reporting and oversight. The President is required to submit an annual report on the operation and activities of the Residual SCSL to the parents—the Secretary-General and the Government of Sierra Leone. The President and Prosecutor are required to submit six-monthly reports in the event of trial or appeal proceedings.[110] This would only be the case in the unlikely event of the remaining fugitive being found alive and arrested, in the event of an order for retrial resulting from any review proceedings, or in the event of contempt proceedings, for example if a protected witness were threatened.

Although these reports are to be sent to the parents of the Residual SCSL, they are in practice considered in its Oversight Committee. The Residual SCSL Agreement expressly provides for this Committee. The text leaves some ambivalence as to whether the Committee is established by the Agreement itself by stating that the Residual SCSL 'shall have an Oversight Committee'.[111] The terms of reference of the Oversight Committee were adopted by the Committee itself in February 2014.[112] It is clear, however, that the Oversight Committee is not established as an organ of the Residual SCSL, and there is no treaty or other legal instrument binding between the members of the Oversight Committee and the Residual SCSL. The same legal disconnect as referred to above for the SCSL Management Committee remains between the Residual SCSL, its oversight body, and the members of that oversight body. The former Management Committee members now comprise the new Oversight Committee and its Terms of Reference largely follow those of the predecessor Management Committee.[113] There is no systematic reporting by the Oversight Committee to any broader group of UN member states nor to a UN organ.

10.4.3 Oversight of the ECCC

The concept underlying the UN's engagement in the ECCC was entirely different to that for the SCSL. As the ECCC was negotiated and established as a national court of Cambodia, the UN's approach from the outset was characterized as technical assistance to the national authorities, delivered by UNAKRT, an office of the UN Secretariat. The international component of the ECCC was thus, unlike the SCSL, not placed outside UN financial and administrative control, but run as a UN project. In accordance with UN practice, it is the UN Department of Economic and Social Affairs (DESA) that manages the project, with the support of other relevant UN departments and offices, in particular the UN Controller and OLA.

The ECCC Agreement did not mention oversight of the ECCC's activities at all, and made no provision for annual reporting by the tribunal. Under the Agreement, the costs of the ECCC fall partly to the Government of Cambodia, but primarily to the UN. At the time of conclusion of the ECCC Agreement, as with the SCSL, there

[110] Residual SCSL Statute (n 48) Art 26.
[111] Residual SCSL Agreement (n 48) Art 4.
[112] Terms of Reference of the Residual SCSL Oversight Committee, as adopted at the meeting of the Oversight Committee at the Permanent Mission of Canada to the UN in New York on 18 February 2014, and the minutes of that meeting (on file with the author).
[113] ibid.

was no agreement as to the source of funding of the UN's portion of the costs. The Secretary-General took the position, as he did consistently during the development of the voluntarily funded tribunals, that UN assessed contributions would provide the only stable and predictable source of financing for a criminal tribunal.[114] In May 2003, however, the General Assembly decided that the UN portion of the costs should be borne through voluntary contributions by states.[115] The ECCC commenced functioning in 2006 without an oversight framework, except for certain UN auditing requirements for funds provided by donor states to the Government of Cambodia to meet its financial obligations under the ECCC Agreement. A 'Group of Friends' had formed in Phnom Penh consisting of the diplomatic representatives of interested states, chaired by Japan and France, but this group received informal briefings on the progress of the ECCC and did not have oversight functions. The lack of oversight was particularly surprising given the long and difficult negotiation process preceding the ECCC's establishment and the publicly stated concerns of the Secretary-General and the General Assembly regarding the lack of independence of the Cambodian judiciary. This lack of oversight proved untenable. The structure of the ECCC established in the ECCC Agreement was unlike that of the other UN criminal tribunals, making no provision for a President of the tribunal or a single Registrar with overall authority over its financial and administrative management. There was thus an inherent lack of a leadership and governance structure within the ECCC. The bifurcated nature of its financial, administrative, and personnel management between the Cambodian component and the UN component, produced inefficiencies, and confused reporting lines.[116] Accusations of widespread corruption in the Cambodian component of the ECCC also emerged.[117] Consequently, dissatisfaction grew among the donors.[118]

A group of about twenty interested states had begun meeting from around 2005 in New York, convened by the UN Controller and the UN Legal Counsel, to discuss budgetary matters.[119] As a result of discussions between this group, the UN Controller, DESA, and OLA, a smaller group of states was formed, known as the Steering Committee. The Steering Committee was convened for the first time in June 2008,

[114] Report of the Secretary-General on Khmer Rouge Trials' (31 March 2003) UN Doc A/57/769, paras 74–76.

[115] UNGA Res 57/228B (22 May 2003) UN Doc A/RES/57/228B.

[116] Report of the Secretary-General on the Khmer Rouge Trials (27 August 2007) UN Doc A/62/304 paras 4–7, which set out the findings of the two independent experts appointed by the Secretary-General who visited the ECCC in May 2007 to examine its management and administration. See also Erika Kinetz, 'Report Finds Flaws in ECCC Administration' (*The Cambodia Daily*, 25 September 2007) <www.cambodiadaily.com/archives/report-finds-flaws-in-eccc-administration-61492>.

[117] Two reports by the UN Development Programme, 'Audit of Human Resources Management at the Extraordinary Chambers in the Courts of Cambodia' (4 June 2007) and 'Update on UNDP Audit of the ECCC' (12 March 2008) have apparently been removed from the ECCC website, but references to the first of these can be found in UN News, 'Audit of UN-Backed Cambodian Tribunal Shows Recruitment Irregularities' (2 October 2007) <https://news.un.org/en/story/2007/10/234452>. The Deputy Director of Administration was reported as confirming in November 2008 that corruption on the national side of the ECCC was a problem that impinged on its functioning: 'ECCC Corruption Report Suppressed' *Phnom Penh Post* (13 October 2007) <www.phnompenhpost.com/national/eccc-corruption-report-suppressed>.

[118] Tortora (n 99) 105.

[119] Report on the use of the commitment authority and request for a subvention to the Extraordinary Chambers in the Courts of Cambodia (15 October 2024) UN Doc A/79/519 <https://docs.un.org/en/A/79/519>.

some three years after the ECCC's commencement.[120] Like the SCSL Management Committee, the Steering Committee was an informal arrangement without any basis in an agreement or other legal instrument. Its terms of reference,[121] refer to it as the Steering Committee for UNAKRT, ie only for the UN component of the ECCC. This reflected the underlying reality that the national component of the ECCC was subject to national financial and staff regulations, not those of the UN.

The terms of reference of the Steering Committee, like those of the SCSL Management Committee, are advisory in nature. Budgetary authority over the UN component of the ECCC was entrusted to the group of interested states, which included the major donors. There is no record of how the membership of the Steering Committee was determined, but the original members, apart from Cambodia, were: Australia, France, Germany, Japan, the UK, and the US.[122] They were later joined by Sweden. The European Union participated in the meetings as a major donor. These states and the EU collectively contributed approximately 58 per cent of the international budget of the ECCC over its life to date, and almost the entirety of the national budget.[123]

A number of issues arose since the ECCC's commencement of operations that necessitated informal discussion among the members of the Steering Committee and the UN Secretariat, without Cambodian presence. These included public statements by senior Cambodian Government officials opposing Cases 003 and 004, which were at the investigation stage before the ECCC[124] and allegations of corruption in the national component of the ECCC.[125] This practice of meeting without Cambodia crystallized in 2010 into an additional informal oversight group—the Principal Donors Group (PDG).[126] It is entirely informal and does not have terms of reference or any

[120] The proposal for a Steering Committee and its terms of reference were accepted by the ECCC group of interested states at a meeting on 27 March 2008 convened by the UN Controller. A note of the GIS meeting is on file with the author.

[121] The undated terms of reference of the Steering Committee agreed at the above meeting are on file with the author.

[122] Tortora (n 99) 105. The author participated in these meetings as the OLA representative until 2014.

[123] See the financing chart on the UNAKRT website at <www.unakrt-online.org/finances>.

[124] For example, Prime Minister Hun Sen was reported as saying in a meeting with the Secretary-General in Phnom Penh on 26 October 2010 that 'he would not allow prosecutions' in Cases 003 and 004. This was stated publicly to the press after the meeting by the Foreign Minister, Hor Namhong, see Cheang Sokha and James O'Toole, 'Hun Sen to Ban Ki-Moon: Case 002 last trial at ECCC' (*The Phnom Penh Post*, 27 October 2010) <www.phnompenhpost.com/national/hun-sen-ban-ki-moon-case-002-last-trial-eccc>. Information Minister Khieu Kanharith was reported as saying in May 2011 that if ECCC investigating judges wanted to pursue Cases 003 and 004, 'they should pack their bags and leave', as reported in Lindsay Murdoch, 'Khmer Rouge trials face collapse as judge quits' (*The Sydney Morning Herald*, 12 October 2011) <www.smh.com.au/world/khmer-rouge-trials-face-collapse-as-judge-quits-20111011-1lj1k.html>.

[125] Cambodian staff were reported as stating that they were required to pay 'kickbacks' to more senior Cambodian officials, and the Deputy Director of Administration was reported as confirming in November 2008 that corruption on the national side of the ECCC was a problem that impinged on its functioning. See Vong Sokheng and James O'Toole, 'ECCC Corruption Report Suppressed' *Phnom Penh Post* (13 October 2007) <www.phnompenhpost.com/national/eccc-corruption-report-suppressed>. Negotiations between the UN and the Government of Cambodia led to the establishment in August 2009 of a post of Independent Counsellor to whom staff could take any complaints of corruption.

[126] Report of the Secretary-General on the Khmer Rouge Trials (19 September 2012) UN Doc A/67/380, para 49; and the Statement by the Principal Donors Group for the ECCC (27 June 2014) <https://www.cambodiatribunal.org/wp-content/uploads/2014/06/ECCC_Statement_140627_Principal_Donors_Group.pdf>.

other basis in an agreed instrument. In practice, from 2010, the PDG has become the primary oversight body in which the major donors and the relevant UN Secretariat officials meet frequently, whenever needed. Like the SCSL Management Committee, a legal officer of the Office of the UN Legal Counsel attends the meetings to provide advice and to liaise with the UN officials of the ECCC.

In 2012, the position of Special Expert of the Secretary-General on the Khmer Rouge trials was established.[127] The Special Expert played an important role in the governance of the ECCC by travelling frequently to Phnom Penh to hear the views of the judges and other senior officials, and by advising the UN Secretariat and the PDG. He met frequently with the Government of Cambodia at the level of the Deputy Prime Minister to ensure a constant and constructive dialogue between the UN and the Government. He had no formal authority in relation to the ECCC or the UN departments and offices concerned, but he played an important and high-level political role in support of the ECCC and its relationship with the Government, the UN, and the oversight bodies, particularly the PDG.

10.4.4 The STL Management Committee

The STL was the most recent of the UN criminal tribunals, and it reverted to the model pioneered by the SCSL, including in respect of its oversight arrangements, while also incorporating a number of lessons learned. Article 6 of the draft STL Agreement annexed to Security Council resolution 1757 (2007) stated that '[t]he parties shall consult concerning the establishment of a Management Committee'.[128] As with the SCSL Management Committee, the STL Management Committee was not established on the basis of an agreement or other legal instrument concluded between the UN and the Government of Lebanon, nor is it an organ of the UN or the STL. The establishment and terms of reference of the Committee were finalized by the Secretary-General in February 2008 after consulting the Government of Lebanon, and after receiving an indication from a broad group of interested states, which included the main donors, that they agreed with the terms thereof.[129]

The terms of reference of the STL Management Committee were easier to locate than those of the SCSL Management Committee.[130] They stated that the Committee is an informal body and identified the members as Lebanon, The Netherlands (both as the host country and as a major donor), France, Germany, the UK, and the US. Canada, Italy, and Japan joined subsequently. Under the terms of the STL Agreement, Lebanon contributed 49 per cent of the annual budget. The remaining 51 per cent

[127] UN, 'Daily Press Briefing by the Spokesperson for the Secretary-General' (18 January 2012) <www.un.org/press/en/2012/db120118.doc.htm>.

[128] STL Agreement, annexed to UNSC Res 1757 (2007) (n 11) Art 6.

[129] Terms of Reference for the Management Committee for the Special Tribunal for Lebanon, as approved on 29 February 2008, on file with the author. Establishment of the Committee by the UN Secretary-General (alone) was in accordance with para 29 of the report of the Secretary-General pursuant to UNSC Res 1757 (2007) (n 11).

[130] Terms of Reference for the Management Committee for the Special Tribunal for Lebanon (as amended on 11 October 2013). The STL website is no longer available at the time of editing this chapter.

came from voluntary financing. No breakdown of financing is available to enable a calculation of the percentage contribution of the Management Committee member states. The terms of reference state that a representative of the Secretary-General (in practice, a legal officer of OLA) participates *ex officio*.

The terms of reference were express regarding the Management Committee's authority over budgetary and other financial decision-making. The Management Committee determined the terms and conditions under which the judges, other senior officials, and all staff served—all except the Registrar, who again was a UN staff member. Like the SCSL, the STL operated outside the UN Financial and Staff Rules,[131] and the Registrar was responsible to the Management Committee for his or her exercise of these management functions. Accountability by the STL Management Committee to the broader STL group of interested states was maintained. The group had a very broad membership, totalling nearly 150 states. The Committee reported to this group and held briefing meetings with them roughly twice per year.[132] The STL Management Committee thus lacked a legal basis for its authority and transparency in respect of the terms on which it operated. The STL had the same legal disconnect with its Management Committee as the SCSL, but it was less pronounced. The UN and the Government of Lebanon had legal obligations regarding the functioning of the STL under the terms of the constituent instruments brought into effect by the Security Council, but in this case, the Government provided 49 per cent of the financial resources for these obligations to be met. The UN and the Government were dependent for the remaining 51 per cent on states that were not subject to any legal obligations in this respect. The Management Committee members had authority and control over various aspects of the STL's functioning, but apart from Lebanon, they did not have any corresponding responsibilities under the provisions of the constituent instruments brought into effect by the Council.

10.5 The Requirement of Independence and Impartiality

10.5.1 Judicial independence and impartiality under general international law

Fundamental to the governance of criminal tribunals is that they are enabled to function independently and impartially. There is an extensive international legal framework of requirements concerning the independence and impartiality of judicial bodies. The starting point is Article 14(1) of the 1966 International Covenant on Civil and Political Rights (ICCPR), which states that everyone is entitled to 'a fair and public hearing by a competent, independent and impartial tribunal established by law'.[133] Further detail as to the content of this right can be found in the jurisprudence

[131] STL Financial Regulations and Rules, approved on 5 June 2008, as last amended on 22 April 2015; Staff Regulations and Rules of the STL, STL/RB/1/Rev. 5, 18 December 2017; and the Code of Conduct for the Staff Members of the STL, STL/RB/2, 26 March 2009 (documents on file with the author).

[132] This information has been provided by the UK Chair of the STL Management Committee. The list of the membership of the STL Group of Interested States is not public, but is on file with the author.

[133] International Covenant on Civil and Political Rights (adopted by the General Assembly of the United Nations on 19 December 1966, entered into force 23 March 1976) 999 UNTS 171.

of the UN Human Rights Committee, in regional human rights treaties and the accompanying jurisprudence, in the case law of international criminal tribunals, and relevant non-binding international principles and guidelines.[134]

The relevant rules and principles relate to three aspects of the functioning of courts: (i) their institutional or constitutional establishment, which must be 'according to law', and must ensure a separation of powers between the judiciary and the other branches of government; (ii) the judicial process—judicial (and prosecutorial) decision-making—must be protected from external interference, pressure or influence; and (iii) judicial administration—the internal management and administration of the tribunal, including case management, assignment of judges to cases, and internal allocation of resources—must also be free from external interference, pressure or influence.

As the UN criminal tribunals are not themselves parties to the relevant international legal instruments, these treaties are not applicable to/before the tribunals as such, and the status of the right to a competent, independent, and impartial tribunal established by law is therefore a key consideration in its applicability to these tribunals. The right is widely considered in the literature to be one of universal application—a rule of customary international law and a general principle of law.[135] It is embedded in all major international human rights instruments, both universal and regional,[136]

[134] Universal Declaration of Human Rights (10 December 1948) UNGA Res 217 A(III) (UDHR), Art 10; UN Basic Principles on the Independence of the Judiciary, adopted by the Seventh United Nations Congress on the Prevention of Crime and the Treatment of Offenders held at Milan from 26 August to 6 September 1985 ('UN Basic Principles') and endorsed by UNGA Res 40/32 (29 November 1985) UN Doc A/RES/40/32 and UNGA Res 40/146 (13 December 1985) UN Doc A/RES 40/146; Judicial Group on Strengthening Judicial Integrity, 'The Bangalore Principles of Judicial Conduct' as revised at the Round Table Meeting of Chief Justices held at the Peace Palace (The Hague, 25–26 November 2002); and the Burgh House Principles on the Independence of the International Judiciary, adopted in 2004 by the Study Group of the International Law Association on the Practice and Procedure of International Courts and Tribunals, in association with the Project on International Courts and Tribunals ('Burgh House Principles').

[135] For a detailed survey of the extent to which the Universal Declaration of Human Rights reflects customary international law and general principles of law, see Hurst Hannum, 'The Status of the Universal Declaration of Human Rights in National and International Law' (1995/1996) 25 GA Journal of International and Comparative Law 287 See also *Human Rights in the Administration of Justice, A Manual on Human Rights for Judges, Prosecutors and Lawyers* (OHCHR and International Bar Association 2003) 118 <www.ohchr.org/Documents/Publications/training9chapter4en.pdf>. See also Michael O'Boyle and Michelle Lafferty, 'General Principles and Constitutions as Sources of Human Rights Law' in Dinah Shelton (ed), *The Oxford Handbook of International Human Rights Law* (OUP 2013) 194; Bertrand G Ramcharan, 'The Law-Making Process: From Declaration to Treaty to Custom to Prevention', in ibid 499. See also, eg, Patrick Robinson, 'The Right to a Fair Trial in International Law with Specific Reference to the Work of the ICTY' (2009) 3 Berkeley Journal of International Law <http://bjil.typepad.com/Robinson_macro.pdf>; and the UN Counter-Terrorism Implementation Task Force Basic Human Rights Reference Guide, *Right to a Fair Trial and Due Process in the Context of Countering Terrorism* (October 2014) para 10 <www.ohchr.org/EN/newyork/Documents/FairTrial.pdf>.

[136] UDHR (n 134) Art 10; ICCPR (n 133) Art 14(1); American Convention of Human Rights (adopted on 22 November 1969, entered into force 18 July 1978) 1144 UNTS 123, Art 8(1); European Convention on Human Rights (adopted 4 November 1950, entered into force 3 September 1953) 213 UNTS 221, Art 6(1) (hereafter, ECHR); African Charter on Human and Peoples' Rights (adopted 27 June 1981, entered into force 21 October 1986) 1520 UNTS 217, Art 7(1); Revised Arab Charter on Human Rights (adopted 22 May 2004, entered into force 2008) 12 IHRR 893, Art 13; and ASEAN Human Rights Declaration (adopted 18 November 2012), Art 20; The essential elements are common to all of these instruments. The requirement that the tribunal be 'competent' is interpreted under the ECHR as being included in the term 'established by law'.

and in international humanitarian law instruments.[137] The universal sources of the right are Article 10 of the UDHR and Article 14(1) ICCPR. The UN Human Rights Committee considers that the 'fundamental principles of fair trial' form part of customary international law and that they are peremptory norms of international law, ie rules of international law from which no derogation is permissible.[138] The requirement that the court be 'established by law' is also enshrined in the regional human rights instruments and is similarly considered by the UN Human Rights Committee to be of universal application and non-derogable.[139]

The Burgh House Principles, which are not legally binding, are the only source of international guidance addressing the international judiciary, confirming the necessary separation of powers between international tribunals and organs of the international organizations under whose auspices they were created.[140] The case law of the UN criminal tribunals supports the applicability of the right of the accused to the fundamentals of a fair trial, including to have the charges determined by an independent and impartial tribunal, by reference to the application of a general principle of law. The Appeals Chamber in the *Tadić* case determined that the ICTY met the requirement of 'establishment by law' because it was 'rooted in the rule of law and offer[s] all guarantees embodied in the relevant international instruments'.[141] It held that '[f]or a tribunal such as this one to be established according to the rule of law, it must be established in accordance with the proper international standards; it must provide all the guarantees of fairness, justice and even-handedness, in full conformity with internationally recognized human rights instruments.'[142] The ICTR Trial Chamber in the *Kanyabashi* case followed the same logic and came to the same conclusion,[143] as did the SCSL Appeals Chamber in the *Kallon and others* case[144] and the STL Appeals Chamber in the *Ayyash and others* case.[145]

The tribunal must be 'independent' in the sense of not being subordinated to any other organ, and being established in a manner that protects it from interference with

[137] Geneva Convention (III) Relative to the Treatment of Prisoners of War (adopted 12 August 1949, entered into force 21 October 1950) 75 UNTS 135, arts 84–87 and 99–108; Geneva Convention (IV) Relative to the Protection of Civilians (adopted 12 August 1949, entered into force 21 October 1950) 75 UNTS 287, arts 5 and 64–76; Protocol Additional to the 1949 Geneva Conventions and Relating to the Protection of Victims of International Armed Conflicts (1979) 1125 UNTS 3, art 75; Protocol Additional to the 1949 Geneva Conventions and Relating to the Protection of Victims of Non-International Armed Conflicts (1979) 1125 UNTS 609, art 6.

[138] UN Human Rights Committee, 'General Comment No. 29' (31 August 2001) UN Doc CCPR/C/21/Rev.1/Add.11, para 11.

[139] UN Human Rights Committee, *Miguel Gonzalez del Rio v. Peru*, Communication No 263/1987 (28 October 1992) UN Doc. CCPR/C/46/D/263/1987, para 5.2.

[140] See the Burgh House Principles (n 134) Principle 1.2.

[141] Decision on the defence motion for interlocutory appeal on jurisdiction, *Prosecutor* v *Tadić*, IT-94-1-AR72, AC, ICTY, 2 October 1995, para 42.

[142] ibid para 45.

[143] Decision on the Defence Motion on Jurisdiction, *Prosecutor* v *Kanyabashi*, ICTR-96-15-T, TC, ICTR, 18 June 1997, paras 37–44.

[144] Decision on Constitutionality and Lack of Jurisdiction, *Prosecutor* v *Kallon and others*, SCSL-2004-15-AR72(E), AC, SCSL, 13 March 2004, paras 54–56.

[145] Decision on the Defence Appeals against the Trial Chamber's Decision on the Defence Challenges to the Jurisdiction and Legality of the Tribunal, *Prosecutor* v *Ayyash and others*, STL-11-01/PT/AC/AR90.1, AC, STL, 24 October 2012, para 44.

the functions of the judges and the prosecutor.[146] The manner of appointment of the judges and the other senior officials, and their terms and conditions of service, including the security of tenure, are important considerations in the constitution of the tribunal in a manner conducive to its independent and impartial functioning.[147] The office of the prosecutor is to be strictly separated from the judicial role.[148] 'Impartiality' is closely related to independence, yet it has a distinct meaning.[149] 'Subjective' impartiality refers to the fact that the judges at the individual and collective level must act without any personal bias towards either party and not harbour preconceptions about the cases before them.[150] 'Objective' impartiality means that the judges must appear to the impartial observer—a reasonable person or an 'ordinary citizen'—to be free from bias.[151] What is at stake is the confidence of both the defendant and the public.[152] Respect for the fair trial rights of the defendant requires that he or she has access to legal services provided by an independent legal professional, free of charge if necessary.[153]

The tribunal should be provided with adequate financial and administrative resources.[154] Judicial administration, including the organization of the judiciary within the court, the planning of the judicial work and schedule, the assignment of cases to judges or sections of the court, and the internal allocation of budgetary expenditure within the court are matters over which control should rest with the chief judicial officer of the court.[155] The Human Rights Committee has determined that legislation authorizing ministry of justice officials to inspect courts and to report to the Minister on 'the smooth running of justice' is a matter of concern and a threat to the independence of the judiciary.[156]

[146] eg UN Human Rights Committee, 'Concluding Observations, *Bahamonde v Equatorial Guinea*' (20 October 1994) CCPR/C/49/D/468/1991.

[147] eg Human Rights Committee, 'Concluding Observations on the Central African Republic' (27 July 2006) UN doc CCPR/C/CAF/CO/2, para 16.

[148] United Nations Guidelines on the Role of Prosecutors, adopted by the Eighth United Nations Congress on the Prevention of Crime and the Treatment of Offenders (Havana, Cuba, 27 August to 7 September 1990) Guideline 11.

[149] Human Rights Committee, 'General Comment No. 32' (27 July 2007) UN Doc CCPR/C/GC/32, para 21; and see, eg, *de Cubber v Belgium*, Judgment, App 9186/80, ECtHR, 26 October 1984 and *Hauschildt* v *Denmark*, Judgment, App no 10486/83, ECtHR, 24 May 1989.

[150] *Piersack* v *Belgium*, Judgment, App no 8692/79, ECtHR, 1 October 1982; *Arvo O Karttunen* v *Finland*, views adopted on 23 October 1992 Communication 387/1989, HRC, UN Doc CCPR/C/46/D/387/1989, para 7.2.

[151] *Piersack* v *Belgium*, ibid.

[152] *Piersack* v *Belgium*, ibid, and *de Cubber v Belgium* (n 149). See also Lord Heward in *R. v Sussex Justices, ex parte McCarthy*, [1924] 1KB 256 and *Belilos* v *Switzerland*, Judgment, App no 10328/83, ECtHR, 29 April 1988, para 70.

[153] UN Basic Principles (n 134) Principle 16; Other relevant instruments are the CoE Recommendation No. R (2000) 21 adopted by the Committee of Ministers on 25 October 2000, and; African Commission on Human and Peoples Rights, 'Principles and Guidelines on the Right to a Fair Trial and Legal Assistance in Africa' (2003), Principle I.

[154] UN Basic Principles (n 134) Principle 7; European Charter on the Statute for Judges, Council of Europe (1998) DAJ/DOC (98) 23, operative paragraph 1.6.

[155] The Burgh House Principles (n 134) Principle 1; LAWASIA, 'Beijing Statement of Principles on the Independence of the Judiciary in the LAWASIA Region' (Beijing, 19 August 1995) para 35.

[156] Human Rights Committee, 'Concluding Observations on Romania' (1999) UN Doc CCPR/C/7 9/ Add.111, para 10, criticizing Article 19 of Romania's Organization of Justice Act.

10.5.2 Protections for the independence and impartiality of the UN criminal tribunals

In addition to the above-mentioned protections arising under general international law (treaty law, customary international law, and general principles of law), legal protections for the UN criminal tribunals' independence and impartiality are contained in their constituent instruments, both express and implied.

The most fundamental protection is implicit in all of the constituent instruments—that their judgments are final, and subject to appeal and review only within the tribunals themselves.[157] Further protections include a number of express references to the need for independence and/or impartiality, usually in connection with the qualifications and qualities of the judges and prosecutors: 'The judges shall be persons of high moral character, impartiality, and integrity who possess the qualifications required in their respective countries for appointment to the highest judicial offices. They shall be independent in the performance of their functions, and shall not accept or seek instructions from any Government or any other source'.[158] Similarly, the prosecutors are required to be of high moral character and integrity, to possess the highest level of professional competence in the investigation and prosecution of international criminal cases, and to be independent in the performance of their functions.[159]

All of the constituent instruments contain protections for the fair trial rights of the defendants before the tribunals, reflecting the minimum guarantees contained in Articles 14 and 15 of the ICCPR, including the right to be informed promptly of the charges; to be presumed innocent; to have adequate time and facilities for the preparation of the defence; to a fair and public hearing, and to have legal assistance of their own choosing.[160] The crimes set out in the various Statutes were chosen to respect the principle *nullum crimen sine lege*, although, in each tribunal, there have been challenges to whether this was indeed the case.

In the ECCC Agreement, aspects of the fair trial guarantees are more explicit than in the constituent instruments of the other tribunals, in the sense that there is express reference to Articles 14 and 15 ICCPR and the rights contained therein, to the fact that Cambodia is a party to this instrument, and to the requirement that the ECCC must function in accordance with international standards of justice, fairness and due process of law. These various provisions reflect the concerns of the Secretary-General and the UN Legal Counsel regarding the ability of the ECCC to do so.[161] A provision unique to the STL concerned trials *in absentia*. The Statute was careful to ensure that the rights of the accused in these circumstances are protected in accordance with

[157] eg ICTY Statute (n 6) Arts 23–26 and UNSG report on the ICTY (n 5) paras 116–20; SCSL Statute (n 9) Arts 19–22.

[158] SCSL Statute (n 9) Art 11(2). See also ICTY Statute (n 5) Arts 12–13, and UNSG report on the ICTY (n 5) paras 74–78, ICTR Statute (n 6) Arts 11–12(1); ECCC Agreement (n 10) Arts 3(3), 5(2), and 5(3); STL Agreement (n 11) Art 2(3) and STL Statute (n 11) Art 9.

[159] SCSL Statute (n 9) Art 14(2); ECCC Agreement (n 10) Art 6(2); STL Agreement (n 11) Art 3(4) and STL Statute (n 11) Art 11(2); ICTY Statute (n 5) Arts 16(2), 16(4) and UNSG report on the ICTY (n 5) paras 88-89; and ICTR Statute (n 6) Art 15(2).

[160] ICTY Statute (n 5) Art 21, and UNSG report on the ICTY (n 5) paras 106-107; ICTR Statute (n 6) Art 20; SCSL Statute (n 9) Art 17; ECCC Agreement (n 10) Art 13; and STL Statute (n 11) Art 16.

[161] ECCC Agreement (n 10) Arts 12 and 13.

established international standards for the conduct of such trials, including representation by counsel, and a right to retrial in the event that the accused later appears before the tribunal.[162]

The manner of selection and appointment of the judges and prosecutors is a critical consideration in the protection of the independent and impartial judicial and prosecutorial process.[163] The selection of judges of the ICTY and the ICTR was based on nominations by states and election by the General Assembly,[164] an increasingly criticized mode of selection against the background of the lack of any UN quality-control of the candidates nominated by states, and the prevalence of vote-trading by states in the elections.[165] In addition, the brevity of the four-year term of office between elections was not ideal, in effect prioritizing the UN need for rotation and geographical representation over security of tenure and the independence of the judges from political processes.

Selection processes for the international judges of the voluntarily funded tribunals moved away from election by a political organ to interviews by a panel consisting of a senior official of OLA with two judges or former judges of other UN criminal tribunals.[166] Selection of the international judges by an expert panel on behalf of the Secretary-General, including peers of the candidates with directly relevant international experience, although less transparent, arguably bolstered the protections for judicial independence and impartiality. The duration of the tenure of the judges, however, remained rather short.[167]

A further source of protection for the independent and impartial functioning of the UN criminal tribunals is implicit in their constituent instruments—'inherent judicial authority'. As described by the ICJ, this authority 'derives from the mere existence of the Court as a judicial organ established by the consent of States, and is conferred upon it in order that its basic judicial functions may be safeguarded'.[168] That international courts and tribunals have such inherent authority is widely accepted,[169] and

[162] STL Statute (n 11) Art 22, and Decision to Hold Trial In Absentia, *Prosecutor* v *Ayyash and others*, STL-11-01/1/TC, TC, STL, 1 February 2012.

[163] For a detailed assessment of the means of selection of the judges, prosecutors, and registrars of the UN criminal tribunals, see Huw Llewellyn, *An Institutional Perspective on the UN Criminal Tribunals: Governance, Independence and Impartiality* (Brill 2021) 201–27.

[164] ICTY Statute (n 5) Art 13*bis*; and ICTR Statute (n 6) Art 12*bis*.

[165] Ruth Mackenzie and Philippe Sands, 'International Courts and Tribunals and the Independence of the International Judge' (2003) 44(1) Harvard International Law Journal 271, 278; Allison Danner and Erik Voeten, 'Who Is Running the International Judicial System?' in Deborah D Avant, Martha Finnemore, and Susan K. Sell (eds), *Who Governs the Globe?* (CUP 2010) 35–71; Davis Robinson, 'The Role of Politics in the Election and the Work of Judges of the International Court of Justice' (2003) 97 American Society of International Law Proceedings 277, 279; and International Service for Human Rights, 'Vote Trading and Sliding Standards Risk Eroding the Credibility of the Human Rights Council' (2016) <www.ishr.ch/news/vote-trading-and-sliding-standards-risk-eroding-credibility-human-rights-council>.

[166] This process is not set out in any public document, but the author was involved in its organization.

[167] For an account of the tenure of the judges, prosecutors and registrars of the UN criminal tribunals, see Llewellyn (n 163) 202–18 (judges), 219–23 (prosecutors), and 223–27 (registrars).

[168] *Nuclear Tests (Australia v France)*, Judgment of 20 December 1974, [1974] ICJ Rep 253 para 23; also cited in Judgment on the Request of the Republic of Croatia for Review of the Decision of Trial Chamber II of 18 July 1997, *Prosecutor* v *Blaškić*, IT-95-14-AR-108*bis*, AC, ICTY, 29 October 1997, para 27.

[169] Chester Brown, 'The Inherent Powers of International Courts and Tribunals' (2005) 76 British Yearbook of International Law 195; Dinah Shelton, 'Form, Function and Powers of International Courts' (2009) 9(2) Chicago Journal of International Law 537.

has been confirmed by the UN criminal tribunals.[170] Inherent judicial authority refers to powers that are not expressly stated in the constituent instruments but have been determined by the tribunals as necessary to their judicial functions.[171] The purpose of these powers as described by the ICJ is broad—to safeguard the Court's basic judicial functions, and to enable it to take 'such action as may be required, on the one hand to ensure that the exercise of its jurisdiction over the merits ... shall not be frustrated, and, on the other, to provide for the orderly settlement of all matters in dispute .... The Court is fully empowered to make whatever findings may be necessary for [these] purposes'.[172]

Inherent judicial authority has been relied on by the UN criminal tribunals in a broad range of areas. It was on this basis that the ICTY Appeals Chamber determined in *Tadić* that it had the competence to determine its own jurisdiction—in effect, the lawfulness of its own establishment (known as *compétence de la compétence*).[173] In the *Blaškić* case, the ICTY determined that it had the authority to make a judicial finding concerning a state's failure to observe the provisions of the Statute or the Rules of Procedure and Evidence. In doing so, it stated: 'The power to make this judicial finding is an inherent power: the International Tribunal must possess the power to make all those judicial determinations that are necessary for the exercise of its primary jurisdiction. This inherent power inures to the benefit of the International Tribunal in order that its basic judicial function may be fully discharged and its judicial role safeguarded.'[174]

10.6 Authority and Control

Counterintuitive though it may seem, the parents' authority and control over the UN criminal tribunals are essential ingredients in their existence. Independence on the part of the tribunals, if completely unchecked, would leave them functioning in a void, not anchored within the legal, political, and financial framework established for their operation. National courts are similarly anchored to, and must function within, the constitutional structure and rules of the state. A separation of powers between the UN criminal tribunals and their parent and oversight bodies is essential,[175] yet some form of residual authority and control by those bodies remains necessary.

[170] eg *Prosecutor* v *Tihomir Blaškić* (n 168); and Appeal Judgement, *Prosecutor* v *Marijačić and Rebić*, IT-95-14-R77.2-A, AC, ICTY, 27 September 2006, para 24; Judgement, *Prosecutor* v *Nahimana and others*, ICTR-99-52-A, AC, ICTR, 28 November 2007, paras 312–14; Decision on the Applications for a Stay of proceedings and Denial of Right to Appeal, *Prosecutor* v *Norman and others* SCSL-2003-08-PT, AC, SCSL, 4 November 2003, paras 5–6.

[171] *Blaškić* (n 168) para 27.

[172] *Nuclear Tests case (Australia v France)* (n 168).

[173] *Tadić* (n 141) paras 37–38.

[174] *Blaškić* (n 168) para 33.

[175] The Burgh House Principles (n 134) Principle 1.2.

10.6.1 The constituent instruments

The constituent instruments of the UN criminal tribunals say little about the authority of their parents beyond assigning them statutory roles, for example in the selection of the judges and prosecutors. The constituent instruments establish the channel through which reporting by the tribunals to the parents is to take place—an annual written report—but they do so in a bare-bones fashion.

The Statutes of the ICTY and the ICTR established a system of annual reporting by the President, not only to the parent organ, the Security Council, but also to the General Assembly.[176] This latter reporting obligation was separate from, and in addition to, budgetary reporting to the Fifth Committee of the Assembly. This is perhaps best understood as a necessary link to the plenary organ of the UN in the political context of the establishment of the ad hoc tribunals directly by the Council, with no multilateral treaty negotiation among the UN member states as might have been expected in ordinary circumstances. Although the ad hoc tribunals were established on behalf of all member states of the UN by virtue of Article 24 of the UN Charter, drawing a visible line of accountability between the tribunals and the UN's plenary organ was a necessary further step to enhance their authority and credibility.

The SCSL Statute established an annual reporting obligation 'on the operation and activities of the Court' by the SCSL President to the parents of the tribunal—the Secretary-General (on behalf of the UN) and the Government of Sierra Leone.[177] The STL followed the SCSL's lead, establishing annual reporting by the President 'on the operation and activities' of the tribunal, but to the 'parties' identified in the draft Agreement and Statute annexed to resolution 1757 (2007), the Secretary-General, and the Government of Lebanon. No reporting was established to the establishing organ of the STL—the Security Council. The ECCC Agreement contains no reporting obligations.

There is no express indication in the constituent instruments of the UN criminal tribunals regarding the budgetary and administrative control of the parents or oversight body. As regards the ICTY and the ICTR, the authority and control of the General Assembly were implicit in the decisions contained in the Statutes that the tribunals would be funded from UN assessed contributions.[178] Under the internal rules of the Organization, UN funding automatically triggers a budgetary reporting cycle to the Fifth Committee of the Assembly. The constituent instruments of the SCSL and the STL, based on voluntary funding from states, referred to the establishment of a management committee for each tribunal, but without actually establishing that committee nor assigning administrative and budgetary control to it.[179] The constituent instruments of the ECCC, also a voluntarily funded tribunal, do not mention any oversight body at all, nor determine where administrative and budgetary control are to lie. The other aspect of authority and control arising from the constituent instruments is the most fundamental one. These instruments are the originating acts through which

[176] ICTY Statute (n 5) Art 34; ICTR Statute (n 6) Art 32.
[177] SCSL Statute (n 9) Art 25.
[178] ICTY Statute (n 5) Art 32; ICTR Statute (n 6) Art 30.
[179] SCSL Agreement (n 9) Art 7; STL Agreement (n 11) Art 6.

the parents exercised their authority to bring the tribunals into existence, and set the parameters within which they are permitted to function. The parameters include the core mandates of the tribunals—the limits of their material, temporal and personal jurisdiction—which together with the fundamental guarantees of fairness for the accused, determine the extent to which the tribunals are regarded as having been lawfully established. After the moment of establishment, the authority and control of the parents of the tribunals continue throughout the life of the tribunals through their authority to amend (and ultimately terminate) the constituent instruments.

The means by which the parents of a tribunal are able to amend and/or terminate its constituent instrument are determined by the form of the original act of creation. The Statutes of the ICTY and the ICTR, adopted by the Security Council under Chapter VII of the UN Charter, were thus susceptible to amendment by the Council by the same means—further resolutions adopted under Chapter VII—and indeed, many such amending resolutions were adopted.[180] Similarly, the Council's ability to terminate the Statutes, and thereby the tribunals themselves, was exercisable by means of resolutions under Chapter VII of the UN Charter. In both cases—amendment and termination—the question is whether the Council's broad authority to act under Chapter VII of the Charter determines the matter, or whether its authority is limited by the rules and principles protecting the independence and impartiality of the tribunals that it created.

The same fundamental question arises in relation to the SCSL and the STL. The SCSL Agreement and annexed Statute, a bilateral treaty, were susceptible to amendment and termination by agreement between the parties—the UN and the Government of Sierra Leone. The parties agreed at the outset that the judicial process should run its full course before termination,[181] but they could of course have agreed otherwise subsequently. The Agreement and Statute were not in fact amended, and were only terminated after all cases were completed (except for one case where the defendant is believed to be deceased).[182] The question nevertheless arises whether the possibility of amendment and termination by the parties would have been determined simply on the basis of the applicable rules of treaty law, or whether the rules and principles protecting the independence and impartiality of the SCSL would have placed limits on the authority of the parents.

The provisions contained in the draft constituent instruments of the STL were brought into effect by a Chapter VII resolution of the Security Council, which is susceptible to amendment or termination by the Council. The STL was also the only tribunal among the UN criminal tribunals that was established with a fixed duration—three years, renewable for further periods to be determined by the Secretary-General in consultation with the Government of Lebanon and the Security Council, if the work of the tribunal was not complete at the end of each such period.[183] In June 2021, the STL Registrar announced that the tribunal was facing an unprecedented financial

[180] See the full list of such resolutions at their respective websites <www.icty.org/en/documents/statute-tribunal> and http://unictr.unmict.org>.
[181] SCSL Agreement (n 9) Art 23.
[182] See the website of the Residual SCSL <https://rscsl.org/the-scsl/cases/other-cases/johnny-paul-koroma/>.
[183] STL Agreement (n 11) Art 21.

crisis that had caused a stay of proceedings in both of its ongoing cases and risked causing the tribunal to be unable to complete its mandate.[184] In June 2022, he announced that the unprecedented financial shortage continued due to the COVID-19 pandemic and the economic crisis in Lebanon, and that the STL would not be able to operate beyond July 2022. The tribunal completed the appeal proceedings *in absentia* in the *Ayyash and others* (Hariri bombing) case on 16 June 2022, and two weeks later, on 1 July 2022, it entered a residual phase. The major donors in the Management Committee were not prepared to provide the necessary funding nor request a further subvention from the UN General Assembly. The proceedings in the *Ayyash case*—the trial of the 'connected cases' concerning three car bombings similar to that in the Hariri attack—were suspended. The trial in that case had been due to begin on 16 June 2022 but it never did, and the STL closed on 31 December 2023.

The following sections will examine the applicable rules and principles of international institutional law to assess the relationship between the Council's powers as the sole 'parent' of the STL and the independence and impartiality of the tribunal. The position is complicated, however, by the powers that have been assigned by the Council to the Secretary-General in respect of the duration of the STL, and also by the role of the UN Organization and the Government of Lebanon, which the Council designated as the 'parties'.[185] As the ECCC is a national court, the view could be taken that amendment and termination of its primary constituent instrument, the ECCC Law, is a matter in the sole hands of the Government of Cambodia. When account is taken of the ECCC Agreement, however, the Government has agreed by treaty with the UN not to amend the ECCC Law without prior consultation and has undertaken not to amend the Law in a way that would affect the ECCC's functioning, including in particular in any way that would undermine its functioning in accordance with the international standards of fairness set out in Articles 14 and 15 ICCPR.[186]

10.6.2 Principles of international institutional law: authority and control by parent organs over subsidiary organs—the ICTY and the ICTR

There are two related principles of international institutional law that are directly relevant to the establishment by the Security Council of the ICTY and the ICTR as its subsidiary judicial organs. They both place limitations on the powers and functions that the principal organ can delegate to the subsidiary organ. These are: first, that the principal organ cannot delegate greater powers to the subsidiary organ than it possesses; and second, that the principal organ cannot divest itself of its responsibility. The latter includes the notion that the principal organ must retain authority and control over its subsidiary organ and the ability to terminate and recover the powers transferred.[187]

[184] STL press release, 'Severe Financial Crisis Threatens the STL's Ability to Fulfil Its Mandate' (2 June 2021). See also Evelyn Anoya, 'Governance of the Special Tribunal for Lebanon', in this volume.

[185] STL Agreement (n 11) preambular paragraphs.

[186] ECCC Agreement (n 10) Arts 12 and 13.

[187] Henry G Schermers and Niels M Blokker, *International Institutional Law: Unity within Diversity* (5th edn, Martinus Nijhoff 2011) 173–76, referring to both restrictions being illustrated by *First Meroni*: Case 9/56 *Meroni* [1958] ECR, 151–52.

The principle that parent organs cannot delegate to subsidiary organs greater powers or functions than they possess themselves has an inherent force of logic and has been cited in a number of international cases.[188] The principle that the principal organs cannot divest themselves of their own responsibility to subsidiary organs, and must retain authority and control, equally has a natural logic and support in international case law—a principal organ cannot delegate away its responsibility.[189] Both principles have been confirmed in the context of the UN, including in opinions of the UN Legal Counsel,[190] which state that: the subsidiary organ must be created by a UN principal organ; it must be under the authority and control of that principal organ; its membership, structure, and terms of reference must be determined by, and modifiable by, the principal organ; and it must be terminable by the principal organ. The latter requirement derives from the principle that powers cannot be 'sacrificed' irrevocably to the subsidiary organ—the powers must be recoverable.[191]

The above principles of international institutional law underlay doubts and criticisms that were at the time of the ICTY's creation voiced within the Security Council,[192] in the literature,[193] and subsequently before the ICTY itself.[194] These centred on the Council's establishment of the ICTY as a subsidiary body with judicial powers—powers that the Council did not itself possess. In the absence of a system of judicial review in the UN analogous to the role of constitutional courts in national jurisdictions, such issues of lawfulness have fallen to be determined by the subsidiary judicial bodies themselves. Both the ICTY and the ICTR were faced with challenges to the lawfulness of their establishment, in the *Tadić* and *Kanyabashi* cases respectively.[195] The current chapter does not rehearse the findings in these cases because they have been extensively analysed in the literature.[196] The second principle is that the principal organ cannot divest itself of responsibility for the exercise of the powers in question to the subsidiary organ; it must retain authority and control.[197] The Secretary-General's 1993 report stated that the Council would not be able to interfere

[188] *Meroni* (n 187) 151–52, discussed in Schermers and Blokker (n 187) 173–76; *Tadić* (n 141) para 37, discussed in José Alvarez, 'Nuremberg Revisited: The Tadic Case' (1996) 7 European Journal of International Law 245; Gaetano Arangio-Ruiz, 'The Establishment of the International Criminal Tribunal for the Former Territory of Yugoslavia and the Doctrine of Implied Powers of the United Nations' in Flavia Lattanzi and Elena Sciso (eds), *Dai Tribunali Penali Internazionali Ad Hoc a Una Corte Permanente* (Pisa University Press 1996) 31–45.

[189] *Meroni* (n 187) and Schermers and Blokker (n 187) 175–230.

[190] 'Summary of internal Secretariat studies of constitutional questions relating to agencies within the framework of the United Nations', referred to in UN Doc A/C 1/758 at 13, paras 1 and 2; *Repertory of Practice of United Nations Organs, vol. 1* (United Nations, New York, 1954–55) 228.

[191] Schermers and Blokker (n 187) 179.

[192] See the doubts expressed by Brazil, China, and Venezuela in the Council meetings leading to the establishment of the ICTY; UNSC Provisional Verbatim Record of the 3175th meeting (22 February 1993) UN Doc S/PV.3175 and UNSC Provisional Verbatim Record of the 3217th meeting (25 May 1993) UN Doc S/PV.3217.

[193] eg Arangio-Ruiz (n 188); Danesh Sarooshi, 'The Legal Framework Governing United Nations Subsidiary Organs' (1996) 67 British Yearbook of International Law 413 and 428.

[194] *Tadić* (n 141).

[195] ibid para 44; and *Kanyabashi* (n 143).

[196] Mohamed Shahabuddeen, *International Criminal Justice at the Yugoslav Tribunal: A Judge's Recollection* (OUP 2012) ch 2; Sonja Boelaert-Suominen, 'The International Criminal Tribunal for the Former Yugoslavia and the Kosovo Conflict' (2000) 837 International Review of the Red Cross 217.

[197] *Meroni* (n 187) 151–52.

in the ICTY's independent exercise of any of its judicial functions, but gave no legal analysis as to why this was the case, nor how the Council would otherwise satisfy the requirement of retaining authority and control over its subsidiary organ.[198] Evidence of practice and related case law concerning this principle is found primarily in the UN and in the European Union. The binding nature of the principle has been confirmed in the context of the UN, including in the opinions of the UN Legal Counsel.[199]

The question of authority to amend or terminate a subsidiary tribunal's constitutional architecture so as to remove its independent judicial status was considered by the ICJ in the *Effect of Awards* Advisory Opinion. The ICJ stated that the Administrative Tribunal, a General Assembly subsidiary organ, was 'subordinate in the sense that the General Assembly can abolish the Tribunal by repealing the Statute, [and] that it can amend the Statute and provide for review of the future decisions of the Tribunal'.[200] In other words, the Assembly had no authority to interfere with or review the Tribunal's judicial decisions—they were final; the Assembly had no power to amend the Statute to change the subsidiary body's independent judicial status in respect of ongoing cases—any case over which the Tribunal had already exercised its jurisdiction. The ICJ determined that the Assembly did, however, retain the right to amend the constitutional relationship between the subsidiary Tribunal and the Assembly in respect of its independent judicial status for future cases.

It is notable that this Advisory Opinion was issued by the ICJ in 1954, before the ICCPR and the relevant regional instruments had been concluded, and therefore arguably before the right to an independent and impartial tribunal had developed its general principle of law status. If the case had been heard a few decades later, it is doubtful that the ICJ would have considered that the employment rights of individual UN staff members could be determined in a manner inconsistent with the right to an independent and impartial tribunal. It is even more doubtful that this ICJ precedent could be relied on to support the notion that the Security Council, although prevented from interfering with or reviewing the findings of the ICTY and ICTR in ongoing criminal cases, could lawfully have removed the tribunals' independent and impartial status by amendment of the tribunals' statutes in respect of future cases.

In reality, irrespective of the legal arguments, it is inconceivable that the Council would have taken any such step to interfere with or terminate either the ongoing or future judicial criminal proceedings. To do so would have undermined the reputation not only of the ICTY and ICTR and their ability to attract essential cooperation for their effective functioning, but also the authority and reputation of the Council itself, which had determined under Chapter VII of the UN Charter that establishing independent and impartial tribunals was a necessary step to deter further violations of international humanitarian law in the former Yugoslavia and Rwanda, and to restore peace.

[198] UNSG report on the ICTY (n 5) para 28.

[199] Summary of internal Secretariat studies of constitutional questions relating to agencies within the framework of the United Nations' (n 190) 13, paras 1 and 2; *Repertory of Practice of United Nations Organs, vol. 1* (n 190) 228.

[200] *Effect of Awards of Compensation Made by the United Nations Administrative Tribunal*, Advisory Opinion of 13 July 1954, [1954] ICJ Reports 61.

10.6.3 Authority and control over an international organization by its members—the SCSL and the STL

The question that arises in relation to the SCSL and STL is whether there is a principle, analogous to that discussed above in relation to UN subsidiary organs, that the parties to the instrument that establishes an international organization are required to maintain authority and control over that organization.

An examination of the case law and literature does not reveal an express principle to this effect. This is not because authority and control play no part in the relationship, but because they are intrinsic to it, and flow from the limits of the organization's authority as defined in its constituent instrument—often a treaty. One of the defining elements of international organizations is their capacity to act with a measure of independent will—a certain degree of autonomy. Yet they are also established with specific functions and for specific purposes. It is inherent in the nature of international organizations, therefore, that some measure of authority and control must be maintained by the establishing parties if the organization is not to expand its competences beyond the intended boundaries.

The limits to the independent exercise of will by an organization are found in its constituent instrument, but also in interpretations of that instrument relied upon in interactions of the member states within the organs of the organization, and in the organization's consequent practice. The interpretation of the constituent instrument is the primary vehicle for the parties to place limitations on the organization's powers and the means for avoiding 'mission creep' or *ultra vires* activities by the organization.[201] Unless the organization in question has a court or tribunal that is competent to review the actions of the organization and its organs (like the European Union), the primary means through which interpretations of the powers attributed to the organization take place are its representative organs. Views expressed by members in these organs, and decisions of the organs, play an important role in defining the limits of the organization's autonomy and maintaining the members' authority and control.[202]

Where the international organization concerned is a UN criminal tribunal, however, the capacity of the parties to its constituent instrument to exercise authority and control through interpretation of that instrument is more constrained than it would be in other types of international organization in three respects. First, those components of the constituent instrument that establish the jurisdiction and other aspects of the judicial competence of the tribunal are within the exclusive competence of the tribunal itself to interpret. The parties to the constituent instrument may only offer their interpretations of the institutional, non-judicial aspects of the constituent instrument. If the parties to the constituent instrument consider that the jurisdictional competence of the tribunal needs to be altered, their means for doing so is not through interpretation of the existing provisions but by formal amendment of the constituent instrument. As discussed in relation to the ICTY and ICTR above, any such amendments

[201] Schermers and Blokker (n 187) 837, para 1342.

[202] Sarooshi identifies the other source of control over an organization by its member states as being their implementation of the organization's decisions within the domestic legal order. Dan Sarooshi, *International Organisations and Their Exercise of Sovereign Powers* (OUP 2007) 29–32.

should neither affect the competence of the tribunal in relation to ongoing cases before it, nor the defendants' right to an independent and impartial tribunal or other aspects of the right to a fair trial in accordance with international standards.

Second, the constitutional construction of the UN criminal tribunals, unlike that of the ICC, does not include any plenary organs in which the parties are represented. The organs of all five tribunals are limited to those necessary to carry out the judicial, investigative, prosecutorial and defence functions associated with the criminal process. The views of the parties to the constituent instruments on the functioning of the tribunals, therefore, have to find other fora for their expression. The ICTY and the ICTR sat within the UN Organization, and accordingly, UN member states were able to express themselves within the representative organs of the UN, in particular, the six-monthly Security Council meetings and the annual General Assembly meetings. The SCSL and the STL, by contrast, were established outside the UN Organization and, with accountability to a small handful of UN member states meeting privately in management committees, with no regular opportunity for other member states to participate and no public record of the views and decisions of the committees and their members.

Third, where one of the parties establishing a tribunal as an international organization is itself an international organization, acting with its own measure of autonomy, the members of the creating organization are unable directly to exert authority and control over the new organization where they are not themselves members of the new organization. This was exactly the situation of the SCSL. Its founding members were the UN Organization and the Government of Sierra Leone. No member states of the UN were party to the SCSL Agreement and Statute except Sierra Leone. The UN membership was therefore dependent on the UN Secretary-General, acting through OLA, and the few states who were members of the SCSL Management Committee, for the management of the tribunal. Authority and control over the voluntarily funded tribunals are therefore concentrated in the hands of a small subset of UN member states, largely to the exclusion of the wider membership of the UN in whose name they were established. The ECCC, as a national court, is neither a subsidiary organ of the UN under the authority and control of a principal organ, nor an international organization with member states to exercise authority and control over it. As a national court, it would be natural to assume that the ECCC forms part of the constitutional structure of Cambodia, and relates to the other branches of the state accordingly.[203] If this were the case, the ECCC would function subject to the residual authority and control of the appropriate branches of the state in the exercise of their responsibility for the administration of justice in Cambodia. The combination of the ECCC Agreement, as the governing treaty between the UN and the Government of Cambodia, and the ECCC Law as amended in 2004, as its national implementing legislation, however, carve out a niche for the ECCC that is quite specific. No measures that would alter the constitutional structure of the ECCC with its mix of international and national participation, nor the way that the ECCC functions in accordance with the provisions of Articles 14 and 15 ICCPR, can be regarded as compatible with the ECCC Agreement.

[203] The ECCC Law (n 55), confirms in its Art 2 new that the ECCC was established within the existing court structure of Cambodia.

In addition, amendments to the ECCC Law may only take place following consultations between the Government and the UN.[204]

10.7 Tensions Arising between Oversight, Independence, and Impartiality during the Life Cycles of the UN Criminal Tribunals

Tensions have arisen in the governance of each of the UN criminal tribunals during the various stages of their lifecycles. In almost all cases, these relate to the unique challenges faced by international criminal courts and to their very different institutional architecture compared to that of their national counterparts.

10.7.1 Prosecutorial independence

As the prosecutors of the UN criminal tribunals are also responsible for investigations, they are in many respects the 'engine' of the tribunals, carrying much of the responsibility for the successful achievement of their mandates. Richard Goldstone, the first Prosecutor of the ICTY and ICTR, stated that, after his arrival at the tribunal, he felt pressured by the weight of international opinion, in particular the Security Council, governments, and international civil society, who were impatient for prosecutions.[205] He has conceded that his initial choices for indictments were strongly influenced by the need to get the ICTY's work underway.[206] These pressures led him to indict a low-level accused, Nikolić, who he later stated: 'was not an appropriate first person for an indictment by the first international war crimes tribunal, but we had no option'.[207] Further indictments of individuals not considered to be among the political and military leadership followed. The judges, led by the President, did not approve of this strategy. They held a meeting with Goldstone to inform him of this,[208] and made a public statement to the effect that 'a programme of indictments should effectively meet the expectations of the Security Council and of the world community at large'.[209] Goldstone considered this to be an interference with the independence of the Prosecutor.[210] Cassese considered it to be a necessary intervention 'to help ensure

204 ECCC Agreement (n 10) Art 2(3).

205 William A Schabas, *The UN International Criminal Tribunals: The Former Yugoslavia, Rwanda and Sierra Leone* (CUP 2006) 352.

206 Richard Goldstone, 'Prosecuting Rape as a War Crime' (2002) 34 Case Western Reserve Journal of International Law 277, 281.

207 ibid.

208 Antonio Cassese, 'The ICTY: A Living and Vital Reality' (2004) 2(2) Journal of International Criminal Justice 585, 587.

209 ICTY press release, 'The Judges of the Tribunal for the former Yugoslavia Express Their Concern Regarding the Substance of Their Programme of Judicial Work for 1995' (CC/PIO/003E, The Hague, 1 February 1995) <www.icty.org/en/press/judges-tribunal-former-yugoslavia-express-their-concern-regarding-substance-their-programme>.

210 Richard Goldstone, 'A View from the Prosecution' (2004) 2(2) Journal of International Criminal Justice 380, 381

that the Prosecutor adhered to the tribunal's goals as set forth in the Statute'.[211] This situation highlights the significant differences and pressures in play when the prosecutorial and judicial functions are brought together in one international judicial institution, the head of which is directly accountable to the parent and oversight bodies for the actions and direction that the tribunal takes.[212] The expectations of those bodies are easily discernible and can be felt palpably by the tribunal's principals. The choices and decisions that are made take place in a highly political and public setting, and concern international crimes of the most serious kind, occurring in situations where global, regional, ethnic and religious fault lines are in play. In the early days of the ICTY and the ICTR, the Security Council, the world's most powerful political organ, and the international community of states, with high expectations, were looking over the shoulders of the tribunals' senior officials. These realities in the international setting cause challenges that are unique to international criminal tribunals, and which it may be unrealistic to think could be neutralized through alternative institutional designs.

10.7.2 Accountability of the oversight body

One of the imperatives for the UN criminal tribunals has been to avoid the types of criticism attracted by the Nuremberg and Tokyo international military tribunals as too closely connected to, and controlled by, the small group of Allied states that established them. The UN, with almost global membership, provided the natural vehicle for the establishment of criminal tribunals and oversight arrangements that meet these aspirations. The establishment of, and oversight arrangements for, the ICTY and the ICTR, carried out by principal organs of the UN acting on behalf of the entire UN membership, moved away from such restricted associations. On the other hand, although the voluntarily funded UN criminal tribunals were mandated for establishment by a UN principal organ, each of them has oversight arrangements that concentrate authority and control in the hands of a small number of the largest donor states ranging from around four to eight states in each committee.

Further, there is significant common membership of the management committees of these three tribunals. The net effect is that the oversight of the three voluntarily funded UN criminal tribunals lay with ten major donor states: Australia, Canada, France, Germany, Italy, Japan, the Netherlands, Sweden, the United Kingdom, and the United States. The European Union was a significant donor that participated in the management committees of the ECCC and the STL. There was thus a strong concentration of authority, control, and influence over the management of the voluntarily funded UN criminal tribunals in the hands of a small number of primarily western states. Against this background, ensuring transparency and accountability of these

[211] Cassese (n 208) 586.

[212] A further example of the Prosecutor feeling such pressures concerned the 1999 NATO bombing of Serbia, in the context of the conflict in Kosovo. Carla del Ponte with Chuck Sudetic, *Madame Prosecutor: Confrontations with Humanity's Worst Criminals and the Culture of Impunity* (Other Press 2009) 60.

management committees to the wider UN membership is particularly important. As discussed in Section 10.4 above, despite the existence of a broad-based 'group of interested states' for each of the voluntarily funded tribunals, such transparency and accountability have been less than ideal.

10.7.3 Unrealistic time and cost estimates

The early phase of the SCSL demonstrated that lessons had been learned from the costly ICTY and ICTR experiences, but also that new challenges faced this smaller, leaner form of tribunal based on voluntary funding by states. The adequacy of budgetary provision for the SCSL was a constant issue throughout its life. The major donors had rejected the UN Legal Counsel's estimates based on ICTY/ICTR-type costing and endorsed instead a three-year total estimate for the anticipated life of the SCSL of $56.8 million.[213] Both the time and the cost estimate proved to be unrealistic,[214] and placed the tribunal, and the Registrar in particular, under pressure. Attracting funds remained a major challenge throughout the life of the SCSL, with the Registrar and Prosecutor spending significant time and energy engaged in fundraising. Audits conducted during this early period expressed concern about the SCSL's 'precarious funding position'.[215] Expectations surrounded the tribunal's establishment, yet resources were extremely limited and unpredictable, forcing short-term planning and inefficiencies.[216] The severe financial crisis faced by the STL that caused it to close without completing all of its judicial proceedings provides a prominent example of the instability caused by even partial reliance on a voluntary-funding basis.

10.7.4 Judicial management

Although the functions of the oversight bodies are characterized as relating to the non-judicial aspects of the tribunals' functioning, they have in practice focused closely on the tribunals' progress in the cases before them and the efficiency of the judicial and administrative handling of those cases. The oversight bodies have commissioned experts to report on efficiency and the working methods, and formulated completion strategies as target dates for the overall completion of the tribunals' cases. These activities of the oversight bodies distinguish them from domestic authorities, which are responsible for the administration of justice at a more general level, and which cannot, in accordance with international standards of independence, engage so directly with the handling of individual cases before the courts. As discussed in Section 10.5, the UN Human Rights Committee has expressly criticized national ministry of justice inspections of courts to report on 'the smooth running of justice'.[217] This qualitative

[213] Tortora (n 99) 104–06.
[214] First annual report of the President of the SCSL (n 98) 29.
[215] ibid 29.
[216] ibid 30–31.
[217] Human Rights Committee, 'Concluding Observations of the Human Rights Committee on Romania' (n 156).

change in the type of oversight being exercised by the oversight bodies began with the General Assembly in 1998 when it requested the Secretary-General to conduct a review of the ICTY and the ICTR, 'without prejudice to ... their independent character', with the objective of ensuring the efficient use of resources.[218] The review, conducted by an expert group appointed by the Secretary-General at the request of the Fifth Committee of the General Assembly, went further into the judicial activities of the tribunals than the budgetary and administrative oversight that the General Assembly had previously engaged in. The expert group expressly focused its attention on the judicial management of the tribunals, looking in-depth at many aspects of the conduct of the pre-trial and trial proceedings by the judges.[219] The expert group received the full cooperation of the tribunals' officials, and no complaints were raised (at least publicly) regarding interference with the independence of judicial management.[220]

These apparent incursions into the judicial management of the ICTY and ICTR, far from undermining the tribunals' authority as judicial institutions, had widespread support among UN member states, civil society, commentators, and the judges of the tribunal themselves.[221] A further prominent review of judicial efficiency happened in 2006 with the SCSL Management Committee's request to Cassese to produce an independent expert report into the tribunal's operation and functioning 'with the objective of ensuring the most efficient use of the Court's resources and the completion of the Court's work in a timely manner'. The tasks of the independent expert included an assessment of 'judicial output and productivity', the efficient use of courtroom space and resources, and factors influencing the duration of judicial proceedings.[222] Notably, three of the judges of the SCSL objected to the review. They argued that it amounted to an interference with the independence of the judges of the tribunal.[223] They highlighted that the Management Committee had been established to 'provide advice and policy direction on all non-judicial aspects of the operation of the Court'.[224] These oversight tensions in judicial management of the ICTY, the ICTR, and the SCSL might on one view be regarded as contrary to the tribunals' independence. But, in reacting to their own wish to control the costs and efficiency of the judicial conduct of the cases before the tribunals, the oversight bodies were also catching the spirit of the broader membership of the UN at the time that the UN's venture into the prosecution of international crimes was in need of an overhaul. There was a widespread notion that it had set off on a course that was too slow and too expensive, and

[218] UNGA Res 53/212 (18 December 1998) UN Doc A/RES/53/212, para 5.

[219] Report of the Expert Group to Conduct a Review of the Effective Operation and Functioning of the ICTY and the ICTR (11 November 1999) UN Doc A/54/634.

[220] ibid paras 89–94.

[221] The General Assembly accepted the Report of the Expert Group and its recommendations in UNGA Res 54/239B (15 June 2000) UN Doc A/RES/54/239B, and requested the Secretary-General to follow up and report on implementation. For an account of this period from the judges' point of view and the need for reform, see eg Gabrielle Kirk McDonald, 'Reflections on the Contributions of the International Tribunal for the former Yugoslavia' (2001) 24(2) Hastings International and Comparative Law Review 155, 162.

[222] Report on the Special Court for Sierra Leone, submitted by the independent expert Antonio Cassese (12 December 2006) <www.rscsl.org/Documents/Cassese%20Report.pdf> ('Cassese Report'). The mandate given by the SCSL Management Committee is set out at 4–5.

[223] ibid para 18 and Annex C.

[224] ibid Annex C, para 2.

losing support for these reasons.[225] The expert reviews increased the tribunals' transparency and accountability to the UN membership, arguably bolstering their credibility and authority.

10.7.5 Completion strategies

Completion strategies are the most prominent example of engagement by the oversight bodies in matters of judicial management. In order to hasten the completion of cases and closure of the UN criminal tribunals, the oversight bodies adopted completion strategies for the ICTY, the ICTR, and the SCSL with a timeline as their central focus. As national courts do not have completion strategies, international instruments addressing the independence and impartiality of courts and tribunals, not surprisingly, do not directly address questions of limitations of time on the judicial process. Considerations that are relevant in trying to assess whether the independence and impartiality of a tribunal are impinged by a completion strategy should, in the author's submission, include: whether the completion timeline is generated by the judges, prosecutor, and other senior officials of the tribunal, or is determined externally for the tribunal; whether the completion dates are regarded as 'deadlines' rather than indicative target dates; whether there is any form of pressure on the tribunal, its judges and/or prosecutor, to meet the completion timeline; and whether the judges and/or prosecutor of the tribunal allow the completion dates to influence their judicial or prosecutorial decision-making.

The ICTY itself led the early stages of consideration of a completion timeline. President Jorda in 2000 stated that the time had come to identify a 'timeframe ... for fulfilling its mission'.[226] He submitted a lengthy report to the Secretary-General in June 2002 that had been prepared by the President, Prosecutor, and Registrar and had been considered and approved by the judges.[227] It set out a strategy for completion of all investigations by the end of 2004, of all trials at first instance by the end of 2008, and of all appeals, reviews, and other judicial proceedings by the end of 2010. The Council adopted these target dates in resolution 1503 (2003) in August 2003[228] and termed these goals 'the completion strategies'.[229] The ICTR's engagement in formulating a completion strategy, by contrast, was a reaction to external events. The Security Council in resolution 1503 (2003) urged the ICTR also to formulate a completion strategy, modelled on that of the ICTY,[230] but did so in the same breath as laying down the 2004, 2008, and 2010 completion timeline for both ad hoc tribunals. This is the background against which the ICTR's internal completion strategy

[225] As ICTY President Meron reported to the Security Council in June 2004, the fact that a number of member states had withheld their payments to the UN in respect of the ICTY and ICTR was impacting the tribunals' ability to function. See UNSC 4999th meeting (29 June 2004) UN Doc S/PV.4999 <https://undocs.org/en/S/PV.4999>; Zacklin (n 38) 542; and Raab (n 38).

[226] ICTY press release (n 14).

[227] Letter from the President of the ICTY to the Secretary-General (10 June 2002) UN Doc S/2002/678.

[228] UNSC Res 1503 (2003) (n 15).

[229] ibid para 7.

[230] ibid eighth preambular paragraph.

document was discussed and prepared among the three organs of the tribunal, going through several iterations between July 2003 and December 2005.[231] The UN Office of Internal Oversight Services (OIOS) criticized the setting of the same completion dates for both tribunals as being unsubstantiated in relation to the ICTR given that the nature, size, and complexity of the crimes committed were not necessarily the same.[232] Addressing the Security Council in October 2003, just two months after the adoption of resolution 1503 (2003), Prosecutor del Ponte informed the Council that seven remaining investigations were underway, involving thirteen suspects, and that five additional trials would be needed before the ICTY.[233] Meron, who had by this time succeeded Jorda as the ICTY President, informed the Council in the same meeting that first-instance trials could not be completed by the end of 2008. Referring to the intended further indictments to be issued by the Prosecutor, he stated that these could not be completed within the completion strategy timeline. He acknowledged the independence of the Prosecutor and therefore her prerogative in this regard, and concluded that the matter was one between her and the Council.[234] The assertiveness of the Council's approach in response can be seen in its reiteration in resolution 1534 (2004)[235] of the resolution 1503 (2003) completion timelines—completion of all trials by the end of 2008 and all appeals by the end of 2010. Although these timelines had originally been worked out within the ICTY, the Council now refuted a clear indication from the ICTY President that they could not be met.

The last act in the story of the ad hoc tribunals' completion strategies is the Security Council's adoption just before the end of 2010 of resolution 1966 (2010). It is best known as the resolution which established the Residual Mechanism for the ICTY and ICTR, but it was also an important measure for their completion and closure. With both tribunals set to run past the end of 2010 by significant margins, the resolution aimed at accelerating their eventual dates of closure by removing their competence over certain appeals, contempt cases, and review proceedings, and transferring these competencies to the Residual Mechanism, as set out in the Transitional Arrangements annexed to resolution 1966 (2010).[236]

Turning to the SCSL, its original three-year time span[237] and subsequent completion strategy were amended a number of times. The President and other senior officials of the SCSL in 2003 developed a heavily caveated estimate that trials and appeals

[231] See an account of this process, including questioning of the extent to which the judges apart from the President were involved in the consultations, in J-P Fomété, 'Countdown to 2010: A Critical Overview of the Completion Strategy of the ICTR' in Emmanuel Decaux, Adama Dieng, and Malick Sow (eds), *From Human Rights to International Criminal Law: Studies in Honour of an African Jurist, the Late Judge Laïty Kama* (Martinus Nijhoff 2007) 345, 363.

[232] Review of the Office of the Prosecutor at the International Criminal Tribunals for Rwanda and the former Yugoslavia (7 January 2004) UN Doc A/58/677, paras 10 and 12.

[233] UNSC Provisional Verbatim Record of the 4838th meeting (9 October 2003) UN Doc S/PV.4838. In resolution 1503 (2003) (n 15), the Council had decided that the ICTY and ICTR should each have a Prosecutor, following which the Council appointed del Ponte as the ICTY Prosecutor, and Hassan Bubacar Jallow as the ICTR Prosecutor.

[234] UNSC meeting of 9 October 2003 (n 233).

[235] UNSC Res 1534 (n 15).

[236] UNSC Res 1966 (n 36).

[237] First annual report of the President of the SCSL (n 98) 31.

might be completed by early to mid-2007.[238] Thereafter, the SCSL Registrar provided the Management Committee with monthly status reports on progress and major judicial decisions influencing this progress.[239] It is clear from this reporting that the challenges of inadequate funding and of pursuing completion absorbed significant time and effort of the SCSL staff and senior officials.[240] Cassese's December 2006 report was highly critical of the SCSL's predictions regarding the timeline for the judicial proceedings and set out 'milestones' running to September 2009.[241] This was approved by the Management Committee, adjusting the overall completion timeline to run until the end of 2009.[242] This also proved to be overambitious, and the completion strategy was consequently amended a number of times during the remaining years of the SCSL.[243] The tribunal eventually closed at the end of 2013, to be succeeded immediately by the Residual SCSL.[244] Surprisingly, the compatibility or otherwise of completion strategies with the independence and impartiality of the UN criminal tribunals is hardly addressed, either in the case law of the tribunals or in the literature. The Burgh House Principles confirm that a tribunal established as an organ of, or under the auspices of, an international organization, must be free to exercise its judicial functions free from interference from organs or authorities of that organization.[245] Judicial administration, including the planning of the judicial work and schedule, are matters over which control should lie with the judiciary and the chief judicial officer (President) of the tribunal.[246] More attention needs to be paid to how these requirements could and should be met in the unique circumstances faced by international criminal tribunals.

10.7.6 The residual phase

Moving to the residual phase of the UN criminal tribunals, the governance challenges faced by the Residual Mechanism and the Residual SCSL are practical, financial, and legal. At present, while the Residual Mechanism is conducting trial and appeal proceedings, it is resourced through UN assessed contributions. It has a full-time President and Prosecutor present at the Mechanism, and a full complement of active judges. It is not yet experiencing the minimal nature of financial and staff resources, a remote President and Prosecutor, and part-time roster-based judges that constitute

238 ibid para 31.
239 Third annual report of the President of the Special Court Sierra Leone (n 15) 27–28.
240 ibid 27–30.
241 Cassese Report (n 222) 53.
242 Fourth annual report of the President of the Special Court Sierra Leone (May 2007) 40 <www.rscsl.org/Documents/AnRpt4.pdf>.
243 Sixth annual report of the President of the Special Court Sierra Leone (May 2009) 33 <https://rscsl.org/the-scsl/scsl-annual-reports/>, which extended the overall completion timeline to October 2010.
244 The Residual SCSL came into existence as a matter of law on 2 October 2010 following notification by the Government of the completion of the domestic ratification process in Sierra Leone, and it commenced functioning on 1 January 2014, at the moment of the SCSL's termination. See the Residual SCSL Agreement (n 48) Art 14 and the Residual SCSL (Ratification) Act 2011, Supplement to the Sierra Leone Gazette, Vol CXLIII No 6 of 9 February 2012.
245 The Burgh House Principles (n 134) Principle 1.2.
246 ibid Principle 1.3; and LAWASIA, 'Beijing Statement' (n 155) para 35.

the Residual SCSL's 'administrative hub'.[247] The Registrar is the only full-time Residual SCSL senior official. The Residual SCSL perhaps represents the form of minimalized institution that the Mechanism could become when it has completed its trial and appeal case-load. The 2006 Cassese report on the SCSL highlighted a number of the difficulties of remote working and the absence of the President from the seat of the tribunal, including delays in decision-making, communication difficulties, and a deficit of judicial leadership and supervision.[248] A direct consequence of the minimalist nature of the Residual SCSL is the lack of a high international profile compared to the Mechanism and the remaining UN criminal tribunals, where trials of serious international crimes are ongoing. It has proven difficult, therefore, for the Residual SCSL to raise funding from the international community, and the financial burden continues to fall primarily on the traditional donors, particularly the key donors within the Oversight Committee.[249] This source of funding for the Residual SCSL has not been adequate, and it has had to seek funding by way of regular subventions from the Fifth Committee during its short existence to date. As experienced by the SCSL during its lifetime, funding inadequacies affect forward planning and staff retention. Such financial and administrative insecurity tends to generate critical media coverage, and to divert attention away from the important message of accountability for the perpetrators of serious international crimes.

A further challenge that can be anticipated is whether the Residual SCSL, and the Residual Mechanism when it reaches a later stage, will be able to react rapidly to urgent events. If any of the remaining fugitives were arrested and transferred to either residual body, for example, an initial hearing would need to be held within a matter of days, and the pre-trial process, or referral proceedings to a national jurisdiction, commenced rapidly. Trial proceedings might also be necessary in other circumstances, for example in the event of review proceedings resulting in an order for retrial. The ability of a residual body to react quickly and effectively, where staffing is minimal and both the President and the Prosecutor are part-time and located remotely from the seat, has not yet been tested. It remains to be seen whether the roster-based design of the residual bodies is such that they are able to operate in accordance with international standards of fairness, independence, and impartiality. The location of the Residual SCSL for the foreseeable future in The Hague, and its small and essentially administrative nature, do not equip it well to continue the extensive outreach and capacity-building activities that the SCSL's senior officials had pioneered before it closed. Nor are such outreach and capacity-building activities mandated in the constituent instrument nor budgeted for by the Oversight Committee. Similarly, outreach and capacity-building activities neither feature among the mandated activities of the

[247] This expression is not used in official documentation, but is commonly and informally used among the legal experts who attend meetings of the Residual SCSL Oversight Committee.

[248] Cassese Report (n 222) sections IV, V, and IX in particular.

[249] The Secretary-General warned about this risk: Letter dated 8 November 2012 to the President of the Security Council, UN Doc S/2012/891. The Advisory Committee on Administrative and Budgetary Questions expressed similar concerns in a report to the General Assembly regarding one of the SCSL subvention requests: Request for a subvention to the Special Court for Sierra Leone (14 December 2012) UN Doc A/67/648, para 22.

Residual Mechanism, nor in its budget. No such activities have been reported by the President as taking place.[250]

10.8 Conclusions

Parenthood, oversight, and ownership are notions that would be unlikely to feature in any discussion of national courts, yet they are essential to an understanding of how the UN criminal tribunals are governed. The proximity and singular nature of the relationships between the tribunals and their parent and oversight bodies mark them out as an entirely different institutional context to the one in which national courts function, with different challenges for the separation of powers. Perceptions of the tribunals' effective governance, including their independence and impartiality, are essential to their authority and credibility in the eyes of the affected populations, and their ability to attract the cooperation that they need from third parties to function effectively.

In addition to budgetary authority and control, the oversight bodies have in practice engaged to a significant extent in the judicial management of the tribunals, striving for their efficiency and cost-effectiveness. Completion strategies, in particular, have been applied to pull the tribunals onto as tight a trajectory as possible so that they travel from their commencement to completion and closure as quickly and cheaply as possible. Once in place, the completion strategies define the oversight relationships. Getting to completion and closure becomes a measure of the tribunal's success. In this tough environment, where legal protections for the tribunal's independent and impartial functioning are patchy and not enforceable, political checks and balances among UN member states are key to regulating the boundary between oversight authority and independence. Choosing the establishment of a criminal tribunal as the means to address a threat to international peace and security invests the interests and reputation of the UN organ and the states concerned in the conspicuous functioning of that tribunal in accordance with international standards for fair trials.

For these checks and balances to play out, lines of accountability should run from the oversight bodies to the broader UN membership. The move away from oversight by UN principal organs to small management committees of the most closely interested major donor states has done much to strengthen the bond of partnership and ownership between the oversight bodies and the tribunals. But it could be further strengthened by providing clear and transparent legal bases for these oversight relationships with express protections for the independence of the judicial functions of the tribunals from their oversight bodies, and through institutionalizing accountability by the management committees to the broader groups of donor states and the UN membership at large.

The completion strategies and other such oversight incursions into the judicial management of the UN criminal tribunals would be difficult to square with the

[250] Report of the President of the International Residual Mechanism for Criminal Tribunals to 16 May 2020, annexed to Letter dated 19 May 2020 from the President of the Residual Mechanism to the President of the Security Council, UN Doc S/2020/416.

requirement of the separation of powers in a national context. Yet such measures have largely been seen as necessary and beneficial—tending to boost the tribunals' credibility and authority rather than diminish it. Judicial management is the primary area where the differences between international criminal tribunals and their national counterparts warrant a fresh examination of the interface between oversight and independence. It is an area that would benefit from international discussion and the formulation of international guidance to add to the body of existing international standards, which are applicable primarily to national courts. The Burgh House Principles make an important start in confirming the applicability of the basic principles of independence, impartiality and the separation of powers to international tribunals and the international judiciary. But after nearly three decades of UN experience of establishing and overseeing international criminal tribunals, there is scope for more detailed consideration of the standards that should be applicable, particularly in matters of judicial management.

As the UN criminal tribunals reach the completion, closure, and residual stages of their life cycles, the spotlight is on assessing their legacies—their contributions to the development of substantive and procedural international criminal law, promoting reconciliation among fractured populations and increasing the capacity of the local judiciary and legal professionals in the affected states to prosecute international crimes. A black hole in these legacy considerations is the lack of any assessment of the governance and institutional lessons learned. There is scope for an examination of the strengths and weaknesses of the various institutional forms of the tribunals and their oversight arrangements, and whether they have been well-run and -managed institutions that function independently and impartially, command respect, and carry authority. It is time for a discussion and assessment of these matters involving the tribunals, the states members of the management committees of the voluntarily funded UN criminal tribunals, the members of the Security Council and its Informal Working Group on International Tribunals, UN member states more broadly including the affected states, the UN Secretariat, and civil society.

11
Governance of the Special Tribunal for Lebanon
An Administrative Perspective

Evelyn Anoya

11.1 Introduction

Understanding the legal framework for the governance and structuring of international organizations is an indispensable step in the assessment of successes and failures of such institutions. This is even more so in the case of international criminal courts and tribunals. These strange creatures are first and foremost courts of law. However, their being part of larger international structures requires the application of the law of international organizations. Whether this design model, especially as embodied in the Special Tribunal for Lebanon (STL, or Tribunal), is viable for a court to be able to function effectively and efficiently is the question that this chapter will address.

The STL was the internationalized tribunal created to respond to the call for justice in Lebanon following the assassination of former Prime Minister Rafik Hariri and twenty-one other persons in a massive explosion, which also injured 226 persons, on 14 February 2005 in downtown Beirut. Numerous other attacks followed, including the killing of prominent anti-Syrian journalists and politicians Samir Kassir, George Hawi, and Gebran Tueini, and the attempted assassination of MP Marwan Hamadeh. On 13 December 2005, the Prime Minister, Fuad Siniora, sent a letter to the UN Secretary-General requesting that the UN Security Council: (1) establish a tribunal of an international character to try all those responsible for the assassination of former Prime Minister Hariri; and (2) expand the mandate of the International Independent Investigation Commission (IIIC) which had been set up in April 2005 or create another independent commission to investigate the numerous assassinations that had taken place in Lebanon since 1 October 2004, the day Hamadeh's motorcade was targeted by a car bomb.[1]

This was a significant attempt to address the culture of impunity for political assassinations in Lebanon since gaining its independence in 1943,[2] sending an emotive

[1] Letter dated 13 December 2005 from the Charge d'affaires a.i. of the Permanent Mission of Lebanon to the United Nations Addressed to the Secretary-General, UN Doc S/2005/783, 13 December 2005.

[2] There have been 220 assassinations and murder attempts since Lebanon gained its independence in 1943, including 125 assassinations of journalists, religious figures, politicians, party members, military officers, judges, and Arab and Foreign Military Officers, politicians, and diplomats.

Evelyn Anoya, *Governance of the Special Tribunal for Lebanon* In: *Governance of International Courts and Tribunals*.
Edited by: Sergey Vasiliev and Niels Blokker, Oxford University Press. © Evelyn Anoya 2026.
DOI: 10.1093/oso/9780198922131.003.0011

message to the formal and informal regional powers that 'impunity will not be tolerated'.[3] Yet, Lebanon's political climate and the sectarian character of its society made the subsequent quest for justice complicated. United Nations (UN) Security Council Resolution 1664 mandated the Secretary-General to negotiate an agreement with the Lebanese government. The negotiations resulted in the drafting of the STL Agreement, which was signed on 23 January and 6 February 2007 by the Government of Lebanon and the UN, respectively; the Statute of the STL was attached to the STL Agreement.[4] The STL Agreement was meant to be formally ratified by the Parliament in accordance with the Lebanese Constitution.[5] However, the Speaker of the Parliament refused to convene the Parliament to vote on it.

To resolve the political deadlock, the UN Security Council relied on Chapter VII of the UN Charter to create the STL through UN Security Council Resolution 1757 that ensured that the provisions of the STL Agreement (and Statute) came into force for Lebanon.[6] Although the Security Council relied on its Chapter VII powers, in terms of the institutional design and governance arrangements, the STL model deviated from that which the United Nations previously relied upon in establishing the ad hoc tribunals for the former Yugoslavia[7] and Rwanda.[8] The STL was created not as a subsidiary organ of the UN Security Council, but it was established in a similar manner. With the creation of the Special Court for Sierra Leone (SCSL) and the Extraordinary Chambers in the Courts of Cambodia (ECCC), the UN had tested a new hybrid model of trying serious crimes. These hybrid tribunals were not created under the Security Council's Chapter VII authority. Although the President of the SCSL informed the Secretary-General about the difficulties the court was facing with third-state cooperation and asked for the SCSL to be 'endowed' with broad Chapter VII powers, the UN disagreed and encouraged the use of bilateral cooperation instead.[9] The establishment of the STL continued the trend of mandating hybrid criminal justice institutions, albeit not through a bilateral treaty between the UN and the relevant state but through the Security Council action bringing the provisions of a draft agreement into

[3] UN, 'Statement Attributable to the Spokesman of the Secretary-General on the Tenth Anniversary of the Assassination of Former Lebanese Prime Minister Rafiq Hariri' (14 February 2015) <www.un.org/sg/en/content/sg/statement/2015-02-14/statement-attributable-spokesman-secretary-general-tenth-anniversary>.

[4] Agreement between the United Nations and the Lebanese Republic on the establishment of a Special Tribunal for Lebanon, annexed to UNSC Res 1757 (2007), UN Doc S/RES/1757 (2007), 30 May 2007 ('STL Agreement') and Statute of the Special Tribunal for Lebanon ('STL Statute').

[5] Letter dated 21 November 2006 from the President of the Security Council addressed to the Secretary-General, S/2006/911. On behalf of the Security Council, the President invited the Secretary-General and the Lebanese government to proceed in accordance with the Constitution of Lebanon in taking 'the final steps for the conclusion of the Agreement'.

[6] UNSC Res 1757 (n 4). UNSC Res 1757 refers to a briefing by the Legal Counsel on 2 May 2007 and states that 'the Constitutional process is facing serious obstacles, but noting also that all parties concerned reaffirmed their agreement in principle to the established of the Tribunal'. See also Bahige Tabbarah, 'The Legal Nature of the Special Tribunal for Lebanon' in Amal Alamuddin, Nidal Nabil Jurdi, and David Tolbert (eds), *The Special Tribunal for Lebanon: Law and Practice* (OUP 2014) 40–41.

[7] UNSC Res 808 (1993), UN Doc S/RES/808 (1993), 22 February 1993, and UNSC Res 827 (1993) UN Doc S/RES/827 (1993), 25 May 1993, which approved the 1993 Report of the Secretary-General, UN Doc 25704 and add 1.

[8] UNSC Res 955 (1994), UN Doc S/RES/955, 8 November 1994.

[9] Letter to the President of the Special Court for Sierra Leone, 14 July 2003, in *UN Juridical Yearbook 2003*, ST/LEG/SER.C/41, 541.

effect. Although heavily disputed, this Chapter VII authority was ultimately applied, but only towards Lebanon and not all the UN member states, as with the UN ad hoc tribunals.

This chapter provides an insider's view of the governance structure of the STL. It references the SCSL and ECCC to the extent needed to highlight how their innovative models impacted the creation and the governance architecture of the STL. Although the STL was created through the Security Council's Chapter VII authority, unlike the SCSL, the design of the Tribunal largely mirrored that of its sister UN tribunals, including in part of the external and executive governance structure.[10] This chapter will first explain the STL's governance and institutional design model as an independent international organization with a judicial mandate. Such a framework presents unique features that do not necessarily provide the safeguards necessary to ensure the effectiveness of the judicial institution. Second, the chapter will set out the STL's organizational structure and critique its effectiveness as the court, especially in relation to the pursuit of the goals to bring about accountability. Third, it will address the Tribunal's oversight mechanism. Fourth, the chapter will review the compliance and reporting obligations upon the STL that have been put in place to ensure its transparent and accountable operation. Finally, the chapter will provide concluding observations highlighting some of the challenges posed by the STL governance structure and suggesting improvements for the benefit of future institutions.

11.2 Institutional Design

Four days after Rafik Hariri's assassination, the UN deployed a fact-finding mission to Lebanon, led by Peter FitzGerald, inquiring into the causes, circumstances, and consequences of the 14 February 2005 Beirut Bombing. Within one month, the fact-finding mission produced a report, which it presented to the Security Council, concluding on the necessity of the establishment of an independent international investigation.[11] The recommendation was endorsed by the Secretary-General, leading to the establishment on 7 April 2005 of the IIIC,[12] which obtained the power to investigate common crimes under Lebanese law.[13] The IIIC was an entity of the UN

[10] 'The terms and conditions of service for both judges and staff will be guided by those of the judges and staff of the Special Court for Sierra Leone, with appropriate modifications.' Report of the Secretary-General submitted pursuant to Security Council Resolution 1757 (2007), UN Doc S/2007/525, 4 September 2007, para 20.

[11] Letter dated 24 March 2005 from the Secretary-General to the President of the Security Council, dated 24 March 2005, forwarding the Report of the Fact-finding Mission to Lebanon inquiring into the causes, circumstances, and consequences of the assassination of former Prime Minister Rafik Hariri (24 February to 24 March 2005, S/2005/203).

[12] UNSC Res 1595, UN Doc S/Res/1595 (2005), 7 April 2005.

[13] The Security Council, in its Resolution 1595, termed the bombing that killed the former Prime Minister Rafik Hariri a terrorist act and stated, 'the Lebanese investigation process suffers from serious flaws and has neither the capacity nor the commitment to reach a satisfactory and credible conclusion'. It referenced the Lebanese government's readiness to cooperate fully and approval of establishing an independent investigation commission. As a result, the IIIC was based in Lebanon and was mandated to report to the Security Council on its progress every two months. See also Amal Alamuddin and Anna Bonini, 'The UN Investigation of the Hariri Assassination' in Amal Alamuddin, Nidal Nabil Jurdi, and David Tolbert (eds), *The Special Tribunal for Lebanon Law and Practice* (OUP 2014) 53–57.

Secretariat established under the responsibility of the Department of Political Affairs as one of the Secretary-General's special political missions and funded from the UN regular budget.[14]

By contrast, the STL was set up as an independent international organization separate from the UN, with its own legal personality and administrative framework. The work of the IIIC was foundational to the STL mandate and resulted in the collection of evidence that led to the creation of the Tribunal, which officially opened its doors on 1 March 2009. The institutional design features of the Tribunal proved contentious, and different models were considered by the UN. On 10 March 2008, the Secretary-General appointed Robin Vincent as the first STL Registrar to lead the advance team, which was responsible for ensuring that the court was ready to begin its work in the Netherlands. The Secretary-General signed the Headquarters Agreement on behalf of the newly created institution on 21 December 2007.[15] Lebanon intended to sign the Headquarters Agreement as well, but ultimately it was signed only between the UN and the representative of the Kingdom of the Netherlands as the host state. This document, *inter alia*, conferred upon the STL its legal personality, privileges and immunities, and ability to function as an international organization in the Netherlands.

In addition, the STL Agreement foresaw in Article 8(3) that the STL would create an office for the conduct of investigations in Lebanon. The Registrar signed a Memorandum of Understanding (MOU) with the Government of Lebanon, which set out how the Lebanon office would function. The MOU specified the Lebanese government's willingness to: (a) cooperate with the STL; (b) allow its organs the ability to function independently; (c) allow STL staff to move freely inside the country; and (d) provide for the security of the staff (including judges, heads of organs, experts, and others invited or required to be present at the Tribunal) and its facilities.[16] In addition, the Prosecutor and the Defence Office signed separate memoranda of understanding defining the modalities of their cooperation with Lebanon.[17]

With respect to its administrative framework, as an independent organization, the Tribunal needed to issue its own internal administrative regulations, instead of applying the already existing UN policies. Nevertheless, the organization became part of the UN Joint Staff Pension Fund (UNJSPF). On 24 November 2008, the UN Legal Counsel submitted an Interoffice Memorandum to the Chief Executive Officer of the UNJSPF regarding the legal status of the STL in view of its application for membership

[14] Giorgia Tortora, 'The Financing of the Special Tribunals for Sierra Leone, Cambodia and Lebanon' (2013) 13 International Criminal Law Review 117.

[15] Agreement between the United Nations and the Kingdom of the Netherlands concerning the Headquarters of the Special Tribunal for Lebanon, New York, 21 December 2007, 2486 UNTS 187 ('Headquarters Agreement').

[16] Memorandum of Understanding between the Government of the Republic of Lebanon and the Special Tribunal for Lebanon concerning the Office of the Special Tribunal in Lebanon, 17 June 2009 ('Lebanon-STL MOU').

[17] Memorandum of Understanding between the Government of the Lebanese Republic and the Office of the Prosecutor of the Special Tribunal for Lebanon on Cooperation, 5 June 2009 and the Memorandum of Understanding between the Government of the Republic of Lebanon and the Defence Office on the Modalities of their Cooperation, 28 July 2010.

of the UNJSPF.[18] The UN provided assurance to the UNJSPF that the STL was an international, intergovernmental organization created through an international instrument governed by international law. The UN relied on the Agreement annexed to UNSC Resolution 1757, which states that the STL was expressly conferred with legal capacity to enter contracts, acquire and dispense of property, institute proceedings, and enter into agreements with states.[19]

The admission to the UNJSPF required the STL to align its staff regulations and rules to those of the UN common system, ensuring that common standards, methods, and arrangements would be applied to salaries, allowances, and benefits. This measure allowed the Registrar to design a legal model for administering staff contracts adhering to the guidance provided by the International Civil Service Commission, which is an independent body, mandated by the UN General Assembly to regulate conditions of service of staff in the UN common system. The STL never entered into a formal relationship agreement with the UN similar to the one reached between the UN and the International Criminal Court.[20] The STL did sign the Inter-Organization Mobility Accord, but only in 2019.[21]

In addition, the Tribunal needed to ensure there was an adequate mechanism enabling its employees to bring internal disputes for resolution. The STL employees did not have standing to bring disputes before the UN Dispute or Appeals Tribunals.[22] Its architects chose not to have the STL recognize the jurisdiction of the International Labor Organization's Administrative Tribunal (ILOAT). Since the STL's mandate was initially intended to be only for three years, the ILOAT process was considered too costly and time-consuming. As a result, there was no external administrative tribunal with the competency to consider complaints by STL staff. Instead, the Tribunal created its own internal mechanism for resolving disputes referred to as the Judge for Staff Appeals, which relied on a roster of STL Judges to hear staff appeals.

Initially, the STL mirrored its internal dispute mechanism to that of the SCSL, but over time this unique framework proved not to be effective. The Judge for Staff Appeals would be supported by designated legal officers who were STL staff members assigned to work in Chambers. As the organization matured, more internal complaints arose

[18] Interoffice Memorandum to Chief Executive Officer, UN Joint Staff Pension Fund regarding the Legal Status of the STL in View of its Application for Membership to the UNJSPF, 24 November 2008 in *UN Juridical Yearbook 2008*, ST/LEG/SER.C/46, 440.

[19] ibid 440 para 6.

[20] Negotiated Relationship Agreement between the International Criminal Court and the United Nations, ICC-ASP/3/Res.1, 4 October 2004. It was approved by the UN General Assembly in its Resolution 58/318 of 13 September 2004, and entered into force on 4 October 2004.

[21] Inter-Organization Agreement concerning Transfer, Secondment or Loan of Staff among the Organizations applying the United Nations Common System of Salaries and Allowances, Annex I, 19 July 2019.

[22] Judgment UNDT/2011/128, *Buckley* v *Secretary-General of the United Nations*, UNDT/GVA/2011/022, UNDT, 13 July 2011 and Judgment UNDT/2012/038, *El Issawi* v *Secretary-General of the United Nations*, UNDT/GVA/2012/007, UNDT, 26 March 2012. The only exception pertained to UNJSPF. Since the STL was a member of the UNJSPF, current and former staff members of the pension fund could appeal decisions taken by a staff pension committee, for example, to the UN Appeals Tribunal. Administrative Rules of the United Nations Joint Staff Pension Fund (Annex I to Regulations, Rules and Pension Adjustment System of the UNJSPF, JSPB/G.4/Rev.27, UN General Assembly res 248 (III), 23 January 1949) Section K; Regulations of the United Nations Joint Staff Pension Fund, Art 48 and the Statute of the United Nations Appeals Tribunal, UNGA res 63/253, 24 December 2008 (as amended).

leading to discontent with the process because staff assigned to work in Chambers felt ill at ease to challenge decisions of the Registrar before a Judge. To address this potential conflict and ensure that all staff members had access to a remedy, the President expanded the roster to include external judges. In addition, the STL administrative regulations were amended and strengthened in line with similar policies promulgated by the UN.[23] For example, the Tribunal adopted new policies, which were guided by those of the UN, on prohibiting discrimination and harassment,[24] and on protection against retaliation for reporting misconduct and for cooperating with authorized audits or investigations.[25]

11.3 Organizational and Accountability Structures

11.3.1 Appointment of officials

The Tribunal's internal governance structure was anchored in a shared leadership model. The Tribunal was made up of four independent organs: Chambers, Office of the Prosecutor, Defence Office, and Registry. The UN Secretary-General appointed the principals responsible for each independent organ for a three-year renewable term. The judges were appointed in a similar manner by the Secretary-General. All the Tribunal's officials were technically accountable to the UN as their appointing body. The Registrar was the only principal appointed as a UN staff member; therefore, he was obligated to adhere to the UN regulatory framework.

The Tribunal's structure was unique in that it created a fourth, independent organ for the defence for the first time in the history of international criminal justice.[26] In the UN ad hoc tribunals, the defence matters, such as the administration of legal aid and oversight of the defence teams, were within the mandate of the Registrar. At the SCSL, a step further was made with the creation of the Office of the Principal Defender, but in institutional terms it remained a part of the Registry.[27]

As a hybrid tribunal, the STL judiciary was composed of both international and Lebanese judges.[28] Article 9 of the Statute required the judges to be 'persons of high moral character, impartiality, and integrity, with extensive judicial experience', to 'be independent in the performance of their functions', and not to 'accept or seek instructions from any government or any other source'. For the Lebanese judges, the STL Agreement required the Secretary-General to appoint a judge from a list of twelve persons presented by the Government upon the proposal of the Lebanese Supreme

[23] Administrative Instruction on Misconduct and Procedure for Staff Appeals of Administration Decisions Taken as a Result of Disciplinary Action, STL/AI/HR/6/Rev.1, 22 June 2015.

[24] Administrative Instruction on Prohibition of Discrimination, Harassment, Including Sexual Harassment, and Abuse of Authority, STL/AI/HR/13, 23 May 2013.

[25] Administrative Instruction on Protection against Retaliation for Reporting Misconduct and for Cooperating with Duly Authorized Audits or Investigations, STL/AI/HR/12, 10 April 2012.

[26] John RWD Jones and Miša Zgonec-Rožej, 'Rights of Suspects and Accused' in Amal Alamuddin, Nidal Nabil Jurdi, and David Tolbert (eds), *The Special Tribunal for Lebanon Law and Practice* (OUP 2014) 191.

[27] Jones and Zgonec-Rožej (n 26) 191.

[28] STL Agreement (n 4) Art 2 (on the composition and appointment of the judges) and Art 2(5) (on the appointment of the Lebanese judges).

Council of the Judiciary.[29] The list was submitted confidentially to the Secretary-General and remained as such. The international judges were appointed upon nominations forwarded by states at the invitation of the Secretary-General, who was also permitted to accept nominations from competent persons, although this possibility was not specifically defined.[30] The STL Agreement required the Secretary-General and the Lebanese Government to consult on the appointment of judges.[31]

In the actual process of selection of the judges, the Secretary-General appointed a selection panel, albeit only after informing the Security Council of his intention, to interview and recommend the judges on his behalf. A similar process was used for the selection of the Prosecutor. The STL Agreement required that the panel be composed of two judges, currently on or retired from an international tribunal, and the representative of the Secretary-General.[32] The judges were appointed for a renewable three-year term. The President of the Tribunal was the Presiding Judge of the Appeals Chamber.[33] The Deputy Prosecutor was the only Tribunal staff member who was appointed directly by the Lebanese government and not the Secretary-General.[34] Legislative decrees were issued by the Government, with the approval of the Lebanese Higher Judicial Council, permitting the secondment of the Lebanese judges and the Deputy Prosecutor to the Special Tribunal.

11.3.2 Accountability mechanisms

The Tribunal functioned legally as an international organization with the juridical capacity to 'institute proceedings'.[35] The President represented the Tribunal in instituting proceedings while the Registrar represented it as the international organization in the Netherlands and in Lebanon.[36] The President was required to report annually on the operation and activities of the Tribunal to the Secretary-General and the Government of Lebanon.[37] The President had both an administrative and judicial role to play at the Tribunal. Under the Rules, the President was also vested

29 ibid Art 2(5)(a).
30 ibid Art 2(5)(b).
31 ibid Art 2(5)(c).
32 The selection panel included Judge Mohamed Amin El Mahdi (Egypt), who served as the ICTY judge from 2001 to 2005, Judge Erik Møse (Norway), a judge and former President of the ICTR, and Nicolas Michel, the UN's Legal Counsel. Letter dated 10 October 2007 from the Secretary-General addressed to the President of the Security Council, UN Doc S/2007/609, 16 October 2007. Prior to the interview process, the Secretary-General asked UN member states to nominate candidates for appointment as international judges. The selection panel interviewed candidates from those who were nominated and then made recommendations to the Secretary-General, who accepted the recommendations, but he did not immediately make the names of the judges known to the public due to security reasons.
33 STL Statute (n 4) Art 8(2) and STL Rules of Procedure and Evidence, adopted on 20 March 2009 (as last corrected on 18 December 2020, STL-BD-2009-01-Rev.11) ('STL RPE') Rule 31(A).
34 STL Agreement (n 4) Art 3(3).
35 ibid Art 7(c) and Headquarters Agreement (n 15) Art 4(1)(c).
36 Headquarters Agreement (n 15) Art 4(2) states that for the purpose of the Tribunal's juridical personality, 'the Tribunal shall be represented by the Registrar'. Lebanon-STL MOU (n 16) Art 3(2) is similar to the Headquarters Agreement provision; however, the Tribunal is represented by an 'Office Administrator', who is a Registry staff member delegated by the Registrar.
37 STL Statute (n 4) Art 10(2) and STL RPE (n 33) Rule 32(I).

with the authority to enter into agreements with national or international entities.[38] One example of such an agreement was the cooperation agreement signed by the late President Cassese with Interpol.[39]

The functions of the President and Registrar complemented and supported each other, but the hierarchal structure led to confusion because the Registrar had two bosses: the President and the Secretary-General. The reporting lines were not clearly demarcated. Since the Registrar was the (only) UN staff member, that position was supposed to be fully integrated within the UN system, including oversight and performance management. However, this was not the case in practice. The Registrar was expected to administer and service the Tribunal under 'the authority of the President'.[40] What this meant led to debate. The powers of the President included judicial functions, representing the Tribunal externally, and responsibility for its 'effective functioning and the good administration of justice'.[41] Rule 32 further specified that the President, *inter alia*, was to 'supervise the activities of the Registry'.[42]

The role of the registrar at international or hybrid tribunals is multi-layered and does not replicate the system that one may find in national courts. Within a national judicial system, it is clear why the registrar should fall under the authority of the President of the Court. However, at an international or hybrid tribunal, the role of the registrar is blurred. How involved should the president be in matters pertaining to the administration and servicing of the tribunal? As the president has both judicial and administrative responsibilities, the president should arguably be cautious not to get too involved with the administration and servicing of the other independent organs because of his or her judicial role. The registrar's role includes oversight, which should be administered independently and not under the supervision or control of the presidency. In fact, although the STL Rules foresaw a supervisory role for the President,[43] it only extended to the activities of the Registry and not to those of the Registrar. This resulted in blurred lines of authority. As the Registrar was also expected to 'assist the Chambers, the Judges, the Prosecutor, and the Head of Defence Office in the performance of their functions',[44] it would have been better to limit the President's role to overseeing the Chambers' functioning and not that of the other organs. This balance was not struck properly in the STL framework, creating tensions in practice.

Although the Secretary-General appointed the STL judges and the Prosecutor, the UN did not play the role of an oversight body. The power to appoint and the oversight authority remained distinct. The oversight framework for the judiciary at the

[38] STL RPE (n 33) Rules 13 and 32(G). Under Rule 39, the President could authorize the Registrar to negotiate agreements on behalf of the Tribunal.

[39] STL Press Release, 'The Special Tribunal for Lebanon and Interpol Have Concluded a Co-operation Agreement', 17 December 2009 (on file with the author). This agreement replaced a previously negotiated and signed interim agreement.

[40] STL Statute (n 4) Art 12(1) states, '[under the authority of the President of the Special Tribunal, the Registry shall be responsible for the administration and servicing of the Tribunal'. See also STL RPE (n 33) Rule 48(A) stating '[u]nder the authority of the President, the Registrar shall be responsible for the administration and servicing of the Tribunal'.

[41] STL Statute (n 4) Art 10(1).

[42] STL RPE (n 33) Rule 32(C).

[43] ibid Rule 32(C).

[44] STL RPE (n 33) Rule 48(A).

STL required a critical review. STL judges and the Prosecutor were paid at the Under-Secretary-General (USG) level but not considered UN officials. The exception was the Registrar who was appointed as an Assistant Secretary-General, a position lower than the USG in the UN hierarchy. As an official of the UN system, the Registrar was accountable to UN oversight bodies. Typically, USGs report to the General Assembly through the Secretary-General, who does not have the authority to remove the official from office without the General Assembly's permission. In the case of the STL, judges were appointed for a three-year term and there was no mention of the Secretary-General's oversight power, for example in suspending or terminating an appointment in cases involving serious breaches of the standards of professional conduct, where such accountability measures would not unduly interfere with judicial independence. This lack of clarity on oversight powers arguably weakened the accountability framework at the STL with respect to those officials appointed by the Secretary-General, including the judges.

To remedy this gap in accountability for the judges, the President of the Tribunal implemented 'a series of policies intended to simplify the administrative work associated with the implementation of Judges' rights and obligations in order to promote consistent and transparent practices'.[45] Such policies were added to the updated conditions of service for the judges including the Code of Professional Conduct for the Judges[46] and the Procedure Establishing a Judicial Accountability Mechanism.[47] The President oversaw the Judicial Accountability Mechanism as complaints were made to her in writing providing the necessary details.[48] The President had the authority to reject or dismiss complaints, resolve them through informal means or constitute an investigative panel of judges to consider them.[49] The investigative panel had the authority to recommend the removal of the judge if the serious misconduct or incapacity was proven.[50] The President, after receiving comments from the respective judge, had the discretion to take no action, admonish the judge, require the judge to participate in counselling, or advise the Secretary-General to remove the judge.[51]

The Judicial Accountability Mechanism had not been relied upon by the Tribunal in practice. However, the debate on any sanction that should be imposed on a judge who commits a serious misconduct is critical and this issue was ignored in the STL's initial governance design. Although the UN created the UN Dispute and Appeals Tribunals to handle staff disputes, there was no organ to handle complaints pertaining to senior officials appointed by the Secretary-General, as they were not considered UN staff members. The institution of the Tribunal's own independent mechanism

[45] STL Ninth Annual Report (2017–18) 19–20.

[46] Code of Professional Conduct for the Judges of the Special Tribunal for Lebanon, STL-CC-2016-04, 27 September 2016.

[47] Procedure Establishing a Judicial Accountability Mechanism, Annex 2 to the Conditions of Service and Compensation of Judges of the Special Tribunal for Lebanon (on file with the author).

[48] ibid Art 1(2) ('Complaints shall be made to the President of the Tribunal ... in writing and shall include the name and contact details of the complainant, the name of the Judge(s) concerned, a description of the alleged misconduct or incapacity and any relevant date(s) and shall be accompanied by any supporting documentation available to the complainant').

[49] ibid Arts 2 and 3.

[50] ibid Art 7(3).

[51] ibid Art 8(3)(a).

became a step forward to addressing the existing gap in the accountability framework. Despite the STL mechanism's flaws, one of which was the lack of the right to appeal, its very establishment can be regarded good practice.

Nevertheless, the process of appointing the principals and the hierarchical structure at the STL as described above still raise questions of accountability. Where performance was at issue, the UN, as the appointing body, did not carry out performance appraisals, which would have been a logical solution. Neither the Registrar nor any other official conducted performance appraisals for the Prosecutor or the Head of the Defence Office. The Prosecutor conducted a performance appraisal of the Deputy Prosecutor. It was unclear whether the appointing authority should be consulted regarding the performance appraisal, especially for the purpose of the extension of appointment. The Registrar, as a UN staff member, did not receive a performance appraisal from the UN, which would normally need to be conducted by the Secretary-General.

If no performance appraisals are done for the principals, what happens in case there is a performance issue, or a misconduct case is filed where termination of service is a possible penalty? Contractually, the Prosecutor, Deputy Prosecutor, and the Head of the Defence Office must adhere to the Tribunal's internal regulatory framework, which includes the Staff Regulations and Staff Rules. This means that Tribunal staff could launch a misconduct case against one of these senior officials before the Registrar.[52] The Prosecutor has the same rank as judges and higher than the Registrar. The Deputy Prosecutor and the Head of the Defence Office are lower in rank. Although legally possible, hierarchically, it is unclear whether the Registrar could exercise authority in entertaining such disciplinary cases. As Tribunal principals are appointed by the Secretary-General (or the Lebanese government in the case of the Deputy Prosecutor), it is of paramount importance that they receive performance appraisals, so that they, too, are accountable to a higher authority, possibly in consultation with their appointing body.

The accountability framework for the four STL principals and the judges was a critical point. Judges' performance was subject to appraisal neither in the STL nor in any other international or hybrid court for that matter. While arguments referring to the principle of judicial independence could be adduced militating against submitting judges to such appraisals, this principle should not be interpreted as ruling out performance appraisals and allowing an effective accountability vacuum. Article 101 of the UN Charter states that the UN staff shall be appointed by the Secretary-General under regulations established by the General Assembly. As the STL was independent from the UN and not its subsidiary organ, its accountability structure was delinked from the General Assembly. It had to be improvised along the way, being an afterthought rather than part and parcel of the STL's original governance design.

[52] The procedure for filing a complaint before the Registrar was set out in the Administrative Instruction STL/AI/HR/6/Rev.1 on Misconduct and Procedure for Staff Appeals of Administrative Decisions Taken as a Result of Disciplinary Action, 22 June 2015 (on file with the author).

11.4 Governance and Oversight Framework

The Tribunal's governance arrangements, including its oversight body and administrative oversight arrangements, were similar to those employed at the SCSL.[53] Like with the SCSL, the STL's main oversight body was the Management Committee. The Registrar, who was a UN staff member appointed by the Secretary-General, also provided (internal) oversight within the Tribunal's administrative structure. Moreover, both the traditional internal and external audit process existed at the Tribunal. The Secretary-General exercised key oversight functions because, even though the Tribunal was independent of the UN, it could not function without an overarching oversight.

11.4.1 Management Committee: membership and powers

Article 6 of the STL Agreement foresees the establishment of a Management Committee as the STL's oversight body. The Management Committee was independent of the UN. However, the establishment and the drafting of the terms of reference of the Committee was the UN's responsibility.[54]

The Management Committee was established on 13 February 2008. It consisted of Lebanon and the Netherlands, as the host state, and significant contributors to the STL, including Canada, France, Germany, Italy, Japan, the United Kingdom, the United States of America, and a representative of the Secretary-General as an *ex officio* member.[55] Typically, a legal officer from the Office of Legal Affairs represented the Secretary-General on the Management Committee. In fact, the UN Legal Counsel, Nicolas Michel, chaired the first STL Management Committee meeting. The United Kingdom was designated as the Chair. On 22 January 2009, the Management Committee appointed the representative of Canada as its Vice-Chair.[56] In 2013, the European Union became the second largest financial contributor to the Tribunal. As a significant contributor, it was accepted as a full member. Its membership of the Committee was important for the EU to be able to monitor how its contribution is being used. The following rules applied to the EU's participation in the Management Committee:

- The EU Delegation to the United Nations in New York served as the representative of the EU in the STL Management Committee;
- The EU was to treat the information dealt with in the Management Committee with due regard to the confidentiality of STL proceedings;

[53] For details: Huw Llewellyn, 'Governance of the United Nations Criminal Tribunals', in this volume.

[54] Second Report of the Secretary-General submitted pursuant to Security council Resolution 1757 (2007), UN Doc S/2008/173, 12 March 2008, para 25.

[55] Third Report of the Secretary-General submitted pursuant to Security Council Resolution 1757 (2007), S/2008/734, 26 November 2008, para 13.

[56] Fourth Report of the Secretary-General submitted pursuant to Security Council Resolution 1757 (2007), UN Doc S/2009/106, 24 February 2009, para 13.

- The European External Action Service, in coordination with the European Commission, was to regularly report to the Mashreq/Maghreb Working Party.[57]

Pursuant to the STL Agreement, Lebanon was to pay 49 per cent of the annual STL budget and the remaining 51 per cent was to be funded through voluntary contributions.[58] This is different from the funding model of the SCSL, which was entirely based on voluntarily contributions. Unfortunately, the UNSC Resolution 1757 does not provide any details with respect to the STL Management Committee's formal authority. Article 6 of the STL Agreement states that '[t]he parties shall consult concerning the establishment of a Management Committee'. In contrast with the STL Agreement, Article 7 of the Agreement between the UN and the Government of Sierra Leone specified that the SCSL Management Committee will assist 'the Secretary-General in obtaining adequate funding, and provide advice and policy direction on all non-judicial aspects of the operation of the Court, including questions of efficiency, and ... perform other functions as agreed by interested States'.[59] It also specified that the Committee shall consist of 'important contributors to the Special Court' and that both the Secretary-General and Government of Sierra Leone shall participate in it. Such provisions were left out of the STL Agreement.

The STL Management Committee's regulatory framework was constituted by its terms of reference, which were adopted by the UN in consultation with the Lebanese government.[60] Pursuant to Section IV of these terms of reference, the Management Committee will, *inter alia*:

(a) receive and consider progress reports of the Special Tribunal and provide policy direction and advice on all non-judicial aspects of its operations, including questions of efficiency;
(b) review and approve the Tribunal's annual budget, take any other necessary financial decisions, and advise the Secretary-General on these matters;
(c) ensure that all organs of the Tribunal are operating in as efficient, effective and accountable a manner as possible, and that optimum use is made of resources contributed by donor States, without prejudice to the principle of judicial independence;
(d) assist the Secretary-General in ensuring that adequate funds are available for operation of the Tribunal including the development of fund-raising strategies, in close consultation with the Registrar;
(e) encourage all States to cooperate with the Tribunal; and
(f) report on a regular basis to meetings of representatives of the Group of Interested States for the Special Tribunal.[61]

[57] Outcome of Proceedings of the Council of the European Union, MED17, PESC 509, CONUN 60, 13 May 2013 <https://data.consilium.europa.eu/doc/document/ST-9442-2013-INIT/en/pdf>.

[58] STL Agreement (n 4) Art 5(1)(a).

[59] Agreement between the United Nations and the Government of Sierra Leone on the Establishment of a Special Court for Sierra Leone (signed 16 January 2002, entered into force 12 April 2002) 2178 UNTS 137.

[60] Second Report of the Secretary-General (n 54) para 25; Terms of Reference for the Management Committee for the Special Tribunal for Lebanon, as amended on 11 October 2013 (on file with the author).

[61] Second Report of the Secretary-General (n 54) para 28.

The terms of reference also stated that the Management Committee would organize regular meetings of representatives of the Group of Interested States.[62] This Group was made up of states interested in the work of the Tribunal. This model was also used at the SCSL. The Management Committee was to meet on a regular basis and to take 'decisions on the following main issues: the Special Tribunal's premises, the financial regulations, aspects of the budgets; and the terms and conditions of service of judges and staff'.[63] The role of the Management Committee became even more crucial during the final stage of the Tribunal's existence.

The Management Committee model was welcomed initially as 'it provided better external management oversight than had previously been the case'.[64] This model also anticipated some of the known challenges the tribunals typically face with respect to funding and cooperation. It is for that reason that the Management Committee's terms of reference included a prerogative of the Committee to 'assist the Secretary-General in ensuring that adequate funds are available'.[65] When speaking about the SCSL funding scheme, Robin Vincent, the first STL Registrar, recognized that the Management Committee 'did not always succeed in securing funding or state cooperation', adding 'Tribunal officials themselves did much of the work on fundraising or enhancing state cooperation through diplomatic channels'.[66] However, when its turn came, the STL faced even more formidable funding challenges as the Management Committee failed to secure funding so that the Tribunal could complete its mandate.[67] Considering the SCSL and STL experience, in particular the continued lack of success in securing funds to ensure the proper functioning of the tribunals, one wonders whether the Management Committee model should be hailed as an advancement.

11.4.2 Registrar as a UN staff member: status and oversight role

The Registrar was appointed by the UN as its employee to oversee the good administration of the STL. As the UN relied on a more cost-effective design model in creating the Tribunal, it was administratively less burdensome and more streamlined with respect to reporting obligations. The Security Council established an international organization with the authority to function as a court, but independent from the UN and the Lebanese judiciary. As such, it was required to build its own administrative framework to implement the good governance standards expected by the UN. Initially, the Registrar led the advance team in assisting the transition from the IIIC to the Tribunal.

Although the UN intended for the STL to be completely independent, there were circumstances, mainly financial, that made it impossible to cut the 'umbilical cord'. For

62 ibid para 29.

63 Third Report of the Secretary-General (n 55) para 14.

64 International Center for Transitional Justice (ICTJ), 'Handbook on the Special Tribunal for Lebanon' (10 April 2008) <www.ictj.org/sites/default/files/ICTJ-Lebanon-STL-Handbook-2008-English.pdf> 16.

65 Terms of Reference (n 60) s IV(d).

66 ICTJ (n 64) 16.

67 Registrar's Submissions Pursuant Trial Chamber Request Dated 24 June 2021, *Prosecutor* v *Ayyash*, STL-18-10/PT/TC, Registrar, SCSL, 30 June 2021, paras 2 and 3.

example, in 2008 the UN considered how best to transfer the money that was donated to a UN Trust Fund directly to the Tribunal. Under the UN Financial Regulations and Rules, the UN Trust Fund is administered by the UN Controller who, as the official in charge of financial oversight, could not transfer the funds to a non-UN entity. In fact, the UN Controller could only delegate his authority to a UN staff member. Therefore, the pragmatic solution for this problem was to transfer the money to the Registrar who, as a UN staff member, could receive the funds and sign contracts on behalf of the Tribunal.[68]

The STL's Financial Regulations and Rules (STL FRR), adopted on 5 June 2008, stated that '[t]he Registrar is responsible and accountable to the Management Committee for the effective and efficient financial administration of the Tribunal'.[69] There is a division of authority with respect to promulgation of such regulations and rules. The Financial Regulations were promulgated by the Management Committee pursuant to Article 6 of the STL Agreement. The Financial Rules were promulgated by the Registrar and approved by the Management Committee. The STL FRR resemble those of the UN, incorporating the necessary checks and balances[70] to guide the Registrar in how best to administer the finances of the international organization. The Tribunal was also guided by the UN Procurement Manual in how it administered contracts and referenced it at such on its (no longer accessible) website.[71]

Internally, the Registrar exercised oversight responsibilities with respect to the financial and risk management. The four heads of organs made up the Senior Management Board, which was responsible for ensuring 'the coordination of the activities of the organs of the Tribunal'.[72] The judges accepted to be bound by separate conditions of service approved by the Management Committee. The Management Committee's terms of reference made it clear that it was not to be involved in judicial matters, and the judges were therefore not answerable to that body. However, the Committee was empowered to address the issues of efficiency, among others, and could provide input with respect to the length of the proceedings or the time it took a judge or Chamber to issue a decision.

11.4.3 Auditing system

The Tribunal was mandated to appoint both external and internal auditors as an instrument of good governance. The two-tiered audit system allows for a better review of the institutional controls and can help identify good practices. In addition, it ensures compliance and good management of the risk register, which is used to identify

[68] Interoffice memorandum (n 18) 445–47. See also UN Financial Regulations and Rules of the United Nations, ST/SGB/2013/4 (1 July 2013, as amended), Regulation 14 and Rule 104.3.

[69] The Special Tribunal for Lebanon Financial Regulations and Rules (approved on 5 June 2008, as last amended on 22 April 2015) Regulation 1.4.

[70] ibid Regulation 5.8 and Rules 105.8.2 to 105.8.7.

[71] The STL website referenced United Nations Procurement Manual, Revision 7; the latest version (Ref No DOS/2020.9, amended 30 June 2024) is available at <www.un.org/Depts/ptd/sites/www.un.org.Depts.ptd/files/files/attachment/page/pdf/pm.pdf>.

[72] STL RPE (n 33) Rule 38. The President chaired the Senior Management Board meetings.

risk in an organization and reduce the possibility of fraud. Unlike the internal audit, the external auditor's annual reports on the Tribunal's finances were directly submitted to the Management Committee. This reporting process provided the members with the assurance that the public funds were being spent in accordance with the objectives and the mandate of the Tribunal.

The external auditors were appointed by the Management Committee and reported directly to this external governance body.[73] The auditors were independent and conducted their work applying the 'generally accepted common auditing standards' and 'any special directions of the Management Committee'.[74] The additional terms of reference for the auditing of the Tribunal stated that the 'External Auditor shall be the sole judge as to the acceptance in whole or in part of certifications and representation by the Registrar and may proceed to such detailed examination and verification as he or she chooses of all financial records, including those relating to supplies and equipment'.[75] The auditors verified the Tribunal's accounts, financial controls, and financial operations on an annual basis.

Under the FRR, the Registrar was required to maintain internal financial controls and to put independent internal audit in place. Regulation 5.13 of the STL FRR provided that he may use the UN Internal Oversight Services for that purpose, but the Tribunal decided to hire an outside company to provide the service. The internal audits enabled the Tribunal to efficiently manage its risk register, internal financial controls, and governance processes and made it possible to identify areas requiring improvement. Using such a two-tiered audit system is good practice.

11.4.4 UN secretary-general's role in STL governance

Although the only form of oversight from the UN was performed by the STL Registrar, the Secretary-General was also expected under the legal framework to carry out the following ongoing governance functions:

1. Appointment and reappointment of the Judges.[76]
2. Appointment and reappointment of the Prosecutor.[77]
3. Appointment of the Registrar as the only UN staff member.[78]

[73] STL FRR (n 69) Art VII (External Auditor), Regulation 7.1 (specifying that the Management Committee shall appoint an External Auditor) and Regulation 7.2 (defining a six-year term of office).

[74] ibid Regulation 7.5 and Annex (providing additional terms of reference governing the audit of the Tribunal).

[75] STL FRR Annex (n 74) para 2.

[76] STL Statute (n 4) Art 9(3) and STL Agreement (n 4) Art 2. The reappointment for a further period after the initial three-year mandate was to be done in consultation with the Government of Lebanon. STL Agreement (n 4) Art 2(5) specifies that the Secretary-General shall appoint the Lebanese judges from a list of twelve persons presented by the Government of Lebanon, upon the proposal of the Lebanese Supreme Council of the Judiciary.

[77] STL Statute (n 4) Art 11(3) and STL Agreement (n 4) Art 3. The reappointment for a further period after the initial three-year mandate was to be done in consultation with the Government of Lebanon. STL Agreement (n 4) Art 3(3) states that the Deputy Prosecutor is appointed by the Government of Lebanon, in consultation with the Secretary-General.

[78] STL Statute (n 4) Art 12(3). The reappointment for a further period following the initial three-year mandate is done in consultation with the Government of Lebanon.

4. Appointment of an Independent Head of the Defence Office.[79]
5. Mandate extension.[80]
6. Funding of the Tribunal.[81]
7. Waiver of privileges and immunities accorded to the judges, Prosecutor, the Deputy Prosecutor, the Registrar, and the Head of the Defence Office.[82]
8. Continuous consultations with the Lebanese government, especially with respect to ensuring that the 49 per cent funding is received.[83]
9. *Ex officio* representation on the Management Committee.

The Tribunal's Rules also foresaw an ongoing role for the Secretary-General in channelling communications to the Security Council concerning an expansion of its jurisdiction. Rule 12 provided that, if the Prosecutor considers that an attack that occurred after 12 December 2005 is a 'connected attack', he should inform the President who would then request the Registrar to transmit the reasoned conclusions to the Secretary-General. Ultimately, the Security Council and the Government of Lebanon decided whether to expand the STL jurisdiction. This shows, yet again, that the Secretary-General played an important governance role in the operations of the STL.

11.5 Reporting, Compliance, and Funding Challenges

The governance practices in dealing with public expenditures are well established within international organizations, including courts and tribunals. Such practices are based on the requirement of transparency in spending and the necessary checks and balances to ensure accountability and prevent fraud. Reporting obligations were in place at the Tribunal to provide such assurances.

11.5.1 Reporting obligations of the principals

The reporting and compliance at the STL represented a two-track system and was an important part of the governance scheme. In accordance with Article 10(2) of the Agreement and Rule 32(I) of the Rules, the presidency was required to submit annual reports to the Secretary-General and the Government of Lebanon. In addition,

[79] STL Statute (n 4) Art 13. The Secretary-General appoints the Head of the Defence Office in consultation with the President of the Tribunal.

[80] STL Agreement (n 4) Art 21(2) states that if the Tribunal's work is not completed follow the three-year mandate, the 'Agreement shall be extended to allow the Tribunal to complete its work, for a further period(s) to be determined by the Secretary-General in consultation with the Government and the Security Council'.

[81] UNSC Res 1757 (n 4) and STL Agreement (n 4) Art 5(2) state: '[s]hould the voluntary contributions be insufficient for the Tribunal to implement its mandate, the Secretary-General and the Security Council shall explore alternate means of financing the Tribunal'.

[82] STL Agreement (n 4) Art 11(2) (the Secretary-General is granted the authority to waive the privileges and immunities, in consultation with the President of the Tribunal).

[83] When the budget was approved by the Management Committee, the UN Secretary-General informed the Government of Lebanon and requested that they pay their mandatory 49 per cent contribution.

pursuant to Rule 32(H), the President, in close consultation with the Registrar, was to inform 'the Management Committee of the activities of the Tribunal that are relevant to the functions of the Committee at any time on the request of the Committee, or on his own initiative'.

The STL FRR required the Registrar to report to the Management Committee and to submit the budget on behalf of the Tribunal organs. The Prosecutor and the Head of the Defence Office must adhere to the Tribunal's Staff Regulations and Staff Rules. The Judges of the Tribunal had their own conditions of service issued by the UN and administered by the STL Registry.

11.5.2 Fraud prevention

As the guardian of the Tribunal's purse, the Registrar exercised a critical role in ensuring that the oversight structures operated effectively, and risks were mitigated. He was also required to put in place ethical rules, such as the code of conduct for staff, which incorporated an obligation to report fraud or any other misconduct.[84] The fraud prevention mechanism included reminding staff regularly of their obligation to report on their own private legal obligations, such as breaches of local laws and failures to honour local court orders, including those pertaining to family support. As a hybrid Tribunal employing both Lebanese and international staff, the institutional culture at the Tribunal was multi-faceted, but it was essential for it to adhere to the principles of international civil service while maintaining the STL's reputation of impartiality, integrity, and probity. Under the fraud prevention scheme, the Registrar was also required to put in place measures to protect whistleblowers from retaliation.[85]

11.5.3 Reporting to the Management Committee

As the STL's main external governance body, the Management Committee's oversight functions were an important element of the Tribunal's governance. The Registrar reported to the Management Committee on the implementation of the budget annually.[86] The external auditors were 'independent and solely responsible for the conduct of the audit'.[87] The Management Committee played an overall role in appointing and directing the external auditors. It also reviewed the external audit reports.[88] The STL FRR do not address the Management Committee's specific role in reviewing the external audit reports. Recognizing this gap, in 2020 the Management Committee established an independent expert Advisory Committee on Finance and Audit to examine

[84] Code of Conduct for Staff Members of the Special Tribunal for Lebanon, STL/RB/2, 26 March 2009, para 18.

[85] Protection Against Retaliation for Reporting Misconduct and for Cooperating with Duly Authorized Audits or Investigations, STL/AI/HR/12, 10 April 2012.

[86] STL FRR (n 69) Regulation 2.1.

[87] ibid Art VII. Regulation 7.11 obligates the external auditor to transmit the reports to the Management Committee. STL FRR Annex (n 74).

[88] STL FRR (n 69) Regulation 7.6.

'the STL's approach to financial management, internal controls and risk management' and advise the Committee accordingly.[89] Previously, reports were sent to capitals for review and comments; yet, the necessary expertise to provide meaningful advice to the Committee was often missing. While areas of risk were flagged at times, substantial action was hardly ever taken. The establishment of the expert Advisory Committee was an important improvement to ensure an effective financial oversight.

11.5.4 Fundraising

The Registrar was required to oversee the financial management of the Tribunal, including the obligation to fundraise for it. The Tribunal's fundraising model was not limited to voluntary contributions and, as noted, the Security Council required that Lebanon contribute 49 per cent of the Tribunal's annual budget. Funding of such temporary institutions as the STL tends to be unpredictable. State contributions are heavily relied upon, but states generally do not include voluntary funding for international institutions in their respective regular budgets. This makes it difficult to secure a consistent budget source for courts such as the STL and limits the viability of such a funding model especially for a criminal tribunal. The control over the pledges and contributions leaves room for interference in the judicial process. Towards the end of the STL's existence, the Management Committee increasingly referenced the financial problems to impede the Tribunal's ability to complete its judicial proceedings. On 1 June 2021, the Registry made a submission to the Tribunal's President, Appeals Chamber, Trial Chamber, and Pre-Trial Judge, stating that 'the imminent exhaustion of the Tribunal's currently available funds would impact the Tribunal's ability to finance the continuation of judicial proceedings beyond 31 July 2021, and ultimately its ability to complete its mandate'.[90] While the political will to fund the STL existed in 2009, it effectively evaporated by 2021.

On 25 February 2021, the Secretary-General's spokesperson announced that the STL's mandate was extended from 1 March 2021 for an additional two-year term.[91] Previously, the STL's mandate was extended in three-year increments with the caveat that the mandate would end sooner if the cases were completed.[92] However, the 2021 mandate extension referred to the completion of the case 'or the exhaustion of available

[89] STL Twelfth Annual Report (2020–21) 22. See also Request for a subvention to the Special Tribunal for Lebanon: Report of the Secretary-General, UN Doc A/75/763, 18 February 2021, para 18.

[90] Registrar's Notice Pursuant to Rule 48(C) of a Shortfall in Funding Impacting the Tribunal's Operations, *Prosecutor* v *Ayyash*, STL-18-10/PT/TC, Registry, STL, 1 June 2021. Numerous filings followed the Registrar's submission in the same case, eg Registrar's Updated Notice Pursuant to Rule 48(C) of a Shortfall in Funding Impacting the Tribunal's Operations, 18 June 2021; Corrected Version of Registrar's Updated Notice Pursuant to Rule 48(C) of a Shortfall in Funding Impacting the Tribunal's Operations 19 June 2021; Registrar's Submissions Pursuant Trial Chamber Request Dated 24 June 2021, 30 June 2021.

[91] UN Press Release, 'Secretary-General Extends Mandate of Special Tribunal for Lebanon, to Last until It Completes Pending Cases or Exhausts Funding', SG/SM/20600, 25 February 2021 <https://press.un.org/en/2021/sgsm20600.doc.htm>.

[92] UN Press Release, 'Secretary General Extends Mandate of Special Tribunal for Lebanon, in Accordance with Security Council Resolution 1757 (2005)', (SG/SM/18837-L/327322 December 2017 <https://press.un.org/en/2017/sgsm18837.doc.htm> (stating that the STL's mandate was extended 'for a period of three years, or upon the completion of the cases before the Special Tribunal if sooner').

funds, if sooner'. This reflected a fundamental shift in approach as the Agreement annexed to the UNSC Resolution 1757 stated that the duration of the Agreement shall be for three years. Afterwards, the UN and the Government of Lebanon were expected to review the progress of the work of the STL, in consultation with the Security Council. Article 21(2) of the Agreement went on to stipulate that '[i]f after the end of this period of three years the activities of the Tribunal have not been completed, the Agreement shall be extended to allow the Tribunal to complete its work, for a further period determined by the Secretary-General in consultation with the Government and the Security Council'. Notably, the availability of funding was not envisaged as a requirement for the mandate extension, but rather the completion of the work was provided the only legal ground for non-extension of the Agreement.

11.5.5 Judicial independence and enforcement powers

The proper balance between the external governance of the Tribunal as a safeguard of its effective and efficient functioning, on the one hand, and its ability to function as a court independently and impartially, on the other, is important for the public trust in the institution. This is even more so when the court is based far away from where the crimes were committed. The independence of the court must be preserved and its officials, especially the judges and the prosecutor, must be protected from any undue interference. Should they experience pressure or interference, they do not have an effective remedy like the possibility of bringing a dispute before an external body, similar to the arrangements found in some of the national system. Judges must be able to ensure that their decisions are complied with and enforced.[93]

While the UN Security Council relied on Chapter VII of the UN Charter in adopting its Resolution 1757, the obligation to cooperate with the Tribunal was only expressly stated in relation to Lebanon and not all the UN member states. This means that the Tribunal had no authority to enforce its decisions through Resolution 1757 vis-à-vis states other than Lebanon. In fact, the STL Rules reflected this difference by creating two separate procedures to address non-compliance with a request or order of the Tribunal. Pursuant to Rule 20, if Lebanon failed to comply with an order, there was a multi-step procedure leading to the President making a judicial finding and referring the matter to the Security Council.[94] Pursuant to Rule 21, should a third state fail to comply with the Tribunal's decision, the Rules offered two different options, depending on whether the Tribunal had entered into an agreement with that state. For cases where such an agreement existed, the Rules referred to the dispute-settlement clause for resolving the matter. Lacking such an agreement, the President was expected to enter into consultations with that state. Under Rule 21, there is no obligation for a third state to cooperate and there was no possibility of referral to the Security Council for non-compliance with the Tribunal orders.

Pursuant to Rule 48(B)(ii) of the Rules, the Registrar was mandated to give effect to judicial decisions. When judicial decisions required the Registrar to serve them

[93] Dorine Nauleau, 'The Enforcement of International Judicial Decisions', in this volume.
[94] STL RPE (n 33) Rule 20(C).

upon the Lebanese authorities, the Registry was to do so based on the MOU, which named the Minister of Justice as the entity representing the Lebanese government. The Minister of Justice also implemented service of process on behalf of the Lebanese authorities. With respect to the continuing obligation to search for, arrest, and transfer accused or convicted persons to the Tribunal, the Lebanese Prosecutor-General was the responsible authority.[95] The Prosecutor-General was also required to submit monthly reports to the Tribunal's President on the efforts to search for, arrest, and transfer accused or convicted persons. The decisions and orders of the judges must be respected, but only by Lebanon; third states' engagement was voluntary and rooted in goodwill rather than a legal obligation to cooperate.

11.6 Concluding Observations and Suggestions for Improvement

The creation of the Special Tribunal for Lebanon brought with it hope and reflected the political will to support Lebanon in ensuring that terrorist offences do not go unpunished and that impunity is not tolerated. However, this political will wavered over time. States, especially those serving on the Tribunal's Management Committee, no longer wanted to fund it. As a result, the institution was not able to complete its judicial proceedings due to lack of funding, which is unprecedented in international criminal justice. Previously, similar tribunals were encouraged, through a formal body, such as the Security Council, to implement a completion strategy to allow for a process of drawing down the court's judicial work in a coordinated and regulated manner. The abruptness with which the Tribunal was expected to shut down raises questions of compliance with the principles of judicial independence and the rule of law.

The hybrid tribunals were seen as innovative because they were not as big or costly as the UN ad hoc tribunals. In fact, through the hybrid tribunals, a new institutional model was tested, and the international criminal justice system learned a lot from those experiences. The leaner mechanism of the STL built upon the SCSL model. The Management Committee model was hailed as a better governance scheme to ensure effective oversight. There is no doubt that elements of good governance could be strengthened further and that informal governance mechanisms should have been formalized. One should not lose sight of the significant lessons to be learned from the STL experience.

Already based on the experience of the SCSL, it was clear that the Management Committee's role as an informal oversight body needed to be better defined. At the STL, the Management Committee's terms of reference were published for the public to understand better its role in overseeing the work of the Tribunal. An independent advisory body was appointed to support the Management Committee in critically reviewing the external audit reports it received directly from the auditors. This new

95 UN Press Release, 'Secretary-General Acknowledges That Special Tribunal for Lebanon Has Handed over Arrest Warrants, Calls for Support of Independent Judicial Process', SG/SM/13683-L/3176, 30 June 2011 (the Secretary-General confirming that the indictment and arrest warrants were delivered to the Prosecutor-General to the Supreme Court in Lebanon).

mechanism, attached to the Management Committee, proved essential and should be built into any future oversight structure.

Both the STL and SCSL experienced challenges with respect to the Tribunal's administrative authority. Appointed by the Secretary-General as the only UN staff member, the Registrar effectively operated as the independent oversight authority of the UN assigned to the STL. As the Registrar supported all the organs of the Tribunal, the division of functions between the Registrar and the President should have been better defined and demarcated, allowing for the Registrar to report directly to the Secretary-General or to the respective delegated authority. Furthermore, for the principals who the Secretary-General appoints, there should have been a well-defined performance appraisal process in place and a mechanism to ensure that claims regarding alleged misconduct could be adequately and effectively addressed by a neutral authority external to the Tribunal. This should have also been the case for the judges.

The Tribunal spent a substantial amount of time in an earlier phase putting in place the policies and procedures separate from those of the UN because it had been created to be independent and having no linkage to the UN. In order to ensure proper checks and balances, and to benefit from a strong accountability mechanism already in place within the UN, institutions such as the STL should not be forced to reinvent the wheel each time. Too much time is unnecessarily wasted in that process—for which they later get criticized. Instead, such tribunals should be established in a manner that would allow for the formal linkage with the UN, so that the regulatory governance frameworks continue to apply and need not be recreated. In the alternative, and at a minimum, the tribunal should sign a relationship agreement with the UN allowing for it to rely on the essential existing UN mechanisms. The STL's experience teaches many important lessons, which could ensure that hybrid tribunals function more efficiently with the required accountability structures in place. A cost-effective system of checks and balances is paramount while respecting the principle of judicial independence. Finding the equilibrium between independence and oversight will also allow these courts of law to function more effectively as international organizations.

PART IV
JUDICIAL GOVERNANCE FUNCTIONS

12

The Election of Judges onto the European Court of Human Rights

Andrew Drzemczewski

12.1 Introductory Remarks

The unique procedure for the election of judges onto the European Court of Human Rights (ECtHR, the Court) by an international parliamentary body, the Parliamentary Assembly of the Council of Europe (PACE) is simple to understand. Yet, its *modus operandi* is relatively complex. Also, this procedure usually takes about twelve months from the moment a state is asked, by the Secretary-General of the Parliamentary Assembly, to furnish the Assembly with a list of three candidates until the newly elected judge terminates his or her previous employment and takes up permanent residence in Strasbourg.

The manner in which this election procedure has evolved since the first elections to the Court, held back in 1958, is well documented and has been the object of considerable scrutiny.[1] The present chapter is limited to a brief description of the selection/election process and an overview of substantive 'criteria for office', followed by a more detailed explanation of how the election procedure *presently* functions in the Parliamentary Assembly, fleshing out a number of issues of particular interest.

This chapter does not deal with the designation of ad hoc judges to the Court (when a judge is unable to sit, withdraws or is exempted from a judicial formation).[2] Nor

[1] eg Andrew Drzemczewski, 'Election of Judges: European Court of Human Rights (ECtHR)', *Max Planck Encyclopedia of International Procedural Law* (OUP 2025) <https://opil.ouplaw.com/view/10.1093/law-mpeipro/e3367.013.3367/law-mpeipro-e3367> and Open Society Justice Initiative and International Commission of Jurists, 'Strengthening from Within: Law and Practice in the Selection of Human Rights Judges and Commissioners' (Open Society Foundations 2017) <www.justiceinitiative.org/publications/strengthening-within-law-and-practice-selection-human-rights-judges-and-commissioners>. See also (guest) editorials on this subject in (2023) 4 European Convention on Human Rights Law Review 231 and Council of Europe (Steering Committee on Human Rights (CDDH)), 'Report on issues relating to judges of the European Court of Human Rights' (issued on 8 February 2024 by the Committee of Ministers) document CM(2024)6-add <https://search.coe.int/cm/Pages/result_details.aspx?ObjectID=0900001680ae1a41>, <https://search.coe.int/cm/Pages/result_details.aspx?ObjectId=0900001680ae5978>.

[2] See on this subject Council of Europe (PACE, Rapporteur Marie-Louise Bemelmans-Videc), '*Ad Hoc* Judges at the European Court of Human Rights: An Overview' (23 January 2012, document 12827) <https://pace.coe.int/en/files/13035/html>, especially paras 9–14, 24–25, and 38–47; Andrew Drzemczewski, 'Revisiting the Issue of Designation of Ad Hoc Judges in the European Court of Human Rights: Some Remarks Following the Case *Wałęsa v. Poland*' (2025) 1(66) Gdańskie Studia Prawnicze/Gdańsk Legal Studies 66 and the Court's portal European Court of Human Rights (Registry of the Court) 'Rules of Court' (15 September 2025), Rule 29 <www.echr.coe.int/rules-of-court> and ECtHR, 'List of *Ad Hoc* Judges for the Year 2024', <www.echr.coe.int/Documents/List_adhoc_judges_BIL.pdf>.

Andrew Drzemczewski, *The Election of Judges onto the European Court of Human Rights* In: *Governance of International Courts and Tribunals*. Edited by: Sergey Vasiliev and Niels Blokker, Oxford University Press. © Andrew Drzemczewski 2026.
DOI: 10.1093/oso/9780198922131.003.0012

does it consider the manner in which a judge will be elected onto the Court in respect of the EU if and when the EU accedes to the European Convention on Human Rights (Convention, or ECHR).[3]

For convenience, the principal texts upon which the election process is based (extracts from the ECHR, key texts on the basis of which the Assembly operates, and the terms of reference of the Assembly's Committee on the Election of Judges to the European Court of Human Rights (AS/Cdh)) can be found at the end of this chapter.

12.2 Brief Description of the Selection/Election Process

Article 21 of the Convention specifies that judges must be of high moral character and possess qualifications required for appointment to high judicial office or be jurisconsults of recognized competence.

In order to ensure that these criteria for office are met, there are two distinct phases in the election process. The first is a national selection procedure, in which each state party to the Convention must provide a list of three appropriately qualified candidates, and the second is the election procedure undertaken by the Assembly, in which a special parliamentary committee (AS/Cdh) assesses the qualifications of the three candidates as well as the fairness of the national selection procedure before the Assembly elects a judge onto the Court.

12.2.1 National selection procedure

In selecting three candidates, states must ensure that their national procedure is fair and transparent by issuing open calls for candidates. All three candidates must possess appropriate legal qualifications and experience and must have an active knowledge of either English or French—the two official languages of the Council of Europe in which Court judgments are drafted—and at least a passive knowledge of the other language.

In order to ensure gender balance in the Court, states are obliged to put forward at least one candidate from the sex that is under-represented (this has almost always been the case with respect to women, ie less than 40 per cent of the total number of judges on the Bench), unless the Assembly can be convinced that 'exceptional circumstances' exist allowing for the possibility of a state not to comply with this requirement.

Since 2011, the names and CVs of candidates are provided by states, in a confidential procedure, to an international Advisory Panel (established by the Committee of Ministers) before a final list is sent to the Assembly. The Advisory Panel provides governments advice as to whether potential candidates comply with the criteria for office, as specified in Article 21 of the Convention.

[3] Andrew Drzemczewski, 'Accession of the EU to the ECHR: A Key Role (to Be) Played by PACE' (2017/2018) 17/18 Revista do Instituto Brasileiro de Direitos Humanos 11, and references therein, available at < https://www.milas.x10host.com/ojs/index.php/ibdh/article/view/371>. For information relating to negotiations on accession, consult the Council of Europe portal: <www.coe.int/en/web/human-rights-intergovernmental-cooperation/accession-of-the-european-union-to-the-european-convention-on-human-rights>.

12.2.2 Election by the Parliamentary Assembly

Once the Assembly has received the list of candidates, the Committee on the Election of Judges to the European Court of Human Rights (AS/Cdh), a special twenty-two-member parliamentary committee whose members have appropriate legal experience, assesses the fairness and transparency of the national procedure used to select them.

The Committee then interviews each of the candidates in person and scrutinizes their CVs, which are submitted in a standardized format, in order to evaluate whether all three persons are sufficiently qualified for the post. If it finds that all the conditions are met, the Committee draws up a recommendation for the Assembly indicating which candidate or candidates it believes to be the strongest. If the conditions are not met, the Committee can recommend that a state be asked to submit a fresh list.

The Parliamentary Assembly, which presently consists of 306 parliamentarians (since Russia was expelled from the Organization in 2022 and credentials of the Azerbaijani delegation were not transmitted), then proceeds to vote on the candidates in a secret ballot, which is held during a plenary session in Strasbourg, in light of the Committee's recommendations. An absolute majority of votes cast is required in the first round. If this is not achieved, a second round is held, and the candidate with the most votes is duly elected to serve on the Court for a single term of nine years.

12.3 Criteria for Office

The Convention itself is the principal source that sets out broad criteria for the office of judge of the Court. As noted, Article 21(1) stipulates that 'judges shall be of high moral character and must either possess the qualifications required for appointment to high judicial office or be jurisconsults of recognised competence'.

Because of the nebulous character of these general criteria *in concreto*, the Assembly has, over the years, refined and elaborated what it understands by these criteria.[4] Thus, it added certain procedural details as well as language proficiency and gender requirements which—as confirmed by the ECtHR in its first advisory opinion—'can be considered to flow implicitly from Article 21.1'.[5] These procedural requirements and selection criteria have been consolidated in Assembly texts; they can also now be found in the Guidelines addressed to states parties by the Committee of Ministers.

[4] Council of Europe (PACE), 'Procedure for the Election of Judges to the European Court of Human Rights', memorandum prepared by the Secretary General of the Assembly, document SG-AS (2025) 01 of 20 October 2025 (updated regularly and available in both English and French on the Assembly's portal: <https://rm.coe.int/procedure-for-the-election-of-judges-to-the-european-court-of-human-ri/1680aa8ddf>) and the Appendix to the present chapter. An appendix providing a list of criteria, used by the AS/Cdh, to evaluate candidatures for the office of Judge on the Court has—regrettably—recently been expunged from the Secretary General's memorandum (but see, in this connection, (2015) 35 Human Rights Law Journal 273–74).

[5] Advisory opinion on certain legal questions concerning the lists of candidates submitted with a view to the election of judges to the European Court of Human Rights, GC, ECtHR, 12 February 2008, para 47. See also para 43 of the said opinion in which the Court acknowledges that the Assembly 'has a certain latitude' in establishing its procedure in electing judges. Text available on the Court's portal: <https://hudoc.echr.coe.int/eng#{%22documentcollectionid2%22:[%22ARTICLE47%22]}>.

Likewise, the Advisory Panel created by the latter has provided a useful set of 'minimum qualifications' required of candidates for the post of judge in Strasbourg.[6]

12.4 The Election Procedure before the Parliamentary Assembly

12.4.1 Commencement of procedure

The Council of Europe's in-house procedure relating to the election process, dating back to 1958, was overhauled and streamlined in 2009. Since 2009, all communications on this subject with state parties are dealt with by the Parliamentary Assembly, replacing the somewhat disorderly procedure which existed up until then (see the text of Article 22, ECHR, in the Appendix).[7]

Approximately one year prior to the expiration of the mandate of the sitting judge, the Secretary-General of the Parliamentary Assembly invites the government concerned, in a formal letter transmitted via its Permanent Representative/Ambassador in Strasbourg, to provide the Assembly with a list of three candidates. In the said letter, the state authorities are requested to submit—usually within a time span of twelve months or so, depending on the scheduling of the Assembly's part-sessions—the list of candidates and their CVs in a pre-determined standardized 'Word model' format. When transmitting the CVs, the state authorities are asked to describe the procedure by which the candidates were selected, ie to indicate clearly that the national selection procedure was fair and transparent, and that the candidates had been interviewed, as specified in relevant Assembly texts and as required by the Assembly's AS/Cdh.[8]

The Secretary-General's letter also draws the state authorities' attention to the need to ensure that lists include at least one candidate of each sex (a subject to be reverted to later), the requirement of prior consultation with the Advisory Panel, and to the fact that candidates must be less than sixty-five years of age at the date by which the transmission of the list is requested by the Assembly. Now that Protocol No 15 has entered into force, the age limit of seventy for judges no longer applies.[9]

An electronic version of the letter is transmitted at the same time to facilitate its immediate transmission to the state's capital and to grant access to a number of relevant documents hyperlinked in a two-page 'information note' appended to the letter. Among the listed documents, one can find the Committee of Ministers' Guidelines addressed to states on the national selection procedure, information pertaining to the status and conditions of service of judges, as well as a specific proposal that candidates

[6] On the Guidelines and the role of the Advisory Panel: Section 12.4.2.

[7] For more details, see an internal *Memorandum* and *Appendix* thereto, dated 22 April 2009, on the transfer of specific administrative functions to the Parliamentary Assembly addressed to the Secretary General (Terry Davis), co-signed by the Assembly's Director General and the Director General of Human Rights & Legal Affairs (on file with the author).

[8] Appendix, Section C, at the end of this chapter as concerns the Assembly texts. See also Council of Europe (PACE) (n 4) *passim*.

[9] In effect, extending the age limit to seventy-four; see Art 21(2) ECHR in the Appendix (text amended by Protocol No 15, ECHR, Art 2, in force since 1 August 2021).

be informed that the person elected may be required to perform additional judicial duties at the European Tribunal in matters of state immunity and/or be asked to be part of the judicial formation when the Court is requested to provide an advisory opinion on the interpretation of the Council of Europe's 1997 Convention on Human Rights and Biomedicine.[10]

12.4.2 Requirements imposed upon states parties and the specific role of the Advisory Panel

The Parliamentary Assembly possesses exclusive competence to elect a judge from a list of three persons provided by a state party, as specified in Article 22 of the Convention (see text in the Appendix). Two interrelated *desiderata* warrant specific mention in this respect: the requirement to have in place an appropriate national selection procedure and the need to ensure that all three candidates comply with the minimum qualifications of eligibility for election to the post of judge on the Court.

The quality of national selection procedures is of crucial importance for the outcome of this process. These procedures must be fair and transparent, the key requirements being, *inter alia*, the existence of an appropriate selection procedure, wide dissemination of the call for candidates, a balanced composition of the body responsible for recommending candidates (which should be free from undue influence) and the need to interview all serious candidates, including an assessment of their linguistic ability. Most of these proposals—now, in effect, considered as requirements which are clearly specified in a text adopted by the Assembly[11]—have also been incorporated into the 2012 Committee of Ministers' 'Guidelines on the [national procedure of] selection of candidates for the post of judge at the European Court of Human Rights',[12] addressed to all states parties. These Guidelines cover all the stages of the national selection procedure, including its establishment, the identification of criteria applicable to the inclusion in a candidates' list, and the composition and procedures of the selection body responsible for proposing candidates, as well as the role of the final decision-maker. The Guidelines, as amended in 2014 and 2024, also refer to the need for a state to present the proposed list of candidates—in a confidential procedure—to the Advisory Panel prior to the submission of its list of three candidates to the Parliamentary Assembly.[13]

Because of concerns as to the quality of certain candidates put forward by states, and upon the initiative of the then-President of the Court, Jean-Paul Costa, in

[10] Council of Europe (PACE) (n 4) 7–9 for further details, and Drzemczewski (n 1) paras 26–28.

[11] An updated and consolidated version of that text is reproduced in the Appendix, Section C.

[12] Council of Europe (Committee of Ministers) 'Guidelines on the [National Procedure of] Selection of Candidates for the Post of Judge at the European Court of Human Rights' (adopted 28 March 2012) CM (2012), <https://rm.coe.int/16805cb1ac>, as amended on 26 November 2014 by CM/Del/Dec (2014)1213/1.5 and on 7 February 2024 by CM/Del/Dec(2024)1488/4.2,<https://search.coe.int/cm/Pages/result_details.aspx?ObjectId=09000016805c49f5>. The Committee of Ministers added, in the criteria listed in the Guidelines, that '[c]andidates need to have knowledge of the national legal system(s) and of public international law' (Point 4 therein).

[13] For details, see the Guidelines and the Explanatory Memorandum appended thereto.

2010 the Committee of Ministers decided to setup an Advisory Panel of Experts on Candidates for Election as Judge to the European Court of Human Rights.[14] This Panel consists of seven persons chosen from among members of the highest national courts, former international judges, and lawyers of recognized competence. Its mandate is to advise states parties confidentially on whether the shortlisted candidates meet the criteria stipulated in Article 21(1) of the Convention, by examining their *curricula vitae*.

When the election procedure is commenced, as explained above, the Advisory Panel receives a copy of the letter sent by the Assembly's Secretary-General to the state's Permanent Representative in Strasbourg. The Panel then invites the government concerned to send it—prior to responding to the Assembly's request—the names and CVs of the candidates proposed, together with information on the national selection procedure. It then determines, in a written procedure or a meeting, and, if necessary, after having obtained additional information about candidates, whether all of the candidates fulfil the requirements, suggesting the replacements of those who do not.[15] The procedure before the Advisory Panel and all its communications with the state authorities remain confidential.[16] States are expected to follow the Advisory Panel's proposals, although they are not duty-bound to do so.

Once the list of candidates is received by the Assembly, the Panel then informs the AS/Cdh in writing, and confidentially, of its views on the candidates. Also, as pointed out earlier, the Assembly will not accept lists submitted to it from states which have not consulted the Advisory Panel beforehand.[17]

The candidates' CVs, together with the accompanying letter, are then published in English and French on the Assembly's website. Once the deadline for transmission has expired, the government can no longer modify or withdraw the list, as was confirmed by the Court in its second advisory opinion provided to the Committee of Ministers in 2010.[18]

[14] Council of Europe (Committee of Ministers) 'Resolution CM/Res(2010)26 on the establishment of an Advisory Panel of Experts on Candidates for Election as Judge to the European Court of Human Rights' (2010) as amended by CM/Res (2014) 44. This text and all other relevant (background) documents relating to the work of the Advisory Panel can be accessed on the Panel's website: <www.coe.int/en/web/dlapil/advisory-panel>. See, in particular, the 'Short Guide' on the Panel's role and the minimum qualifications required of a candidate (2020) <https://assembly.coe.int/LifeRay/CDH/Pdf/GuideRoleQualification-EN.pdf>.

[15] In a letter with which the CVs of Croatia's candidates were transmitted to the Assembly, it was explained that the Advisory Panel had suggested to the Croatian authorities that they envisage shortlisting a 'reserve' candidate, so that if the Panel were to consider that the initial list of proposed candidates did not meet the necessary requirements, a reserve candidate could replace a candidate on a new list to be submitted to the Advisory Panel without a need to repeat the (often complex and time-consuming) national selection procedure: Council of Europe (PACE) 'Election of Judges to the ECtHR: List and Curricula Vitae of Candidates Submitted by the Government of Croatia' (21 May 2021) document 15295 <https://pace.coe.int/en/files/29196> 4.

[16] For more details, consult texts referred to in footnote 14.

[17] This requirement is in force since 2019: Council of Europe (PACE) 'Assembly Resolution 2278 (2019) of 10 April 2019' <https://pace.coe.int/en/files/27665>, para 4; text in Appendix, Section C.

[18] Advisory opinion on certain legal questions concerning the lists of candidates submitted with a view to the election of judges to the European Court of Human Rights (No 2), GC, ECtHR, 22 January 2010, para 49. See also Assembly text in the Appendix, Section D.

12.4.3 Principal tasks of the Assembly's Committee on the Election of Judges

Created in 2015, the Committee on the Election of Judges to the European Court of Human Rights (AS/Cdh) is a specialist committee whose members must have the appropriate knowledge or practical experience in the legal field. The AS/Cdh, specifically constituted by the Assembly on the basis of proposals put forward by political groups, is mandated by the plenary Assembly to scrutinize the CVs of candidates, interview all candidates in person, and make specific recommendations to the Assembly concerning their qualifications. Based on its recommendations, the Assembly proceeds with the election or rejects the list.

Detailed information relating to the AS/Cdh's composition, the quorum requirement, and specific rules as to how the Committee functions, including voting arrangements, can be found in the Appendix to this chapter, in Section E. Committee meetings follow a well-established procedure. The meetings are held *in camera*, and all participants are subject to strict confidentiality. Prior to the interview of each of the three candidates, the Committee holds a briefing session during which a number of issues are discussed, including the 'position' taken by the Advisory Panel based on its prior confidential consultations with a state party,[19] as well as communications received if deemed appropriate, from, eg, respected associations of judges or civil society representatives. Also, since 2019, the chairperson or a representative of the Advisory Panel is invited to attend the briefing sessions in order to explain the reasons for the Panel's views on the candidates.

The Committee must then decide whether there are any reasons to reject a list, such as inadequate or inappropriate national selection procedures (which need to include interviews with candidates), or the fact that the Advisory Panel had not been consulted, or the failure to include in the list a candidate belonging to the sex which is under-represented in the Court (see Section 12.4.4). A list can also be rejected if the Committee considers that one or more of the candidates is so weak—even on paper, upon the examination of his or her CV—that it would be pointless to interview the respective candidate(s). A proposal to reject a list at this stage requires a simple majority vote, whereas the (possible) acceptance of a single-sex list, in exceptional circumstances, necessitates a two-thirds majority.

When no grounds exist to reject a list for reasons indicated above (or when there is no majority to accept a proposal to reject a list), the candidates are interviewed. Each candidate is interviewed for 30 minutes, with the first 5 minutes of the interview being allotted for a short self-presentation, if the candidate so wishes. Candidates are informed of the possibility of making such a presentation by the Secretary-General of the Assembly in the letter inviting him or her for the interview. The Committee members then pose questions, in English or French, and the candidate responds in either or both of these languages; simultaneous interpretation between English and French

[19] States have not always accepted the Advisory Panel's proposals to withdraw one or more persons from a list submitted to the Assembly; in several instances written (confidential) explanations for doing so have been provided by the state authorities to the Committee.

is provided. The interviews are carried out in the alphabetical order of the names of candidates.

After the interviews, the Committee engages in an exchange of views on the merits of each candidate and must first decide (ie confirm) that all three candidates fulfil the criteria for election as a judge. A proposal to reject the list may be made if the areas of competence of candidates are unduly restricted, if one or more of the candidates do(es) not comply with the Assembly's linguistic requirements or if, after the interviews, it transpires that not all the candidates fulfil the eligibility requirements of Article 21(1) of the Convention. If there is no proposal to reject the list, a vote by secret ballot is then taken on preferences among candidates.[20]

The Committee's report, addressed to the plenary Assembly, is prepared by its chairperson and is transmitted to the Assembly via its Bureau in good time before the part-session during which the election is scheduled to take place. The said report contains recommendations in which succinct reasons are provided to explain the ranking of candidates.[21] The AS/Cdh's report is made public and placed on the Assembly's portal prior to the commencement of the election procedure.

If rejection of a list is recommended to the Assembly, the reason(s) must be specified. The Assembly must then ratify, ie endorse, the proposal to reject a list at a plenary session.

12.4.4 Issues of particular interest

The need to ensure a balanced representation of women and men is a specific concern of the Assembly. The Assembly has consistently taken measures to ensure a gender-balanced Court, especially since the mid-1990s, in the period leading up to the entry into force of Protocol No 11 to the Convention with the establishment of a (new) full-time Court in Strasbourg: the percentage of women on the Court increased dramatically from 2.7 per cent in 1997 to 20 per cent in 1998, and since 2007 has consistently been above 30 per cent.[22]

Without the need, at this juncture, to provide a historical account of (at times contentious) developments to secure gender balance on the Court, suffice is to note that this objective is now uncontested.[23] The Assembly obliges states parties to include at least one candidate of each sex in the list submitted to it, except when the

[20] For more details, see Sections C and E in the Appendix to this chapter. Recent statistical data are provided in the 2024 CDDH report (n 1) paras 31–34.

[21] Council of Europe (PACE) (n 4) para 29, and Drzemczewski (n 1) para 32. A recommendation of a candidate can be made eg 'unanimously' or 'with an overwhelming [or large, or clear, or narrow] majority', sometimes 'over' a second candidate, if there is only a small difference in support between two of the three candidates.

[22] Helen Keller, Corina Heri, and Myriam Christ, 'Fifty Years of Women at the European Court of Human Rights: Success and Failures of the Council of Europe's Gender Agenda' in Freya Baetens (ed), *Who Is the Judge? Identity and Diversity on the International Bench* (OUP 2021) 179–205, *passim*. See also blogpost and comments thereto: Cecilia M Bailliet, 'Launch of GQUAL!—A Global Campaign for Gender Parity in International Tribunals and Monitoring Bodies' (*EJIL:Talk!*, 8 October 2015) <www.ejiltalk.org/launch-of-gqual-a-global-campaign-for-gender-parity-in-international-tribunals-and-monitoring-bodies>.

[23] ECtHR (n 5) para 54 and subsequent developments referred to by Keller and others above.

candidates belong to the sex which is under-represented in the Court, ie the sex to which under 40 per cent of the total number of judges belong,[24] or if exceptional circumstances exist to derogate from this rule (see Appendix, Section C, for the exact wording of the text). When a state invokes 'exceptional circumstances' when transmitting an exclusively male list, as was done in respect of Malta, Belgium, Croatia, Moldova, and Denmark, the Committee will invite the Minister of Justice of the state concerned, or a person designated by him or her, to a hearing in order to obtain an explanation of the circumstances that prompted the respective state's authorities to transmit such a single-sex list. As noted, the acceptance, by the Committee, of such a list necessitates a two-thirds majority vote and subsequent endorsement by the plenary Assembly.[25]

The Advisory Panel, functioning independently from the Assembly, has come to play a complementary, preparatory role in the parliamentary process of electing judges.[26] The relationship with the Panel has evolved positively after initial 'teething problems' dating back to 2013, when the latter proposed, *inter alia*, that its confidential opinions (*sic*!) be distributed to all members of the Assembly and that the Committee of Ministers be implicated in the procedure.[27] Closer ties have now been forged between the Assembly's Committee on the Election of Judges and the Advisory Panel, as exemplified by the presence of a representative of the Panel at the Committee's briefing sessions and the Committee's refusal to consider a list of candidates if a state has not consulted the Panel beforehand.[28] These and related developments have been the subject of an in-depth analysis in which the creation and working methods of the Advisory Panel have been compared with that of the EU Panel instituted by Article 255 of the Treaty on the Functioning of the European Union.[29]

When the Assembly last adjusted its election procedure in 2018, consideration was given to a number of matters, among which figured proposals to increase transparency by, for example, providing for live transmission of interviews with

[24] This was the case with respect to Latvian and Croatian lists a number of years ago and more recently the Maltese list of three women candidates, submitted in March 2019: see country-by-country 'table of progress' of the election procedure, available on the Assembly's portal: <https://rm.coe.int/forthcoming-elections-for-judges-country-by-country-december-2025-/1680aa06ac>.

[25] See text in Appendix, Section C, and Council of Europe (PACE) (n 4) paras 22–24. The tenor of this Assembly text is reflected in the Committee of Ministers' Guidelines as well as in state practice: Explanatory Memorandum thereto (n 12) Section II. 8 and para 34.

[26] See the Panel's 'Short Guide' (n 14) 5. See also Paul Mahoney 'Guest Editorial' (2023) 4 European Convention on Human Rights Law Review 231, 250–58.

[27] Appendix 2 in the Panel's first Report for 2010–13, of 12 December 2013, available on the Advisory Panel's portal <www.coe.int/en/web/dlapil/advisory-panel>. For obvious reasons, such confidential opinions are provided *only* to members of the AS/Cdh who interview candidates with respect to the state concerned.

[28] 4th Activity Report of the Advisory Panel of Experts on Candidates for Election as Judge to the ECtHR, (2019) 39 Human Rights Law Journal 464, *passim*, and especially comments by its then chairperson N Vajić, at 471–72. See also the Panel's 5th Activity Report (and related documents) in (2023) 43 Human Rights Law Journal 323, 323–35.

[29] Mitchel de S-O L'E Lasser, *Judicial Dis-Appointments: Judicial Appointments Reform and Rise of European Judicial Independence* (OUP 2020) especially chapters 4, 5, 10, and 11. These two Panels are of a completely different nature, as explained in the book. On the Article 255 Panel: Christiaan Timmermans, 'The Procedure for Nominating Members of the EU Courts', in this volume.

candidates, as well as the idea mooted by the CDDH, an intergovernmental committee of the Council of Europe,[30] suggesting that the AS/Cdh could be mandated to forward only the names of two candidates for election by the plenary Assembly (in contradiction with the wording of Article 22 of the Convention). Both of these suggestions were given short shrift in the report presented to the Assembly.[31]

The serious manner in which the Assembly undertakes its task to elect judges of the highest calibre cannot be doubted. This can be discerned from a perusal of lists with respect to which the AS/Cdh has found candidates insufficiently qualified and/or has determined that national selection procedures did not comply with standards required by the Assembly and the Committee of Ministers. Thus, it has proposed the rejection of lists submitted by Albania (twice), Andorra, Azerbaijan (twice), France, Georgia, Hungary, Poland (three times), Serbia, Slovakia (twice), Turkey (twice), and Ukraine. This information is in the public domain and is accessible on the Assembly's portal.[32]

When the Committee decides to recommend the rejection of a list, an 'unseen' yet highly significant aspect of the procedure is activated. This relates to a confidential procedure whereby the Secretary-General of the Assembly and the Committee's Chairperson provide to the Permanent Representative or Ambassador of the state concerned and the chairperson of said state's parliamentary delegation, respectively, details as to why rejection of the list was proposed. This allows the authorities of the state to know exactly which candidate(s) appeared not to comply with specific eligibility requirements and/or any other reasons as to why rejection of the list was proposed.[33] Such confidential discussions enable states to know which person(s) on the original list can re-apply, assuming their credentials comply with the eligibility requirements and/or what measures must be taken by the state concerned to ensure that a new list is not rejected, assuming that the plenary Assembly endorsed the recommendation to reject the list.[34]

[30] Council of Europe (Steering Committee on Human Rights (CDDH)), 'Report on the Process of Selection and Election of Judges of the European Court of Human Rights' (11 December 2017) document CDDH(2017)R88addI, especially paras 25–26 and 135 <https://rm.coe.int/report-on-the-process-of-selection-and-election-of-judges-of-the-europ/1680772e4d>.

[31] Council of Europe (Committee on the Election of Judges to the European Court of Human Rights, rapporteur Boris Cilevičs)'Procedure for the election of judges to the European Court of Human Rights' (2 November 2018) document 14662, especially sections 2 and 3 in the appendix therein, available at <https://pace.coe.int/en/files/25083>. This report led to the adoption of Assembly Resolution 2248 (2018), with the same title. See also in this connection the Court's first advisory opinion (n 5) para 44.

[32] Committee on the Election of Judges to the European Court of Human Rights, 'Elections: Table of Progress' <https://pace.coe.int/en/pages/committee-30/AS-CDH>, <https://rm.coe.int/forthcoming-elections-for-judges-country-by-country-december-2025-/1680aa06ac>.

[33] Such a confidential communication is of added importance in a situation in which rejection is proposed without interview, as has occurred in respect to lists submitted by Austria, Azerbaijan, France, Monaco, and Poland (three times): see, in this connection, 'Dokumentation' rubric 'Parlamentarische Versammlung des Europarats, Strasburg' (2021) 48 Europäische Grundrechte Zeitschrift 325, 325–26.

[34] On a number of occasions, candidates have decided to withdraw after such 'confidential discussions' have been held, with the (face-saving) result that no recommendation to reject a list could be made to the plenary Assembly: appendix to Assembly Resolution 1432 (2005) (text in Appendix, Section D).

12.4.5 Election by plenary Assembly

The election by the Assembly is by secret ballot, usually on the Tuesday or Wednesday morning of a plenary session in Strasbourg. An absolute majority of votes cast by parliamentarians is required in the first round of voting (50 per cent +1). If this is not obtained, a second vote takes place in the afternoon on the same day, when a simple majority of votes is sufficient; the names of all three candidates remain on the ballot. Election results are announced publicly by the President of the Assembly on the day of the election.[35] The results are also published in the form of a press release on the Assembly's website shortly afterwards.

Strictly speaking, the Assembly is not bound by the AS/Cdh's recommendations, but there must be strong reasons for parliamentarians not to follow the Commission's proposal(s). In this connection, comments have been made that the election process is sometimes politicized and marked by unpredictability. It can be accepted that political considerations may come into play as the Assembly is, by definition, a political body of parliamentarians who take political decisions.[36] However, the argument of unpredictability needs to be seen in the context of recommendations provided to the Assembly by its specialized Committee: since its inception in January 2015, the Assembly has followed the Committee's recommendations in fifty-eight out of fifty-nine cases.[37]

When rejection of a list is proposed, this must be ratified by the plenary Assembly in the framework of a Progress Report submitted to it by the Bureau. Ratification of the Committee's proposal signifies definitive rejection of the list. If the recommendation to reject a list were not accepted in plenary, the list would need to be referred back to the Committee.[38]

12.5 Conclusions

As indicated at the outset of this chapter, the processes of selecting candidates at the national level and electing judges onto the Court by the Assembly appear quite straightforward, although their implementation is complex and time-consuming.

[35] For the manner in which the terms of office are determined, see Council of Europe, 'Resolution 1726 on the Effective Implementation of the ECHR: The Interlaken Process', para 8 (text available in the Appendix, Section D). This procedure needed 'codification' by the Assembly so as to prevent ad hoc arrangements—occasionally agreed to by the Court's President—to permit a sitting judge to stay in office for a (much) longer period of time when this suited both the incumbent and the newly elected judge.

[36] This subject of 'political lobbying' is broached by B. Cilevičs, in Explanatory Memorandum, PACE document 14662 (n 31) paras 18, 26–31 and appendix, section 2, points 1–6.

[37] The one exception relates to the judge elected in respect of Spain in 2018. See also, in this context, Drzemczewski (n 1) para 34 and Cilevičs (n 31) para 18. This figure of fifty-nine recommendations includes the election, in late 2021, of the judge in respect of the Russian Federation whose short-lived term of office ceased on 16 September 2022, after the country's expulsion from the Council of Europe on 16 March 2022. For more information on this subject, see Andrew Drzemczewski and Rick Lawson, 'Exclusion of the Russian Federation from the Council of Europe and the ECHR: An Overview' (2023) 21 Baltic Yearbook of International Law 38, 66–69 and 97–98.

[38] See Appendix, Section C, for details. This has not yet happened. For a proposal to do so, with respect to a list submitted by Poland, see Council of Europe (PACE) Verbatim Record of the PACE Spring Session 2021 (Monday afternoon, 19 April 2021) <https://pace.coe.int/en/verbatim/2021-04-19/pm/en>.

That said, this procedure provides a unique example—now in operation for nearly seventy years—of how a parliamentary body *elects* members of an international judicial body, conferring on the office-holders democratic legitimacy in a relatively open and transparent manner.

Certainly, the procedure has 'improved beyond recognition'.[39] But it is not perfect; it has necessitated and will continue to necessitate amelioration and refinement so as to ensure that highly qualified and respected judges are elected. Among the important steps taken, in this context, was the creation of the Assembly's dedicated Committee on the Election of Judges and the placing, on the Assembly's portal, of detailed, up-to-date and easily accessible information explaining how the election process functions.[40]

The quality and coherence of the Court's caselaw are contingent on the stature of its judges, which, in turn, is dependent on the selection and subsequent election of appropriately qualified persons. The Assembly and, in particular, states parties are invested with a heavy responsibility in this respect. As Jean-Paul Costa, a former President of the Court, has said: 'the system will fail if judges do not have the necessary experience and authority'.[41]

Appendix: Key Texts Relating to the Election Process

A. Relevant Extracts from the European Convention on Human Rights (signed at Rome on 4 November 1950, as amended by Protocol Nos 11, 14, and 15, supplemented by Protocol Nos 1, 4, 6, 7, 12, 13, and 16)

Article 20

Number of judges

The Court shall consist of a number of judges equal to that of the High Contracting Parties.

Article 21

Criteria for office

1. The judges shall be of high moral character and must either possess the qualifications required for appointment to high judicial office or be jurisconsults of recognised competence.

[39] Sir Nicolas Bratza, former President of the Court; citation taken from publication of the Open Society/International Commission of Jurists (n 1) 81.

[40] The consolidation and further improvement of the procedure for the election of judges are again on the Assembly's agenda: see AS/Cdh Motion for a resolution (document 16011, 17 June 2024, ratified by the plenary Assembly on 28 June 2024) <https://pace.coe.int/en/files/33587>.

[41] Quotation taken from a letter appended to Council of Europe (PACE) 'National Procedures for the Selection of Candidates for the European Court of Human Rights' (2010) document 12391, at 7 <https://pace.coe.int/en/files/12764>. See also, in this context, comments made by former ECtHR Judge Lech Garlicki, 'How Should the New ECtHR Judge from Poland Be?' (*Rule of Law*, 20 January 2021) <https://ruleoflaw.pl/how-should-the-new-european-court-of-human-rights-judge-from-poland-be-lech-garlicki-explains> (interview initially published in Polish by OKO.press on 2 December 2020: <https://oko.press/kandydaci-europejski-trybunal-praw-czlowieka>).

2. Candidates shall be less than 65 years of age at the date by which the list of three candidates has been requested by the Parliamentary Assembly, further to Article 22.
3. The judges shall sit on the Court in their individual capacity.
4. During their term of office the judges shall not engage in any activity which is incompatible with their independence, impartiality or with the demands of a full-time office; all questions arising from the application of this paragraph shall be decided by the Court.

Article 22

Election of judges

The judges shall be elected by the Parliamentary Assembly with respect to each High Contracting Party by a majority of votes cast from a list of three candidates nominated by the High Contracting Party.

Article 23

Terms of office and dismissal

1. The judges shall be elected for a period of nine years. They may not be re-elected.
2. The judges shall hold office until replaced. They shall, however, continue to deal with such cases as they already have under consideration.
3. No judge may be dismissed from office unless the other judges decide by a majority of two-thirds that that judge has ceased to fulfil the required conditions.

B. Extracts from the Assembly's Rules of Procedure

PART VII Languages and records [as determined by the Assembly: Article 12 of the Statute of the Council of Europe, 1949]

[...]

Rule 30—Interpretation in Committees

30.1. [...] Interpretation at meetings of the Committee on the Election of Judges to the European Court of Human Rights and in sub-committees shall be limited to official languages [of the Council of Europe, ie English and French].

[...]

PART X: Committees [establishment thereof, by the Assembly, as specified in Article 24 of the Statute of the Council of Europe, 1949]

Rule 44—Appointment of Committees

44.1. At the beginning of each ordinary session, the Assembly shall set up the following [9] general committees:

[...]

9. Committee on the Election of Judges to the European Court of Human Rights (20 seats).[Footnote: Plus the chairpersons of the Committee on Legal Affairs and Human Rights and the Committee on Equality and Non-Discrimination as *ex officio* members, or, in their absence, a vice-chairperson.]

[...]

44.3.a. On the basis of the candidatures presented by the political groups and taking into account gender balance and regional balance, the Bureau shall appoint [...] 20 members (and their alternates) of the Committee on the Election of Judges to the European Court of Human Rights by applying the apportionment ratio based on the so-called 'D'Hondt principle'. At the beginning of each ordinary session, the candidatures presented by each political group to each of these committees must include at least one-third women where the group holds at least three seats. The Bureau shall appoint members, ensuring that the committees concerned always include at least one-third women.

[...]

Rule 48—Meetings of Committees

[...]

48.3. Unless a Committee decides otherwise, Committee meetings shall be held in private. The Monitoring Committee and the Committee on the Election of Judges to the European Court of Human Rights meet in camera [ie in secret, the latter, in essence, only in the presence of the Secretary General of the Assembly and the Committee's Secretariat].

48.4. Members of the Assembly may attend meetings of Committees of which they are not members but without the right to speak or vote. However, only members of the Monitoring Committee and members of the Committee on the Election of Judges to the European Court of Human Rights may attend meetings of their respective Committees.

[...]

48.6. Meetings of the [...] Committee on the Election of Judges to the European Court of Human Rights shall not be open to members of special guest, observer and partner for democracy delegations.

48.7. The conditions on which any person who is not covered by sub-paragraphs 4 to 6 above may be heard by a Committee shall be decided by that Committee.

48.8. Secretaries of national delegations and secretaries of political groups may attend the meetings of Committees of the Assembly, except for those of the Monitoring Committee and the Committee on the Election of Judges to the European Court of Human Rights.

[Appendix XXI to the Rules specifies that a Committee may, once a year, meet elsewhere than in Paris or Strasbourg when so authorised by the Bureau. The AS/Cdh has done so once, in Riga, Latvia, in October 2017. The AS/Cdh has also recently held a joint meeting with the Advisory Panel of Experts for Election as Judge to the European Court of Human Rights in Vienna, Austria, on 13 May 2024, subsequent to a similar meeting held in Paris on 7 June 2022.]

C. Candidates for the European Court of Human Rights

Assembly Resolution 1366 (2004) as modified by Resolutions 1426 (2005), 1627 (2008), 1841 (2011), 2002 (2014), and 2278 (2019)

1. The Parliamentary Assembly, referring to its Recommendation 1649 (2004), continues to support the procedure by which candidates are asked to complete a standard curriculum vitae [available in appendix to Assembly Resolution 1646 (2009)]; it believes that the model to be used should be reviewed by the Committee on the Election of Judges to the European Court of Human Rights and that proposals for modification should be reported to the Committee for adoption by the Assembly.

2. The Assembly remains convinced that the twelve-month timetable it has adopted provides a practical model for all participants, but resolves nevertheless to keep its targets under review.
3. The Assembly decides not to consider lists of candidates where:
   i. the areas of competence of the candidates appear to be unduly restricted;
   ii. not all of the candidates fulfil each of the conditions laid down by Article 21, paragraph 1, of the European Convention on Human Rights;
   iii. one of the candidates does not appear to have an active knowledge of one of the official languages of the Council of Europe and a passive knowledge of the other;
   iv. the national selection procedure did not satisfy the minimum requirements of fairness and transparency;
   v. the Advisory Panel was not duly consulted. [A footnote to paragraph 3. v. specifies: The mandate of the Advisory Panel of Experts on Candidates for Election as Judges to the European Court of Human Rights is to advise the High Contracting Parties whether candidates meet the criteria stipulated in Article 21, paragraph 1, of the Convention. See [Committee of Ministers] Resolution CM/Res (2010) 26, as amended by Resolution CM/Res (2014) 44].

In such cases, the Committee on the Election of Judges to the European Court of Human Rights shall decide on a proposal to reject a list of candidates by a majority of the votes cast. This proposal shall be endorsed by the Assembly in the Progress Report of the Bureau of the Assembly and the Standing Committee. The Assembly's endorsement of the proposal to reject a list entails its definitive rejection; the State concerned is invited to submit a new list. Rejection by the Assembly of the Committee's proposal to reject a list shall entail the referral of the list back to the Committee.

4. Moreover, the Assembly decides to consider single-sex lists of candidates when the candidates belong to the sex which is under-represented in the Court (i.e. the sex to which under 40% of the total number of judges belong), or in exceptional circumstances where a Contracting Party has taken all the necessary and appropriate steps to ensure that the list contains candidates of both sexes meeting the requirements of paragraph 1 of Article 21 of the European Convention on Human Rights.
   Such exceptional circumstances must be duly so considered by a two-thirds majority of the votes cast by members of the Committee on the Election of Judges to the European Court of Human Rights. If the required majority has not been achieved, the Committee shall recommend that the Assembly reject the list concerned. This position shall be endorsed by the Assembly in the Progress Report of the Bureau of the Assembly and the Standing Committee.
5. The Assembly continues to believe that the process of interview provides additional insight into the qualities of the candidates and decides:
   i. that nominated candidates should be informed as far as possible of the purpose of the interview and procedures for its conduct;
   ii. that alternative locations for interviews should be considered if there is a valid reason for holding interviews outside Strasbourg and Paris;
   iii. that further staggering or additional sessions of the Committee might permit an extension of the time available for each interview;
   iv. that the political groups, when nominating their representatives to the Committee, should aim to include at least 40% women, which is the parity threshold deemed necessary by the Council of Europe to exclude possible gender bias in decision-making processes;
   v. that candidates should be made aware of the criteria employed by the Committee in reaching its decision;

vi. that one of the criteria used by the Committee should be that, in the case of equal merit, preference should be given to a candidate of the sex under-represented at the Court;
vii. that a fair and efficient interview process requires a continuous process of training and re-assessment of the members and staff involved in selection panels;
viii. that the obligation to promote an open and transparent process might require the Committee to give reasons for its recommendations and ranking of candidates and in particular to give positive reasons for its recommendation in favour of a particular candidate;
ix. that it would be desirable to provide timely feedback to both the individual candidate and the nominating State.

6. The Chairperson or a representative of the Advisory Panel shall be invited by the Chairperson of the Committee on the Election of Judges to explain the reasons for the Panel's views on candidates, during the briefing sessions scheduled before each set of interviews.

D. Modalities for the Election of Judges to the European Court of Human Rights

Appendix to Assembly Resolution 1432 (2005)

1. In principle, the list of candidates for the election of judges, once submitted to the Parliamentary Assembly, should not be modified. The Assembly shall only exceptionally accept partial or complete modification of the list on the initiative of the government concerned.
2. The Assembly shall interrupt the procedure if one of the three candidates on a list for the post of judge [. . .] withdraws before the first ballot. It shall ask the government concerned [. . .] to complete the list of candidates.
3. The Assembly confirms its practice of listing candidates for the post of judge in alphabetical order [the words 'on the ballot paper' were deleted from this text by Resolution 2551 (2024) para 6.1]. This shall also remain the practice in those cases where the government, disregarding the Assembly's position as set out in Recommendations 1429 (1999) and 1649 (2004), has expressed a preference for one of the candidates. Any such expressions of governmental preference shall play no role in the deliberations of the Committee on the election of judges to the European Court of Human Rights where only the criteria provided for in the European Convention on Human Rights and those established by the Assembly itself shall be relevant.

[. . .]

Paragraph 8 of Assembly Resolution 1726 (2010) on effective implementation of the ECHR: the Interlaken process

8. [. . .] the nine-year term of office of a judge elected by the Assembly to the Court shall commence from the date of taking up of his or her duties, and in any event no later than three months after his or her election. However, if the election takes place more than three months before the seat of the outgoing judge becomes vacant, the term of office shall commence the day the seat becomes vacant. If the election takes place less than three months before the seat of the outgoing judge becomes vacant, the elected judge shall take up his or her duties as soon as possible after the seat becomes vacant and the term of office shall commence as from then and in any event no later than three months after his or her election.

E. Terms of Reference of the Committee on the Election of Judges to the European Court of Human Rights (AS/Cdh)

(Assembly Resolution 1842 (2011), as modified by Resolution 2002 (2014))

Number of seats: 20 plus the two chairpersons of the Assembly's Committee on Legal Affairs and Human Rights (AS/Jur) and the Committee on Equality and Non-Discrimination (AS/Ega), as *ex officio* members, or, in their absence, a vice-chairperson thereof, as stipulated in the Assembly's Rules of Procedure, Rule 44.1 and footnote thereto. *Quorum*: presence of one-third, i.e., 7 members (Rule 47.3).

Terms of reference of the AS/Cdh:

1. In the framework of the procedure for the election of judges to the European Court of Human Rights, in accordance with Article 22 of the European Convention on Human Rights, the Committee shall examine the candidatures and make recommendations to the Assembly.
2. The Committee shall:
   i. study the curricula vitae and interview all candidates for posts of judge of the European Court of Human Rights, before their election by the Assembly;
   ii. under the authority of its chairperson, prepare a report to the Assembly on the election of each judge to the European Court of Human Rights, which shall include its recommendations. Whenever possible, the reasons for its recommendations and ranking of candidates shall be indicated in the report;
   iii. review, when necessary, the standard curriculum vitae sent to candidates for the post of judge of the European Court of Human Rights;
   iv. seek to ensure that the national procedure for the nomination of candidates complies with the criteria which the Assembly has drawn up for the establishment of lists, and in particular the presence of candidates of both sexes.
3. The Committee may report to the Assembly on any question related to the procedure for the selection of candidates and the procedure for the election of judges to the European Court of Human Rights.
4. In addition to the general regulations or as an exception thereto, the Committee shall apply the following rules:
   i. the Committee shall vote by a majority of the votes cast. A decision to consider a single-sex list of candidates in exceptional circumstances shall require a two-thirds majority of the votes cast. The Committee shall vote on candidates by secret ballot. Only members who have attended in full the interview procedure for a post of judge may vote. Members of the Committee from the country whose list is under consideration shall not have the right to vote, either on the possible rejection of their country's list or on the expression of preferences among candidates. For any other decision, voting shall take place by a show of hands. However, voting may be by secret ballot if requested by at least one-third of the members present. The chairperson shall be entitled to vote;
   ii. when rejection of a list of candidates is recommended to the Assembly, the reason(s) must be specified.
5. In order to be able to evaluate the qualifications and skills of candidates, Committee members shall have appropriate knowledge or practical experience in the legal field.

13
The Procedure for Nominating Members of the EU Courts
The Role of the 255 Panel

Christiaan Timmermans[*]

13.1 Introduction

The initiators of this project on the Governance of International Courts and Tribunals should be congratulated. A comparative analysis of the various aspects of this governance will not only be of academic interest but also has the potential to be of practical significance. Conclusions sketching out optimal structures, general principles, and best practices of governance might be of direct importance for these courts and for the creation of future international courts. Even without major changes requiring amendment of their founding statutes or secondary rules of an organizational and procedural nature, these conclusions might possibly also become a source of inspiration for their daily functioning and management.

This chapter will discuss the genesis and functioning of the so-called 255 Panel, the panel set up under Article 255 of the Treaty on the Functioning of the European Union (TFEU).[1] It is mandated to issue non-binding opinions about the suitability of candidates proposed by EU member states to be appointed as a judge or an advocate-general of the Court of Justice of the European Union (CJEU) or as a judge of the General Court of the European Union (GCEU).

The following issues will be discussed successively in this chapter: the genesis of the panel, institutional aspects (mandate and national selection procedures), assessment procedure and criteria, the character of its opinions, and the reasons why they are not published. The final part of the chapter will focus on a number of general issues and critical questions raised in academic writing about the functioning of the panel, namely the question of the panel's accountability and democratic legitimacy, the question of judicial self-governance, of co-optation and finally also the issue of the Courts' working language.

In discussing these issues, the main source of reference will be the Activity Reports.[2] The panel has published these reports from its inception on its own initiative. As of now, six reports have been published, covering the almost ten years of its existence.

[*] This contribution was finished in March 2021. Subsequent developments have not been taken into account.

[1] Consolidated version of the Treaty of the Functioning of the European Union [2012] OJ C 326/47.

[2] These Reports are available on the website of the panel: <https://comite255.europa.eu>.

Christiaan Timmermans, *The Procedure for Nominating Members of the EU Courts* In: *Governance of International Courts and Tribunals*. Edited by: Sergey Vasiliev and Niels Blokker, Oxford University Press. © Christiaan Timmermans 2026.
DOI: 10.1093/oso/9780198922131.003.0013

The stated aim of the Activity Reports is to better inform member states' governments, EU institutions, potential future candidates, and the citizens (the reference added in the Fifth Report) about the panel's working methods, the criteria it applies, and its expectations vis-à-vis those whose suitability it is called upon to assess.[3] For some of the issues to be discussed, a comparison will be made with the panel set up in 2010 by the Council of Europe to advise about the qualifications of candidates proposed by its member states for nomination to the European Court of Human Rights (ECtHR).[4]

13.2 Genesis of the Panel

The appointment of members of the EU courts is in the hands of the member states. A candidate for nomination is selected by each member state and appointed by the member states acting collectively as the Conference of the Representatives of the Governments of the Member States. Before the Treaty of Lisbon, which provided for the 255 Panel, there normally was no debate about the qualifications of a proposed candidate. Member states respected and accepted each other's choices. It was well known that in some member states the selection of candidates was politically motivated. This did not necessarily imply that the legal qualifications of those candidates were insufficient, but it did mean that sometimes the mandate of a well-functioning judge was not renewed because he or she had to be replaced by a candidate of another political family. Nevertheless, the risk of an insufficiently qualified candidate being nominated did exist, the more so since most member states did not apply an open and independent selection procedure.

It might be that the perspective of a substantial enlargement of the Union during the second half of the 1990s increased anxieties in this respect. The Court of Justice itself, in its Reflexion Document of March 1999 on the Future of the Judicial System of the EU, a document which explicitly discussed necessary reforms in view of future enlargements, remained silent on this question. However, the Report on the Future of the Judicial System of the European Communities ('The Due Report'), produced in January 2000 by a Study Group set up by the European Commission and composed of a majority of former members of the EU courts, considered it 'useful' that the member states, when deciding about nominations at the courts, would dispose of an Advisory Committee composed of highly qualified and independent lawyers, capable to assess the legal competence of candidates proposed.[5]

This suggestion was discussed and accepted by the Discussion Circle on the Court of Justice, set up by the European Convention responsible for designing a draft Treaty establishing a Constitution for Europe. Indeed, a proposal to that effect was included

[3] For example, 255 Panel, 'Second Activity Report' (26 December 2012) 5091/13, 15.

[4] On 10 November 2010 the Committee of Ministers of the Council of Europe adopted a resolution to establish an advisory panel, see Council of Europe (Council of Ministers), 'Resolution CM/Res (2010) 26 on the Establishment of an Advisory Panel of Experts on Candidates for Election as Judge to the European Court of Human Rights' (2010) CM/Res (2010) 26. See Andrew Drzemczewski, 'The Election of Judges onto the European Court of Human Rights', in this volume.

[5] Report by the Working Party on the Future of the European Communities' Court System ('The Due Report'), 19 January 2000.

in the draft Constitution (Article III-262) and ended up in the Treaty of Lisbon. The Discussion Circle considered it appropriate to set up an advisory panel, which 'would have the task of giving the member states an opinion on whether a candidate's profile was suited to the performance of his/her duties, particularly on the basis of objective criteria relating to professional qualifications.'[6] The panel's deliberations should not be public; there would be no hearings. Further, it should be made up of former members of the EU Court and representatives of national Supreme Courts. The European Parliament was to be allowed to appoint a legal expert. Such a panel 'might make Member States more demanding in the choice of candidates they put forward.'[7]

In this context, mention should be made of the independent Advisory Committee established by the Council of the EU to give an opinion on the suitability of candidates for appointment as a judge at the Civil Service Tribunal, a special judicial panel with jurisdiction at first instance for European civil service disputes. This panel was established in 2004 and attached to what then was the EC Court of first instance.[8] This Committee had a much more prominent position than the 255 Panel because it had to first select the most qualified candidates after a public call for applications and then provide the Council with a list comprising twice as many candidates as there were judges to be appointed. This Tribunal, and the Advisory Committee with it, were abolished in 2016 when the jurisdiction for civil service cases was retransferred to what now is the General Court.[9]

13.3 Institutional Aspects

According to Article 255 TFEU, 'A panel shall be set up in order to give an opinion on candidates' suitability to perform the duties of Judge and Advocate-General of the Court of Justice and the General Court before the governments of the member states make the appointments.' Albeit that the Treaties are not explicitly saying so, in practice member states propose only one candidate for an appointment. Consequently, the 255 Panel has nothing to say about the selection of that candidate. This is exclusively a matter for the member states to decide. As a member of the 255 Panel, I was once criticized for a favourable opinion being given on a candidate with the argument that there were much more suitable candidates in the member state in question. Such criticism should of course be addressed to the government of that member state.

Article 255 TFEU further states: 'The panel shall comprise seven persons chosen from among former members of the Court of Justice and the General Court, members of national supreme courts and lawyers of recognised competence, one of whom shall be proposed by the European Parliament.' The Council on a proposal from the

[6] The European Convention, 'Final Report of the Discussion Circle on the Court of Justice' (25 March 2003) CONV 636/03, para 6.

[7] ibid.

[8] Council Decision 2004/752/EC, EURATOM of 2 November 2004 establishing the EU Civil Service Tribunal, [2004] OJ L 333/7.

[9] Regulation (EU, Euratom) 2016/1192 of the European Parliament and of the Council of 6 July 2016 on the transfer to the General Court of jurisdiction at first instance in disputes between the European Union and its servants [2016] OJ L200/137.

President of the Court of Justice appoints the members of the panel. From the start, the panel has been composed of a majority of (former) members of national supreme courts, one or two former members of the EU courts, and one member proposed by the European Parliament. The present members are the Chief Justice of Ireland, a former member of the Polish Constitutional Court, a former President of the German Constitutional Court, the President of the Spanish Supreme Court, a former member of the European Parliament,[10] a former member of the EU General Court, and a former member of the EU Court of Justice, who is also the President of the panel.

The Council, on a proposal of the President of the Court of Justice, establishes the operating rules of the panel.[11] According to these rules, the General Secretariat of the Council is responsible for the panel's secretariat and the deliberations of the panel take place *in camera*.

13.3.1 Mandate of the panel

The panel is mandated by the Treaty to 'give an opinion on candidates' suitability to perform the duties' related to the function for which they are to be nominated. Articles 253 and 254 TFEU define different conditions in that respect for nominations to the Court of Justice and the General Court. To be appointed as judge or advocate-general at the Court of Justice (Article 253 TFEU), apart from being independent beyond doubt, candidates must 'possess the qualifications required for appointment to the highest judicial offices in their respective countries' or be 'jurisconsults of recognised competence'. A literal interpretation of the first condition would oblige the panel to verify whether the *national* criteria for appointment to the highest judicial offices are being satisfied. Apart from the practical problem of being fully informed of these criteria, this interpretation would entail a more fundamental difficulty. These criteria will vary by member state. The result would risk subjecting candidates to unequal treatment. Moreover, limiting the assessment to the suitability for highest judicial office in the member state of origin would ignore the important additional qualifications (international experience, language requirements, knowledge of EU law) required for being able to function adequately at the EU courts.

In my view, this first condition of Article 253 for an appointment at the Court of Justice should be read as being addressed to the member states when selecting their candidates. This text of Article 253 originates from the founding Treaties and has remained unchanged ever since. Apparently, the authors of the Lisbon Treaty, when providing for the 255 Panel, did not see reasons for adapting the Article in this respect or overlooked the potential problem.

The panel has not followed this literal interpretation. It has developed, on the basis of the treaty conditions, uniform assessment criteria, indiscriminately applied to all candidates for appointment at the Court of Justice whatever their member state of origin.[12]

10 At the time of writing this member had resigned and not yet been replaced.

11 Council Decision 2010/124/EU of 25 February 2010 relating to the operating rules of the panel provided for in Article 255 of the Treaty on the Functioning of the European Union [2010] OJ L 50/18.

12 Section 13.4.1.

The corresponding condition for an appointment at the General Court is more neutrally drafted as it does not refer to conditions applying in the member state of origin of the candidate. To be suitable for an appointment the candidate must, according to Article 254 TFEU, 'possess the ability required for appointment to high judicial office'.

Strangely enough, contrary to what the treaty provides for appointments at the Court of Justice, Article 254 TFEU does not include for the General Court the alternative condition of being a lawyer of recognized competence.[13] The panel has not drawn any specific conclusion therefrom. Its assessment criteria as applied to candidatures for the General Court in no way exclude lawyers of recognized competence. On the contrary, it has stated repeatedly in the Activity Reports that no preference is given for appointments at the EU courts to any particular type of occupational background, whether that of a judge, university professor, jurisconsult, lawyer, or high-level official specialized in the field of law.[14]

As the panel's mandate is clearly limited to assessing the suitability of a candidate, it has felt obliged to exclude a certain number of additional assessments from its remit. Thus the panel will not enter into considerations about a balanced composition of the EU courts in terms of legal expertise represented, gender, professional, socio-cultural, let alone political, backgrounds of its members, due to a lack of competence.[15] The representation of legal expertise in the Court's composition or about gender balance is a matter for the member states, not for the panel, to consider. Indeed, the Council has insisted, in its motivation of the 2015 Regulation doubling the number of judges of the General Court, on the high importance of ensuring gender balance within the General Court.[16] To achieve that objective, the Council stated that partial replacements in that Court should be organized in such a way that the governments of member states gradually begin to nominate two judges for the same partial replacement with the aim of choosing one woman and one man. By comparison, the selection procedure for appointments at the ECtHR is stricter in this regard. The list of candidates submitted by a member state must generally comprise one woman and one man. Exceptions are possible but only if the member state, when submitting a single list of candidates of the overrepresented sex, is able to demonstrate that it has taken all the necessary and appropriate steps in trying to respect the principle.[17]

[13] According to Dumbrovsky and others, this criterion adds nuance more readily associated with selection criteria for constitutional court judges: Tomas Dumbrovsky, Bilyana Petkova, and Marijn van der Sluis, 'Judicial Appointments: The Article 255 TFEU Advisory Panel and Selection Procedures in the Member States' (2014) 51(2) Common Market Law Review 455, 465.

[14] eg 255 Panel, 'First Activity Report' (17 February 2011) 6509/11, 10; 255 Panel, 'Third Activity Report' (13 December 2013) SN 1118/2014, 11.

[15] 255 Panel, 'First Activity Report' (n 14) 4; also Jean-Marc Sauvé, 'Le rôle du comité 255 dans la sélection du juge de l'Union' in *The Court of Justice and the Construction of Europe: Analyses and Perspectives on Sixty Years of Case-Law—La Cour de Justice et la Construction de l'Europe: Analyses et Perspectives de Soixante Ans de Jurisprudence* (TMC Asser Press 2013) 99, 117.

[16] Regulation (EU, Euratom) 2015/2422 of the European Parliament and of the Council of 16 December 2015 amending Protocol No 3 on the statute of the Court of Justice of the European Union, [2014] OJ L 341/14.

[17] Parliamentary Assembly of the Council of Europe, 'Procedure for the election of judges to the European Court of Human Rights' (30 September 2020) Information document, SG-AS (2020) 03 rev 3, para 10; also Andrew Drzemczewski, 'The Election of Judges onto the European Court of Human Rights', in this volume.

In one case the panel did not consider itself competent to oppose a candidature submitted to replace a judge, who had been on the bench only for a few months and had asked his/her term to be renewed. In the context of the increase of the number of judges of the General Court in 2015, five new judges, all having received a favourable opinion from the panel, had been appointed in 2016 for a term of less than five months because of the need to integrate them into the three-year rotation system of the judges at the Court. The members of the EU courts are appointed for a six-year term, half of them coming up for renewal after three years. For the renewal of the term of office of these five judges the panel had given a favourable opinion noting that there were no reasons whatsoever to decide otherwise and expressly stating that the non-renewal of their terms of office 'could undermine or appear to undermine the independence of Judges of the Courts of the Union and call into question the proper functioning and continuity of justice in the European Union'.[18] Nevertheless, when the panel received a new candidature to replace one of these five judges, it considered that it could not refuse to assess the new candidate. However, it decided to send a letter to the Conference of the Representatives of the Governments of the member states firmly expressing its serious concerns about this unprecedented situation. In the end, the new candidate withdrew his candidature.[19]

Problems resulting from the refusal of member states to propose the renewal of a mandate would, of course, be resolved if the six-year term of nomination were extended, for instance, to twelve years and become non-renewable. A treaty amendment to that effect was proposed by the Due Report, but it found no consensus in the Discussion Circle on the Court of Justice of the European Convention.[20]

13.3.2 National selection procedures

Although the selection of a candidate is a matter for the member states, the panel attaches much importance to the nature and quality of national selection procedures. When submitting a candidature, the member states are requested to explain how and according to what procedure the candidate was selected, whether a public call for candidatures was published, whether a selection committee was set up and how it was composed, and which candidates were proposed by the committee.[21] The panel will not hold the absence of a transparent and objective selection procedure against the candidate. Previously, the panel has given a favourable opinion on candidates selected without such a procedure. However, in case of doubts about the suitability of a candidate, the fact that he or she has been selected according to an objective procedure will be considered an argument in his or her favour.[22] More generally, the panel has stressed in its Activity Reports the importance of a transparent and objective selection procedure. In that regard, it appears to attach great value to the composition of a

[18] 255 Panel, 'Sixth Activity Report' (Publications Office of the European Union, October 2019) 15.
[19] ibid.
[20] Final Report of the Discussion Circle (n 6) para 7.
[21] 255 Panel, 'Second Activity Report' (n 3) 9.
[22] ibid.

selection committee, where it exists and more particularly to the question of whether, in case of a mixed composition, the majority of the members is independent.[23] Finally, the panel 'attaches the greatest importance' to member states complying with the rules on selection procedures where adopted.[24]

Comparative studies about the evolution of the selection processes in the member states clearly demonstrate a positive trend in terms of more transparency (through, for example, public calls for candidatures) and greater objectivity (the emergence of more or less independent selection committees).[25] The panel itself concluded from the information provided by the member states since 2016 that eighteen of them systematically hold open calls for applications; however, only in nine member states are applications examined by a national panel in which the majority of the members are independent and qualified persons.[26]

Some authors consider that this positive evolution may also be attributed to the practice and recommendations of the 255 Panel and speak of a harmonizing effect in this regard. If true, this might also be due to the much stricter approach followed by the Council of Europe for the selection of judges of the ECtHR. The aforementioned Guidelines adopted by the Council's Committee of Ministers set out requirements which also cover the procedure to be followed by the Contracting Parties for that selection. To mention a few: a public call for applications; the body responsible for recommending candidates should have a balanced composition, its members should have sufficient technical knowledge and be free from undue influence; all serious candidates must be interviewed based upon a standardized format; any departure by the final decision-maker from the selection body's recommendation should be justified by reference to the criteria for the establishment of lists of candidates.[27] The Committee for the selection of judges set up by the Parliamentary Assembly of the Council of Europe (PACE), when assessing a list of candidates, will, first of all, examine the fairness and transparency of the national selection procedure. If the Committee is not satisfied, it can recommend to the PACE to ask the state to submit a new list. In the past lists of candidates have been rejected because of an absence of a public call for candidatures or because no interviews were held.[28]

In this context, mention should also be made of an important recent judgment of the Grand Chamber of the ECtHR in the case *Gudmundur* v *Iceland*.[29] The right to 'an independent and impartial tribunal established by law' under Article 6 of the Convention (right to a fair trial) also covers the legitimacy of the appointment procedure. This right implies the right to a tribunal composed of judges fulfilling the requirements of technical competence, moral integrity, and being free from undue interference.[30]

[23] eg 255 Panel, 'Sixth Activity Report' (n 18) 11.

[24] ibid.

[25] Henri De Waele, 'Not Quite the Bed That Procrustes Built' in Michal Bobek (ed), *Selecting Europe's Judges: A Critical Review of the Appointment Procedures to the European Courts* (OUP 2015) 24, 32ff; Dumbrovski, Petkova, and van der Sluis (n 13) 466ff.

[26] 255 Panel, 'Sixth Activity Report' (n 18) 11.

[27] Parliamentary Assembly (n 17) para 7.

[28] ibid paras 8 and 17; also Andrew Drzemczewski, 'The Election of Judges onto the European Court of Human Rights', in this volume.

[29] *Gudmundur* v *Iceland*, App no 26374/18 (ECtHR, 1 December 2020).

[30] ibid paras 220–22, 226.

13.4 Assessment Procedure and Criteria

The procedure before the panel consists of three stages:

- a preparatory written procedure to obtain the necessary information from both the national government and the candidate;
- a preliminary discussion on the suitability of the candidate based on the file followed by a hearing. However, there will be no hearing in case of a candidature for the renewal of a mandate; and
- a deliberation and drafting of the opinion.

Before examining each stage in more detail, let us first briefly discuss the assessment criteria applied by the panel.

13.4.1 Criteria

Although the First Activity Report states that the criteria established by the Treaty are exhaustive, the panel nevertheless considers that the criteria can be more clearly and precisely explained.[31] Six criteria are distinguished. The first four of these criteria may without difficulty be related to the Treaty conditions of aptitude for the highest judicial offices in the respective member states (Article 253 TFEU) or high judicial office (Article 254 TFEU).

13.4.1.1 Legal capabilities

These capabilities must be 'very extensive' for candidates for the Court of Justice and 'extensive' for the General Court.[32] The panel is not submitting the candidate to an examination of his or her legal knowledge. It is much more probing the analytical capacities, the capability of the candidate to handle and argue complex legal questions related in the first place to his or her professional experience. This criterion also covers EU law. Candidates are not required to be experts or specialists in EU law. However, they must demonstrate to have 'an adequate basic knowledge of, and ability to analyse and reflect on the general issues of EU law'.[33] What counts 'is the candidate's ability to engage, in a thoughtful way, with the conditions and mechanisms of application of EU law'.[34] The panel also noted that 'these requirements can be met without difficulty by a high-level generalist who is not specialised in Union law'.[35]

13.4.1.2 Professional experience

Candidates must possess extensive high-level professional experience: in principle, at least twenty years for an appointment at the Court of Justice and twelve to fifteen

[31] 255 Panel, 'First Activity Report' (n 14) 8
[32] 255 Panel, 'Fourth Activity Report' (10 February 2017) 23.
[33] 255 Panel, 'Second Activity Report' (n 3) 13.
[34] ibid.
[35] ibid.

years for the General Court. In case a candidate's experience is of a lesser duration, an unfavourable opinion is presumed to be justified. However, that presumption may be rebutted if the candidate 'demonstrates exceptional legal capabilities'.[36]

As already mentioned, no preference is given to any particular professional profile, whether judicial, academic, jurisconsult, lawyer or senior official.[37]

13.4.1.3 Ability to perform the duties of a judge or an advocate-general

Do the candidates fully appreciate the extent of the responsibilities and challenges of the function envisaged and the requirements it involves in terms of independence and impartiality, workload, and the ability to take positions well reasoned in law? This criterion focuses in particular on a candidate's capacity to reason and argue.[38]

13.4.1.4 Independence, impartiality, probity, and integrity beyond any doubt

Obviously, this is one of the most essential conditions for being allowed to assume judicial responsibilities. The Activity Reports mention one case in which the panel, because of serious doubts about the probity and integrity of a candidate, decided to issue a negative opinion.[39] These doubts were triggered by information received from third persons. In such cases, the information will only be taken into consideration after having confronted the government concerned and the candidate with it and after having invited them to submit observations.[40]

13.4.1.5 Language skills

A candidate should be able to speak, or at least understand, a number of official languages of the EU. As far as French, the working language of the EU courts, is concerned, fluency is not required. However, candidates must be able to acquire proficiency in that language, to be in a position to make an effective personal contribution after a period of adjustment of a number of months, rather than a number of years, to the judicial role for which they aspire.[41]

13.4.1.6 Aptitude for working in an international environment in which several legal systems are represented

Apart from language skills, this criterion requires an openness to different legal systems and cultures.

The panel has considered introducing an additional criterion requiring candidates to submit a medical certificate attesting to their physical capacity to carry out taxing judicial duties.[42] However, since it appeared from a comparative analysis that member states follow highly different approaches in this regard and the implementation of

[36] eg 255 Panel, 'Sixth Activity Report' (n 18) 18.
[37] eg 255 Panel, 'Third Activity Report' (n 14) 11.
[38] eg 255 Panel, 'Sixth Activity Report' (n 18) 18.
[39] ibid 20.
[40] ibid 15.
[41] ibid 18 and 20.
[42] 255 Panel, 'Fifth Activity Report' (28 February 2018) 22 and 25.

such a criterion could create difficulties on matters of principle in some legal systems, the idea was ultimately abandoned.[43] This does not exclude that the panel, when assessing a candidature for renewal of the term of office, could conclude that the candidate no longer has the ability to continue performing his/her duties.[44] In my view, this could also concern physical ability.

In academic writing, the panel has been criticized for having defined these assessment criteria, at least some of them *praeter legem*, and for having arrogated regulatory powers by doing so. Michal Bobek has argued this more particularly with regard to the duration of high-level professional experience required for appointment at the Court of Justice.[45] In his view, this goes beyond the condition imposed by Article 253 TFEU (the requirement to be qualified for the highest judicial offices in the member state of origin the difficulty of a mere textual interpretation of which has already been discussed above). If one follows Bobek's line of reasoning, it could be argued that the various criteria specifically related to the characteristics of the EU courts as international courts (language skills and experience with international environment) and to the law they interpret and apply (knowledge of EU law), find no legal basis in the Treaty. In its First Activity Report, the panel justified the condition concerning the duration of professional experience by invoking an analogy between offices of judge or advocate-general of the Court of Justice or judge of the General Court and staff of equivalent level in the European civil service along with reference to the national practices of which the panel was aware.[46]

Also, a reverse criticism has been voiced related to the panel's failure to establish more specific criteria for the appointment as advocate-general or as judge of the General Court; the latter in view of the more specialized, non-constitutional nature of that Court's jurisdiction.[47] The easy answer would be to use Michal Bobek's argument: the Treaty does not provide a basis for such distinct criteria. To introduce a specific criterion for the function of advocate-general and distinguish it from the function of a judge might not be so obvious since the judges of the General Court are authorized to function as an advocate-general. Indeed, according to its Rules of Procedure, this Court may in particular cases designate one of its judges to function as advocate-general if it feels the need to benefit from an independent opinion. As far as the jurisdiction of the General Court is concerned, it should not be forgotten that this Court may also be confronted with constitutional issues (as was the case, for instance, with the Kadi saga or with the case law on general principles and fundamental rights).[48]

[43] 255 Panel, 'Sixth Activity Report' (n 18) 6.
[44] ibid 14.
[45] Michal Bobek, 'Epilogue' in Michal Bobek (ed), *Selecting Europe's Judges: A Critical Review of the Appointment Procedures to the European Courts* (OUP 2015) 290, 294; also Dumbrovsky and others (n 13) 466.
[46] 255 Panel, 'First Activity Report' (n 14) 9.
[47] Bobek (n 45) 292; Dumbrovsky and others (n 13) 466.
[48] Case T-315/01 *Yassin Abdullah Kadi* v *Council and Commission*, EU:T:2005:332; Joined Cases C-402/05 P and 415/05 P, *Yassin Abdullah Kadi and Al Barakaat International Foundation* v *Council and Commission*, EU:C:2008:461.

13.4.2 Assessment procedure

13.4.2.1 The preparatory written procedure

The purpose of the preparatory written procedure is more particularly to obtain the necessary information from the member state's government and the candidate allowing the panel a full assessment of his or her qualifications.

For a *first-term candidate* the government is requested to submit:

- the essential reasons for proposing the candidate;
- the information on the national selection procedure as already mentioned.

The candidate should provide:

- a letter of motivation explaining the reasons for applying;
- a CV in the harmonized format defined by the panel, including a list of publications;[49]
- the text of one to three recent publications from the candidate, where possible written in or translated into English or French. As already explained, the panel does not give preference to certain professional profiles. Therefore, a lack of publications cannot in and of itself penalize a candidate;
- a presentation of one to three complex legal cases which the candidate has handled in his or her professional practice, not exceeding five pages per case.

In case of a *candidature for renewal of the term of office*, the CV in the standardized format with the list of publications should be submitted. Moreover, specific information is requested enabling the panel to assess the productivity of the candidate:

- candidates for the function of a judge at the courts are requested to submit a list of closed cases for which they acted as rapporteurs indicating among others the formation of the court, the subject-matter concerned, the date of initiating the proceedings, and the date of the final judgment, as well as a list of the pending cases for which they are rapporteur, indicating the same but instead of the final judgment the status of the proceedings;
- candidates for the function of an advocate-general are requested to submit the list of cases in which they delivered an opinion, distinguishing between the different formations of the court.

According to the 6th Activity Report, the panel will request, beginning with candidatures for renewal at the Court of Justice in 2021, additional data allowing a more detailed comparative analysis of a candidate's productivity such as the expected duration of proceedings in comparable cases and the indicative internal deadlines of the two courts.[50] Until now the panel has not given an unfavourable opinion on a candidature for renewal. However, as previously mentioned, it will not refrain from doing so if it

[49] The format is annexed to the Activity Reports.
[50] 255 Panel, 'Sixth Activity Report' (n 18) 14, 15.

considers that a candidate proposed for renewal does not have, or no longer has the ability required. In such a case the panel will ask the candidate for any explanations they wish to provide, including in the context of a hearing.[51]

13.4.2.2 Preliminary discussion and the hearing

Only candidates for a first term will be requested to participate in a hearing, unlike candidates for a renewal of their term of office.[52] Before the hearing starts, the panel will first have a discussion on the suitability of the candidate based on all the information submitted in the file, aiming at formulating preliminary conclusions. The hearing is intended to supplement that first assessment and test the soundness of the preliminary conclusions. As the panel put it in its First Activity report, 'the hearing enables the initial analysis of the dossier to be confirmed, supplemented or refuted'.[53] Therefore, the hearing must not and cannot be seen as a kind of entry-exam, a *concours d'entrée* in the best French tradition. Decisive for the success of a candidature is in the first place the solidity of the file. The hearing serves to test that solidity. An assessment will never be based on the performance during the hearing alone.[54]

The hearing, which lasts for an hour, starts with an introduction of ten minutes by the candidate presenting his or her candidature and addressing one of the complex legal cases submitted in the written procedure. Candidates may speak in English, French, or any other official language of the EU. After the presentation, the members of the panel will ask questions in English or French which the candidates are supposed to answer in the same language as the question was asked. If the candidates consider their mastery of English and French insufficient, they may answer in any other official language of the EU. Questions may be asked to clarify aspects of the CV; to probe the reasons why the candidates consider themselves suited to performing the duties of a judge or advocate-general at the EU courts and more generally to assess candidates' analytical abilities and capacity for reasoning with regard to the conditions and mechanisms for applying the law, particularly as regards EU law.[55]

13.4.2.3 Deliberation and drafting of the opinion

The deliberation, as a rule, takes place immediately after the hearing. The overall assessment is based on the six criteria listed above. A favourable opinion requires that a candidate has demonstrated the ability to make an effective and personal contribution to the work of the court, after a period of adjustment of several months rather than years.[56] If a candidate is clearly failing on a particular criterion, that could be a ground for an unfavourable opinion.[57] The panel has given in its successive Activity Reports examples of typical cases, in which an unfavourable opinion was given: insufficient length of professional experience not compensated with an otherwise excellent profile; complete absence of any professional experience relevant to EU law; inadequate

[51] ibid.
[52] Operating Rules of the Panel (n 11) point 7.
[53] 255 Panel, 'First Activity Report' (n 14) 9.
[54] 255 Panel, 'Sixth Activity Report' (n 18) 19.
[55] For more details, 255 Panel, 'Sixth Activity Report' (n 18) 13.
[56] 255 Panel, 'Second Activity Report' (n 3) 14.
[57] 255 Panel, 'First Activity Report' (n 14) 9.

legal abilities in the light of the requirements of the office of an advocate-general or a judge; a clear lack of knowledge of the EU legal system and insufficient familiarity with EU law.[58] Since its 2nd Activity Report the panel publishes the number of unfavourable opinions related to the total of opinions issued on first-term candidatures during the reporting period as well as for the entire period of its operation since 2010. For the period from March 2010 to October 2019, 20.8 per cent of the first-term opinions were unfavourable.[59]

According to point 8 of the panel's Operating Rules, the panel must state the reasons for its opinions. That statement must set out the principal grounds on which the panel's opinion is based. Consequently, the panel has felt bound to explain in the motivation of its opinions the weak and the strong points of a candidate with regard to the fulfilment of the various criteria applied for its assessment, not only in the case of an unfavourable opinion but also in the case of favourable ones. As Jean-Marc Sauvé, the first President of the panel, has put it: 'the opinions are extensively motivated, not only to inform the member states about the precise criteria for the assessment but also their application in each individual case. More generally, the motivations may contribute to guiding the governments in choosing candidates and orientate their definition of national selection procedures'.[60] He added that '[t]he usefulness of the opinions may also consist in having both a dissuasive and a virtuous effect on member states' selection of effectively the most suitable candidates'.[61]

The opinions are not binding, but until now the Conference of the Representatives of the Member States' Governments has always followed them, including the unfavourable ones.

13.5 Transparency

According to Curtin and Weimar, '[c]urrently, the selection panel is shrouded in secrecy both in terms of their input and their output'.[62] Likewise, Bobek asserted that '[e]verything in and around the 255 Panel's work is confidential'[63]

But is that so? Working methods and procedures followed by the panel are extensively explained in the Activity Reports. This chapter has illustrated that. However, it is true that the hearing is not public and the opinions remain confidential. This has met with fierce criticisms in academic writing.[64]

[58] 255 Panel, 'Second Activity Report' (n 3) 13; 255 Panel, 'Fourth Activity Report' (n 32) 25.
[59] 255 Panel, 'Sixth Activity Report' (n 18) 10.
[60] Sauvé (n 15) 113. The translation is by the author.
[61] ibid 116.
[62] Deirdre Curtin and Maria Weimer, 'The Court of Justice of the European Union: Supranational Adjudicator and Accountability Forum' in Pieter Jan Kuijper and others (eds), *The Law of the European Union* (Kluwer Law International 2018) 402.
[63] Michal Bobek, 'Prologue' in Michal Bobek (ed), *Selecting Europe's Judges: A Critical Review of the Appointment Procedures to the European Courts* (OUP 2015) 20.
[64] Apart from the authors referred to in the two previous footnotes, see more particularly Alberto Alemanno, 'How Transparent Is Transparent Enough?' in Michal Bobek (ed), *Selecting Europe's Judges: A Critical Review of the Appointment Procedures to the European Courts* (OUP 2015) 202ff; also Dumbrovsky and others (n 13) 482; Henri de Waele, 'Not All That Glitters Is Gold: The Covert Failings of the EU's Court of Justice', MPILux Research Paper 2019, 4.

The reasons for this confidentiality are, first of all, of a legal nature. The Operating Rules of the panel explicitly state that the hearing shall take place in private (point 7). According to point 8, the panel's opinion shall be forwarded to the representatives of the governments of the member states. As announced since its 1st Activity Report, the panel has interpreted the latter provision as excluding public access to its opinions. But in the panel's view, also other more fundamental legal reasons militate against public access: protection of the panel's decision-making procedure and protection of privacy, both recognized by Union legislation as legitimate exceptions to public disclosure.

According to Article 4(1)(b) of Regulation 1049/2001 on access to documents, access shall be refused 'where disclosure would undermine the protection of privacy and the integrity of the individual, in particular, in accordance with Community legislation regarding the protection of personal data'.[65] According to Article 9(1) of the new data protection Regulation 2018/1725, which applies to the Union institutions, bodies, offices, and agencies, personal data may notably be transmitted to a recipient established in the Union if that recipient establishes that the transmission is necessary for a specific purpose in the public interest and the controller, where there is any reason to assume that the data subject's legitimate interests might be prejudiced, establishes that it is proportionate to transmit the personal data for that specific purpose after having demonstrably weighed the various competing interests.[66] Both provisions should be read and applied together, as follows from the *Bavaria Lager* judgment.[67] Of the exceptions to disclosure provided for by the Regulation on the access to documents, also a second one is relevant in this context: access 'shall be refused if the disclosure of the document would seriously undermine the institution's decision-making process unless there is an overriding public interest in disclosure' (Article 4(3)).

The Council receives the opinions of the panel through the latter's secretariat, which is provided by the Council. The Council, after consultation with the panel, has refused to give access to the opinions for the legal reasons just mentioned. Notably, it has argued that access would risk impacting negatively on the panel's working methods; the panel might become restrained and more guarded in the drafting of its opinions.

In a Decision of 23 May 2019, the European Ombudsman rejected a complaint against the Council because it refused to give access to the favourable opinions of the panel.[68] The complainant insisted on the overriding public interest to strengthen public confidence and trust in the legitimate choice of members of the courts and permit the public to scrutinize the functioning of the panel, thus increasing citizens' trust. The Ombudsman accepted the arguments based on the protection of the decision-making process of the panel and the protection of privacy. It qualified the

[65] Regulation (EC) 1049/2001 of the European Parliament and of the Council of 30 May 2001 regarding public access to European Parliament, Council and Commission documents [2001] OJ L 145/43.

[66] Regulation (EU) 2018/1725 of the European Parliament and of the Council of 23 October 2018 on the protection of natural persons with regard to the processing of personal data by the Union institutions, bodies, offices, and agencies and on the free movement of such data [2018] OJ L 295/39. This Regulation replaced Regulation 45/2001 on the protection of personal data.

[67] Case C-28/08 P *European Commission* v *The Bavarian Lager Co Ltd*, EU:C:2010:378.

[68] Decision of 23 May 2019 (European Ombudsman) in case 1955/2017/THH on the Council of the European Union's refusal to grant public access to opinions evaluating the merits of candidates for appointment to the Court of Justice and the General Court of the European Union.

panel's decision-making process as robust considering the opinions thorough and frank as regards the relative strengths and weaknesses of all candidates. 'Opinions cannot be categorised as wholly positive or negative. Fullness and objectivity are such that it would be simplistic to suggest that disclosure of favourable opinions would not be prejudicial.'[69] Full public access would risk resulting in less frank and less thorough opinions, depriving member states of the information they need. This would not serve the public interest. Furthermore, the Ombudsman held that full disclosure would undermine the protection of privacy and that the necessity of disclosure had not been established. The overarching public interest was rather that the system of review by the panel remained robust.

It will be for the EU courts to decide whether these legal arguments are sound and sufficient. In my personal view, there would be real risks that public access to the opinions would prompt the panel to become more cautious and less frank in its drafting in order to protect the privacy of the candidates and their reputation. Standardized texts, even skeleton opinions, could be the result. That would mean much less transparency for the member states and no transparency for the public. The argument is also valid for the positive opinions. Those opinions are rarely entirely positive. They mention the strong but also the weak points of a candidate. The motivation sometimes makes it clear that a candidate is considered apt even in the absence of a high score. Making these opinions public might affect the functioning of the persons concerned as members of the Court as they would risk being qualified as second or third class.

13.6 Further Criticisms

While the lack of transparency is the main critique levelled at the 255 Panel, other criticisms mentioned in the limited literature available include lack of democratic legitimacy and accountability, judicial self-government, risk of de facto co-optation, and French as the elephant in the room. A few comments on each will be discussed below.

13.6.1 Lack of democratic legitimacy and accountability

It is sometimes claimed that the 255 Panel is not subject to any form of democratic oversight;[70] and that, as far as its functioning and decision-making are concerned, there is no accountability at all.[71] The panel is free in how it interprets the treaty criteria for the suitability for appointment and is even free to alter them, it is said. In this respect, it cannot be made accountable to anyone.

These statements lack nuance, to say the least. Indeed, there exist ways to make the panel accountable for its decision-making. According to the Operating Rules

[69] ibid para. 24.

[70] Alemanno (n 64) 204, 212.

[71] Bobek (n 63) 20; Bobek (n 45) 294; also Armin von Bogdandy and Christoph Krenn, 'On the Democratic Legitimacy of Europe's Judges' in Michal Bobek (ed), *Selecting Europe's Judges: A Critical Review of the Appointment Procedures to the European Courts* (OUP 2015) 162.

(point 8), the President of the panel may be invited to present the panel's opinion to the representatives of the governments of the member states. On that occasion, the representatives could also raise more general questions about the functioning of the panel, for instance concerning the assessment criteria it applies and give their views in that regard. Until now this has happened only once, in 2012.[72] Moreover, the President together with the member of the panel designated by the European Parliament had a discussion regarding the functioning of the panel with the Legal Affairs Committee of the Parliament in 2011 and 2013.[73] The subsequent Activity Reports systematically report that there had been no invitation from the institutions for the President to give an account of the panel's activities. This illustrates the willingness of the panel to provide such accounts if need be. Consequently, if there were queries about the operation of the panel, the President of the panel could be invited both before the Conference of Member States' representatives and the European Parliament to give explanations and be confronted with critique and suggestions. If there were to be a more general dissatisfaction about the assessment criteria as applied by the panel, the Council could amend the panel's Operating Rules to give more guidance in that respect. This would require an initiative of the President of the Court of Justice but it is not to be expected that the President would reject reasonable suggestions in that regard.

13.6.2 Judicial self-government

In view of the important role the panel plays in the appointment procedure and because of the composition of the panel and the way in which that composition is decided, the appointment procedure entails a form of judicial self-government, so it is suggested. Reference is more particularly made to a 'substantial' number of the panel members being former members of the EU courts and the circumstance that the majority of the panel members are chosen by the President of the Court of Justice.[74]

If the argument is addressing judicial self-government by the EU courts, as it seems to be, then it is seriously flawed. First of all, the one or two former members of the EU courts who have participated until now in the panel of seven members can hardly be qualified as forming a substantial number of its composition. Additionally, the mere suggestion that the President of the Court, because of having proposed the members of the panel (with the exception of the member proposed by the European Parliament), actually controls the panel and its functioning, appears surrealistic. How would he or she ever be able to control, for example, the two presidents of national supreme courts, the former President and the former member of a national Constitutional Court, who are presently members of the panel? Finally, this argument overlooks the fact that it is not the panel which selects the candidate but the member state.

72 255 Panel, 'Second Activity Report' (n 3) 14.
73 ibid; 255 Panel, 'Third Activity report' (n 14) 23.
74 Alemanno (n 64) 204, 218; Dumbrovsky and others (n 13) 481, 482.

13.6.3 High risk of de facto co-optation

I understand the possible co-optation critique in the sense that the panel would systematically prefer candidates with a judicial profile similar to that of the majority of its members.[75] This critique does not convince me either. A first argument is linked to the third assessment criterion mentioned above: 'Ability to perform the duties of a judge'. This criterion is said to allow for opinion checking, that is, to check the views of a candidate about the nature, role, and scope of the office of a judge. However, instead of 'opinion checking', this criterion aims at assessing the ability to perform the duties of a judge or an advocate-general. One just needs to read the explanations given above and the information provided by the Activity Reports. The second argument invokes the empirically established fact—which I was not able to verify—that a majority of the candidates accepted by the panel have a judicial profile. However, this is insufficient to conclude that there is a de facto co-optation because again this ignores that candidates are selected by the member states and not by the panel. The beginning of an argument in that regard might be for instance that the percentage of candidatures rejected by the panel is systematically lower for candidates with a judicial profile than for the others. Whether that is actually the case, I was not able to verify either.

13.6.4 French as the elephant in the room

Michal Bobek writes in the epilogue of the book he edited, *Selecting Europe's Judges*, that one aspect not discussed in that book is the working language of the Court. This is striking because of its importance in terms of the best candidates likely to apply.[76] Bobek calls it the elephant in the room, and I agree.

The qualities of the French language as a legal language are beyond praise. In the European Communities of the original six member states, French was an official language in three member states and widely mastered as a foreign language in the other member states. Moreover, French at that time still was the language of international diplomacy, at least in Europe. All that has dramatically changed since.

The continuing use of French as the working language of the Court of Justice in spite of the successive enlargements over the last two decades excludes an increasing number of highly qualified potential candidates from appointment at the EU courts. The time has come to recognize that this exclusion is becoming excessive and not without risks for the Court itself. There is, first of all, the question of fairness towards the many member states where the French language does not (anymore) have a place in the curricula of secondary schools or is underrepresented. In the end, this is also becoming a question of equality of treatment. According to Article 4(2) TEU, the Union shall respect the equality of member states before the Treaties. But changing the working language into the new *lingua franca* seems to me also

[75] Alemanno (n 64) 219.
[76] Bobek (n 45) 308.

highly important for the Court itself. What is at stake, is guaranteeing the continuity and the quality of the case law of the EU courts for the future. Of course, such a fundamental change would require a highly complex restructuring of the Court's internal services. Currently, the staffing of the translation service and the composition of the cabinets of the members are based on French being the working language. Naturally, such a reorganization would require sound preparation and an adequately structured transition period. But, at least in my view, the time has come to start this operation.

13.7 Final Remarks

The Council of Europe established in 2010 an Advisory Panel giving advice about the suitability of candidates for an appointment as a judge at the European Court for Human Rights.[77] This panel is composed of members of highest national courts, former judges of international courts, including the ECHR, and other lawyers of recognized competence. For the appointment of judges at the ECHR the Contracting Parties of the Council of Europe must submit a list of three candidates. The Advisory Panel gives its confidential opinion on the three candidates to the government of the State concerned before the final list is sent to the Parliamentary Assembly, which appoints the judges on a recommendation of the Parliamentary Committee on the Selection of Judges.[78] This gives that government, in case of an unfavourable opinion, the possibility to replace the candidature (and for the candidate to withdraw). This procedure could be considered less painful both for the candidate and for the government concerned than the one followed by the 255 Panel. An unfavourable opinion of that panel is addressed to the Conference of the Representatives of the Member States' Governments. The rejection of a candidature by the member states collectively might be seen as more damaging for the reputation of the candidate and for the government. Of course, the candidate or the government concerned might withdraw the candidature when being confronted with a negative opinion. However, member states would all be informed by then, so the damage would already have been done. Addressing the opinion in a first stage only to the member state in question and giving it in case of an unfavourable opinion, the opportunity to replace the candidature or for the candidate to withdraw may be considered a more elegant solution. This would not require an amendment of the Treaty but only a modification of the panel's Operating Rules (point 8).

[77] Resolution of the Committee of Ministers of 10 November 2010 on the establishment of an Advisory Panel of Experts on Candidates for Election as a Judge to the ECHR [2010] CM/Res (2010) 26, as amended by Resolution CM/Res (2014)44 of 26 November 2014. Koen Lemmens, '(S)electing Judges for Strasbourg' in Michal Bobek (ed), *Selecting Europe's Judges: A Critical Review of the Appointment Procedures to the European Courts* (OUP 2015) 95; David Kosař, 'Selecting Strasbourg Judges' in Michal Bobek (ed), *Selecting Europe's Judges: A Critical Review of the Appointment Procedures to the European Courts* (OUP 2015) 120.

[78] Andrew Drzemczewski, 'The Election of Judges onto the European Court of Human Rights', in this volume.

14
Financial Governance of International Courts and Tribunals

Adriana-Maria Manolescu[*]

14.1 Introduction

A great amount of money and time has been and continues to be invested around the world in the funding of international courts and tribunals (ICTs). Even leaving aside such efforts, financial governance can make or break a court. Where the manner in which states decide on a court's budget and fund it makes it clear that its judicial independence is respected, more parties will be likely to trust the court and bring their disputes before it for resolution. Similarly, a court that demonstrates sound financial management will be in a much better position to obtain the funds it needs to implement its mandate. In extreme scenarios, a court that is not trusted by its stakeholders, be it with cases or the funds needed to sustain its activities, will not be able to carry out the mandate it was created to implement. Therefore, the financial governance framework of a court must both safeguard judicial independence and promote the court's accountability to enable its effective functioning and bolster its legitimacy.

The general contours of ICTs' financial governance are drawn when they are created. At this stage, states have freedom to design the new institutions as they see fit. Once the ink has dried on the constituent instruments, the envisaged setup cannot easily be altered, as they are characteristically difficult to amend, frequently requiring consensus to do so.[1] However, states retain the power to shape the ICTs' operations on a regular and dynamic basis by, among others, deciding on their annual budgets.

The power to draw up and control the budget is one of the most effective 'sticks and carrots' states have over ICTs, and it can be used as both a positive and a negative incentive, to influence, punish, or reward it. States may be understandably reluctant to continue spending their taxpayers' money on an institution they think does not make adequate use of said funds. This reinforces the need for the court to demonstrate sound and accountable financial management. States may also have less legitimate reasons to withhold funding in cases, for example, of disagreement with a specific judgment. Budgetary decisions can be at odds with ICTs' judicial independence, which is why their statutes often include provisions that aim to limit or restrict states'

[*] This chapter is written in a personal capacity and is based on the research carried out for the purpose of a doctoral thesis on the same topic.

[1] For further on this, see Tom Ginsburg, 'Political Constraints on International Courts' in Cesare PR Romano, Karen J Alter, and Yuval Shany (eds), *The Oxford Handbook of International Adjudication* (OUP 2013) 492.

Adriana-Maria Manolescu, *Financial Governance of International Courts and Tribunals* In: *Governance of International Courts and Tribunals*. Edited by: Sergey Vasiliev and Niels Blokker, Oxford University Press.
 DOI: 10.1093/oso/9780198922131.003.0014

ability to use their budgetary authority as a tool of influence and control.[2] This set of rules related to budgetary decision-making, income, expenditure, and oversight, and the manner in which they are implemented in practice, including institutional arrangements and processes, is understood as financial governance.

While every ICT is different, with its own characteristics, and operates in a distinct institutional context, many of the key institutional design choices made in terms of financial governance are similar across the majority of courts. Moreover, many such choices can be traced back to the 1920s, to the rules and early practice of the Permanent Court of International Justice (PCIJ). This is due to the process of 'diffusion by emulation', meaning the tendency to replicate the institutional design of existing institutions when establishing new ones.[3] This approach is neither bad nor good in and of itself, but it can be unfortunate if we consider the following.

Firstly, there is limited in-depth research on individual courts' financial governance and hence an insufficient understanding of whether a certain rule or the way it has developed through practice was successful, and thus whether or not it should be replicated. When financial aspects of an ICT are discussed, the focus is mostly on costs and benefits, looking at whether its results were 'worth' the investment or whether the court had the funds needed to carry out its mandate. Even fewer are the works engaging in a comparative analysis of ICTs' financial governance,[4] that enable an assessment of whether a rule or practice that has been successful in a certain context might have the same effects in another. Similarly, where the same rule has been applied differently in practice in various courts, informed decisions on what approach would best fit a new court cannot be made without comparative research.

Secondly, shaping ICTs' financial governance without data on other courts' experience increases the risks of making wrong choices given that financial governance schemes do not receive a lot of attention when new courts are being set up. For example, many elements of the International Criminal Court's (ICC's) institutional design have evolved over decades of reflection in various fora.[5] But how the ICC was to be funded was mostly discussed only at the conference of plenipotentiaries where its Statute was adopted.[6] Even there, the topic was 'on the backburner, completely

[2] Karen J Alter, 'Delegation to International Courts and the Limits of Re-Contracting Political Power' in Darren G Hawkins and others (eds), *Delegation and Agency in International Organizations* (CUP 2006) 321.

[3] Theresa Squatrito, 'Resourcing Global Justice: The Resource Management Design of International Courts' (2017) 8 Global Policy 62, 64.

[4] eg Thordis Ingadottir, 'The Financing of International Adjudication' in Romano, Alter, and Shany (n 4); Thordis Ingadottir, 'Financing of Internationalized Criminal Courts' in Cesare PR Romano, André Nollkaemper, and Jann K Kleffner (eds), *Internationalized Criminal Courts and Tribunals: Sierra Leone, East Timor, Kosovo and Cambodia* (OUP 2004); Giorgia Tortora, 'The Financing of the Special Tribunals for Sierra Leone, Cambodia and Lebanon' (2013) 13 International Criminal Law Review 93.

[5] A draft code of offences against the peace and security of mankind was considered by the International Law Commission from as early as 1949 onwards, and the UNGA discussed the establishment of an international criminal court in 1989. UN Codification Division Publications, 'UN Diplomatic Conference of Plenipotentiaries on the Establishment of an International Criminal Court' <https://legal.un.org/diplomaticconferences/1998_icc>.

[6] Rome Report of the Coalition for an International Criminal Court (Center for Development of International Law, Center for UN Reform Education and the World Federalist Movement/Institute for Global Policy, 2018) ('CICC Rome Report'), Team Reports & Questionnaires, 2.11, B., 283.

overshadowed by the more controversial issues of jurisdiction and definitions',[7] until the approaching end of the meeting and the resulting time pressure brought attention to the issue.[8] Similarly, across some 800 pages of minutes covering discussions of the Advisory Committee of Jurists tasked with preparing the Statute of the PCIJ,[9] there is a record of one sole discussion related to finances. Even more telling is that it concludes with the following remark: considering the aim of the PCIJ, namely the prevention of wars, the question of expenses was, in comparison, of too little significance.[10]

As a contribution to addressing the research gap outlined previously, this chapter offers a comparative presentation and analysis of financial governance frameworks of several ICTs, identifying systemic challenges and how they were addressed, in four key areas:

(a) the internal and external actors involved in financial governance and budgetary process;
(b) financial accountability and oversight;
(c) sources of funding; and
(d) expenditure.

The chapter mostly draws from the relevant frameworks (or schemes) of seven permanent international courts,[11] with practices from other tribunals, such as the ad hoc tribunals[12] and hybrid tribunals[13] referenced where the approaches employed differ from that of the permanent courts. The seven permanent ICTs have been selected to cover a representative sample of different *ratione materiae*[14] and *personae*[15] jurisdictional regimes, as well as the courts' variation in terms of their institutional-legal nature.[16]

In the following section, the two main elements identified as essential for a legally viable and legitimate financial governance framework, namely judicial independence and accountability, will be defined (Section 14.2). Sections 14.3–14.5 provide

[7] 'Three Proposals, One Deadlock' in CICC Rome Report (n 6), the Rome Treaty Conference Monitor, Special Issue of the NGO CICC, Issue 23—15 July 1998, 1.

[8] ibid 282–83.

[9] On the governance of the PCIJ: Henri de Waele, 'Managing the Realization of "The Hope of Ages"', in this volume.

[10] Advisory Committee of Jurists, *Procès-Verbaux of the Proceedings of the Committee (June 16th to July 26th 1920* (Van Langenhuysen Brothers 1929)' <www.icj-cij.org/sites/default/files/permanent-court-of-international-justice/serie_D/D_proceedings_of_committee_annexes_16june_24july_1920.pdf> 222.

[11] The PCIJ, the International Court of Justice (ICJ), the International Tribunal for the Law of the Sea (ITLOS), the ICC, the Inter-American Court for Human Rights (IACtHR), the World Trade Organization Appellate Body (WTO AB), and the Court of Justice of the European Union (CJEU).

[12] International Criminal Tribunals for the Former Yugoslavia (ICTY) and Rwanda (ICTR).

[13] The Special Panels for Serious Crimes in East Timor (SPSC), the Special Court for Sierra Leone (SCSL), the Extraordinary Chambers in the Courts of Cambodia (ECCC), and the Special Tribunal for Lebanon (STL).

[14] General jurisdiction (PCIJ and ICJ) and specialized jurisdictions: law of the sea (ITLOS), trade, commerce and investments (WTO AB), criminal law (ICC), human rights (IACtHR), and regional economic and/or political integration (CJEU).

[15] Inter-state (PCIJ, ICJ, ITLOS, and WTO AB), individual responsibility (ICC), and mixed jurisdiction (IACtHR and CJEU).

[16] Independent international organizations, or IOs (ICC, ITLOS), organs of a parent IO (ICJ, WTO AB, and CJEU), and bodies otherwise affiliated with an IO (PCIJ and IACtHR).

a systematic comparative presentation of the rules and practices in place in the key areas outlined previously: financial decision-making entities and budgetary process (Section 14.3); sources of funding (Section 14.4); and expenditure (Section 14.5). Lessons learned, suggestions for further research, and concluding remarks are contained in Section 14.6. The chapter proceeds in a comparative manner as it presents the main approaches adopted in the ICTs it covers, the systemic challenges to their respective financial governance schemes, and how they were addressed. This survey aims to be exhaustive neither in its coverage of ICTs, nor in the aspects of financial governance. Instead, it outlines in broad strokes the most salient issues and gauges the impact finances exert on ICTs' judicial independence and accountability.

14.2 Judicial Independence and Accountability of ICTs

14.2.1 Judicial independence

It is undisputed that judicial independence is an essential component for a court of law. Put succinctly, the principle refers to a judge's freedom to decide on a case by applying the law to the facts before him/her, without any undue interference. This interference—its existence or absence—is the key element in assessing judicial independence. It is thus a relational rather than behavioural concept, referring to the relation between judges and third parties, be they internal court actors (such as other judges) or external ones (political bodies, media representatives, and the public).[17] Consequently, when assessing judicial independence, one has to look at whether the institutional and operational arrangements in place in a specific court safeguard the independence of judicial decision-making.[18] For the purpose of this chapter, it is the institutional and operational arrangements falling under financial governance of ICTs that are of particular interest, and that could, by virtue of their nature or effect, constitute undue interference with judicial independence.

Absent binding international law instruments elaborating on specific requirements flowing from the principle of judicial independence relevant to ICTs' financing schemes, soft-law instruments provide important normative insights and can serve as guidance. Most of those address four themes that fall within the scope of financial governance:

(1) *Relation with governance actors*: courts and judges should be able to carry out their judicial activities free from interference.[19] The entities playing a role in the management of a court should not engage in actions, including statements,

[17] Kate Malleson, 'Promoting Judicial Independence in the International Courts: Lessons from the Caribbean' (2009) 58 International and Comparative Law Quarterly 671.

[18] Also UN Office on Drugs and Crime (UNODC), 'Commentary on The Bangalore Principles of Judicial Conduct' (2007) para 23.

[19] The Burgh House Principles on the Independence of the International Judiciary, published in Philippe Sands, Campbell McLachlan, and Ruth MacKenzie, 'The Burgh House Principles on the Independence of the International Judiciary' (2005) 4 The Law and Practice of International Courts and Tribunals 251 ('Burgh House Principles') paras 1.1 and 1.2.

that would threaten or pressure judges,[20] or that would undermine judicial independence or the public's confidence in the judiciary.[21] That being said, the judiciary can and should sustain constructive working relations with such entities.[22]

(2) *Budget preparation, decision-making, and administration*: where courts do not prepare their own budgets or participate in the process, they should at a minimum be heard and have their needs considered in both budget preparation[23] and decision-making.[24] This latter process should not be used by authorities to exert any pressure or influence over the judiciary[25] or any 'improper control' over the court.[26] Budgetary decisions should be taken on 'objective and transparent criteria', and not in a discretionary manner[27] or in a way that makes courts vulnerable to political fluctuations.[28] The freedom of judges and courts to exercise their functions without undue interference also extends to the operation of the court and its registry.[29]

[20] LAWASIA, 'Beijing Statement of Principles of the Independence of the Judiciary in the LAWASIA Region' (adopted 19 August 1995, amended 28 August 1997) ('Beijing Statement') para 38; Judicial Integrity Group, 'Measures for the Effective Implementation of The Bangalore Principles of Judicial Conduct (The Implementation Measures)' (adopted on 21-22 January 2010) ('Bangalore Principles Implementation Measures') para 10.1(h).

[21] Council of Europe (CoE), Committee of Ministers, 'Judges: Independence, Efficiency and Responsibilities', Recommendation CM/Rec(2010)12 and explanatory memorandum (adopted 17 November 2010) para 18; International Bar Association (IBA), 'Minimum Standards of Judicial Independence' (1982) paras 16 and 18.

[22] Recommendation CM/Rec(2010)12 (n 21) para 12.

[23] International Commission of Jurists, 'International Principles on the Independence and Accountability of Judges, Lawyers and Prosecutors, Practitioners Guide No.1' (2007) ('ICJ Practitioners Guide') 33; Bangalore Principles Implementation Measures (n 20) para 17.1; Council of Europe, Consultative Council of European Judges (CCJE), Opinion No. 2 (2001) of the CCJE for the attention of the Committee of Ministers of the CoE on the Funding and Management of Courts with reference to the Efficiency of the Judiciary and to Art 6 of the European Convention on Human Rights ('CCJE Opinion No.2(2001)') para 10; European Commission for Democracy through Law, 'Report on the Independence of the Judicial System', Part I: The Independence of Judges (adopted 12-13 March 2010) ('Venice Commission Report on Independence of Judges') para 55; Beijing Statement (n 20) para 37; African Union, African Commission on Human and Peoples' Rights, 'Principles and Guidelines on the Right to a Fair Trial and Legal Assistance in Africa' (adopted 29 May 2003) 203 para A(4)(v); Consultative Council of European Judges, 'Magna Carta of Judges (Fundamental Principles)' (2010) ('Magna Carta of Judges') Art 7 ('*Following consultations with the judiciary*, the State shall ensure the ... resources necessary' (emphasis added).

[24] CCJE Opinion No 2(2001) (n 23) para 10; International Association of Judges, 'The Universal Charter of the Judge' (adopted 1999 and updated 2017) ('Universal Charter of the Judge') Arts 2–4; Venice Commission Report on Independence of Judges (n 23) para 55; Magna Carta of Judges (n 23) Art 7; Principles and Guidelines on the Right to a Fair Trial and Legal Assistance in Africa (n 23), para A(4)(v).

[25] Bangalore Principles Implementation Measures (n 20) para 17.1; CCJE Opinion No 2 (2001) (n 23) para 5.

[26] ICJ Practitioners Guide (n 23) 34, citing Latimer House Guidelines for the Commonwealth on Parliamentary Supremacy and Judicial Independence (adopted 19 June 1998) Guideline II.2.

[27] Venice Commission Report on Independence of Judges (n 23) para 53.

[28] CCJE Opinion No. 2(2001) (n 23) para 5.

[29] International Project of Judicial Independence of the International Association of Judicial Independence and World Peace, 'Mount Scopus International Standards of Judicial Independence' (approved in 2008, consolidated in 2015) ('Mount Scopus International Standards') para 10.2; similarly, Burgh House Principles (n 19) Art 1.3.

(3) *Conditions of service of judges*: judges should benefit from financial security, so that they are shielded from any attempts to have their decisions influenced.[30] They should receive an 'adequate'[31] or 'appropriate remuneration',[32] in line with their status, duties, and dignity of the office,[33] that enables them to 'secure true economic independence'.[34] Remuneration should be periodically adjusted according to potential increases in the cost of living at the seat of the court,[35] and paid on time.[36] Judges should also be provided with an adequate pension, at a level close to their salary,[37] and with social welfare.[38] No financial or non-financial benefits should be allocated based on discretionary elements.[39]

(4) *Level of resources*: courts should be endowed with the necessary resources to enable judges to properly, efficiently, and effectively fulfil their role.[40] Not only does an inadequate level of resources make it harder, if not impossible, for a court to carry out its mandate, but it also renders the institution vulnerable to corruption, which would undermine its independence and impartiality.[41] Where economic constraints dictate allocation of resources below the level considered as adequate by the court, decision-making bodies should give high priority to the needs of the judiciary in the allocation of resources.[42]

14.2.2 Accountability

The existence of appropriate accountability mechanisms is an essential reassurance for states when deciding whether or not to transfer powers to an international

30 Council of Europe, European Charter on the Statute for Judges, DAJ/DOC(98) 23 (adopted 8–10 July 1998) para 6.1; for a similar phrasing, Recommendation CM/Rec(2010)12 (n 21) para 54; ICJ Practitioners Guide (n 23) 33–34.

31 UN Congress on the Prevention of Crime and the Treatment of Offenders, 'Basic Principles on the Independence of the Judiciary' (adopted 6 September 1985) Art 11; Mount Scopus International Standards (n 29) para 13.3.

32 Magna Carta of Judges (n 23) Art 7; Burgh House Principles (n 19) para 4.3.

33 Venice Commission Report on Independence of Judges (n 23), para 51; Bangalore Principles Implementation Measures (n 20) para 14.1.

34 Universal Charter of the Judge (n 24) Art 8-1.

35 Burgh House Principles (n 19) para 4.3; Mount Scopus International Standards (n 29) para 13.3.

36 ICJ Practitioners' Guide (n 23) 22.

37 Magna Carta of Judges (n 23) Art 7; Burgh House Principles (n 19) para 4.4; Universal Charter of the Judge (n 24) Art 8-3; Mount Scopus International Standards (n 29) para 13.4; European Charter on the Statute for Judges (n 30) para 6.4.

38 European Charter on the Statute for Judges (n 30) para 6.3 (guarantee for judges acting in a professional capacity 'against social risks linked with illness, maternity, invalidity, old age and death'); Universal Charter of the Judge (n 24) Art 8-2; similarly, Recommendation CM/Rec(2010)12 (n 21) para 54.

39 Venice Commission Report on Independence of Judges (n 23) para 51.

40 European Charter on the Statute for Judges (n 30) para 1.6; Beijing Statement (n 20) paras 37 and 41; Basic Principles on the Independence of the Judiciary (n 32) Art 7; Burgh House Principles (n 19) Art 6; Mount Scopus International Standards (n 29) para 15.1; Recommendation CM/Rec(2010)12 (n 21) paras 32–33; Minimum standards of judicial independence (n 22) para 10; European Charter on the Statute for Judges (n 30) para 1.6; Universal Charter of the Judge (n 24) Art 2-4; Principles and Guidelines on the Right to a Fair Trial and Legal Assistance in Africa (n 23) para A(4)(v) 33.

41 ICJ Practitioners Guide (n 23) 33.

42 Beijing Statement (n 20) para 42.

organization (IO).[43] As noted by the International Law Association, 'accountability has been congenital to [IOs'] very first appearance on the international scene. Forms and modalities may have been embryonic or more elaborated, but accountability was there'.[44] Accountability is indispensable to IOs' mission, as it increases their efficiency and authority; it is also an unavoidable consequence of such entities becoming major actors on the international scene.[45]

In simple terms, 'accountability' entails accepting responsibility for one's own actions. It encompasses 'an obligation to report, explain and justify conduct, so that information can be monitored, questions can be posed, and depending on the form of accountability, consequences may ensue'.[46] 'Oversight' refers to reviewing someone else's actions. The term 'oversight body' is usually employed to refer to the budgetary and administrative authority of an ICT, as established in its statutory framework. Oversight may be carried out through a broad range of measures from monitoring of activity to regulatory control. 'Accountability' and 'oversight' thus refer to the same processes, and describe the same relation between the court and its external governance body. The difference is in the entity that performs the action: the *court* is the one accountable, and the *external governance bodies* are the ones to oversee (certain aspects) of the court's work.

The first and essential component of accountability is the availability and proper functioning of mechanisms to monitor the conduct of IOs. Monitoring can be carried out through (i) submission of reports; (ii) collection and dissemination of data; and (iii) inspections or audits. Monitoring enables stakeholders to decide whether to maintain or adjust their course of conduct,[47] and whether and how to hold the IO accountable. Accountability can be pursued through five main mechanisms:

(i) control over executive and secretariat organs based upon their regular or special reports;
(ii) adoption of the budget of the organization and monitoring of its execution;
(iii) withholding (re-)appointment of senior officials;
(iv) restricting, suspending or revoking the delegation of powers; and
(v) annual or special parliamentary debate over the functioning of the international organization.[48]

States also have further means of redress available, namely: refusal to pay their financial contribution to the IO's budget, withholding the payment of any voluntary contributions, suspending active cooperation with the IO, temporarily or permanently

[43] International Law Association (ILA), 'Accountability of International Organisations', Final Report, Berlin Conference (2004) ('ILA Berlin Report') 6.
[44] ILA, 'Accountability of International Organisations', First Report, Taipei Conference (1998) ('ILA Taipei Report') 598.
[45] ibid 610.
[46] Huw Llewellyn, *An Institutional Perspective on the United Nations Criminal Tribunals: Governance, Independence and Impartiality* (Brill 2021) 47.
[47] ILA Taipei Report (n 44) 600.
[48] ibid 606.

withdrawing from the IO, instituting legal proceedings against the IO before ICTs, and, finally, dissolution of the organization.[49]

Accountability is not a uniform notion to be rigidly and indiscriminately applied to every IO.[50] Rather, in the interest of operationality, states tailor accountability mechanisms to each IO's characteristics and specificities. In the case of ICTs, one such specificity that must be considered is the need to safeguard independence in judicial decision-making.

The interaction between judicial independence, on the one hand, and accountability on the other, has been subject to debate. It has at times been suggested that the two are opposite concepts, which can only exist at the other's expense.[51] Rolf Einar Fife remarked that such a view was rooted in Western culture, focused on an antagonistic perspective of 'either–or', whereas a more appropriate lens would be that of Chinese philosophy, where even two opposite concepts, such as *ying* and *yang*, can co-exist and can complement each other without losing their essence.[52]

In practice, the two phenomena indeed co-exist, although tensions can arise between them as part of the regular interactions between internal and external governance entities due to ambiguities of the concepts, which are not clearly delineated in ICTs' statutory documents. This leaves room for judicial independence to be used as a shield against accountability, in response to a perceived risk that accountability mechanisms may be misused by states to interfere in specific cases. In turn, this can trigger states employing increasingly intrusive instruments of control as a way to ensure accountability, which ultimately, in an unconstructive and divisive cycle, may end up endangering judicial independence.[53] To address this problem, stakeholders need to identify and agree on the required level of independence and appropriate mechanisms for accountability for every type (or layer) of activity of the court. This chapter attempts to provide clarity, as it discusses the interaction between judicial independence and accountability in the specific areas of financial governance of ICTs from a comparative perspective.

14.3 Financial Decision-Making Actors and Processes

14.3.1 Internal financial governance actors

The financial management of an ICT is the key responsibility of a Registrar, who is the chief administrative officer, similar to secretaries-general in other IOs. This role may

[49] ibid 608.

[50] ibid 598.

[51] eg Miroslava Scholten, 'Independence vs. Accountability: Proving the Negative Correlation' (2014) 21(1) Maastricht Journal of European and Comparative Law 197.

[52] Remarks by Mr Rolf Einar Fife, then Ambassador of Norway to the EU during a roundtable discussion on 'Ensuring effective governance and judicial independence—potential challenges', Leiden University's 'Inaugural Conference on the Governance of International Courts and Tribunals: Ensuring judicial independence and accountability', Leiden, 20–21 September 2019 (hereafter 'Leiden University Conference') (on file with the author).

[53] For further on this, see Nicolas Guillou and Adriana-Maria Manolescu, 'The Three-Layered Governance Model', in this volume.

have different titles in some courts, such as Director at the ECCC and WTO AB or Secretary at the IACtHR, but the mandates entrusted to such officials are nonetheless very similar. Registries, headed by the Registrar, are broadly responsible for providing the judicial support and administrative services required for judicial proceedings to take place. As part of this mandate, Registrars are responsible for the financial management of the court's funds and assets, including the budget process and its implementation. The Registrar is in some instances appointed by the plenary of judges, who also has the power to dismiss her/him, but that is not the case for all courts. For instance, at the Kosovo Specialist Chambers, the Registrar is appointed by the Head of the EU Common Security and Defence Policy Mission, as are the President, Judges, and Prosecutor.[54] The UN Secretary-General appointed the Registrars of the STL,[55] ICTY, and ICTR, though in the latter two cases in consultation with the presidents of the tribunals.[56] At the Special Criminal Chambers for the Central African Republic, the (national) Chief Registrar is appointed by the state, while the (international) Deputy Registrar by the UN mission in the country, MINUSCA.[57]

In carrying out her/his mandate, the Registrar works closely with the President of the ICT, who is the head of the court. Presidents are responsible for the judicial administration of the court,[58] which involves, among other things, assigning judges to cases[59] and dealing with absences, recusals, and disqualification of judges.[60] In most courts, judges elect the President (and one or two vice-presidents) from among their ranks. In some ICTs, Presidents are appointed by external bodies, as is the case at the KSC[61] and the Caribbean Court of Justice.[62] The ECCC was a notable exception, with statutory documents not foreseeing a President at all.

In terms of the relationship between the Registrar and the President, in some cases, statutory documents foresee that registrars carry out their responsibilities under the guidance of the judges or of the President.[63] As a consequence, while the Registrar is responsible for preparing the budget, in certain courts the budget must be approved by either the Plenary or the President before it is submitted to the external

[54] Law on the Kosovo Specialist Chambers and Specialist Prosecutor's Office, Law No.05/L-053, 3 August 2015 (Law on the KSC-SPO) Art 34(4); also Arts 28(3), 32(1), and 35(7).

[55] Agreement between the UN and the Lebanese Republic on the Establishment of a Special Tribunal for Lebanon, Annex to UNSC Res 1757, S/RES/1757, 30 May 2007, Art 4.

[56] Updated Statute of the ICTY, adopted 1993, last amended 2009 ('ICTY Statute') Art 17; ICTR Statute, adopted 1994, last amended 2002, Art 16.

[57] Loi organique no 15.003 du 3 juin 2015, portant création organisation et fonctionnement de la Cour Pénale Spéciale (2015), Arts 22 and 24.

[58] Law on the KSC-SPO (n55), Art 32(2); Statute of the Special Tribunal for Lebanon, Attachment to STL Statute, UNSC Res 1757, S/RES/1757, 30 May 2007, Art 10.

[59] ICTY Statute, Art 14(3).

[60] Statute of the International Court of Justice (adopted on 26 June 1945, entered into force on 24 October 1945) (ICJ Statute) Arts 23(3) and 24(1)–(2); ITLOS Statute, Annex VI to UN Convention on the Law of the Sea (adopted on 30 April 1982, entered into force on 16 November 1994) Art 8(2)–(3); Consolidated version of the Treaty on the Functioning of the European Union, Protocol (No 3) on the Statute of the Court of Justice of the European Union, Art 18.

[61] Namely by the Head of the EU Common Security and Defence Policy Mission. Law on the KSC-SPO (n 54) Art 32(1).

[62] Agreement establishing the Caribbean Court of Justice (adopted on 14 February 2001, entered into force on 23 July 2002) Art IV(6). The President is the only Judge appointed by States at this Court.

[63] eg ICJ, Rules of the Court (adopted on 14 April 1978, last amended 1 July 2020) Art 26(3): 'In the discharge of his functions the Registrar shall be responsible to the Court.'

governance bodies for adoption. In parallel with the Registrar's responsibility towards the President in this regard, financial regulations often indicate that the Registrar is (also) accountable to the states parties.[64] The report of the Independent Expert Review of the ICC and the Rome Statute System (IER) addresses the duality in roles as the Registrar being accountable to judges/presidency for matters falling under the judicial function of the Court and to the Assembly of States Parties (ASP) for matters related to non-judicial aspects of the administration and servicing of the Court.[65] Registrars play a pivotal role in ensuring that all services required for the smooth continuation of judicial activities are provided. This task inherently depends on, and is under the overall responsibility, of the judges, normally acting through the President of the Court. This responsibility has to be implemented in such a way as to ensure sound management of funds and demonstrating accountability to the states parties. It is thus a matter not of competing but of simultaneous responsibilities.

14.3.2 External financial governance actors

With the exception of the Caribbean Court of Justice, the final decision-making power on ICTs' budgets lies with states parties gathering in a general congress or meeting of the organization. For instance, the function is carried out by the UN General Assembly (UNGA) for the ICJ, the States Parties to the American Convention in the OAS General Assembly for the IACtHR, Meeting of States Parties (SPLOS) for ITLOS, and the ASP for ICC. SPLOS stands out from the list, as it was not formally created and established as the ITLOS governance body, but developed as such in practice. It has been referred to as a 'specialized mini General Assembly'.[66] By contrast, states parties to the American Convention attempted to gather during three conferences to discuss reforming the inter-American system.[67] With delegations repeatedly reserving their position on the conclusions reached, in view of the informal character of the meeting, and until they were to be examined by the competent OAS organs, the fourth such conference was ultimately cancelled and never rescheduled.[68] Decisions of states parties to the American Convention are thus taken in the framework of the OAS General Assembly.

[64] eg ITLOS, Rules of the Tribunal (adopted 1997, last amended 2021) Art 36(3) and ITLOS, Financial Regulations and Rules (adopted on 12 June 2003, last amended 2021) Rule 4.7; ICC, Rome Statute (adopted on 17 July 1998, entered into force on 1 July 2002) Art 43(2) and ICC Financial Regulations and Rules (adopted on 21 November 2008) ICC-ASP/7/5 (Part II-D) Rules 101.1(b) and 110.20.

[65] Independent Expert Review of the International Criminal Court and the Rome Statute System, Final Report, 30 September 2020 <https://asp.icc-cpi.int/iccdocs/asp_docs/ASP19/IER-Final-Report-ENG.pdf> ('IER Report') para 37.

[66] Niels Blokker, 'Governance of the International Tribunal of the Law of the Sea: The Role of the Meeting of States Parties to the Law of the Sea Convention' in Angela Del Vecchio and Roberto Virzo (eds), *Interpretations of the United Nations Convention on the Law of the Sea by International Courts and Tribunals* (Springer 2019) 85.

[67] 'Las razones de la crisis del Sistema Interamericano de Derechos Humanos y las respuestas elaboradas en el marco de la Organización de Estados Americanos' in Sebastián Alejandro Rey (ed), *Los Desafíos Del Sistema Interamericano de Protección de Derechos Humanos en el Siglo XXI. Una Mirada Crítica Para (Re) pensar Su Funcionamiento* (Ediciones de la Universidad Nacional de Lanús 2015) 91 *et seq.*

[68] ibid 94.

The plenary bodies deciding on the court's budget and allocating the share of expenses among the members are often supported by subsidiary bodies. The constellations differ from one ICT to another, with the ICTs that are embedded in an IO seeing a higher number of such bodies involved in the budgetary process. These subsidiary bodies are divided into two categories: (i) financial experts carrying out the technical examination of the court-proposed budget; and (ii) political subsidiary bodies that meet either in smaller constellations than in the assembly, or with representatives at a lower working level, to prepare the decision for the assembly. Examples of technical review bodies are UNGA's Advisory Committee on Administrative and Budgetary Questions (ACABQ) for the ICJ and the ASP's Committee on Budget and Finance for the ICC. Following their review, the court-proposed budgets are reviewed by the UNGA's Fifth Committee on Administrative and Budgetary Matters and discussed in the ASP The Hague Working Group, respectively.

For ICTs that are embedded in an IO, an important role is also played by the entity responsible with preparing the IO's overall budget. For instance, the ICJ budget proposal is submitted to the UN Secretary-General, who cannot modify the proposal, but can attach comments and recommendations.[69] The budget is also reviewed by a Controller (Assistant Secretary-General) who can adapt the draft with the agreement of the Court.[70] By contrast, the EU Commission can amend the CJEU's budget proposal, even without the latter's agreement.[71] In terms of budget implementation, the OAS Secretary-General has the authority to retain, without prior consultation, up to 5 per cent of the IACtHR's budget (as well as of all OAS entities), in case of budgetary difficulties in the General Secretariat's budget. By way of example, in 2018, over 25 per cent of the approved budget for the Court was used for the General Secretariat's expenses rather than transferred to the Court, and less than half of the amount was reimbursed by the following year.[72]

14.3.3 Budget process

The general flow of the budget process is broadly similar across ICTs and IOs generally. Assisted by a finance and budget unit, the Registrar is responsible for preparing the budget. After consultation with relevant internal actors or with such actors' approval, the budget is submitted to external governance bodies. For courts that are

[69] UN Financial Regulations and Rules, ST/SGB/2013/4, 1 July 2013 Regulation 2.14; 'Finance and Administration' in Shabtai Rosenne and Malcolm N Shaw QC (eds), *Rosenne's Law and Practice of the International Court: 1920–2015. Vol I* (5th edn, Brill Nijhoff 2016) 452, para 108.

[70] Rosalyn Higgins and others, *Oppenheim's International Law: United Nations. Vol II* (OUP 2017) 1194, para 29.246.

[71] Consolidated version of the Treaty on the Functioning of the European Union (13 December 2007), 2008/C 115/01 (TFEU), Art 314(1) ('The Commission shall consolidate [the received] estimates in a draft budget, which may contain different estimates'). There is no mention in the applicable texts of the need for the EU entity to agree with the changes made by the Commission to the estimates received from the former. Eg EU, Regulation (EU, Euratom) 2018/1046 of the European Parliament and of the Council of 18 July 2018 on the financial rules applicable to the general budget of the Union ... PE/13/2018/Rev/1, Arts 41(1), (3)(a), and 42.

[72] IACtHR, Annual Report 2018, 131. Annual reports of the IACtHR are available at <https://corteidh.or.cr/informes_anuales.cfm?lang=en>.

embedded in an IO, the budget is transmitted to the IO for inclusion in its overall budget.

Research on the seven permanent courts shows that, although budgetary processes are often where tensions between internal and external governance bodies can flare up, both sides have an interest in ensuring an efficient and constructive process, and both have their own crucial role to play in this regard.

Firstly, the *sine qua non* condition for a successful budgetary process is for the court to present a clear, convincing, and reasonable budget proposal. This requires as realistic assumptions as possible for the upcoming budgetary period,[73] demonstrating sound financial management for use of public funds, and requesting only those resources that are reasonably required for the court to carry out its mandate.

Secondly, there needs to be constructive and open dialogue between the court and the external bodies reviewing the budget on the court proposal. This is, on the one hand, so that the court can be heard in budget discussions, in line with judicial independence requirements,[74] and, on the other hand, for external governance bodies to be able to carry out their financial oversight role.

For the court to be heard, it must also speak with a clear voice. At the ICC, the practice has developed for a number of court representatives to attend ASP budget discussions, such as the President, Registrar and Prosecutor, judges, and other staff members. Presumably in relation to this, CBF amended its working methods to require that presence of a Court representative in its meetings be on a needs-only basis, after the Registrar had reported on the budget.[75] Reports also point to discontent within ASP bodies on account of receiving contradictory information from different organ representatives,[76] with anecdotal evidence of one organ pushing for cuts to be made in another organ's budget, as a way of saving their own. Such practices are in no one's interest and harm not only the budgetary process itself, but also the external governance bodies' trust in the court and its representatives. In principle, and particularly for courts that have several organs, it is best to ensure that the court communicates with one voice, and that its representative has a 'helicopter' view of the entire organization and its budget needs, and particularly of how changes in one budget line or one organ's budget may impact the others. As the chief administrative officer, this task should fall on the Registrar. Having the Registrar represent the ICT before external governance bodies would not only benefit the process but also serve to further shield the judges (and prosecutors, where applicable) from such discussions. Judges and prosecutors, who must remain independent in their decision-making, should not be negotiating budgets, justifying decisions they made that led to expenses being incurred, or advocating for additional resources to enable implementation of their decisions. Such involvement risks giving the appearance of exposure to improper interference.

[73] For instance, in 2006, the ICC requested resources for two trial proceedings, though at that point, nobody had been arrested yet. Jonathan O'Donohue, 'Financing the International Criminal Court' (2013) 13 International Criminal Law Review 269, 278–79.

[74] Section 14.2.1.

[75] Coalition for the ICC (CICC), Report on the 13th Session of the ASP, 8–17 December 2014, 41.

[76] IER Report (n 65) para 335.

External governance bodies must also play their part in ensuring the effectiveness of the budget process. As a starting point, relevant members of such bodies must be familiar with the specificity of the court. Levels of familiarity may be lower for review bodies that examine the budget of a complex IO constituted by several organs, with an ICT as one of many budget lines. For instance, former ICJ President, Dame Higgins suggested that certain members in UNGA subsidiary bodies reviewing the budget did not fully grasp the particularities of the ICJ as a court and the differences from other UN organs and subsidiary bodies. She referred to examples such as the ACABQ's request to the Court for 'programs it could axe'[77] and the Fifth Committee's inquiry regarding updates on the ICJ prosecutor's activity,[78] while, of course, the ICJ has neither.

Respect for the court's judicial independence requires that its views be taken into account when deciding on the budget. When the UNGA rejected the ICJ requested budget (showing an increase of 2.2 per cent from the previous biennium) and further reduced it by 10 per cent without any prior consultation with the Court, the latter noted that exchanges between the UNGA and the ICJ

> have always enabled the Assembly to gain a better understanding of the specific needs of the Court, which is not subject to the same budgetary rationale as other organs .... Without such exchanges, measures may be taken which, while making marginal savings in the Organization's budget, could jeopardize the Court's work and thus prove severely counterproductive.[79]

Part of the challenge for external governance bodies, particularly those governing courts that are not self-standing IOs, is the increased workload involved in reviewing budgets of ever more bodies, missions, and programs within the universe of the organization, often with only limited time available. This may explain the difficulty of capturing the particularities of each one of them but does not justify it. To ensure respect of an ICT's judicial independence, the governing body must be aware that the entity whose budget is before it is a court of law and understand what that entails.

From this perspective, courts that are self-standing IOs are in a more beneficial situation, as budgetary discussions are focused solely on their own needs as judicial institutions, and state representatives dedicate their attention to the court for the duration of the relevant meeting. The downside may be too much attention, with a risk of gearing towards micromanagement. In this regard, a stark difference in process is noteworthy between the budget review for ITLOS and the ICC, both IOs in their own right.

At the ICC, the court-proposed budget is discussed and examined throughout the year, first by the CBF, that meets at least twice annually. Between the moment the Court shares its proposed budget and the issuance of the CBF report, the CBF sends an average of 100 inquiries to the Court.[80] By way of illustration, for the 29th

[77] Higgins and others (n 70), vol II, 1195, para 22.248.

[78] ibid.

[79] UN GA, Report of the ICJ, 1 August 2015 to 31 July 2016, A/71/4, para 33. Higgins and others (n 70), vol I, 1196, para 29.252 and n274.

[80] IER Report (n 65) para 340. This is not a recent phenomenon—in 2017, the ICC Registrar indicated having received 127 queries from the CBF: ICC ASP, Remarks of Herman von Hebel, Registrar of the ICC to the 16th Session of the ASP, 5–6.

to the 30th CBF sessions, the Court submitted to it almost forty reports and papers per session, totalling an average of over 500 pages per session.[81] The court-proposed budget is also discussed by The Hague Working Group of the ASP several times during the year, where states reportedly on occasion repeat CBF's scrutiny of even minor budget lines,[82] prior to discussions at the ASP itself. By contrast, ITLOS' court-approved budget is presented to states parties that discuss and decide on it at their annual meeting. No subsidiary bodies are involved in the process. The addition of a technical examination body was considered (and dismissed) in the preparatory phase of the Tribunal.[83] Similar proposals were on the SPLOS' agenda every year between 2010 and 2014, all stemming from one state, namely the UK. The proposals put forward aimed to facilitate financial and budgetary discussions, ensure a more detailed and effective examination of the budget, and improve states' understanding of the Tribunal's budget by organizing discussions in additional groups or fora.[84] In all cases, the majority of states expressed concern about the additional complexity the changes would bring, duplication of work, and financial implications.[85] Simply put, states noted their satisfaction with the system in place and saw no need for a change.[86] Why is such a straightforward process suitable for ITLOS, but not for the ICC? This may be explained by the difference in budgets, as the ICC's budget for 2023 was almost fifteen times bigger than that of ITLOS.[87] Understandably, the more states invest in an entity, the more ensuring oversight becomes a priority for them. On the other hand, the ICC deals with individual criminal responsibility, whereas ITLOS' decisions may more directly affect states' interests regarding, for instance, the delimitation of their maritime zones. One would thus expect states to wish to be involved in the work of the ITLOS, more than in that of the ICC, considering the potential impact of ITLOS judgments.

Two other aspects may also explain the difference in approaches towards the two courts. Firstly, it is the composition of the external governance bodies. SPLOS meetings take place at the UN headquarters, with state delegations often composed of a mix of representatives from New York and capitals. For the state representatives at the UN headquarters, SPLOS is but one of the many bodies they are responsible for, and likely not ranking high on their priority list. For the other delegates, it is a small part

[81] IER Report (n 65) n212.

[82] ibid para 340.

[83] UN, Preparatory Commission for the International Seabed Authority and for the International Tribunal for the Law of the Sea, LOS/PCN/152 (Vol 1) (1995) para 77.

[84] SPLOS, Report of the 20th Meeting of States Parties (2010), SPLOS/218, 2010, paras 41, 53; Report of the 21st Meeting of States Parties (2011), SPLOS/231, 2011, para 46; Report of the 22nd Meeting of States Parties (2012), SPLOS/251, 2012, para 45; Report of the 23rd Meeting of States Parties (2013), SPLOS/263, 2013, paras 37–41; Report of the 24th Meeting of States Parties (2014), SPLOS/277, 2014, paras 60–65.

[85] SPLOS, Report of the 21st Meeting of States Parties (2011), SPLOS/231, 2011, para 46; Report of the 22nd Meeting of States Parties (2012), SPLOS/251, 2012, para 45; Report of the 24th Meeting of States Parties (2014), SPLOS/277, 2014, paras 60–65.

[86] SPLOS, Report of the 21st Meeting of States Parties (2011), SPLOS/231, 2011, para 46; Report of the 22nd Meeting of States Parties (2012), SPLOS/251, 2012, para 45; Report of the 23rd Meeting of States Parties (2013), SPLOS/263, 2013, paras 37–41.

[87] ICC's budget for 2023 was approved at EUR 173.234.300—ASP Resolution ICC/ASP/21/Res.1, 9 December 2022, para 1—and ITLOS' budget for 2023–24 at EUR 23.443.900—SPLOS, SPLOS/32/12, 15 June 2022, para 1 (and assuming, for the sake of calculation, an equal division of the biennial budget for the two years, ie EUR 11,721,500 per year).

of their daily work carried out in capitals. The Hague Working Group of the ASP, that traditionally is assigned with budget review, is made up of embassy representatives, most often legal advisers or liaison officers responsible for the international courts in The Hague, which are few and have differing levels of activity. The number of meetings with states' participation convened for the ICC is unlike any other in the city, with a multitude of working groups on various topics states can take part in. To a great extent, the ASP is a 'playground' for diplomats, who—even if with the best intentions—create more work for themselves.

The second explanation concerns the relationship between the ICTs and their respective external governance bodies. The ITLOS and SPLOS' relationship has been described as constructive and based on trust, with states generally granting the Tribunal's increases in budget, when requested, and praising the Tribunal's efforts to optimize costs and reduce expenses.[88] By contrast, ICC–ASP relations have not benefitted from the same degree of trust. The review of the whole Rome Statute system that states set in motion, due to their 'grave ... concern ... with the multifaceted challenges' facing the ICC attests to this.[89]

One of the key ways to build institutional trust between the court and external governance bodies is effective accountability and oversight measures, as will be outlined in the following sub-section.

14.3.4 Accountability and oversight mechanisms

In practice, accountability of ICTs is pursued in three main ways: (i) reporting; (ii) budget processes; and (iii) audits. These will be addressed in turn.

14.3.4.1 Reporting

ICTs report regularly to external governance bodies, for instance by conveying monthly and/or quarterly financial and administrative updates. These reports indicate how much of the allocated budget has been spent, how much of the financial contributions owed have been received, how many funds remain available for the budgetary period, and the level of staffing. Annual reports on financial and administrative management are also submitted, often as part of the budget negotiation process. Further, ICTs also present annual reports on their activity, usually delivered by the president of the court during the annual general meeting of states parties. In recognition of the courts' judicial independence, resolutions of external governance bodies generally simply 'welcome' the activity report of the court, without venturing into further details, unlike in respect of financial and administrative matters. The meeting of states parties also offers an opportunity for them to exchange with court principals and share their views on the court's activity. It is also a moment where care must be exercised to ensure that such commentary does not pressure the judges or undermine the court's independence and the public's confidence in it in any way.

[88] Blokker (n 66) 87-88, 90-91; eg SPLOS, Report of the 28th Meeting of States Parties (2018), SPLOS/324, para 36.
[89] ASP, Resolution ICC/ASP/18/Res.7, 6 December 2019, preamble.

14.3.4.2 Budget process

Courts can demonstrate their accountability in the budget process, firstly, through results in the implementation of previous budget exercises and, secondly, through reasonable and professional budget proposals. Simultaneously, states should not use the oversight role they have in this process to inappropriately interfere with the ICT's work. An example of such interference is the now infamous refusal by the UNGA's Fifth Committee of the ICJ's request for additional resources for unforeseen expenses due to dissatisfaction with the ICJ's decision in the *South West Africa* case. Fifth Committee members stated that 'a vote could not be taken … on a purely financial basis' and that a 'shameful decision' such as the one in the *South West Africa* case was important enough to block additional resources being awarded to the Court.[90] Such comments alone suffice to be seen as exerting undue pressure on the judiciary, let alone the decision to reject the ICJ request on such basis. While this is an extreme case, and not representative of the practice of oversight bodies, it illustrates the sensitivities the interplay between judicial independence and accountability in the budget process entails, and the need for adequate safeguards.

14.3.4.3 Audits

In line with international standards, ICTs undergo external and internal audit processes. Internal auditors support the registrars in the exercise of their responsibility over the financial management of the ICTs' accounts. The internal audit consists of reviewing 'transactions that have financial implications as to the regularity of the receipt, custody and disposal of all funds and other financial resources of the organization, the conformity of obligations and expenditures with the appropriations made in the budget, and the effective, efficient and economic use of the resources of the organization'.[91] As internal audit is a management and oversight tool for the registrar, internal auditors normally report to that official. At the ICC, the Office of Internal Audit (OIA) was placed under the direct authority of the Audit Committee,[92] a subsidiary body of the ASP and thus an organ of the external oversight body. This links internal with external oversight processes and may consequently lower the effectiveness of the support that the Internal Auditor can provide to the Registrar, as well as reduce the openness of various Court units or organs vis-à-vis the OIA. In this regard, the IER Report concluded that it would be more appropriate for the OIA to report to the Court principals, and for the Audit Committee to no longer oversee the substance of the OIA's work.[93]

External auditors are normally appointed by the external governance bodies for a fixed period of time from among internationally recognized firms of auditors or auditors-general of a state party.[94] The aim of external audit is to determine whether an ICT's financial transactions respect the generally accepted accounting principles. The

[90] UNGA 21st session, Official Records, Fifth Committee, 1124th meeting, UN Doc A/6631, 10 October 1966.

[91] Henry G Schermers and Niels M. Blokker, *International Institutional Law: Unity within* Diversity (6th edn, Brill Nijhoff 2018) 741, para 1123.

[92] ICC ASP, ICC-ASP/14/Res.1, 26 November 2015, K, para 1.

[93] IER Report (n 65) para 957 and Recommendation 367.

[94] eg ICC Financial Regulations (n 64), Regulation 12; ITLOS Financial Regulations (n 64), Rule 12.1.

external auditor's reports should contain, among others, 'expenditures not properly substantiated, cases of fraud or wasteful expenditure, defects in the system governing financial control, expenditure likely to commit the organization to further outlay on a large scale, and expenditure in excess of appropriations or not in accordance with the intentions of the [external governance body]'.[95] Such reports are submitted to the external governance body, but the court, through the registry, is usually given an opportunity to review it first, and attach any comments it may deem necessary.[96] For both internal and external audits, the registrar is responsible for implementing the measures suggested or recommended.

Audits, as an accountability and oversight tool, must also be carried out in such a way as to not improperly interfere with judicial decision-making. Unclarity as to the extent to which audits can be carried out, the activities that are covered, and the bodies that have the power to perform them, can lead to tensions between the court and its external governance body, as demonstrated by two examples from the ICJ and the CJEU. Further to the audits performed by the UN External Board of Auditors, ICJ management and administration activities have also been reviewed by the UN Joint Inspection Unit (JIU) and the UN Office of Internal Oversight Services (OIOS). Former ICJ President Higgins recounted tensions between the UN and the Court, due to the former's insistence on asserting administrative oversight over the Court, while the latter considered such aspects to be in its exclusive competence.[97] Higgins further indicates that JIU's 2000 report misunderstood the functions of the ICJ and interfered with its autonomy,[98] and that the same year, the OIOS also performed an audit, often asking for the same information, causing confusion as to the mandates of the two entities.[99] This illustrates the need for agreement and clarity as to the division of responsibilities and the allocation of an oversight role for the ICT, which is necessary to avoid duplication of work and prevent the appearance that repeated audits are used to either micromanage or inappropriately interfere with the court's work.

In terms of the scope of the audit, in 2017 the EU Court of Auditors (CoA) evaluated the CJEU's performance in terms of case management, looking at whether the procedures in place facilitated an efficient handling of cases and whether cases could be dealt with more expeditiously.[100] The CoA asked for access to all case documents and deplored the Court's refusal to grant it invoking its obligation to maintain secrecy of deliberations.[101] Judicial management of proceedings is part of judges' responsibility for the administration of justice, and the interference by auditors in this area does not appear warranted. It is not that activities falling under the administration of justice cannot be audited, but to safeguard judicial independence while enabling accountability, the audit ought to be performed by independent, external peers and the results submitted to the judges themselves for consideration and potential follow-up.

[95] Schermers and Blokker (n 91) 742 para 1125.
[96] eg IACtHR, Annual Report 1993, 16.
[97] Higgins and others (n 70) 1188–90 paras 29.219–29.228.
[98] ibid para 29.221.
[99] ibid 1190, n253 and paras 29.225–29.228.
[100] European Court of Auditors, Special Report: Performance review of case management at the Court of Justice of the European Union (pursuant to Article 287(4), second subparagraph, TFEU), No 14/2017.
[101] ibid paras 11–14, n15.

This would enable an objective assessment and provide assurances against inappropriate interference.[102]

Audits are an important instrument to ensure responsible use of public funds. To achieve that objective, they must be adequately employed and not used in a way that might amount to interference with judicial independence. Audits are also a way for the court to demonstrate sound financial management to its funders. Positive results indicate to all stakeholders that the court can be trusted with taxpayers' money and is a reliable partner in this regard. Audits are the main instrument through which institutional trust between the court and its external governance body is built. A court that has a positive track record in this regard is also in a much better position to negotiate requests for additional resources.

14.4 Sources of Funding

While states have been expressing concerns over the ever-increasing costs of ICTs since the PCIJ era, the great majority of tribunals continue to be financed directly by states through regular contributions (Section 14.4.1). There has been some experimentation with voluntary contributions (Section 14.4.2) but the appetite to go beyond these models and seriously consider alternatives proved rather limited. Successful outliers do exist but have not been replicated in other regimes (Section 14.4.4). In part, that may be because continuing to fund ICTs directly means that states retain the 'power of the purse' and thus a degree of control over such institutions.

14.4.1 Regular contributions

Expenses of courts that are organs of an IO or operate in the universe of an IO are funded from the budget of the organization. The UN, WTO, OAS, and the EU bear the costs of the ICJ, WTO AB, IACtHR, and the CJEU, respectively. For courts that are self-standing IOs, the contracting parties to their statutes cover the costs. This is the case for parties to the UN Convention on the Law of the Sea and the Rome Statute with regards to the ITLOS and ICC's costs, respectively. For these tribunals, the contribution of each state to the budget is determined based on a scale of appropriations.

The UN scale of assessed contributions is set by the UNGA, broadly according to capacity to pay.[103] The scales used for the ITLOS, ICC, and the OAS budgets are calculated based on the UN scale, adjusted to reflect the difference in membership,[104] and

[102] In this regard, the IER recommended that the ASP establish a Judicial Audit Committee for the ICC that could in the long-term also service several ICTs, and that would be composed of current or former national or international judges with relevant experience. IER Report (n 65) para 34, R3 and R113; also Nicolas Guillou and Adriana-Maria Manolescu, 'The Three-Layered Governance Model', in this volume.

[103] ICJ Statute (n 60) Art 33: 'The expenses of the Court shall be borne by the United Nations in such a manner as shall be decided by the General Assembly.'

[104] For the ICC, Rome Statute Art 117 and eg ASP, Resolution ICC-ASP/1/Res.14, 3 September 2002, ASP, ICC-ASP/17/Res.4, 12 December 2018, E. For the ITLOS, Gudmundur Eiriksson, *The International Tribunal for the Law of the Sea* (Martinus Nijhoff 2000) 106. For the OAS, Charter of the Organization

in some instances, applying different minimum and maximum rates. For example, while the minimum contribution to the UN budget is set at 0.001 per cent from the overall budget and the highest share is capped at 22 per cent,[105] the OAS member states' shares of the budget cannot be lower than 0.044 per cent or higher than 49.990 per cent.[106]

Depending on the nature of the IO, the approaches to such scales may differ. For example, the WTO AB's expenses were included in the WTO budget, which works with a scale of contributions based on members' and observers' share in international trade (imports plus exports) in relation to the total international trade of all WTO members.[107]

For a non-negligible number of ICTs, states contribute in equal share to their budgets or to those of the relevant IO. That is the case, for example, for the Judicial Tribunal of the Organization of Arab Petroleum Exporting Countries,[108] the Court of Justice of the Central African Monetary Community,[109] the East African Community Court of Justice,[110] the Permanent Review Tribunal of MERCOSUR,[111] and the Central American Court of Justice.[112]

This was the approach foreseen in the Convention establishing the Central American Court of Justice—the first international court—which foresaw that the five contracting parties would contribute in equal parts to the Court's budget.[113] The Advisory Committee of Jurists that drafted the PCIJ Statute considered whether every state should have to contribute equally to the Court's budget, but expressed concern that doing so would place too heavy a burden on smaller states.[114] Ultimately, the model of scales of appropriations was used for the overall budget of the League of Nations.

For the courts affiliated with regional integration IOs, a different funding scheme has been employed. The EU's budget, that covers the CJEU expenses, is financed from contributions from EU member states from different sources: Gross National Income-based contributions (over 70 per cent of all EU revenue), custom duties on imports from outside the EU, levy on countries' value-added tax (VAT), and a contribution based on the non-recycled plastic packaging waste.[115] A key difference

of American States (signed 30 April 1948, entered into force 13 December 1951) Art 55; OAS General Standards OAS, AG/RES.1 (XXXIV-E/07), 13 November 2007, Art 95.

105 For minimum and maximum assessment rates for the regular budget at UN: Committee on Contributions, 'Regular Budget and Working Capital Fund' <www.un.org/en/ga/contributions/budget.shtml>.

106 OAS AG/RES.1 (XXXIV-E/07), 13 November 2007, Appendix with OAS Permanent Council, CP/RES.1103 (2168/18), 19 June 2018.

107 WTO Financial Regulations, WT/L/156/Rev.3, Regulation 12.

108 Agreement of the Organization of Arab Petroleum Exporting Countries (1968) Art 27.

109 Revised CEMAC Treaty (2009) Art 50.

110 Treaty on the establishment of the Eastern African Community (1999, as amended in 2006 and 2007) Art 132.

111 Protocolo de Olivos para la solución de controversias en el MERCOSUR (2002) Art 36(2).

112 Statute of the Court (Convenio de Estatuto de la Corte Centroamericana de Justicia (1992)) Art 41.

113 Convención para el establecimento de una Corte de Justicia Centroamericana (signed 20 December 1907, entered into force 25 May 1908) Art VII.

114 Procès-Verbaux of the Proceedings of the Committee (n 10) 495, para 1.

115 EU, 'Revenue' <https://european-union.europa.eu/institutions-law-budget/budget/revenue_en>.

from the assessed contributions model is that rather than states having to effect payment once per budgetary period, the EU's own resources are credited monthly to the European Commission's accounts held with member states treasuries or central banks.[116] The African Court of Human and People's Rights, as well as the Courts of Justice of ECOWAS, the African Economic and Monetary Union, and the Economic and Monetary Community of Central Africa (CEMAC) are also financed through a form of community levy. For the African Union, the assessed contributions are to be financed through a 0.2 per cent levy that member states must apply on eligible goods imported from non-members of the African Union.[117] Members of the CEMAC can opt to contribute to the organization's budget through a 0.5 per cent community levy on external imports, but also make a direct contribution or a levy (existing or to be created) on alcoholic beverages, tobacco, cosmetics, and perfumes.[118] This model is more akin to how domestic courts are financed, namely through a taxation-like system. It provides a stable source of income to the organization and, where automatic and regular collection of funds is foreseen, non-payment of contributions—on time or in full—is less of an issue. However, collecting taxes from citizens is a corollary of sovereignty, and ceding part of it to supranational organizations is expectably accompanied by the heightened level of control states have over the IO's operations and expenditure.

14.4.2 Voluntary contributions

States can supplement their regular contributions to an ICT's budget with voluntary contributions. For some judicial entities, though, voluntary contributions have been envisaged as a sole or main form of funding.

14.4.2.1 Additions to regular contributions

Voluntary contributions are irregular payments made by donors, be they states, international organizations, or private persons, to the budget of an organization. There is no obligation for states to provide such a contribution and no specific timelines for making it. Most often, donors can choose whether to earmark it for a specific purpose, meaning to specify what project or category of expenses the funds should be used for, or to leave it to the relevant budgetary authority to decide.

ICT budgets benefit on a regular basis from voluntary contributions. It is a way for states to support a specific agenda or an aspect of the mandate if and when they so desire, without having to commit to such payments in advance and for a longer

[116] Council Regulation (EU, Euratom) No 609/2014 on the methods and procedure for making available the traditional, VAT and GNI-based on resources and on measures to meet cash requirements, OJEU L 168/39, 7.06.2014, arts 6, 10; EUR-Lex, EU Member States' contributions to the EU budget, https://eur-lex.europa.eu/legal-content/EN/TXT/HTML/?uri=LEGISSUM:0601_2. Consult also, for instance, an explanation of the process in EU Commission, EU Budget 2018—Financial Report <https://commission.europa.eu/publications/eu-budget-2018-financial-report_en> 44.

[117] African Union, Assembly/AU/Dec.605 (XXVII) (2016) Art 5.

[118] Union Douanière et Economique de l'Afrique Centrale (UDEAC), Acte no 1/93-UDEAC-573-CD-SE1 portant adoption du système des ressources permanentes de l'Union.

period of time. Voluntary contributions are also a way for states party to an ICT to (further) support its activities where there is no agreement among funders to cover certain expenses (at all or not to the full amount needed). Thus they may support the court where the budget allocated or the level of received regular contributions is either insufficient or not timely paid. For instance, after ICC states parties decided on the Court's budget in December 2021, the ICC Prosecutor called on states in March of the following year to provide assistance to the Prosecutor's Trust Fund for Advanced Technology and Specialized Capacity, to address 'its urgent resource needs'.[119] While not explicitly referenced, this call came days after the Prosecutor's announcement that he had opened an investigation into the situation in Ukraine following Russia's February 2022 invasion.[120] The Prosecutor stated that 'the funds received will be deployed based on [the Prosecutor's] assessment of needs across all situations' the Office was investigating or prosecuting, and that he would not accept earmarking for a specific situation.[121] A former US Ambassador for Global Criminal Justice noted that 'from the ICC's perspective, earmarked funding can create at least the perception that the justice that ensues was not arrived at impartially'.[122] In spite of the Prosecutor's position on earmarked funds, several states that responded to his call (at least) publicly linked their donation to the investigation in the Ukraine situation.[123] Civil society organizations expressed concerns with the approach, suggesting that it risked 'exacerbating perceptions of politicization of and selecting in the Court's work' and

[119] ICC, 'Statement of ICC Prosecutor, Karim A.A. Khan QC: Contributions and Support from States Parties Will Accelerate Action across Our Investigations', 28 March 2022 <www.icc-cpi.int/news/statement-icc-prosecutor-karim-aa-khan-qc-contributions-and-support-states-parties-will-0>.

[120] ICC, Statement of ICC Prosecutor, Karim AA Khan QC, on the situation in Ukraine: Receipt of Referrals from 29 States Parties and the Opening of an Investigation, 2 March 2022 <www.icc-cpi.int/news/statement-icc-prosecutor-karim-aa-khan-qc-situation-ukraine-receipt-referrals-39-states>.

[121] 'I am pleased that since the 7 March when I sent a Note Verbale to all State Parties, we have about 20 countries that have pledged financial support and/or secondment of personnel. We will not earmark for Ukraine, I can't accept that, but we'll use across the situations to help international justice be more meaningful': Karim Khan, 'US Institute of Peace, Pursuing Justice for Mass Atrocities: A Conversation with ICC Prosecutor Karim Khan', 26 April 2022 <www.youtube.com/watch?v=-SQbqoGRgvM>, 34:24–34:42.

[122] Ryan Goodman, 'How Best to Fund the International Criminal Court' (*Just Security*, 27 May 2022) <www.justsecurity.org/81676/how-best-to-fund-the-international-criminal-court>.

[123] eg Government of Canada, 'Canada Provides Funding to International Criminal Court to Strengthen Accountability for Conflict-Related Sexual Violence', 26 May 2022 (statement explicitly refers to the Trust Fund and that 'to respect the independence and impartiality of the ICC and its proceedings, resources will be allocated to specific investigations determined by the prosecutor of the ICC', while simultaneously indicating that the contribution will 'allow the ICC to redirect much-needed resources to support the investigation of reported atrocities committed by the Russian forces in Ukraine') <www.canada.ca/en/global-affairs/news/2022/05/canada-provides-funding-to-international-criminal-court-to-strengthen-accountability-for-conflict-related-sexual-violence.html>; French Ministry of Justice, 'Enquête de la CPI sur les crimes commis en Ukraine', 23 March 2022 <www.presse.justice.gouv.fr/communiques-de-presse-10095/archives-des-communiques-de-2022-13011/enquete-de-la-cpi-sur-les-crimes-commis-en-ukraine-34363.html> (announcing France's contribution with secondments and a financial contribution); Australian Department of Foreign Affairs and Trade, Invasion of Ukraine by Russia, 'As part of the coordinated international effort to hold Russia accountable for its actions, Australia has … [c]ommitted AUD 1 million and three staff to support the [ICC] investigation into reported Russian war crimes' <www.dfat.gov.au/crisis-hub/invasion-ukraine-russia>. Furthermore, an international conference in London raised $4.9 million for the ICC, with media reporting that officials stated that the funds were for the Court's 'investigations into alleged war crimes in Ukraine and its work to hold Russia to account'. Sylvia Hui, 'Millions in Extra Funding Pledged for ICC Work in Ukraine' (*Associated Press News*, 21 March 2023) <https://apnews.com/article/ukraine-uk-war-crimes-conference-icc-2facdba93e4dae9bb4d27027c6aadbe8>.

'sen[t] the unfortunate signal that justice for some victims should be prioritized over others, depending on political will'.[124] A state's decision to enhance the resources at the Court's disposal with an earmarked voluntary contribution can be motivated by the expected potential increase in approval ratings of a government when it is seen as helping a cause that has wide support among its citizens, as would be the case for investigations into crimes allegedly perpetrated in the context of the war of aggression by Russia against Ukraine. Earmarked contributions may thus be more appealing to a state and garner more media coverage. 'State pays its annual contribution to the ICT's budget, just as it committed to' is not exactly breaking news.

Earmarked voluntary contributions can also be seen as disrupting the careful balance of the system foreseen for regular budget negotiations. Normally, there has to be agreement among all funders as regards both the activities that will be funded and the level at which they will be covered. Further to diplomatic negotiations, this process already necessitates a lot of care to ensure that in reviewing, cutting, and approving the budget, states do not interfere with judicial (or prosecutorial) independence, while fulfilling their responsibility to only cover reasonable expenses. An earmarked voluntary donation is a unilateral decision as to which activity of the court should be prioritized and 'deserves' more funding, independent of the decision reached in the multilateral fora. States choose what they want to earmark the donation for based on their political agenda, and by linking their additional financial support to the court to one identified activity, they essentially direct the court to focus on that point on the state's agenda. It can thus also be seen as a more intense way of intervening with the court's operations, exposing it to claims of interference with its judicial/prosecutorial work and making it harder to defend its judicial independence and credibility towards critics. Of course, ICTs have procedures in place to avoid appearance of interference, by—for example—only accepting donations that are in line with the court's nature and mandate and that would not affect the court's independence.[125] Nonetheless, if voluntary contributions are needed, non-earmarked ones, that allow the court to direct the resources where it considers them to be most needed, are on safer ground in terms of respecting judicial independence. The safest and ideal option, however, is ensuring that the court has the needed funds to sustain its operations through the regular budgetary process, so that the court is not in a position of needing to accept extrabudgetary contributions.[126]

In the case of the IACtHR, voluntary contributions enabled the Court to remain afloat when OAS member states failed to cover its full expenses. That was the case for a number of years, with regular funding covering only around 50 per cent of the Court's expenses between 2010 and 2014, reaching a record low of 47.73 per cent in 2014. The need to secure such contributions left the Court functioning in a state of

[124] For a critique of this approach, see Sergey Vasiliev, 'Watershed Moment or Same Old? Ukraine and the Future of International Criminal Justice' (2022) 20 Journal of International Criminal Justice 893, section 4; CICC, 'Victims Could Lose Out with States' Double-Standard on International Criminal Court Resources: Open Letter to the ICC and ASP', 30 March 2022 <https://coalitionfortheicc.org/news/20220330/OpenLetter_ICCresources>.

[125] eg ICC Financial Regulations and Rules (n 64), Rule 107.1, 7.2–7.4; ASP, ICC-ASP/1/Res.11, 3.09.2002, paras 1–2.

[126] Similarly, Vasiliev (n 124) section 5.

uncertainty due to reliance on the willingness of states—most often with no relation to its mandate, such as Norway and Denmark—hampering its long-term planning and with Court officials having to dedicate a considerable amount of time to fundraising. The risks posed by voluntary contributions to the Court's appearance of judicial independence was shown, for example, in the case of Colombia and Mexico, when each made substantial voluntary contributions days before hearings in cases they were involved in, exposing the Court to criticism.[127]

14.4.2.2 Main source of funding

Voluntary contributions have not only been employed as extrabudgetary income, but also as main source of income for hybrid tribunals. In the early 2000s, a hybrid model of ICTs developed, as a result of UN member states' reluctance to fund new international tribunals, given the growing dissatisfaction with ICTY and ICTR's financial efficiency.[128] Already after the first few years of the ad hoc tribunals' operation, states reportedly became averse to funding ICTs based on assessed contributions due to a perception that the increases in the two tribunals' budgets was not justified by the progress achieved in proceedings.[129] Coupled with concerns regarding their financial accountability and efficiency based on audit and expert reports, this led to states' insistence on de-linking any new courts from the UN, including in terms of funding and administrative arrangements.[130]

The funding schemes employed for the SPSC in East Timor, SCSL, ECCC, and the STL all relied on voluntary funding either as the only source of income or as a way of complementing funding provided by the state in relation to which the ICT had jurisdiction. The SPSC and the SCSL were (envisaged to be) fully funded from voluntary contributions,[131] while the ECCC and STL were financed through a mixed system, whereby Cambodia and Lebanon, respectively, would bear part of the costs. How this model worked in practice brings to light the dangers and downsides of reliance on voluntary contributions as the main source of ICT funding. The decision to opt for such a model in both the SCSL and the ECCC case was done against the explicit recommendation of the UN Secretary-General who noted that:

> A financial mechanism based entirely on voluntary contributions will not provide the assured and continuous source of funding which would be required .... The risks associated with the establishment of an operation of this kind with insufficient funds, or without long-term assurances of continuous availability of funds, are very high, in terms of both moral responsibility and loss of credibility of the Organization, and its

127 'El (des)financiamiento de los órganos de protección del Sistema Interamericano de Derechos Humanos: la madre de todas las batallas' in Rey (n 67) 165–66.

128 David Cohen, 'Seeking Justice on the Cheap: Is the East Timor Tribunal Really a Model for the Future?' (2002) 61 Asia Pacific Issues 2; Tortora (n 4), 93–95.

129 Tortora (n 4) 94–95 and n6–7.

130 ibid 94–96.

131 Funding for the SPSC came from the voluntary trust fund set up to support the national judicial system, while the prosecution (Special Crimes Unit) received funding from the general UN peacekeeping budget through UNTAET and later UNMISET, which was based on assessed contributions. International Center for Transitional Justice (ICTJ), 'The Serious Crimes Process in Timor-Leste: In Retrospect' (2006) 29–30.

> exposure to legal liability.... A special court based on voluntary contributions would be neither viable, nor sustainable.[132]

To mitigate the uncertainty inherent in voluntary contributions, the UN Secretary-General was tasked to proceed with setting up the SCSL only after receiving funds for at least the first twelve months and pledges for a second year.[133] While this may have been a more effective solution if the Court's envisaged three-year lifespan had been realistic, in practice it was not sufficient to provide the same degree of certainty that stable and regular funding would. Throughout its existence, the SCSL 'faced constant and serious financial uncertainty', and the irregularity with which funds were received often left the Court with resources for only a few weeks ahead, compelling it to slow down activities and expenditures.[134] The UN had to intervene on several occasions to supplement the SCSL's resources and thus provide help without which the Court would not have been able to continue operations.[135] The pressure of having to continuously fundraise also took a substantial amount of time from the Court's officials who, for example, during two years only had to hold over 174 fundraising meetings and sent 225 fundraising requests to potential donors.[136]

While SCSL is broadly considered to have effectively carried out its mandate, in spite of the challenges posed by its funding scheme, the SPSC reportedly had neither the resources required to enable it to meet international fair trial standards, nor effective oversight. No registrar[137] or internationalized registry was foreseen, and there was no clear management or policy development in the initial phase of the Court.[138] Judges had no legal or support staff, there were no case managers, no court calendar and thus uncertainty for the parties as to whether and when hearings would take place. By the time thirteen trials reached a verdict, there was still no transcription for the proceedings; witnesses and accused were often transported together to hearings; and the public defender's office lacked financial means and adequate staff, leading to the defence not calling any witness during the first fourteen trials.[139] This led Cohen to conclude that

> the deeply flawed process in East Timor makes clear that the United Nations should not proceed 'on the cheap' so as to avoid the excessive expenditures of the ICTY and ICTR. In doing so, it does an injustice to those individuals convicted without a fair

[132] UN, Report of the Secretary-General on the establishment of a Special Court for Sierra Leone, UN Doc S/2000/915, 4 October 2000, para 70. Similar conclusions were reached with regard to the ECCC: UNGA Report of the Secretary-General on Khmer Rouge Trials, 31 March 2003, UN Doc A/57/769, paras 74–75.

[133] UN, Letter dated 22 December 2000 from the President of the Security Council addressed to the Secretary-General, S/2000/1234, 22 December 2000, para 2.

[134] Tortora (n 4) 102 and 104.

[135] ibid 102–03.

[136] ibid 104.

[137] The position of Registrar was only created in mid-2002, and at a rather junior level.

[138] ICTJ (n 131) 28.

[139] Cohen (n 128) 5–6; Rupert Skilbeck, 'Funding Justice: The Price of War Crimes Trials' (2008) 15 Human Rights Brief 3, 2.

trial and undermines the very standards of the justice and the rule of law that the tribunals are supposed to advance.[140]

However, such calls and experiences did not deter the UN from proceeding with a voluntary contribution-based system for the ECCC and STL. While both of them were intended to be partially funded by the state that had called for their establishment, ie Cambodia and Lebanon respectively, they did not manage to fully or consistently fulfil this obligation.[141] The gap was covered also through voluntary contributions.[142] The absence of available funds led to the abrupt end of the STL, and almost prompted the stay of investigations at the ECCC.

In 2021, the STL Registrar informed the judges of an 'unprecedented financial crisis' that left the Tribunal unable to operate for longer than one more month.[143] While a UN subvention had covered 75 per cent of Lebanon's contribution to the budget, other contributions remained outstanding; Lebanon's share of the budget was 49 per cent, with the remaining to be covered through voluntary donations. This led to the Tribunal suspending proceedings in a new *Ayyash* case that was due to commence that same month,[144] while additional funding was secured last minute so that the appeal in the main case before the STL could be finalized.[145] It is important to mention in this context that the willingness of states to contribute with voluntary funding to the STL decreased gradually. The Tribunal operated for almost fifteen years, with a very limited mandate over one incident, which understandably tested the patience and commitment of donors.

In the case of the ECCC, the two Co-Investigating Judges went on the record in May 2017 that they would order a stay of proceedings unless they were provided with 'sufficiently specific and reliable information that the funding situation will improve drastically', as they found it would have been unacceptable to proceed with an investigation without sufficient funding to complete it.[146] It was similarly deemed unacceptable to close the investigation phase, while uncertainty remained whether there was funding to enable an appellate review of a closing order or proceed to trial in case of a valid indictment.[147] At the time the request was filed, the Chambers only had sufficient funding to operate for little over one month.[148] In a twenty-four-page-long document,

[140] Cohen (n 128) 7.

[141] For example, voluntary contributions supplemented Lebanon's contributions when the latter could not pay its own share in full or in time in 2011 and 2012: Tortora (n 4) 122.

[142] Tortora (n 4) 111 and 122.

[143] STL, 'Severe Financial Crisis Threatens the STL's Ability to Fulfil Its Mandate', 2 June 2021 <https://web.archive.org/web/20231018130512/www.stl-tsl.org/en/media/press-releases/severe-financial-crisis-threatens-the-stls-ability-to-fulfil-its-mandate>. On this, see Evelyn Anoya, 'Governance of the Special Tribunal for Lebanon', in this volume.

[144] STL, 'Start of Trial in the Ayyash Case (STL-18-10) on 16 June Cancelled Due to Lack of Funds', 3 June 2021 <https://web.archive.org/web/20231018120749/www.stl-tsl.org/en/media/press-releases/start-of-trial-in-the-ayyash-case-stl-18-10-on-16-june-cancelled-due-to-lack-of-funds>.

[145] Reuters, 'Lebanon Tribunal Secures Funding to Hold Hariri Case Appeal', 13 September 2021, <www.reuters.com/world/middle-east/lebanon-tribunal-secures-funding-hold-hariri-case-appeal-2021-09-13>.

[146] Request for Submissions on the Budgetary Situation of the ECCC and its Impact on Cases 003, 004, and 004/2, *Ao An*, 004/2/07-09-2009-ECCC-OCIJ, OCIJ, ECCC, 5 May 2017, paras 53 and 79.

[147] ibid para 53.

[148] ibid para 76.

the judges outlined the significant financial challenges the ECCC faced since it started its work and the donors' 'drip-feed approach to the provision of funding', leading to a situation that potentially forced certain judicial decisions 'in violation of international standards of judicial independence and the effective administration of justice'.[149] Ultimately, the judges did not find it necessary to order a stay of proceedings, in great part due to the 'rapid increase in funding' being made available to the Chambers following their request for submissions.[150] Their decision, however, is a rare record of the interaction between judges and the governance body on the issue of finances.

Two aspects of the decision are particularly relevant for this chapter. Firstly, the judges outlined at what stage the issue of financing becomes a matter for the court. More specifically, they noted that when lack of funding encroaches or risks encroaching 'on the conduct, substance, fairness, and integrity of judicial proceedings ... these matters cease to be purely administrative and trigger the competent judicial body's responsibility to take those measures that are necessary to avoid injustice'.[151] In essence, as long as the funding of the court is provided as expected, there is no need for judicial intervention in an otherwise administrative matter. Secondly, the UN and the Principal Donor Group reportedly indicated in their submissions that the situation the ECCC found itself in was not out of the ordinary, both because its funding had always been a difficult issue, and because other international courts, regardless of their funding mechanism, were affected by similar problems.[152] The judges replied that this statement was an admission of states' failure to fulfil their obligations under the treaties or resolutions that created those courts.[153] It pointed to the systemic challenge of adequately funding ICTs, and the fact that it affected several courts did not make it less of a problem in each particular instance. On the contrary, it underlined the importance of finding systemic solutions and fundamentally different approaches.

If voluntary contributions as extrabudgetary income expose a court to criticism of (an appearance of) bias, as was seen with the ICC and the IACtHR, the risk is even higher for courts that fully depend on voluntary contributions to cover their expenses. For example, a draft US budget proposal that included a contribution to the ECCC conditioned the disbursement of funds on whether the court would consider a specific case, and indicating that contributions would cease if a closing order was issued in that case.[154] The phrasing in the document that was ultimately adopted was less specific, yet still foresaw the need for the US Secretary of State to certify that the contribution to the ECCC was in the national interest of the US and that it would support the prosecution and punishment of perpetrators of genocide in Cambodia.[155] The Co-Investigating Judges noted that this placed the court in a difficult position: if they were to file an indictment in the case, 'court observers may say that we caved in to US

[149] ibid paras 6, 24–33, 45, and 75.
[150] Combined Decision on the Impact of the Budgetary Situation on Cases 003, 004, and 004/2 and Related Submissions by the Defence for Yim Tith, *Ao An*, 004/2/07-09-2009-ECCC-OCIJ, OCIJ, ECCC, 11 August 2017 ('ECCC Combined Decision') para 62.
[151] ibid paras 14 and 17 ('we most certainly do have jurisdiction to adjudicate on the impact the financial situation may have on the fairness of the proceedings').
[152] ibid para 7(d).
[153] ibid para 28.
[154] ibid para 45.
[155] ibid para 47.

demands; if we dismiss the case or do not indict ... we risk the loss of a major donor to the ECCC. ... This is at least a *prima facie* case of implied influence on the actual outcome of the case'.[156] As a further example, a former SCSL Prosecutor explained that the decision not to indict Colonel Gaddafi was made in consideration of donor states' likely disapproval of such a decision: 'It was my political sense, dealing with senior leadership in the United Kingdom, United States, Canada, United Nations and the Netherlands, that this would not be welcome. ... Indicting Gaddafi would have been the 'death knell' for the court as the countries objecting would have pulled funding'.[157] As these examples demonstrate, voluntary contributions have not been a wholly successful funding mechanism. Rather than providing the financial stability and sufficient funding that a court needs to operate smoothly, they tend to endanger judicial independence or at least make it more challenging for the courts to meet the underlying standards. At the same time, the assessed contributions system has its own deficiencies, mostly in view of the consistent failure by states to pay their contributions on time and in full.

14.4.3 Systemic challenge of delays in payment of contributions

State arrears are as old an issue as international organizations themselves. Concerns regarding delays in the payment of owed contributions were raised already in the first year of the OAS[158] and the ITLOS.[159] Despite the prevalence of the problem, no systemic solutions have been implemented. The most common approach revolves around bilateral efforts to engage with the indebted states, both through their embassy at the seat of the IO and in the capital; distributing the list of states in arrears at the annual meetings of states parties; and, in some cases, the loss of vote in the assembly for those states with arrears equalling or exceeding the amount owed for a certain number of years.[160]

The persistence of the problem indicates that such measures are insufficient, if not mostly ineffective. The sanction of the loss of voting rights was considered an improvement when introduced in the UN Charter, being a lesson learned from the League of Nations' struggles. However, as highlighted by ECCC judges, one cannot put 'too much stock by the effectiveness of a threat to lose the right to vote in an organization one is not willing to support financially in the first place and that has no powers to take any enforcement action'.[161] This points to what potentially more effective measures could look like: they should either provide incentives to states to

[156] ibid para 48.

[157] Soraya Kishtwari, 'Prosecutor Reveals How Britain Let Gaddafi Off' (*Times*, 25 February 2011) in SCSL, press clippings, 28 February 2011 <https://s3.eu-west-1.amazonaws.com/rscsl.org/Clippings/2011/2011-02/pc2011-2-28.pdf> 11.

[158] Already at its first session, the OAS General Assembly deplored the continued delay in the payment of contributions, and warned of the impact it would have in the future: OAS GA, AG/RES.34 (I-O/71), 22 April 1971, Art 3.

[159] In the first year of the Tribunal, only thirteen of the eighty-five states parties paid their advance contributions: Report of the Fifth Meeting of States Parties (1996), SPLOS/14, SPLOS, 28 July 2006, para 32.

[160] eg UN Charter Art 19; ICC Rome Statute Art 112(8).

[161] ECCC Combined Decision (n 150) fn 44.

finance the organization or foresee ways to enforce the rules. Measures fulfilling these criteria have been considered but not (yet) implemented. For instance, the inability of states in arrears to nominate their nationals for elected positions was suggested in the IER Report for the ICC ASP and considered by the General Assembly for the OAS, but neither forum has adopted it.[162] Some organizations credit directly the financial contributions owed by states from specific accounts, removing to a great extent the freedom to decide whether to make a payment or not. There are also examples of organizations that have adopted more extensive measures. For instance, the OAS and WTO have an early payment encouragement scheme.[163] WTO also has a catalogue of consequences that apply gradually to delays in the payment of contributions from one to three years. By way of illustration, after a year of delay, states in arrears can no longer nominate representatives to preside over WTO bodies; after two years, they no longer have access to the members' platform; and after three years, they are declared inactive.[164] These WTO measures have explicitly been recommended also for the ICC, but not adopted.[165] This shows that it is not a matter of states being short of options or solutions, but rather they are not willing to adopt them. Implementing measures that would force them to pay their contributions in full and on time would limit the freedom and flexibility they currently have. It would also reduce the power that comes with deciding when and whether one wants to pay, delay, or withhold funds from an IO.

While arrears are not unique to ICTs, the impact on ICTs is different in view of their unique characteristics. As the PCIJ Registrar explained, core activities of a court cannot not be restricted: 'the judges are always at the disposal of the Court, which is always at the disposal of the litigants'.[166] Once an admissible case is brought before it, the court does not have the power to choose not to engage with it. Delays in funding lead to delays in proceedings which, depending on the court, may hamper the chances of an effective and peaceful resolution of disputes,[167] deprive individuals of a recourse they are entitled to in case of breaches of their human rights, and delay justice for victims. From a financial perspective, delays prolong the duration of proceedings, leading to an increase of costs in the long term.

Another risk specific to the ICTs is posed to their judicial independence when they are placed in a position of having judges fundraise for the court. Such efforts may be laudable from the point of view of judges' commitment to their court's mandate, but

162 IER Report (n 65) para 350 and R140; OAS GA, AG/RES.1757 (XXX-O/00), 6 June 2000, appendix B.

163 Members are refunded *pro rata* the interest earned from investing the funds received, whereas OAS applies discounts to the upcoming year's quota depending on the timing of payment (between January and end of April): WTO Financial Regulations, WT/L/156/Rev.3 (2015), Regulation 13, and Annex A 'WTO Early Payment Encouragement Scheme'; OAS, AG/RES.1757 (XXX-O/00), 6 June 2000, appendix A.

164 WTO Financial Regulations, Annex B 'Administrative Measures for Members and Observers in Arrears'.

165 IER Report (n 65) para 350 and n220.

166 PCIJ, Eighth Annual Report of the Permanent Court of International Justice (June 15th, 1931 to June 15th, 1932), Series E, No 8, 327.

167 As a former ICJ President once noted, 'such long delays will impinge not only on the Court's role in resolving disputes, but also its function in preventing and resolving international crisis and, to be frank, in maintaining peace and security'. Address by HE Judge Gilbert Guillaume, President of the International Court of Justice, to the United Nations General Assembly, 26 October 2000 <www.icj-cij.org/public/files/press-releases/9/2999.pdf> 3.

they also expose the court to criticism that it has invited states' interference in their work, eroding the public and parties' trust in the institution. For instance, the ECCC Co-Investigating Judges took the initiative of meeting with representatives of donor states to make a case for adequate funding.[168] The comments reportedly received from states on that occasion included criticism over the delays in investigations and dilatory tactics by the defence.[169] Both issues relate directly to the judges' management of proceedings and decision-making and, if anything, should be dealt with in the courtroom, and not in a debate between judges and states. The IACtHR judges have also at times supported fundraising efforts directed at states, raising concerns about the influence states play in the Court's handling of cases before them. To safeguard a court's judicial independence, as well as the appearance thereof, states should not place it in such a situation that judges would have to justify or explain their decisions, let alone be confronted with states' attempts to direct or influence future decisions. States must provide stable funding that enables the court to carry out its mandate.

Part of the reason why more effective measures to deal with arrears have not been adopted in ICTs is states' wish to retain power over ICTs' budgets without imposing hard obligations upon themselves. States' wish to do that may be understandable, considering they are accountable to their citizens for the decisions they make to fund (or not) IOs. But a corollary of this power is the responsibility to fulfil their obligations in good faith. By becoming a party to the court's treaty that foresees states' obligation to cover its expenses, states commit themselves financially and should deliver on that commitment in good faith in accordance with the *pacta sunt servanda* principle.[170] The same is true for UNSC resolutions that are binding on member states of the UN. Courts have no power to enforce such state obligations themselves. This responsibility falls on the other states parties, in a 'self-regulated' and 'self-policed' system, to either pressure states in arrears to pay their dues or to adopt rules that would have that effect. Another alternative is to establish a financial governance framework where arrears cannot be an issue—as is the case for the Caribbean Court of Justice (CCJ), that will be outlined next.

14.4.4 Outlier: the Caribbean Court of Justice

The assessed contributions model has mostly been replicated through diffusion by emulation, and funding through voluntary contributions arose in response to concerns regarding financial inefficiency of the UN ad hoc tribunals. But the approach to financing the CCJ came from one individual, Justice Duke Pollard, who—together with Sir David Simmons—the Chief Justice of Barbados, convinced the relevant Caribbean Community (CARICOM) committee of it.[171]

[168] ECCC Combined Decision (n 150) para 23.

[169] ibid.

[170] 'Every treaty in force is binding upon the parties to it and must be performed by them in good faith': Vienna Convention on the Law of Treaties (signed 23 May 1969, entered in force in 1980) 1155 UNTS 331, Art 26.

[171] David Simmons, 'The Caribbean Court of Justice: A Unique Institution of Caribbean Creativity' (2005) 29 Nova Law Review fn. 65.

Having estimated that US$100 million would be needed to fund the Court's operations, states took out a long-term loan for this amount with the Caribbean Development Bank and endowed a newly established trust fund with the borrowed funds.[172] A group of trustees is tasked with investing in securities to yield income that is used to finance the Court's expenses.[173] This solution was aimed to provide the Court with funding on a secure and sustainable basis, based on experiences of regional institutions that had 'suffered from fiscal disequilibrium owing to the delinquency of some governments in paying their contributions in a timely manner' and the wish to ensure that the CCJ would 'not be subjected to fiscal uncertainty or embarrassment'.[174] The Court's website states that this approach responded to concerns that judges 'would be paid by governments which can exert decisive informal pressure on them to deliver judgments favourable to this or that government'.[175]

The CCJ Trust Fund is managed by a Board of Trustees, made up of high-ranking officials of CARICOM institutions of a non-political character or their nominees.[176] In 2020, the Trust Fund generated approximately 13 per cent return in investment, bringing the cumulative return since inception, in 2005, to approximately 138 per cent.[177] By the end of 2020, the Fund had accumulated over US $81 million, with its asset portfolio consisting mostly of US and non-US markets equity (45.6 per cent).[178]

With states not involved in appointing the judges sitting on the bench (with the exception of the CCJ President), not approving the budget of the Court, and not directly funding its expenses, the CCJ is the only court that is, in its own words, 'financially independent of the largesse of governments and free from their administrative control'.[179]

The same model was proposed to the OAS, as a way of funding the expenses of the Inter-American Court and Commission of Human Rights. The OAS Secretary-General proposed states to take a US$100 million loan to be repaid in instalments over twenty years, proportionally with their OAS quota assessments.[180] The suggestion has not been implemented, and it does not seem to have been given serious consideration by the OAS states.

172 ibid 87.
173 ibid.
174 ibid.
175 CCJ, 'CCJ Trust Fund' <https://ccj.org/about-the-ccj/ccj-trust-fund>.
176 Revised Agreement Establishing the Caribbean Court of Justice Trust Fund (2004) Art VI: Secretary-General of CARICOM, Vice-Chancellor of the University of the West Indies, the President of the Insurance Association of the Caribbean, the Chairman of the Association of Indigenous Banks of the Caribbean, the President of the Caribbean Institute of Chartered Accountants, the President of the Organization of Commonwealth Caribbean Bar Associations, the Chairman of the Conference of Heads of Judiciary of Member States of the Caribbean Community, the President of the Caribbean Association of Industry and Commerce, and the President of the Caribbean Congress of Labour.
177 CCJ Trust Fund, Annual Report 2020 <https://ccj.org/wp-content/uploads/2022/02/CCJTF-2020-Annual-Report_Website.pdf> 4. The 2020 Report was the latest one publicly available at the time of writing.
178 Further to equity, the asset portfolio consists of hedge funds (22.2 per cent), private equity (12.5 per cent), cash (8.5 per cent), emerging market equity (7 per cent), real assets (3.8 per cent), and global fixed income (0.6 per cent). ibid 7 and 10.
179 CCJ, CCJ Trust Fund (n 175).
180 OAS Permanent Council, Document on 'Financially Strengthening the Inter-American Human Rights System' (Presented by the Secretary General of the OAS), OEA/Ser.G, CP/INF.6585/12, 15 November 2012, appendix, 2.

14.5 Expenses

14.5.1 General remarks

Many of a court's expenses are similar to those of an average IO. Salaries and personnel costs are often the highest percentage of the budget. The mandate of an ICT entails specific categories of expenses which will further differ from one court to another depending on the jurisdiction and institutional setup. In inter-state courts, parties cover the costs of their own representation in the proceedings. By contrast, budgets of criminal courts include expenses of the parties to trials (prosecution costs and legal aid for indigent accused). Since criminal courts also incur expenses related to witness protection, detention management, and, where applicable, victim participation, their budgets may be higher than those of an inter-state court.

Similarly, courts that operate within the universe of an IO may benefit from certain services of the organization, and thus do not need to include such expenses into their own budget. For example, recruitment of staff for the WTO AB is handled by the WTO human resources unit, in contrast to ITLOS or the ICC that need to have their own units and cover the respective costs. Operating in the context of an IO can—in theory—be a safety net, not only in terms of reliance on certain services, but also in terms of the availability of funding. In practice, the example of the IACtHR shows that this is not always the case. While the Court does not benefit from any services within the OAS, as it is administratively independent from it, even where the OAS General Assembly decided that the Court's translation costs should be covered from the OAS budget, the decision was never implemented.[181] Operating within a broader IO also exposes the court to institution-wide approaches, that may not always take into account the specificities of the court. That is for example the case of the CJEU which was affected by an EU-wide decision to reduce personnel by 5 per cent across Union institutions by 2017. While the Court was handling an increased caseload and preparing to double the number of judges as of 2019, it achieved the targeted goal and cut ninety-eight posts.[182] Shortly thereafter, the Council of the EU deemed this methodology not suitable for the purpose of reducing administrative expenditure as the expected gains of the financial cuts were not met.[183]

ICTs often dispose of a working capital fund and a contingency fund. The former is meant to cover short-term liquidity problems, pending receipt of regular income, while the latter is used to cover unforeseen expenses. Such funds—eg the Special Guarantee Fund (the equivalent of a contingency fund)—were in place already at the time of the League of Nations, and thus available to the PCIJ. Contingency funds are particularly useful to courts, as they have limited control over the level of their activity. For instance, inter-state courts such as the ICJ and ITLOS must be available to states whenever they decide to bring their disputes for resolution. There is nothing in the

[181] IACtHR, Annual Report 2011, 69; IACtHR, Annual Report 2012, 88.

[182] European Court of Auditors, 'Rapid Case Review on the Implementation of the 5% Reduction of Staff Posts', <www.eca.europa.eu/Lists/ECADocuments/RCR_STAFF/RCR_STAFF_EN.pdf> table 1, 9.

[183] Council of the European Union, Council Conclusions on the Budget Guidelines for 2019 (20 February 2018) <https://data.consilium.europa.eu/doc/document/ST-6315-2018-INIT/en/pdf> para 32.

ICJ Statute or the ITLOS Statute that would enable the judges not to handle an admissible case submitted before them that falls under their jurisdiction.

14.5.2 Remuneration of judges

One type of expense from ICTs' budgets that merits elaboration is judges' remuneration. Conditions of service of judges are decided by the funders, and are thus a type of direct interaction between the courts and their governance institutions. To ensure that the power over the conditions of service is not abused to influence judicial decision-making, certain safeguards are mentioned in the ICTs' statutory documents and outlined in soft-law instruments on judicial independence.[184]

In practice, judges receive an annual salary, either as a fixed sum or with a dual component, where the fixed monthly sum is complemented by a flexible component, titled post-adjustment, that can be modified depending on increases in the cost of living at the seat of the court. Presidents receive a special allowance, as do vice-presidents of courts when fulfilling the duties of presidents.

At the WTO AB, IACtHR, and ITLOS, judges do not serve full time and, consequently, have different schemes of remuneration. WTO AB members received a monthly retainer fee, a fee for every day worked, and a monthly allowance for administrative expenses (travel and subsistence allowance).[185] IACtHR judges are also paid per day of work, with a maximum monthly emolument set, further to a *per diem* and, where appropriate, travel allowance.[186] The ITLOS has a complex three-element remuneration system, with judges receiving an annual allowance, a special allowance for each day that they are engaged in Tribunal-related work, and a subsistence allowance for every day of ITLOS meetings.[187] The maximum salary a judge can receive is equivalent to the salary of an ICJ judge. The ITLOS and the WTO AB cover judges' work from home, whereas IACtHR judges are only paid for work carried out during judicial sessions at the Court.

The model of remuneration for non-full-time judges relies, in part, on the notion that busier periods or years are offset by calmer ones, in which case, for example, the costs incurred on account of the WTO AB members' remuneration are balanced off. However, while the AB was functioning, it had few—if any—calm periods in the years prior to its paralysis. The ITLOS and IACtHR approaches have a maximum threshold (for the total remuneration and, for the IACtHR, also the number of days) that can be compensated. This may be a financially wise approach in the early years of a court, but once activity intensifies, states should evaluate whether the model needs to be rethought and the limits extended or removed. The IACtHR has long been advocating

184 Section 14.2.1.
185 WTO, Establishment of the Appellate Body, WT/DSB/1, 19 June 1995, para 12.
186 Program-Budget of the Organization for 2020, AG/RES.2940 (XLIX-O/19), 27 June 2019, IV (2019), para 14.
187 ITLOS Statute (n 60) Art 18; SPLOS, Report of the Second Meeting of States Parties (1995), SPLOS/4, para 25(iv).

for becoming a 'full time Court' to enable it to more efficiently manage its increasing workload.[188]

In terms of how salaries are calculated, several ICTs' judicial salaries have been intertwined. For example, the Statutes of the ICTY and ICTR foresaw that the conditions of service of judges were those set for the ICJ members of the bench.[189] Though not a UN body, ITLOS judges' salaries are also linked to those at the ICJ. The maximum salary an ITLOS judge can receive equals the salary of an ICJ judge. In practice, however, this has been interpreted as full equivalence.[190] Over time, SPLOS approved the automatic adjustment of ITLOS judges' salaries upon review of the annual net base salaries of ICJ judges.[191] This approach is essentially similar to a delegation of authority to the UNGA, as changes to ITLOS judges' salaries can be made even without a confirmation by SPLOS of the UNGA decision. Some states opposed this approach, arguing that it would undermine the SPLOS' authority.[192] On the other hand, this model is efficient as it removes the need to regularly review judges' remuneration from the SPLOS agenda.

While ICJ judges' salaries determine conditions of service at other courts as well, the mechanism through which the former are set warrants further attention. Presented with proposals to link the ICJ judges' salaries to other posts or levels in the UN system, UN bodies have insisted on the importance of considering them as *sui generis*, meaning that

> the General Assembly applies to them an element of judgment which is independent of the considerations that enter into the determination of the salary scales of international officials. A corollary of the *sui generis* nature of the salaries of the Members of the Court is that they cannot be used for purposes of comparison with or as reference points for other salaries or honoraria.[193]

The advantage of linking the judicial salaries to those related to other posts or levels in the UN system, is that organization-wide reviews of salaries would automatically trigger the adjustment of judges' salaries as well, complying with the judicial independence requirement to have judges' remuneration periodically adjusted.[194] Such reviews would ensure that judges are not 'forgotten' and remove the need for the judges to ask states for an increase in their remuneration. This is what happened at the ICJ in 1985 and 1990, when judges had to make such requests referring to the difference

[188] Manuel E Ventura Robles, 'El Compromiso de La Comunidad Internacional Con La Protección Internacional Efectiva de Los Derechos Humanos Y Las Implicaciones Financieras Del Fortalecimiento Del Sistema Interamericano: El Caso de La Corte Interamericana de Derechos Humanos' in *Memoria del Seminario: El sistema interamericana de protección de los derechos humanos en el umbral del siglo XXI, San José, Costa Rica, 23 y 24 de noviembre de 1999* (Corte Interamericana de Derechos Humanos 2001) 270.

[189] ICTY Statute, annexed to UNSC Res 827 (25 May 1993) UN Doc S/RES/827, Art 13*bis*(3); ICTR Statute annexed to UNSC Res 955 (8 November 1994) UN Doc S/RES/955, Art 12*bis*(3).

[190] SPLOS, Fourth Meeting of States Parties, SPLOS/203, 2009, para 53.

[191] SPLOS, Decision on the adjustment mechanism for the remuneration of members of the ITLOS, SPLOS/230, *in fine*.

[192] SPLOS, Report of the 20th Meeting of States Parties (2010), SPLOS/218, paras 52 and 55; SPLOS, Report of the 21st Meeting of States Parties (2011), SPLOS/231, para 44.

[193] Rosenne and Shaw (n 69) para 117.

[194] As discussed in n 35.

between their salaries and those of senior officials in the UN Secretariat, as well as the remuneration of judges in national courts, the European Court of Justice, and the Iran-US Claims Tribunal.[195] Moreover, applying 'an element of judgment' that is separate from considerations applied to other posts, in absence of defined quantitative criteria, qualifies as a discretionary approach, that is discouraged by certain soft-law instruments on judicial independence.[196] It is unclear why it would be inappropriate for ICJ judges' salaries to be linked with a post/level in the UN system, considering that this model is used in other courts. For example, ICC judges' salaries have been linked to the level of UN Under-Secretary-General package, including participation in the UN Staff Pension Fund.[197] The decision came after eighteen years without any adjustment made to ICC judges' salaries, and no formal system foreseeing changes to judges' remunerations and allowances, and likely as a consequence of a number of judges suing the Court on this matter.[198] Linking does not necessarily mean equivalence—for instance, CJEU judges' salaries are determined as a percentage of the basic salary of an EU official at the highest level. Thus, the salary of the Court of Justice President is 138 per cent of the basic salary of an EU official at the highest level (third step, grade 16).[199]

ICJ and ITLOS judges receive an annual pension equal to half the annual base salary.[200] CJEU judges' pensions are 3.6 per cent of the final basic salary last received for each year of service.[201] By contrast, WTO AB members and IACtHR judges receive neither pension nor social welfare, contrary to judicial independence considerations. While the difference may be justified by the fact that judges do not serve full time and can engage in other professional activities, that is also the case for ITLOS judges, who do receive a pension.

14.5.3 Pressure to contain ICTs' budgets

A prevalent discussion in the context of financial governance concerns states' attempts to keep ICTs' costs under control. While this is not unique to ICTs and applies to all IOs, for courts of law such measures often trigger concerns of states' interference with judicial independence. With the multiplication of ICTs and the so-called crisis of multilateralism, this discourse has become more prevalent. Yet it is not new, and

[195] ibid paras 119–20.

[196] eg Venice Commission Report on Independence of Judges (n 23) para 53.

[197] ASP, Resolution ICC-ASP/18/Res.2, 6 December 2019.

[198] ICC ASP, Report of the Judicial Remuneration Panel, ICC-ASP/19/18, 01.12.2020, para 11; *New York Times*, 'In the Hague's Lofty Judicial Halls, Judges Wrangle over Pay' (20 January 2019) <www.nytimes.com/2019/01/20/world/europe/hague-judges-pay.html>.

[199] Council Regulation 2016/300 determining the emoluments of EU high-level public office holders (29 February 2016) Art 2. The basic salary of EU officials is established through Regulation (EU) No 423/2014 of the EP and Council adjusting with effect from 1 July 2012 the remuneration and pensions of officials and other servants of the EU and the correction coefficients applied thereto (16 April 2014) Art 2.

[200] UN, Report of the International Court of Justice, 1 August 2020 to 31 July 2021, para 227; Eiriksson (n 104) 104.

[201] Council Regulation (EU) 2016/300, 29 February 2016 determining the emoluments of EU high-level public office holders, Art. 12, read together with Regulation 31 (EEC), 11 (EAEC), laying down the Staff Regulations of Officials and the Conditions of Employment of Other Servants of the European Economic Community and the European Atomic Energy Community (version of 1 January 2024) Art 77.

can be traced, for instance, to the first years of the PCIJ. In response to a state's call for the establishment of a committee to consider potential reductions to the 1933 budget of the League of Nations organizations, the PCIJ Registrar suggested that political agendas to hire nationals of certain states and other non-financial reasons were behind the financial pressures on the Court at the time.[202] This statement illustrates the longstanding character of this problem.

Two main approaches have been used to contain ICTs' budgets: zero-growth budgeting and financial envelopes. Firstly, a zero-growth budget implies that the budget for the upcoming year is set at the same level as the previous year's budget, with adjustments accounting for inflation or currency adjustments. ITLOS budgets are prepared based on this principle,[203] even though no explicit rule has been adopted by SPLOS in this regard.[204] States have also advocated for zero *nominal* growth,[205] which does not leave room for any adjustments, resulting in practice in a reduction of the budget, as increases in costs due to inflation or currency changes have to be absorbed from the budget. This approach has been applied across IOs, and for long periods at a time.[206] For some states, it can be a policy adopted for all IOs they are part of.[207] Therefore, in pushing for zero (nominal) growth for courts' budgets, states do not necessarily intend to interfere with the court's judicial independence, but may rather simply aim to apply the same approach as to all other IOs. However, the same approach may have a different impact on different IOs, and the scheme should rather be tailored to the specific mandate of the ICT.

The push for courts' budgets to be resource-driven can also be observed in proposals to employ a 'financial envelope' approach by setting a threshold for the upcoming budgetary period that the court-proposed budget would have to respect. In essence, this means determining the level of activity the court can carry out depending on the funds states are willing to commit to it. This was proposed by the CBF in 2014 for the ICC and met with strong criticism from civil society, which deplored that the financial envelope could be used as a justification by states to block those activities of the Court they politically opposed.[208] The issue was discussed for several years by the ASP,[209] but no consensus was reached. States favouring the financial envelope

[202] PCIJ, Eighth Annual Report of the PCIJ (June 15th, 1931 to June 15th, 1932), Series E No 8, 329–30.

[203] Philippe Gautier, 'The International Tribunal for the Law of the Sea: Activities in 2002' (2003) 2 Chinese Journal of International Law 341, 344; also eg SPLOS, Report of the 12th Meeting (2002), SPLOS/91, para 37: 'maintaining a zero-growth budget ... was indicative of an efficiently run organization'; SPLOS, Report of the 26th Meeting (2016), SPLOS/303, paras 38 and 41.

[204] One delegation pointed out in 2007 that SPLOS had never decided that the budget should be based on such a principle: SPLOS, Report of the 28th Meeting of States Parties (2018), SPLOS/164, 2007, para 40.

[205] In 2018, some delegations in SPLOS stressed that the point of departure in budget discussions should be zero nominal growth: SPLOS, Report of the 28th Meeting of States Parties (2018), SPLOS/324, para 36.

[206] For instance, 2019 was the tenth year in a row of zero nominal growth for the WTO: WTO 2019 Financial Performance Report, WT/BFA/527, 7 September 2020, para 3.

[207] eg the US's indication in WTO budget discussions that this country was following a general policy of zero nominal growth in the budgets of international organisations: WT/GC/M/61, 2nd section.

[208] CICC, 'Budget and Finance Team, Recommendations to The Hague Working Group on the Budget' (18 November 2014) item 4 <http://iccnow.org/documents/CICC_BudgetandFinance__HWG_submission_18Nov2014.pdf>.

[209] eg ASP, Resolution ICC-ASP/13/Res.1, 17 December 2014, Section I, para 5, and CICC, Report on the 14th Session of the ASP, 18–26 November 2015, 30 and 41; ICC-ASP/15/Res.5, paras 70–72 and CICC, Report of the 15th ASP, 16–24 November 2016, 30–31.

noted the limitations they faced in receiving authorization from capital for budget increases; states opposed to this approach shared concerns that it would undermine the Court's independence, as states would essentially be prioritizing situations and cases before the Court, rather than letting the Court do so itself.[210] A financial envelope is, however, in place at the OAS, and thus for the IACtHR. Alongside the proposed OAS budget for the upcoming year, the Secretary-General submits a proposal for the overall budget level for the following year and a tentative budget level for the year after. The Court is not consulted in this process, and the budget it submits to the OAS has to respect the preset maximum level of expenses.[211]

Among the main arguments against both approaches are that court budgets should be mandate-driven and not resource-driven, and that an increase in activity requires an increase in funding. Courts cannot be expected to do more with the same amount of money. Furthermore, financial regulations task courts with preparing budgets based on their needs. Neither the court, nor its registrar can prioritize among the mandates entrusted to it by the statute and states parties.[212] As suggested by a former ICC President, two sets of interests have to be balanced: the task-driven needs of the court and the requirements of economy and efficiency.[213]

While approaches to containing courts' budgets may be part of states' policies towards IOs, in some cases they may be a sign of states' unwillingness to support an increased or continued level of activity for the court. For instance, in discussing the WTO AB's budget in 2000, a few member states were reluctant to increase the AB's funding due to a perceived risk that this would encourage frivolous litigation and transform the WTO into a litigation forum.[214] The STL's abrupt end ensued after the gradual loss of interest by states to continue funding its activities.[215] For the IACtHR, the persistent failure of states to cover the Court's expenses was criticised as part of a 'deliberate strategy from States to financially asphyxiate the organs of the inter-American system of human rights, restrict its freedom of action and exercise a major influence on their agendas through specific earmarked funds'.[216]

Decisions to lower the expenses related to a specific budget item can be seen as interfering with the court's independence, either by micromanaging its activities or by failing to consider its needs and applying arbitrary cuts to its budget. To give only two examples, the CBF at one point recommended the ICC Prosecutor to delay an investigation by proposing to refer resources requested for such an activity planned to

[210] Osvaldo Zavala, 'The Budgetary Efficiency of the International Criminal Court' (2018) 18 International Criminal Law Review 461, 483–84.

[211] References to the Court submitting budgets 'in accordance with the Secretary General's decision on maximum level of expenses' in eg IACtHR Annual Report 1983, 7; IACtHR Annual Report 1985, 7.

[212] ICC Registrar, Presentation to the ASP in its consideration of the 2012 Proposed Programme Budget, 10th Session of the ASP <https://asp.icc-cpi.int/sites/asp/files/asp_docs/ASP10/Statements/ASP10-ST-Reg-Arbia-Remarks-ENG.pdf> 8.

[213] Judge Sang-Hyun Song, President of the ICC, Remarks to the 10th Session of the ASP <https://asp.icc-cpi.int/sites/asp/files/asp_docs/ASP10/Statements/ASP10-ST-Pres-Song-Remarks-ENG.pdf> 4.

[214] WTO General Council, Minutes of Meeting, WT/GC/M/61, 7 February 2001, para 45; also paras 42, 52, 54, and 57.

[215] Section 14.4.2.2.

[216] 'El (des)financiamiento de los órganos de protección del Sistema Interamericano de Derechos Humanos: la madre de todas las batallas' in Rey (n 67) 160.

start in 2004 to 2005.[217] In 2011, after the CBF recommended cuts that according to the Committee itself had pushed the Court to its limit, the ASP adopted an even lower budget than recommended.[218]

However, not every decision to adopt a lower budget is an inappropriate use of states' oversight role. The delegation of authority to state representatives to negotiate and decide on the court's budget implies a power to commit the state's public funds up to a certain amount and a responsibility for ensuring that the funds are spent to cover reasonable expenses required for the furtherance of the court's mandate. Hence states' scrutiny of the ICTs' budget and decisions not to approve the requested level of expenditure for certain budget lines is not in and of itself an improper interference with the court's independence. Civil society often criticizes states' decisions approving a lower budget than requested for the court. Yet, more often than not, the public, including civil society organizations, does not have all information available to states when ICT budgets are negotiated. It would not be fair or accurate to assume budget cuts always stem from states not performing their oversight role in good faith. It is also possible that courts do not present carefully considered budgets that cover only reasonable expenses. For instance, the ASP's push for zero growth came as a result of the pattern of underspending by the ICC.[219] It may also be that, faced with repeated cuts to proposed budgets, courts seek to put forward inflated budgets, as a way of guaranteeing the funds they deem necessary.

What often becomes evident from budget negotiations is a mismatch between the stakeholders' expectations for the court. This can be seen in somewhat contradictory statements from states, some suggesting that courts ought to have a higher level of activity,[220] while pushing for lower budgets or not endowing the ICTs with the funds required to sustain or increase their work. Similarly, with the UN ad hocs and the STL, all temporary institutions, concerns soon arose among states regarding their high budgets and extended lifespan. To begin to address this issue, it is essential that stakeholders are on the same page as to the ideal, desired level of activity for an ICT and the level of resources estimated to be required to reach it. This would facilitate longer-term planning, as well as smoother budgetary negotiations. Such discussion should ideally take place before the court is set up, to enable states to decide on the financial governance framework with full awareness of the financial commitment it entails. Such a discussion was also recommended for the ICC stakeholders for the following ten years, as a way to ensure that all of them focus their efforts on achieving the same goals.[221]

[217] O'Donohue (n 73) 276.

[218] CICC, Report on the Tenth Session of the ASP, 12–21 December 2011, 13.

[219] O'Donohue (n 73) 279–80.

[220] For instance, while employing—in practice—a zero-growth budget, SPLOS members regularly call for increased use of ITLOS for it to fully reach its potential. SPLOS, Reports of the 12th Meeting (2002), SPLOS/91, para 22; 13th Meeting (2003), SPLOS/103, para 26; 23rd Meeting (2013), SPLOS/263, para 18; 24th Meeting (2014), SPLOS/277, para 27; UNGA, Oceans and the law of the sea, UNGA Res 57/141 (2002). Janet H Anderson, 'Money Matters at the ICC' (*JusticeInfo.Net*, 14 December 2018) <www.justiceinfo.net/en/tribunals/icc/39771-money-matters-at-the-icc.html>.

[221] IER Report (n 65) R363.

14.6 Conclusions and Way Forward

The overview of financial governance rules and practices in ICTs provided in this chapter shows that, as in all other institutional areas, there is unity in diversity.[222] Many of the rules adopted are similar, though at times they have developed differently in practice. Systemic and recurrent challenges can be found across the board; yet, they have not always been addressed in a systemic and effective manner. Alternative successful practices that merit further attention exist, but there has been limited appetite to experiment with them.

The preparation, adoption, and implementation of an ICT budget, as well as financial oversight, are all key processes in the governance of courts. This is also where the two cornerstone principles of judicial independence and accountability must be carefully applied and respected. Perceptions that one of them comes under threat can lead to disruptions hampering effective governance, and ultimately the functioning of the court. Both internal and external governance bodies have their share of responsibility for preventing such outcomes. Firstly, the court must prepare a carefully considered budget, where only necessary and reasonable expenses are included. In both the budget preparation and the budget implementation phase, the court should demonstrate sound financial management and have in place adequate internal and external audit processes. The budget review process should be based on a constructive and transparent dialogue between the court and its external governance bodies. The court should speak with one clear voice and be represented by its chief administrative officer, the registrar. Review of a court's budget should be based on the understanding of the specificities of an ICT, its functioning, mandate, and contours of judicial independence. It should take into account the court's needs, and external governance bodies should consult it when considering changes to the court-proposed budget.

In reflecting on potential amendments to the budget process, states should be guided by the need to ensure an efficient process, which implies avoiding duplication of work for both the court and the external governance bodies. While states have a duty to carefully review the budget and approve only those expenses that are reasonable, the process should not amount to micromanagement. Nor should it place unduly cumbersome reporting burdens on the court or pressure that can be seen as threatening its judicial independence. The more intrusive the oversight exercised over the court is perceived to be, the wider the scope of judicial independence is likely to be claimed by the court as a shield from that oversight. This is to be avoided in the interest of constructive and efficient financial decision-making. Courts have limited power themselves to influence states' behaviour in the process. Self-regulation is the answer to the question *quis custodiet ipsos custodes?* (who will guard the guards themselves?), in the sense that the responsibility falls on states to constrain themselves (and other states) in that regard. States are required to advocate for respect of the applicable rules in their political negotiations and to push for the adoption of necessary safeguards.

In terms of sources of funding, courts should be endowed with stable, regular, and secure funding. Voluntary contributions as a main way of covering a court's expenses

[222] Schermers and Blokker (n 91) paras 22–25.

is not a reliable system of funding. Arrears are the main challenge of funding schemes based on assessed contributions. No impactful method to deal with arrears has been implemented because states prefer to keep the flexibility of deciding whether and when to pay their contribution to a court's budget. Such freedom may come at odds with states' responsibility to fulfil their obligation to fund ICTs in good faith. The international community has not yet found the ideal funding mechanism for ICTs. Models such as the one employed by the CCJ merit further consideration, and efforts should be put in contemplating other potential alternatives. Further research is needed both in-depth, zooming in on individual courts' rules and practices, and comparatively across ICTs. This would enable a fuller understanding of the impact and benefits of, and challenges posed by, certain rules and practices, as the foundation for developing new approaches that would allow strengthening the judicial independence and accountability of ICTs and designing more effective and resilient financial governance schemes of any future ICTs.

At the time when drafters of the PCIJ Statute opined that in view of the ultimate goal of the Court, namely the prevention of war, the matter of its costs was of too little significance, the world knew one prior international court and was creating its second ever such court.[223] Some one hundred years later, and with dozens of ICTs operating across the world, perspectives have surely changed. It has been argued that it is no longer the case that 'justice has no price'; there is a price for justice, and it is exactly how much states are willing to pay for it.[224] Undeniably, with the proliferation of ICTs in the twentieth and twenty-first centuries, the international justice playing field has become increasingly crowded, and with that, 'the days of endless resources for justice' have come to an end.[225] However, as long as states decide to create ICTs and endow them with mandates, it is also their responsibility to enable them to function adequately, which includes setting up budget processes and oversight mechanisms that safeguard ICTs' independence and accountability.

[223] The Central American Court of Justice (1907–18) was the first international court to be established, followed by the PCIJ. Christian Tomuschat, 'International Courts and Tribunals', *Max Planck Encyclopedia of Public International Law* (Oxford Public International Law, OUP, article updated 2011) paras 8–9. Its Statute was reconfigured in 1991, and it has since been operating as the judicial organ of the Central American Integration System.

[224] Remarks by Ms Carolina Fernández Opazo (CBF member 2008–20), panel on 'Financial Governance of International Courts: Budgetary Issues and Audit', the Leiden University Conference (on file with the author).

[225] Remarks by Mr Kees Sterk, then Vice-Chair of the Dutch *Raad voor de Rechtspraak*, and Chair of the European Network of Councils for the Judiciary, at Leiden University Conference (on file with the author).

15
The Enforcement of International Judicial Decisions

Dorine Nauleau

15.1 Introduction

The enforcement of international judicial decisions is often seen as 'executive or political in nature'.[1] It is a highly politicized process that may feed critiques against international courts according to which the enforcement would be subject to states' interests, or even give rise to claims that it is about 'siding with one of the parties to a dispute'.[2] International judicial decisions are, however, not sufficient in and by themselves for enforcing the law. Justice without the binding force that allows its enforcement is not credible: Themis, the Goddess of Justice, is often depicted not only with a scale but also with a sword—the symbol of authority. Even though the enforcement of international judicial decisions has been studied extensively,[3] it is often assumed

[1] Richard Frimpong Oppong and Angela M Barreto, 'Enforcement' in William A Schabas and Shannonbrooke Murphy (eds), *Research Handbook on International Courts and Tribunals* (Edward Elgar Publishing 2017) 276.

[2] ibid 278.

[3] eg Alexandra Huneeus, 'Compliance with Judgments and Decisions' in Cesare PR Romano, Karen J Alter, and Yuval Shany (eds), *The Oxford Handbook on International Adjudication* (OUP 2014) 437; Oscar Schachter, 'Invisible College of International Lawyers' (1977–78) 72(2) Northwestern University Law Review 217; Robert Jennings, 'The Judicial Enforcement of International Obligations' (1987) 47 Max-Planck-Institut für Ausländisches Öffentliches Recht und Völkerrecht 3; Attila Tanzi, 'Problems of Enforcement of Decisions of the International Court of Justice and the Law of the United Nations' (1995) 6 European Journal of International Law 539; Steve Charnovitz, 'The Enforcement of WTO Judgments' (2009) 34 The Yale Journal of International Law 558; Veronika Fikfak, 'Reinforcing the ICJ's Central International Role? Domestic Courts' Enforcement of ICJ Decisions and Opinions' in Mads Andenas and Eirik Bjørge (eds), *A Farewell to Fragmentation Reassertion and Convergence in International Law* (CUP 2015) 343; Chiara Giorgetti, 'What Happens after a Judgment Is Given? Judgment Compliance and the Performance of International Courts and Tribunals' in Theresa Squatrito and others (eds), *The Performance of International Courts and Tribunals* (CUP 2018) 324; Amuda-Kannike Abiodun San and Abila Sylvanus, 'A Critical Examination of the Enforcement of ICJ Decisions through the Organs of the United Nations' (2018) 6(1) Journal of Law and Criminal Justice 21; Zlata Durdevic, 'Legal and Political Limitations of the ICC Enforcement System: Blurring the Distinctive Features of the Criminal Court' in Bruce Ackerman, Kai Ambos, and Hrvoje Sikirić (eds), *Visions of Justice* (Duncker & Humbolt 2016) 163; Yuval Shany, 'Assessing the Effectiveness of International Courts: A Goal-Based Approach' (2012) 106(2) American Journal of International Law 225; Frimpong Oppong and Barreto (n 1); Jean d'Aspremont, 'The Collective Security System and the Enforcement of International Law' in Marc Weller (ed), *The Oxford Handbook of the Use of Force in International Law* (OUP 2016); Sergey Vasiliev, 'Judicial Governance Entities as Power-Holders in International Criminal Justice: A Plea for a Socio-Legal Enquiry' in Morten Bergsmo and others (eds), *Power in International Criminal Justice* (Torkel Opsahl Academic EPublisher 2020) 483.

Dorine Nauleau, *The Enforcement of International Judicial Decisions* In: *Governance of International Courts and Tribunals*. Edited by: Sergey Vasiliev and Niels Blokker, Oxford University Press. © Dorine Nauleau 2026.
DOI: 10.1093/oso/9780198922131.003.0015

that enforcement—that is, the execution of a court's order[4]—lies in the hands of international courts themselves.[5] But as Karen Alter rightly puts it, '[i]nternational courts are participants in international law enforcement, they do not themselves enforce the law'.[6] Scholars have identified several ways to enforce international judicial decisions: self-help, diplomacy, and negotiations, among others.[7] But international courts' governance institutions (*injugovins*) also have a role to play in the enforcement of judicial decisions, although they have remained under the radar for too long.[8]

In the final report of the Independent Expert Review of the International Criminal Court (ICC), the experts found that the enforcement of arrests was among the main challenges faced by the Court.[9] They referred to two examples: the failure to arrest the President of Sudan Omar Al-Bashir and the withdrawal of charges against the Kenyan President Uhuru Kenyatta.[10] In her statement following the Office of the Prosecutor's (OTP's) decision to withdraw charges against Kenyatta, the then ICC Prosecutor, Fatou Bensouda, explained that one of the reasons why she decided to withdraw said charges was the fact that 'the Kenyan Government's non-compliance compromised the Prosecution's ability to thoroughly investigate the charges'.[11] The ICC is not the only international court facing this challenge of non-enforcement of decisions. This is also an issue for other international courts, that even suffer from a political backlash on account of their rulings. For instance, the Southern African Development Community's tribunal (SADC tribunal) was dissolved after its ruling against Zimbabwe,[12] and the International Court of Justice (ICJ) saw the United States withdrawing from the proceedings initiated by Nicaragua after the Court found that it had jurisdiction to hear the dispute.[13] This is highly problematic, especially considering that judicial decisions of international courts are binding.[14] A judgment needs to be enforced to be given effect and the role of *injugovins* is crucial here: a proper enforcement of these decisions upholds the authority of the court.

While it is important that *injugovins* take an active role in the enforcement of judicial decisions, their relationship with the states that created them may be difficult.

[4] William M Reisman, 'The Enforcement of International Judgments' (1969) 63(1) The American Journal of International Law 1.

[5] Karen J Alter, *The New Terrain of International Law* (Princeton University Press 2014) 244.

[6] ibid 245.

[7] Frimpong Oppong and Barreto (n 1).

[8] Niels Blokker, 'The Governance of International Courts and Tribunals: Organizing and Guaranteeing Independence and Accountability: An Appeal for Research' in Geir Ulfstein and Andreas Føllesdal (eds), *The Judicialization of International Law: A Mixed Blessing?* (OUP 2018) 26.

[9] Independent Expert Review of the International Criminal Court and the Rome Statute System, Final Report, 30 September 2020 <https://asp.icc-cpi.int/iccdocs/asp_docs/ASP19/IER-Final-Report-ENG.pdf> (IER Report) 215.

[10] ibid fn 458.

[11] Statement of the Prosecutor of the International Criminal Court, Fatou Bensouda, on the Withdrawal of Charges Against Mr. Uhuru Muigai Kenyatta, 5 December 2014 <www.icc-cpi.int/Pages/item.aspx?name=otp-statement-05-12-2014-2>.

[12] Frederick Cowell, 'The Death of the Southern African Development Community Tribunal's Human Rights Jurisdiction' (2013) 13(1) Human Rights Law Review 153; *Mike Campbell (Pvt) Ltd and Others* v *Republic of Zimbabwe (Judgment)* (SADC Tribunal, 28 November 2008).

[13] *Military and Paramilitary Activities in and against Nicaragua (Nicaragua* v *United States of America) (Judgment)* (ICJ Reports, 1984); The New York Times Archives, 'Text of US Statement on Withdrawal from Case before the World Court' (19 January 1985) <www.nytimes.com/1985/01/19/world/text-of-us-statement-on-withdrawal-from-case-before-the-world-court.html>; Giorgetti (n 3) 331.

[14] ICC Statute Art 105(1); UN Charter Art 94(1); ECHR Art 46(1).

Injugovins cannot be fully independent from international politics: they are made of states. The system of the Council of Europe, however, proves that *injugovins* can be effective in the enforcement of the respective court's decisions. The Committee of Ministers which oversees the execution of judgments of the European Court of Human Rights (ECtHR) ensured enforcement in 2,048 cases in 2019, therefore reducing the number of cases under its watch from 6,151 to 5,246.[15]

This chapter argues that it is a crucial function of *injugovins* to contribute to the proper enforcement of decisions of international courts and tribunals. The chapter will first examine the enforcement of judicial decisions as such: why this function is important and what it means for the effectiveness of international courts and tribunals (Section 15.2). It will then survey the arrangements adopted for, and the main challenges to, the effective enforcement of judicial decisions using the examples of three international courts and tribunals: the ICJ, ICC, and the ECtHR (Section 15.3). Finally, it will provide some concluding remarks (Section 15.4).

15.2 Significance of the Enforcement of International Judicial Decisions

International judicial decisions are scrutinized by various actors and from various angles, but the post-adjudication phase has remained understudied.[16] This is problematic: the enforcement of judicial decisions is a significant indicator of the degree of an international court's authority[17] and effectiveness.[18]

15.2.1 Enforcement of international judicial decision: a measure of a court's authority and effectiveness

In his declaration regarding the Order of the ICJ on 1 July 2000 in the *Case Concerning Armed Activities on the Territory of the Congo*, Judge Oda wrote that 'the repeated disregard of the judgments or orders of the Court by the parties will inevitably impair the dignity of the Court and raise doubt as to the judicial role to be played by the Court in the international community'.[19] A court's decision will in fact have more chances to

[15] Council of Europe, *Communication on the Activities of the Committee of Ministers* (Rapport, CM/AS(2020)1, 24 January 2020), <https://search.coe.int/cm/Pages/result_details.aspx?ObjectId=090000168099916f>. See also Council of Europe, Décisions Adoptées (CM/Del/Dec(2019)1362, 5 December 2019) <https://search.coe.int/cm/Pages/result_details.aspx?ObjectID=0900001680990a37>. On the enforcement function of the Committee of Ministers: Hanneke Palm and Roeland Böcker, 'Implementation of Judgments of the European Court of Human Rights', in this volume.

[16] Giorgetti (n 3) 324.

[17] ibid 324; David C Baluarte, 'From Judgment to Justice: Implementing International and Regional Human Rights Decisions' (2010) Open Society Foundations 12, <www.srji.org/upload/medialibrary/694/implementation-report-osi.pdf>; Committee of Ministers, Implementation of Decisions of the European Court of Human Rights by Turkey Parliamentary Assembly Recommendation 1576 (2002), CM/AS (2003) Rec1576 (31 March 2003).

[18] Baluarte (n 17) 11; Committee of Ministers, Implementation of Decisions of the European Court of Human Rights by Turkey Parliamentary Assembly Recommendation 1576 (2002), CM/AS (2003) Rec1576 (31 March 2003).

[19] *Armed Activities on the Territory of the Congo (Democratic Republic of the Congo v. Uganda)* (Provisional Measures), Order of 1 July 2000 [2000] ICJ Rep 111, Judge Oda declaration, 132.

be enforced if said court is perceived as being legitimate.[20] International courts have authority 'when the litigants, the court's compliance partners, and the legal field recognize the binding nature of international court rulings and undertake meaningful steps to give effect to those rulings'.[21]

However, the issue 'is not in arriving at an answer in law, but in *enforcing* an answer in law'.[22] In a report on the implementation of international human rights decisions, David Baluarte argued that the enforcement of a judicial decision is 'the central measure of a Court's efficacy'.[23] He explains that the authority of a court cannot be assessed on the basis of a judgment it released itself: no matter how good the judgment is, if not enforced, it does not have an impact on states or people victimized by a violation of international law.[24] While it is true that the proper enforcement of decisions will boost the authority of the court, the lack of enforcement tools available to these courts will rather tend to undermine it.

15.2.2 Lack of enforcement tools in the international judicial system

Laurence Helfer is of the view that international courts lack 'strong enforcement mechanisms'.[25] States can disregard international judicial decisions as much as they can neglect 'the obligations of the treaty that established it'.[26]

Back in 1945, when the ICJ was established, international courts may have been considered as a 'sovereign risk' for states: international courts may shape international law in a way that disregards national interests.[27] Some argue that one of the reasons why the Heads of State of the member states of the Southern African Development Community (SADC) decided to dissolve the SADC Tribunal was that the Tribunal issued a decision 'that was too independent from their wishes'.[28] Laurence Helfer's theory of constrained independence is helpful in that regard: he argues that states create international courts that are formally independent to enhance the credibility of their commitment to the international legal order, all the while using 'formal, structural, political and discursive' mechanisms to constrain judicial independence.[29]

International courts have indeed been provided with what can be referred to as 'soft tools' to enforce their decisions. Their constitutive acts provide them with various

[20] Yvonne M Dutton, 'Bridging the Legitimacy Divide: The International Criminal Court's Domestic Perception Challenge' (2017) 56(1) Columbia Journal of Transnational Law 71, 85.

[21] Karen J Alter, Laurence R Helfer, and Mikael R Madsen, 'How Context Shapes the Authority of International Courts' (2016) 79(1) Law and Contemporary Problems 1, 35.

[22] Reisman (n 4) 1 (emphasis added).

[23] Baluarte (n 17) 11.

[24] ibid.

[25] Laurence R Helfer, 'Why States Create International Tribunals: A Theory of Constrained Independence' in Stefan Voigt, Max Albert, and Dieter Schmidtchen (eds), *International Conflict Resolution* (Mohr Siebeck 2006) 258.

[26] ibid.

[27] Alter and others (n 21) 9.

[28] Cowell (n 12) citing Jan Norlander, 'The SADC Tribunal – Regional Organisations, Human Security, Human Rights and International Law' (2011) 57 Development Dialogue .

[29] Helfer (n 25) 254.

enforcement mechanisms,[30] such as monitoring,[31] reporting,[32] and referral of non-cooperation to *injugovins*.[33]

15.3 Enforcement of Judicial Decisions: A Distinct Function of *Injugovins*

In the international arena, some *injugovins* were given a role in the enforcement of decisions in accordance with the court statutes or other instruments. This is the case for the UN Security Council (UNSC) for decisions of the ICJ,[34] the Assembly of States Parties (ASP) for decisions issued by the ICC,[35] and the Committee of Ministers of the Council of Europe, which supervises the execution of ECtHR's decisions.[36]

15.3.1 Role of *injugovins* in the enforcement of ICJ judicial decisions

The ICJ's *injugovins*—the UN General Assembly (UNGA) and the UNSC—are responsible for the governance of the ICJ: they elect its judges, adopt its budget, and fix the judges' salary.[37] As the principal judicial organ of the UN, the ICJ addresses a wide variety of disputes, from maritime law to diplomatic and consular law to genocide.[38] However, the ICJ Statute did not provide the Court with tools to guarantee the enforcement of its judgments.[39] Rather, the power to enforce ICJ decisions is in the hands of the UNSC (3.1.1), as well as, to a certain extent, in the hands of the UNGA (3.1.2).

15.3.1.1 Role of the UNSC in the enforcement of ICJ decisions

Article 94(2) of the UN Charter provides that:

> If any party to a case fails to perform the obligations incumbent upon it under a judgment rendered by the Court, the other party may have recourse to the Security Council, which *may, if it deems necessary*, make recommendations or decide upon measures to be taken to give effect to the judgment. (Emphasis added)

[30] Giorgetti (n 3) 328.

[31] For example, Art 46 of the ECHR provides that the Committee of Ministers supervises the execution of the Court's judgments.

[32] ICC Statute Art 87(7) providing that the ICC may report a matter of non-cooperation to the UNSC.

[33] For example, UN Charter Art 94(2) refers to the Security Council when it comes to issues of non-enforcement.

[34] UN Charter Art 94(2).

[35] ICC Statute Art 87(7).

[36] ECHR Art 46(2).

[37] ICJ Statute Arts 8, 32, and 33; United Nations, 'Security Council Elects 5 Judges to International Court of Justice after Single Round of Voting' (Meeting Coverage, Security Council 8773rd Meeting SC/14/357, 12 November 2020), <https://press.un.org/en/2020/sc14357.doc.htm >.

[38] The list of cases is on the ICJ website, <www.icj-cij.org/en/list-of-all-cases>.

[39] Giorgetti (n 3) 328–29.

At first sight, the UN Charter provides the ICJ with an effective enforcement mechanism: if a party fails to comply with an ICJ judgment, the UNSC has the power to take measures to enforce it. However, one cannot fail to notice the weakness of this wording: the use of the power to enforce is not mandatory. The UNSC has full discretion in these matters: it '*may, if it deems necessary* ... give effect to the judgment'. This wording is weaker than the language used in the Covenant of the League of Nations, whereby the Council was under an obligation to propose solutions to give effect to the judgment. Article 13(4) of the League Covenant read as follows: 'In the event of any failure to carry out such an award or decision, the Council shall propose what steps should be taken to give effect thereto.'[40]

This broad discretion given to the UNSC partly explains why some states bypass ICJ decisions.[41] The *Nicaragua* case is one of the most striking examples.[42] Nicaragua referred to Article 94(2) of the UN Charter requesting the UNSC to 'consider the non-compliance' with the judgment of 27 June 1986 regarding the *Military and Paramilitary Activities in and against Nicaragua* case.[43] The US, a permanent member of the UNSC, used its veto power against a draft UNSC resolution, arguing that the ICJ had no jurisdiction to give such a judgment.[44] This sheds light on the limits of Article 94(2) of the UN Charter and the choice of the UNSC, and therewith states holding the power to veto its resolutions, as actors authorized to enforce ICJ decisions. The veto can jeopardize the orderly enforcement if ICJ decisions are contrary to veto-holders' interests.

By giving the UNSC the enforcement power, the UN created an imbalance within the international community: veto-holders can prevent the enforcement of ICJ judgments. The impact of the veto on the enforcement should not be underestimated: it is one of the 'bottle-necks' of the system which undermines states' compliance with international law.[45] Some scholars have referred to Article 94(2) as a 'negative clog in the progressive wheel of international justice'.[46]

That being said, scholars tend to agree that ICJ judgments are mostly complied with.[47] In her 2006 speech, the then-President of the ICJ Dame Rosalyn Higgins stated that '[o]f nearly 100 contentious cases the Court has dealt with, no more than a handful have presented problems of compliance. Of this handful, the problems of compliance have mostly turned out to be temporary'.[48] However, and this is

[40] Covenant of the League of Nations, 28 April 1919.
[41] San and Sylvanus (n 3) 23.
[42] *Military and Paramilitary Activities In and Against Nicaragua (Nicaragua v. United States of America)* (Merits), Judgment of 27 June 1986 [1986] ICJ Rep 14.
[43] United Nations Security Council, *Letter Dated 17 October 1986 from the Permanent Representative of Nicaragua to the United Nations addressed to the President of the Security Council*, S/18415 (20 October 1986), available at <www.securitycouncilreport.org/atf/cf/%7B65BFCF9B-6D27-4E9C-8CD3-CF6E4FF96FF9%7D/s_18415.pdf>.
[44] UNSC, 'In Hindsight: The Security Council and the International Court of Justice', Security Council Report (28 September 2016) <www.securitycouncilreport.org/monthly-forecast/2017-01/in_hindsight_the_security_council_and_the_international_court_of_justice.php>; San and Sylvanus (n 3) 27; The New York Times Archives (n 13).
[45] San and Sylvanus (n 3) 28.
[46] ibid.
[47] eg Paulson Colter, 'Compliance with Final Judgments of the International Court of Justice since 1987' (2004) 98(3) American Journal of International Law 434.
[48] UN Doc S/PV.5474, 7 (22 June 2006).

very telling, she also said that 'the Council, faced with the massive problems in its agenda, might be forgiven for wondering whether judgments by a Court with no enforcement powers of its own—indeed, the Charter provides that enforcement of Court judgments lies ultimately with the Security Council—will, in fact, be complied with'.[49]

Even though ICJ judgments are generally observed, this is not necessarily due to the measures taken by the UNSC. Often, an ICJ decision triggers further negotiation between states. If a state decides to refer the issue of non-enforcement to the UNSC, the effectiveness of this procedure will depend on the interests of the veto-holders at stake. As noted, the UNSC is not the only *injugovin* of the UN system and its role regarding the enforcement of ICJ decisions is not exclusive;[50] the UNGA also has a role to play.[51]

15.3.1.2 Role of the UNGA in the enforcement of ICJ decisions

The UNGA consists of all the members of the United Nations.[52] It is the organ partly responsible for admitting states as members of the UN,[53] that 'may discuss any question or any matters ... relating to the powers and functions of any organs provided for in the ... Charter'.[54] It also has the power to act when the UNSC fails to do so under the so-called Uniting for Peace resolution.[55] Furthermore, the UNGA may 'recommend measures for the peaceful adjustment of any situation' which may impair the general welfare or friendly relations between states.[56] The UNGA could therefore discuss a matter relating to relations between states affected by non-enforcement of an ICJ decision and adopt a recommendation, requesting states to enforce the ICJ judgment—provided that the UNSC has not been seized of the matter.[57] The power of the UNGA is, however, not to be overestimated: its recommendations are not binding.[58] That said, a formal decision from the UNGA addressing the issue of non-enforcement could certainly have a weight and put pressure on states to act. It could even lead the UNSC to seize itself of the matter or, at least, prod states involved in the dispute to commence negotiations.

15.3.2 Role of *injugovins* and the enforcement of ICC judicial decisions

The ASP oversees the administration of the ICC by the Presidency, the Prosecutor, and the Registrar.[59] Over recent years, the ASP has been receiving much attention due

49 ibid.
50 Frimpong Oppong and Barreto (n 1) 277.
51 San and Sylvanus (n 3) 30.
52 UN Charter Art 9.
53 ibid Art 4.
54 ibid Art 10.
55 *Uniting for Peace*, GA Res 377, 5th session, 302nd plenary meeting (3 November 1950) 10.
56 ibid Art 14.
57 ibid Art 12.
58 UN Charter Art 10.
59 ICC Statute Art 112(2)(b). Silvia Fernández de Gurmendi, 'Challenges to the Governance of the International Criminal Court', in this volume.

to the 'crisis' the ICC has been facing on account of criticisms in relation to its performance.[60] Four former ASP presidents published a joint letter claiming that the ICC 'needs fixing'.[61] But does the ASP not need fixing too?

The track record of the ASP as the ICC's governing body was questioned, among others, during the election of the third ICC Prosecutor in 2020–21.[62] This is certainly due to the complex relationship between the ASP and the Court,[63] which has been characterized by 'mutual distrust' between organs of the ICC and the ASP.[64] An Independent Expert Review was carried out in 2020 to 'identify ways to strengthen the ICC and the Rome Statute system'.[65] The ASP, as an *injugovin* of the ICC, has a role to play in the enforcement of the Court's decisions (Section 15.3.2.1). A special relationship was also established with the UNSC which has the power of enforcement when it refers a situation to the Prosecutor of the Court (Section 15.3.2.2).[66]

15.3.2.1 Enforcement of ICC decisions as a distinct function of the ASP

Enforcement of ICC judicial decisions refers here to the enforcement of the ICC's requests for cooperation addressed to states parties.[67] The scope of the enforcement of ICC decisions is thus understood as going beyond enforcement of final judgments and extending to interlocutory decisions, in particular decisions on the issuance of arrest warrants and requests for surrender, which are crucial for the work of the Court.[68] Under the Rome Statute, states parties must cooperate with the ICC 'in its investigation and prosecution of crimes within [its] jurisdiction';[69] non-cooperation by states parties negatively impacts the work of the Court.[70]

Even though the ICC acts independently, it remains an international organization governed by the ASP, its 'management oversight and legislative body'.[71] As part of its governance functions, the ASP shall consider 'any question relating to non-cooperation'.[72] This wording is vague, particularly the word 'consider', and does not give any clarification as to which measures the ASP is supposed to take when a state does not cooperate with the Court.[73] It conveys, however, that (i) if a state party to the Rome Statute fails to comply with the ICC's decision, the Court, by itself, is

60 Vasiliev (n 3) 487.

61 Prince Zeid Raad Al Hussein and others, 'The International Criminal Court Needs Fixing' (*New Atlanticist*, 24 April 2019) <www.atlanticcouncil.org/blogs/new-atlanticist/the-international-criminal-court-needs-fixing>.

62 eg Open Society Justice Initiative, 'ASP Presidency Fails to Protect the Integrity of the Election of the Next ICC Prosecutor', Press Release, 10 February 2021, <www.justiceinitiative.org/newsroom/asp-presidency-fails-to-protect-the-integrity-of-the-election-of-the-next-icc-prosecutor>.

63 eg Blokker (n 8).

64 IER Report (n 9) 312 para 950.

65 IER Report (n 9) 7 para 1.

66 ICC Statute Art 87(5)(b).

67 ibid Art 87(1)(a).

68 ibid Art 58.

69 ICC Statute Art 86.

70 Resolution ICC-ASP/10/Res.5 (Adopted at the 9th plenary meeting, on 21 December 2011) para 9 where the ASP 'welcomes the report of the Bureau on potential Assembly procedures relating to non-cooperation'.

71 ICC Statute Arts 112(1) and (6).

72 ibid Art 112(2)(f).

73 Göran Sluiter and Stanislas Talontsi, 'Credible and Authoritative Enforcement of State Cooperation with the International Criminal Court' in Olympia Bekou and Daley J Birkett (eds), *Cooperation and the International Criminal Court* (Brill 2016) 80, 105.

not responsible for the enforcement of its decision; and (ii) the Court can refer the matter to the ASP which is responsible for the enforcement of the Court's decisions. Article 87(7) of the Rome Statute explicitly endows the Court with the power to make requests for cooperation to the ASP, 'where a State Party fails to comply with a request to cooperate by the Court contrary to the provisions of this Statute'.[74] Despite this nominal power, the failure of the ASP to enforce cooperation obligations of ICC states parties shows the weakness of the ICC's governance model. The most striking example is the non-execution of the 2009 and 2010 arrest warrants against the then-President of Sudan, Omar Al-Bashir. The referrals of non-cooperation made by the Court to the ASP were not met with 'any meaningful action on the part of the Assembly'.[75] This even led the Court to decide not to refer the matter to the ASP when it found that South Africa had failed to fulfil its obligation of cooperation with the Court by not arresting Al-Bashir when he was on its territory.[76] The Chamber considered this to be unnecessary and not warranted.[77] The arguments put forward by the Court are telling:

> [T]he Chamber observes that States Parties have been referred to both the Assembly of States Parties and the United Nations Security Council in six instances in relation to failures to arrest and surrender Omar Al-Bashir. However, the past 24 meetings of the Security Council of the United Nations following the adoption of Resolution 1593 (2005), including meetings held on the occasion of the biannual reports made by the Prosecutor to the Security Council of the United Nationals, have not resulted in measures against States Parties.[78]

In other words, referring the issue to the ASP and the UNSC led nowhere. As Sergey Vasiliev bluntly observed: 'This is the judges' way of saying that the ASP … ha[s] proven to be of no assistance in enforcing co-operation'.[79] This is highly problematic. The Rome Statute implies that the Court cannot act alone in enforcing cooperation. The Statute distinguishes between the responsibilities of the Court and those of the ASP, with the responsibility to ensure state cooperation with the Court being entrusted to the Assembly.[80]

[74] ICC Statute Art 87(7).

[75] eg Decision on the non-compliance by the Republic of Djibouti with the request to arrest and surrender Omar Al-Bashir to the Court and referring the matter to the United Nations Security Council and the Assembly of the State Parties to the Rome Statute, *Prosecutor* v *Al Bashir*, *Situation in Darfur*, ICC-02/05-01/09-266, PTC II, ICC, 11 July 2016; Decision on the non-compliance by the Republic of Uganda with the request to arrest and surrender Omar Al-Bashir to the Court and referring the matter to the United Nations Security Council and the Assembly of States Parties to the Rome Statute, *Prosecutor* v *Al Bashir*, *Situation in Darfur*, ICC-02/05-01/09-267, PTC II, ICC, 11 July 2016); Decision under article 87(7) of the Rome Statute on the non-compliance by South Africa with the request by the Court for the arrest and surrender of Omar Al-Bashir, *Prosecutor* v *Al Bashir*, *Situation in Darfur*, ICC-02/05-01/09-302, PTC II, ICC, 6 July 2017. ICC website, *Al Bashir Case* <www.icc-cpi.int/darfur/albashir>; Vasiliev (n 3) 545.

[76] Decision under Art 87(7) of the Rome Statute on the non-compliance by South Africa (n 75) para 123.

[77] ibid paras 135–38; Göran Sluiter, 'Enforcing Cooperation: Did the Drafters Approach It the Wrong Way?' (2018) 16 Journal of International Criminal Justice 383, 392; Vasiliev (n 3) 545.

[78] Decision under Art 87(7) of the Rome Statute on the non-compliance by South Africa (n 75) para 138.

[79] Vasiliev (n 3) 546.

[80] ICC Statute Art 87(7); Sluiter (n 77) 391.

Article 87(7) of the Rome Statute also provides the Court with the ability to refer an issue of non-cooperation to the UNSC, when the Council has referred the situation to the Court.

15.3.2.2 Enforcement of ICC decisions as a distinct function of the UNSC

Even though the Rome Statute system is independent from the UN system, the UNSC was vested with the power to enforce ICC decisions. Contained in part 9 of the Rome Statute, entitled 'International cooperation and judicial assistance', Article 87(7) provides the Court with the power to refer matters of non-cooperation to the UNSC in situations it has referred to it:

> Where a State Party fails to comply with a request to cooperate by the Court contrary to the provisions of this Statute, thereby preventing the Court from exercising its functions and powers under this Statute, the Court may make a finding to that effect and refer the matter to the Assembly of States Parties or, where the Security Council referred the matter to the Court, to the Security Council.

Considering that the UNSC is the organ primarily responsible for 'the maintenance of international peace and security',[81] it is understandable that if non-enforcement of an ICC decision is found to threaten international peace and security, the UNSC would be competent to adopt the appropriate measures. That being said, it has been argued that a number of ICC decisions referring non-cooperation matters to the UNSC have remained a dead letter.[82] To date, the Court has referred issues of non-cooperation several times to the UNSC.[83] One example is UNSC Resolution 1593, in which the Council requested that the Sudanese Government and all other parties involved in the conflict 'cooperate fully with the Court'.[84] However, when addressing the UNSC in 2016, Prosecutor Fatou Bensouda stated the following regarding the situation in Darfur: 'A further aggravating factor is this Council's inaction. It is no surprise then that victims and witnesses of the Office are slowly but surely losing faith in the process

[81] UN Charter Art 24(1).

[82] Sluiter (n 77) 388, citing as examples the Libya and Sudan situations.

[83] ASP website, 'Non-cooperation', <https://asp.icc-cpi.int/non-cooperation>; Decision informing the UNSC about the lack of cooperation by the Republic of Sudan, *Prosecutor* v *Ahmed Harun and Ali Kushayb, Situation in Darfur*, ICC-02/05-01/07-57, PTC I, ICC, 25 May 2010; Decision pursuant to article 87(7) of the Rome Statute on the failure by the Republic of Malawi to comply with the cooperation requests issued by the Court with respect to the arrest and surrender of Omar Hassan Ahmad Al Bashir, *Prosecutor* v *Al Bashir, Situation in Darfur*, ICC-02/05-01/09-139-Corr, PTC I, ICC, 13 December 2011; Decision on the non-compliance by the Republic of Djibouti with the request to arrest and surrender Omar Al-Bashir to the Court and referring the matter to the United Nations Security Council and the Assembly of the State Parties to the Rome Statute, *Prosecutor* v *Al Bashir, Situation in Darfur*, ICC-02/05-01/09-266, PTC II, ICC, 11 July 2016; Decision on the non-compliance by the Republic of Uganda with the request to arrest and surrender Omar Al-Bashir to the Court and referring the matter to the United Nations Security Council and the Assembly of State Parties to the Rome Statute, *Prosecutor* v *Al Bashir, Situation in Darfur*, ICC-02/05-01/09-267, PTC II, ICC 11 July 2016; Decision on the non-compliance by Libya with requests for cooperation by the Court and referring the matter to the United Nations Security Council, *Prosecutor* v *Saif Al-Islam Gaddafi, Situation in Libya*, ICC-01/11-01/11-577, PTC I, ICC, 10 December 2014.

[84] SC Res 1593, 5158th meeting, UN Doc S/RES/1593 (31 March 2005).

of international criminal justice in Darfur.'[85] Another example is the situation in Libya, referred to the ICC Prosecutor in 2011.[86] In 2014, the ICC decided to refer the matter to the UNSC following its decision on the non-compliance by Libya with requests for cooperation.[87] However, in 2020 the Prosecutor was still reminding the UNSC that it has a 'special responsibility to support and urge cooperation with the Court' with regard to the situation in Libya.[88]

The UNSC's lack of effective action threatens the process of international criminal justice. What is more, the UNSC's lack of action is rooted in political reasons. Reports of the Bureau of the ICC on non-cooperation indicate that the UNSC was unwilling to use its powers under Chapter VII of the UN Charter despite the request from the ICC Prosecutor to address the issue of non-compliance with the Court's decisions.[89] In its 2020 Report, the Bureau mentioned again that the ICC Prosecutor had called for 'greater support' from the UNSC.[90]

One way for the UNSC to become more effective in enforcing ICC decisions would be to rule out the use of the veto when it comes to ICC cooperation matters. But that may be too idealistic as all or some permanent members of the UNSC would be against this measure. The ASP, along with the ICC Prosecutor, could nonetheless address the matter with the UNSC. As such, the mandate of the third ICC Prosecutor, Karim Khan, will be determinative of the path the ICC will be taking in attempting to remedy this situation.

15.3.3 Role of *injugovins* and the enforcement of ECtHR judicial decisions

Under Article 46(1) of the European Convention on Human Rights (ECHR), member states 'undertake to abide by the final judgment of the Court in any case to which they are parties'. In addition, the ECHR envisages that the execution of judgments is supervised by the Council of Europe's Committee of Ministers.[91] This Committee is assisted by the Department for the Execution of Judgments of the European Court of Human Rights, whose mandate is to 'provide support to the member states in their efforts to

[85] 'Statement of ICC Prosecutor, Fatou Bensouda, before the United Nations Security Council on the Situation in Darfur, pursuant to UNSCR 1593 (2005)' (13 December 2016) <www.icc-cpi.int/Pages/item.aspx?name=161213-otp-stat-unsc-darfur>.

[86] SC Res 1970, 6491th meeting, UN Doc S/RES/1970 (26 February 2011).

[87] Decision on the Non-Compliance by Libya with Requests for Cooperation by the Court and Referring the Matter to the United Nations Security Council, *Prosecutor v Saif Al-Islam Gaddafi, Situation in Libya*, ICC-01/11-01/11, PTC I, ICC, 10 December 2014).

[88] Statement to the United Nations Security Council on the Situation in Libya, pursuant to UNSCR 1970 (2011), 5 May 2020 <www.icc-cpi.int/Pages/item.aspx?name=200505-statement-prosecutor-unsc-libya>.

[89] Sluiter and Talontsi (n 73) 105; ASP, Report of the Bureau on Non-Cooperation (ICC-ASP/12/34, 7 November 2013) para 14; ASP, Report of the Bureau on Non-Cooperation (ICC-ASP/13/40, 5 December 2014) paras 25–30.

[90] Report of the Bureau on Non-Cooperation, ICC-ASP/19/23, 10 December 2020, para 29.

[91] ECHR Art 46(2). Hanneke Palm and Roeland Böcker, 'Implementation of Judgments of the European Court of Human Rights', in this volume.

achieve full, effective and prompt execution of the judgments of the European Court of Human Rights, in the cases to which they are parties'.[92]

Clare Ovey, the Head of the Department of the Execution of Judgments at the Council of Europe, considers that having vested the Committee with the power of enforcement is a 'massive strength' of the system.[93] According to her, entrusting a political body with the execution of judgments allows putting political pressure on states while providing some needed flexibility.[94] In fact, the Committee of Ministers can go as far as triggering an infringement procedure, therefore referring the matter of non-implementation of judgments to the Court.[95] What also differs from other systems is that enforcement forms part of the right to a fair trial.[96] The Committee of Ministers adopted a series of recommendations on enforcement and highlighted that 'respect for the judgments of the ECtHR is a condition *sine qua non* for membership of the Organization'.[97] In 2008, the European Commission for the Efficiency of Justice (a Council of Europe organ) even established a group of experts on the enforcement of judicial decisions,[98] which resulted in the adoption of the 'Guidelines for a better implementation of the existing Council of Europe recommendation on enforcement'.[99] In 2010, the Council of Europe then adopted the Interlaken Declaration which 'stresses that full, effective and rapid execution of the final judgments of the Court is indispensable'.[100]

Therefore, in the ECHR system the enforcement of its Court's decisions is explicitly made a function of its *injugovin*. The Committee of Ministers stressed the importance of 'strengthening exchanges of information with other bodies', such as the Parliamentary Assembly and the Commissioner for Human Rights in order to speed up the execution of judgments.[101] This does not mean, however, that enforcement of

[92] Council of Europe, 'Mandate of the Department for the Execution of Judgments of the European Court of Human Rights', <www.coe.int/en/web/execution/presentation-of-the-department>.

[93] Jan Lhotský, 'How Are Judgments of the Strasbourg Court implemented? Interview on the Work of the Department for the Execution of Judgments', Czech Centre for Human Rights and Democracy (Interview, 21 December 2021) <www.humanrightscentre.org/how-are-judgments-strasbourg-court-implemented-interview-work-department-execution-judgments>.

[94] ibid.

[95] ECHR Art 46(4); Rules of the Committee of Ministers for the Supervision of the Execution of Judgments and of the Terms of Friendly Settlements, adopted on 10 May 2006, amended in January 2017, Rule 11.1.

[96] *Hornsby* v *Greece*, App no 18357/91, ECtHR, 19 March 1997, in which the Court found that the right of access to a court 'would be illusory if a Contracting State's domestic legal system allowed a final, binding judicial decision to remain inoperative to the detriment of one party. It would be inconceivable that Article 6§1 should describe in detail procedural guarantees afforded to litigants ... without protecting the implementation of judicial decisions. ... Execution of a judgment given by any court must therefore be regarded as an integral part of the 'trial' for the purposes of Article 6'.

[97] Committee of Ministers, 'Supervision of the Execution of Judgments of the European Court of Human Rights, First Annual Report, 2007' (Council of Europe Strasbourg 2008) 9 <https://rm.coe.int/090000168051e1a2>.

[98] Commission Européenne pour l'Efficacité de la Justice (CEPEJ), 'Mandat Spécifique du Groupe de Travail sur l'Exécution des Décisions de Justice' (CEPEJ 2008, 10–11 December 2008).

[99] Council of Europe, 'European Commission on the Efficiency of Justice (CEPEJ) Guidelines for a Better Implementation of the Existing Council of Europe's Recommendation on Enforcement' (Strasbourg, 17 December 2009) CEPEJ (2009) 11REV2.

[100] Interlaken Declaration, High Level Conference on the Future of the European Court of Human Rights, 19 February 2010.

[101] *Supervision of the Execution of Judgments of the European Court of Human Rights* (n 97).

decisions will be automatic. Russia, Ukraine, Hungary, Romania, Turkey, Azerbaijan, and Italy are examples of member states which have shown the 'highest rate of unimplemented judgments'.[102]

15.4 Concluding Remarks

The survey of international adjudicatory regimes in this chapter has shown that the enforcement of international judicial decisions constitutes an essential and distinct function of *injugovins*. The latter are the arms and legs of international courts; international courts cannot function without those bodies.[103] International courts' authority is jeopardized by the unwillingness or inability of their *injugovins* to support them when it comes to the enforcement of judgments. This, in turn, threatens not only the enforcement but also the reputation of said decisions and the courts themselves. Some scholars argue that it 'increases and confirms the impression that there is no harm in refusing cooperation with the Court'.[104]

Injugovins should adopt a firm position reaffirming the obligation of states to ensure the enforcement of judicial decisions and take effective measures following courts' findings on non-enforcement, 'without room for discretion'.[105] They should act as a collective body and in the interest of the respective court, the same way the Committee of Ministers is acting for the benefit of the ECHR system. This is crucial to the authority and effectiveness of international courts.

102 Lhotský (n 93).
103 eg Blokker (n 8) 83, who argues that '[i]nternational courts and tribunals can only perform their dispute settlement function if they are well "governed"'.
104 Sluiter and Talontsi (n 73) 108.
105 ibid.

16
Implementation of Judgments of the European Court of Human Rights
The Supervisory Role of the Committee of Ministers

*Hanneke Palm and Roeland Böcker**

16.1 Introduction

The European Convention on Human Rights (ECHR, or Convention), widely regarded as the most effective human rights system in the world,[1] tasks the Committee of Ministers of the Council of Europe (CM) with the supervision of the member states' compliance with the judgments of the European Court of Human Rights (ECtHR, or Court). Ensuring an effective implementation of its judgments constitutes a key function the CM exercises as part of the governance of the Court. Article 46 of the ECHR deals with binding force and the execution of judgments. The High Contracting Parties to the Convention have a legally binding obligation to abide by the Court's judgments in any case to which they are parties. They have a certain discretion in deciding which measures to take for the full execution of judgments. Recent developments in the use of the so-called infringement proceedings under Article 46(4) of the ECHR have clarified how the competences of the CM and the Court relate to each other. This concerns in particular the question of who is competent to decide whether a state[2] has taken sufficient measures to execute a judgment.

In Section 16.2 of this chapter, we describe the working methods of the CM when supervising the execution of the Court's judgments. In Section 16.3, we pay attention to the interaction between the CM and the Court on the implementation of judgments. Section 16.4 is concerned with challenges to the supervision process. Section 16.5 deals with the reference to domestic procedures, occasionally used as an excuse for non-execution of judgments, and discusses some examples of relevant cases. In Section 16.6, we discuss the infringement proceedings under Article 46(4) of the ECHR, resulting in judgments in the cases of *Ilgar Mammadov* v *Azerbaijan*[3]

* The authors wrote this chapter in their personal capacity. The current text reflects developments up to August 2024.

[1] Advisory Council of International Affairs (AIV), 'Human Rights: A Core Interest in the Current Geopolitical Context' (Advisory Report 122, 28 June 2022) 16.

[2] While the foreseen accession of the European Union to the Convention will render the term 'state' obsolete in this context, the term will be used in this chapter alongside the term 'party', as is currently the case in the Convention itself.

[3] *Ilgar Mammadov* v *Azerbaijan (Article 46 para 4)*, App no 15172/13, GC, ECtHR, 29 May 2019 ('*Mammadov* Art 46(4) judgment').

Hanneke Palm and Roeland Böcker, *Implementation of Judgments of the European Court of Human Rights* In: *Governance of International Courts and Tribunals*. Edited by: Sergey Vasiliev and Niels Blokker, Oxford University Press.
 DOI: 10.1093/oso/9780198922131.003.0016

and *Kavala* v *Türkiye*.[4] The CM decisions leading up to these procedures and the respective judgments of the Court provide insight into the separate, but complementary roles of the Court and the CM within the Convention system. Finally, in Section 16.7, we conclude with some remarks on how to preserve the balance in the relationship between the Court and the CM and how to ensure complementarity between these bodies.

16.2 Working Methods of the CM When Supervising the Execution of the Court's Judgments

Final judgments of the Court are transmitted to the CM on the basis of Article 46(2) of the ECHR with a view to the supervision of their execution.[5] The Rules of the Committee of Ministers for the supervision of the execution of judgments and of the terms of friendly settlements ('Rules'),[6] adopted by the CM on 10 May 2006 and updated several times since, govern the functioning of the CM with regard to its supervisory task. The current working methods of the CM are mainly shaped by the Interlaken Declaration and Action Plan adopted in 2010[7] and by the entry into force of Protocol 14 to the ECHR in the same year.[8] In the following years, further political declarations were adopted to improve the execution of judgments.[9]

On average, the CM meets once a year at the ministerial level and three times each month at the Ministers' Deputies level, ie at the level of Permanent Representatives to the Council of Europe. Every three months, a Deputies' meeting, under the heading CM-DH, is specifically devoted to the supervision of the execution of judgments, while leaving open the possibility to discuss execution at every other CM meeting, including the yearly ministerial meeting, if the circumstances so require. In cases in which the Court has found a violation of the Convention by a state party, the latter must submit an action plan within six months from the date on which the judgment has become final under Article 44 of the ECHR. In its action plan, the state must clarify which individual and general measures it will take to fully execute the Court's judgment, including payment of any just satisfaction awarded by the Court in its

[4] *Kavala* v *Türkiye (Article 46 para 4)*, Judgment, App no 28749/18, ECtHR, 11 July 2022 ('*Kavala* Art 46(4) judgment').

[5] For a summary of relevant international legislation underpinning the CM's practice of supervision as well as a brief description of practice in Dutch cases, see Roeland Böcker, 'Taru's tiental, of het lot van EHRM-uitspraken' in Thom Dieben, JIMG Jahae, and Petra van Kampen (eds), *Advocaat(-generaal): Liber amicorum Taru Spronken* (Wolters Kluwer 2015).

[6] CoE Committee of Ministers, Rules of the Committee of Ministers for the supervision of the execution of judgments and of the terms of friendly settlements, CM/Del/Dec(2006)964/4.4-app4consolidated (adopted 10 May 2006 and last amended on 6 July 2022).

[7] Interlaken Declaration—High Level Conference on the Future of the European Court of Human Rights (adopted on 19 February 2010) <https://prd-echr.coe.int/documents/d/echr/2010_Interlaken_FinalDeclaration_ENG>.

[8] Since then, the CM has also been tasked with the supervision of the execution of the terms of friendly settlements on the basis of ECHR Art 39(4). In the context of this chapter, we will leave this task aside.

[9] CoE Committee of Ministers, Brussels Declaration (adopted 27 March 2015) <www.echr.coe.int/documents/d/echr/brussels_declaration_eng> and CoE Committee of Ministers, Decision 'Securing the long-term effectiveness of the system of the European Convention on Human Rights' CM/Del/Dec(2021)131/3 (adopted 21 May 2021, Hamburg).

judgment. When the state has taken all measures required to execute the judgment, it must inform the CM in an action report.

In accordance with general principles of international law,[10] the state's obligation under Article 46(1) of the ECHR to ensure the full execution of a final judgment with regard to individual measures is to end the violation(s) established and achieve *restitutio in integrum*: to bring the injured party, as far as possible, in the same situation as he or she enjoyed prior to the violation of the Convention. This may be achieved, for example, by reopening domestic proceedings found to be in violation of the right to a fair trial.[11]

In addition, general measures are required to stop continuing violations or prevent similar violations from occurring, for example by abolishing discriminatory legislation or by using alternatives to detention in case of overcrowding in prisons. This ensures the subsidiarity of the Convention's supervisory mechanism: human rights protection should first and foremost be secured at the national level. Taking general measures will swiftly and comprehensively prevent similar complaints from reaching the Court, thus preventing unnecessary workload. The CM takes into account the discretion of states to choose the means necessary to comply with the Court's judgments.[12]

A twin-track procedure is applicable to the supervision of judgments: cases are dealt with under a standard supervision procedure, unless their specific nature necessitates consideration under an enhanced supervision procedure. Standard supervision is based on the principle that the state is itself responsible for ensuring effective implementation of judgments. The involvement of the CM in the standard supervision procedure is limited to ensuring that action plans and reports are presented and that any measures are taken appropriately and in a timely fashion. Enhanced supervision is applicable to judgments requiring urgent individual measures, pilot judgments, and judgments revealing important, structural, and/or complex problems as identified by the Court and/or by the CM, as well as inter-state cases.[13] Enhanced supervision implies a much more rigorous scrutiny by the CM of measures taken by the state. Therefore, cases are tabled for examination at the CM-DH meetings. This examination may lead to the adoption of decisions or interim resolutions in order to encourage the state concerned to speed up the implementation, or to give directions on what is expected of the state for full implementation of a judgment. The enhanced

[10] Roeland Böcker and Herman Von Hebel, 'The Enforcement of Strasbourg and Geneva Decisions: The International Law Context' in Tom Barkhuysen, Michiel van Emmerik, and Piet Hein van Kempen (eds), *The Execution of Strasbourg and Geneva Human Rights Decisions in the National Legal Order* (Martinus Nijhoff 1999) 235–41.

[11] CoE Committee of Ministers, Recommendation No R(2000)2 of the Committee of Ministers to member states on the re-examination or reopening of certain cases at domestic level following judgments of the European Court of Human Rights, adopted 19 January 2000, 694th meeting.

[12] CoE Committee of Ministers, 'Rules of the Committee of Ministers for the supervision of the execution of judgments and of the terms of friendly settlements' (adopted on 10 May 2006 and amended on 18 January 2017) Rule 6(2)b.

[13] CoE Committee of Ministers, Document CM/Inf/DH(2010)37 (adopted on 6 September 2010) para 8. See also iGuide on the procedures and working methods of the Committee of Ministers, Committee of Ministers at Deputy level, Article 19 Human Rights (DH) Meetings under 'standard and enhanced procedure'.

procedure is not punitive but is intended to assist national authorities in the execution process and allows the CM to follow the progress more closely.[14]

In supervising the execution of judgments, the CM relies to a large extent on the assistance of the Department for the Execution of Judgments, which is part of the Directorate General of Human Rights and Rule of Law of the Council of Europe. The Department also supports member states in achieving full, effective, and rapid execution of judgments of the Court in cases to which they are party.[15] It closely follows the progress in cases under standard supervision and may propose to the CM to put a case under enhanced supervision if the pace of the progress so requires.

One important aspect of the supervisory process, particularly with a view to its transparency, is the involvement of non-governmental organizations.[16] On the basis of Rule 9, civil society organizations (CSOs), national human rights institutions (NHRIs), and the Council of Europe Commissioner for Human Rights may send communications to the CM on the execution of judgments under Article 46(2) of the ECHR. In 2023, a record number of 239 such communications were submitted by CSOs and NHRIs concerning thirty-three states.[17] Each year the CM publishes an annual report on its supervisory activities, which it transmits to the Court, as well as to the Secretary-General, the Parliamentary Assembly, and the Commissioner for Human Rights.[18] This annual report contributes to accountability and transparency of the work of the CM.[19]

16.3 Interaction between the CM and the Court on the Implementation of Judgments

Given the large number of pending cases requiring supervision, rising to the extremely high number of 11,000 cases in 2012, the CM decided upon a priority policy, which was developed in dialogue with the Court.[20] In its Resolution (2004)3 on judgments revealing an underlying systemic problem, the CM requested the Court to identify such problems in its judgments.[21] The Court responded to this request in its Grand Chamber judgment of 22 June 2004 in *Broniowski* v *Poland*,[22] in which it introduced

[14] CoE Committee of Ministers, 'Supervision of the Execution of the Judgments and Decisions of the European Court of Human Rights: Implementation of the Interlaken Action Plan—Outstanding Issues Concerning the Practical Modalities of Implementation of the New Twin Track Supervision System', CM/Inf/DH(2010)45 (adopted on 7 December 2010) para 17.

[15] 'Presentation of the Department' <www.coe.int/en/web/execution/presentation-of-the-department>.

[16] Copenhagen Declaration (adopted on 12 April 2018) <https://rm.coe.int/copenhagen-declaration/16807b915c>.

[17] CoE Committee of Ministers, 'Supervision of the Execution of Judgments and Decisions of the European Court of Human Rights: 17th Annual Report of the Committee of Ministers 2023' 78.

[18] 'Rules of the Committee of Ministers for the Supervision of the Execution of Judgments and of the Terms of Friendly Settlements' (n 12) Rule 5.

[19] 'Annual Reports of the Committee of Ministers: Supervision of the Execution of Judgments and Decisions of the European Court of Human Rights' <www.coe.int/en/web/execution/annual-reports>.

[20] Rules of the Committee of Ministers for the supervision of the execution of judgments and of the terms of friendly settlements (n 12) Rule 4.

[21] CoE Committee of Ministers, Resolution (2004)3 of the Committee of Ministers on judgments revealing an underlying systemic problem (adopted 12 May 2004).

[22] *Broniowski* v *Poland*, Judgment, App no 31443/96, GC, ECtHR, 22 June 2004.

the pilot-judgment procedure for major structural problems. With this procedure, the Court means to facilitate the execution process by identifying the structural problems underlying recurrent cases and by imposing an obligation on states to effectively address those problems.[23] The Court not only decides whether the Convention has been violated, but also provides clear indications as to the type of measures the state needs to take in order to remedy the situation.[24] This greatly helps the CM in its supervisory task.

In other cases, as well, the Court regularly provides indications under Article 46 or 41 of the ECHR on the nature of the required measures. A telling example is the (original) judgment in the case of *Kavala* v *Turkey*,[25] in which the Court ordered the applicant's immediate release, based on the finding of violations of Article 5 of the ECHR, read separately and in conjunction with Article 18. While these indications in the Court's judgment do not contradict the state's prerogative to choose the appropriate means to execute a judgment and are primarily aimed at assisting it in doing so, it also serves to signal to the CM that it needs to give priority to the case given the urgent individual measures required.

Article 46(3) of the ECHR allows for a request by the CM to the Court for interpretation of a judgment, in case supervision is hindered by differing views on the meaning of the judgment. This provision has not been applied yet. Article 46(4) and (5) of the ECHR provide for a formal procedure for interaction between the CM and the Court on the execution of specific judgments, the infringement proceedings.[26] More informal ways of interaction between the CM and the Court also exist. The President of the Court visits the CM twice a year for an exchange of views on issues not related to specific cases. The Department for the Execution of Judgments also has regular meetings with the Court's Registry.[27]

16.4 Challenges to the Supervision Process

In 2023, the total number of judgments pending execution was just over 6,300, including cases pending against the Russian Federation. While this is a significant decrease since 2012, the pace of closure cannot keep up with the number of new judgments sent to the CM by the Court.[28] In the CM's annual report of 2023, the Director General of Human Rights and Rule of Law of the Council of Europe pointed out the continuing high number of new Court judgments against member states transmitted

[23] ECtHR, 'Factsheet—Pilot Judgments', November 2023 <www.echr.coe.int/documents/d/echr/fs_pilot_judgments_eng>.

[24] In February 2011 the European Court codified the existing pilot-judgment procedure in its Rules of Court: ECtHR, Rules of Court (last edition entered into force on 22 January 2024) <www.echr.coe.int/Documents/Rules_Court_ENG.pdf>.

[25] *Kavala* v *Turkey*, Judgment, App no 28749/18, ECtHR, 10 December 2019. The Kavala case will be discussed in greater detail under the infringement proceedings.

[26] Section 16.6.

[27] eg Committee of Ministers' reply to Parliamentary Assembly Recommendation 2110 (2017), Doc. 14502, 16 February 2018 <www.assembly.coe.int/nw/xml/XRef/Xref-XML2HTML-en.asp?fileid=24511&lang=en>.

[28] 17th Annual Report of the Committee of Ministers 2023 (n 17) 12.

to the CM after a 6 per cent increase in 2022 and a 40 per cent increase in 2021.[29] The number of leading cases under supervision—cases in which the Court has identified a systemic/structural issue which has not already been identified in another judgment—has also risen over the past years,[30] while 47 per cent of leading cases have been pending for at least ten years.[31] If leading cases are not executed speedily, new cases concerning the same issues will keep coming to the Court.

There is a clear dynamic between the output of the Court and the workload of the CM and the Department for the Execution of Judgments. When the Court changes its working methods, or its case law for that matter, this will have implications for how the CM and the Department should organize their work.

A case in point is the effect of Article 28(1)(b) of the ECHR, which allows the Court to render judgment on the merits by a committee of three judges, if the issues raised by the case are already the subject of well-established case law of the Court (the so-called WECL-cases). For the Court, this provides a means to deal with applications more rapidly. However, from an execution perspective, a WECL-case cannot as easily be dealt with by referring to previous case law. For each WECL-case, it must still be determined whether just satisfaction has been paid and whether the required individual measures have been taken.[32]

Whereas the supervisory role of the CM is crucial to ensure the execution of judgments, thus contributing to the credibility and authority of the Court, resources of the two institutions must be in balance in order to avoid bottlenecks. A High-Level Reflection Group, set up at the initiative of the ministerial session of the CM in Turin in May 2022, identified the challenge of the increase in judgments delivered by the Court and the need to enhance the capacities of the Department for the Execution of Judgments, if this trend continues.[33]

The High-Level Reflection Group noted that the long duration of the execution process reveals obstacles that either have to do with the state's ability to choose, adopt, and implement effectively the appropriate measures, or with a lack of co-ordination among the national authorities, or, finally, with political difficulties, in particular when the judgment at stake touches upon financial, societal, or security issues.[34] This led the High-Level Reflection Group to recommend a more political approach to the supervision by the CM, beyond the CM-DH, in particular with regard to cases where the political will to implement the judgment is lacking.[35] It recommends,

[29] ibid 13.

[30] On 1 January 2022, 1,300 leading judgments were pending implementation. In the 2023 Annual Report the statistics are for the first time separated into cases related to member states and the Russian Federation: 1,088 leading cases regarding member states were pending implementation and 238 leading cases regarding the Russian Federation. CoE Committee of Ministers, 'Supervision of the Execution of Judgments and Decisions of the European Court of Human Rights: 17th Annual Report of the Committee of Ministers 2023'.

[31] Letter from European Implementation Network to Secretary-General of the Council of Europe and the Committee of Ministers, 16 May 2022 <www.einnetwork.org/blog-five/2022/5/16/open-letter-by-ein-calling-for-a-public-strategy-to-address-the-systemic-problem-of-non-implementation-of-ecthr-judgments>.

[32] 17th Annual Report of the Committee of Ministers (n 17) 139 (Appendix F: Additional Statistics).

[33] CoE, 'Report of the High-Level Reflection Group to the Council of Europe', October 2022 <https://rm.coe.int/report-of-the-high-level-reflection-group-of-the-council-of-europe-/1680a85cf1> para 19.

[34] ibid.

[35] ibid para 22.

among other things, to consider the issuing of graduated sanctions in cases of persistent non-compliance with a judgment by a state.[36] The Dutch Advisory Council on International Affairs equally recommends to strengthen the role of the CM with regard to the enforcement of judgments of the Court in general, including through the use of infringement proceedings.[37]

Finally, when discussing challenges to the supervision process, the situation of the Russian Federation cannot be ignored. By virtue of Article 58 of the ECHR, Russia ceased to be a party to the Convention on 16 September 2022, following its expulsion from the Council of Europe six months earlier. Article 58(2) stipulates that this does not release the state from its obligations under the Convention in respect of any act which, being capable of constituting a violation of such obligations, was performed by it before the date at which the Convention ceased to apply to that state. This means that the enormous caseload of Russian cases, including those that emanate from the first semester after the brutal and illegal invasion of Ukraine, remains in the Court's docket and, when concluded by judgments finding one or more violations, in the hands of the CM. This constitutes a challenge for both the Court and the CM, which are obligated to pursue their procedures in the absence of a respondent state, since Russia has refused to communicate on pending applications and even has enacted legislation aimed at obstructing the execution of the Court's judgments. At the time this chapter was being finalized, the Council of Europe Committee of Legal Advisers on Public International Law (CAHDI), upon request by the Committee of Ministers,[38] was examining the challenges in securing the payment of just satisfaction by the Russian Federation focusing on issues such as state immunity from jurisdiction and execution and state-owned property. CAHDI assessed the scope of state immunity, determining whether it encompasses legislative or executive actions, or is confined solely to judicial actions. It also explored ways to overcome immunity, notably the exception for cases where a state fails to execute an international court decision to which it has voluntarily submitted, and when the collective enforcement mechanisms established by the Convention prove ineffective. Additionally, it examined the possible justification for countermeasures.

16.5 Reference to Domestic Proceedings as an Excuse for Non-Execution

Challenges to the role and mandate of the CM in the supervision process arise particularly where the CM calls upon a state to implement certain measures, while the latter is of the view that the matter is under consideration by domestic courts and cannot be interfered with. This is illustrated by the supervision of the *Bekir Ousta and*

36 ibid para 27, l.

37 AIV (n 1) recommendation 7. In more general terms, the Council recommends cherishing the Council of Europe ('koester de Raad van Europa').

38 Decision CM/Del/Dec(2024)1488/10.5, adopted on 7–8 February 2024, at the 1488th meeting of the Ministers' Deputies.

others group of cases against Greece, which also includes *Emin and others* v *Greece* and *Tourkiki Enosi Xanthis and others* v *Greece*.[39]

This group of cases concerns violations of the right to freedom of association set out in Article 11 of the ECHR.[40] Some cases concern a refusal to register, or the dissolution of, associations which Greece believes aim at the promotion of the idea that an ethnic Turkish minority exists in Greece. This is not in conformity with the 1923 Treaty of Lausanne which merely recognizes religious minorities, not national or ethnic minorities.[41] The interference with the right to freedom of association was therefore justified, according to Greece.

The Court considered in its judgment in 2007 that, even assuming that the true aim of the association was to promote the idea that an ethnic minority existed in Greece, this could not in itself be considered a threat to a democratic society.[42] The refusal of registration and the dissolution of the associations were therefore disproportionate, according to the Court. On the dissolution, the Court also stressed the radical nature of the measure.

Given these findings, the way to achieve *restitutio in integrum* for the applicants would be to have their registration re-examined at the domestic level, taking into account the Court's judgment. While Greece amended its legislation in 2017 to allow for reopening of the relevant procedures, the violations suffered by the associations have not yet been remedied.[43] The Court of Cassation rejected the appeal of *Tourkiki Enosi Xanthis* concerning dissolution in June 2021 and the appeal in the *Bekir Ousta and others* and *Emin and others* cases concerning refusal of registration in August 2022.[44]

In order to examine whether adequate redress has been provided to applicants, the CM must take into account any reopened, continuing, or new procedures at the domestic level that affect the situation of applicants. However, these proceedings may lead to new cases before the Court. While the CM's role is to supervise whether measures taken—such as reopening a domestic procedure—adequately remedy the established violation, the Court may have to consider a new issue that has not yet been decided.[45] The Department for the Execution of Judgments has published an information document on the supervisory role of the CM under Article 46 of the ECHR in respect of developments subsequent to a judgment of the Court.[46] This document

[39] *Bekir Ousta and others* v *Greece*, Judgment, App no 35151/05, ECtHR, 11 October 2007; *Emin and others* v *Greece*, Judgment, App no 34144/05, 27 March 2008; *Tourkiki Enosi Xanthis and others* v *Greece*, Judgment, App no 26698/05, 27 March 2008.

[40] This chapter leaves aside the finding of a violation of Art 6(1) ECHR on account of the excessive length of civil proceedings to dissolve the association *Tourkiki Enosi Xanthis and others*.

[41] *Bekir Ousta and others* v *Greece* (n 39) para 49.

[42] ibid para 44.

[43] Notes of the Secretariat regarding 1436th CM-DH meeting, 8–10 June 2022 <https://hudoc.exec.coe.int/eng?i=004-15567>.

[44] Decisions H46-15 *Bekir-Ousta and others group* v *Greece* (App No 35151/05) CM/Del/Dec(2022)1451/H46-15 (1451st meeting CM-DH, 6–8 December 2022) paras 5–8.

[45] *Moreira Ferreira v Portugal (No 2)*, Judgment, App no 19867/12, GC, ECtHR, 11 July 2017, para 47.

[46] CoE Committee of Ministers, 'Supervisory Role of the Committee of Ministers under Article 46 of the European Convention on Human Rights in Respect of Developments Subsequent to a Judgment of the European Court of Human Rights' (Information document prepared by the Department for the Execution of Judgments of the European Court of Human Rights, 4 March 2022) CM/Inf/DH(2022)9 <https://search.coe.int/cm/Pages/result_details.aspx?ObjectID=0900001680a5b600>.

provides examples of supervision of cases entailing developments at the national level following the Court's judgment, including cases in which the CM and the Court examine the same domestic proceedings launched in response to a judgment of the Court.

In the *Bekir Ousta* group of cases, the CM assessed in detail the reopening of proceedings before the Greek court of cassation and deeply regretted that it rejected the appeal brought by the applicant association and found its dissolution to be lawful on grounds expressly impugned by the Court in its judgment.[47] Greece argued, however, that the judgment had been fully executed, since the court of cassation re-examined the status of the applicant association, and that the applicant association should have complained to the Court if it was not satisfied with the outcome of the procedure.[48] By the time this chapter was finalized, the Greek authorities had established a Committee of Experts to study the matter and advise them on the next steps to take.[49] No further measures have been taken by Greece to remedy the situation. The CM therefore remains seized of the matter.

The case of *Navalnyy and Ofitserov* v *Russia*[50] is an illustrative example of a situation in which the CM and the Court examined the same domestic procedure initiated in response to an earlier judgment of the Court. New criminal proceedings were brought against Aleksey Navalnyy after that judgment. Russia argued that a new application regarding these proceedings was pending before the Court and, thus, the CM would have no competence to supervise the matter.[51] However, the CM insisted on its competence under Article 46 of the ECHR to examine whether the violations established in the Court's earlier judgment were remedied with these new proceedings.[52] Since the Russian Federation, as demonstrated above, remains bound by its obligation to implement judgments of the Court even after it ceased to be a party to the Convention, the CM continued its supervision and strongly condemned the Russian authorities in March 2024 for the death of Aleksey Navalnyy in detention.[53]

[47] Decisions H46-8 *Bekir-Ousta and others group* v *Greece* (App No 35151/05) CM/Del/Dec(2022)1436/H46-8 (1436th meeting, 8–10 June 2022) para 5.

[48] Communication of the authorities under Rule 8.2a (21 July 2021) on the *Bekir Ousta and others* v *Greece* (App no 35151/05) for 1411th DH-meeting September 2021, DH-DD(2021)735 [French only].

[49] Decisions H46-14 *Bekir-Ousta and others group* v *Greece* (App No 35151/05) CM/Del/Dec(2024)1501/H46-14 (1501st meeting CM-DH, 11–13 June 2024) para 4.

[50] *Navalnyy and Ofitserov* v *Russia*, Judgment, App no 46632/13, ECtHR, 4 July 2016.

[51] Action report submitted by the authorities of the Russian Federation on *Navalnyy and Ofitserov* v *Russia*, 19 October 2021, DH-DD(2021)1076.

[52] Decisions H46-34 Navalnyy and Ofitserov (App No 46632/13) Navalnyye (App No 101/15) v Russian Federation, CM/Del/Dec(2021)1419/H46-34 (1419th meeting CM-DH, 30 November to 2 December 2021) paras 2–4.

[53] Decisions H46-40 *Navalnyy and Ofitserov group* v *Russian Federation* (App No 46632/13) CM/Del/Dec(2024)1492/H46-40 (1492nd meeting CM-DH, 12–14 March 2024), para 2: Interim Resolution CM/ResDH(2024)49.

16.6 Infringement Proceedings

16.6.1 General observations

With the entry into force of Protocol 14 to the ECHR in 2010, an important tool was added to the Convention's supervisory mechanism: Article 46(4) of the ECHR grants the CM the power to refer to the Court's Grand Chamber the question of whether a state has failed to fulfil its obligations to comply with a judgment.[54] Extending the competences of the CM was deemed necessary as a way to put more pressure on states and ensure the rapid and full execution of the Court's judgments.[55] The infringement proceedings were intended to be used solely in exceptional circumstances.[56] They should help avoid the ultimate step of suspension or even expulsion of a member state from the Council of Europe under Article 8 of the organization's Statute.[57] Recourse to Article 8 is regarded in the Explanatory Report to Protocol 14 as counterproductive in most cases. The Explanatory Report highlights the collective duty of the parties to the Convention to preserve the Court's authority—and thus the Convention system's credibility and effectiveness—whenever the CM considers that a state refuses, expressly or through its conduct, to comply with the Court's final judgment in a case to which it is a party.[58] As the Explanatory Report clarifies, the aim is *not* to reopen the question of violation which has already been decided by the Court in its initial judgment; nor are financial penalties at stake. To exert political pressure by bringing a case to the Grand Chamber and the subsequent judgment of the Court on compliance should do the trick of securing execution of the Court's initial judgment by the state.[59]

In order to start infringement proceedings, the CM must first serve formal notice on the state urging it to comply with the judgment. If this does not lead to the required measures, the CM will adopt a second decision to refer the case to the Court. For both decisions, the CM needs to adopt an interim resolution with a qualified majority of two-thirds of the representatives entitled to sit on the CM.[60] While the Explanatory Report states that the procedure's mere existence, and the threat of using it, should serve as an effective new incentive to execute the Court's judgments,[61] the procedure has already been used twice so far, with regard to Azerbaijan[62] and

[54] Explanatory report to Protocol 14 to the Convention for the Protection of Human Rights and Fundamental Freedoms, amending the control system of the Convention (Strasbourg, 30 May 2004) CETS no 194 <https://rm.coe.int/16800d380f>.

[55] European Ministerial Conference on Human Rights (Rome 3–4 November 2000), CM(2000)172 <https://rm.coe.int/16805e2eec> paras 19–20.

[56] Explanatory report to Protocol 14 to the ECHR (n 54) para 100.

[57] Statute of the Council of Europe (5 May 1949, London) ETS no 1.

[58] ibid para 98.

[59] ibid para 99.

[60] With forty-seven member states, this required thirty-two votes in favour of the adoption of the interim measures. Since the expulsion from the organization of the Russian Federation on 16 March 2022, thirty-one votes are required.

[61] Explanatory report to Protocol 14 to the ECHR (n 54) para 100.

[62] CoE Committee of Ministers, Interim Resolution CM/ResDH(2017)379 'Execution of the judgment of the European Court of Human Rights—Ilgar Mammadov against Azerbaijan' (1298th meeting, 25 October 2017) and Interim Resolution CM/ResDH(2017)429, 'Execution of the judgment of the European Court of Human Rights—Ilgar Mammadov against Azerbaijan' (1302nd meeting CM(DH), 5–7 December 2017).

Türkiye,[63] both cases concerning the issue of the required release of a political prisoner.

We will now discuss both these cases. Since the focus of this chapter is on the interaction between the Court and the CM, we will not go too much into the (factual) details. Our focus is on the arguments provided by the relevant state, the CM, the Court, and other actors, as well as on the dynamics between the Court and the CM in securing the credibility and effectiveness of the Convention's supervisory mechanism and their respective and sometimes overlapping mandates.

16.6.2 *Ilgar Mammadov* v *Azerbaijan*

16.6.2.1 Events leading up to the referral request

In its initial judgment in the case of *Ilgar Mammadov* v *Azerbaijan*,[64] the Court found a violation of Article 5 of the ECHR, read separately and in conjunction with Article 18 of the ECHR, in that, given the lack of reasonable suspicion, the actual purpose of the applicant's arrest and pre-trial detention was to silence or punish him for criticizing the Azerbaijani government. The applicant's detention was based on charges of 'organising public disorder' and 'violent resistance to the police'. The first charge was later replaced by the more serious charge of 'organising mass disorder'.[65] The Court found that the applicant's liberty was not restricted with the aim of bringing him before a competent legal authority on the basis of a reasonable suspicion, but to punish or silence him for criticizing the government and for his attempt to share information which he believed to be true and which the government was trying to hide.[66]

According to the CM, this judgment required from Azerbaijan to release the applicant immediately and unconditionally. The criminal proceedings against the applicant were concluded on 18 November 2016 before the supreme court of Azerbaijan, but did not take into account the conclusions that should have been drawn from the violations found by the Court, particularly with regard to Article 18 in conjunction with Article 5 of the ECHR.[67] However, Azerbaijan argued that it had implemented the necessary measures having regard to the absence in the Court's judgment of a specific instruction to secure the applicant's immediate release, and to the discretion of the state to choose the means necessary to comply with the Court's judgment.[68]

[63] CoE Committee of Ministers, Interim Resolution CM/ResDH(2021)432 'Execution of the Judgment of the European Court of Human Rights—Kavala against Turkey' (1419th meeting CM(DH), 30 November to 2 December 2021, and Interim Resolution CM/Res/DH(2022)21 'Execution of the Judgment of the European Court of Human Rights—Kavala against Turkey' (1423rd meeting, 2 February 2022). In conformity with Dutch foreign policy, the name Türkiye is used throughout this chapter, except in references to existing documents using the name Turkey, notably the Court's judgment in the first *Kavala* case.

[64] *Ilgar Mammadov* v *Azerbaijan*, Judgment, App no 15172/13, ECtHR, 22 May 2014.

[65] ibid para 91.

[66] ibid para 143.

[67] Decisions H46-3 Ilgar Mammadov v Azerbaijan (App No 15172/13) CM/Del/Dec(2016)1273/H46-3 (1273rd meeting (DH), 6–8 December 2016) para 3.

[68] 'Appendix: Views of the Republic of Azerbaijan', CM/ResDH(2017)429 (1302nd meeting CM(DH), 5–7 December 2017).

The referral to the Court by the CM-DH under Article 46(4) of the ECHR in December 2017 did not come out of the blue: since the date on which the judgment became final, the CM urged Azerbaijan repeatedly and with growing concern to release the applicant. In the first instance, this occurred in each CM-DH meeting. From 8 June 2016 onwards, the case was also placed on the agenda of each regular CM meeting.[69] During the CM meeting on 13 September 2017, the Secretary-General of the Council of Europe called upon the CM to trigger infringement proceedings if the applicant's situation remained unchanged.[70] The CM then served formal notice on Azerbaijan by an interim resolution adopted on 25 October 2017[71] and subsequently launched infringement proceedings.

In the weeks between the service of the formal notice and the actual launch of infringement proceedings by the CM, the Court delivered a second judgment regarding the applicant in which it found a violation of Article 6(1) of the Convention.[72] The Court held that the criminal proceedings against the applicant did not comply with fair trial guarantees: his conviction was based on flawed or misrepresented evidence and any favourable evidence for the applicant was put aside with inadequate reasoning or in a manifestly unreasonable manner.[73]

While the infringement proceedings were pending before the Court, the applicant was released on 13 August 2018, subject to certain conditions imposed on him by the Shaki court of appeal.[74] On 28 March 2019 the supreme court ruled on the applicant's appeal. It partially upheld the appeal and reduced the sentences imposed on the applicant. In light of the time he already served in prison, the supreme court considered that the applicant had fully served his sentence.[75] After the applicant's release, the CM decided to continue examining the case in the context of its CM-DH meetings.[76]

16.6.2.2 Submissions by the CM and by Azerbaijan

In its referral to the Court under the infringement proceedings, the CM requested the Court to conclude that Azerbaijan had not executed the Court's initial judgment in the absence of the applicant's release, and to order such release. In response, Azerbaijan argued that the CM's position would imply that the applicant had to be released notwithstanding the fact that the national court's judgment had become final and in the absence of any direct indication by the Court to that effect.[77] After the applicant's release, Azerbaijan argued that, given the aim of infringement proceedings and their exceptional nature, the matter had been resolved and there was no need for the Court to continue to examine the question.[78] According to the applicant and the CM, however, the conditions imposed on the applicant by the Shaki court of appeal still interfered with his civil and political rights, in particular his right to stand for election.[79] The CM

69 For an overview of the execution process, see <https://hudoc.exec.coe.int/eng?i=004-1866>.
70 *Mammadov* Art 46(4) judgment (n 3) para 63.
71 CM/ResDH(2017)379 (n 62).
72 *Ilgar Mammadov* v *Azerbaijan (no 2)*, Judgment, App no 919/15, ECtHR, 16 November 2017.
73 ibid para 237. See also *Mammadov* Art 46(4) judgment (n 3) para 210.
74 *Mammadov* Art 46(4) judgment (n 3) para 71.
75 ibid para 73.
76 ibid para 132.
77 ibid.
78 ibid para 134.
79 ibid para 199.

therefore did not withdraw the case and provided further written submissions to the Court following the applicant's conditional release.[80]

16.6.2.3 The Court's judgment in the infringement proceedings

In its judgment, the Court sets out the rules and practice of the CM concerning its supervisory task. It pays particular attention to cases in which violations of Article 18 of the ECHR in conjunction with Article 5 were established.[81] The Court also clarifies that the supervisory mechanism established under Article 46 of the ECHR is reinforced by the practice of the CM. The supervisory work of the CM is characterized as having a political character even though it consists in the application of the relevant legal rules.[82] Rule 6 is considered by the Court as reflecting the principles of international law set out in the Articles on Responsibility of States for Internationally Wrongful Acts.[83]

The Court furthermore holds that the infringement proceedings were not intended to upset the fundamental institutional balance between the Court and the CM.[84] The CM has a supervisory role, and this is not diminished with the introduction of infringement proceedings:

> 167. The Court has emphasised the competence of the Committee of Ministers to assess the specific measures to be taken by a State to ensure the maximum possible reparation for the violations found .... It has also found that the question of compliance by the High Contracting Parties with its judgments falls outside its jurisdiction if it is not raised in the context of the 'infringement procedure' provided for in Article 46 §§ 4 and 5 of the Convention ....
>
> 168. However, in infringement proceedings the Court is required to make a definitive legal assessment of the question of compliance. In so doing, the Court will take into consideration all aspects of the procedure before the Committee of Ministers, including the measures indicated by the Committee. The Court will conduct its assessment having due regard to the Committee's conclusions in the supervision process, the position of the respondent Government and the submissions of the victim of the violation. In the context of infringement proceedings, the Court will have to identify the legal obligations flowing from the final judgment, as well as the conclusions and spirit of that judgment ... with a view to determining whether the respondent State has failed to fulfil its obligations under Article 46 § 1.

On the question of whether Azerbaijan has refused to take the required individual measures, the Court first dealt with its argument that the absence of an indication in the Court's judgment concerning individual measures meant that no such measures were required.[85] The institutional balance between the CM and the Court means that in principle it is for the state to choose the measures to be taken, under the supervision

80 ibid para 145.
81 ibid paras 89–116.
82 ibid para 164.
83 ibid.
84 ibid para 166.
85 ibid para 181.

of the CM, on the condition that the measures are compatible with the conclusions and spirit of the Court's judgment.[86] Otherwise, the supervision would be limited to explicit indications by the Court and remove the flexibility the CM needs for its supervisory task, enabling it to take new developments into account.[87]

Furthermore, the Court held that by the time the CM referred the case under Article 46(4) of the ECHR, it was clear that no redress had been provided and that it was not possible to conclude that the state acted in good faith. This is in line with the position of the CM that the domestic courts had not achieved *restitutio in integrum* for the applicant. On the question of whether it was appropriate for the CM to call for the release of the applicant while the domestic procedures had not yet been terminated, the Court confirms that it was logical to seek the applicant's release urgently[88] in the light of its finding that the violation of Article 18 in conjunction with Article 5 of the ECHR vitiated any action resulting from the imposition of the charges.[89] The Court also referred to the fact that the second *Mammadov* judgment later confirmed the defects identified in the first *Mammadov* judgment[90] and did not displace that judgment. In fact, the Court considers that the second judgment confirmed the need for the individual measures required by the first one.[91] Thus, the state had failed to fulfil its obligation under Article 46(4) of the ECHR to abide by the judgment of 22 May 2014.[92]

16.6.2.4 Concurring opinions

The Court's judgment concluding the infringement proceedings was accompanied by concurring opinions of seven judges with direct relevance to the relationship between the CM and the Court in the supervisory process. Given their substance, it could be argued that these opinions are in fact dissenting in their nature: the judges concerned opined that the CM's call for the applicant's immediate release interfered with ongoing domestic proceedings. According to those judges, such interference should not be allowed as it is difficult to reconcile with the independence of the judiciary.[93] They were also of the view that the CM could be seen as having interfered with the case pending before the Court by holding that the domestic criminal proceedings against the applicant were fundamentally flawed, whereas a second application by Ilgar Mammadov, on the fairness of proceedings, was still pending before the Court at the time.[94] According to these judges, the supervisory powers of the CM under Article 46 of the ECHR are not unlimited, and measures indicated by the CM within its supervision mandate should be compatible with the Court's finding. In their view, the CM could not have demanded the immediate and unconditional release of the applicant while proceedings were still pending at the domestic level.[95] They even held that there

[86] ibid para 186.
[87] ibid para 184.
[88] ibid para 208.
[89] ibid para 189.
[90] ibid para 209.
[91] ibid para 211.
[92] ibid para 218.
[93] Joint Concurring Opinion of Judges Yudkivska, Pinto de Albuquerque, Wojtyczek, Dedov, Motoc, Poláckova and Hüseynov, *Mammadov* Art 46(4) judgment (n 3) para 17.
[94] ibid para 18.
[95] According to their conclusion, the second judgment required the applicant's release only implicitly. ibid paras 19–21.

is a need to put adequate safeguards in place ensuring that the supervisory powers of the CM within the execution process do not interfere with pending proceedings before domestic courts or before the Court.[96]

It is difficult to reconcile these separate opinions with the CM's responsibility—as a political body—to supervise the execution of the Court's judgments, or with the aim of infringement proceedings to improve the efficiency of the supervisory mechanism and enhance the execution of judgments. This line of 'concurring' reasoning has not found any support in the Court's second judgment in infringement proceedings, which we will now discuss.

16.6.3 *Kavala* v *Turkey*

16.6.3.1 Events leading up to the referral request

As in the case of Ilgar Mammadov, the Court ruled in its initial judgment on the detention of Osman Kavala that the state, in this case Türkiye, violated Article 5 of the ECHR, read separately and in conjunction with Article 18 of the ECHR.[97] Kavala's detention was based on attempting to overthrow the government through force and violence (the Gezi Park events) and on attempting to overthrow the constitutional order in the context of the failed coup attempt of 15 July 2016, but in reality 'pursued an ulterior purpose … namely that of reducing the applicant to silence'.[98] A noteworthy difference between the *Kavala* and *Mammadov* judgments is the explicit indication by the Court under Article 46 of the ECHR in the former case that the state is to put an end to the detention of the applicant and immediately release him.[99] The Court reiterates that its judgments are declaratory in nature and that it is primarily for the state, subject to the CM's supervision, to choose the means to implement a judgment.[100] However, if there is no real choice in measures to be taken in light of the established violation, the Court may indicate an individual measure. In the case of Kavala, the Court considered that the continuation of the applicant's pre-trial detention would entail a prolongation of the established violations.[101] It is not too far-fetched to think that the Court has learned, so to say, from Azerbaijan's reliance in *Mammadov* on the fact that it did not specifically indicate the applicant's release.

On 18 February 2020, Kavala was acquitted of the charge related to the Gezi Park events. On the same day, however, he was put in pre-trial detention in relation to the attempted coup. From 9 March 2020 onwards, the applicant's pre-trial detention was based on charges related to military or political espionage.[102] The initial judgment became final on 11 May 2020 and was first examined by the CM in its meeting on 1–3 September 2020.

[96] ibid paras 19–22.
[97] *Kavala* v *Turkey* (n 25).
[98] ibid para 232.
[99] ibid para 240.
[100] ibid para 238.
[101] ibid para 239.
[102] *Kavala* Art 46(4) judgment (n 4) para 10.

Türkiye argued before the CM that since 9 March 2020 the applicant's detention was based on a different ground, not covered by the Court's judgment. The CM considers in its first decision that the information available to it raises a strong presumption that the applicant's current detention is a continuation of the violations found by the Court.[103] The CM urges the state, pending a decision from the constitutional court, to ensure the applicant's immediate release.[104] Given the urgency of the required individual measures, the CM decided to examine the case at each CM-DH meeting and from 11 March 2021 onwards at each regular CM meeting as well.[105] Almost a year later, on 2 February 2022, the CM launched infringement proceedings under Article 46(4) against Türkiye,[106] after having served formal notice by an interim resolution adopted in the CM-DH meeting.[107] Türkiye maintained its position that the applicant's continued detention was not covered by the Court's judgment, since his detention order was lifted on 18 February 2020 and he was released in that respect.[108] In a press release of 2 December 2021 regarding the formal notice by the CM of infringement proceedings, the Turkish Ministry of Foreign Affairs stated the following on interfering with national proceedings:

> In line with the principle of respect for pending judicial proceedings, we call on the Council of Europe to avoid taking further steps, which would mean interference in the independent judiciary. Everyone, and above all the Committee of Ministers of the Council of Europe should respect and trust in legal proceedings conducted by independent and impartial courts.[109]

The Secretary-General of the Council of Europe did not repeat her predecessor's urgent call on the CM, made in the context of the *Mammadov* case, to take stronger measures against the state concerned. She did, however, call on the Turkish Minister of Foreign Affairs to release the applicant.[110]

16.6.3.2 Submissions by the CM and by Türkiye

In its referral of the case to the Court as part of infringement proceedings, the CM recalled that since 11 May 2020, the date on which the initial judgment became final, the applicant remained in detention on the basis of proceedings criticized by the Court

[103] Decisions H46-38 Mergen and Others (App No 44062/09) and Kavala (App No 28749/18) v Turkey, CM/Del/Dec(2020)1377bis/H46-38 (1377bis meeting, 1–3 September 2020) para 3.

[104] ibid para 4.

[105] Decisions H46-33 Kavala v Turkey (App No 28749/18), CM/Del/Dec(2021)1398/H46-33 (1398th meeting, 9–11 March 2021).

[106] CoE Committee of Ministers, Interim Resolution CM/ResDH(2022)21 'Execution of the Judgment of the European Court of Human Rights—Kavala against Turkey' (1423rd meeting, 2 February 2022).

[107] CoE Committee of Ministers, Interim Resolution CM/ResDH(2021)432 'Execution of the Judgment of the European Court of Human Rights: Kavala against Turkey (App No 28749/18)' (1419th meeting, 30 November to 2 December 2021).

[108] eg Communication from Türkiye concerning the case of *Kavala* v *Turkey* (App no 28749/18), Action Plan of 17 November 2021, DH-DD(2021)1212.

[109] Republic of Türkiye, Ministry of Foreign Affairs, No 402, 2 December 2021, Press Release Regarding the Decision Adopted by the Committee of Ministers at its 1419th Session on the Execution of the ECtHR Judgment of Kavala v Turkey (No 28749/18).

[110] *Kavala* Art 46(4) judgment (n 4) para 75.

or based on evidence which it found insufficient to justify his detention.[111] The CM held on the basis of the Court's indications under Article 46 of the ECHR that the state must take every measure to put an end to the applicant's detention and secure his immediate release.[112] Therefore the CM was of the view that Türkiye refused to abide by the final judgment of the Court.

Türkiye, on the other hand, argued that the conditions for bringing infringement proceedings by the CM had not been met. On the basis of Article 46(4) of the ECHR and the Explanatory Report to Protocol 14 to the ECHR, Türkiye identified two conditions: refusal of the state to implement a judgment and exceptional circumstances.[113] Türkiye held that it never refused to execute any Court judgment and that it did not refuse to abide by the *Kavala* judgment either.[114] Instead, it had engaged in a constructive dialogue with the CM and provided all the relevant information in line with Rule 6. In addition, Türkiye referred to the concurring opinions of seven judges in the *Mammadov* judgment in the infringement proceedings and argued that the CM was overstepping its supervisory mandate.[115] The Court had considered in its initial judgment that any continuation of the applicant's detention *in the present case* would entail a prolongation of the violation. Since the applicant's detention was based on other charges, Türkiye was of the view that the CM not only interfered with ongoing judicial procedures at the domestic level, but also took a position on a matter that could be brought before the Court in a separate application.[116] The CM would therefore, according to Türkiye, go beyond its mandate and authority to assess evidence that is being examined in a pending case at the domestic level. Türkiye underlined that the CM initiated infringement proceedings on the basis of a presumption, instead of a refusal by the state.[117] Furthermore, the criterion of exceptionality had not been fulfilled in its view. Infringement proceedings should only be initiated when all tools available to the CM in the context of the supervision process have been exhausted in an effective manner. Türkiye submitted that no more than twenty-six days elapsed between two consecutive CM-DH meetings at both of which the case was discussed.[118] It also indicated there was (only) a year and a half between the date of 11 May 2020, when the initial judgment became final, and the referral under infringement proceedings, leaving Türkiye without adequate time to react to the measures of the CM in the supervision process.

On 11 May 2022, Türkiye proposed the withdrawal of the case from the Court since the applicant had been sentenced to aggravated life imprisonment by the Istanbul 13th assize court on 25 April 2022.[119] His detention was therefore no longer pre-trial but based on a conviction. However, the CM saw no justification for such a withdrawal.[120]

[111] Interim Resolution CM/ResDH(2022)21 (n 106) para (e).
[112] ibid para (b).
[113] 'Appendix: Views of the Republic of Türkiye', CM/ResDH(2022)21 (1423rd meeting, 2 February 2022).
[114] ibid para 29.
[115] ibid para 52.
[116] ibid para 54.
[117] ibid para 60.
[118] ibid para 65.
[119] *Kavala* Art 46(4) judgment (n 4) para 99.
[120] Decisions H46-31 Kavala v Turkey (App No 28749/18), CM/Del/Dec(2022)1436/H46-31 (1436th meeting, 8–10 June 2022) para 2.

It requested Türkiye to provide a copy of the domestic judgment, which the chair of the CM would then send to the Court.

16.6.3.3 The Court's judgment in the infringement proceedings

The Court first dealt with the preliminary objection raised by Türkiye, notably that the CM could not yet refer the case to the Court under infringement proceedings. The argument made by Türkiye, according to the Court, is closely linked to the substance of the question raised by the CM and it should therefore be examined. It is up to the Court in the context of the Article 46(4) proceedings to decide whether the initial judgment is implemented in good faith and compatible with the conclusions and spirit of that judgment. The Court referred to its general considerations on the infringement proceedings in the *Mammadov* judgment:

> 128. The Court reiterates that, according to its settled case-law, the ultimate choice of the measures to be taken to execute a judgment remains with the States under the supervision of the Committee of Ministers, provided the measures are compatible with the 'conclusions and spirit' set out in the Court's judgment .... The Rules for the supervision of the execution of judgments also define the procedure to be followed with regard to the infringement proceedings provided for in Article 46 § 4 of the Convention .... Accordingly, the supervision mechanism now established under Article 46 of the Convention provides a comprehensive framework for the execution of the Court's judgments, reinforced by the Committee of Ministers' practice ....
>
> 129. With more specific regard to infringement proceedings, paragraphs 4 and 5 of Article 46 empower the Committee of Ministers to trigger infringement proceedings where it considers that a High Contracting Party refuses to abide by a final judgment in a case to which it is a party. This procedure does not aim to reopen the question of violation, already decided in the Court's first judgment. When introducing this procedure, it was felt that the political pressure exerted by proceedings for non-compliance before the Grand Chamber and by the latter's judgment should suffice to secure execution of the Court's initial judgment by the State concerned .... Indeed, infringement proceedings should be brought only in 'exceptional circumstances', as provided for by Rule No. 11 and the Explanatory Report to Protocol No. 14 .... This criterion is intended to indicate that the Committee of Ministers should apply a high threshold before launching this procedure. Infringement proceedings should therefore be viewed as a measure of last resort, where the Committee of Ministers considers that the other means to secure the execution of a judgment have ultimately proved unsuccessful and are no longer adapted to the situation. Moreover, infringement proceedings are not intended to upset the fundamental institutional balance between the Court and the Committee of Ministers .... The right to initiate a referral is a procedural prerogative which comes within the responsibility of the Committee of Ministers .... In consequence, where this procedure has been duly initiated, it is not the Court's task to express a view on the desirability of such a decision by the Committee of Ministers.[121]

[121] *Kavala* Art 46(4) judgment (n 4) paras 128–29.

The key issue for the Court in these infringement proceedings is the required individual measure, as emphasized by the CM in its submissions for referral.[122] The Court explained that its finding in the initial judgment of a violation of Article 5 of the ECHR, read separately and in conjunction with Article 18, vitiated any action resulting from the charges relating to the Gezi Park events and the attempted coup.[123] In addition, the Court pointed at its explicit indication on how the initial judgment should have been executed. The established violation did not leave any real choice to the state on how to remedy it and achieve *restitutio in integrum*. The urgency of ending the violation is highlighted in relation to unjustified detention, even more so where the violation has also been held contrary to Article 18 of the ECHR.[124] According to the Court, the usefulness of giving indications under Article 46 of the ECHR is twofold: it should ensure that the protection afforded by the Court is effective and prevent the continuation of the violation. Thus, it assists the CM in its supervision of the execution of the final judgment.[125]

On the relationship between the Court and the CM in the supervision process, in particular with regard to follow-up cases or reopened proceedings, the Court explained that both organs may have to examine the same domestic proceedings in the context of their different tasks. This does not upset the fundamental institutional balance between them.[126] The Court notes that the applicant was detained for more than four years on the date of the CM's referral under infringement proceedings. The proceedings in which he was convicted on 25 April 2022 did not remedy the shortcomings found in the initial judgment.[127] The measures taken by Türkiye were insufficient to conclude that it acted in good faith and in a manner compatible with the conclusions and spirit of the initial judgment. Therefore, according to the Court, Türkiye failed to fulfil its obligation under Article 46(1) of the ECHR.[128]

16.6.3.4 Then what ...?

After the publication of the Court's judgment on 11 July 2022, the CM once again urged Türkiye to ensure the immediate release of the applicant.[129] Türkiye stated, however, that the judgment did not examine the applicant's conviction of 25 April 2022. It pointed to the fact that the Grand Chamber last convened on 9 June 2022 and that the translated version of the judgment from the assize court of 25 April 2022 was not sent to the Court before 20 June 2022. According to Türkiye, the applicant's conviction and life imprisonment sentence fell within the scope of neither the initial judgment nor the judgment in infringement proceedings.[130] This position is in clear

[122] ibid para 139.
[123] ibid para 145.
[124] ibid para 147.
[125] ibid para 148.
[126] ibid para 155.
[127] ibid para 172.
[128] In a partly dissenting opinion Judge Yüksel, as the only dissenter, expressed serious concerns regarding how the CM had referred the case to the ECtHR under Article 46(4) ECHR.
[129] Decisions H46-1 *Kavala* v *Türkiye* (App No 28749/18), CM/Del/Dec(2022)1440/H46-1 (1440th meeting, 13 July 2022).
[130] Communication from the authorities (06/09/2022) concerning the case of *Kavala* v *Türkiye* (App no 28749/18), DH-DD(2022)928E, para 8.2a.

contrast to the Court's considerations in its judgment in infringement proceedings.[131] In its CM-DH meeting of September 2022, the CM deeply regretted that the applicant still had not been released, despite the clear and unequivocal conclusions of the Court.[132]

At the time this chapter was finalized, Osman Kavala was still in detention and the CM continued to insist on his immediate release. In the past two years, the CM intensified its engagement with the Turkish authorities, high-level technical dialogue with the Secretariat continued, and a visit of the co-rapporteurs of the Parliamentary Assembly to Türkiye took place. This leads to the question of what comes next: how to convince Türkiye to abide by the judgments of the Court? Clearly, political will is required to achieve the release of the applicant, since the launch of infringement proceedings itself did not lead to his release. Under Article 46(5) of the ECHR, the CM needs to consider the measures to be taken with regard to the Court's finding of a violation of Article 46(1) of the ECHR. With regard to individual measures, the CM held as follows at its first CM-DH meeting after the publication of the Court's judgment:

> 6. stressing, in this respect, that it is the shared responsibility of all competent authorities, including the judiciary, to achieve *restitutio in integrum*, urged the competent Turkish authorities to eliminate all the negative consequences of the criminal charges brought against the applicant, in particular by ensuring that he is immediately released;
>
> 7. welcomed the high-level meetings which have recently taken place between the Chair of the Committee of Ministers and his counterpart, the Minister of Foreign Affairs of Türkiye, and encouraged them to meet again at the earliest possible opportunity; called upon all member States, the Secretary General as well as other relevant Council of Europe bodies and Observer States to intensify their high-level contacts with Türkiye to raise this case; ...
>
> 9. encouraged the Chair of the Committee of Ministers to discuss with the President of the Parliamentary Assembly of the Council of Europe on further steps that could be taken by the Committee if the applicant remains in detention ...[133]

The importance of political will is clearly acknowledged in paragraph 7 by calling upon various actors to intensify their high-level contacts to raise issues related to this case with Türkiye. Paragraph 9 hints at the so-called joint complementary procedure, adopted by the CM in February 2020. A similar wording is used by the Parliamentary Assembly of the Council of Europe in its October 2022 resolution on the honouring of obligations and commitments by Türkiye. While acknowledging that the solution to the *Kavala* case lies in the hands of the Turkish judicial system, which has the capacity to adopt appropriate legal measures and show a more diligent interpretation of the Court's judgment in compliance with international law, the Assembly invited its

[131] *Kavala* Art 46(4) judgment (n 4) paras 145 and 172.
[132] Decisions, H46-30 Kavala v Türkiye (App No 28749/18), CM/Del/Dec(2022)1443/H46-30 (1443rd meeting, 20–22 September 2022) para 5.
[133] ibid.

President and the Chair of the CM to maintain close contacts and make full use of the means at their disposal, if Türkiye's failure to comply with its obligations should persist.[134]

The joint complementary procedure is intended to be applied solely with regard to the most serious violations of fundamental principles and values of the Council of Europe under Article 3 of its Statute.[135] The aim of this procedure is for the statutory organs of the Council of Europe to enter into a constructive dialogue with the state concerned and to put the state back on the path of respect for its obligations towards, and the principles of, the Council of Europe.[136] The joint complementary procedure may be initiated by the CM, the Parliamentary Assembly, or the Secretary-General of the Council of Europe. While the procedure does not have the aim of imposing sanctions, it might ultimately, depending on the state's response to the procedure, lead to a decision under Article 8 of the Statute to suspend or expel a member state from the organization.[137]

Since the infringement proceedings in the *Mammadov* case, there has been a growing call on the CM to resort to these proceedings also in other cases. It remains to be seen whether the absence of a swift response by Türkiye to the infringement proceedings in the *Kavala* case will diminish this appetite. Whereas Mammadov was released pending infringement proceedings before the Court, these proceedings have not yet achieved such result for Kavala.

16.7 Concluding Remarks

For the credibility and authority of the Court, it is crucial that its judgments are implemented. While there are many challenges in the execution process, the CM was able to close 180 leading cases in 2023.[138] It is up to the CM as a political body to ensure the full implementation of the Court's judgments by exercising its collective responsibility.

The Court's judgments in infringement proceedings have confirmed the CM's competence and practice relating to the supervision of domestic proceedings, thus enabling the CM to play its key role in redressing violations established by the Court, even if these proceedings are still pending, as well as in case a follow-up application is lodged with the Court itself. To enhance the effectiveness and credibility of the system, it is crucial that the CM examines whether any measures taken by the respondent state

[134] PACE, Resolution 2459 (2022) 'The honouring of obligations and commitments by Türkiye', paras 8.3 and 8.4.

[135] CoE Committee of Ministers, 'Complementary Procedure between the Committee of Ministers and the Parliamentary Assembly in Response to a Serious Violation by a Member State of Its Statutory Obligations', CM/Del/Dec(2020)1366/1.7, 5 February 2020 and 'Practical Modalities for a Complementary Procedure between the Committee of Ministers and the Parliamentary Assembly in Response to a Serious Violation by a Member State of Its Statutory Obligations', CM/Del/Dec(2020)1366/1.7-app., 5 February 2020.

[136] PACE Resolution 2319(2020) 'Complementary Joint Procedure between the Committee of Ministers and the Parliamentary Assembly in Response to a Serious Violation by a Member State of Its Statutory Obligations', 29 January 2020.

[137] CM/Del/Dec(2020)1366/1.7-app. (n 135).

[138] 17th Annual Report of the Committee of Ministers 2023 (n 30) 12.

are in line with the conclusions and spirit of the Court's judgment. As held by the Court in the infringement proceedings in the *Kavala* case,

> [w]ere it otherwise, the judicial authorities could continue to deprive individuals of their liberty simply by opening new criminal investigations in respect of the same facts. Such a situation would amount to permitting the law to be circumvented and might lead to results incompatible with the object and purpose of the Convention.[139]

The reopening of domestic proceedings that have violated the Convention is not an end in itself. It is simply a means of achieving a full and proper execution of the Court's judgment. However, the fact that domestic proceedings are reopened does not bring them outside the scope of the CM's supervision. Otherwise, it would create Kafkaesque situations whereby a state can simply reopen a case at the domestic level in bad faith, meaning that no redress would be provided and the applicant would have to seek justice at the Court again. Such an understanding of the Convention's supervisory mechanism cannot be reconciled with the specific task entrusted to the CM by Article 46 of the ECHR, or with the required effectiveness of the system.

Furthermore, the independence of judges and courts cannot be used by a state as an excuse for not executing judgments of the Court. This principle does not in any way alleviate the responsibilities of the state under the Convention to act in good faith in executing the Court's judgments.

Do infringement proceedings deliver on their intended purpose to increase the efficiency of the supervision process, by improving and accelerating the execution?[140] After all, the saying 'justice delayed is justice denied' not only applies to lengthy judicial proceedings but also to the execution of judgments. In the *Mammadov* case, the launch of infringement proceedings undoubtedly contributed to the applicant's release, although this was not officially recognized by Azerbaijan. In the case of Osman Kavala, however, Türkiye did not act swiftly upon the Court's respective judgments, thereby denying redress for the applicant and at the same time damaging the authority of the Court and the credibility of the Convention's supervisory mechanism.

In any case, given the exceptional nature of infringement proceedings, it seems unlikely that the CM would resort easily to this step outside of the context of urgently required individual measures and/or without the finding of an Article 18 violation. On a more general note, while the Convention's supervisory mechanism remains a unique tool at the international level and while it has, in the course of decades, to a large extent demonstrated its effectiveness, there is nevertheless reason for concern. Although the cases discussed above may not be indicative of the wider caseload of the CM, their continued non-execution or delayed execution still threatens not only the authority of the Court but also the core values of the Council of Europe. Non-governmental organizations such as the European Implementation Network have argued that the Council of Europe should formulate an effective public strategy to address the systemic non-execution of judgments with sufficient funding and political will.[141] The

[139] *Kavala* Art 46(4) judgment (n 4) para 143.
[140] *Mammadov* Art 46(4) judgment (n 3) para 160.
[141] European Implementation Network, 'EIN Board Writes to the CoE Secretary General and Committee of Ministers to Call for Action on the Implementation of ECtHR Judgments', 16 May 2022 <www.einnetw

Court has also underlined the 'paramount importance that the member States reaffirm their commitment to the execution of the Court's judgments and decisions, given their binding nature and the States' parties obligations under the Convention.'[142] Although the CM has stressed the importance of implementation of Court judgments and of the Convention at the national level,[143] the budget of the Department for the Execution of Judgments remained the same for the period 2022–25 as compared to 2021.[144] However, following the Fourth Summit of heads of state and of government of the Council of Europe in Reykjavík on 16 and 17 May 2023, the CM increased the funding for the Department in the 2024–27 budget.

At that Summit, the heads of state and of government recommitted to the Convention system as the cornerstone of the Council of Europe's protection of human rights. They stressed the need to develop a more cooperative, inclusive, and political approach based on dialogue. While they expressed their concern about 'the lack of engagement, delays and failings in implementing certain judgments, undermining the authority of the Court and seriously threatening the effectiveness of the Convention',[145] the continued detention of Osman Kavala was not explicitly mentioned.

We can only support the calls by the High-Level Reflection Group and the Dutch Advisory Council on International Affairs for strengthening the supervision process. This could be done, for instance, by taking a more political approach to the supervision by the CM, beyond the CM-DH, in particular with regard to cases where political will to implement is lacking,[146] by issuing graduated sanctions in cases of persistent non-compliance with a judgment by a state,[147] by making a more frequent use of infringement proceedings of Article 46(4) of the ECHR,[148] or by any other means. The choice of the avenues should at least become the subject of further discussion, both at the domestic and at the European level. While perhaps not as far reaching as needed, this discussion did take place in the run-up to the Reykjavík Summit and needs to be continued. The call at the Summit to enhance the tools available to the CM in the supervision of the execution of judgments in the event of non-execution or persistent refusal to execute the final judgments of the Court should be followed up on. One of these methods—or their combination—can hopefully put the CM in an even better position to perform its governance functions vis-à-vis the Court as effectively as possible.

ork.org/blog-five/2022/5/16/open-letter-by-ein-calling-for-a-public-strategy-to-address-the-systemic-problem-of-non-implementation-of-ecthr-judgments> ('EIN letter').

[142] European Court of Human Rights, Memorandum 'Fourth Summit of Heads of State and Government of the Council of Europe', 20 March 2023.

[143] CoE Committee of Ministers, 'Securing the Long-Term Effectiveness of the System of the European Convention on Human Rights', CM/Del/Dec (2021)131/3 (131st session, Hamburg, 21 May 2021). See also Council of Europe Programme and Budget 2022–25 <https://rm.coe.int/0900001680a4d5de>.

[144] EIN letter (n 141) 3.

[145] Fourth Summit Heads of State and Government of the Council of Europe, Reykjavík Declaration 'United around Our Values' (Reykjavik Summit, 16–17 May 2023), appendix IV <https://rm.coe.int/4th-summit-of-heads-of-state-and-government-of-the-council-of-europe/1680ab40c1> 17–19.

[146] Report of the High-Level Reflection Group (n 33) para 22.

[147] ibid para 27, l.

[148] AIV (n 1) recommendation 7.

PART V
CRISES AND SOLUTIONS

17

The Demise of the WTO Appellate Body

Lessons for the Governance of International Adjudication?

Peter Van den Bossche[*]

17.1 Introduction

In spite of its successful functioning over the past twenty-five years, the World Trade Organization (WTO) dispute settlement system is today in crisis due to the demise of the WTO Appellate Body, its appeals tribunal. While the WTO dispute settlement system has a number of atypical features, including appellate review, its crisis nevertheless holds useful lessons for the governance of international courts and tribunals in general. In this chapter, I first discuss the genesis of the WTO dispute settlement system and the use made of this system to date. Next, I describe how and why a decade-long looming crisis of the system developed into an acute crisis in 2019 and discuss the rules and procedures for the governance of WTO appellate review, which have contributed to this crisis. Subsequently, I examine the multiple aspects of misgovernance of WTO dispute settlement in general and WTO appellate review in particular. I conclude with some reflections on the lessons to be drawn for the governance of international adjudication in general.

17.2 The WTO Dispute Settlement System

The multilateral trading system, which aims at bringing a degree of security and predictability to international trade, has a long history of incremental and pragmatic development. It started in 1948 with the provisional entry into force of the General Agreement on Tariffs and Trade (GATT) and only in 1995 cumulated in the establishment of the WTO. One of the most noted features of the WTO is its dispute settlement system, which is to ensure the rule of law in trade relations and to avoid everyday trade disputes escalating into destructive trade wars. While the 1990s saw a proliferation of international courts and tribunals, the WTO dispute settlement system stood out as being highly innovative and, arguably, the most significant advance in interstate dispute resolution since the establishment of the Permanent Court of International Justice in 1920.

[*] This chapter reflects institutional and case-law developments up to 1 October 2021. My thanks go to Mishael Wambua for his able research assistance.

Peter Van den Bossche, *The Demise of the WTO Appellate Body* In: *Governance of International Courts and Tribunals*.
Edited by: Sergey Vasiliev and Niels Blokker, Oxford University Press. © Peter Van den Bossche 2026.
DOI: 10.1093/oso/9780198922131.003.0017

17.2.1 The genesis of the WTO dispute settlement system

The WTO dispute settlement system was negotiated during the Uruguay Round of Multilateral Trade Negotiations (1986–93) to address the United States' unilateral approach to the settlement of trade disputes, which it had increasingly adopted since the early 1980s. The WTO dispute settlement system is set out in the Understanding on Rules and Procedures for the Settlement of Disputes, commonly referred to as the Dispute Settlement Understanding (DSU). It replaced the dispute settlement system of the GATT, the WTO's de facto predecessor.[1] The GATT dispute settlement system had become dysfunctional due to the requirement that GATT panel reports ('reports' is GATT/WTO parlance for 'judgments') had to be adopted by consensus among all GATT Contracting Parties in order to become legally binding. As from the early 1980s onwards, increasingly GATT panel reports did not become legally binding because the losing party refused to join the consensus to adopt the report. The new WTO dispute settlement system resolved this problem by providing that panel reports be adopted by negative consensus (ie a report is adopted unless there is a consensus *not* to adopt the report). This, for all practical purposes, means that the adoption is quasi-automatic. As a safeguard against flawed panel reports, the WTO dispute settlement system provides for the possibility of appellate review of panel reports by a standing Appellate Body, an appeals tribunal composed of seven judges.

17.2.2 WTO dispute settlement to date

The WTO dispute settlement system is in many respects unique among international dispute resolution systems, due to its compulsory jurisdiction, mandatory pre-litigation consultations, appellate review, strict time frames for proceedings, and its surveillance and enforcement of compliance. Since its initiation in 1995, it has also been the most frequently used system for the resolution of state-to-state disputes. To date, WTO Members have brought 606 new disputes (and sixty-six compliance disputes) to the WTO for resolution.[2] In 2018, a near-record number of thirty-nine new disputes (and six compliance disputes) were brought to the WTO. As of 1 October 2021, there were thirty-two cases pending before first-instance dispute settlement panels and twenty-one cases were before the Appellate Body.

To date, the WTO dispute settlement system has been used by 110 out of the 164 WTO Members, as parties to the proceedings or as third parties, and it has been used by developed and developing countries alike.[3] While the United States and the European Union have been the most frequent complainants (as well as the most

[1] Understanding on Rules and Procedures Governing the Settlement of Disputes (DSU), Annex 2 to the Marrakesh Agreement Establishing the World Trade Organization (the WTO Agreement), 1867 UNTS 154, 33 ILM 1144.

[2] This reflects the number of requests for consultations on 1 October 2021. For up-to-date statistical information on WTO dispute settlement, see <www.wto.org> or <http://worldtradelaw.net>.

[3] WTO, 'Dispute Settlement Activity—Some Figures' <www.wto.org/english/tratop_e/dispu_e/dispu stats_e.htm>.

frequent respondents), the system has often been used by other WTO Members to see legal right prevail over economic and other might. As of 1 October 2021, a total of 235 panel reports and 148 Appellate Body reports have been adopted by the WTO Dispute Settlement Body (DSB).[4]

When compared with other interstate dispute resolution systems, such as the International Court of Justice (ICJ) or the International Tribunal for the Law of the Sea (ITLOS), this reveals a very high level of activity. In the period from 1 January 1995 to 1 October 2021, the ICJ rendered eighty-two judgments and seven advisory opinions.[5] The ITLOS, an international tribunal with jurisdiction limited to a specific field of international law like the WTO dispute settlement system, rendered fourteen judgments and two advisory opinions between its inauguration in 1996 and 1 October 2021.[6]

While the law applied by WTO panels and the Appellate Body is highly technical, the issues raised in many WTO disputes are often politically sensitive, as they concern the legality under WTO law of national legislation and policies for the protection of core societal values and interests, such as public health, public morals, the environment, employment, economic development, and national security. The rulings in many WTO disputes have attracted much interest and received high praise as well as sharp criticism from WTO Member governments, economic operators, and civil society. Finally, and most importantly, the WTO dispute settlement system has not only been used frequently and has produced many rulings on politically sensitive issues, but it also has an excellent record of compliance with its rulings. In nine out of ten disputes in which the respondent had to withdraw or amend a WTO-inconsistent measure, it did so.[7]

17.3 From a Looming to an Acute Crisis

For many years, the WTO dispute settlement system was referred to as the 'jewel in the crown' of the WTO. It was also admired and coveted by international law scholars and practitioners active in other fields of international law, and it stood as the model for the system of international investment dispute settlement now advocated by the European Union.[8] At present, however, WTO dispute settlement is in an existential crisis. Due to the demise of the Appellate Body, it is not fully operational from 11 December 2019 and has been withering away since.

[4] WorldTradeLaw.net, 'WTO Panel Reports' <www.worldtradelaw.net/databases/wtopanels.php> and 'WTO Appellate Body Reports' <www.worldtradelaw.net/databases/abreports.php>.

[5] ICJ, 'Judgments, Advisory Opinions and Orders' < www.icj-cij.org/decisions?type=4&from=1995&to=2021&sort_bef_combine=order_ASC> and < www.icj-cij.org/decisions?type=2&from=1995&to=2021&sort_bef_combine=order_ASC>.

[6] ITLOS, 'Contentious Cases' <www.itlos.org/en/main/cases/contentious-cases> and <www.itlos.org/en/main/cases/advisory-proceedings>.

[7] Peter Van den Bossche and Werner Zdouc, *The Law and Policy of the World Trade Organization* (5th edn, CUP 2022) 215.

[8] eg the Comprehensive and Economic Trade Agreement (CETA) between the European Union and Canada (Opened for signature on 30 October 2016, entered into force provisionally on 21 September 2017) Document 22017A0114(01), Art 8.28.

17.3.1 A decade-long looming crisis

The current crisis, while unprecedented in its gravity, did not come unexpectedly. While in the early years of the system, WTO Members often expressed their satisfaction with its functioning, there were already a number of crisis moments then (eg the *Helms-Burton Act* national security crisis in 1997, the Articles 21.5/22.6 DSU sequencing crisis in 1999, and the *amicus curiae* brief crisis in 2000).[9] Moreover, while expressing satisfaction with the operation of the dispute settlement system, WTO Members made a multitude of DSU reform proposals both before and in the early stages of Doha Round negotiations in the first half of 2000s. More recently, and certainly from the early 2010s on, the WTO dispute settlement came under ever-increasing pressure.

A major crisis was looming large for several related reasons. First, the workload of panels and the Appellate Body grew significantly due to the increased size and complexity of the disputes brought to the WTO for resolution, while the financial and other resources made available for dispute settlement fell short. Second, the paralysis of the 'legislative' branch of the WTO made Members seek changes to WTO law through adjudication, rather than negotiations.[10] The paralysis of the 'legislative' branch of the WTO also made it impossible for Members to 'correct' alleged errors by the Appellate Body in the interpretation of WTO law. Third, some Members, and in particular the United States, increasingly made antagonistic allegations of judicial overreach by the Appellate Body and accused it of unacceptable disregard of procedural rules, in particular the ninety-day timeframe for appellate review. Fourth and finally, the United States took both overt and covert action affecting the independence and impartiality of Appellate Body members, primarily in the context of the process of reappointment.[11]

17.3.2 The existential crisis

The looming existential crisis became acute because of the blockage by the first Trump administration of the appointment (or reappointment) of Appellate Body members. Because of this blockage, the Appellate Body, ordinarily seven strong, had on 11 December 2019 only one member left, and was, as from that date, no longer able

[9] Van den Bossche and Zdouc (n 7) 674–75 (on the *Helms-Burton Act* national security crisis), 310–11 (on the sequencing crisis) and 279–83 (on the *amicus curiae* brief issue).

[10] Apart from dispute settlement, another main function of the WTO is to act as a forum for the negotiation and adoption of new trade rules. This function is referred to as the 'legislative' function of the WTO and is performed by the WTO's political bodies. While there have been a few negotiation successes since 1995 (eg the Trade Facilitation Agreement and the decision on the prohibition of agricultural export subsidies), the 'legislative' branch of the WTO has been unable to adopt new trade rules and adapt the WTO rulebook to the changing nature of international trade. The 'legislative' branch has been paralyzed by the fact that all decisions need to be taken by consensus.

[11] The United States' blockage of the reappointment of Jennifer Hillman (US) in 2022 and Seung Waha Chang (Korea) in 2016 are highly publicized examples of such action. See Van den Bossche and Zdouc (n 7) 318.

to hear and decide any new appeals.[12] The term of the last sitting member expired on 30 November 2020. The Appellate Body is currently a court without judges. The United States blocked, and continues to block, the appointment (or reappointment) of members because it has fundamental concerns regarding the Appellate Body and its functioning.[13]

The most significant concern of the United States is that the Appellate Body added to or diminished the rights and obligations of WTO Members under the WTO agreements. The United States accuses the Appellate Body of 'judicial activism' on matters relating to anti-dumping measures, subsidies, countervailing measures, safeguard measures and technical barriers to trade. The United States argues, in particular, that the Appellate Body's case law limits its ability to counteract the importation of goods, which harm its domestic industry. In addition, according to the United States, the Appellate Body disregarded the rules on WTO dispute settlement by: (1) exceeding the mandatory ninety-day time limit for appellate review (without the consent of the parties); (2) allowing outgoing Appellate Body members to complete work on appeals to which they had been assigned before the end of their term; (3) issuing 'advisory opinions' on issues not necessary to resolve the dispute; (4) reviewing factual findings of panels and, in particular, panel findings on the meaning of the respondent's domestic law; and (5) treating its rulings as binding precedent. It should be noted that most of these concerns regarding the functioning of the Appellate Body had already been raised by the United States under the Obama and the George W. Bush administrations. However, only the Trump administration saw fit to plunge the WTO dispute settlement system into an existential crisis over these concerns.

Faced with a possible collapse of the WTO dispute settlement system, WTO Members tabled in late 2018 and throughout 2019 a number of proposals for reform of the Appellate Body to address the concerns raised by the United States. On 26 November 2018, the European Union, China, Canada, India, Norway, New Zealand, Switzerland, Australia, Korea, Iceland, Singapore, and Mexico submitted a communication to the WTO General Council (WT/GC/W/752) setting out proposals for amendments to WTO appellate review. On the same day, the European Union, China, and India submitted a second communication to the General Council (WT/GC/W/

[12] Of the thirteen appeals pending before the Appellate Body on 11 December 2019, only three were decided. The other ten appeals remained pending.

[13] The United States set out its concerns in detail in a February 2020 report: Office of the United States Trade Representative, Report on the Appellate Body of the World Trade Organization, February 2020 <https://ustr.gov/sites/default/files/Report_on_the_Appellate_Body_of_the_World_Trade_Organization.pdf>. However, see also US President's 2018 Trade Policy Agenda and 2017 Annual Report of the President of the United States on the Trade Agreements Program <https://ustr.gov/sites/default/files/files/Press/Reports/2018/AR/2018%20Annual%20Report%20FINAL.PDF> 22 *et seq*. Statement by the United States at the Meeting of the WTO Dispute Settlement Body of 22 July 2019 on Transparency in WTO Dispute Settlement < https://geneva.usmission.gov/2019/07/22/statement-by-the-united-states-on-transparency-in-wto-dispute-settlement>; Statement by the United States at the Meeting of the WTO Dispute Settlement Body on 22 June 2018 concerning Article 17.5 of the Understanding on Rules and Procedures regarding the Settlement of Disputes <https://ustr.gov/sites/default/files/enforcement/DS/Jun22.DSB.Stmt.(Item%205_90%20days).(public).pdf> 9–21; Statement by the United States at the Meeting of the WTO Dispute Settlement Body on 29 October 2018 concerning the Issuance of Advisory Opinions on Issues not Necessary to Resolve a Dispute <https://ustr.gov/sites/default/files/enforcement/DS/Oct29.DSB.Stmt.(Item%204_Advisory%20opinions).(public).pdf> 10–26.

753) setting out proposals for additional amendments, particularly with regard to institutional issues concerning the Appellate Body. However, at the General Council meeting of 12 December 2018, the United States curtly rejected these proposals as not addressing the concerns it had raised.

Subsequently, Honduras (in January and February 2019, WT/GC/W/758, /759, /760 and /761), Chinese Taipei (in February 2019, WT/GC/W/763 and /763/Rev.), Brazil, Paraguay and Uruguay (in March and April 2019, WT/GC/W/767 and /767/Rev.), Japan, Australia and Chile (in April 2019, WT/GC/W/768 and /768/Rev), Thailand (in April 2019, WT/GC/W/769) and the African Group (in June 2019, WT/GC/W/776) submitted communications to the General Council setting out further proposals, varying in detail and approach, for amending WTO appellate review. In parallel with formal discussions on these proposals in the General Council, Members engaged in 2019 in frequent informal and confidential discussions under the leadership of Ambassador David Walker of New Zealand, the Chair of the WTO Dispute Settlement Body.

However, the United States did not actively participate in these discussions and did not put forward any specific proposal for changes to address its concerns regarding the functioning of the Appellate Body. In October 2019, the discussions among the other WTO Members on amending WTO appellate review resulted in a draft General Council Decision on the Functioning of the Appellate Body.[14] As stated by Ambassador Walker, this draft Decision was aimed at 'seeking workable and agreeable solutions to improve the functioning of the Appellate Body', in the hope to avoid the paralysis of the Appellate Body as from December 2019.[15] The draft Decision was a carefully constructed compromise, which preserved the core features of WTO appellate review while addressing US concerns. However, the hope that the draft Decision would allow the WTO to avoid the paralysis of the Appellate Body was short-lived. At the General Council meeting of 15 October 2019, the United States rejected off-hand the draft Decision as insufficient to address its concerns. With this, the impasse was complete and the paralysis of the Appellate Body on 11 December 2019 unavoidable.

In 2020 and 2021, WTO Members made no new concerted efforts to reform WTO appellate review in order to address US concerns.[16] Most Members, including the European Union, China, India and Canada, disagree with the United States that the Appellate Body systematically engaged in judicial overreach and demonstrated

[14] General Council, Informal Process on Matters related to the Functioning of the Appellate Body—Report by the Facilitator, H.E. Dr. David Walker (New Zealand), JOB/GC/222, 15 October 2019, Annex.

[15] ibid para 1.22.

[16] However, on 27 March 2020, sixteen WTO Members, including Australia, Brazil, Canada, China, the European Union, and Mexico, announced that they had reached an agreement on the Multi-Party Interim Appeal Arbitration Arrangement under Art 25 of the DSU, commonly referred to as the 'MPIA', which became effective on 30 April 2020, when it was notified to the DSB. See Statement on a Mechanism for Developing, Documenting and Sharing Practices and Procedures in the Conduct of WTO Disputes, Addendum, JOB/DSB/1/Add. 12, 30 April 2020. At the DSB meeting of 28 June 2020, the European Union delivered a statement explaining that the MPIA is an interim arrangement intended 'to preserve, in disputes among Members participating in the MPIA, a functioning and two-step dispute settlement process, as envisaged by the DSU'. According to the United States, the MPIA 'incorporates and exacerbates some of the worst aspects of the Appellate Body's practices'. The MPIA currently has twenty-five parties, representing WTO Members, but to date no appeal of a panel report has been heard and decided under the MPIA.

consistent and malicious disregard for procedural and institutional rules.[17] In the course of 2020 and 2021, 120 and more WTO Members repeatedly tabled a draft decision for the DSB to commence the process for the appointment of Appellate Body members.[18] However, the United States has consistently blocked the adoption of such decision. To date, the Biden administration has continued the Trump administration's obstruction of the appointment process and has left the Appellate Body paralyzed.

The paralysis of the Appellate Body has not only deprived WTO Members of appellate review of first-instance panel reports. It has also undermined the whole WTO dispute settlement system. Pursuant to Article 16.4 of the DSU, when a panel report is appealed, it can only be adopted by the DSB and become legally binding once the Appellate Body has completed its review. As was to be expected, since 11 December 2019 only one panel report has been adopted by the DSB. All other panel reports have been appealed to the paralyzed Appellate Body by the losing party, thus ensuring that an unfavourable panel report would not become legally binding.

In such circumstances, complainants have few incentives to have recourse to the WTO dispute settlement system. Not surprisingly, the number of new disputes brought to the WTO for resolution in 2020 and 2021 fell to five and eight respectively, while, as mentioned above, in 2018 it was thirty-nine.[19] The unavailability of appellate review has undermined the whole WTO dispute settlement system. The system, which is 'a glorious experiment with the rule of law in international relations',[20] is falling apart and unlikely to overcome its current state of crisis any time soon.

17.4 Rules and Procedures for the Governance of WTO Appellate Review

While the underlying causes of the current crisis of WTO dispute settlement and the demise of the Appellate Body are political in nature and closely related to the rise of unilateralism and economic nationalism, the crisis is an immediate result of the rules and procedures for the governance of WTO dispute settlement, and in particular the governance of WTO appellate review. These rules and procedures are set out in the WTO Agreement, the Dispute Settlement Understanding (DSU), the 1995 Decision of the Dispute Settlement Body on the Establishment of the Appellate

[17] eg Statement by Amb João Aguiar Machado (European Union) at the WTO General Council meeting on 15 and 16 October 2019 on Informal Process on Matters Related to the Functioning of the Appellate Body—Report by the Facilitator <https://eeas.europa.eu/delegations/world-trade-organization-wto/68955/eu-statement-ambassador-joão-aguiar-machado-general-council-meeting-15-and-16-october-2019_en>; and Statement by Amb Zhang Xiangchen (China) at the WTO General Council meeting on 15 and 16 October 2019 on Informal Process on Matters Related to the Functioning of the Appellate Body—Report by the Facilitator.

[18] WTO, 'Dispute Settlement Body' <www.wto.org/english/tratop_e/dispu_e/dispu_body_e.htm>.

[19] WTO, 'Dispute Settlement Activity—Some Figures' <www.wto.org/english/tratop_e/dispu_e/dispustats_e.htm>.

[20] Farewell speech of Appellate Body member Peter Van den Bossche delivered to the WTO Dispute Settlement Body on 28 May 2019 <www.wto.org/english/tratop_e/dispu_e/farwellspeech_peter_van_den_bossche_e.htm>.

Body (1995 DSB Decision),[21] the Rules of Conduct for the Understanding on Rules and Procedures Governing the Settlement of Disputes (Rules of Conduct),[22] and the Working Procedures for Appellate Review (Appellate Body Working Procedures).[23] This section will address the role of, and the rules applicable to, the different actors in the governance of WTO appellate review. These actors can be divided into four groups: (1) political actors, such as the WTO Dispute Settlement Body and the WTO General Council; (2) executive actors, such as the WTO Director-General; (3) the parties in the disputes; and (4) the Appellate Body and its Secretariat.

17.4.1 WTO Dispute Settlement Body

According to Article 2 of the DSU, the WTO Dispute Settlement Body (DSB), which is composed of senior representatives of all 164 WTO Members, is established to 'administer' the rules and procedures of WTO dispute settlement. This 'administration' includes: (1) the establishment of the ad hoc WTO dispute settlement panels; (2) the adoption of panel and Appellate Body reports (which renders recommendations and rulings of these reports legally binding); and (3) the authorization of retaliation measures in case of non-compliance with the recommendations and rulings of adopted panel and Appellate Body reports.[24] The DSB takes the decisions on these matters by reverse consensus, which means—as explained above—that the decision is taken unless Members decide by consensus not to take the proposed decision.[25] As there is always at least one Member that wants the decision to be taken (eg the Member requesting the establishment of a panel or the Member that is the 'winning' party in a dispute), a consensus not to take the decision is highly unlikely. There has never been such an instance to date.

While decisions on the three matters referred to above are taken by reverse consensus, the DSB takes all other decisions by 'normal' consensus.[26] As stated in footnote 1 of the DSU, a decision is taken by consensus 'if no Member, present at the meeting of the DSB when the decision is taken, formally objects to the proposed decision'. While for other bodies of the WTO (including the General Council), there is—at least in theory—the possibility of recourse to voting if consensus cannot be reached,[27] the DSB can only take decisions by (normal or reverse) consensus, and never by voting.

[21] Establishment of the Appellate Body, Recommendations by the Preparatory Committee for the WTO approved by the Dispute Settlement Body on 10 February 1995, WT/DSB/1, 19 June 1995 <https://docs.wto.org/dol2fe/Pages/FE_Search/FE_S_S009-DP.aspx?language=E&CatalogueIdList=13919&CurrentCatalogueIdIndex=0&FullTextSearch>.

[22] Rules of Conduct for the Understanding on Rules and Procedures Governing the Settlement of Disputes adopted by the Dispute Settlement Body, WT/DSB/RC/1, 11 December 1996 <www.wto.org/english/tratop_e/dispu_e/rc_e.htm>.

[23] Working Procedures for Appellate Review, WT/AB/WP/6, 16 August 2010.

[24] DSU (n 2) Art 2.1. This provision also states that the DSB maintains surveillance of the implementation of the recommendations and rulings, as is further elaborated in DSU (n 2) Art 21.

[25] DSU (n 2) Arts 6.1 (on the establishment of a panel), 16.4 and 17.14 (on the adoption of panel and Appellate Body reports), and 22.6 (on the authorization to retaliate).

[26] ibid Art 2.4.

[27] WTO Agreement (n 2) Art IX:1.

Most important among the decisions that the DSB must take by 'normal' consensus is, pursuant to Article 17.2 of the DSU, the decision on the appointment of Appellate Body members. In deciding on these appointments, the DSB is to be guided by the relevant requirements set out in Article 17.3 of the DSU, namely that: (1) the Appellate Body 'shall comprise persons of recognized authority, with demonstrated expertise in law, international trade and the subject matter of the covered agreements generally';[28] (2) Appellate Body members shall be unaffiliated with any government; and (3) the Appellate Body membership shall be broadly representative of membership in the WTO.[29] The 1995 DSB Decision on the Establishment of the Appellate Body explicitly states that 'the success of the WTO will depend greatly on the proper composition of the Appellate Body'.[30]

As regards the procedure for the appointment of Appellate Body members, in order to facilitate the decision-making process, a Selection Committee, composed of the five ambassadors chairing the most important WTO political bodies and the WTO Director-General, make—after intensive consultations with the WTO membership and interviewing the candidates—a proposal to the DSB on whom to appoint.[31] While the appointment process became increasingly acrimonious and politicized, the work of the Selection Committee allowed the DSB to come to consensus decisions on appointments until and including the appointment of Hyun Chong Kim (Korea) in 2016. Before 2017, only once a WTO Member objected, at least initially, to an appointment proposed by the Selection Committee.[32]

The DSB not only appoints Appellate Body members, but it also decides on their conditions of employment. It did so in the 1995 DSB Decision on the Establishment of the Appellate Body. While Article 17.3, fourth sentence, of the DSU requires Appellate Body members 'to be available at all times and on short notice', it was the expectation of WTO Members in 1995 that parties would only occasionally have recourse to appellate review and that the Appellate Body would not be very busy.[33] Therefore, the DSB decided not to offer Appellate Body members full-time contracts, but contracts based on a monthly retainer and a fee for actual days worked.

This expectation of only occasional recourse to appellate review proved to be quite wrong. In the first few years of WTO dispute settlement all panel reports were appealed and over the last twenty-five years more than two out three panel reports were appealed.[34] While the 1995 DSB Decision stated that the employment conditions 'could be kept under review by the DSB ... to determine whether a move to full-time employment was warranted',[35] the DSB never amended the conditions of employment

[28] As stated in 1995 DSB Decision (n 18) para 10, DSU Art 17.3, fourth sentence, suggests that Appellate Body members have 'a priority working relationship with the WTO' but may 'have other activities'.

[29] 1995 DSB Decision (n 18) para 6 states that while the 'overriding concern is to provide highly-qualified members for the Appellate Body', 'factors such as different geographical areas, levels of development, and legal systems shall be duly taken into account'.

[30] ibid para 4.

[31] ibid para 12.

[32] In 2008, Chinese Taipei objected to the proposal of the Selection Committee to appoint Yuejiao Zhang, a national of China, as Appellate Body Member.

[33] 1995 DSB Decision (n 18) para 2 refers to '*sporadic* trips to Geneva' (emphasis added).

[34] See WorldTradeLaw.net, 'WTO Panel Reports' <http://worldtradelaw.net/databases/appealcount.php>.

[35] 1995 DSB Decision (n 18) para 11.

of Appellate Body members it adopted in 1995. In view of the heavy workload of the Appellate Body in many of the past twenty-five years, full-time employment of Appellate Body members would most probably have imposed a lesser financial burden on the WTO than the 'retainer plus daily fee' arrangement.

17.4.2 WTO General Council

The other political actor in the governance of WTO appellate review is the WTO General Council, which is also composed of senior representatives of all WTO Members, but which has a much broader competence than the DSB. In the intervals between the meetings of the WTO Ministerial Conference, the supreme political organ of the WTO, it is the WTO General Council, which has the authority to take decisions on all WTO matters. In the context of the governance of WTO appellate review, the most important decision for the General Council to take is the adoption of the WTO annual budget, including the budget of the Appellate Body.[36] As noted above, the General Council has also been involved, albeit unsuccessfully, in discussions in 2019 on ways to avoid the impending paralysis of the Appellate Body as a result of the US blockage of the appointment of its members.[37] The General Council can take decisions by voting if consensus cannot be reached.[38] However, since 1995, only a handful of decisions of the General Council have been taken by voting, and this never concerned matters relating to dispute settlement.

17.4.3 WTO Director-General

The most important executive actor in the governance of WTO appellate review is the WTO Director-General. Article VI:1 of the WTO Agreement provides that the WTO Secretariat shall be headed by a Director-General. Pursuant to Article VI:3, the Director-General appoints the staff of the WTO Secretariat and determines their duties and conditions. While paragraph 17 of the 1995 DSB Decision on the Establishment of the Appellate Body explicitly states that the staff of the Appellate Body should be independent from the WTO Secretariat and answerable to the Appellate Body only, it is—pursuant to the same paragraph 17—the Director-General who appoints the Appellate Body staff and determines their employment conditions, including promotions and terminations. Another task of the Director-General relating to the governance of WTO appellate review is the preparation of the annual WTO budget, including the Appellate Body budget.[39] Finally, as already noted, the

[36] See WTO Agreement (n 2) Art VII:3. Pursuant to the Financial Regulations of the WTO, expenditure specific to the functioning of the Appellate Body and its Secretariat shall be identified and subject to a specific recommendation to the General Council by the Committee on Budget, Finance and Administration. See Financial Regulations of the World Trade Organization, WT/L/156/Rev. 3, dated 27 February 1995, Regulation 7.

[37] As discussed above, this involvement resulted in the draft General Council Decision on the Functioning of the Appellate Body of 15 October 2019.

[38] WTO Agreement (n 2) Art IX:1.

[39] WTO Agreement (n 2) Art VII:1 and Financial Regulations (n 33).

Director-General is, as a member of the Selection Committee, involved in the appointment process of Appellate Body members.

17.4.4 Parties to the dispute

In addition to the political actors, such as the DSB and the General Council, and executive actors, such as the Director-General, the parties to a dispute obviously also play an important role in the governance of WTO appellate review. It is one of the parties that initiates an appeal while the other party may follow up with an 'other appeal' (which is WTO speak for a cross-appeal). The appellant and other appellant are free in deciding the extent and subject-matter of their appeal of the issues of law covered in a panel report and legal interpretations developed by a panel. Once initiated, the conduct of the appellant(s), appellee(s) and third participant(s) in the appellate proceedings is regulated by the Appellate Body Working Procedures, which are quite detailed. At the request of the appellant(s), appellee(s) or third participant(s), the Appellate Body may, in the interest of fairness and orderly procedure, adopt additional procedural rules for the purpose of a specific appeal or may allow deviation from the standard timetable for appeals.[40]

However, parties have only in few cases requested the Appellate Body to adopt additional procedural rules or allow deviation from the standard timetable. The most common additional procedural rules relate to the protection of business confidential information during the appellate proceedings. Pursuant to DSU Article 17.14, parties must accept 'unconditionally' the recommendations and rulings of Appellate Body reports once they are adopted by the DSB. However, this obligation is without prejudice to the right of parties, and all other WTO Members, to express their views on an Appellate Body report.[41] The latter is usually done when the DSB meets to adopt the report concerned. Generally, this is a politically useful feature of WTO dispute settlement, as it allows the losing party to 'let off steam' in a procedurally 'controlled' context.

17.4.5 Appellate Body

Arguably the most important actor in the governance of WTO appellate review is the Appellate Body itself. Article 17.1 of the DSU provides that a standing Appellate Body shall be established by the DSB, which the latter did in its Decision of 10 February 1995, already referred to above. The overall mandate of the WTO dispute settlement system, and thus of the Appellate Body, is set out in Article 3.2 of the DSU. According to Article 3.2 of the DSU, the WTO dispute settlement system is 'a central element in providing security and predictability to the multilateral trading system'. As further stated in this core provision, the WTO dispute settlement system serves 'to preserve the rights and obligations' of Members under the WTO agreements, *and* 'to clarify the

[40] Appellate Body Working Procedures (n 20) para 16(1) and (2).
[41] DSU (n 2) Art 17.14, last sentence.

existing provisions under those agreements'. The latter is to be done 'in accordance with customary rules of interpretation of public international law'. The last sentence of Article 3.2. of the DSU explicitly warns against judicial activism when it states that WTO dispute settlement rulings 'cannot add to or diminish the rights and obligations' provided for in the WTO agreements. This warning is repeated in Article 19.2 of the DSU. It is also important that Article 3.3 of the DSU states that the 'prompt settlement' of disputes is 'essential to the effective functioning of the WTO'. Several DSU provisions therefore provide for exacting time frames.

The more specific mandate of the Appellate Body is set out in paragraphs 1, 6, 12, and 13 of Article 17 of the DSU. Pursuant to paragraph 1, the Appellate Body 'shall hear appeals from panel cases', but as stated in paragraph 6, it can only hear appeals concerning 'issues of law in the panel report and legal interpretations developed by the panel'. Pursuant to paragraph 12, the Appellate Body is required to address all issues raised in accordance with paragraph 6 during the appellate proceedings. Paragraph 13 stipulates that the Appellate Body 'may uphold, modify or reverse' the legal findings and conclusions of a panel. In practice, the Appellate Body has interpreted its mandate broadly and, as already referred to above, has been strongly criticized for doing so by the United States. It has heard appeals with respect to factual findings which were allegedly inconsistent with the legal obligation of the panel to make an objective assessment of the facts and therefore constituted a legal issue subject to appellate review. Also, the Appellate Body has, in addition to upholding, modifying, and reversing panel findings and conclusions, on occasion, and under specific conditions, completed the legal analysis of a panel, and has thus acted as a first-instance adjudicator and not as an appeals tribunal. It did so in order not to leave a dispute unresolved.

Pursuant to Article 17.1 of the DSU, the Appellate Body shall be composed of seven persons. When compared with other international courts, such as the ICJ (fifteen judges) or the ITLOS (twenty-one judges), the modest size of the Appellate Body stands out. As to the composition of the Appellate Body, Article 17.3, first sentence, of the DSU further provides that 'the Appellate Body shall comprise persons of recognized authority, with demonstrated expertise in law, international trade and the subject matter of the covered agreements generally'. Paragraph 5 of the 1995 Decision on the Establishment of the Appellate Body further stipulates that the required expertise of Appellate Body members 'should be a type that allows [them] to resolve "issues of law covered in the panel report and legal interpretations developed by the panel"'. This is a rather self-evident, and therefore not very useful, clarification of who is fit to serve on the Appellate Body. More informative is the requirement set out in Article 17.3, second sentence, that Appellate Body members 'shall be unaffiliated with any government'. The 1995 DSB Decision on the Establishment of the Appellate Body further elaborates on this requirement by stating that Appellate Body members 'should not ... have any attachment to a government that would compromise their independence of judgment'.[42] This requirement would not necessarily rule out persons who, although paid by a government, serve in a function rigorously and are demonstrably

[42] 1995 DSB Decision (n 18) para 7.

independent from that government, such as those holding academic positions at government-funded universities.

Reflecting the same concern regarding the independence and impartiality of Appellate Body members, Article 17.3, fifth sentence, of the DSU states that Appellate Body members 'shall not participate in the consideration of any disputes that would create a direct or indirect conflict of interest'. To clarify the scope of this requirement, the DSB adopted in 1996 the Rules of Conduct for the Understanding on Rules and Procedures Governing the Settlement of Disputes (Rules of Conduct). These Rules apply to everybody involved in WTO dispute settlement but have some specific provisions for the Appellate Body members. The governing principle of the Rules is that all those covered by them 'shall be independent and impartial, shall avoid direct or indirect conflicts of interest and shall respect the confidentiality of proceedings ... so that through the observance of such standards of conduct the integrity and impartiality of that mechanism are preserved'.[43]

To ensure observance of this governing principle, the Rules require any person subject to them *inter alia*: (1) 'to disclose the existence or development of any interest, relationship or matter that that person could reasonably be expected to know and that is likely to affect, or give rise to justifiable doubts as to, that person's independence or impartiality';[44] and (2) to 'not incur any obligation or accept any benefit that would in any way interfere with, or which could give rise to, justifiable doubts as to the proper performance of that person's dispute settlement duties'.[45] With regard to the disclosure requirement, an Appellate Body member should disclose any interest, relationship or matter of the kind referred to above, to his or her fellow Appellate Body members, and not, as others involved in WTO dispute settlement, to the Chair of the DSB. It is the Appellate Body, and not a political WTO entity, which decides whether the disclosure made would justify recusal from an appeal. The Appellate Body is thus protected from political interference.

While the Appellate Body never made public a decision to recuse one of its members from an appeal, this has been a more common occurrence than often thought. Parties may request the disqualification of an Appellate Body member on grounds of a material violation of the Rules of Conduct. It is for the Appellate Body, and not for the Chair of the DSB (as is the case for others involved in WTO dispute settlement), to decide on whether such violation has occurred and, if so, to take appropriate action.[46] To date, no WTO Member has ever formally requested the disqualification of an Appellate Body member on grounds of a material violation of the Rules of Conduct.[47]

[43] Rules of Conduct (n 19) para II(1).
[44] ibid para III(1). See also ibid para VI.
[45] ibid para III(2).
[46] ibid para VIII(14)–(17).
[47] Note, however, that in March 2020, the United States contended that Hong Zhao was not 'a member of the Appellate Body because she has not eligible under the DSU'. According to the United States, Hong Zhao, who had been on the Appellate Body since 2016, was ineligible because of her affiliation with China's Academy of International Trade and Economic Cooperation. See Steve Charnovitz, 'The Trump Administration's Shameful Attack on Appellator Zhao' (International Law and Policy Blog, 5 March 2020) <https://ielp.worldtradelaw.net/2020/03/the-trump-administrations-shameful-attack-on-appellator-zhao.html>.

Appellate Body members serve for a four-year term which is renewable once.[48] When compared with the term in office of judges in other international courts, such as the ICJ or the ITLOS (nine-year terms), the four-year term of Appellate Body members is short. As ICJ and ITLOS judges, Appellate Body members can be reappointed, albeit only once.

Finally, it should be noted that the Appellate Body has detailed working procedures. As provided for in Article 17.9 of the DSU, the Appellate Body draws up its own working procedures and communicates them to the WTO Members for their information. While the Appellate Body is to consult with the Chair of the DSB and the WTO Director-General when drawing up its working procedures, WTO Members gave the Appellate Body a large degree of freedom in this regard. Some Members would now argue that the Appellate Body 'abused' this freedom when adopting its Working Procedures in February 1996. These Working Procedures reflect some fundamental choices with regard to the nature of Appellate Body proceedings and the conduct of WTO appellate review.

As to the nature of Appellate Body proceedings, the Working Procedures provide for judicial-type proceedings and reveal that the Appellate Body considers itself to be a court, rather than an arbitral tribunal. The Appellate Body made clear that it wanted to break with the party-controlled GATT panel proceedings. The Working Procedures describe the appellate review process in detail and with particular concern for due process. Of particular concern to the Appellate Body is to provide for procedures that would allow hearing and deciding appeals in no more than ninety days, as required under Article 17.5 of the DSU.

Another notable feature of the Working Procedures is the introduction of the exchange of views. Pursuant to Article 17.1 of the DSU, an appeal is not heard and decided by the Appellate Body *en banc*, but, instead, by a division of three members serving in rotation. It is clear that such an approach to appellate review would make it more difficult for a consistent body of case law to arise. To address this, Rule 4 of the Working Procedures, entitled 'Collegiality', requires the division responsible for deciding an appeal 'to exchange views' with the four other Appellate Body members, before it finalizes its report. Such an 'exchange of views' is quite unique in international (or national) dispute resolution but has been of significant benefit to the work of the Appellate Body. It has contributed to the quality and authority of its decisions and ensured consistency and coherence in its case law.

17.4.6 Appellate Body Secretariat

Pursuant to Article 17.7 of the DSU, the WTO is to provide the Appellate Body 'with appropriate administrative and legal support as it requires'. On the basis of the expected workload of the Appellate Body, the DSB considered in its 1995 Decision that 'a reasonable level of support in the initial stages of operation of the Appellate Body would be one registrar, three professional assistants with legal training, and sufficient

[48] DSU (n 2) Art 17.2.

clerical staff'.[49] In 1997, the Appellate Body Secretariat had one Director, acting as registrar, one senior and two junior legal advisors, as well as two support staff. From the beginning, it was clear that the Appellate Body Secretariat was considerably understaffed. Over the years it grew in size and had in December 2019, in addition to the Director, seven senior and ten junior legal advisors and five support staff. But the legal and administrative support given to the Appellate Body was, in most years, less than what was required to handle the workload.

Apart from the administrative and legal support to the Appellate Body, the 1995 DSB Decision also addressed the issue of the independence of the Appellate Body Secretariat. Paragraph 17 of the Decision states that the Appellate Body Secretariat should be independent from the WTO Secretariat.[50] This makes eminent sense since, pursuant to Article 27.1 of the DSU, the WTO Secretariat (with the WTO Director-General at its head) assists and gives legal advice to the panels. Therefore, the WTO Secretariat cannot be called up to assist and give legal advice to the Appellate Body, which hears and decides on appeals of panel findings and conclusions. The task of assisting and advising the Appellate Body must be entrusted to an entity which is separate and independent from the entity that assisted and advised the panel whose findings are on appeal. Paragraph 17 of the 1995 DBS Decision recognizes this need but leaves the decision on the appointment of the staff of the Appellate Body Secretariat, as well as decisions on their promotion and termination, to the WTO Director-General.

17.5 Aspects of Misgovernance

WTO dispute settlement in general, and WTO appellate review in particular, undoubtedly have governance features which contribute to effective adjudication of international disputes. Some of these features are uncommon in international adjudication, and the introduction of such features in other international dispute resolution systems might well enhance the effectiveness of the latter. Among these features are the provision of appellate review itself, but also, for example, the 'exchange of views' among judges when cases are not heard and decided *en banc*. However, the governance of WTO dispute settlement, including WTO appellate review, also has features that have resulted in the current Appellate Body crisis and undermined the credibility and effectiveness of WTO dispute settlement. This section focuses on five aspects of the misgovernance of WTO appellate review: (1) the blockage of the appointment of Appellate Body members; (2) persistent and unfounded allegations of 'overreach' by the Appellate Body; (3) inadequate protection of the independence and impartiality of the Appellate Body and its Secretariat; (4) unrealistic timeframes for appellate review; and (5) the size of the Appellate Body and its Secretariat.

[49] 1995 DSB Decision (n 18) para 16.
[50] 1995 DSB Decision (n 18) para 17.

17.5.1 Blockage of the appointment of Appellate Body members

As explained above, the immediate cause of the current crisis of the Appellate Body is the blockage by the United States of the appointment of Appellate Body members. The appointment of members requires a consensus decision by the DSB, and the United States has made clear that it will veto such decision as long as its 'concerns' regarding the Appellate Body and its functioning are left unaddressed. Moreover, the United States indicated that it would not agree to the appointment of members as long as broader reforms of the WTO and its law are not agreed on. As the then United States Trade Representative Robert Lighthizer said to the US Senate Finance Committee in March 2019, the Appellate Body crisis was 'leverage' for such broader reforms.[51] Hence, the process for the (re)appointment of Appellate Body members has been blocked since 2017. The appointment of judges is often a contentious matter in the governance of many international courts or tribunals. The appointment of ICJ judges is a good example in this regard. However, while it may be cumbersome, the appointment process of judges in other international courts cannot be blocked by one or a few countries. The appointment of ICJ judges, for example, 'only' requires majority support in the Security Council and the General Assembly.[52]

It has been suggested that the WTO should break the blockage of the appointment of Appellate Body members by referring this matter to the WTO General Council, which can take decisions by majority vote. As noted above, dispute settlement matters have on occasion been discussed in the General Council. In 2018 and 2019, the Appellate Body crisis was on the agenda of many meetings of the General Council. However, it is questionable whether, formally speaking, the General Council could take a decision on the appointment of Appellate Body members, ie a matter explicitly entrusted, pursuant to Article 17.2 of the DSU, to the DSB. Article IV:3 of the WTO Agreement states: 'The General Council shall convene as appropriate to discharge the responsibilities of the Dispute Settlement Body provided for in the Dispute Settlement Understanding'. This means that whenever the General Council discusses dispute settlement matters it convenes as the DSB (and not as the General Council) and decisions can only be taken by consensus. To overcome the current blockage, the decision on the appointment of Appellate Body members could be referred to the Ministerial Conference, the WTO's supreme body, which, pursuant to Article IX:1 of the WTO Agreement, can take all its decisions by majority vote. It is, however, highly unlikely that the Ministerial Conference will adopt any important decision by majority vote, certainly in the face of strong US opposition. The blockage of the appointment of Appellate Body members, and the failure to address this blockage, is a first aspect of the misgovernance of the WTO appellate review.

[51] US Senate Committee on Finance, 'Approaching 25: The Road Ahead for the World Trade Organization' <www.finance.senate.gov/hearings/approaching-25-the-road-ahead-for-the-world-trade-organization>.

[52] Note that the permanent members of the UN Security Council have no veto power regarding decisions on the appointment of ICJ judges.

17.5.2 Persistent and unfounded allegations of 'overreach' by the Appellate Body

As noted above, the blockage by the United States of the appointment of Appellate Body members is motivated by its concerns regarding the functioning of the Appellate Body. The United States considers *inter alia* that the Appellate Body 'overreached', ie exceeded, its mandate under the DSU in several ways. This section will evaluate some of the arguments advanced to support this claim.

17.5.2.1 Judicial activism

According to the United States, the Appellate Body has, through its interpretation of WTO provisions, created obligations to which the United States never agreed. In other words, the United States accuses the Appellate Body of judicial activism. In this context, the United States refers in particular to the Appellate Body case law on 'zeroing', on 'public body', on 'unforeseen developments', and on 'legitimate regulatory distinctions'.[53]

Whether this case law indeed reflects judicial activism is contested by many other WTO Members. As one of the Appellate Body members in *US—Continued Zeroing (2009)* stated in a concurring opinion, 'a treaty bears the imprint of many hands. And what is left behind is a text, sometimes negotiated to a point where an agreement to regulate a matter could only be reached on the basis of constructive ambiguity, carrying both the hopes and fears of the parties'.[54] This is definitely true for the WTO agreements, which are a masterpiece of 'constructive ambiguity' with many provisions that Members understand differently and which thus give rise to disputes. As a result, there is much need for 'clarification', a task which Article 3.2, second sentence, of the DSU explicitly assigns to the WTO dispute settlement system, and thus ultimately to the Appellate Body. The scope of this mandate to clarify is circumscribed by Articles 3.2, third sentence, and 19.2 of the DSU, which state that the WTO dispute settlement system, and thus the Appellate Body, 'cannot add to or diminish the rights and obligations provided in the covered agreements'.[55] The DSU thus clearly does not condone judicial activism. The Appellate Body is definitely not to take on the role of 'legislator'.

The line that divides 'clarification of WTO provisions' from 'adding to or diminishing the rights and obligations of Members' is, however, not always easy to draw. For panels and the Appellate Body to stay within their mandate to clarify existing provisions, it is important that they clarify them as instructed by Article 3.2, second sentence, of the DSU, namely 'in accordance with the customary rules of interpretation of public international law'. As the Appellate Body already noted in 1996, the rules of interpretation set out in Articles 31 and 32 of the Vienna Convention on the Law of Treaties (VCLT) are such customary rules of interpretation.[56] To avoid adding

[53] See Office of the United States Trade Representative, Report on the Appellate Body of the World Trade Organization, February 2020 <https://ustr.gov/sites/default/files/Report_on_the_Appellate_Body_of_the_World_Trade_Organization.pdf>.

[54] Appellate Body Report, *US—Continued Zeroing (2009)* para 306.

[55] The constituent instruments of other international courts and tribunals seldom have provisions prohibiting judicial activism, although it is obviously disallowed.

[56] See Appellate Body Report, *US—Gasoline (1996)* 15–16; and Appellate Body Report, *Japan—Alcoholic Beverages II (1996)* at 104.

to or diminishing the rights and obligations of Members, ie to avoid judicial activism, the clarification of WTO provisions requires rigorous adherence to the rules of interpretation contained in Articles 31 and 32 of the VCLT. As the Appellate Body stated in *Chile—Alcoholic Beverages (2000)*, '[w]e have difficulty in envisaging circumstances in which a panel could add to the rights and obligations of a Member of the WTO if its conclusions reflected a correct interpretation and application of provisions of the covered agreements'.[57] Article 31 of the VCLT provides that the words of the treaty form the foundation for the interpretative process.[58] The results of an interpretative approach which gives primary importance to the wording actually used, are more easily accepted by the parties to the treaty than the often 'surprising' results of interpretative approaches that, for example, give more importance to the object and purpose of the treaty. If most WTO Members hold the Appellate Body in high esteem, this is to a large extent due to the Appellate Body's choice for, and near-consistent application of, a 'text first' approach to interpretation.[59]

While it is not uncommon for a WTO Member in the immediate aftermath of an unfavourable ruling to accuse the Appellate Body of having added to or diminished that Member's WTO rights and obligations, in most instances this accusation is primarily for domestic consumption and short-lived. However, the latter is not the case for the United States, which has, with regard to case law with which it does not agree, maintained its strongly worded accusations of judicial activism. As noted earlier, for the United States, the alleged judicial activism of the Appellate Body is the main reason for its obstruction of the appointment of Appellate Body members and thus its undermining of the whole WTO dispute settlement system. To be clear, if the Appellate Body had indeed systematically engaged in judicial activism, it would have been acting inconsistently with its mandate and the United States' action would have been justified. However, while the United States continues to make antagonistic allegations of judicial activism regarding Appellate Body case law it does not agree with, it has not convincingly demonstrated that the Appellate Body's interpretation in these instances was not in accordance with Articles 31 and 32 of the VCLT.[60]

To address the United States' concern regarding judicial activism, it has been suggested to institute an annual 'dialogue' between the Appellate Body and the WTO Dispute Settlement Body on developments in the case law. Article 17.14, second sentence, of the DSU already provides for 'the right of Members to express their view on an Appellate Body report'. The parties to a dispute, and to a lesser degree also other WTO Members, make use of this right at the DSB meeting at which the report is adopted. At this meeting, the winning party usually limits itself to thanking the Appellate Body for 'a job well done' and the losing party seldom does more than repeating in detail the arguments it unsuccessfully made during the appellate proceedings. These statements seldom shed new light on the matter at issue. Whether an annual meeting between the

[57] Appellate Body Report, *Chile—Alcoholic Beverages (2000)* para 79.

[58] See Appellate Body Report, *Japan—Alcoholic Beverages (1996)* at 11.

[59] See Peter Van den Bossche, 'The Making of the "World Trade Court": The Origins and Development of the Appellate Body of the World Trade Organization' in Rufus Yerxa and Bruce Wilson (eds), *Key Issues in WTO Dispute Settlement: The First Ten Years* (CUP 2005) at 72.

[60] Disagreeing with the Appellate Body's interpretations is something else than demonstrating that the Appellate Body erred in its application of Arts 31 and 32 of the VCLT when making these interpretations.

Appellate Body and the DSB will be any different in character is doubtful. However, as noted, an additional opportunity for Members to vent their disagreement with developments in the Appellate Body's case law is useful, especially if the discussion on these developments can be conducted at a general, non-case-specific level (where that is at all possible).

17.5.2.2 Rendering advisory opinions

The United States also argues that the Appellate Body 'overreaches' its mandate by rendering advisory opinions, ie rulings on issues which need not be addressed to resolve the dispute.[61] As noted above, Article 17.12 of the DSU, however, explicitly requires that the Appellate Body addresses 'each of the issues raised ... during the appellate proceedings'. To address the United States' objection regarding what it considers to be advisory opinions, other WTO Members have proposed to amend Article 17.12 by including language explicitly instructing the Appellate Body not to address issues that need not be addressed to resolve the dispute. However, parties may disagree on what is needed to resolve the dispute and therefore there may be merit in giving both parties their 'day in court' by addressing all issues raised and related arguments made. While an international adjudicator should be cautious not to rule on more issues than is strictly needed to resolve the dispute, there is virtue in considering all issues and arguments and explaining a ruling carefully so that the high quality of decision-making can be ensured.

17.5.2.3 Appellate review of factual findings

Another concern raised by the United States regarding the 'overreach' of the Appellate Body relates to the scope of appellate review. The United States alleges that the Appellate Body erroneously reviews factual findings of the panel, and in particular its findings on the meaning of municipal law, thereby acting *ultra vires*. As noted above, Article 17.6 of the DSU limits appellate review to 'issues of law covered in the panel report and legal interpretations developed by the panel'. Factual issues are therefore clearly beyond the scope of appellate review. As the Appellate Body stated in *EC—Hormones (1998)*, 'findings of fact, as distinguished from legal interpretations and legal conclusions, by a panel are, *in principle*, not subject to review by the Appellate Body'.[62] However, the panel's discretion in the determination of the facts is *not* unlimited; it must be consistent with Article 11 of the DSU. Under Article 11, the panel is under the legal obligation 'to make an objective assessment of the matter before it, including an objective assessment of the fact of the case'. As the Appellate Body ruled in *EC—Hormones (1998)*, 'whether or not a panel made an objective assessment of the facts before it ... is ... a legal question, which, if properly raised on appeal, would fall within the scope of appellate review'.[63] The standard applied by the Appellate Body for finding that a panel failed to make an objective assessment of the facts is quite high. Not every error of the panel in the determination of the facts amounts to a violation of Article 11. Under the current case law, the error must be such that it casts doubt on the

[61] Note that the United States uses the concept of 'advisory opinions' in a 'novel' way.
[62] Appellate Body Report, *EC—Hormones (1998)* para 132 (emphasis added).
[63] ibid.

objectivity of the panel's factual assessment.[64] While the United States expresses concern regarding the Appellate Body's review of factual findings, one wonders whether the United States would object to the review of factual findings which raise questions regarding the objectivity of the panel's assessment of the facts, for example because the findings by the panel were made in blatant violation of due process. Limiting appellate review of such findings would significantly undermine the credibility of WTO dispute settlement. The US concern regarding the review of factual findings often focusses on panel findings on the meaning of US municipal law. Such panel findings are factual findings and—if they are not alleged to be inconsistent with Article 11—should, indeed, not be subject to appellate review. To the extent that the Appellate Body has reviewed such findings, it did so in error.[65]

17.5.2.4 Giving precedential value to case law

Finally, the United States contends that the Appellate Body has 'overreached' its mandate by giving precedential value to its case law. The United States objects to any obligation on panels to consider prior Appellate Body rulings as precedent, ie as binding on them. The Appellate Body has consistently held that the doctrine of binding precedent (*stare decisis*) does not apply in WTO dispute settlement. However, it has also noted that Article 3.2 of the DSU states that WTO dispute settlement is a central element in providing security and predictability to the multilateral trading system, and that WTO Members have a legitimate expectation that the same legal issue is decided in the same way in later disputes. Therefore, panels cannot be free to deviate from established case law absent 'cogent reasons'.[66]

17.5.2.5 Impact of persistent and unfounded allegations of judicial overreach

Persistent and unfounded allegations of judicial activism and other forms of overreach undermine the authority and the effective operation of the court or tribunal concerned. Such allegations are therefore a second aspect of the misgovernance of WTO appellate review.

17.5.3 Inadequate protection of the independence and impartiality of the Appellate Body and its Secretariat

As regards the independence and impartiality of the Appellate Body, two issues give cause for apprehension—one relating to its members and the other to its staff. As noted above, Appellate Body members are appointed for a four-year term, which is renewable once. As the first term is short, many Appellate Body members may be expected to seek a second term. It is this possibility of reappointment which may cast doubt on the independence and impartiality of those Appellate Body members wishing to secure a second term. Like the initial appointment, reappointment requires a consensus decision of the DSB. This gives any WTO Member the power to deny an Appellate

[64] Appellate Body Report, *US—COOL (2012)* para 300.
[65] eg Appellate Body Report, *US—Countervailing and Anti-Dumping Measures (2014)* para 4.101.
[66] Appellate Body Report, *US—Stainless Steel (Mexico) (2008)*, para 160.

Body member reappointment because of its displeasure with rulings by the Appellate Body in which that member was involved.

The United States twice prevented the reappointment of Appellate Body members for this reason. In 2011, it did not nominate Jennifer Hillman, a US national, for re-appointment, allegedly because she had not been sufficiently proactive and/or successful in defending US positions.[67] In 2016, the United States blocked the reappointment of Seung Wha Chang, a Korean national, primarily because of Chang's involvement in four Appellate Body rulings, which the United States considered erroneous.[68] The US decision to block the reappointment of Chang, and in particular the reason given for this decision, was strongly criticized by other WTO Members.[69]

While DSU Article 17.2 makes it clear that reappointment requires consensus in the DSB, there was no procedure for reappointment set out in either the DSU or the 1995 DSB Decision. However, for the first time in 2013 and then again in 2015 and 2016, WTO Members agreed on an ad hoc procedure which involved submitting the member nominated for reappointment to questioning by a group of ambassadors of frequent users of the dispute settlement system (2013) or by the DSB (2015 and 2016).[70] In the context of the discussion on the reform of WTO appellate review, China, the European Union, India, and Montenegro proposed to amend Article 17.2 of the DSU and appoint Appellate Body members for a single, non-renewable six- or eight-year term.[71] This proposal was motivated by the perceived need to better ensure the independence and impartiality of Appellate Body members. The United States rejected this proposal arguing that it would make Appellate Body members less accountable.[72]

A second issue regarding the independence and impartiality of the Appellate Body concerns the staff of the Appellate Body. As discussed above, paragraph 17 of the 1995 DSB Decision on the Establishment of the Appellate Body states, for good reason, that the support staff of the Appellate Body 'should be independent from the [WTO] Secretariat'.[73] However, while paragraph 17 explicitly states that the staff of the

[67] Gary Clyde Hufbauer, 'WTO Judicial Appointments: Bad Omen for the Trading System' (Realtime Economic Issues Watch, Peterson Institute for International Economics, 13 June 2011) <www.piie.com/blogs/realtime-economic-issues-watch/wto-judicial-appointments-bad-omen-trading-system>. Note that in 2007 also Merit E Janow, the Appellate Body member from the United States (2003–07) and a professor of law at Columbia University, was not reappointed, although she did, after some initial hesitation, seek reappointment. She was replaced by Jennifer Hillman, who as a former US Trade Representative General Counsel and member of the US International Trade Commission was seen as more of an insider.

[68] See Statement by the United States at the meeting of the WTO Dispute Settlement Body of 23 May 2016, item 7 <www.wto.org/english/news_e/news16_e/us_statment_dsbmay16_e.pdf>. Seung Wha Chang, a professor of law at Seoul National University, was subsequently replaced by Hyun Chong Kim, who was a former trade minister for Korea. The latter resigned in August 2017, when he was again appointed trade minister for Korea.

[69] See WTO, 'WTO Members Debate Appointment/Reappointment of Appellate Body Members' <www.wto.org/english/news_e/news16_e/dsb_23may16_e.htm>.

[70] The Appellate Body members seeking reappointment in 2013 were Peter Van den Bossche of the European Union; in 2015, Ujal Singh Bhatia of India and Thomas Graham of the United States, and in 2016, Seung Wha Chang of Korea.

[71] See Communication from the European Union, China, India, and Montenegro to the General Council, WT/GC/W/753, 26 November 2018, WT/GC/W/753/Rev. 1, 11 December 2018.

[72] See Laura von Daniels, Susanne Dröge, and Alexandra Bögner, 'Ways Out of the WTO's December Crisis: How to Prevent the Open Global Trade Order from Unravelling' (Stiftung Wissenschaft und Politik, 12 April 2019) <www.swp-berlin.org/10.18449/2019C46>.

[73] 1995 DSB Decision (n 18) para 17.

Appellate Body is 'answerable to the Appellate Body' (and not to the WTO Director-General), the staff is to be appointed (and can presumably also be dismissed) by the WTO Director-General (and not by the Appellate Body).[74] The Director-General also decides on the conditions of employment of the staff, including promotions in rank. Successive Directors-General have, to different degrees, sought to influence the operation of the Appellate Body Secretariat by requiring the Director of the Appellate Body Secretariat to report to them. The 'hold' of the WTO Director-General over the Appellate Body staff is difficult to reconcile with the intended independence of the Appellate Body Secretariat.

The inadequate protection of the independence and impartiality of the Appellate Body and its Secretariat is a third aspect of the misgovernance of WTO appellate review.

17.5.4 Unrealistic timeframe for appellate review

Article 17.5 of the DSU stipulates regarding appellate review that 'in no case shall the proceedings exceed 90 days'. No other international court or tribunal works with a time frame of a similar nature and severity. Until 2011 the Appellate Body was able to keep to this very demanding timeframe in most cases. However, over the last decade, the vastly increased complexity and size of many appeals have made it unrealistic.[75]

While the length of Appellate Body proceedings is still limited when compared with the length of the proceedings in some other international courts and tribunals, the Appellate Body's failure to complete its proceedings within 90 days has been criticized harshly by some WTO Members. According to the United States, the Appellate Body may only exceed the ninety-day timeframe if the parties have agreed to an extension. Before 2010 the Appellate Body invited the parties to a dispute to communicate to it that they would deem a report circulated after ninety days to be a report circulated within that period (the so-called deeming letters).

However, from 2010 onwards the Appellate Body stopped this practice of inviting deeming letters. Such practice could be seen as a recognition by the Appellate Body that the ninety-day timeframe could only be exceeded with the agreement of the parties. This cannot be so because it would allow an appellee to frustrate proper appellate review in appeals which—due to the complexity or size of the appeal or due to the number of appeals before the Appellate Body at a given time—could not possibly be disposed of within ninety days. The Appellate Body refused to interpret and apply Article 17.5 of the DSU in a manner that would effectively deny an appellant its right

[74] The WTO Director-General takes decisions on staff appointments on the advice of a selection committee. The selection committees for Appellate Body staff have always included a majority of WTO Secretariat staff and only in selection committees for the Director or (in recent years) senior legal advisors, the Appellate Body would be represented by one of its members.

[75] To date, Appellate Body proceedings have taken on average 141 days: <http://worldtradelaw.net/databases/abtiming.php>. However, if the appeals in three very large cases, namely *EU and Certain member States—Large Civil Aircraft (2010, 2018)*, *US—Large Civil Aircraft (2012, 2019)* and *Australia—Tobacco Plain Packaging (2020)* are not included in the calculation, the average time for Appellate Body proceedings exceeds the ninety-day limit by less.

to proper appellate review by compromising the quality and thoroughness of such review.

The United States and others have taken the position that Appellate Body reports circulated after ninety days, without the agreement of the parties, are no longer reports which the DSB could adopt by reverse consensus. Such reports would, according to the United States, require adoption by 'normal' consensus in the DSB, which would give any Member, and in particular the losing party, the possibility of blocking the adoption of the report (and thus prevent it from becoming legally binding). Other WTO Members, and foremost the European Union, disagreed with the United States' position on the consequences of exceeding the ninety-day time frame. The uncompromising insistence on an unrealistic timeframe and allowing the resolution of a dispute to be frustrated if the timeframe is exceeded is a fourth aspect of the misgovernance of WTO appellate review.

17.5.5 Size of the Appellate Body and its Secretariat

As noted above, the Appellate Body is composed of seven members, which is a small number compared with other international courts or tribunals, especially when one considers that the workload and output of the Appellate Body has by far exceeded that of those other international courts and tribunals. The small number Appellate Body members is a reflection of the initial expectation that parties would only occasionally have recourse to appellate review. Although this expectation very soon turned out be quite wrong, the number of Appellate Body members was not adjusted.

In the context of the discussion on the reform of WTO appellate review, China, the European Union, India, and Montenegro proposed to increase the number of Appellate Body members from seven to nine in order to 'improve the efficiency and internal organization of the Appellate Body' as well as the 'geographical balance on the Appellate Body'.[76] These WTO Members also suggested to provide that 'membership of the Appellate Body is the exclusive occupation of Appellate Body members' and replace the current part-time with full-time employment conditions. While the proposed enlargement of the Appellate Body from seven to nine members would indeed allow it to handle a somewhat larger workload, the proposed change in the employment conditions will not have the same effect. As required by Article 17.2 of the DSU, Appellate Body members 'shall be available at all times and on short notice'. In view of this obligation regarding availability, Appellate Body membership was over the past ten years, due to the large workload, often more than a full-time job, regardless the part-time employment conditions. All proposals to amend Appellate Body members' part-time employment conditions have in the past met with fierce resistance from WTO Members, including the United States, that object to, and challenge, the court-like nature of the Appellate Body.

[76] General Council—Communication from the European Union, China, India, and Montenegro to the General Council, WT/GC/W/753, 26 November 2018, WT/GC/W/753/Rev. 1, 11 December 2018.

Not only is the Appellate Body undersized, but also its Secretariat. As discussed above, Article 17.7 of the DSU states: 'The Appellate Body shall be provided with appropriate administrative and legal support as it requires.' While the Secretariat grew considerably in size over the years, it always had less staff than the workload required. Constraints on the growth of the WTO budget were the most important but not the only explanation for the understaffing. In recent years, some WTO Members, and in particular the United States, objected to any increase in the staff of the Appellate Body Secretariat and they did so to express their dissatisfaction with the Appellate Body, its functioning and part of its case law. According to the United States, an Appellate Body with an understaffed Secretariat would be less likely/able to engage in judicial activism or other forms of judicial overreach.

Therefore, the undersized Appellate Body and its understaffed Secretariat constitute the fifth aspect of the misgovernance of WTO appellate review.

17.6 Lessons for the Governance of International Adjudication

An international adjudicative body, court, or tribunal can only function effectively as such when three essential conditions are met, namely:

- it acts, and is allowed to act, within its mandate as an adjudicator;
- it is independent and impartial, and its independence and impartiality are respected; and
- it settles disputes in a timely manner, consistent with the requirements of due process, and is endowed with the financial and human resources to do so.

For the WTO Appellate Body, these conditions have not been met for some time or have never been met. The rules and procedures for the governance of WTO appellate review and the manner in which these rules and procedures have been (ab)used, have resulted in the current profound crisis of WTO appellate review and the undermining of the credibility and effectiveness of the whole WTO dispute settlement system.

The crisis of WTO appellate review holds some crucial lessons for the governance of international adjudication. These lessons, which concern all actors in international adjudication, consist in reaffirming the need to: (1) ensure that the appointment of judges cannot be blocked *sine die*; (2) ensure that the term in office of adjudicators as well as the legal position and terms of employment of their support staff do not adversely affect the adjudicators' independence and impartiality; (3) provide for the timeframe for adjudication that is realistic and allows for a proper consideration of all the issues raised in a dispute; (4) give the adjudicative body sufficient human and financial resources to perform its task well; and (5) avoid making persistently unfounded allegations of judicial overreach by losing parties with the sole aim of undermining the authority and credibility of the adjudicative body. The demise of the WTO Appellate Body is a sad example of what may happen if these lessons are not taken seriously.

17.7 Post Scriptum

Since finishing this chapter some time has passed, but little has changed. The crisis of WTO appellate review remains unresolved and the credibility and effectiveness of the WTO dispute settlement seriously undermined. At the Twelfth WTO Ministerial Conference in June 2022, WTO Members 'recognize[d] the importance and urgency of addressing' the 'challenges and concerns with respect of the dispute settlement system' and 'commit[ted] to conduct discussions with the view of having a fully and well-functioning dispute settlement system accessible to all Members by 2024'. At the request of key Members, Mr Marco Molina, the then Deputy Permanent Representative of Guatemala to the WTO, initiated in February 2023 informal discussions on dispute settlement reform, referred to as the 'Molina Process'.

Unlike in the 2019 Walker Process, the United States actively engaged in the Molina Process, which resulted in February 2024 in the Consolidated Text of a draft Ministerial Decision on Dispute Settlement. The Consolidated Text contains a large number of proposed changes to the WTO dispute settlement system but was criticized by a group of key developing countries, including Bangladesh, Egypt, India, Indonesia, and South Africa. Most importantly, the Consolidated Text did not address the issue of appellate review, which is at the core of the current crisis. The positions of the United States, which is opposed to meaningful appellate review, and most other WTO Members, which consider appellate review indispensable, are so far apart that it is unlikely that any middle ground can be found any time soon. The crisis of the Appellate Body and of WTO dispute settlement as a whole thus persists. The lessons for the governance of international adjudication that can be drawn from this crisis remain as relevant as ever.

18
Challenges to the Governance of the International Criminal Court

Silvia Fernández de Gurmendi

18.1 Introduction

After the entry into force of the Rome Statute of the International Criminal Court (ICC, or the Court), the enthusiasm of the early years gradually turned into disappointment. During two decades of operations, there were threats of withdrawals, politically motivated attacks, and good-faith criticism of the Court's functioning by internal and external observers, including among its strongest supporters.

The Assembly of States Parties (ASP, or the Assembly) and the Court multiplied measures to respond to mounting concerns about inefficient governance and slow proceedings, some of them resulting in structural reorganization, new strategies and policies, improved methods of work, and discrete amendments to the legal framework. These efforts were, however, not sufficient to dispel the perception that the Court was not delivering to its full potential. In 2019, the Assembly, with the agreement of the Court, launched an initiative to engage in a broad review of the entire Rome Statute system, addressing not only the Court's own performance but also the obligations of states parties as well as their commitment to provide sufficient cooperation and support to the ICC. This ambitious review, aimed at strengthening the system as a whole, was given the highest priority by the Assembly and, during the three years that followed, the Court, the Assembly, and civil society engaged in a transparent and inclusive dialogue on all aspects of the system; the review was completed in December 2024.

These are all welcome and extremely necessary efforts, which have gone a long way in enhancing the performance of the Court. Some of the reforms implemented throughout more than a decade of initiatives have indeed produced some positive and tangible results. However, without prejudice to these significant outcomes, the review process has been particularly useful to help recognize that matters of governance and performance cannot be addressed in isolation but need to be considered holistically. To achieve systemic improvements, it is required to look not only into the challenges derived from the Court's architecture, legal framework, and methods of work, but also to take into account the external challenges arising from the powers and obligations of states parties under the Rome Statute and, more broadly, from the risks and constraints imposed by our increasingly polarized world.

This chapter attempts to contribute to the understanding of these challenges and the efforts undertaken by the Court and the Assembly to overcome them.

Silvia Fernández de Gurmendi, *Challenges to the Governance of the International Criminal Court* In: *Governance of International Courts and Tribunals*. Edited by: Sergey Vasiliev and Niels Blokker, Oxford University Press.
 DOI: 10.1093/oso/9780198922131.003.0018

18.2 The Fragmented Architecture of the Court

The main and overarching challenge conspiring against unified governance is the fragmented architecture of the Court. There is no single authority at the Court with responsibility for the overall administration. Outside the Court, there is no overall authority either because the Assembly only has limited oversight powers. The Court is an international organization of a special character due to its judicial functions that must be exercised independently and impartially. Therefore, the Assembly does not have direct management responsibilities at the Court and must fulfil its oversight role with due respect for such independence as well as due regard to the various and sometimes opposing interests and goals of its 125 members.

18.2.1 Co-existence at the Court of multiple independent organs and functions

The Court is not only a tribunal, but rather a combination of multiple organs and entities with independent or autonomous functions. The proper functioning of the Court depends on decentralized management efforts by many internal actors and, therefore, on the collective capacity of those in charge to align different mandates and goals around a common vision.

Article 34 of the Rome Statute of the International Criminal Court (Statute, or Rome Statute) lists the four organs that constitute the Court, namely the Presidency, the Appeals, Trial and Pre-Trial Divisions, the Office of the Prosecutor, and the Registry.

Therefore, in addition to the Judges, who perform the judicial functions, the Court also comprises the Registry, which services all organs, and the Office of the Prosecutor, which 'shall act independently as a separate organ of the Court'.[1]

The Presidency and the Registry bear the greatest responsibility for the administration of the Court but must exercise it without prejudice to the functions and powers of the Office of the Prosecutor, which is a fully independent and separate organ. In addition to their core judicial role, the eighteen Judges exercise important non-judicial managerial functions, either collectively in plenary sessions or separately as part of their work in their respective divisions, chambers, and in individual cases.

As demonstrated by two decades of operations of the Court, the demarcation of the respective competencies, responsibilities, and reporting lines is not sufficiently clear. The Registry, pursuant to Article 43(1), is responsible for the non-judicial aspects of the administration and servicing of the Court but needs to perform these responsibilities 'without prejudice to the functions and powers of the Prosecutor'. Indeed, while being serviced by the Registry, the Prosecutor has 'full authority over the management and administration of the Office including the staff, facilities and other resources thereof'.[2] However, the legal and material separation of the Office of the Prosecutor is

[1] Rome Statute of the International Criminal Court (opened for signature 17 July 1998, entered into force on 1 July 2002) 2187 UNTS 3 (ICC Statute), Art 42(1).

[2] ibid Art 42(2).

not absolute. This constantly requires striking a balance between independence and co-existence.

Considering this and related provisions, there is a potential for conflict, confusion, and overlap between some of the powers of the Prosecutor and the administrative functions of the Registry. Determining whether the Registrar or the Prosecutor is entitled to perform certain functions or decide on certain matters is not always an easy task and there is also no one at the Court with sufficient authority to arbitrate in case a dispute arises. Indeed, the Registrar exercises his or her duties under the authority of the President of the Court.[3] But also the President, together with the two Vice-Presidents, is responsible for the administration of the Court 'with the exception of the Office of the Prosecutor'.[4]

Adding to the complexity, besides the Prosecutor and the Judges, the Registry also services the independent work of defence counsel and legal representatives of victims. That work may be performed by external lawyers or by the staff members of the Office of Public Counsel for the Defence (OPCD) and the Office of Public Counsel for the Victims (OPCV). The functioning of these two autonomous offices established within the Registry has also raised questions of authority and reporting lines. In order to clarify the situation, Judges amended the Regulations of the Court in 2011,[5] explicitly indicating that both offices fall within the remit of the Registry solely for administrative purposes but function in their substantive work as wholly independent offices.[6]

18.2.2 Co-existence of non-judicial functions of the Presidency and the Judges

Pursuant to Article 34 of the Statute, the Presidency—composed of three Judges elected as President and Vice-Presidents—and the three judicial divisions constitute two separate organs of the Court with distinct functions.[7]

While the Presidency is responsible for the exercise of non-judicial functions of the Court, Judges working collectively in plenary sessions or within Divisions and Chambers, also perform important non-judicial functions under the legal framework.

18.2.2.1 Presidency

In accordance with Article 38(1) of the Statute and the Rules of Procedure and Evidence (Rules),[8] a new Presidency is elected every three years after the election of six new judges. The election of the members of the Presidency is done in a plenary session of Judges convened immediately after the swearing-in ceremony of the new judges.[9]

[3] ibid Art 43(2).
[4] ibid Art 38(3)(a).
[5] Regulations of the Court, adopted on 26 May 2004, as amended on 2 November 2011, amendments entered into force on 29 June 2012.
[6] ibid Regulations 77(2) and 81(2).
[7] ibid Art 34(a) and (b).
[8] ibid Arts 38 and 39; Rules of Procedure and Evidence of the International Criminal Court, Official Records of the Assembly of States Parties to the Rome Statute of the International Criminal Court, First Session (New York, 3–10 September 2002) ICC-ASP/1/3 and Corr.1 (ICC RPE).
[9] ICC RPE Rule 4(1).

Judges elect—separately by simply majority and by secret ballot—the President, followed by the First Vice-President, and finally the Second Vice-President. They take office on the same day as their election.

This is an event of major importance for the life and governance of the Court. While the Presidency does not have full authority over the entire Court, its powers to lead the institution, promote its efficiency and effectiveness and garner external cooperation and support cannot be underestimated. In particular, by exercising authority over the Registrar as well as by playing a crucial external relations role, the President has great potential to impact positively (or negatively) the governance, credibility, and legitimacy of the institution.

And yet, the election of the President and Vice-Presidents is done by the Judges alone and without formal or informal consultation with other organs of the Court, and at a time when six newly elected Judges have hardly had the chance of getting acquainted with their colleagues at the Court and get apprised of the institutional challenges facing it.

While all Judges agree that the election of the members of the Presidency should be done by consensus, it is the product of at times bitter competition. This may result in lasting interpersonal tensions and divisions within the judiciary. As discussed further below, Judges have most recently sought to improve the system through amendments to the Code of Judicial Ethics and the adoption of Guidelines to regulate the election process.[10]

The pool of potential candidates for the position of President is very small, which does not guarantee that the person most qualified for such role is elected. Indeed, the interpretative practice so far has been that only those assigned to the Appeals or Pre-Trial Divisions may aspire to the position of President, which is due to the combined effect of paragraphs 1, 4 and 3(a) of Article 39 of the Statute. Paragraph 1 indicates that the President shall be part of the Appeals Division, while paragraph 4 states that Judges assigned to the Appeals Division shall serve only in that Division. In turn, paragraph 3(a) and principles of fair trial imply that, once hearings have started, a Judge must remain on the bench in any ongoing trial until its completion. Therefore, and bearing in mind also the practical difficulties of exercising the functions of the Presidency while sitting daily in the courtroom, Judges involved in trials have traditionally been excluded from the pool of potential candidates. The universe of eligible candidates was narrowed even further since a new practice was adopted in 2015, namely that only those commencing their last three years of mandate may be considered. This practice also precludes re-election, which is otherwise allowed under Article 38 of the Statute, and three years may be too short to implement some measures.

As noted, the Presidency is responsible for the non-judicial administration of the Court while the Judges exercise judicial functions within their respective Chambers and Divisions. The Presidency takes non-judicial decisions that are, however, crucial for the conduct of judicial proceedings, such as the assignment of Judges to Divisions, and the constitution of Chambers. In accordance with Article 39 of the Rome Statute, as soon as possible after each election of the Judges and their swearing-in, the Court

[10] Section 18.4.4.4.

needs to organize itself into three divisions, i.e. the Appeals, Trial, and Pre-Trial Divisions. While some criteria to carry out the assignment are set out in this provision, they leave ample room for discretion.

In accordance with Rule 199 of the Rules, the Presidency also has important responsibilities, that could be qualified as quasi-judicial, under Part 10 of the Statute related to the enforcement of sentences.

The distinction between the functions of Judges and those of the Presidency is not always easy to draw, considering that the Judges also have management responsibilities that are described below.

18.2.2.2 Plenary of Judges

The Judges have important responsibilities affecting the functioning of the Court that they exercise collectively in plenary meetings convened to that end.[11]

In addition to the election of the Presidency, the Judges have legislative and disciplinary powers. They adopt the Regulations of the Court (Regulations) necessary for the routine functioning of the Court and any amendments thereof,[12] and may also propose amendments to the Rules to be submitted to the Assembly of States Parties.[13]

With regard to disciplinary matters, it is for the Judges to recommend to the Assembly of States Parties, by a two-thirds majority, the removal of a Judge[14] or decide themselves, by simple majority, upon the removal of the Registrar and Deputy Registrar.[15] Other disciplinary measures against a Judge, the Registrar, or a Deputy Registrar may be taken by the Presidency.[16] The Plenary of Judges decides on the disqualifications of Judges[17] while the Presidency may, at the request of a Judge, excuse that Judge from the exercise of a function under the Statute.[18]

The rationale for attributing some management functions to the Judges instead of the Presidency may be questionable both from a legal and governance perspective. In the initial years, it was the Plenary of Judges which decided upon the assignment of Judges to Divisions, while the Presidency could only determine their appointment to specific Chambers within the Divisions. This anomaly was corrected by the Assembly through the adoption of Rule 4 *bis* by which it transferred from the Plenary of Judges to each newly established Presidency the function of assigning Judges to Divisions, in consultation with the Judges.[19] Further, with a view to enhancing efficiency, the Assembly adopted another amendment in 2013, this time upon request of the Judges themselves, transferring from the Plenary to the Presidency the power to decide whether to hold proceedings in a state other than the host state.[20]

[11] ICC RPE Rule 4.
[12] ICC Statute Art 52(1).
[13] ibid Art 51(2).
[14] ibid Art 46(2)(a).
[15] ibid Art 46(3).
[16] ICC RPE Rule 30(1).
[17] ICC Statute Art 41(2)(c).
[18] ibid Art 41(1).
[19] ICC RPE Rule 4 *bis* (as amended by Resolution ICC-ASP/10/Res.1, 20 December 2011).
[20] Study Group on Governance, Working Group on Lessons Learnt: Second Report of the Court to the Assembly of States Parties (The Hague, 20–28 November 2013) ICC-ASP/12/37/Add.1, 31 October 2013.

18.2.2.3 Divisions and Chambers

The Appeals, Trial, and Pre-Trial Divisions constitute a separate organ of the Court. The Judges exercise judicial functions of the Court while distributed in Chambers within these Divisions. The Appeals Chamber is composed of all five Judges of the Division. Judges assigned to the Trial and Pre-Trial Divisions fulfil their judicial work within Chambers composed of three Judges each, which are constituted by the Presidency according to the workload.

While the Judges do not have administrative functions of a general kind, they are responsible for the management of their cases. This management has, in turn, a tremendous impact on the functioning of the Court itself. Indeed, the performance of the Court ultimately depends on the efficient conduct of judicial proceedings.

While all Judges are responsible for the efficiency of proceedings, Presidents of Divisions as well as presiding Judges of Chambers and Judges appointed as Single Judge at pre-trial or trial proceedings bear greater responsibility and have ample opportunity to contribute to the management of the Court.

Presidents of Divisions are elected on a yearly basis by the Judges of the respective Division from among its members in order to oversee its administration.[21] With regard to the presiding Judges, the Judges of the Appeals Chamber decide on a presiding Judge for each appeal while the Judges of each Trial and Pre-Trial Chamber elect by majority a presiding Judge of the Chamber, to carry out the functions set forth in the Statute, the Rules, and other instruments.[22] In carrying out these functions, it is expected that they not only organize and conduct the legal proceedings efficiently and expeditiously but also ensure an effective use of staff assigned to support them as well as other resources and services.

Single judges, both in pre-trial and trial proceedings, also carry a significant responsibility and fundamental managerial role. While the assignment of single pre-trial Judges is foreseen in Article 57 of the Statute, Single Judges for trial were first introduced by an amendment to the Rules proposed by the Judges, to expedite the preparatory phase of trial proceedings.[23]

18.3 Oversight Role of the Assembly of States Parties

18.3.1 Organization of the Assembly

The Assembly, composed of the states that have ratified the Statute or acceded to it, is not an organ of the Court but a separate body with management oversight, legislative, and other important functions for the governance of the Court.[24]

Among others, the Assembly approves the budget, elects the Judges, Prosecutor, and Deputy Prosecutors of the Court, as well as members of other autonomous and

[21] Regulations of the Court, adopted on 26 May 2004, ICC-BD/01-01-04, last amended on 12 November 2018, ICC-BD/01-05-16, amendments entered into force on 15 November 2018 (ICC RoC), Regulation 14. This version of the ICC RoC will be referred to throughout in this chapter, unless otherwise provided.

[22] ICC RoC Regulation 13.

[23] ICC RPE Rule 132 *bis* (ASP Res ICC-ASP/11/Res.2, 21 November 2012).

[24] ICC Statute Art 112.

subsidiary bodies, such as the Board of Directors of the Trust Fund for Victims, the Advisory Committee on Nominations of Judges, the Committee on Budget and Finance, and the Independent Oversight Mechanism.

As already indicated, the Assembly does not have management responsibilities at the Court itself but can seriously impact its governance with its own actions or inactions. The Assembly has a multi-layered structure which includes a Bureau consisting of the President and two Vice-Presidents and eighteen members elected every three years by the Assembly.[25] In addition, various representatives of the Bureau or other states parties are appointed by the Bureau every year to facilitate discussions and foster progress in the consideration of specific matters. While some of these mandates assigned to one or more representatives of states parties expire once completed, most of them are renewed yearly and have thus become a permanent feature of the Assembly's structure.[26] Among these facilitations, focal points, and groups, the Study Group on Governance is of particular importance. This Group was established by the Assembly for the first time in 2010[27] to conduct a structured dialogue between states parties and the Court with a view to strengthening the institutional framework of the Rome Statute system and enhancing the efficiency and effectiveness of the Court. Its creation brought about an extremely important first process to improve the performance of the Court, known as 'Lessons Learned process'. In 2019, in addition to this Group and other mandate-holders of the Bureau, the ASP established a Review Mechanism to deal with the Review process of the entire Rome Statute system.[28] Both processes are further addressed below.

The multiplicity of mandates and facilitations requires a regular involvement of states, civil society, and the Court in meetings of various kinds and formats all year round both in The Hague and New York, certainly beyond what was initially envisaged in the legal framework. Pursuant to Rule 29 of the Rules of Procedure of the Assembly, the Bureau, which assists the Assembly in the discharge of its responsibility, must meet to that end as often as needed and at least once a year. In the practice that has been developed, the Presidency and the Bureau hold regular meetings every month.

Further, while regular sessions of the Assembly take place only once a year pursuant to Rule 4 of the Assembly's Rules of Procedure, its members meet regularly in monthly meetings of the Working Groups of New York and The Hague, each of them chaired by one Vice-President. The meetings of those Working Groups are open to states parties, observers from non-parties, and civil society. Representatives of the Court are invited to participate in all meetings of the Bureau, Working Groups, and formal sessions of the Assembly.

[25] ICC Rules of Procedure of the Assembly of States Parties (New York, 3–10 September 2002) ICC-ASP/1/3, Rule 29.

[26] These include the facilitations, focal points, and groups for: Governance; Complementarity; Cooperation; Plan of Action for achieving universality and full implementation of the Rome Statute; Non Cooperation; Budget; Budget Management Oversight; Review of the work and operational mandate of the Independent Oversight Mechanism; Amendments; Geographical representation and gender balance in the recruitment of the staff of the Court; Arrears; Review of the procedure for the nomination and election of judges; and Scheduling of Assembly sessions.

[27] Resolution ICC-ASP/9/Res.2, 10 December 2010.

[28] Resolution ICC-ASP/19/Res.7, 18 December 2020.

There is no clear division of labour between The Hague and the New York Working Groups. There is thus a potential of generating duplication, contradictions, and unnecessarily protracted discussions. This risk has been mitigated to some extent through the recent practice of holding Bureau meetings virtually, thus allowing both communities to participate jointly in its discussions.

18.3.2 Legislative functions of the Assembly

Among the powers of the Assembly, its legislative functions are of paramount and unprecedented importance. Within the Rome Statute system, the adoption and amendment of the legal framework of the Court is a prerogative of states parties and the Judges have only limited powers in this regard. Indeed, contrary to the practice of other courts and tribunals, states decided early on in the negotiations that they would not only draft and adopt the Statute of the Court but also its main complementary substantive and procedural instruments, namely the Elements of Crimes (Elements) and the Rules.[29] The Judges were entrusted solely with the task of drafting and amending the Regulations, a third tier of legal provisions necessary for the Court's routine functioning, and even these provisions would require some involvement of states.[30]

The first Judges, who were sworn in on 10 March 2003, adopted the Regulations at their fifth plenary session on 26 May 2004, after a process that allowed the participation of representatives of the Prosecutor and the Registrar.[31] While most provisions do relate to the routine aspects of proceedings, some Regulations go beyond that and provide for important institutional mechanisms and legal tools with a significant impact on the work of the Court. Among those most relevant to governance are the provisions for the establishment of the Office of the Public Counsel for the Defence and the Office of the Public Counsel for the Victims already referred to above.[32] Through the Regulations, the Judges also created an Advisory Committee on Legal Texts, composed of representatives of the Judges, the Office of the Prosecutor, the Registry, and Counsel included in the list of counsel, to consider and report on proposed amendments to the Rules, Elements, and Regulations.[33]

The legal framework of the Court relies on a unique, innovative, and hybrid legal system, which combines elements of the main legal systems of the world, predominantly the common law and the civil law. The potential risks of imposing on the future institution a comprehensive and untested legal scheme were recognized by the drafters, who agreed that the amendment procedure for the Rules, as opposed to the one required for the Statute, needed to be more flexible and open to the concerns of the Court. Accordingly, Article 51 of the Statute allows amendments to be proposed not only by states parties, but also by the Judges and the Prosecutor. Furthermore, in

[29] For a detailed history of the negotiations, see Silvia Fernández de Gurmendi, 'Enhancing the Court's Efficiency: From the Drafting of the Procedural Provisions by States to Their Revision by Judges' (2018) 16(2) Journal of International Criminal Justice 341–61.
[30] ICC Statute Art 52(3).
[31] ICC RoC, as adopted on 26 May 2004, ICC-BD/01-01-04.
[32] ICC RoC Regulations 77 and 81.
[33] ibid Regulation 4.

accordance with Article 51(3), the Judges may draw up provisional rules by a two-thirds majority to be applied in urgent cases where the Rules do not provide for a specific situation before the Court.

While Regulations and Rule amendment proposals are adopted by the Judges by an absolute majority in accordance with Article 50(2)(b) of the Statute, they are the product of a collective consideration by representatives of all organs of the Court and defence counsel sitting in the Advisory Committee on Legal Texts. At the Assembly, amendments to the Rules need to be adopted by a two-thirds majority of its members, in accordance with Article 51(2) of the Statute. In practice, states have opted to adopt amendments only by consensus, what may allow amendments to be blocked by a few states or even one. Experience has demonstrated that this practice frustrates the margin of flexibility envisaged in the Statute. It may politicize discussions and end up making it very difficult to seek improvements to the ICC proceedings through amendments to the Rules. Indeed, as further explained below, this practice ended up generating a deadlock at the Assembly, which was unable to agree on the adoption of any of the proposals for amendments submitted by the Court. This deadlock could only be overcome in 2022, as part of the Review process.

For this and other reasons, from 2014 onwards, proposals for amendments of the legal framework were kept to a minimum and addressed almost exclusively by way of Regulations or practice changes, which are the sole instruments in the hands of Judges. Indeed, Judges may only draw provisional Rules themselves in urgent cases, where the existing ones do not provide for a specific situation before the Court. This possibility, that only addresses urgent unforeseen problems, does not provide an effective instrument to enhance the legal framework as may be necessary. As demonstrated by twenty years of operations, most if not all the procedural problems identified until now do not derive from 'lacunae' or unforeseen situations but rather from flawed or ambiguous provisions that are inapt to facilitate expeditious proceedings. In addition, provisional Rules can only be adopted in urgent cases, raising questions about the appropriate timing for their adoption. It may be difficult to justify the urgency of drawing new Rules in the absence of specific proceedings. But it may be too late for Judges to draw such provisional Rules once such proceedings have already started, considering the prohibition of their retroactive application to the detriment of the suspect of the accused contained in Article 53(4) of the Statute.

Not surprisingly, the Judges have drawn a provisional Rule only once in twenty years of operations. This was done in 2016, when considering ongoing trials and information available on expected new proceedings, Judges had reasons to believe that there would not be enough of them to handle all cases in an efficient manner. Therefore, they decided to adopt a rule amendment provisionally that would allow them to enhance the overall efficiency of proceedings by enabling the Court to focus its judicial resources on core crimes while preserving the fairness of proceedings on offences against administration of justice under Article 70.[34] Therefore, they decided to draw

[34] 'The ICC judges provisionally amend the Rules of Procedure and Evidence and adopt a new regulation in the Regulations of the Court' (ICC press release, 1 March 2016) <www.icc-cpi.int/Pages/item.aspx?name=pr1194>.

up Rule 165 as a provisional amendment along with an accompanying Regulation 66 *bis*. The provisionally amended Rule 165 allows the respective functions of the Pre-Trial and the Trial Chamber, including the confirmation of charges and the trial, to be exercised by one Judge instead of a Chamber of three Judges in cases related to offences against the administration of justice. It further allows for appeal proceedings in the same cases to be conducted by a panel of three Judges instead of the entire Appeals Chamber composed of five Judges. The adoption of Regulation 66 *bis* of the Regulations complemented the provisionally amended Rule 165 by establishing the modalities for the constitution of Chambers and the panel of three Judges in such proceedings.

In accordance with Article 53(3) of the Statute, a provisional Rule may be applied until adopted, amended or rejected by states at the next special or ordinary session of the Assembly of States Parties. When Rule 165 was adopted in 2016, some states considered it an unjustified initiative in detriment of the legislative prerogatives of the Assembly. However, there was no consensus to adopt, amend or reject it, and the Assembly did neither, providing yet another example of the difficulties it faces in exercising its legislative powers. The amendment, which is still valid due to the inaction of the Assembly since its provisional adoption, was applied for the first time in the case against Paul Gicheru for offences against the administration of justice consisting of corruptly influencing witnesses of the Court in Kenya.[35]

18.4 Efforts to Promote Coordination and Cohesion

18.4.1 One-Court Principle

As already indicated, no single Court's organ has full authority and responsibility for its governance. Decision-making requires consultation and coordination among, and a collegial attitude of, all officials involved.

While acknowledging the need to respect the independence of the Court organs under the Statute, the Assembly has repeatedly stressed the need to pursue the 'One-Court Principle' as an integral part of institution-building.[36] This is an important principle considering that the need for concerted action is not only a policy aspiration but also a legal obligation under the Statute. Article 38(4) explicitly mandates the Presidency to 'coordinate with and seek the concurrence of the Prosecutor on all matters of mutual concern' in discharging its responsibility.

The Court has taken steps to implement this statutory requirement through the establishment of cross-organ platforms to discuss and promote coordination on issues

35 Public Redacted Version of Decision on the confirmation of charges against Paul Gicheru, *Prosecutor v Paul Gicheru*, Situation in the Republic of Kenya, ICC-01/09-01/20-153-Red, Pre-Trial Chamber A, ICC, 15 July 2021.

36 See eg Resolutions ICC-ASP/2/Res.7, 12 September 2003, ASP/4/Res.4 of 3 December 2005, ICC-ASP/5/Res.3, 1 December 2006.

of common concern – not only internal administration matters but also external relations and communications of the Court.[37] The Presidency and the Judges have also strived to enhance cohesion within the Judiciary with the aim of expediting and improving pre-trial, trial, and appeal proceedings.

18.4.2 Dialogue between organs: the Coordination Council

Most important among the coordinating structures is the Coordination Council (CoCo), comprising the President, the Prosecutor, and the Registrar. The CoCo was established in 2004 under the Regulations,[38] following the example of other international tribunals. The CoCo provides a platform for regular formal encounters between the ICC principals. It meets at least once a month or on any other occasion, at the request of one of its members, in order to discuss and coordinate the administrative activities of the organs of the Court. It is therefore a key mechanism for fostering strategy and policy alignment.

One key area requiring coordination and unity of purpose is the drafting of the proposed budget. It is essential that it reflects the Court-wide strategic priorities rather than an aggregate of individual organs' requests. Several concrete measures have been taken at the Court to improve this process for it to reflect a 'One-Court' approach more clearly, following the comments and guidance provided by the Assembly of States Parties and its Committee on Budget and Finance. The overall defining feature of the efforts to revise the process has been an earlier and greater involvement of the three heads of organs in the development of the budget proposals in ensuring that they reflect a coherent common vision. The final proposed budget submission is approved by the three heads of organs at the CoCo, who remain involved in the subsequent exchanges with the Assembly of States Parties and its subsidiary bodies. In 2017, the Assembly recognized the improvements of the budgetary process within the Court that had resulted from these inter-organ coordinating efforts.[39] However, the formulation and approval of the budget continue to constitute the most contentious and difficult exercise undertaken at the Court and the Assembly each year. Despite some institutional improvements already taken to foster coordination, it is clear that they cannot fully counter the tendency of each organ to seek to maximize its own capabilities to exercise its separate mandate. Unfortunately, the collegial approach to the Court's budget is still very much dependent on the personal relations between principals and their willingness to cooperate with each other.

[37] There is an inter-organ external relations working group where teams of the three organs share information, design external relations and communications strategies, and seek to coordinate the representation of the Court at international events.

[38] ICC RoC Regulation 3.

[39] See eg Resolution ICC-ASP/16/Res.1, 14 December 2017, part I, para 5, where the Assembly '[w]elcomes the Court's continued efforts to fully implement the "One-Court principle" when establishing the proposed programme budget, which has resulted in improvements to the budgetary process such as more efficient use of the Coordination Council and other inter-organ mechanisms'.

18.4.3 Dialogue between Judges and the Assembly: the lessons learned process

Judges deliberate and decide collectively on certain matters but exercise their judicial functions independently in separate Chambers and Divisions, supported by legal support staff. Judicial independence was initially interpreted as precluding discussions on case proceedings with Judges not belonging to the respective Chamber. This lack of dialogue between Judges and Chambers resulted in divergent responses to common procedural problems. Inconsistent and unsatisfactory solutions in key areas such as the confirmation of charges and the pre-trial phase, generated considerable delays in the Court's proceedings.

In 2010, in order to counter criticism and take into account mounting concerns about the Court's performance, states parties stressed the need to conduct a structured dialogue between the Assembly of States Parties and the Court with a view to expediting proceedings and enhancing the efficiency and effectiveness of the Court. For this purpose, as indicated above, they created a Study Group on Governance within the Assembly to engage with the Court.[40] In response, the Court created a Working Group on Lessons Learned composed of five Judges to act as interlocutor of the Study Group. The Group led efforts at the Court to take stock of experience and propose measures to improve the procedural practice, including through amendments to the legal framework.[41] There was particular interest and indeed pressure from the Assembly's Study Group on Governance to obtain from the Court as many proposed amendments to the Rules as possible.[42]

The Court submitted its first report in October 2012.[43] It proposed a 'roadmap' outlining the actions to be taken. Among other matters, the roadmap contained nine clusters and twenty-four sub-clusters that the Court identified as requiring discussion with a view to expediting proceedings and enhancing their quality.[44] In addition, it included the promise that amendment proposals that received support of at least five Judges would be submitted for consideration of the Advisory Committee on Legal Texts of the Court.

In November 2012, the Assembly of States Parties endorsed the nine clusters of issues,[45] and adopted by consensus the first amendment to the Rules proposed by the Judges, namely Rule 132 *bis* on the designation by the Trial Chamber of one or more of its judges to handle the preparation of the trial.[46] Under the continuing pressure of the Study Group of the Assembly, two more amendment proposals were presented by the Court. These included Rule 100, which transferred from the Plenary of Judges to

40 Resolution ICC-ASP/9/Res.2, 10 December 2010, paras 1–3.

41 The Working Group was chaired by former Vice-President Judge Monageng and composed of Judges Kuenyehia, Trendafilova, Aluoch, and Fernández de Gurmendi.

42 Resolution ICC-ASP/11/31 Add.1, 23 October 2012, para 6.

43 ibid.

44 The nine clusters were as follows: Pre-Trial; Pre-Trial and Trial Relationship and Common Issues; Trial, Victims Participation and Reparations; Appeals; Interim Release; Seat of the Court; Language Issues; and Organizational Matters.

45 Resolution ICC-ASP/11/Res.8, 21 November 2013, para 41.

46 Resolution ICC-ASP/11/Res.2, 21 November 2012. See also Report of the Study Group on Governance on rule 132 bis of the Rules of Procedure and Evidence, 1 November 2012, ICC-ASP/11/41, Annex I.

the Presidency of the Court the power to decide on whether to hold proceedings in a state other than the Host State; and Rule 68, which expanded the circumstances in which a prior recorded testimony may be admitted at trial.[47]

All three amendments have had a positive impact on the performance of the Court. In particular Rules 132 *bis* and 68 are applied regularly in the Court's proceedings with tangible excellent results. However, while discrete amendments may indeed be necessary to expedite proceedings, the excessive focus of the 'Lessons Learned' process on obtaining amendments was based on the questionable premise that all inefficiencies were caused by flaws of the legal framework, which could be fixed through a piecemeal approach and scattered amendments to individual Rules. In addition, as already said, the amendment process, which was complex and cumbersome at the Court, became virtually paralysed at the Assembly from 2014 onwards.

Therefore, in its 2014 report to the Study Group on Governance, the Court stressed that many of the problems experienced in the first years of the Court could be addressed through practice changes without the need for amendments to the Rules. It also announced that the identification and consolidation of best practices would be sought in other ways, including, where necessary, through amendments to the Regulations instead of amendments to the Rules.[48] Most importantly, it indicated that it was important to abandon a piecemeal approach to procedural amendments and conduct instead an overall revision of all issues common to pre-trial and trial proceedings so as to provide the necessary solutions as part of a coherent package of proposals.[49] Accordingly, subsequent efforts, as described below, sought to modify both the process and output of the 'Lessons Learned' process.

18.4.4 Dialogue among Judges

18.4.4.1 Judicial retreats

Since their election in 2012 and 2013, the previous Prosecutor and Registrar had taken important steps to restructure and improve the functioning of their respective organs. The 'Lessons Learned' process initiated by the Assembly in 2010, which focused on expediting judicial proceedings, led to an important change of attitude within the Judiciary, which had been until then less proactive in efforts to enhance efficiency.

By the time of the inauguration of that cohort of Judges and the election of the Presidency in March 2015, the need to expedite and improve judicial proceedings was generally recognized and the ICC Presidency promoted the participation of all Judges in initiatives to that effect. The composition of the Working Group on Lessons Learned—until then composed of five Judges—was expanded to incorporate all interested Judges and the first Judges' retreat was convened to discuss collectively a common approach to improving proceedings and methods of work. The retreat was

[47] Working Group on Lessons Learnt: Second Report of the Court to the Assembly of States Parties (n 22).

[48] Report of the Bureau on Study Group on Governance, ICC-ASP/13/28, 28 November 2014, Annex II, para 31.

[49] ibid para 32.

to be held within three months to ensure the swift integration of the six newly elected Judges into the work of the Court.

The earlier piecemeal approach to amending the legal framework was substituted by a holistic revision of the whole clusters of issues with a view to diagnosing practical problems and proposing comprehensive remedies. Based on such diagnoses, Judges could decide whether amendments to the Rules or to the Regulations were at all necessary or whether they could implement coherent solutions in some other manner, such as by way of directives or written understandings to consolidate best practices.[50]

The first judicial retreat was hosted by the International Nuremberg Principles Academy from 18 to 21 June 2015. It focused on pre-trial confirmation of charges proceedings, which had generally been recognized as the most problematic procedural phase at the ICC. The two-day gathering proved to be enormously useful for integrating the new Judges and for agreeing on improvements to the working methods as well as best practices to be followed at the pre-trial phase.

Such open collective discussions on problems encountered by Chambers across all divisions during their work were without precedent. For the first time, Judges accepted that judicial independence was in no way incompatible with their exchanging views on matters of law and procedure with a view to identifying collegially a common response to some challenges.

Considering these excellent results, a new retreat was held in 2016 for the Judges to consult on trial proceedings and a third one in 2017 dedicated to appeal matters.

The practice of holding retreats to discuss entire clusters of procedural issues as well as other institutional issues of common concern was preserved by the Presidencies successively elected in 2018 and 2021 and retreats have continued to be held on a yearly basis at the seat of the Court or other venues until today. The retreats continue to be supplemented by meetings at the seat of the Court among Judges of a particular Division or Judges interested in specific clusters of issues. In addition to these gatherings, individual Judges may be appointed as focal points for specific matters.

In sum, all Judges, as well as some legal officers, have increasingly become involved in reviewing proceedings and institutional matters with a view to expediting, streamlining, and improving the quality of justice the ICC delivers. These collective efforts that seek to enhance judicial cohesion are essential for the legitimacy of the Court. Undoubtedly, Judges within Chambers have the primary responsibility of interpreting and applying the law, taking into account the views of the parties and participants and the particular circumstances of their respective cases. However, a fragmented approach that multiplies divergent responses to the same procedural questions is not conducive to an efficient and predictable system and undermines the authority and impact of the Court's jurisprudence.

The product of this collective effort by ICC Judges to enhance cohesion may take various forms, including the development of the Chambers Practice Manual and discrete proposed amendments to the Rules or Regulations of the Court. It can also result in practical measures meant to improve the organization and methods of work of the

[50] On this initiative to promote understanding among Judges on ways of enhancing judicial proceedings, see Presidency 2015–2018: End of Mandate Report by President Silvia Fernández de Gurmendi, 9 March 2018 <www.icc-cpi.int/sites/default/files/itemsDocuments/180309-pres-report_ENG.pdf>.

Chambers legal staff. In this regard, at their first retreat in 2015, Judges decided to propose the creation of the position of the Head of Chambers intended to improve the oversight, coordination, and flexible assignment of the legal support of staff to Chambers. The position was established upon approval of the Assembly of States Parties in November 2015.[51]

18.4.4.2 Chambers Practice Manual

The Chambers Practice Manual is an important instrument reflecting the common understanding of Judges on entire clusters of issues. It was developed by the Judges following their first retreat in 2015 and has continued to be updated ever since. The Manual is a non-binding living document containing the best practices identified by the judges, which is made available on the Court's website.

The Chambers Practice Manual first took the form of a Pre-Trial Practice Manual, relating exclusively to pre trial issues, which were tackled as a matter of priority in order to enhance the efficiency of the Court. These proceedings were at the time the phase of the process which had generated the greatest number of questions, multiple responses, and unsatisfactory solutions. The endorsement in 2015 of the best practices for the pre-trial phase was therefore a major breakthrough in terms of enhancing the speed and quality of the proceedings. It was agreed that the document was to be extended to other issues and phases of the proceedings as further agreements were achieved on the best practices in other areas.[52]

Accordingly, the Pre-Trial Practice Manual, that was first made available on 4 September 2015, was expanded by the Judges in subsequent editions issued in following years to include other aspects of the proceedings. Already in its second edition, the Pre-Trial Manual became the Chambers Practice Manual, as the document went beyond the pre-trial phase to cover issues related to various stages of proceedings.

These additions to the Manual incorporated significant changes aimed at expediting proceedings and enhancing cohesion of jurisprudence and increasing collegiality of deliberations. For instance, in the 2019 fourth edition of the Chambers Practice Manual, the Judges established deadlines for key judicial decisions and internal guidelines on trial judgment drafting and structure. With regard to the judicial deadlines, the Manual explicitly underlines the need for a holistic approach to proceedings. Deadlines are recommended for various proceedings pertaining to all three judicial Divisions 'with it being recognized that improvements in the efficiency of one phase of the proceedings will be little noticed unless complemented by equal efficiency in the other phases'.[53] In the seventh edition adopted on 13 July 2023, Judges added a new section on principles and procedures governing the issuance of dissenting and separate opinions, a topic that had been a subject of external criticism and taken up during the Review process. The principles agreed by the Judges include that dissenting and separate opinions should be a measure of last resort. Other issues

[51] Resolution ICC-ASP/14/Res.1, 26 November 2015.

[52] Annex II, Working Group on Lessons Learnt to the Study Group on Governance, Report, Cluster I: Expediting the Criminal Process: Progress Report on Clusters A, B, C, and E (The Hague, 18–26 November) ICC-ASP/14/30, 30 September 2015, para 11.

[53] See introduction to the *Fourth Edition of the Chambers Practice Manual* issued on 29 November 2019 <www.icc-cpi.int/iccdocs/other/191129-chamber-manual-eng.pdf>.

addressed are the length of dissenting and separate opinions and their issuance together with the majority judgment, decision, or order. Where appropriate, dissenting or separate views may be included together with that of the majority in a single document. The new section also devises an internal procedure reflecting best practices on the preparation of dissenting and separate opinions.[54]

18.4.4.3 Amendments to the legal framework: focus on the Regulations

As already indicated, Judges decided to avoid amendments to the Rules as much as possible from 2014 onwards, bearing in mind the difficulties of securing amendments to the Rules at the Assembly but also and most importantly to favour a holistic approach to clusters of issues instead of focusing on scattered amendments to single provisions. Accordingly, Judges have focused since then on alternative ways of acting on their collective agreements, the Chambers Practice Manual being the preferred instrument until today. However, there are still instances in which binding provisions are required which are to be respected by all parties and participants in proceedings and cannot be replaced by common understandings among Judges. Therefore, in parallel to developing the Manual, the Judges have continued to resort to discrete amendments to the Regulations when strictly necessary.

Following subsequent retreats and further collective discussions among Judges, more amendments to the Regulations followed in 2017 and 2018. Such amendments were meant to expedite and streamline appeal proceedings[55] and address procedural issues arising in connection with the activation of the jurisdiction of the Court over the crime of aggression in July 2018 by the Assembly of States Parties.[56]

The Judges' emphasis on expediting and streamlining judicial proceedings was soon emulated by the Prosecutor, whose representatives sit in the Advisory Committee on Legal Texts. Based upon the Prosecutor's proposal and following consideration by the Committee, in 2016 the Judges adopted several amendments to Regulations which aimed at clarifying a range of procedural and technical matters.[57] Most importantly, as further developed below, in January 2021, following their 2020 retreat, Judges amended the Code of Judicial Ethics, in accordance with Regulation 126.

18.4.4.4 Amendments to the Code of Judicial Ethics: efforts to improve the election of the Presidency

While the need to update the Code of Judicial Ethics, had long been recognized, recommendations made within the Review process also served as an incentive for actions in this regard. Judges acted accordingly at the end of 2020, taking into account recommendations of the Independent Experts.[58]

[54] 'ICC Judges Update Chambers Practice Manual to Include Guidelines on Dissenting and Separate Opinions' (ICC press release, 13 July 2023) <www.icc-cpi.int/news/icc-judges-update-chambers-practice-manual-include-guidelines-dissenting-and-separate-opinions>.

[55] Amendments to ICC RoC Regulations 57, 58, 59, 61, 63, 64, and 65.

[56] Amendments to ICC RoC Regulations 13, 45, and 46.

[57] These issues concerned page limits, time limits and other procedural matters: amendments to regulations 20(2), 24(5), 33(1)(d), 34, 36, 38, and 44(1).

[58] Independent Expert Review of the International Criminal Court and the Rome Statute System, Final Report, 30 September 2020, ICC-ASP/19/16 <https://asp.icc-cpi.int/iccdocs/asp_docs/ASP19/IER-Final-Report-ENG.pdf> (IER Report), recommendations 181–84.

The revised Code of Judicial Ethics clarifies that certain ethical obligations continue to apply to former Judges, for instance in respecting the secrecy of deliberations or maintaining confidentiality.[59] It also adds important concepts such as loyalty to the Court,[60] and further elaborates on judicial independence.[61]

Key amendments were made to Article 5 of the Code of Judicial Ethics concerning integrity, such as adding an express reference to judicial collegiality. The Code now requires that 'Judges shall act at all times towards one another in a spirit of collegiality and professionalism'. The amendments to this provision also include a welcome explicit prohibition on any form of discrimination, harassment, and abuse of authority.[62]

Most importantly from the perspective of governance, the new detailed paragraph on ethical obligations in connection with the election of the Presidency requests Judges, among other things, to 'refrain from any action that might, in the context of the election, be reasonably perceived as an inappropriate promise, gift, advantage, privilege or reward of a personal nature'. It also clarifies that 'all limitations on electoral campaigning established in the Guidelines on the Procedure for the Election of the Presidency must be respected, any violation of which shall be a violation of this Code'.[63]

Accordingly, the Judges also adopted the Guidelines on the Procedure for the Election of the Presidency, which reaffirms the principles and concepts included in the Code of Judicial Ethics and sets out provisions to guide the electoral campaign.[64]

Without prejudice to these amendments by the Judges to their own Code, the President of the ICC Court also participated in discussions of the 'Ethica' project promoted by several institutions aimed at identifying common ethical principles for all international criminal judges.[65]

18.5 Efforts to Strengthen the Rome Statute System: The Review Process

Efforts deployed at the Court from 2010 onwards, including as part of the 'Lessons Learned' process initiated by the Assembly, went a long way in improving the

[59] Code of Judicial Ethics, adopted on 9 March 2005, as amended on 19 January 2021 <www.icc-cpi.int/Publications/Code-of-Judicial-Ethics.pdf> (CoJE) Art 12(1).

[60] ibid Art 8.

[61] ibid Art 3.

[62] ibid Art 5(5).

[63] ibid.

[64] Guidelines on the Procedure for the Election of the Presidency, 19 January 2021, ICC <www.icc-cpi.int/sites/default/files/itemsDocuments/Guidelines-on-the-Procedure-for-the-Election-of-the-Presidency.pdf> section 6(3): 'No discussion or communication amongst judges concerning the potential outcome of a Presidency election may occur unless all judges who will vote in the Presidency election are given the opportunity in good faith to participate in any such discussion or communication. This does not preclude a newly elected judge, at her or his own initiative only, from speaking privately with outgoing judges only, in order to seek information about one or more candidate. Guided by the ethics of collegiality, any such discussion should be constructive and neutral in nature.'

[65] 'ETHICA: Ethical Principles for International Criminal Judges' (Paris, 15 May 2023) <www.diplomatie.gouv.fr/IMG/pdf/ethical_principes_-_ethica-ang_cle02f837.pdf>. The ASP took note of this project in its Resolution ICC-ASP/22/Res.3on Strengthening the International Criminal Court and the Assembly of States Parties, 13 December 2023, para 14.

governance of the Court through ensuring the better functioning of each organ, more coordination between them, and enhanced judicial cohesion. Judges' initiatives to harmonize, accelerate, and streamline proceedings, including through written collective understandings and some amendments to the Rules and Regulations had a tangible positive impact on criminal proceedings. However, these measures by the Court to improve internal structures, working methods, and procedural issues, while extremely necessary and welcomed, were not sufficient to bring about radical systemic changes in the functioning and working culture of the Court. Furthermore, the 2018 inauguration of new Judges and the change of the Court's leadership brought about a shift in priorities and some initiatives lost momentum, were slowed down, or discontinued altogether. Strong concerns re-emerged about the Court's performance and, more generally, about the vitality of the Rome Statute system.

18.5.1 The conduct of the Review process

In 2019, four former Presidents of the Assembly of States Parties voiced their concerns in an unprecedented public letter, noting that

> the powerful impact of the Court's central message is too often not matched by its performance as a judicial institution. We are disappointed by the quality of some of its judicial proceedings, frustrated by some of the results, and exasperated by the management deficiencies that prevent the Court from living up to its full potential.[66]

According to them, it was time to make a 'new deal' between the ICC and its states parties, in the spirit that made them succeed in Rome. Importantly, they acknowledged that this new deal required not only the efforts on the part of the Court to improve its own performance but also implied an obligation on states to 'fully embrace the potential of the ICC as the central institution in the fight against impunity'. States, they said, 'have to stand up for the ICC in its mission to be judicially independent, even, or in particular, in situations where that may be politically inconvenient. And states need to give the Court the resources it needs to do the job'. As a first step towards this new deal, the former Presidents of the Assembly suggested that an independent assessment of the Court's functioning should be undertaken to provide Court officials and all stakeholders with a common point of reference going forward.[67]

The Assembly, in consultation with the Court, accepted the recommendation and launched a process of review of the entire Rome Statute system that same year. During its 2019 session, the Assembly established an Independent Expert Review with the overall mandate of making 'concrete, achievable and actionable recommendations aimed at enhancing the performance, efficiency and effectiveness of the Court and the Rome Statute system as a whole'.[68] To this end, nine Independent Experts were

[66] Zeid Raad Al Hussein and others, 'The International Criminal Court Needs Fixing' (Atlantic Council, 24 April 2019) <www.atlanticcouncil.org/blogs/new-atlanticist/the-international-criminal-court-needs-fixing>.

[67] ibid.

[68] Resolution ICC-ASP/18/Res.7, 6 December 2019.

appointed from various regions of the world to take charge of the three clusters of issues to be reviewed, namely Governance; Judiciary; and Preliminary Investigations, Investigations and Prosecutions.[69]

The Independent Experts submitted their Report to the Assembly by the end of 2020 (IER).[70] It was based on painstaking research and hundreds of written submissions, interviews, and meetings with all relevant stakeholders, including ICC former and current elected officials and staff members, legal representatives of victims and accused persons, civil society organizations, and academia. It contained 384 recommendations, both short-term and long-term, with varying degrees of complexity, and urgency of implementation. Having regard to the many recommendations included in this Report, the Independent Experts drew special attention to those recommendations that needed, in their view, to be implemented as a matter of priority. Therefore, they included a summarized list of these recommendations in Annex I to their report.[71]

Upon its reception, the Assembly established a Review Mechanism to lead the process of assessing and implementing, as appropriate, the recommendations contained therein, through an inclusive and transparent dialogue open to the Court, the Assembly, civil society organizations, and all other relevant stakeholders of the international community.[72] The Review Mechanism was to be led by two state party representatives, assisted by representatives of three countries acting as focal points appointed by the Bureau of the Assembly of States Parties in consultation with the regional groups.[73]

On 28 July 2021, the Assembly's Bureau adopted a Comprehensive Action Plan proposed by the Review Mechanism for the assessment of the recommendations of the Independent Experts, including requirements for possible further action.[74] The Action Plan included the allocation of the recommendations to the relevant organ of the Assembly, the Court, or both, the prioritization of some of them, based on the proposal annexed to the IER and very short timelines for the consideration of the recommendations.[75]

In the introductory note to the Action Plan, the Review Mechanism pointed out that the Plan provided an ambitious roadmap for the assessment of the recommendations,

[69] Cluster 1: Governance: Mr Nicolas Guillou (France), Ms Mónica Pinto (Argentina), Mr Mike Smith (Australia). Cluster 2: Judiciary: Ms Anna Bednarek (Poland), Mr Iain Bonomy (United Kingdom of Great Britain and Northern Ireland), Mr Mohamed Chande Othman (United Republic of Tanzania). Cluster 3: Preliminary Examinations, Investigations and Prosecution: Mr Richard Goldstone (South Africa), Mr Hassan Jallow (The Gambia), Ms Cristina Schwansee Romano (Brazil).

[70] IER Report (n 58).

[71] ibid.

[72] Resolution ICC-ASP/19/Res.7 of 18 December 2020.

[73] The two state party representatives appointed to lead the Review Mechanism were HE Ambassador Paul van den IJssel (Netherlands) and HE Ambassador Michael Imran Kanu (Sierra Leone). Countries serving as focal points were Bangladesh, Chile, and Poland.

[74] 'Review Mechanism: Comprehensive Action Plan for the Assessment of the Recommendations of the Group of Independent Experts, Including Requirements For Possible Further Action' (ASP, 30 June 2021) <https://asp.icc-cpi.int/sites/asp/files/asp_docs/ASP20/RM-Comprehensive%20Action%20Plan-ENG.pdf>.

[75] ibid.

whereby many of the recommendations would be assessed within a year.[76] It recognized that this plan was indeed intended to match the utmost importance and high priority assigned by the Assembly to this process and keep its momentum. Its execution would translate into the Court, the state parties, Assembly mandates, and other stakeholders undertaking much work in the process at a particularly difficult time in which new authorities at the Judiciary and the Office of the Prosecutor were still settling in:

> We realize this is putting a lot on the plate of the Court after transitions in the Judiciary and Office of the Prosecutor. However, given the importance of the review process to the Assembly and the Court, the Review Mechanism thinks a fine balance has to be struck between making progress with the review and continuing the core work of the Court. Consequently we have to be ambitious in the process to strengthen the Court and improve its performance.[77]

As anticipated, during the years that followed, the execution of this Action Plan implied a heavy extra workload for all those involved, in particular for the Court, which had to devote much time to providing its input, sometimes by way of written reports, and take an active part in the discussions. To this end, each of its organ appointed focal points responsible for transmitting the Court's views and ensuring the appropriate follow-up within the institution. States and civil society representatives were also active participants in this vibrant and inclusive dialogue, which was conducted in existing working groups and other ad hoc platforms for discussions. The goal of these discussions was to assess—positively or negatively—each one of the 384 recommendations submitted by the Independent Experts and, in case of a positive assessment, determine the way forward to ensure appropriate implementation. The ASP Presidency and Bureau were regularly briefed by the Review Mechanism and provided guidance and assistance as needed. As further developed below, the Bureau was itself responsible for the implementation of certain recommendations, such as the one pertaining to the protection of the Court and others cooperating with it from political threats and attacks.[78]

By December 2023, the bulk of recommendations by the Experts were assessed according to schedule, many of them accepted, and some of them already implemented by the Court or the Assembly. An important pending issue was the tenure policy recommended by the Independent Experts, aimed at establishing a time limit for the occupation of the highest positions of staff (P5 and above).[79] Such a policy had been assessed positively but no agreement could be reached on the modalities of implementation. At its December 2023 session, the Assembly commended the Review Mechanism for the significant progress towards the completion of its mandate and decided to extend it, for one additional year, until December 2024.[80] It also decided

[76] 'Proposal for a Comprehensive Action Plan for the assessment of the recommendations of the Group of Independent Experts, including requirements for possible further action' (ASP, 30 June 2021) <https://asp.icc-cpi.int/sites/asp/files/asp_docs/ASP20/RM-CAP-Introductory-Note-ENG.pdf>.
[77] ibid.
[78] Section 18.5.4.
[79] IER Report (n 58) Recommendation 104.
[80] Resolution ICC-ASP/22/Res.6, 14 December 2023.

to implement a tenure policy as of 1 January 2025 and to consider further the Court's proposal on how to implement it within this timeframe.[81]

18.5.2 Recommendations by the Independent Experts to the Court and the Assembly

The recommendations issued by the Independent Experts were holistic by nature. They related not only to specific issues of governance, structure, and decision-making and legal-technical intricacies of the criminal proceedings, but also to matters that affect the very soul of the system, such as ethics, prevention of conflict of interests, and working culture. They were also holistic in the sense that they were not only addressed to the Court but also to the Assembly of States Parties in order to achieve an overhaul of the Rome Statute system as a whole.

Recognizing the difficulties posed by the fragmented architecture of the Court, many of the Independent Experts' recommendations also aimed at strengthening cohesion and coordination within and between organs of the Court. This included encouraging the judiciary to go further and deeper in some of the initiatives already taken to allow for a more collegial judicial approach as well as a more coherent and predictable jurisprudence. In this regard, the Independent Experts acknowledged the positive impact of several of the judge-driven measures to enhance collegiality and improve efficiency referred to above, namely the Judges' annual retreats, the Chambers Practice Manual, including the recent additions of guidelines for ICC judgment drafting and for judgment structure, and proposals on amendments to the Rules and Regulations.[82]

Consistent with the spirit of the initiative triggering the review, the recommendations also referred to the obligations of states parties to perform their own duties to contribute to enhancing the Court's functioning. Importantly, among other problems attributable to states themselves, the Independent Experts noted that the Assembly's practice of adopting amendments to the Rules by consensus had resulted in a deadlock that disabled the Court from 'steadily introducing measures to improve the multifarious aspects of its procedures'.[83] They recommended the Assembly to amend the Rome Statute transferring to the Plenary of Judges the Assembly's power to amend rules and, in the meantime, to apply the two-thirds majority foreseen in Article 51(3) of the Statute.[84] This encouraged the Assembly to recognize the need to address such deadlock and expedite decision-making processes related to amendment proposals. At its twentieth session, the Assembly decided that, in accordance with Articles 112(7) and 51(2) of the Rome Statute, a decision on the adoption of a rule amendment proposal should be taken at the session of the Assembly of States Parties that followed the submission of this proposal to the Working Group on Amendments.[85] As a result of this important decision, the Assembly adopted long-awaited amendments proposals,

81 Resolution ICC-ASP/22/Res.7, 14 December 2023.
82 IER Report (n 58) para 468.
83 ibid para 983.
84 ibid Recommendation 381.
85 Resolution ICC-ASP/20/Res.4, Review of the International Criminal Court and the Rome Statute system, 9 December 2021.

as well as new ones, in 2022 and 2023.[86] This is a positive outcome of the Review process as the strengthening of the system is indeed likely to require additional changes to its legal framework in the future.

18.5.3 Improvements to the selection of elected officials: due diligence procedures

Improvements to the institutional structures and methods of work, together with reforms of the legal framework, can go a long way in enhancing the governance and overall performance of the Court. However, the Court can only be as good as the individuals working in it. In particular, the professional and personal competences and moral character of those elected to occupy its highest positions are of paramount importance to guide the institution, manage the cases efficiently, and ensure that all those involved in the work of the Court align behind a common vision and share its fundamental values. This is an area in which the states bear the greatest and, in the case of Judges and Prosecutor, sole responsibility, since it is for states to nominate the candidates that may be then elected by secret ballot at the Assembly of States Parties.[87]

In light of its importance for the governance and functioning of the Court, it is not surprising that, going beyond the topics specifically indicated to them, the Independent Experts decided to also address the nomination and election of Judges. They rightly considered that it was impossible for them to ignore the comments received, according to which some of the Court's problems may in part be the result of the quality of some of the Judges and the belief that some of them may have been elected because of trading of votes rather than their competence:

> [f]aced with the suggestion that the quality of the Judiciary may be part of the problem, and having regard to the fundamental importance of the calibre of the Judiciary to the performance, efficiency and effectiveness of the Court and the Rome Statute system as a whole, it was considered impossible to say that the Experts' review was complete without looking at the method by which the Judges are appointed, to see whether measures to improve the process could be identified with a view to ensuring the appointment of the best candidates.[88]

This general comment on the election process was accompanied by concrete recommendations to improve the selection process, addressing, *inter alia*, the nomination procedures at the national level, the assessment of the candidates' competences by way of roundtables and interviews with the Advisory Committee on Nominations (ACN).[89]

It must be recognized that the Assembly has been slow in undertaking the appropriate actions to ensure the selection of the best possible candidates for Judges. Only in

86 See Rule 140 *bis* adopted by Resolution ICC-ASP/21/Res.5, 9 December 2022; Rules 69 *bis* and 140 *ter* adopted by Resolution ICC-ASP/22/Res.1, 13 December 2023; and amendment of Article 39.2 (b) of the Statute adopted by Res. ICC-ASP/22/Res.2 of 13 December 2023

87 ICC Statute Arts 36 and 42.

88 IER Report (n 58) para 962.

89 ibid Recommendations 371 to 380.

2012 did the Assembly agree to establish the ACN foreseen in the Statute, that is twelve years after its entry into force. Before that, it was the civil society—in particular, the Coalition for the ICC (CICC)—who undertook the task of ensuring some measure of quality control and transparency in the selection process, including by submitting questionnaires to candidates and hosting public debates among them. Most importantly, in 2010 the CICC established an Independent Panel on ICC Judicial Election to provide expert assessment of the candidates for the 2011 elections. This initiative undoubtedly pushed the ASP to establish the ACN the following year to scrutinize the candidates' competences and qualifications required by the Statute.[90] This is an important body to assist states in the judicial selection, although its conclusions, which now include a welcome 'ranking' of candidates, are not binding on states.

The Assembly has not always followed the assessment by the ACN and, most importantly, it has not been able to eliminate the detrimental practice of exchanging votes referred to by the Independent Experts. However, the ASP has acknowledged its existence and encouraged states parties 'to refrain from the trading of votes'.[91] Furthermore, it has undertaken steps to improve the election process. This includes the adoption of measures to enhance the mandate of the ACN and to improve other modalities of the process. Interviews of all candidates by the ACN have now become customary and were indeed conducted for the 2023 election of Judges, together with improved roundtables among candidates led by representatives of states and civil society. As mandated by the Assembly, the format of these roundtables was modified to enable a more effective assessment of candidates regarding the aspects highlighted in the report of the ACN.[92] In addition, the Assembly requested the ACN to prepare guidelines for national-level nomination procedures and to bring them to the attention of state parties at its 2024 session.[93]

Most importantly, at the 2023 election, judicial candidates were submitted for the first time to a so-called due diligence procedure. This innovative vetting procedure had been adopted by the Bureau earlier that year,[94] in consultation with the Independent Oversight Mechanism (IOM), an ASP subordinate body in charge of internal investigations and evaluations of the Court. The procedure intended to assess the requirement of 'high moral character' contained in Article 36 of the Statute, does not only allow for an in-depth background check of all candidates but also opens a confidential channel for the submission of any allegations of misconduct by a candidate. The procedure defines misconduct for its purposes and details the steps to be followed in case of the submission of allegations against any candidate. The procedure that was applied in the Judges' elections benefitted from the experience garnered from the two previous ad hoc due diligence procedures applied for the elections of the Deputy Prosecutors and Registrar of the Court in 2021 and 2023, respectively.[95]

90 For a detailed analysis of the selection process, see Silvia Fernández de Gurmendi, 'Judges: Selection, Competence, Collegiality' (2018) 112 AJIL Unbound 163.

91 Resolution ICC-ASP/18/Res.4, 6 December 2019, para 10.

92 Oral report on the activities of the Bureau, presented by the President of the Assembly at the first plenary meeting of the twenty-second session of the Assembly, on 4 December 2023, para 25.

93 ICC-ASP/21/Res.2, 9 December 2022, Annex III.

94 Oral Report (n 92) para 24.

95 ibid.

Taking stock of the accumulated experience regarding this matter, the Assembly adopted in December 2023 a permanent due diligence process emphasizing that it would need to be taken into account in any future decision on the process for the election of the Judges, Prosecutor, Deputy Prosecutor(s), Registrar, and Deputy Registrar.[96] The procedure based on the one already applied, will be conducted by the IOM, with the assistance of the Registry of the Court and the Secretariat of the Assembly of States Parties, as appropriate. Like its precursors, this procedure is intended only to assist states parties and/or the authority in charge of the election process to assess whether there might be relevant concerns as to whether such candidates possess 'high moral character' as required by the Rome Statute. It is without prejudice to other efforts or mechanisms to assess the professional skills and competencies of such candidates.[97]

18.5.4 Protection of the Court and those involved in its work against threats and attacks

Obtaining sufficient cooperation, political support, and financial resources is essential for the Court's operations and a constant challenge for the institution, particularly so in current circumstances of an increasingly divided international community. Furthermore, being involved in highly sensitive situations, the Court has been the target of threats and political attacks, including by way of unprecedented sanctions and criminal proceedings against elected officials and members of staff.

The Independent Experts also addressed these challenges and proposed recommendations in their Report. In particular, considering previous attacks, the Independent Experts stressed that the Assembly and state parties should develop a strategy for responding to such attacks in the future and be prepared to speak up in the Court's defence, given that its dignity and judicial independence and impartiality seriously inhibit its ability to defend itself against unsubstantiated and biased attacks.[98]

This recommendation was implemented by the Bureau on 29 July 2022 through the adoption of a mechanism to enhance the protection of the Court, its officials, and those cooperating with it, from any threat or attack, which has the potential to undermine its integrity, effectiveness, or impartiality. It is clear that the mechanism cannot be expected by itself to produce a robust collective response to any such attack. The nature of the response, if any, will depend on the political will of state parties in the specific circumstances at hand. However, taking stock of experience, the mechanism is useful to clarify who bears the responsibility to coordinate such response, indicate the type of measures that may be taken, and detail the procedures to be followed. To this effect, while recognizing that the Assembly of States Parties and the Court have a shared responsibility to promote and protect the goals and work of the Court, the mechanism explicitly states that the Presidency of the Assembly bears the main responsibility for coordinating an appropriate response in consultation with the Court, the Bureau, state parties and those cooperating with the Court, as appropriate. The ASP Presidency may,

[96] Resolution ICC-ASP/22/Res.3, 13 December 2023, Annex II.
[97] ibid.
[98] IER Report (n 58) Recommendation 169.

in consultation with the Court, issue a statement to ensure a prompt reply, but it is for the Bureau to determine the additional measures that may be taken to respond to such threats or attacks. Measures adopted by the Bureau under the mechanism shall be without prejudice to any initiative undertaken by other stakeholder.[99] On 2 December 2022, a compilation of good practices was added as an annex to this mechanism. The compilation, prepared by the Secretariat on the basis of inputs received from states and civil society, had the purpose of taking stock of actions undertaken on previous occasions when the Court had been under political attack, and to serve for future reference. It contains a non-exhaustive list of potential measures as well as examples of past statements and initiatives to counter threats and attacks.[100]

The mechanism adopted by the Bureau does not refer only to threats and attacks against the Court and its officials, but also against those cooperating with the Court. Human rights defenders and others have become increasingly vulnerable to reprisals for their contributions to the Court's work as well as for their participation in the work of the Assembly. Drawing on consultations by the ASP Presidency with the United Nations as well as representatives of non-governmental organizations, on 4 October 2023, the Bureau adopted the 'Guidelines for enhancing the security of participants in the regular sessions of the Assembly of States Parties and its side events', aiming at ensuring a safe, secure, and open space and a fruitful dialogue at Assembly sessions and side-events.[101] The guidelines stress the importance of ensuring a free and inclusive expression of views, before, during, and following the Assembly sessions, including for participants attending side-events. They also provide several concrete measures to mitigate risks for participants during meetings. These Bureau guidelines, that were applied at the 2023 December session, were intended only as a first step towards enhancing the protection of those involved in the work of the Assembly. At the end of the session, the Assembly called upon all states to refrain from any acts constituting attacks, threats, intimidation, or reprisals against participants in the work of the Assembly and, taking note of the Guidelines already adopted, requested the Bureau to continue developing measures to enhance their protection with states parties, the Court, and civil society, and to report to the Assembly in December 2024.[102]

[99] Bureau of the Assembly of States Parties, 'Implementation of IER Recommendation 169', 12 August 2022 <https://asp.icc-cpi.int/sites/asp/files/2022-08/Bureau-Proposal-Rec-169-ENG.pdf>.

[100] Bureau of the Assembly of States Parties, 'Proposed Annex to Bureau Decision on the Implementation of IER Recommendation 169', 2 December 2022, <https://asp.icc-cpi.int/sites/asp/files/2022-12/PASP-Request-R169-Good-Practices.pdf>. In 2023, in application of the mechanism, the Presidency of the Assembly, in consultation with the Court, issued several statements expressing serious concern regarding the attacks faced by the Court and repeatedly rejected the proceedings initiated against the Prosecutor, the President, and six Judges of the Court, as well as the cybersecurity incident that affected the Court in September 2023.

[101] The Guidelines for enhancing the security of participants in the regular sessions of the Assembly and side-events were integrated to the Guidelines for the preparation and conduct of sessions of the Assembly of States Parties. See Bureau of the Assembly of States Parties, 'Guidelines for the Preparation and Conduct of Sessions of the Assembly', 29 September 2023 <https://asp.icc-cpi.int/sites/default/files/asp_docs/Guidelines-preparation-conduct-ASP-with-appendix-ENG.pdf>.

[102] Resolution ICC-ASP/22/Res.3, 13 December 2023.

18.6 Conclusion

The Court and the Assembly have dedicated more than a decade to seeking ways to improve the governance and overall performance of the Court. Initiatives undertaken thus far have included commendable efforts to promote concerted action and increased coordination and cohesion within the inherently complex and fragmented architecture of the Court. Concrete steps taken to nurture a more collegial culture, accompanied by measures to reform specific aspects of the ICC's structure and improve its working methods have already had a positive, tangible effect on the functioning of the Court and on the pace of proceedings. The focus on improving the performance through articulation of common understanding on best practices is commendable, although experience has also shown that the possibility of adopting discrete amendments to the innovative legal framework of the Court, including the Rules of Procedure and Evidence and the Statute itself, should not be foreclosed. For this reason, the ASP must ensure that it exercises its legislative powers, as foreseen in the Statute.

The Review process initiated in 2019 has been useful to help understand that the Court and the Assembly have a shared responsibility in enhancing the functioning of the institution by exercising their respective duties appropriately and addressing internal and external challenges in a comprehensive manner. These are all intrinsically linked, as the Court's improvements to governance and proceedings cannot be sustained without external cooperation, political support, and protection of the Court, its officials, and all those cooperating with it against threats and attacks. Furthermore, the Court can only be as good as the officials working in it, and their selection by the Assembly, in the exercise of its powers, remains crucial.

The Review process is still ongoing at the time of writing, but some of its concrete positive outcomes have become apparent. Most importantly, beyond the impressive set of recommendations produced by the Independent Experts, the Review has been a catalyst for change and dialogue that should continue far beyond its formal closure in December 2024. Many of the recommendations will take years to be fully implemented and some, such as those related to working culture, are of the kind that require perpetual vigilance. After the end of the Review, we can also expect that the enhanced collegiality at the Court and the renewed and open dialogue between the Court, the Assembly, and civil society, will bring about additional reforms as well as new ideas on how to strengthen the Court's system.

In 2023, the Assembly celebrated the twenty-fifth anniversary of the adoption of the Rome Statute through a series of discussions on a theme recommended by the Independent Experts: 'a strategic vision for the next decade of the Court: how to ensure consistent and sustainable support for the Court'. These fundamental questions have no obvious answers and must always be part of discussions on governance. As the Experts realized, any reflection on how to improve the Court needs to go hand in hand with a reflection on how best to support it.

19
Electing the Best? Process and Politics in the Nomination and Election of International Judges

*Christian M De Vos, Mariana Pena, and Yassir Khudayri**

19.1 Introduction

The standards and procedures for nominating and electing judges are among the cornerstones on which judicial independence and trust in the rule of law are built. This is as true for domestic courts as it is for their international counterparts. But, for a long time, the processes by which candidates are chosen to serve on international courts and tribunals have remained largely unknown and shrouded in secrecy. As the authors of an early treatise on the subject noted, 'the international selection and appointments processes have attracted almost no attention outside a narrow circle of lawyers, officials, and judges who are directly involved'.[1] And yet, judges have a critical role to play not only in the competent exercise of their adjudicatory duties, but also in securing the longer-term health of international judicial institutions: leading them well, steering their trajectories wisely and strategically, and providing an overall sense of mission and purpose. In short, good governance of international courts and tribunals begins with who the judges are and how they are chosen.

The non-governmental organization (NGO) Open Society Justice Initiative ('Justice Initiative') has worked on the challenge of strengthening international judicial institutions for many years—improving their performance, while also defending them from increasing attempts at political subversion—both in the context of criminal justice bodies, as well as regional human rights courts and commissions. Ensuring fair, merit-based elections is crucial to the improved performance of these bodies. The Justice Initiative previously published jointly with the International Commission of Jurists a report titled *Strengthening from Within: Law and Practice in the Selection of Human Rights Judges and Commissioners*, which, for the first time, examined the nomination practices in twenty-two countries from across the three regional human rights systems (African, European, and Inter-American). The report concluded that, while states employ a wide range of practices in their nomination and selection procedures,

* The authors wrote this chapter while employees of the Open Society Justice Initiative. While this chapter builds on the work the Justice Initiative has done on the nomination and elections of judges, the authors write here in their personal capacity. The views expressed should be attributed to them alone.

[1] Daniel Terris, Cesare PR Romano, and Leigh Swigart, *The International Judge: An Introduction to the Men and Women Who Decide the World's Cases* (Brandeis University Press 2007) 1.

Christian M De Vos, Mariana Pena, and Yassir Khudayri, *Electing the Best? Process and Politics in the Nomination and Election of International Judges* In: *Governance of International Courts and Tribunals*. Edited by: Sergey Vasiliev and Niels Blokker, Oxford University Press.
DOI: 10.1093/oso/9780198922131.003.0019

'in almost all countries it is clear that the standards for nominations that are set out in a growing body of international norms and jurisprudence have yet to be met domestically'.[2] This study also made a series of recommendations on how to strengthen these procedures. Later, the Justice Initiative published *Raising the Bar: Improving the Nomination and Election of Judges to the International Criminal Court*, which included an evaluation of nomination procedures and other stages of the election process. It too concluded that '[s]tates have not been consistently good stewards of their duty to responsibly nominate and elect ICC judges.'[3]

Some might ask if this is the most pressing issue to address now, particularly as attacks against judges—both domestic and international—are growing in frequency and severity globally, from threats to their safety to punishing, state-sanctioned financial sanctions and even criminal liability.[4] But if protecting judicial independence is vital, so too is the assurance of independence. And the process by which judges are selected and appointed, as well as their qualifications, are critical elements of judicial independence. This framework is rooted in the fundamental principle of the rule of law, as well as in the international right to a fair trial, which guarantees not only judicial freedom from political interference but also encompasses 'the procedure and qualifications for the appointment of judges'.[5] The European Court of Human Rights (ECtHR) has identified a number of factors to assess the independence of the judiciary, namely 'the manner of appointment of its members and the duration of their term of office, the existence of guarantees against outside pressures and the question whether the body presents an appearance of independence'.[6] Similarly, the Inter-American Court of Human Rights (IACtHR) has emphasized that 'the independence of any judge presumes that there is an appropriate appointment process, a fixed term in the position and a guarantee against external pressures.'[7] International instruments on the independence of the judiciary further detail normative standards relevant to the international bench. These include the United Nations (UN) Basic Principles on the Independence of the Judiciary (endorsed by the UN General Assembly in 1985), the Universal Charter of the Judge (1999), the Bangalore Principles of Judicial Conduct (2002) and their Implementation Measures (2010), and the International

[2] Open Society Justice Initiative and International Commission of Jurists, 'Strengthening from Within: Law and Practice in the Selection of Human Rights Judges and Commissioners' (Open Society Justice Initiative 2017) 83.

[3] Open Society Justice Initiative, 'Raising the Bar: Improving the Nomination and Election of Judges to the International Criminal Court' (Open Society Justice Initiative 2019) 5.

[4] For example, at the time of publication, the United States under the second Trump administration had already designated the ICC Prosecutor and four ICC Judges for sanctions, as well as the UN Special Rapporteur on the Occupied Palestinian Territories. 'The International Criminal Court Deplores New Sanctions from the US Administration against ICC Officials' (5 June 2025) <www.icc-cpi.int/news/international-criminal-court-deplores-new-sanctions-us-administration-against-icc-officials>. Threats against judges in the United States also increased sharply during this time: eg 'Escalating Online Rhetoric Reflects a Violent Authoritarian Turn Against the Judiciary' (Global Project Against Hate and Extremism, 8 May 2025) <https://globalextremism.org/post/violent-authoritarian-turn-against-the-judiciary>.

[5] UN Human Rights Committee, 'General Comment No. 32, Article 14: Right to Equality before Courts and Tribunals and to a Fair Trial' (23 August 2007) UN Doc CCPR/C/GC/32 (2007) para 19.

[6] *Campbell and Fell* v *The United Kingdom*, App no 7819/77; 7878/77, 28 June 1984, para 78.

[7] *Case of the Constitutional Court* v *Peru*, Judgment (merits, reparations, and costs), Series C No. 71, IACtHR, 31 January 2001, para 75.

Law Association's Burgh House Principles on the International Judiciary (2004).[8] Together these instruments form the bedrock of principles governing judicial qualifications, election and nomination procedures, and appropriate judicial conduct once judges are in office.

How the judges of a given international court or tribunal are elected differs depending on the system in question. To name but a few examples: in the regional human rights context, these systems include the Parliamentary Assembly of the Council of Europe (PACE), the General Assembly of the Organization of American States (OAS), and the African Union Assembly (AU Assembly). For the ICC, it is the Assembly of States Parties (ASP); and for the International Court of Justice (ICJ), it is the UN General Assembly and the UN Security Council. But as this chapter illustrates, across all these different fora, judicial selection shares a common affliction: too often, personal political connections, patronage, and a worrisome culture of vote-trading prevail over transparent, merit-based procedures.

This chapter proceeds in five parts. The next section focuses on nominations at the national level as a critical point of entry for understanding and improving the selection process for international judges. It summarizes key findings from the Justice Initiative's reports, which tracked the nomination practices of over twenty-five countries to the regional human rights courts and the ICC. Section 19.3 details how nominated candidates are scrutinized by some systems, including the different methodologies that are employed to assess (or not assess, as the case may be) both candidates' qualifications and professional experience, as well as their 'high moral character'. Section 19.4 delves more deeply into the politics of elections and considers rotational regional practices, vote-trading, and campaigning. Section 19.5 considers what role continuing judicial education, together with improved selection procedures, can play in both ensuring the quality of international adjudicators and mitigating the harmful effects of procedures that are insufficiently rigorous, before conclusions are drawn (Section 19.6).

19.2 Nominating Candidates at the National Level

Nominations of candidates at the national level constitute the first in two broad but distinct phases of the selection process, the second being election by intergovernmental or parliamentary political bodies from among the pool of candidates that states have nominated.[9] There are many factors that may influence a state's decision to nominate

[8] UN General Assembly, 'UN Basic Principles on the Independence of the Judiciary' (13 December 1985) Principles 10 and 13; International Association of Judges, 'Universal Charter of the Judge, adopted by the International Association of Judges' (Santiago De Chile, 17 November 1999); Round Table Meeting of Chief Justices (Judicial Group on Strengthening Judicial Integrity), 'Bangalore Principles of Judicial Conduct' (The Hague, 25–26 November 2002); UN Human Rights Council, 'Independence and Impartiality of the Judiciary, Jurors and Assessors, and the Independence of Lawyers' (10 July 2017) UN Doc A/HRC/RES/35/12; Judicial Integrity Group, 'Measures for the Effective Implementation of the Bangalore Principles of Judicial Conduct' (Lusaka, Zambia, 21–22 January 2010); ILA Study Group on the Practice and Procedure of International Courts and Tribunals, 'Burgh House Principles on the International Judiciary' (2004).

[9] The content of this section draws upon data presented in OSJI/ICJ, 'Strengthening from Within' (n 2) and OSJI, 'Raising the Bar' (n 3).

a candidate for international judicial office, including the prestige associated with certain courts, a desire to contribute—and be seen as contributing—to the international legal order, and the ability to influence and shape that order. The decision to nominate a candidate will often depend on the availability of resources to run a judicial election campaign, the state's political and diplomatic leverage at a given moment, and the candidate's prospect of success. Candidates' international experience and recognition, as well as their ability to carry out effective election campaigns, may also influence whether they are considered 'viable' to nominate. Indeed, governments sometimes use these posts to reward long-term service to a government or former head of state, or to 'remove' controversial political personalities without causing an internal uproar.

As the principal authors of the Justice Initiative's two reports on judicial nominations and elections, we conducted interviews with government officials, civil society, judges, and academics from across almost thirty states. Our findings were remarkably similar, namely:

- *There is a lack of standardized criteria to guide the nomination of qualified candidates at the national level.*

States have broad discretion determining which candidates to nominate for judicial office and the process by which they do so. However, regional standards offer some guidance on how these procedures should be conducted. The European human rights system offers the most detailed criteria governing national selection processes. The ECtHR is the only 'full panel' court amongst the regional human rights systems, with one judge from each of the current forty-six member states (following the expulsion of Russia from the Council of Europe (CoE) in March 2022). PACE and the Committee of Ministers of the CoE have each issued a series of directives and guidelines that are meant to ensure common nomination procedures across all CoE member states.[10] Other systems have similarly acknowledged the desirability of taking 'into account good practices at the national and international level when conducting their national procedures or the nomination of candidates', but have been less prescriptive as to what those practices should entail.[11] Regional organizations such as the AU or the OAS, have not yet issued similar directives or guidelines on the nomination of candidates to their regional commissions and courts.

[10] Committee of Ministers, 'Guidelines of the Committee of Ministers on the selection of candidates for the post of judge at the European Court of Human Rights' (28 March 2012) CM(2012)40-final, section II, para 4; PACE, 'Nomination of candidates and election of judges to the European Court of Human Rights' (27 January 2009) Resolution 1646 and PACE, 'National procedures for nominating candidates for election to the European Court of Human Rights' (24 September 1999) Recommendation 1429.

[11] While abstaining from indicating what such practices should entail, the ICC Assembly of States Parties now mandates its Advisory Committee on Nominations to produce a compendium based on the practice of states parties: Assembly of States Parties (ICC), 'Resolution on the review of the procedure for the nomination and election of judges' (6 December 2019) ICC-ASP/18/Res.4 para 7 as amended by 'Strengthening the International Criminal Court and the Assembly of States Parties (9 December 2022) ICC-ASP/21/Res.2, annex III, para B. As a further layer of control, the ICC also requests that the nominating states include an acknowledgement by a senior member of the states' judiciary or authority overseeing the process that the candidate meets the substantive and procedural requirements for nomination: Assembly of State Parties (ICC), 'Procedure for the Nomination and Election of Judges of the International Criminal Court' (10 September 2004) ICC-ASP/3/Res.6, as amended by ICC-ASP/21/Res.2, annex II.

In determining what national criteria should guide the selection of candidates, some countries (eg Norway and the United Kingdom) have adopted a useful general rule for nominating international judges: applying the same criteria as those for appointment to the country's highest national court. However, such practice is the exception rather than the norm. Some states (eg South Africa and Argentina) have adopted legislation that provides for ICC judicial nominations under the same process used for domestic judicial appointments, which the ICC Statute explicitly provides for, but this appears to be relatively rare in practice. Furthermore, it presumes that the nomination processes for national judicial service are themselves merit-based.

- *Most states lack a national legal framework or even a clear procedure for nominating judicial candidates and seldom publicize international judicial vacancies.*

Only a handful of states have a legal framework in place for the nomination of international judges. The lack of a legal framework—or even an established practice—for nomination, in turn, makes the process less transparent and more susceptible to political influence. Generally speaking, a transparent process is one that, at a minimum, seeks candidates through an open and public call for applications, selects a qualified candidate according to established criteria, and follows a decision-making procedure that is made clear to the candidates and the larger public. In practice, however, these three phases are often merged into one undifferentiated political decision.

Typically, international judicial postings are only accessible to individuals within certain elite social and political circles. Numerous anecdotal illustrations of this emerged in researching the Justice Initiative's two reports. For instance, one ICC judge, who had neither applied nor been interviewed by their government, was nominated after receiving a phone call from a personal friend at the Ministry of Foreign Affairs. Another was a senior advisor to the President of the country's Senate, who reportedly made a request to be nominated by the Foreign Ministry.[12] Of those ICC judges interviewed by the Justice Initiative, several indicated that they were not even aware whether an application process took place in their nominating countries; indeed, many of them were either directly contacted or lobbied for their own nomination.[13] Moreover, in other cases where domestic legislation provides for an evaluation of qualifications, the selected candidate was the only one considered, further suggesting the lack of a competitive process.

In the context of regional human rights systems, European countries have a practice of publicly circulating a call for applications. However, the degree to which CoE member states ensure effective, timely dissemination of such calls varies. Among countries surveyed in the African and Americas regions, only very few issue open calls for applications and none appear to have a legal framework—or even a clearly identified procedure—in place to guide the nomination process. Efforts to involve or engage professional networks and/or civil society more broadly in circulating vacancy notices are similarly limited. This lack of transparency and consultation reinforces

[12] OSJI, 'Raising the Bar' (n 3) 32.
[13] ibid 31–32; see also OSJI/ICJ, 'Strengthening from Within' (n 2) 54.

the view that judicial nominations are often largely meant to reward political connections, or that the secrecy surrounding the process is one way for states to indirectly exert control over the institutions.

- *Nominations rarely take place under the coordination of an independent selection body, and candidates seldom undergo interviews or assessments at the national level.*

A crucial function that a formal nomination or review body can serve is the practice of interviewing candidates and/or administering some form of written assessment. All CoE states considered in *Strengthening from Within* carried out interviews with prospective nominees as they are required to do, but this appeared to be only occasionally practised elsewhere. Furthermore, in most cases, these interview panels are not standing entities but created on an ad hoc basis, while their independence (and/or that of their members) is not always evident.[14] Panels with members appointed solely by the executive, for instance, or who are themselves servants of a political institution, raise questions about sufficient independence.

Similar concerns arise in the context of the ICJ, where the involvement of the Permanent Court of Arbitration (PCA) national group was, in principle, intended to constitute an independent nomination body. A PCA national group is generally constituted by the four jurists of that state who can be called upon to serve as members of an arbitral tribunal under the Hague Conventions of 1899 and 1907. Many members of these groups are themselves government representatives, which hinders independent, merit-based appointments. As one diplomat remarked, 'I am unsure if any state actually uses the PCA system as it should. ... Even at the ICJ-level, national groups are not periodically updated, and countries often lose membership because they do not pay contribution.'[15] Some of the countries assessed by the Justice Initiative in *Raising the Bar* have established some kind of entity to coordinate applications for ICC judicial elections. But interlocutors noted that even when they exist, these bodies often operate as branches of foreign ministries, rather than as effectively independent entities. These concerns underscore the value of establishing a legal framework for nominations.

- *Not all states nominate enough judicial candidates to assure competitive, merit-based elections.*

Research into judicial nominations confirms a consistent practice: outside of the CoE (where states are required to nominate three candidates), states seldom nominate more than one candidate to a regional human rights commission or court. Both the African Court Protocol and the American Convention on Human Rights grant states the right to nominate up to three candidates to the African Court and the

[14] cf, in this volume, Andrew Drzemczewski, 'The Election of Judges onto the European Court of Human Rights', on the nomination of the ECtHR judges and Christiaan Timmermans, 'The Procedure for Nominating Members of the EU Courts', on the 255 Panel in the EU context.

[15] OSJI, 'Raising the Bar' (n 3) 32.

Inter-American Commission and Court, respectively.[16] However, states rarely exercise this right. Similarly, only a small—and decreasing—number of ICC states parties have nominated candidates for election.[17] The effect of this practice is two-fold: (1) it suggests a worrisome concentration of the international judiciary amongst a small handful of states;[18] and (2) it leads to a growing phenomenon of near clean-slate elections where the number of nominated candidates is only barely above the number of open seats, further increasing the likelihood that unqualified nominees will be elected.[19] A related concern is that many successful candidates—judges and commissioners alike—have previously served as government officials, particularly in a diplomatic capacity.[20]

- *A lack of gender parity and inclusivity in national selection procedures contributes to the under-representation of women on international courts and tribunals.*

Finally, sub-optimal nomination practices also mean that very few states have made affirmative efforts to ensure gender balance in their national selection bodies; a troubling disparity broadly consistent with the low number of women serving on international courts and tribunals overall. For instance, of the 102 international bodies monitored by GQUAL—a global campaign that seeks gender parity in international representation—43 per cent of positions are currently occupied by women at the time of writing (261 out of 614).[21] Amongst the three regional human rights courts, only 39 per cent of open positions are currently held by women.

These deficiencies in representation at the international level underscore the need to develop national-level nomination bodies and practices that are themselves sex-representative and gender-conscious. The risk of subconscious bias also reinforces the need for greater transparency in the nomination process, ie ensuring that actual criteria exist to guide the process and that public calls for applications are widely circulated to national bar and civic associations, many of whom are likely better positioned to reach out to under-represented groups.[22] A low number of candidates overall also leads, as noted, to limited competition at the regional level, which further

[16] Protocol on the Statute of the African Court of Justice and Human Rights (adopted 1 July 2008, not yet in force) Assembly/AU/Dec.196(XI) reprinted in Olufemi Elias, 'Introductory Note to the Protocol on the Statute of the African Court of Justice and Human Rights' [2009] 48 ILM 334, Art 12(1); Statute of the Inter-American Court (adopted 1 October 1979, entered into force 1 January 1980) 1144 UNTS 143, Art 7; Statute of the Inter-American Commission (adopted 1 November 1979, entered into force 1 November 1979) OAS OR OEA/Ser.P/IX.0.2/80, Vol 1 at 88, Art 3.

[17] OSJI, 'Raising the Bar' (n 3) 30–31; OSJI/ICJ, 'Strengthening from Within' (n 2) 71–73.

[18] On this point, see Section 19.4.1 and Anthea Roberts, *Is International Law International?* (OUP 2017).

[19] Christian De Vos and Liliana Gamboa, 'Elections for the Inter-American Commission on Human Rights: A Line States Should Not Cross' (*Justicia en las Américas*, 18 June 2019) <https://dplfblog.com/2019/06/18/elections-for-the-inter-american-commission-on-human-rights-a-line-states-should-not-cross>.

[20] OSJI, 'Raising the Bar' (n 3) 35.

[21] 'GQUAL Data—Composition of International Organizations and Tribunals' <www.gqualcampaign.org/current-composition> (statistics up to April 2025).

[22] One important example of this is that of Judge Bossa of Uganda who noted that she only became aware of a vacancy on the African Court on Human and Peoples' Rights through the Association of Female Judges, which then supported her candidacy alongside the government's efforts. OSJI/ICJ, 'Strengthening from Within' (n 2) 77.

contributes to gender disparities, as well as under-representation among other social groups and geographic regions on the international bench. As one scholar has put it, 'nonmeritorious selection procedures are the main problem, and the gender imbalance that we see across international courts and tribunals is a manifestation of it'.[23]

19.3 Scrutinizing Candidates: Merit and 'High Moral Character'

Moving from the national level (where nominations occur) to the supranational level (where candidates are elected), at least two important moments in the selection process deserve scrutiny: (1) assessing whether candidates are indeed qualified for election because of their record of professional achievement; and (2) ensuring that all candidates meet the 'high moral character' required for international judicial office. This section considers each in turn.

19.3.1 Assessing qualifications and experience

In some cases, a formal international assessment body has been established to evaluate judicial candidates prior to their election; however, such a process does not always exist. For example, there is no evaluation of the candidates' qualifications for ICJ elections. Where those bodies exist, some have a role in pre-selecting or 'filtering' the best pool of candidates for consideration. Yet, most bodies only possess non-binding, advisory powers that, at a minimum, seek to ensure that voting member states are aware of candidates' qualifications for office. Their mandates are typically regulated through terms of reference that lay out the body's working methods, the criteria to consider in evaluating candidates, and any reporting requirements. Some of the reports produced by these bodies are confidential; this, in turn, affects the public's ability to evaluate the quality of their assessments.[24]

The practices of three systems in this regard—regional human rights courts, the Court of Justice of the European Union, and the ICC—are detailed below.

19.3.1.1 Regional human rights courts

ECtHR candidates are assessed by an Advisory Panel that the Committee of Ministers established in 2010, as well as by a PACE Committee on the Election of Judges (AS/Cdh).[25] The Advisory Panel privately informs the nominating state and the AS/Cdh

[23] Cecily Rose, 'Justifying Arguments about Selection Procedures for Judges at International Courts and Tribunals: A Response to Nienke Grossman' (2017) 110 AJIL Unbound 86.

[24] While public reports might arguably deter panel members from discussing candidates' qualifications more candidly, it is important that assessment bodies provide the public with a report describing—at a minimum—the reasoning for, and the methodology leading to, its findings. cf Christiaan Timmermans, 'The Procedure for Nominating Members of the EU Courts', in this volume.

[25] Committee of Ministers (Council of Europe), 'Resolution CM/Res(2010)26 on the establishment of an Advisory Panel of Experts on Candidates for Election as Judge to the European Court of Human Rights' (10 November 2010) Resolution CM/Res(2010)26; PACE, 'Nomination of candidates and election of judges to the European Court of Human Rights' (27 January 2009), Resolution 1646; also Andrew Drzemczewski, 'The Election of Judges onto the European Court of Human Rights', in this volume.

on whether the three nominated candidates satisfy, in its view, the criteria for election prior to their formal nomination. However, the Panel does not have the authority to reject a state's list. Moreover, it does not interview any of the candidates directly, and its working methods are less than clear. When scrutinizing candidates' qualifications, the AS/Cdh conducts interviews with each nominee in advance of sending a report with its recommendations to the Parliamentary Assembly.[26] Critically, the Committee, unlike the Panel, does possess the authority to reject a state's list on the grounds that one (or all) of the candidates are unqualified, requiring the nominating state to submit a new list of candidates.

Neither the African nor the Inter-American human rights system has a formal assessment body for evaluating judicial candidates. Since 2015, however, an independent panel of experts—the Inter-American Panel of Experts (Inter-American Panel)—has assessed nominees standing for election to the Inter-American Court of Human Rights and the Inter-American Commission of Human Rights.[27] For several years, the Panel has been convened by the Centre for Human Rights and Humanitarian Law at American University, with the support of many civil society organizations throughout the region. This initiative sought to address the OAS's own failure to create an independent advisory committee, like the one found in the European system, by producing nuanced assessments of each nominee in a public report that is released prior to elections.[28]

19.3.1.2 Court of Justice of the European Union

In the Court of Justice of the European Union (CJEU), the panel provided for by Article 255 of the Treaty on the Functioning of the European Union ('Article 255 Panel') evaluates candidates' suitability to perform the duties of judges and advocates-general at the CJEU.[29] While member states are charged with making appointments, the Article 255 Panel reviews candidates' materials, conducts hearings with them, and provides an opinion on each candidate in a report.[30] These reports are not public, but the Panel issues activity reports that can provide guidance to member states on the requirements that candidates are expected to meet.

The materials the Article 255 Panel reviews support its evaluation of candidates' thought processes, analytical skills, and their ability to relay thoughts into writing. The Panel then provides 'favourable' or 'unfavourable' opinions on each candidate's

[26] Committee on the Election of Judges to the European Court of Human Rights, 'Procedure for electing judges to the European Court of Human Rights' (27 April 2017) AS/Cdh/Inf (2017) 01 rev 4.

[27] Open Society Justice Initiative, 'New Independent Panel Will Monitor Election of Inter-American Human Rights Commissioners and Judges' (Open Society Justice Initiative, 29 April 2015) <www.justiceinitiative.org/newsroom/new-independent-panel-will-monitor-election-inter-american-human-rights-commissioners>.

[28] Independent Panel of Experts, 'Report from the Independent Panel of Experts for the Evaluation of Candidates for the Inter-American Commission on Human Rights' (American University Washington College of Law Center for Human Rights & Humanitarian Law, 5 June 2019).

[29] For a detailed discussion: Christiaan Timmermans, 'The Procedure for Nominating Members of the EU Courts', in this volume.

[30] Panel provided for by Article 255 of the Treaty on the Functioning of the European Union ('255 Panel'), 'Seventh Activity Report of the panel provided for by Article 255 of the Treaty on the Functioning of the European Union' (October 2022) <https://curia.europa.eu/jcms/upload/docs/application/pdf/2022-07/2022.2597-qcar22002enn_002.pdf>.

suitability for appointment to the Court. To date, member states have followed the Panel's opinions, whether favourable or unfavourable.[31]

19.3.1.3 International Criminal Court

The ICC did not initially have a body that assessed judicial candidates prior to election, but the ASP established one in 2011, building on the work of an informal panel then coordinated by the Coalition for the International Criminal Court (CICC Independent Panel). At present, once states parties nominate their candidates, the ICC's Advisory Committee on Nominations of Judges (ACN) assesses, interviews, and reports on each nominee. The Advisory Committee is mandated to 'facilitate that the highest-qualified individuals are appointed as judges of the International Criminal Court' and conducts mandatory interviews with all nominated candidates.[32]

The ACN's initial mandate restrained it from providing critical and sufficiently nuanced assessments, which led to civil society criticism and recognition by the Committee itself that it required additional powers.[33] In December 2019, following concerted advocacy by the Justice Initiative and other civil society groups, the ASP amended the ACN's governing framework, granting it a more expansive and proactive role, including the power to check references and request that nominees substantiate their knowledge, for example by filling out detailed questionnaires.[34] The 2019 resolution also conferred upon the ACN the ability, upon request, to provide a provisional, confidential assessment of the suitability of candidates prior to a state's formal nomination.[35] The Committee's first report after the mandate was amended represented substantial progress, but room for improvement remained, as an Independent Expert Review (IER) of the ICC convened in 2020 also concluded.[36] Further progress was made by the ACN in 2023, when, for example, it introduced optional language tests for candidates to ensure their competency in the ICC's working languages.[37]

The Committee is required to prepare a 'thorough and detailed report' and make it available to states parties at least sixteen weeks prior to the elections.[38] The report provides a qualitative evaluation and analysis on the suitability or unsuitability of each candidate in accordance with the Rome Statute's requirements, and includes an indication of the national nomination procedure used.[39] Importantly, in 2020 the

[31] ibid.

[32] Assembly of States Parties (ICC), 'Terms of Reference for the Establishment of an Advisory Committee on Nominations of Judges of the International Criminal Court' (New York, 30 November 2011) ICC-ASP/10/36 Annex, para 5. The Committee has highlighted the importance of conducting interviews given the limitations of the written information provided by States Parties, stating that they reveal 'important elements relating to how [candidates] fulfill the requirements of... the Rome Statute and to the relevance of their professional experience to the work of the Court.' OSJI, 'Raising the Bar' (n 3) 44.

[33] OSJI, 'Raising the Bar' (n 3) 15–19.

[34] Assembly of States Parties (ICC), 'Resolution on the review of the procedure for the nomination and election of judges' (6 December 2019) Res ICC-ASP/18/Res.4.

[35] ACN Terms of Reference, ICC-ASP/10/36 as amended by ICC-ASP/13/Res.5 annex III, and ICC-ASP/18/Res.4, para 8*bis*.

[36] 'Independent Expert Review of the International Criminal Court and the Rome Statute System: Final Report' (30 September 2020) ('IER Report') 316–25.

[37] Assembly of State Parties (ICC), 'Report of the Advisory Committee on the Nominations of Judges on work of its ninth session' (21 July 2023) ICC-ASP/22/4, paras 14–16.

[38] ACN Terms of Reference (n 35) para 11.

[39] ibid para 10(*bis*).

Committee introduced a four-tier formulation to designate candidates' qualifications: 'highly qualified'; '(well) qualified'; 'formally qualified'; and 'not qualified'. To date, the Committee has never ranked a candidate as 'not qualified'.[40]

19.3.2 Assessing 'high moral character'

19.3.2.1 Content of the requirement

'High moral character' or 'high(est) moral authority' are common requirements for election at international and regional tribunals.[41] The Rome Statute specifically establishes that judges must embody impartiality and integrity.[42] Similarly, the judges and advocates-general of the Court of Justice, as well as the judges of the General Court 'shall be chosen from persons whose independence is beyond doubt'.[43] The CoE Advisory Panel has noted the following as key components of high moral character: 'integrity, a high sense of responsibility, courage, dignity, diligence, honesty, discretion, respect for others and the absence of convictions for crimes ... as well as (obviously) independence and impartiality'.[44]

Checking that candidates possess 'high moral character' is crucial for several reasons. International judgments exert not only legal but also moral authority. Exercising that authority requires that judges do not have a history of misbehaviour, such as corruption or financial mismanagement, or workplace misconduct, including bullying, sexual and other types of harassment, discrimination, or abuse of power. Lack of high moral character could bring the relevant court into disrepute.

These risks are far from theoretical. A 2019 survey by the International Bar Association (IBA) concluded that bullying and sexual harassment are rampant in the legal profession.[45] A 2020 independent expert report on the ICC similarly noted that some judges had engaged in bullying and harassment, thereby adversely affecting the work environment.[46] And as of May 2025, the current ICC Prosecutor, Karim

[40] Since 2017, the Advisory Committee had started designating candidates as 'formally qualified' or 'particularly well qualified', while shying away from differentiating between candidates who were qualified and those who were not, and from providing a nuanced explanation for their designation. For more on the Advisory Committee's 2020 report: Angela Mudukuti and Yassir Al-Khudayri, 'Electing the Next ICC Judges: How Did the Advisory Committee Fare This Time Around?' (*International Justice Monitor*, 3 November 2020) <www.ijmonitor.org/2019/11/electing-the-next-icc-prosecutor-assessing-sexual-misconduct-as-part-of-the-high-moral-character-requirement>.

[41] Rome Statute (adopted 17 July 1998, entered into force 1 July 2002) 2187 UNTS 3, Art 36(3)(a); ICJ Statute (adopted 26 June 1945, 24 October 1945) 33 UNTS 993, Art 2; European Convention on Human Rights (adopted 4 November 1950, entered into force 3 September 1953) 213 UNTS 221, Art 21; Statute of the Inter-American Court of Human Rights (n 16) Art 24.

[42] Rome Statute (n 41) Art. 36(3)(a).

[43] Treaty on the Functioning of the European Union (consolidated version 26 October 2012) OJ L 326/47-326/390, Arts 253-254.

[44] Advisory Panel of Experts on Candidates for Election as Judge to the European Court of Human Rights, 'Fourth activity report for the attention of the Committee of Ministers' (2019)REV (31 July 2019) para 40.

[45] See International Bar Association (IBA), 'Us Too? Bullying and Sexual Harassment in the Legal Profession' (IBA Report, 2019).

[46] IER Report (n 36) para 72. A December 2019 statement by the ICC Staff Council called on ICC states parties to pay more attention, within the framework of elections, to judges' compliance with the requirement of high moral character, impartiality, and integrity: Taegin Reisman, 'ICC Staff Union Council Calls on States to Give Full Meaning to the Provisions on High Moral Character of Elected Officials' (*International*

Khan placed himself on administrative leave following credible allegations of sexual misconduct.[47]

Overall, the #MeToo movement has helped unearth instances of sexual exploitation and harassment scandals in a variety of sectors, including in humanitarian and intergovernmental organizations.[48] There is therefore increasing awareness that practices such as bullying and harassment are extremely harmful and serious, and that they must no longer be tolerated. Abuses such as those described in the IBA survey are not new, but those who commit and tolerate misconduct, including sexual harassment, have largely escaped accountability, especially when in positions of authority.[49]

19.3.2.2 Informal verification by some courts

Although limited attention has been paid to evaluating judicial candidates' integrity in the context of election processes at different courts to date, there is increasing pressure to do so.[50] Some selecting and advisory panels have undertaken efforts to assert, to the extent possible, that candidates fulfil this requirement. For example, the Inter-American Panel supported by civil society has analysed whether candidates received sanctions, warnings, or denunciations.[51] The panel has undertaken such assessments based on information provided by the candidates, publicly available materials 'issued by an official source', and reports shared by civil society following a call for information.[52]

Justice Monitor, 8 January 2020) <www.ijmonitor.org/2020/01/icc-staff-union-council-calls-on-states-to-give-full-meaning-to-the-provisions-on-high-moral-character-of-elected-officials>. In 2024, following complaints received, the ICC's Independent Oversight Mechanism found that 'the behaviour of [one] elected official could reasonably be expected or perceived to create an intimidating, hostile, and offensive work environment'. Assembly of States Parties (ICC), 'Annual Report of the Head of the Independent Oversight Mechanism' (18 October 2024, ICC-ASP/23/18) paras 11–15.

47 At the time of publication, an investigation by the UN's Office of International Oversight Services remains pending. Majd Al-Waheidi, 'ICC Chief Prosecutor Karim Khan Is on Leave amid a Sexual Misconduct Investigation' (NPR, 16 May 2025) <www.npr.org/2025/05/16/g-s1-67183/icc-karim-khan-sexual-misconduct-investigation-leave>.

48 Eric Witte, 'By Failing to Screen ICC Prosecutor Candidates for Sexual Misconduct, States Put Court at Risk', (*International Justice Monitor*, 9 March 2020) <www.ijmonitor.org/2020/03/by-failing-to-screen-icc-prosecutor-candidates-for-sexual-misconduct-states-put-court-at-risk>.

49 The IBA Report explains that the profile or status of the perpetrator is the main reason why victims do not report bullying and sexual harassment, as well as the fear of repercussions for self, endemic misconduct in the workplace, lack of confidence in reporting procedures, and fear of not being believed: IBA Report (n 45) 45 and 64. The IER Report notes that bullying and harassment committed by some judges have not been addressed 'due to the perceived unaccountability of judges': IER Report (n 36) para 72.

50 In 2019–20, civil society groups including the Open Society Justice Initiative and the Women's Initiatives for Gender Justice, initiated a campaign to ensure that the next ICC Prosecutor was formally vetted. Coline Schupfer and Taegin Reisman, 'Electing the Next ICC Prosecutor: Assessing Sexual Misconduct as Part of the High Moral Character Requirement' (*International Justice Monitor*, 13 November 2019) <www.ijmonitor.org/2019/11/electing-the-next-icc-prosecutor-assessing-sexual-misconduct-as-part-of-the-high-moral-character-requirement>.

51 Open Society Justice Initiative, 'Final Report of the Independent Panel for the Election of Judges to the Inter-American Court of Human Rights' (31 May 2018) 9 <www.american.edu/wcl/impact/initiatives-programs/center/documents/upload/independent-panel-final-report-2018.pdf>.

52 ibid 10. In order to ensure transparency and due process, the panel shared the communications received with the candidates concerned and afforded them an opportunity to respond.

The EU's Article 255 Panel has stated that in addition to the requirements of impartiality and independence, it attaches 'particular importance to the integrity and probity of candidates'.[53] The Panel strives to 'establish whether there are factors of any kind which are likely to lead it to express reservations as to the ability of candidates to perform the duties of judge with independence, impartiality, integrity and probity'. The Panel's public reports, however, do not elaborate on how it goes about that task.[54]

By contrast, the CoE Advisory Panel has stated that it has no mechanism to assess the candidates' character 'unless it is otherwise manifestly apparent'.[55] As already explained, this panel does not interview candidates, which makes producing such judgements even more difficult. The panel believes that it has no option but to 'assume that a judge or jurist presented as a candidate by a Government is of high moral character, absent any objective element, such as a record of disciplinary or criminal offence, in the material provided to it'.[56] While the AS/Cdh does interview candidates, there is no publicly available information on whether—and if so, how—it goes about assessing the candidates' moral character.

19.3.2.3 Experiences of national systems

In certain countries, vetting is a common practice for judicial and other governmental appointments.

- In the United Kingdom, the Judicial Appointments Commission conducts comprehensive character checks prior to judicial appointments. The assessments are based on a broad interpretation of the term 'good character' and include enquiries into professional conduct, as well as criminal records and financial management. In addition to considering the information disclosed by the candidate, the commission conducts checks with government agencies and professional regulatory bodies.[57]
- Other countries also vet public officials either at the regional or federal level. For example, in Canada, judicial appointments at the federal level are preceded by a background check,[58] 'including, where applicable, information respecting complaints against [candidates'] professional conduct, [their] insurance record, reports on [their] practice ... and any disciplinary proceedings taken against [them]'.[59] In the Province of British Columbia, the Judicial Council screens

[53] 255 Panel (n 30) 19.
[54] ibid and 255 Panel, 'Second Activity Report' 5091/13 (26 December 2012) 26.
[55] Advisory Panel (n 44) para 40.
[56] ibid.
[57] UK Judicial Appointments Commission, 'Good Character Guidance for 2021' (Judicial Appointments Commission, November 2020) <https://judicialappointments.gov.uk/guidance-on-the-application-process-2/good-character/good-character-guidance>.
[58] Federal Judicial Affairs Canada, 'Overview of Federal Judicial Appointments' <www.fja.gc.ca/appointments-nominations/index-eng.html>.
[59] ibid. 'Appointments to superior courts, Authorization and Release Forms' (Office of the Commissioner for Federal Judicial Affairs Canada, 26 October 2016) <www.fja.gc.ca/appointments-nominations/forms-formulaires/ar-ac/index-eng.html>.

applicants seeking judicial appointment. Checks include credit, driving, and criminal records,[60] and can also involve reference verification with professional regulatory bodies, current and former employers, colleagues, law firm partners or associates; and other colleagues in the community and professional organizations the applicant has been affiliated with.[61]

- Kenya adopted the Vetting of Judges and Magistrates Act in 2011, which provides ample powers to a vetting board, including the ability to gather written information from a variety of sources, compel production of information, interview individuals and members of organizations, and conduct other inquiries.[62] The vetting board's evaluation extends beyond ethical considerations and can also comprise an assessment of the candidates' professional competence, communication skills, and legal and life experience, in addition to their integrity, fairness, temperament, good judgement, and commitment to public service.[63] While promising in theory, the vetting board has faced challenges and its standing and decisions have been brought into question.[64]
- In the United States, until 2025, the American Bar Association (ABA) had established a longstanding practice of evaluating the professional qualifications of nominees to the federal bench through its Standing Committee on the Federal Judiciary.[65] Such an evaluation included an assessment of the candidates' integrity and 'judicial temperament',[66] as well as an investigation into any disciplinary action against candidates and a broad range of confidential interviews with 'lawyers and judges who may know the nominee'.[67]

Vetting is also practised for other appointments and professional roles. For example, moral character checks are undertaken to assert applicants' fitness to practice law in

[60] Provincial Court of British Columbia, 'Judge Applications' <https://provincialcourt.bc.ca/judicial-council/judge-applications>.

[61] Judicial Council of British Columbia, 'Judicial Candidate Application Worksheet' (Provincial Court of British Columbia) <https://apply.provincialcourt.bc.ca/documents/Judicial%20Candidate%20Worksheet.pdf>.

[62] Vetting of Judges and Magistrates Act (Kenya) 2011, Art 14(1).

[63] ibid Art 18(2).

[64] Jan van Zyl Smit, 'Kenya's New Chief Justice Must Press on with Cleaning Up the Judiciary' (*The Conversation*, 6 October 2016) <https://theconversation.com/kenyas-new-chief-justice-must-press-on-with-cleaning-up-the-judiciary-66372>.

[65] 'Standing Committee on the Federal Judiciary: Evaluations of Nominees to the Supreme Court of the United States' (American Bar Association, November 2019) <www.americanbar.org/groups/committees/federal_judiciary/ratings/supreme-court-evaluation-process>.

[66] Angela Mudukuti, 'Searching for the Next ICC Prosecutor: Where to From Here?' (*International Justice Monitor*, 15 September 2020) <www.ijmonitor.org/2020/09/searching-for-the-next-icc-prosecutor-where-to-from-here>

[67] ibid. Historically, this was an informal process that resulted in advice to the White House and the Senate, and the ABA's recommendations were not binding. Attorney General Pam Bondi, alleging without evidence partisan bias against Republican judicial nominees, announced as of June 2025 that the Department of Justice would block the ABA Standing Committee on the Federal Judiciary's access to judicial nominees and restrict its access to relevant information in evaluating them. As such, this vetting practice is now greatly diminished. Amanda Robert, 'DOJ Restricts AB's Access to Vet and Rate Judicial Nominees' (*ABA Journal*, 2 June 2025) <www.abajournal.com/web/article/doj-restricts-abas-work-to-vet-and-rate-judicial-nominees>.

several American states.[68] Specific checks in relation to employees' past misconduct involving sexual harassment are likewise being implemented at the United Nations and within humanitarian organizations' networks.[69]

19.3.2.4 Developing a vetting system for international judicial elections
Good governance of international courts and tribunals means ensuring the judiciary's good character as well. As noted, there is significant pressure for international courts to establish formal and permanent vetting procedures in the near future.[70] As of 2020, the ICC has introduced the following steps to certify high moral character, which might provide a blueprint for other institutions. First, following directions from the ASP, the ACN drew up a declaration to be signed by candidates certifying that they fulfil a series of requirements in relation to high moral character.[71] Second, in 2023 it established a 'due diligence' process for elected officials including judges.[72] The process consists of (a) an in-depth background check of criminal, academic, and employment record of the candidates through analysis of open-source materials and contacts with former employers/employees; and (b) a review of allegations of misconduct received through the establishment of a confidential channel and response by the candidate concerned. At the conclusion of the process, a report is addressed to the ASP president. If the process yields concerns as to the candidates' high moral character, the ASP president shall propose a course of action.

19.4 The Politics of Elections

International elections are a product of international politics, and the outcome is often determined by reasons other than merit.[73] In some cases, there are unspoken rules that certain seats 'belong' to certain countries, regions, or sub-regions either permanently or at specific periodic elections. That impacts the way in which countries nominate and vote—for example, a country may abstain from nominating a candidate if it is not its region's 'turn'.[74] In addition, rather than voting based on the

[68] eg the State Bar of California, 'Instructions for Application for Determination of Moral Character and Application for Extension of Determination of Moral Character' <www.calbar.ca.gov/Portals/0/documents/admissions/Moral-Character-Determination-Application-Instructions.pdf>.

[69] United Nations System Chief Executive Board for Coordination, 'Briefing Note on Clear Check' (CEB) <https://unsceb.org/sites/default/files/2021-05/2021%20-%20Briefing%20Note%20on%20Clear%20Check.pdf>; Steering Committee for Humanitarian Response, 'The Inter-Agency Misconduct Disclosure Scheme' <www.schr.info/the-misconduct-disclosure-scheme>.

[70] Following the failure by the ICC ASP to set up a procedure for the election of the ICC Prosecutor in 2020–21, there was increasing pressure from civil society to establish a permanent vetting mechanism. Mariana Pena, 'IER Blog Series: The Shocking Findings on Bullying and Harassment' (*International Justice Monitor*, 2 February 2021) <www.ijmonitor.org/2021/02/ier-blog-series-the-shocking-findings-on-bullying-and-harassment>; Angela Mudukuti, 'Continued Concerns about the ICC Prosecutor Election: No Election without Vetting' (*International Justice Monitor*, 3 February 2021) <www.ijmonitor.org/2021/02/continued-concerns-about-the-icc-prosecutor-election-no-election-without-vetting>.

[71] ACN Terms of Reference (n 35) para 5*bis*.

[72] Assembly of States Parties (ICC), 'Strengthening the International Criminal Court and the Assembly of States Parties' (13 December 2023) ICC-ASP/22/Res.3, para 81 and annex II.

[73] Ruth Mackenzie and others, *Selecting International Judges: Principles, Process and Politics* (OUP 2010) 101.

[74] ibid 105–06.

candidates' qualifications, states often make deals whereby they undertake to support another state in a different international election[75] in exchange for the latter's vote for their candidate at the election at hand.[76] These deals are called 'vote-trading', 'vote-swapping', 'mutual support', 'reciprocals', or 'horse-trading'. Vote-trading requires extensive outreach to other countries, which is normally combined with intense campaigning by and on behalf of candidates.[77] The politicization of elections has an undeniable impact on the state's decision to nominate and the way in which the nomination is undertaken,[78] and it often prevails over solely merit-based considerations. When a state decides to nominate a candidate, it often weighs factors such as regional considerations, the political suitability of the candidate, and whether it intends to seek another international position in the near future.[79]

These practices have less of an impact on elections at 'full panel' courts, where every member state has a judge represented at the institution. More commonly, however, elections at courts where seats are limited, and where the number of voting member states is large (the ICJ and the ICC, for instance) are more vulnerable to vote-trading. The posts in both these courts are also traditionally regarded as amongst the most prestigious international judicial positions.[80]

19.4.1 Assigned seats

According to Article 2 of the ICJ Statute, the court 'shall be composed of a body of independent judges, elected *regardless of their nationality*'. In practice, however, since the ICJ's founding, there have been strong traditions according to which each of the five permanent members of the UN Security Council always had a seat at the Court and the remaining ten seats are elected in accordance with 'a long-standing, negotiated compromise that governs the mix of the United Nations Security Council as well'.[81] In 2017, however, the UK lost an election and thus no longer has a seat it had held since the Court's creation in 1945.[82] Likewise, Russia lost 'its' seat at the ICJ bench in the 2023 elections, following its full-scale invasion of Ukraine.[83] This suggests that,

[75] This can be the appointment of an expert to a position within another organization, or, as it often is the case for trades in relation to judicial elections, the election of the country as a member of an international body, such as non-permanent membership in the United Nations Security Council. Mackenzie and others (n 73) 26.

[76] Ofer Eldar, 'Vote-Trading in International Institutions' (2008) 19(3) European Journal of International Law 3, 24.

[77] 'Selecting International Judges: Principle, Process and Politics', Discussion Paper (University College London Centre for International Courts and Tribunals, 2019) 7.

[78] ibid 11.

[79] ibid 5.

[80] Mackenzie and others (n 73) 123.

[81] Davis Robinson, 'The Role of Politics in the Election and the Work of Judges of the International Court of Justice' (2003) 97 Proceedings of the Annual Meeting (American Society of International Law) 277, 278.

[82] 'Britain Loses Seat on the International Court of Justice for First Time Ever' (*Deutsche Welle*, 21 November 2017) <www.dw.com/en/britain-loses-seat-on-international-court-of-justice-for-first-time-ever/a-41460450>.

[83] Andreas Zimmerman, 'Five, Four, Three… and Counting Down?—The Outcome of the Recent Triennial Elections at the International Court of Justice' (*EJIL:Talk!*, 17 November 2023) <www.ejiltalk.org/five-four-three-and-counting-down-the-outcome-of-the-recent-triennial-elections-at-the-international-court-of-justice>.

for certain courts, even permanent Security Council members need, at a minimum, to actively campaign to obtain or keep a seat and that, in certain instances, custom can yield to political condemnation.[84]

The Rome Statute endeavours to achieve equitable regional attribution in a more transparent way, through a system of 'minimum voting requirements' that allocate a minimum number of seats to each region.[85] However, other unwritten rules apply to these elections. For example, the main contributors to the ICC budget have always or nearly always had a judge at the ICC since they joined the court.[86] In addition, as noted in *Raising the Bar*, there appears to be an 'understanding' that out of the three seats allocated to the Group of Latin American and Caribbean States, at least one should be assigned to a Caribbean state.[87]

19.4.2 Vote-trading

In order to win an election, states engage in intense negotiations within and outside their regional groups. These negotiations start early on, sometimes as early as two years before the election. Traded votes appear to be available on a first-come-first-served basis,[88] so a delay in vote-swapping can lead to a lost election. When merit does play a role in deciding whom to vote for, it is often a factor along vote-trading. For example, a state will exchange votes when it would vote for the candidate anyhow based on their qualifications, or may refuse to do so when the candidate is clearly unqualified.[89] Some states do not engage in reciprocals for ICJ and ICC elections, either because they prioritize merit for such crucial elections or because they find it unacceptable to trade individual seats for such positions.[90] Those states, however, are in the minority, and horse-trading remains a widespread practice.[91]

While vote-trading is formally frowned upon, it is difficult to curb in practice. Governments do not have an incentive to abstain from reciprocals if other states continue to swap votes. At the ICC, however, there are signs of recognition that horse-trading is a harmful practice. For example, in its 2019 resolution, the ASP, '[e]ncourage[d] States Parties to refrain from the trading of votes'.[92] This flowed from an acknowledgement that the quality of ICC judges needed to improve.[93] It suggests

84 Mackenzie and others (n 73) 111.
85 ICC-ASP/3/Res.6 (n 10), para 20.
86 Japan, the United Kingdom, and Italy nominated candidates three times to the ICC and have never failed to have a candidate elected. Germany also always had a judge until 2024.
87 OSJI, 'Raising the Bar' (n 3) 42.
88 Mackenzie and others (n 73) 123.
89 ibid 126; OSJI, 'Raising the Bar' (n 3) 40.
90 Selecting International Judges (Discussion Paper) (n 77) 26; Mackenzie and others (n 73) 123.
91 Selecting International Judges (Discussion Paper) (n 77) 27.
92 Assembly of States Parties (ICC), 'Resolution on the Review of the Procedure for the Nomination and Election of Judges' (6 December 2019) ICC-ASP/18/Res.4, para 10. Before the first election of ICC judges in 2003, the Bureau of the ASP, had also appealed to states parties but vote-trading has persisted. OSJI, 'Raising the Bar' (n 3) 38.
93 ICC-ASP/18/Res.4 (n 92) para 1. OSJI, 'Raising the Bar' (n 3) 11–13; Assembly of State Parties (ICC), 'Report to the Bureau on the review of the procedure for the nomination and election of judges' (2 December 2019) ICC-ASP/18/31; IER Report (n 36) paras 962–63.

that vote-trading may change in time with more pressure for merit to be the only basis for voting, but the more conventional wisdom appears to be that vote-trading will never cease. The best solution, then, is to improve national nomination procedures so as to ensure that, at a minimum, vote exchanges occur amongst a pool of sufficiently qualified candidates.[94]

19.4.3 Campaigns

In principle, campaigning and vote-swapping have different goals. Campaigning aims at promoting a candidate, while exchanges of votes seek to secure a victory through political arrangements. However, in practice, campaigning is an integral part of vote-trading deals.[95]

Campaigns start early on, often months and even years before the election, and can run through the election day.[96] Their intensity depends on the court in question. They can involve 'a wide range of different strategies', including preparation of pamphlets and flyers to promote the candidate, sending of *notes verbales*, visits to governments in capital cities as well as embassies and permanent missions, lobbying at the UN Headquarters in New York, social media campaigns, and holding of receptions and other events.[97]

Campaigning for judicial elections has professionalized over time.[98] States sometimes deploy full-time staff to run the campaign, especially close to the election.[99] Government advisors often devise strategies to gain other states' support through campaign activities. This may include advice or instructions to the candidate to secure a vote.[100] In short, campaigns demand significant financial and political commitment to succeed: candidates with the strongest campaign, rather than those most qualified, are most likely to be elected. The opposite also holds true: if the state concerned does not invest significant capital, its nominee is unlikely to win.[101] The cost and length of campaigns—and the pressure to engage in them in order to succeed—often discourage states who lack the necessary resources from putting a candidate forward.[102]

The fact that campaigning, much like vote-trading, runs counter to the notion of merit-based election is no secret. However, unless concrete steps are taken to criticize the process and reduce the resort to campaigning and vote-trading, these practices will continue to adversely impact the quality of elected adjudicators.

[94] IER Report (n 36) paras 963–64.

[95] OSJI, 'Raising the Bar' (n 3) 38.

[96] Mackenzie and others (n 73) 112 and 119.

[97] ibid 113–14, 116; OSJI, 'Raising the Bar' (n 3) 27. When facing constraints, states may find other ways to campaign. For example, in 2020, during the COVID-19 pandemic, states 'found creative ways to promote their candidates, ranging from online meeting requests to Twitter campaigns and having candidates featured extensively in virtual events'. Mariana Pena, 'ICC Judicial Elections Reform: Some Progress but Still a Long Way to Go' (*International Justice Monitor*, 15 January 2021) <www.ijmonitor.org/2021/01/icc-judicial-elections-reform-some-progress-but-still-a-long-way-to-go>.

[98] Mackenzie and others (n 73) 115.

[99] Selecting International Judges (Discussion Paper) (n 83) 20–21.

[100] OSJI, 'Raising the Bar' (n 3) 37.

[101] Mackenzie and others (n 73).

[102] OSJI, 'Raising the Bar' (n 3) 3 and 37.

19.5 Continuing Judicial Education

Judicial trainings can play an important role in complementing appointment processes to ensure the quality of adjudicators. Professional development is a common practice in many jurisdictions' highest courts, and an integral part of judicial life in civil law and common law jurisdictions alike.[103] Still, in the international sphere, judges may have an apprehension towards legal education programmes, presuming that they could reflect a wrong public perception about their level of knowledge. For example, it could be considered 'anathema to the standing of a judge of an international criminal court'.[104] Despite such perceptions, some legal texts, in fact, require that judges undergo professional trainings. The ICC Code of Judicial Ethics provides, for instance, that 'judges shall take reasonable steps to maintain and enhance the knowledge, skills and personal qualities necessary for judicial office'.[105] Similarly, the Paris Declaration on the Effectiveness of International Criminal Justice, adopted by representatives of international courts and tribunals, calls for the promotion of 'continuous education of Judges and Legal Officers, including through partnerships with national academies for the training of judges'.[106]

Induction programmes seek to integrate newly appointed judges and facilitate their transition into their roles, while continuing professional development programmes typically aim to support sitting members of the judiciary in enhancing relevant skills and keeping up with important developments. In the context of international courts and tribunals, inductions and continuing legal education can help address challenges inevitably arising from judges' diverse backgrounds, legal systems, and professional working cultures. When the International Criminal Tribunal for the former Yugoslavia was established, for instance, judges across the board had no experience in conducting international criminal trials. The tribunal therefore coordinated weeklong training sessions for newly appointed judges on criminal law and procedure. Similarly, the Kosovo Specialist Chambers has organized roundtable discussions to encourage debate on potentially contentious issues that may arise during proceedings among judges.[107] This is good practice.

The ICC has traditionally had limited experience with any centralized or mandatory programme for continuing professional development, but the IER report of 2020 notably recommended that the court significantly reinforce both. It urged that the ICC Presidency organize a compulsory, intensive, and comprehensive induction

[103] For example, trainings are provided by the National Training Academy in Egypt, the Canadian Judicial Council in Canada, the Judicial Commission of New South Wales in New South Wales, Australia, the National School for the Judiciary in France, the National Judicial Academy in India, the National School for Formation and Development in Brazil, the Judicial Institute in New York, NY, and the Judicial Training Center in Slovenia.

[104] IER Report (n 36) para 430.

[105] ICC Code of Judicial Ethics, as amended ICC-BD/02-03-22 (adopted 18 September 2022, entered into force 7 October 2022) Art 7(2).

[106] Paris Declaration on the Effectiveness of International Criminal Justice (16 October 2017) <https://enm.justice.fr/sites/default/files/publications/Declaration_Paris_EN.pdf>, Art 31; IER Report (n 36) para 432.

[107] Open Society Justice Initiative, 'Raising the Bar Further: Professional Development for ICC Judges' (*International Justice Monitor*, 10 June 2020) <www.ijmonitor.org/2020/06/raising-the-bar-further-professional-development-for-icc-judges>.

programme of sufficient duration for incoming judges with the support of partners and stakeholders. Experts further urged a tailored approach that considers each judge's specific background and profile.[108] Following that recommendation, the ICC has started implementing induction courses, judicial trainings, and annual judges' retreats.[109] Operating in an ever-changing environment, international judges could undoubtedly benefit from participating in programmes aimed at furthering their knowledge of developing areas of law, exchanging judicial practices and court management methodologies, and expanding their knowledge on the use of new technologies. While not a panacea for all the judiciary's shortcomings, the value of such programmes for incoming and sitting judges is significant.

19.6 Conclusion

Until recently, relatively little attention had been paid to how international judges were nominated and elected. As international courts face increasing scrutiny, however, scholars and NGOs have started paying greater attention to these processes, highlighting the secrecy in which most of them are shrouded. While practices vary from one court and regional system to another, there is a shared need for improvement in the following areas:

- *National nomination procedures.* For international courts to thrive, the judicial candidates must be nominated through a transparent, merit-based, open, and competitive process. If judges are to be genuinely elected, they cannot be anointed.
- *Scrutinizing candidates.* An independent advisory committee/group of experts should be created for each international court to evaluate the suitability of nominated candidates for judicial office, including that they be of 'high moral character'. Such bodies should further be empowered to reject, where necessary, candidates who are unqualified or unsuitable for service. The quality of the assessments depends largely on the powers with which the relevant body is entrusted, as well as the level of transparency of the process. Unfortunately, most of the extant review bodies' assessments remain only advisory and non-binding in nature.
- *Responsible voting.* While it would be naive to think that judicial elections are immune from political considerations, at present political expediency and vote-trading exert an overwhelming, corrosive influence on how elections are conducted. There are limited signs that governments intend to curb these practices in a meaningful way, but ongoing public discouragement of vote-trading and campaigning should continue, alongside the sort of safeguards at the national and international level identified above.

[108] IER Report (n 36) Recommendation 174.

[109] Assembly of States Parties (ICC), Report of the Review Mechanism on the overall progress of its work (30 June 2022) para 24.

- *Judicial education and trainings.* Induction and continuing education can help prepare judges with different backgrounds in the law and practice of the court to which they have been elected, as well as other relevant legal and non-legal developments. These efforts not only facilitate onboarding but also promote new thinking and help build a culture of collegiality on the bench.

Effective governance of international courts demands competent judicial leaders of high moral character who are prepared and qualified to serve the mandates with which they are endowed. International courts and tribunals have benefited from many such leaders, but more can and must be done to ensure that states nominate candidates befitting of those institutions. To be sure, while there is no perfect nominations process or model, in almost all cases, the standards for nominations at the national level and for rigorous, transparent scrutiny at the international level have yet to be met. While judicial independence and the rule of law must be defended against growing partisan attacks, more can and should be done to ensure that the international bench itself benefits from improved procedures.

20

Deficient Protection of the Independence of International Judges by International Judicial Governance Institutions

The Case of Judge Akay

Zsuzsanna Deen-Racsmány

20.1 Introduction

Mr Aydın Sefa Akay, a Turkish international lawyer and diplomat, had been a judge of the United Nations International Residual Mechanism for Criminal Tribunals (IRMCT, or Mechanism) since its establishment in 2012.[1] On 21 September 2016, he was arrested in his home in Turkey, and Turkish police searched his home. A week later, Akay was charged with membership of the Fetullah Terrorist Organization (FETÖ) which Turkish authorities consider responsible for the 15 July 2016 attempted coup d'état in Turkey and placed in pre-trial detention.

At the time of these events, Judge Akay was working for the IRMCT, on the review proceedings in the *Ngirabatware* case,[2] remotely from the seats of the Mechanism as envisaged in its Statute.[3] Because of his arrest, those proceedings came to a halt, jeopardizing the ability of the Mechanism to respect fair trial rights.[4]

On 25 October 2016, the UN Legal Counsel asserted Judge Akay's immunities, but Turkey denied their applicability to the proceedings before Turkish courts. Yet, in the face of non-compliance by Turkey with an order issued by the Mechanism in January 2017 for the release of Judge Akay[5] and despite referral of Turkey's non-compliance

[1] Judge Akay's IRMCT profile <www.irmct.org/en/about/judges/judge-dr-aydin-sefa-akay>. From January 2009 through December 2011, Akay was a judge of the International Criminal Tribunal for Rwanda (ICTR).

[2] *Prosecutor* v *Augustin Ngirabatware*, MICT-12-29-R.

[3] Statute of the International Residual Mechanism for Criminal Tribunals, UNSC Res 1966 (22 December 2010) UN Doc S/Res/1966, Annex (IRMCT Statute) Art 8(3).

[4] For a brief summary of relevant facts and early developments concerning Akay's status, arrest and the consequences thereof for the Mechanism, 'Letter dated 5 October 2016 from the President of the International Residual Mechanism for Criminal Tribunals addressed to the President of the Security Council', UN Doc S/2016/841, 5 October 2016. For a detailed account of facts concerning Akay's arrest, detention, and related domestic legal proceedings: *Aydın Sefa Akay* v *Türkiye*, Judgment, App no 59/17, ECtHR, 23 April 2024, paras 15–75.

[5] Order to the government of Turkey for the release of judge Aydin Sefa Akay, *Prosecutor* v *Ngirabatware*, MICT-12-29-R, 31 January 2017 ('*Ngirabatware* order').

Zsuzsanna Deen-Racsmány, *Deficient Protection of the Independence of International Judges by International Judicial Governance Institutions* In: *Governance of International Courts and Tribunals*. Edited by: Sergey Vasiliev and Niels Blokker, Oxford University Press. DOI: 10.1093/oso/9780198922131.003.0020

with that order to the UN Security Council (UNSC),[6] the Council and the General Assembly (UNGA)—the IRMCT's *injugovins*[7]—failed to intervene to ensure Turkey's respect for Judge Akay's immunities. Moreover, when his second term at the Mechanism was about to expire in June 2018, the Security Council and the (President of the) General Assembly conveniently—but, in the view of this author, from a legal as well as from a policy perspective erroneously—went along with UN Secretary-General Guterres' proposal not to reappoint him.

Against this background, the present contribution scrutinizes the conduct of the IRMCT's governance institutions (the UNSC and the UNGA) in two specific contexts: a) their failure to safeguard Judge Akay's immunities; and b) his non-reappointment and the election of new judges. Following this introduction, in Section 20.2, the author will provide a succinct overview and evaluation of the IRMCT's establishment, the role of its *injugovins*, and some relevant features of the Mechanism, including rules pertaining to the appointment and independence of its judges. Section 20.3, in turn, sketches the factual background, from Judge Akay's election as an IRMCT judge up to his non-reappointment. Section 20.4 assesses the (lack of) efforts by the governance institutions to ensure respect for Judge Akay's immunities, while Section 20.5 considers the role of the governance institutions (including also the President of the General Assembly) in the non-reappointment of Judge Akay and the election of a new Turkish judge. The chapter ends with a brief discussion, presenting conclusions regarding the case of Judge Akay and the role of *injugovins* of international courts and tribunals in safeguarding the independence of 'their' court or tribunal.

20.2 The Mechanism and Its Judges

In 2010, acting under Chapter VII of the UN Charter,[8] the Security Council resolved to establish the Mechanism to carry out the residual functions of the International Criminal Tribunal for the former Yugoslavia (ICTY) and of the ICTR.[9] The Council emphasized that 'in view of the substantially reduced nature of the residual functions, the international residual mechanism should be a small, temporary and efficient structure, whose functions and size will diminish over time, with a small number of staff commensurate with its reduced functions'.[10] These considerations—together with

[6] Decision on Republic of Turkey's non-compliance with its obligation to cooperate with the Mechanism, *Prosecutor* v *Ngirabatware*, MICT-12-29-R, 6 March 2017 ('*Ngirabatware* decision').

[7] In his seminal study calling for research regarding such bodies, Blokker introduced the term 'international judicial governance institutions', or *injugovins* (Niels M Blokker, 'The Governance of International Courts and Tribunals: Organizing and Guaranteeing Independence and Accountability' in Andreas Føllesdal and Geir Ulfstein (eds), *The Judicialization of International Law: A Mixed Blessing?* (OUP 2018) 26). The present study adopts that designation (referring in short to *injugovins* or governance institutions). However, the author wishes to emphasize that the adjective 'judicial' pertains to the governed rather than to the governing body. International judicial governance institutions, often organs of the same international organization as the court or tribunal that they govern (ibid 34) are commonly—like in the case of the Mechanism—political organs.

[8] Charter of the United Nations (opened for signature 26 June 1945, entered into force 24 October 1945) 1 UNTS XVI (UN Charter).

[9] IRMCT Statute (n 3) Art 2. For a brief background, see Olufemi Elias, 'International Residual Mechanism for Criminal Tribunals (IRMCT)', *Max Planck Encyclopedia of International Procedural Law*, January 2019.

[10] UNSC Res 1966 (n 3) preambular para 7.

Russia's abstention on the vote on Resolution 1966[11] and its consistent disapproval of the Mechanism ever since—have (had) a significant impact on the legal framework guiding the IRMCT's operation as well as on its actual functioning. They potentially also explain certain aspects of the ensuing relationship between the Mechanism and its *injugovins* addressed in this chapter.[12]

The Mechanism is a subsidiary organ of the Security Council. However, the IRMCT Statute endows—next to the Council—also the General Assembly with certain governance functions, rendering the Council and the Assembly the Mechanism's twin governance institutions. This arrangement creates a situation resembling that of the IRMCT's predecessors and of the International Court of Justice (ICJ).[13] The powers of these *injugovins* as specified in the Statute relate in part to the election (and reappointment) of the judges and the prosecutor of the Mechanism.[14] In addition, both organs receive regular reports from the President of the Mechanism (the Security Council also from the Prosecutor).[15] However, on balance, the Council has a more prominent role than the UNGA, retaining even the key to the IRMCT's continued existence.[16]

In addition to these *injugovins*, other UN organs exercise certain other tasks in relation to the Mechanism, flowing from the UN Charter and/or consistent with their responsibilities within the UN. Most relevantly for this chapter, reflecting his role as the UN's chief administrative officer,[17] the Secretary-General plays a role in the appointment of the highest officials of the Mechanism, including its judges.[18]

The Mechanism has a roster of twenty-five judges, 'elected by the General Assembly from a list submitted by the Security Council' in accordance with the procedure prescribed in the Statute,[19] based on nominations by member states. The successful candidates must 'be persons of high moral character, impartiality, and integrity who possess the qualifications required in their respective countries for appointment to the highest judicial offices'.[20]

11 UNSC Provisional Verbatim Record of the 6463rd meeting (22 December 2010), UN Doc S/PV.6463.

12 For a discussion, see 'Council to Vote on the International Residual Mechanism for Criminal Tribunals' (*What's in Blue*, 25 June 2020) <www.whatsinblue.org>.

13 Statute of the International Tribunal for Prosecution of Persons Responsible for Serious Violations of International Humanitarian Law Committed in the Territory of the Former Yugoslavia, UNSC Res 827 (25 May 1993) UN Doc S/Res/827, Annex (ICTY Statute); Statute of the International Criminal Tribunal for Rwanda, UNSC Res 955 (8 November 1994) UN Doc S/Res/955, Annex (ICTR Statute); and Statute of the International Court of Justice (opened for signature 26 June 1945, entered into force 24 October 1945) 33 UNTS 993 (ICJ Statute).

14 IRMCT Statute (n 3) Arts 10, 11, and 14. The UNGA elects the judges from a list submitted to it by the UNSC (ibid Art 10) while the UNSC appoints the Prosecutor (following nomination by the Secretary-General) (ibid Art 14). In turn, the Secretary-General appoints the Registrar (ibid Art 15(3)).

15 Ibid Art 32. While the President of the Mechanism reports annually to both organs, the President and the Prosecutor must additionally submit six-monthly progress reports to the Council.

16 UNSC Res 1966 (n 3) para 17; also ibid paras 6, 7, 14, and 16 on the role of the UNSC. Moreover, under IRMCT Statute (n 3) Art 13, the Council was granted discretion regarding the (entry into force of) the Mechanism's Rules of Procedure and amendments thereto.

17 UN Charter (n 8) Art 97.

18 IRMCT Statute (n 3) Arts 10, 11, 14, 15.

19 Ibid Art 10(1); also Arts 8–9.

20 Ibid Art 9(1). On the significance of these requirements, eg Henry G Schermers and Niels M Blokker, *International Institutional Law: Unity within Diversity* (6th revised edn, Brill Nijhoff 2018) para 679 and Chittharanjan F Amerasinghe, 'Judges of the International Court of Justice: Election and Qualifications' (2001) 14 Leiden Journal of International Law 335.

In 2011, the first IRMCT judges were elected for a period of four years.[21] However, as envisaged already in 2010 and confirmed by the Security Council nearing the expiry of the first four-year term, the Mechanism—a residual body—was soon to 'continue to operate for subsequent periods of two years',[22] leading to a corresponding reduction of the judges' term of appointment.[23]

For international judges, a two-year tenure is unusually short.[24] However, IRMCT judges are 'eligible for reappointment by the Secretary-General after consultation with the Presidents of the Security Council and of the General Assembly', without renomination or re-election.[25] This arrangement does not appear fully conducive to independence and impartiality. It is commonly acknowledged that that goal 'is best served by judges who have security of tenure than by judges appointed for short terms, who are thus subject to frequent reelection or reappointment'.[26] A relevant concern relates to the fact that, as Schermers and Blokker have warned—concededly in the context of courts with jurisdiction over interstate disputes—states may attempt to 'block reappointment of judges who are considered too "activist" or "independent", although they will generally not say so explicitly'.[27] This prospect can make judges wishing to be reappointed hesitant to support certain decisions.

In the context of the Mechanism, the absence of a requirement of renomination and re-election (ie the fact that the nominating state and/or other states do not have a pronounced role in the process) appears to help eliminate such negative effects. However, regarding the Mechanism's predecessors—where judges were eligible for re-election by the UNGA[28]—it has been argued that, as 'the UN [was], derivatively, at least, a party in the proceedings before the tribunals', the possibility of re-election ('reappointment') of judges posed relevant risks.[29] While IRMCT judges may be reappointed without re-election, (the presidents of) the *injugovins* (ie the UN itself) retain a role in that process. The concerns regarding the impact of their short-term appointment, coupled with the possibility of reappointment, on their independence thus still pertain to some extent to the IRMCT as well. Fortunately, such threats seldom materialize: records show that IRMCT judges who indicate their availability for another term are routinely reappointed.[30]

[21] UNGA Decision 66/416, 20 December 2011, reproduced in UN Doc A/66/49 (Vol II) 11; also IRMCT Statute (n 3) Art 10(3).

[22] UNSC Res 2256 (22 December 2015), UN Doc S/Res/2256 preambular para 14; also UNSC Res 1966 (n 3) para 17.

[23] UNSC Res 2269 (29 February 2016), UN Doc S/Res/2269, para 2.

[24] Dinah Shelton, 'Legal Norms to Promote the Independence and Accountability of International Tribunals' (2003) 2 Law and Practice of International Courts and Tribunals 27, 37–39; Theodor Meron, 'Judicial Independence and Impartiality in International Criminal Tribunals' (2005) 99 American Journal of International Law 359, 361–62; Karin Oellers-Frahm, 'International Courts and Tribunals, Judges and Arbitrators', *Max Planck Encyclopedias of International Law Online*, March 2019, para 16.

[25] IRMCT Statute (n 3) Art 10(3).

[26] Remarks by Maritza Struyvenberg, 'Proceedings of the Annual Meeting' (2012) 106 American Society of International Law Proceedings 353, 354.

[27] Schermers and Blokker (n 20) para 682A.

[28] ICTY Statute (n 13) Art 13(4) and ICTR Statute (n 13) Art 12(5).

[29] Chittharanjan F Amerasinghe, *Principles of the Institutional Law of International Organizations* (2nd edn, CUP 2005) 249–50.

[30] Consult nn 122–23 and accompanying text.

Moreover, the judges—UN officials not members of the UN Secretariat—are entitled to privileges and immunities; an important safeguard of their independence. As the Statute renders the Convention on the Privileges and Immunities of the United Nations (Convention or CPIUN)[31] applicable *inter alia* to the judges of the Mechanism,[32] like all UN officials they, too, enjoy immunity from jurisdiction in relation to their official conduct.[33] Furthermore, the Statute specifically endows the judges with privileges and immunities 'as accorded to diplomatic envoys, in accordance with international law' which include, relevantly, personal inviolability, freedom from arrest and detention, immunity from criminal proceeding regarding any—ie even private—conduct and inviolability of their private residence.[34]

The importance of this provision is not limited to its explicit contents. Coupled with the general reference to the Convention in Article 29(1), it links IRMCT judges' diplomatic immunity to Article V, Section 19 of the Convention.[35] Significantly, however, in the case of IRMCT judges such privileges and immunities do not apply for their entire tenure (ie when a judge is on the roster) but only when (s)he is 'engaged on the business of the Mechanism'.[36] Judges' diplomatic immunity is thus conditional on their being assigned to a case.[37]

International judges regularly enjoy such far-reaching privileges and immunities.[38] While the likelihood that states would attempt to influence the outcome of IRMCT proceedings is admittedly smaller than in interstate dispute settlement, such protection still appears crucial for IRMCT judges. First, the functions of the Mechanism (ie criminal proceedings whereby the independence of judges is essential from the perspective of the right to a fair trial)[39] necessitate extensive and effective protection of impartiality and independence. Secondly, the determination of the Security Council

31 Convention on the Privileges and Immunities of the United Nations (adopted 13 February 1946, entered into force 17 September 1946) 1 UNTS 15 (CPIUN).

32 IRMCT Statute (n 3) Art 29(1).

33 CPIUN (n 31) Section V, Art 18.

34 IRMCT Statute (n 3) Art 29(2). The specific privileges and immunities enjoyed by diplomatic envoys under customary international law correspond to those stated in the Vienna Convention on Diplomatic Relations (signed 18 April 1961, entered into force 24 April 1964) 500 UNTS 95, in particular Arts 29–31.

35 Section 19 provides that: 'In addition to the immunities and privileges specified in Section 18, the Secretary-General and all Assistant Secretaries-general shall be accorded in respect of themselves, their spouses and minor children, the privileges and immunities, exemptions and facilities accorded to diplomatic envoys, in accordance with international law.' cf Ronja Bandyopadhyay and Tomoko Iwata, 'Officials (Article V Sections 17-21 General Convention)' in August Reinisch and Peter Bachmeyer (eds), *The Conventions on the Privileges and Immunities of the United Nations and Its Specialized Agencies* (OUP 2016) 313, 373 and Rosalyn Higgins and others, *Oppenheim's International Law: United Nations* (OUP 2017) 602 n 257, noting that IRMCT judges are covered by this provision.

36 IRMCT Statute (n 3) Art 29(3). This limitation is not unusual; it pertains for example also to the immunities of ICJ judges (ICJ Statute (n 13) Art 19). Moreover, it corresponds to IRMCT judges' terms and conditions of service (motivated by cost-efficiency) which—for each day when they exercise their functions for the Mechanism—are equal to those of judges *ad hoc* of the ICJ (IRMCT Statute (n 3) Art 8(4)). ICJ Statute (n 13) Art 31(2)–(6) and <www.icj-cij.org/en/judges-ad-hoc>.

37 eg *Ngirabatware* order (n 5) para 5 (referring to ibid para 3). Consult also IRMCT Statute (n 3) Art 12 on the assignment procedure; and Higgins and others, *Oppenheim's International Law* (n 35) 602 n 257, confirming that IRMCT judges' diplomatic immunity commences upon their assignment to a bench.

38 Shelton, 'Legal Norms to Promote' (n 24) 30, 41, 45; Oellers-Frahm, 'International Courts and Tribunals' (n 24) para 23.

39 Consult n 136 and accompanying text.

to ensure IRMCT's cost-efficiency[40] has resulted in an arrangement whereby judges may, as far as possible and as decided by the President of the Mechanism, exercise their functions 'remotely, away from the seats of the branches of the Mechanism'.[41] They are only to be 'present at the seats of the branches of the Mechanism as necessary at the request of the President to exercise the functions requiring their presence'.[42] Judges thus regularly perform functions for the Mechanism at locations other than its seats, not infrequently in their state of nationality.[43] This arrangement exposes them to a heightened risk of influence by authorities of the respective state, not covered by the additional protections guaranteed under the IRMCT's headquarters agreements.[44]

20.3 Factual Background up to Judge Akay's Non-Reappointment

Upon nomination by Turkey, Mr Aydın Sefa Akay was elected by a sweeping majority of the members of the General Assembly and he was appointed as one of the first twenty-five IRMCT judges in July 2012.[45] Following his reappointment in June 2016 for a period of two years,[46] President Meron of the Mechanism assigned him to the *Ngirabatware* case on 25 July 2016.[47]

On 21 September 2016, Judge Akay was arrested at his residence in Istanbul. On 21 September 2016, he was charged with membership of the FETÖ, the organization which, according to Turkish authorities, has been behind the July 2016 attempted coup d'état and which they consider an armed terrorist organization. Judge Akay was placed in pre-trial detention. His indictment states that the evidence underlying the charge of his links with this organization concerned the fact that he had used ByLock—an application which Turkish authorities allege is exclusively used by FETÖ members—and two books written by FETÖ leaders, seized by Turkish police following the search of his residence on the day of his arrest. Judge Akay admitted that he was a user of ByLock but denied having used it for communicating with(in) the FETÖ. While he

[40] Text accompanying n 10.

[41] IRMCT Statute (n 3) Art 8(3).

[42] ibid. Owing to its dual legacy, the Mechanism has two branches and two seats: one in Arusha (Tanzania), opened in 2012 to carry out residual functions of the ICTR, and one in the Hague (The Netherlands), opened in 2013 inheriting relevant functions from the ICTY <www.irmct.org/en/about>.

[43] Consult n 59. Significantly, no more than two judges may be nationals of the same state (IRMCT Statute (n 3) Art 8(1)).

[44] Agreement between the United Nations and the Kingdom of the Netherlands concerning the Headquarters of the International Residual Mechanism for Criminal Tribunals (signed 23 February 2015, entered into force 1 September 2016); ('Netherlands Seat Agreement') and Agreement between the United Nations and the United Republic of Tanzania concerning the Headquarters of the International Residual Mechanism for Criminal Tribunals (signed 26 November 2013, entered into force 1 April 2014) <www.irmct.org/en/documents/member-states-agreements>.

[45] UNGA, Provisional Verbatim Record of the 87th Plenary Meeting, Sixty-Sixth Session (16 December 2011) UN Doc A/66/PV.87. UNGA, Provisional Verbatim Record of the 44th Plenary Meeting, Seventy-First Session (9 November 2016) UN Doc A/71/PV.44, 15.

[46] 'Letter dated 24 June 2016 from the Secretary-General addressed to the President of the Security Council' (27 June 2016), UN Doc S/2016/574, Annex II; also nn 21–23 above and accompanying text.

[47] UNGA, '71/44th Plenary Meeting' (n 45) 5; also IRMCT Statute (n 3) Art 12(4).

did not deny that the said books belonged to his personal library, he submitted that he read all kinds of books.[48]

On 5 October 2016, IRMCT President Meron reported Judge Akay's arrest by Turkish authorities to the Security Council, requesting it to consider the matter promptly and to effectuate Akay's speedy release.[49] On 25 October 2016, the UN Legal Counsel asserted Judge Akay's diplomatic immunity on behalf of Secretary-General Ban Ki-Moon, requesting Turkey to release him and to cease legal proceedings against him.[50] Akay's immunity has not been waived.[51] However, Turkey disputed whether the diplomatic immunity enjoyed by Judge Akay under the Statute and the Convention also applied in the state of nationality.[52]

Akay's detention brought the review proceedings in the *Ngirabatware* case—on which he was working, remotely, at the time of his arrest—to a standstill, with obvious consequences for the efficiency of the Mechanism. Concerned about this problem as

[48] Indictment against Aydın Sefa Akay, Investigation No 2017/20886, Case No 2017/3498, Indictment No 2017/313 (unofficial English translation, on file with the author). Significantly, with regard to the use of ByLock, the ECtHR found in a different case that 'the uniform and global approach adopted by the Turkish judiciary vis-à-vis the ByLock evidence in convictions for membership of the FETÖ/PDY' was inconsistent with various provisions of the European Convention on Human Rights (ECHR) (Convention for the Protection of Human Rights and Fundamental Freedoms, as amended by Protocols No 11 and 14 (signed 4 November 1950, entered into force 3 September 1953) 213 UNTS 222; ETS No 5. *Yüksel Yalçinkaya v Türkiye*, Judgment, App no 15669/20, GC, ECtHR, 23 September 2023, para 364. It ordered the Respondent to adopt general measures, reaching beyond the case in question, to eliminate this problem 'in order to avoid [the ECtHR] having to establish similar violations in numerous cases in the future' (ibid para 418).

[49] IRMCT President's letter dated 5 October 2016 (n 4). This request was 'without prejudice to the determination of immunity in the case under the Statute of the Mechanism and the Convention'.

[50] Request for Invitation to United Nations Office of Legal Affairs, *Prosecutor* v *Augustin Ngirabatware*, MICT-12-29-R, 22 December 2016, Annex B; International Law Commission, Provisional Records, 'Statement by the Under-Secretary-General for Legal Affairs, the Legal Counsel: Cooperation with Other Bodies', UN Doc A/CN.4/SR.3371, 3 August 2017, 4–5. As Judge Akay was a member of the *Ngirabatware* bench—exercising his judicial functions in relation to that case remotely in Turkey at the time of his detention—he was entitled to privileges and immunities pertaining to diplomatic envoys under international law at the relevant time under Art 29(2) of the IRMCT Statute (n 3) and under Art V, Section 19 of the Convention (n 31). Consult nn 31–34 and accompanying text. Relevantly, Turkey acceded to the CPIUN in 1950 without a relevant reservation (United Nations Treaty Collection ratification information at <https://treaties.un.org/Pages/ViewDetails.aspx?src=TREATY&mtdsg_no=III-1&chapter=3&lang=en>).

[51] *Ngirabatware* order (n 5) para 6; also CPIUN (n 31) Art V Section 20, endowing the Secretary-General with 'the right and *the duty* to waive the immunity of any official in any case where, in his opinion, the immunity would impede the course of justice and can be waived without prejudice to the interests of the United Nations' (emphasis added).

[52] UNSC, 'Letter dated 10 March 2017 from the Permanent Representative of Turkey to the United Nations addressed to the President of the Security Council' (10 March 2017) UN Doc S/2017/210, para 3; also Statement by the Under-Secretary-General for Legal Affairs (n 50) 5; cf Bandyopadhyay and Iwata, 'Officials (Article V Sections 17–21 General Convention)' (n 35) 376–77; Higgins and others, *Oppenheim's International Law* (n 35) 596–97; and Anthony J Miller, 'Privileges and Immunities of United Nations Officials' (2007) 4 International Organizations Law Review 169, 227 on the opposability of such immunities towards authorities of the UN official's state of nationality in general; and Ady Niv, 'The Immunity of Judge Akay in Turkey: A Test Case for International Judges' Immunity and Independence' (2018) 22(14) ASIL Insights <www.asil.org/insights/volume/22/issue/14/immunity-judge-akay-turkey-test-case-international-judges-immunity-and>; Bilge Erson Asar, 'Prosecuting a Judge that Enjoys Diplomatic Immunity: The Case of Judge Aydın Sefa Akay' (*Verfassungsblog*, 30 August 2018) <https://verfassungsblog.de/prosecuting-a-judge-that-enjoys-diplomatic-immunity-the-case-of-judge-aydin-sefa-akay> and, in less categorical terms, *Akay v Türkiye* (n 4) paras 120–30 on this question in the context of Judge Akay's case. In any event, the significance of Turkey's position appears limited: text accompanying n 67.

well as about the rights of the accused, the independence of international judges, and the interests of justice, President Meron raised Judge Akay's case in the UNSC and the UNGA in November-December 2016. He referred to Judge Akay's immunities, requesting the Council to seek to resolve the situation swiftly,[53] and called upon Turkey to release him. He submitted in particular that, by detaining Judge Akay, Turkey was violating the IRMCT Statute and UNSC Resolution 1966.[54] While certain states (permanent and non-permanent members) voiced concerns about Judge Akay's fate and/or the functioning of the Mechanism, expressing their hope for a speedy resolution of the situation, they appeared content to leave the matter in the hands of the UN Secretariat's Office of Legal Affairs (OLA) and the Security Council's own Informal Working Group on International Tribunals (IWGIT).[55]

As no solution was forthcoming, on 31 January 2017, following a request by Ngirabatware to that effect, acting as pre-review judge of the Mechanism, President Meron ordered Turkey to 'cease all legal proceedings against Judge Akay; and (ii) take all necessary measures to ensure Judge Akay's release from detention as soon as practicable, but no later than Tuesday, 14 February 2017, so that he can resume his judicial function in this case'.[56]

The Order emphasized *inter alia* that '[t]o uphold [the absolute right to an independent and impartial tribunal], in the exercise of their judicial functions, the judges of the Mechanism shall be independent of all external authority and influence, including from their own States of nationality or residence'.[57]

On 9 March 2017, President Meron notified the UNSC of Turkey's non-compliance with the Order.[58] However, the Council and the Assembly still failed to take steps to ensure respect for Akay's immunity (and thus for the independence of the Mechanism and its judges) and towards his release. In vain, President Meron kept raising the prevailing situation before the Mechanism's *injugovins*. For instance, in June 2017 he reminded the Security Council that 'the failure to resolve the matter in a manner that respected the privileges and immunities of Judge Akay ... places in jeopardy the integrity of the remote model of judging'.[59] Noting that Judge Akay's detention of nearly

[53] UNSC Provisional Verbatim Record of the 7829th meeting (8 December 2016) UN Doc S/PV.7829, 6–7.

[54] UNGA, 71/44th meeting (n 45) 5–6.

[55] ibid, statement by the representative of the United States of America; also UNSC 7829th meeting (n 53), statements by the representatives of Angola, Bolivia, Egypt, Senegal, the United Kingdom, the USA, and Uruguay, and the reaction of Turkey. There are unfortunately no public records available indicating whether and how the OLA and the IWGIT have attempted to tackle this problem. In any event, the IWGIT reports presented to the UNSC in the relevant period do not contain references to Turkey and/or to Judge Akay. (UNSC, 'Report of the Informal Working Group on International Tribunals for 2016', UN Doc S/2016/1110 (29 December 2016), Annex; UNSC, 'Report of the Informal Working Group on International Tribunals for 2017', UN Doc S/2017/1102 (27 December 2017), Annex; UNSC, 'Report of the Informal Working Group on International Tribunals for 2017', UN Doc S/2018/1172 (31 December 2018), Annex.)

[56] *Ngirabatware* order (n 5) para 18.

[57] ibid para 11.

[58] UNSC, 'Letter dated 9 March 2017 from the President of the International Residual Mechanism for Criminal Tribunals addressed to the President of the Security Council' (9 March 2017), UN Doc S/2017/204; also *Ngirabatware* decision (n 6).

[59] UNSC Provisional Verbatim Record of the 7960th meeting (7 June 2017) UN Doc S/PV.7960, 7. Already in his letter of 17 November 2016 to the President of the Security Council (UN Doc S/2016/975), President Meron referred to the 'serious implications [of the situation] for the Mechanism's ability to carry out its core judicial functions in accordance with the remote-judging model ... pursuant to which, for the

nine months was 'an extraordinarily long period for the resolution of the detention of an international judge, whatever the legal complexities may be' and considering the *status quo* 'untenable', he 'call[ed] upon the Council to take such measures as may be necessary to achieve an appropriate resolution to that unprecedented situation'.[60]

At the same meeting, Uruguay, the Chair of the IWGIT called for collective or individual action by the members of the Council 'to ensure that the principles essential to the effectiveness of the work of those institutions ... are respected'.[61] While several other states (Bolivia, Egypt, Ethiopia, Japan, Senegal, the UK, and the USA) also voiced concerns about the situation, no concrete (public) steps by the Council ensued.

However, in the same month—upon being sentenced to seven years and sixth months in prison—Judge Akay was provisionally released pending his appeal. With his passport forfeited and subject to a travel ban, he resumed his work on the *Ngirabatware* bench, remotely, from Turkey.[62]

The immediate concerns about the functioning of the Mechanism were thus removed, but the questions concerning the effect of Turkey's non-compliance with the immunity of an IRMCT judge on the independence of the Mechanism have not been resolved. The difference of (legal) opinion between the IRMCT/UN and Turkey regarding Judge Akay's immunities and Turkey's obligations endured as well. In light of the threat posed by Judge Akay's pending appeal, this disagreement was far from immaterial. As aptly noted by President Meron, Judge Akay's conviction at first instance constituted 'further breach of Judge Akay's protected status under the international legal framework'.[63] While welcoming his release, President Meron emphasized, again, the need for urgent resolution of the situation in accordance with international law. Nevertheless, the issue was not given further consideration in subsequent meetings of the Security Council.

In the General Assembly, only the European Union (EU) raised the matter again, on the occasion of the discussion of the IRMCT's annual report in October 2017: having noted Judge Akay's release and the resumption of proceedings in the *Ngirabatware* proceedings,[64] Mr Chaboureau hinted at the still prevailing disagreement between the IRMCT and Turkey, 'call[ing] for new measures to resolve that matter with full respect for international law'.[65] Unsurprisingly, no (public) efforts towards resolving the situation followed.

most part, judges carry out their functions in their State of nationality'. For a similar statement, see 'Letter dated 17 May 2017 from the President of the International Residual Mechanism for Criminal Tribunals addressed to the President of the Security Council' (17 May 2017) UN Doc S/2017/434, para 14 and UNGA, 71/44th meeting (n 45) 5.

[60] UNSC, 7960th meeting (n 59) 7.

[61] ibid 11.

[62] IRMCT Press release, 'Statement of the Mechanism on Conviction of Judge Aydin Sefa Akay by Turkish Criminal Court of First Instance' (15 June 2017) <www.IRMCT.org/en/news/statement-mechanism-conviction-judge-aydin-sefa-akay-turkish-criminal-court-first-instance>; Note by the Secretary-General, 'International Residual Mechanism for Criminal Tribunals', UN Doc A/72/261–S/2017/661, 1 August 2017, para 26; and UNGA, Provisional Verbatim Record of the 32nd Plenary Meeting, Seventy-Second Session (18 October 2017) UN Doc A/72/PV.32, 8.

[63] Statement of the Mechanism (n 62).

[64] *Ngirabatware* (n 2).

[65] UNGA, 72/32nd meeting (n 62) 8.

The difference concerning Judge Akay's immunities was eventually rendered moot in June 2018 through his non-reappointment.[66]

20.4 Relevant Obligations and the Failure of the *Injugovins* to Protect Judge Akay's Immunities

By asserting Judge Akay's immunity from detention, arrest and legal proceedings in Turkey, the UN Legal Counsel, acting on behalf of the Secretary-General, invoked the application of the Convention. As noted by the ICJ in 1999, the underlying determination that immunities under the Convention apply 'creates a presumption which can only be set aside for the most compelling reasons and is thus to be given the greatest weight by national courts'.[67] Moreover, the Mechanism itself has ordered Turkey to respect Judge Akay's immunities.[68] All in vain. What could and should the Security Council and the General Assembly have done to safeguard Akay's immunities (and thus the independence of the Mechanism they govern)?

In the *Cumaraswamy* advisory opinion, the ICJ unmistakably linked immunities to the concept of (functional) protection.[69] In turn, it confirmed already in 1949 in its *Reparation for Injuries* advisory opinion that the UN has the *right* and the *capacity* to exercise functional protection on behalf of its agents when they (are at risk of) suffer(ing) damage or injury as a result of a breach of an obligation owed to the Organization:

> In order that the agent may perform his duties satisfactorily, he must feel that this protection is assured to him by the Organization, and that he may count on it. To ensure the independence of the agent, and, consequently, the independent action of the Organization itself, it is essential that in performing his duties he need not have to rely on any other protection than that of the Organization (save of course for the more direct and immediate protection due from the State in whose territory he may be). In particular, he should not have to rely on the protection of his own State. If he had to rely on that State, his independence might well be compromised, contrary to the principle applied by Article 100 of the Charter. And lastly, it is essential that—whether the agent belongs to a powerful or to a weak State; to one more affected or less affected, by the complications of international life; to one in sympathy or not in

[66] Upon the expiry of his term as an IRMCT judge not followed by his reappointment (discussed in Section 20.5), Akay ceased to enjoy the immunities underlying the dispute.

[67] *Difference relating to Immunity from Legal Process of a Special Rapporteur of the Commission on Human Rights*, Advisory opinion of 29 April 1999, ICJ Reports (1999) 62 ('*Cumaraswamy*') para 61; also *Akay* v *Türkiye* (n 4) para 123, referring to the presumption thus created regarding Akay's immunity.

[68] *Ngirabatware* order (n 5). For an analysis of this order, Zsuzsanna Deen-Racsmány, '*Prosecutor v Ngirabatware*, Order to the government of the Republic of Turkey for the release of Judge Aydin Sefa Akay, 31st January 2017 (Case no MICT-12-29-R)', OXIO 585.

[69] *Cumaraswamy* (n 67) paras 50–51. On functional protection, eg Myriam Benlolo Carabot and Muriel Ubéda-Saillard, 'Functional Protection' in James Crawford and others (eds), *The Law of International Responsibility* (OUP 2010) 1073. Consult also ibid 1077–78 on the relationship between functional protection and privileges and immunities.

> sympathy with the mission of the agent—he should know that in the performance of his duties he is under the protection of the Organization. . . .
>
> Upon examination of the character of the functions entrusted to the Organization and of the nature of the missions of its agents, it becomes clear that the capacity of the Organization to exercise a measure of functional protection of its agents arises by necessary intendment out of the Charter.[70]

It is admittedly not entirely clear whether the ICJ meant to identify a relevant obligation of the UN under international law or whether these statements merely serve to support its conclusion that 'it is necessary that, when an infringement occurs, the Organization should be able to call upon the responsible State to remedy its default'.[71] In any event, functional protection is increasingly perceived of as a (legal) duty on the part of the international organization.[72]

Judge Akay's case beyond doubt concerns a situation wherein functional protection could and ought to have been exercised. Regarding the reach of functional protection *ratione personae*, the ICJ has explicitly stated that the UN could protect its officials even towards their state of nationality.[73] At the same time, relying on an earlier passage of *Reparation for Injuries*, commentators tend to limit the *material* scope of functional protection, considering in general that 'it extends only to acts and omissions linked to the official mission, not to private acts of the agent'.[74] However, the ICJ's position cited above shows that the right to exercise functional protection is justified by the need '[t]o ensure the independence of the agent, and, consequently, the independent action of the Organization itself'. This very need is what underlies the grant of immunities as well. While for most agents immunity from jurisdiction in relation to official acts is considered sufficient, in some exceptional cases (ie in relation to certain high-ranking officials) such immunities are recognized as being indispensable also concerning private acts, owing to a heightened need of their protection. It is submitted that in relation to such individuals (including the judges of the Mechanism) the same

70 *Reparation for Injuries Suffered in the Service of the United Nations* (Advisory Opinion) 11 April 1949, ICJ Reports (1949) 174 at 183–84.

71 ibid 183.

72 In a 1964 judgment, the International Labour Organization's Administrative Tribunal (ILOAT) noted, referring to *Reparation for Injuries* (n 70), that 'it is the duty of the [International Labour Organization] to protect and assist its officials in the performance of their functions and in connection therewith'. *In re Jurado*, ILOAT, Judgment No 70 (11 September 1964) para II(3); cf Benlolo Carabot and Ubéda-Saillard (n 69) 1076 and 1078, referring to relevant due diligence obligations of the organization to prevent harm and noting that 'functional protection covers certain obligations of the international organization'; and James Crawford, *State Responsibility: The General Part* (CUP 2013) 594, positing that 'where [diplomatic protection] is recognized as a right or entitlement of the state, [functional protection] is closer to a duty on the part of the international organization'.

73 *Reparation for Injuries* (n 70) 186.

74 eg Robert Kolb, *The International Law of State Responsibility: An Introduction* (Edward Elgar Publishing 2017) 202; *In re Jurado* (n 72) para II(3); Crawford (n 72) 595; Benlolo Carabot and Ubéda-Saillard (n 69) 1079–80, reaching this conclusion based on the ICJ's explicit distinction between situations where 'the injury for which the reparation is demanded arises from a breach of an obligation designed to help an agent of the Organization in the performance of his duties' and 'a case in which the wrongful act or omission would merely constitute a breach of the general obligations of a State concerning the position of aliens; claims made under this head would be within the competence of the national State and not, as a general rule, within that of the Organization'. *Reparation for Injuries* (n 70) 182.

considerations justify the exercise of functional protection more broadly as well, ie also in the broader context of violations of their diplomatic immunity rather than only regarding conduct in performance of their official duties. After all, in such cases too, the underlying wrong concerns a breach of an obligation towards the Organization itself, one 'designed to help an agent of the Organization in the performance of his duties'.[75]

Moreover—while not specifically designed for that purpose—as evidenced by the *Cumaraswamy* and *Mazilu* proceedings, functional protection may clearly be exercised in situations where the underlying wrong concerns violation of immunities of an agent.[76] It should thus have been exercised regarding Judge Akay, to ensure that he could carry out his functions as intended. Concededly, privileges and immunities are granted under the Convention in the interest of the UN rather than for the personal benefit of the individual concerned.[77] It is thus for the Secretary-General to determine whether they are applicable and whether to assert or waive them.[78] Consequently, there is no general or absolute obligation on the UN to invoke the immunities of its agents. However, the UN had asserted Judge Akay's immunity, thus confirming that it applied and could not be waived in the circumstances. If one accepts that the ICJ has perceived functional protection as an obligation (at least one of conduct) on the part of the Organization, it may thus be concluded that the UN had a duty to follow through and at least attempt to ensure that Turkey ceased violating Judge Akay's immunity.

Pertinently, in *Reparation for Injuries*, the ICJ did not clarify which UN organs have a role to play in this context. However, fifty years later in *Cumaraswamy*, the Court specified—based on extensive practice—that '[t]he Secretary-General, as the chief administrative officer of the Organization, has the authority and the responsibility to exercise the necessary protection where required'.[79] It added that 'the Secretary-General has the *primary* responsibility and authority to protect the interests of the Organization and its agents'.[80] Accordingly, it was in the first place for Secretary-Generals Ban Ki-Moon and his successor Antonio Guterres to intervene with Turkey to safeguard Judge Akay's immunity.

However, the ICJ's formulation ('primary') indicates that the Secretary-General is not the sole holder of that authority and responsibility. Other organs may play a role in functional protection as well, on their own right (eg through adopting a statement, decision or resolution addressed to the state concerned) or through requesting the Secretary-General or others to undertake relevant steps.

This position gains support from the cases of Mr Dumitru Mazilu (Special Rapporteur on human rights and youth of the Sub-Commission on Prevention of

75 *Reparation for Injuries* (n 70) 182.

76 Benlolo Carabot and Ubéda-Saillard (n 69) 1078. Consult also *Cumaraswamy* (n 69); *Applicability of Article VI, Section 22, of the Convention on the Privileges and Immunities of the United Nations*, Advisory Opinion of 15 December 1989, ICJ Reports (1989) 177 ('*Mazilu*').

77 eg CPIUN (n 31) Art V, Section 20.

78 ibid; *Cumaraswamy* (n 67) para 60. Consult also n 51.

79 *Cumaraswamy* (n 67) para 50.

80 ibid para 51 (emphasis added).

Discrimination and Protection of Minorities)[81] and Mr Dato Param Cumaraswamy (Special Rapporteur on the independence of judges and lawyers of the Commission on Human Rights).[82] In both cases, the principal UN organ—the Economic and Social Council (ECOSOC)—under whose authority these bodies fell undertook the ultimate steps towards resolving the dispute regarding the immunities of these UN agents. Admittedly, even in those cases, it took considerable time before the Secretary-General and ECOSOC became actively involved; but they did. First, they resorted to diplomatic channels, and when those proved insufficient, ECOSOC—in cooperation with the Secretary-General who lacks the competence to initiate such proceedings[83]—requested an ICJ advisory opinion in both cases.[84]

In relation to Judge Akay, next to the Secretary-General, the Security Council and the General Assembly had the authority and possibility to intervene and seek to resolve the matter. As the Mechanism's *injugovins*, they regularly had IRMCT business on their agenda. Yet, beyond the assertion of Judge Akay's immunities by the Secretariat, there are no indications of any intervention by these organs, with the possible exception of the IWGIT.[85] Member states apparently have not considered it necessary and/or suitable to press the matter in these bodies beyond noting that they deplored the situation and hoped for its quick resolution. In the Security Council, Judge Akay's situation and its implications for the independence of the Mechanism have not been discussed at all after his release from prison awaiting his appeal, even though IRMCT business regularly featured on the Council's agenda and member states had the right to request the issue to be put on the Council's agenda on additional occasions.[86]

Significantly, as Blokker rightly posited,

> International courts and tribunals can only perform their dispute settlement function if they are well 'governed', or rather 'governanced'. ... [S]ince it is generally agreed that international courts and tribunals must be independent, just like and perhaps even

[81] *Mazilu* (n 76) paras 10–25 and ibid, Request for Advisory Opinion (including the dossier of documents transmitted to the Court pursuant to article 65, paragraph 2 of the Statute) (13 June 1989) <www.icj-cij.org/public/files/case-related/81/9703.pdf>.

[82] *Cumarswamy* (n 67) paras 5–20 and ibid, Request for Advisory Opinion (including the dossier of documents transmitted to the Court pursuant to article 65, paragraph 2 of the Statute) (10 August 1998) <www.icj-cij.org/public/files/case-related/100/7644.pdf>.

[83] Under Article 96 UN Charter (n 8), the UNGA and the UNSC may seek ICJ advisory opinions 'on any legal question'. Consult also ICJ Statute (n 13) Art 65. Conversely, the Secretary-General and UN member states cannot (directly) request ICJ advisory opinions. Cf Theodor Meron, 'Status and Independence of the International Civil Servant' (1980) 167 Collected Courses of the Hague Academy of International Law 285, 337 for a proposal that the Secretary-General should be authorized to do so.

[84] Regarding Mr Mazilu—owing to a possibly relevant reservation by Romania—the ECOSOC did so acting under its general competence to request an advisory opinion rather than under Section 30 of the Convention (n 31). Consult text accompanying n 99 and *Applicability of Article VI, Section 22* (n 76) paras 29–31.

[85] While diplomatic efforts may have taken place behind the scenes, the wealth of evidence of efforts by ECOSOC and the UN Secretariat to ensure respect for the immunities of Special Rapporteurs Mazilu and Cumaraswamy as opposed to the lack thereof in relation to Judge Akay remains remarkable.

[86] UNSC, 'Provisional Rules of Procedure of the Security Council', UN Doc S/96/Rev.7 (UNSC RoP), Rules 6–7. Member states also had the possibility to initiate further discussions of the matter in the General Assembly; UNGA, 'Rules of Procedure of the General Assembly (with amendments until September 2016)', UN Doc A/520/Rev.18* (UNGA RoP), Rules 13(e), 14–19.

more than their national colleagues, it is important that injugovins should provide the necessary guarantees for their independence.[87]

Accordingly, owing to its particular nature, in relation to the IRMCT and its staff the governance institutions arguably ought to have played a prominent role in this context. Moreover, as explained in Section 20.2, the need for such guarantees and protection (of immunities and independence) by the governance institutions is particularly pronounced in the case of the IRMCT and its judges.[88] It may thus be submitted that the Security Council and the General Assembly, as the Mechanism's *injugovins*, had at least a responsibility or moral duty (possibly even a legal obligation) to safeguard the independence of the Mechanism and the immunities of Judge Akay through adopting an active role in the context of functional protection. In addition, flowing from the principle of functional necessity, governing institutions appear at the very least to be under an obligation of good faith not to undermine the independence and impartiality of the judicial institution they govern or that of its judges. Yet, they failed even to consider exercising the requisite protection.

Admittedly, the Security Council and the General Assembly are political rather than judicial organs. Moreover, while the Mechanism was established by the Council in fulfilment of their shared responsibility for maintaining peace and security,[89] at the time of Judge Akay's arrest the conflicts in Rwanda and the former Yugoslavia were part of history. As the violation of Judge Akay's immunity clearly did not pose a direct threat to international peace and security, the Council and the Assembly may have been more inclined to tend to other matters.

Moreover, the Mechanism's *injugovins* (and governance institutions in general) have their own Achilles heel: whereas they (as organs of an international organization) are more than a sum of their members, the organ's ability to undertake concrete action depends on the stance of its membership on the particular issue. As indicated by the overview of the events and discussions that took place in the relevant period in the previous section, member states were overall not keen on ensuring that the governing institutions would play an active role in this context. They preferred to leave the matter to the OLA or the IWGIT. Furthermore, Judge Akay's return to the bench pending his appeal appears to have satisfied the Security Council and tempered the tone of the discussion (further) in the General Assembly as well, suggesting that the majority of their members were only (or mainly) concerned about the *functioning* of the Mechanism. They were apparently not as interested in safeguarding the IRMCT's *independence* and, for that purpose or in general, in ensuring compliance with member states' obligations regarding the immunity of its judges.

A closer look at the members renders the inactivity of the Security Council unsurprising: at least two permanent members (the USA and the UK)—and for a significant part of the relevant period even at least one non-permanent member (Italy in 2017

[87] Niels M Blokker, 'Governance of the International Tribunal of the Law of the Sea: The Role of the Meeting of States Parties to the Law of the Sea Convention' in Angela del Vecchio and Roberto Virzo (eds), *Interpretations of the United Nations Convention on the Law of the Sea by International Courts and Tribunals* (Springer 2019) 83.

[88] Text accompanying nn 39–44.

[89] UN Charter (n 8) Chapters IV–VII.

followed by the Netherlands in 2018)—are known to deny the applicability of diplomatic immunity of high-ranking UN officials in the state of nationality.[90] While the USA and the UK did emphasize the importance of a quick solution, they may have been wary to support efforts specifically aimed at convincing Turkey to recognize the applicability of Judge Akay's diplomatic immunity in his state of nationality and thus to create a precedent in conflict with their own position. In addition, the fact that charges against Judge Akay related to participation in a coup d'état and other topical political considerations undoubtedly influenced the position of certain member states, including permanent members. After all, Turkey cooperated closely with Russia at the time in an attempt to end the Syrian civil war, was seen as a key to the European Union's attempts to curb refugee flows and manoeuvred ingeniously in the context of the tragic case of Jamal Khashoggi.[91] Moreover, the uneasy relationship between the Mechanism and the Security Council (and in particular Russia) that manifested itself already at the IRMCT's inception was likely not beneficial either.[92] Many states thus appear to have had weighty reasons not to seek confrontation with Turkey—ie not to adopt a hard line in the IRMCT's *injugovins* against Turkey regarding its violation of Judge Akay's asserted immunity—even after the Mechanism reported Turkey's non-compliance with its order for the release of Judge Akay to the Security Council.[93] Most importantly, as the election of a new Turkish judge in 2018[94] demonstrated, Turkish diplomacy was apparently very effective in that period.

Admittedly, the fact that three UN organs (including two *injugovins*) had a potential role to play in protecting Judge Akay and the independence of the Mechanism—without a clear division of relevant responsibilities—may not have been conducive of a solution. However, member states' demonstrated lack of initiative and of support for Judge Akay and the independence of the Mechanism in both *injugovins* suggests that this factor did not play a significant role.

To readers familiar with the circumstances which eventually led to the requests for the advisory opinions in the *Mazilu* and *Cumaraswamy* proceedings,[95] the lack of concrete action by these organs is probably not surprising. In those instances too, it proved easier to initiate (any) action via the ECOSOC—a relatively small organ with favourable decision-making rules and with a membership that has a relatively strong affinity for human rights—than through the General Assembly.

Moreover, these two cases, where the matter was eventually pressed to the highest level (ie the ICJ) in an effort to reach a solution, represent the tip of the iceberg. When it comes to protecting UN agents against their states of nationality, inaction seems to be the rule rather than the exception. As noted by a commentator in relation to the

[90] eg Miller, 'Privileges and Immunities of UN Officials' (n 52) 227 in relation to the USA and the UK. In relation to Italy: Felice Morgenstern, *Legal Problems of International Organizations* (Grotius Publications 1986) 9. In turn, the Dutch stance on this issue is indicated eg by Article 16 of the Netherlands Seat Agreement (n 44) which explicitly deprives Dutch judges of the benefit of diplomatic immunity in The Netherlands.

[91] eg Tom Lansford, *Political Handbook of the World 2018–2019* (Sage 2019) Vol 1, 1621.

[92] Text accompanying nn 10–12.

[93] *Ngirabatware* decision (n 6).

[94] Section 20.5.3.

[95] The factual and procedural background of these proceedings is well illustrated and documented in the dossiers attached to the request for the advisory opinions in these cases (nn 81 and 82, respectively).

latest request by the General Assembly for an ICJ advisory opinion, lobbying, 'concerted diplomatic efforts', 'persuasion and political will' are indispensable to success.[96] This observation likely has a broader validity, not limited to requests for advisory opinions.

In the cases of Messrs Mazilu and Cumaraswamy, decisive pressure was forthcoming, from non-state actors. It is quite telling that, in relation to Mr Cumaraswamy, the Assistant Secretary-General for Legal Affairs informed the Permanent Representative of Malaysia in mid-June 1998 as follows:

> the Secretary-General is under considerable pressure from the international human rights and legal community to have this matter resolved. It is clear that the Secretary-General cannot avoid the issue, should it remain without a negotiated settlement, during the upcoming session of the Economic and Social Council which commences on 6 July 1998. Accordingly, unless the Government of Malaysia formally responds to the draft settlement agreement, we will have to resort to the International Court of Justice and will thus proceed to submit to you the questions we intend to present to the Economic and Social Council to request an advisory opinion.[97]

In relation to Judge Akay, a similar degree of pressure and activism was lacking. The media and NGOs barely noticed the incident. Although President Meron frequently and forcefully called for a solution in the Mechanism's *injugovins*,[98] the international judicial and human rights community was not successfully mobilized. Admittedly, while the Secretary-General (and ECOSOC in the case of Mazilu and Cumaraswamy) may have proved responsive to such activism, it is questionable whether any degree of public pressure would have sufficed in relation to the Mechanism's *injugovins*, in particular the Security Council. However, UN documents including meeting records do not contain evidence of *any* initiative by the Secretary-General or by member states to discuss the matter in general or to try to convince the *injugovins* to undertake specific action in relation to Judge Akay.

In any event, while these considerations are important for understanding the process and for drawing lessons, they fall short of providing a valid excuse for the governance institutions' passivity in the face of their responsibility to protect the independence of the Mechanism.

Admittedly, the existence and scope of the UN's *legal* duty to exercise functional protection may not be sufficiently clearly established and defined so as to rule out all perceivable justifications. However, in relation to the specific case of Judge Akay, the Convention imposed a categorical obligation on the UN:

[96] Priya Pillai, 'The African Union, the International Criminal Court and the International Court of Justice: At the Fault Lines of International Accountability' (2018) 22 ASIL Insights (22 August 2018) <www.asil.org/insights/volume/22/issue/10/african-union-international-criminal-court-and-international-court>.

[97] *Cumaraswamy*, Request for Advisory Opinion (including the dossier) (n 82) Document No 58, 330.

[98] On the efforts by President Meron to ensure Turkey's respect for Judge Akay's immunities: Theodor Meron, *Standing Up for Justice: The Challenges of Trying Atrocity Crimes* (OUP 2021) 137–39.

> If a difference arises between the United Nations on the one hand and a Member on the other hand [out of the interpretation or application of the present convention], *a request shall be made for an advisory opinion on any legal question involved* in accordance with Article 96 of the Charter and Article 65 of the Statute of the Court. The opinion given by the Court shall be accepted as decisive by the parties.[99]

The divergence of views between the UN/IRMCT and Turkey concerning the applicability of Akay's diplomatic immunity in Turkey most plausibly qualified as a difference in the sense of this provision.[100] Accordingly, the UN was under a legal obligation to seek a (decisive) advisory opinion. Whereas in the context of functional protection they could theoretically hide behind the Secretary-General, here only the *injugovins* were endowed with a relevant competence.[101] This obligation was thus in effect directed to them, without even a theoretical possibility to fall back on the Secretary-General. Yet, the UNGA and the UNSC failed to act. In the absence of transparency, the reasons for the failure of the General Assembly and the Security Council to protect Judge Akay and the independence of the Mechanism, including through a request for an ICJ advisory opinion, may only be guessed. However, the fact remains that they have failed to fulfil their responsibility and duty as governance institutions or even the UN's obligation under the Convention. By condoning Akay's non-reappointment, they opted for a solution at variance with fundamental legal principles including judicial independence.

20.5 Judge Akay's Non-Reappointment and Beyond

As explained in Section 20.2, IRMCT judges' reappointment does not necessitate their re-election or even renomination, limiting the influence of individual states in that process.[102] However, when Judge Akay's second term at the Mechanism was about to expire in 2018, Turkey used a backdoor provided by the requirements in the Statute concerning the eligibility and qualifications of the judges[103] to prevent his reappointment. As noted by the Secretary-General in his letter addressed to the President of the UNSC, conveying the list of IRMCT judges he intended to reappoint,

> [t]he Government of Turkey has informed the Secretariat that Judge Aydin Sefa Akay is no longer eligible to be a judge in Turkey and *does not possess the qualifications for appointment to the highest judicial office in Turkey under the applicable law.* The

[99] CPIUN (n 31) Section 30 (emphasis added).

[100] Akay's immunity was asserted by the UN Legal Counsel on behalf of the Secretary-General, with specific reference to the applicability of diplomatic immunity under the Convention even in the official's state of nationality (Statement by the Under-Secretary-General for Legal Affairs (n 50) 5), and was not waived or rectified. At the same time, Turkey persistently denied that Akay's conduct was covered by immunities, even in the face of an order by the IRMCT (Section 20.3). For a recent discussion of the requirement of the existence of a dispute (or 'difference') in the ICJ's jurisprudence: Aniruddha Rajput, 'Necessity of "Objective Awareness" for the "Existence of Dispute"' (2018) 58 Indian Journal of International Law 85.

[101] Consult n 83.

[102] Text accompanying n 25.

[103] IRMCT Statute (n 3) Art 9(1).

> Government has provided supporting material in this regard. In the light of the information furnished by the Government and a review of the relevant material, it is considered that Judge Akay *does not currently meet the qualification requirements* for judges of the Mechanism ... and, consequently, cannot be considered for reappointment.[104]

Consequently, Secretary-General Guterres did not propose to reappoint Judge Akay, and the Office of Legal Affairs did not approach him regarding his availability for re-appointment.[105] Since the UNSC and the UNGA (or at least the latter's President) concurred, the Secretary-General proceeded to appoint the judges as proposed, ie excluding Judge Akay.[106]

In the Security Council, no reference was made to Judge Akay anymore. In the General Assembly, two representatives—of the EU and Serbia—drew attention to 'the circumstances that led to the non-reappointment of former Judge Akay of the Mechanism'. They expressed concern and regret,[107] apparently without any effect.

20.5.1 Judge Akay's 'lack of qualifications'

Since Article 9(1) of the IRMCT Statute on the required qualifications of judges features in a provision distinct from the rule on elections, and in light of its wording, it appears to impose continuing conditions regarding judges' qualifications. It thus follows that judges must fulfil the criteria stated therein, including the requirement of eligibility for appointment for the highest legal posts in their respective countries, not only in the context of their nomination but also as a precondition of their reappointment.

One relevant condition concerns age.[108] In accordance with Articles 139-140 of the Turkish Constitution,[109] judges in Turkey must retire having reached the mandatory retirement age of sixty-five years. Judge Akay was born in 1950. Turkey could thus legitimately have invoked his age and this rule to prevent his reappointment. However, if Turkey's objections to his reappointment in 2018 concerned Judge Akay's age, this

[104] UNSC, 'Letter dated 22 June 2018 from the Secretary-General addressed to the President of the Security Council' (26 June 2018) UN Doc S/2018/626, emphases added. Consult also IRMCT Press release, 'Statement of the President on the Non-Reappointment of Judge Akay' (Arusha/The Hague, 3 July 2018) <www.irmct.org/en/news/statement-president-non-reappointment-judge-akay>, noting that '[i]t is understood that the decision not to reappoint Judge Akay was based on information provided by the Government of Turkey to the UN Secretariat that Judge Akay no longer satisfies the qualifications for Judges identified in Article 9 of the Mechanism's Statute *by virtue of his conviction*'. (Emphasis added.)

[105] Secretary-General's letter dated 22 June 2018 (n 104).

[106] Twenty-three of the twenty-five judges were reappointed. 'Of the two remaining judges, one declined to seek reappointment *while the other's reappointment was denied*'. UNGA, 'Sixth Annual Report of the International Residual Mechanism for Criminal Tribunals' (1 August 2018) UN Doc A/73/289-S/2018/569, para 9 (emphasis added).

[107] UNGA, Provisional Verbatim Record of the 21st Plenary Meeting, Seventy-Third Session (18 October 2018) UN Doc A/73/PV.21.

[108] On the observance of this requirement in the context of the judges of the ICJ: Amerasinghe, 'Judges of the International Court of Justice' (n 20) 337–38.

[109] 2019 Constitution the Republic of Turkey ('Constitution') <www.anayasa.gov.tr/media/7258/anayasa_eng.pdf>. The relevant provisions have not been amended since 2010.

issue should have been raised against his reappointment already in 2016, rendering its possible invocation in 2018 controversial.

In any event, the Secretary-General's letter and President Meron's July 2018 statement[110] suggest that Turkey's objections concerned Akay's conviction at first instance rather than his age. Turkey appears to have relied on the rule of the Constitution which provides that judges may not be dismissed or retire, except upon their own request, before the age of 65, adding that '[e]xceptions indicated in law relating to those convicted for an offence requiring dismissal from the profession, those who are definitely established as unable to perform their duties because of illhealth, or those determined as unsuitable to remain in the profession, are reserved'.[111]

It is quite plausible that due to his conviction at first instance (and pending his appeal) Akay did not 'possess the qualifications required in [Turkey] for appointment to the highest judicial offices'.[112] However, as observed by President Meron, 'the acquiescence to the position advanced by the Government of Turkey represents a de facto acceptance of a State's action in contravention of the diplomatic immunity asserted by the United Nations, a dangerous precedent to set'.[113] It was thus far from evident for the Organization—and in particular for the IRMCT's governance institutions expected to safeguard the independence of the judges of a judicial institution—to uncritically go along with Turkey's allegations.

Because of IRMCT judges' diplomatic immunity it may admittedly appear difficult to demonstrate—even in case of well-founded accusations—that a judge no longer meets the requirements of integrity and high moral character stated in Article 9(1) of the IRMCT Statute.[114] However, relevant allegations may be verified through two appropriate paths. First, the Secretary-General has the right and duty to waive immunities where this is possible without prejudice to the interests of the Organization.[115] He routinely does so in relation to immunities flowing from Section 19 of the Convention.[116] Secondly, a complaint may be brought under the Mechanism's own Code of Professional Conduct for the Judges of the Mechanism.[117]

However, the situation that prevailed between Judge Akay's conviction and his non-reappointment was undeniably precarious: the case of an individual convicted *inter alia* of direct and public incitement to commit genocide was about to be reviewed by

[110] Consult n 104 and accompanying text.

[111] Constitution (n 109) Art 139.

[112] IRMCT Statute (n 3) Art 9(1). Cf *Yalçinkaya* v *Türkiye* (n 48) on the ECtHR's conclusions on the use of ByLock evidence.

[113] Statement of the IRMCT President (n 104).

[114] IRMCT Statute (n 3) Art 9(1).

[115] CPIUN (n 31) Art V, Section 20.

[116] 'Note to the Executive Office of the Secretary-General concerning the issuance of an arrest warrant' (6 March 2006) *United Nations Juridical Yearbook* 2006, Special edition, 1 at 3.

[117] UN Doc MICT/14/Rev.1 (revised 9 April 2018) <www.irmct.org/sites/default/files/documents/180409-judges-code-of-conduct-mict-14.pdf>. Article 11 of the Code on the complaint procedure and Articles 4.1 and 9 on possible relevant substantive grounds. Significantly, the 2015 version of this Code (<www.irmct.org/sites/default/files/documents/pd_mict14_en.pdf>) did not contain a complaint mechanism and the 2018 text envisages that the complaint must be received within sixty days from the alleged conduct, in the absence of good cause to deviate from this requirement (Code of Professional Conduct for the Judges of the Mechanism (2018), Art 11(4)). It is, however, plausible that, considering the lack of a complaint procedure in the 2015 version, Turkey could have demonstrated such a cause under the revised code in 2018.

a bench including a judge convicted (at first instance) of membership of an armed terrorist organization. While Ngirabatware himself insisted on Judge Akay's return and opposed his replacement on the bench proposed by the Office of the Prosecutor,[118] it is conceivable that due to the sensitivity of this situation—with a potential to undermine the IRMCT's reputation—relevant UN organs were relieved to have been offered a simple and seemingly legally sound way out. Yet, it is peculiar that concerns regarding his conviction at first instance—and more broadly those concerning Judge Akay's qualifications—did not surface or were not given decisive weight at the moment when Judge Akay recommenced his work for the Mechanism following his conviction, to become a major issue upon the expiry of his term in 2018.

20.5.2 The role of the *injugovins*' presidents

In the context of Judge Akay's non-reappointment, the procedure followed by (the presidents of) the governance institutions in concurring with the Secretary-General's proposal is worth considering as well. As evidenced by a letter by the UNSC President to the Secretary-General, the Secretary-General's reappointment proposals have 'been brought to the attention of the members of the Security Council. *They take note* of the intentions and nomination'.[119] Notably, whereas the Council dealt with IRMCT business in an open session on the next day,[120] there are no public records of any discussion of the reappointment of the Mechanism's judges in this period.[121] Judge Akay's non-reappointment thus did not raise (public) controversies in the Council.

The approach followed by the President of the Council on this occasion appears consistent with the practice of previous UNSC Presidents.[122] Conversely, the UNGA President responded, ostensibly on his own behalf rather than that of the Assembly's members—also consistently with the practice of succeeding UNGA Presidents in the context of the IRMCT[123]—as follows: '[p]ursuant to article 10, paragraph 3, of the

[118] *Ngirabatware* order (n 5) paras 9-10.

[119] UNSC, 'Letter dated 26 June 2018 from the President of the Security Council addressed to the Secretary-General' (26 June 2018) UN Doc S/2018/627 (emphasis added).

[120] UNSC Resolution 2422 (27 June 2018), UN Doc S/Res/2422, reappointing the IRMCT Prosecutor.

[121] UNSC provisional records <www.un.org/en/sc/meetings/records/2018.shtml>.

[122] eg 'Letter dated 9 June 2016 from the President of the Security Council addressed to the Secretary-General' (9 June 2016) UN Doc S/2016/527 and 'Letter dated 25 June 2020 from the President of the Security Council addressed to the Secretary-General' (25 June 2020) UN Doc S/2020/581. In the context of the ICTR: eg 'Letter dated 4 August 2009 from the President of the Security Council addressed to the Secretary-General' (5 August 2009) UN Doc S/2009/404.

[123] eg 'Letter dated 24 June 2016 from the Secretary-General addressed to the President of the Security Council' (n 46) Annex I and 'Letter dated 26 June 2020 from the Secretary-General addressed to the President of the Security Council' (30 June 2020) UN Doc S/2020/616, Annex I. This reaction is also consistent with the practice concerning eg the appointment of ICTY and ICTR judges to fill temporary vacancies in accordance with Article 13 *bis* 2 and 12 *bis* 2 of the respective Statute (n 13). Consult eg 'Letter dated 11 September 2013 from the Secretary-General addressed to the President of the Security Council' (13 September 2013) UN Doc S/2013/550, Annex I. Due to the comparable formulation contained in Article 10(4) IRMCT Statute (n 3), the considerations discussed in this section regarding the competence of the UNGA President appear applicable in relation to that provision as well.

statute of the Mechanism ... *I hereby concur* with the proposed reappointment of the 23 judges.'[124]

The author has not been able to find evidence (eg a UN document) of the matter having been brought to the attention of the members of the Assembly. In any event, the UNGA meeting records[125] confirm that no public discussion of the Secretary-General's proposal has taken place in the Assembly.

Considering the identical role of the presidents of the UNGA and the UNSC under Article 10(3) IRMCT Statute, the question arises whether—through his (more autonomous) conduct—the President of the General Assembly may have acted *ultra vires*. Admittedly, as observed by the ICJ, it is in the first place for each organ to ascertain its own competence.[126] However, this does not mean that the organ's own interpretation is necessarily correct. In light of the divergent interpretations adopted by the presidents of these organs of their own role, it thus appears useful to consider this issue briefly.

The phrasing of Article 10(3) of the Mechanism's Statute, permitting judges' 'reappointment by the Secretary-General after consultation with the Presidents of the Security Council and of the General Assembly'[127] is admittedly capable of accommodating the competence assumed by subsequent UNGA Presidents to *unilaterally* approve the Secretary-General's proposed list for reappointment. However, this specific power is not explicitly granted under that provision. Moreover, it should not be readily presumed that the Security Council intended to endow the President of the General Assembly (but not its own President) with such a significant independent competence. It is, in any event, unlikely that the Council would have opted for doing so in a provision which ostensibly places the presidents of these two organs on an equal footing.

The IRMCT Statute as a whole, and the nature of the functions of the UNGA President thereunder, does not support the conclusion that (s)he may play such an independent role in this context either. First, the governance of the Mechanism is in the hands of the UNSC and the UNGA, rather than of their presidents.[128] In light of the role of the Council and the Assembly in the context of elections, Article 10(3) of the IRMCT Statute appears to reflect the Council's intention to ensure that reappointment takes place with the support of both *injugovins* (rather than merely of their presidents).

Admittedly, looking beyond the IRMCT Statute it becomes clear that the substantive competences, working methods, and rules of procedure of the UNGA and the UNSC and the specific functions of their presidents thereunder—including the means available to them to consult members of the organ—differ and could in some cases justify divergent practices under the same rule. It is, for instance, much simpler for the UNSC President to gain speedy approval from the fifteen members of the

124 'Letter dated 27 June 2018 from the President of the General Assembly addressed to the Secretary-General' (3 July 2018) UN Doc S/2018/652, Annex I (emphasis added).

125 UN General Assembly Documentation <https://research.un.org/en/docs/ga/meetings>.

126 *Certain Expenses of the United Nations* (Article 17, paragraph 2, of the Charter) (Advisory Opinion) 20 July 1962, ICJ Reports (1962) 151, 168.

127 IRMCT Statute (n 3).

128 Section 20.2.

Council than it is for the UNGA President to obtain the views of the 193 members of the Assembly. Yet, this fact appears irrelevant for the interpretation of the scope of the powers of the UNGA President in relation to the IRMCT. More significantly, the General Assembly increasingly adopts decisions by consensus (ie the lack of a formal objection).[129] Yet, even in such cases, the members are at least informed of the draft decision and the lack of their objection results in a decision *of the Assembly*, rather than in a decision (or formal position) of the UNGA President ('I concur'). Moreover, the *nature* of the tasks and competences of these presidents as set out in the rules of procedure of the respective organ are in essence similar,[130] rendering it unlikely that Article 10(3) of the IRMCT Statute can yield different yet correct interpretations of their authority in relation to the IRMCT's two *injugovins* on this specific (non-procedural) issue.

Significantly, whereas the Rules of Procedure of the General Assembly entrust the President with a varied set of tasks, his or her competence is limited to procedural matters.[131] Moreover, Rule 36 specifically states that '[t]he President, in the exercise of his functions, remains under the authority of the General Assembly'.[132] The position of the President of the Council is similar: (s)he 'shall preside over the meetings of the Security Council and, *under the authority of the Security Council*, shall represent it in its capacity as an organ of the United Nations'.[133] However, the UNGA President does not even have a similar representative function.

The (nature of the) tasks and competences of the UNGA President (under the IRMCT Statute or in general) thus do not support or serve as a source of (substantive) inherent or implied powers which could explain the different role assumed by them in this context. Concededly, the existence of similar precedents (whereby UNGA Presidents approved the Secretary-General's list on their own behalf rather than on behalf of the UNGA membership) may at least appear to substantiate the position that the UNGA President's relevant conduct rests on 'established practice' and is, therefore, *intra vires*. However, the role of established practice of the organization in interpreting existing rules and (constitutional) provisions is not entirely beyond controversy and its parameters are not clearly defined.[134] Moreover, albeit that this practice has not raised objections, it has equally *not obtained explicit support* from members of the General Assembly while it appears inconsistent with the President's role as described above. In concurring with the Secretary-General's list (hence with the implicit proposal not to reappoint Judge Akay) without having consulted the membership of the Assembly, its President may thus have acted *ultra vires*. However, his conduct evidently did not exceed the competence of the UN as a whole. Hence, following the ICJ's pronouncements in the *Certain Expenses* advisory opinion,[135] it

[129] Schermers and Blokker (n 20) para 775.
[130] UNSC RoP (n 86) Rules 1–3, 7, 18–20, 27, 29–30 and 36 on the tasks and competences of the UNSC President and UNGA RoP (n 86) Rules 23, 28, 35, 38, 41, 62, 67–68, 71–76, 78, 87–88, 93 concerning the UNGA President.
[131] Consult n 130.
[132] UNGA RoP (n 86) Rule 36.
[133] UNSC RoP (n 86) Rule 19 (emphasis added).
[134] For some pertinent questions, see Schermers and Blokker (n 20) paras 1144B and 1350B, 1350E-H.
[135] *Certain Expenses* (n 126) 168.

may be concluded that while his conduct may have been 'irregular', this fact would not impair its external validity.

Nevertheless, the UNGA President's course of action may affect the status of the Mechanism as 'a competent, independent and impartial tribunal established by law', a fundamental guarantee of the right to a fair trial.[136] Considering the lack of specificity of Article 10(3) of the Statute, the procedure followed regarding Akay's non-reappointment is not likely to disqualify the Mechanism as a 'tribunal established by law'. Yet, procedural irregularities concerning the (re)appointment of judges and/or disregard for the intentions of the Security Council behind certain rules, together with deficient protection of the integrity of the reappointment procedure, may be relevant when assessing judges' independence and that of the IRMCT.[137]

From this perspective, the conduct of the Secretary-General, the UNSC, and (the President of) the UNGA regarding the reappointment procedure is disconcerting. It is submitted that also in relation to Judge Akay's non-reappointment the Secretary-General has, again, failed to exercise the requisite diligence and care to protect a judge of the Mechanism and the integrity of the reappointment procedure. The fact that the UNGA President went along with his proposal, supposedly without having consulted the membership of the Assembly—and that the Assembly and Security Council did not object to this—does not score well in the context of the responsibility of these *injugovins* to guarantee the independence of 'their' Mechanism.[138] Irrespective of the correctness of the procedure followed, Judge Akay's non-reappointment based on uncritical reliance on Turkey's position provides ample reason to conclude that the governance institutions did not take that task sufficiently seriously. In light of the heightened importance of independence in this context due to the obligation to ensure the right to a fair trial and the remote judging model, their conduct is particularly deplorable.

20.5.3 Election of new judges

To make things even worse, on 21 December 2018 the General Assembly elected a candidate nominated by Turkey (Mr Yusuf Aksar) as a judge of the Mechanism, thus filling one of the two vacancies on the judicial roster of the IRMCT. Out of the eleven candidates nominated by member states,[139] Aksar was the only nominee who

[136] eg International Covenant on Political and Civil Rights (adopted 16 December 1966, entered into force 23 March 1976) 999 UNTS 171, Art 14; African (Banjul) Charter on Human and Peoples' Rights (adopted 27 June 1981, entered into force 21 October 1986) OAU Doc CAB/LEG/67/3 Rev.5, 21 ILM 58 (1982), Art 7; and European Convention on Human Rights (adopted 4 November 1950, entered into force 3 September 1953) ETS No 005, Art 6(1).

[137] eg Human Right Committee, General Comment No 32, 'Article 14: Right to Equality before Courts and Tribunals and to a Fair Trial' (23 August 2007) paras 19–20 <https://tbinternet.ohchr.org/_layouts/15/treatybodyexternal/Download.aspx?symbolno=CCPR%2fC%2fGC%2f32&Lang=en> and European Court of Human Rights, 'Guide on Article 6 of the European Convention on Human Rights, Right to a Fair Trial (Criminal Limb)' (31 August 2022) paras 78–89 and 90–104 <https://icct.nl/sites/default/files/import/publication/guide_art_6_criminal_eng.pdf>.

[138] Section 20.4.

[139] UNGA, 'Election of two judges to the roster of the International Residual Mechanism for Criminal Tribunals: Memorandum by the Secretary-General' (19 November 2018) UN Doc A/73/599, para 11. The list of candidates was prepared by the UNSC, ibid para 9.

obtained the support of the requisite majority of UNGA members on this occasion.[140] Irrespective of Judge Aksar's competence and qualifications, his election was arguably inopportune as it sent the wrong message to states regarding the permissibility of disrespecting the independence of an international judicial body and of violating the diplomatic immunity of international judges (and of high-ranking UN officials in general). Besides, Judge Akay's case had just demonstrated the vulnerability of Turkish nationals occupying (top) UN positions.

The reaction of Judge Christoph Flügge—like Judge Akay one of the original judges of the Mechanism—highlights the severity of this move: he resigned in protest. He saw Judge Akay's non-reappointment as a breach of judicial independence. He found it particularly lamentable, fearing that allowing Turkey to block Judge Akay's re-appointment on spurious grounds may have created a precedent. Furthermore, he complained that, through Judge Aksar's election and appointment as a judge of the Mechanism, the UN in effect even rewarded Turkey.[141]

20.6 Conclusion

This chapter has reviewed the conduct of the governance institutions of the United Nations International Residual Mechanism for Criminal Tribunals—the Security Council and the General Assembly—in relation to (the protection of) the immunities and non-reappointment of Judge Akay, followed by the appointment of another Turkish national as a judge of the Mechanism. While the functioning of the IRMCT's *injugovins* is far from fully transparent (ie diplomatic efforts may have taken place behind the scenes), this study offers a clear picture: for whatever (political) reasons, the Security Council and the General Assembly opted—time and time again—for avoiding confrontation with Turkey on this issue, even though this choice further endangered the independence of the Mechanism and its judges.

This case-study underscores the crucial role of organs entrusted with the governance of international courts and tribunals in ensuring their effective functioning.[142] Although the Mechanism's status as an 'unwanted child'[143] may have worsened the situation, Judge Akay's case appears just another example of the 'delicate' and at times even conflict-prone nature of the relationship between international judicial institutions and their *injugovins*.[144]

This chapter suggests that that relationship may be particularly precarious when the *injugovins* are organs whose primary functions and concerns are located in the political arena. In the present context, even picturing the conduct of the UNSC and the

[140] UNGA Provisional Verbatim Record of the 65th Plenary Meeting, Seventy-Third Session (21 December 2018), UN Doc A/73/PV.65, 3.

[141] Stefan Willeke, 'Ich bin zutiefst beunruhigt' (*Die Zeit*, 24 January 2019) <www.zeit.de/2019/05/christoph-fluegge-internationaler-strafrichter-unabhaengigkeit-justiz> and Judge Flügge's IRMCT profile <www.irmct.org/en/about/judges/judge-christoph-fl%C3%BCgge>.

[142] Blokker, 'Governance of ITLOS' (n 87) 81 (abstract).

[143] Text accompanying nn 10–12.

[144] Blokker, 'Governance of ITLOS' (n 87) 83–84; Blokker, 'The Governance of International Courts and Tribunals' (n 7).

UNGA (President) in the most positive light possible, it appears that the broader (but short-term) interests at stake in maintaining peace and security—possibly coupled with political self-interest—have prevailed over the independence of the Mechanism and its judges.[145] The unique political responsibilities of the IRMCT's governance institutions and the prevailing diplomatic-political context could perhaps serve to (partially) explain neglect of their overall responsibility to protect the IRMCT and its judges. Nonetheless, these considerations fall short of excusing non-compliance with the UN's (and derivatively of these two organs') obligation to request a (binding) ICJ advisory opinion on the underlying difference concerning the interpretation and application of the Convention and the failure to exercise functional protection.

The external validity of Judge Akay's non-reappointment, although procedurally tainted, and of Judge Aksar's election, may strictly speaking still hold. However, owing to its impact on the (perceived) independence of the IRMCT and its judges—which is highly significant in the context of fair trial guarantees—the conduct of the IRMCT's *injugovins* and Secretary-General Guterres is deplorable. The severity of the potential impact of failing to hold Turkey responsible for non-compliance with the Convention on the effectiveness of the measures agreed upon therein—in order to safeguard the independence of UN officials and agents—is not to be underestimated. To contain the damage to the extent it is possible at all at this stage, it is imperative for the UN organs involved to emphasize at the very least that this case was unique and by no means can be seen as a precedent. Moreover, the role of the President(s) of the General Assembly (and of the Security Council) under Article 10(3) of the IRMCT Statute ought to be clarified.

In conclusion, it is submitted that the exclusive focus by (the membership of) the IRMCT's *injugovins* on the prevailing political context and on their own priorities and interests—and, above all, the subordination of judicial independence to such considerations—was at best short-sighted. The effective functioning of international institutions is premised on the independence of their officials, explaining the grant of privileges and immunities and implying a need for their uniform application and interpretation. This premise and its necessity are particularly pronounced in the context of international courts and tribunals. In turn, considering their unique functions (to ensure accountability and thus contribute to deterring the most heinous international crimes) and the importance of judicial independence in the context of the right to a fair trial, the need for independence and impartiality is even more pronounced with respect to international *criminal* courts and tribunals.

The failure of the UNGA and the UNSC to protect the independence of the Mechanism was undoubtedly attributable to the lack of initiative and support by the members of these organs and by the Secretary-General. Beyond some brief and empty calls for swift action by representatives of a few members of these organs, states have not been inclined to contribute to a solution. They apparently failed to understand that '[w]hile sovereign states play an essential role in these governance institutions, they do not act as individual states, but within a collective body',[146] with a collective mandate. In addition, the international human rights and judicial community was clearly

[145] Section 20.4.
[146] Blokker, 'The Governance of International Courts and Tribunals' (n 7) 37.

not (sufficiently) mobilized, leaving member states disinterested and/or free to pursue their own political-diplomatic agendas. Without initiative and the requisite support by their members for a particular course of action, the *injugovins* were paralyzed.

The observations of departing IRMCT President Meron in the Security Council concerning the fate of Judge Akay aptly sum up some of the most fundamental conclusions and recommendations that may be drawn from Judge Akay's case:

> At a time when the world is facing deeply troubling trends related to the undermining of independent judiciaries and the weakening of the rule of law, we at the United Nations simply cannot afford to be anything less than exemplary when it comes to our own handling of interference with judicial independence and actions undertaken in contravention of United Nations immunities. At the very least, it is imperative that, going forward, fair and transparent processes be developed to determine whether any proposed non-reappointment of a Judge accords with the fundamental principles of the rule of law.[147]

While the Secretary-General has a prominent role in safeguarding immunities, the responsibility for ensuring the IRMCT's independence was and remains in the hands of its governance institutions and their members. In relation to Judge Akay, their conduct was clearly 'less than exemplary'.

20.7 Epilogue

In September 2019, the Constitutional Court of the Republic of Turkey confirmed the position of lower courts that the CPIUN and the Statute did not grant Judge Akay immunity in his state of nationality from arrest, detention and search of his private residence. With domestic legal remedies having thus been exhausted, Akay's application before the ECtHR on these issues, like his appeal before domestic courts concerning his conviction, could move forward.

In February 2021, the Turkish Court of Cassation confirmed Akay's conviction. He then had to return to prison to serve the remainder of his sentence. At the time of writing, Akay's application against this decision was still pending before the Constitutional Court.[148] However, on 23 April 2024, the ECtHR ruled in Akay's favour on his application regarding his arrest, pre-trial detention, and search of his Istanbul residence by Turkish police.[149] While noting its lack of competence to decide on Akay's immunity, the ECtHR considered even that matter briefly, to the extent necessary for assessing the compatibility of Turkish authorities' conduct with the ECHR. It concluded that the more than seven months' delay before Turkish courts could address the issue of Akay's immunity and their reading of Akay's immunity were neither foreseeable nor consistent with legal certainty, thus breaching

[147] UNSC Provisional Verbatim Record of the 8416th meeting (11 December 2018) UN Doc S/PV.8416, 4.

[148] *Akay* v *Türkiye* (n 4) paras 74–75.

[149] ibid.

Article 5(1) of the ECHR.[150] Additionally, regarding the search of Akay's home and person on the day of his arrest—an issue that apparently has not raised concerns within the IRMCT's *injugovins*, likely as it did not directly impede the Mechanism's functioning—the ECtHR found that this conduct constituted a breach of Akay's right to 'his private and family life, his home and his correspondence' enshrined in Article 8(1) of the ECHR. Those acts were namely prohibited by applicable rules related to his status as an IRMCT judge, and Akay or the UN had not consented to the search. Pertinently, as Akay worked remotely for the IRMCT at that time from his private residence, his home—which thus served as his office—was to enjoy 'heightened protection'. The search could thus not be seen as 'prescribed by law' in the sense of Article 8(2) of the ECHR.[151]

Furthermore, the ECtHR found that the breaches of both provisions were not justifiable under the Respondent's notice of derogation, since the underlying conduct was inconsistent with its obligations under international law flowing from sources other than the ECHR.[152] Nevertheless, although thus accepting Akay's complaints, as his application concerned his arrest and pre-trial detention while his current detention is prescribed by his conviction, the ECtHR found itself unable to order Akay's release. Instead, it ordered—next to reparations—*restitutio in integrum*, leaving the choice of means to the Respondent 'to restore as far as possible the situation existing before the breach'.[153] In this context, it is worth citing the Concurring opinion of Judge Krenc joined by Judge Schembri Orland, noting that 'reparation should aim to restore the applicant *to the position in which he would have been* had [the ECHR] not been violated'.[154]

In conclusion, in the face of the IRMCT's *injugovins*' blatant failure to exercise their responsibility to protect the independence of the Mechanism, ultimately the ECtHR rather than the ICJ had to address the applicability in his state of nationality of Akay's immunities flowing from his status as an IRMCT judge, and Turkey's violations thereof, on Akay's own motion. The UN does not even appear to have attempted to intervene as *amicus curiae*.[155] Admittedly, by the time the ECtHR entertained Akay's application in 2021, Akay was no longer an IRMCT judge.[156] Yet, the ECtHR recognized the significance of Akay's case before it to safeguarding the IRMCT's independence and its unimpeded functioning, repeatedly invoking relevant considerations.[157]

At the time of writing, it is unknown whether and how Türkiye will implement this judgment. In light of their previous stance, and short-sighted as they appear to be regarding the (temporal and personal) limits of their responsibility concerning the Mechanism and its judges, it is unlikely that the IRMCT's *injugovins* would undertake any action to ensure Akay's release and *restitutio in integrum* in any way.

150 ibid paras 116–29.
151 ibid paras 140–44.
152 ibid paras 130 and 144.
153 ibid paras 146–50.
154 Concurring opinion of Judge Krenc joined by Judge Schembri Orland, ibid para 4 (emphasis added).
155 On this possibility: ECHR (n 48) Art 36.
156 Section 20.5.
157 *Akay* v *Türkiye* (n 4) paras 116, 122, 125, 128, and 142.

PART VI
FUTURE OUTLOOK

21

The Three-Layered Governance Model

The Truce between Independence and Accountability

Nicolas Guillou and Adriana-Maria Manolescu[*]

21.1 Introduction

The very idea of governance of international courts and tribunals (ICTs)[1] is not self-evident and not without controversy. Governance implies a hierarchical relationship that at first sight may appear to contradict the principle of independence of judges and prosecutors. However, ICTs are not only courts of law the judicial independence of which must be upheld; they are also international organizations (IOs) created by states and endowed with a budget, staff, and, for some of them, a board or other form of governance structure representing their main donors. As a corollary of the powers entrusted to them, any IOs, and thus also ICTs, are expected to be accountable to their funders, further to the accountability owed to the international community, and to other stakeholders relevant to their mandate. Without the funders' financial support, ICTs simply cannot exist. While ICTs need to have the independence of their judicial function respected, such complex organizations also need transparent processes, consistent practices, and an accountable management.

Both judicial independence and accountability must be secured in what are continuous and ongoing processes. Too often, the two are seen as mutually exclusive concepts, where priority is given to one versus the other at any given moment. For example, oversight may be seen at its highest and judicial independence at its lowest when establishing the court, and deciding on its dissolution,[2] which is a move often perceived as a response to the judicial body's ineffectiveness or overreach. In these phases, states' involvement and control are much broader and in-depth in matters concerning the management of the ICT as an institution. For example, in some cases they adopt rules of procedure that judges should follow in their judicial work or set

[*] This chapter is written in the authors' personal capacity and not as former member and research assistant, respectively, of the Independent Expert Review committee of the International Criminal Court. The contents hereof do not necessarily represent the views of the Independent Expert Review committee, or of the authors' employers.

[1] The chapter refers to international judicial bodies broadly, whether they are self-standing international organizations or bodies in the institutional system of another international organization, and whether they are permanent and international or hybrid and temporary. Unless otherwise explicitly indicated, the terms 'court' and 'tribunal' are used interchangeably and understood as referring to a court of law. For a typology of *injugovins*, see Niels Blokker, 'International Judicial Governance Institutions', in this volume.

[2] Bingham has referred to an inherent paradox of an independent terminable tribunal: Laura M Bingham, 'Strategy or Process—Closing the International Criminal Tribunals for the Former Yugoslavia and Rwanda' (2006) 24(2) Berkeley Journal of International Law 687, 691.

Nicolas Guillou and Adriana-Maria Manolescu, *The Three-Layered Governance Model* In: *Governance of International Courts and Tribunals*. Edited by: Sergey Vasiliev and Niels Blokker, Oxford University Press.
 DOI: 10.1093/oso/9780198922131.003.0021

deadlines by when the ICT's work should be finalized. In between, state oversight also occurs in the context of elections of principals and budgetary processes, instances that often cause tensions due to their perceived impact on judicial independence.

We argue that accountability mechanisms and bodies entrusted with oversight should be instituted with regard to all operations of an ICT throughout its functioning. The process through which oversight is exercised should be determined taking into account the need to avoid interferences in judicial decision-making.

This chapter introduces a model of multi-layered governance for ICTs that aims to enable effective and efficient governance, by ensuring both independence and accountability, as necessary, in all areas of operations of ICTs. While the following analysis includes examples from a variety of ICTs and may apply to all tribunals generally, the International Criminal Court (ICC) features most prominently in this chapter, due to the rare availability of a comprehensive analysis of its governance in the form of the 2020 Independent Expert Review.[3] The Three-Layered Governance Model developed by the Independent Experts therefore serves as a starting point for the discussion.[4] The model identifies, for each of the three main types (or layers) of activities that an ICT carries out, the relevant authority, the corresponding accountability tools, and the responsible oversight bodies. By distinguishing these three elements per type of activity, the governance model ensures that independence is safeguarded where and to the extent necessary, and that the appropriate form of accountability exists with respect to each type of an ICT's activity. In doing so, the model contributes to clarifying reporting lines and improving cooperation among relevant stakeholders, thus facilitating a better and smoother functioning of courts.

The chapter expands on the need for a governance model for ICTs and demonstrates that viewing judicial independence and accountability as mutually exclusive can be harmful to the effective and efficient governance of an ICT. The key elements of judicial independence and accountability first need to be defined (Section 21.2). The Three-Layered Governance Model for ICTs is then introduced (Section 21.3), before elaborating on its implementation for one court, namely the ICC (Section 21.4).

21.2 Independence versus Accountability

21.2.1 Principles of judicial independence and accountability

Judicial independence is a customary international law principle,[5] a human right,[6] and an important requirement enshrined in statutory texts of international

[3] Independent Expert Review of the International Criminal Court and the Rome Statute System, Final Report, 30 September 2020, ICC-ASP/19/16 <https://asp.icc-cpi.int/iccdocs/asp_docs/ASP19/IER-Final-Report-ENG.pdf> (IER Report).

[4] ibid 12–19.

[5] Dato' Param Cumaraswamy, Report of the Special Rapporteur on Independence and impartiality of the judiciary, jurors and assessors and the independence of lawyers (1995), UN Doc E/CN.4/1995/39, paras 32–35.

[6] International Covenant on Civil and Political Rights (opened for signature 16 December 1966, entered into force 23 March 1976), 999 UNTS 171, Art 14(1); UNGA, Universal Declaration of Human Rights (adopted 10 December 1948), 217 A (III), Art 10.

courts,[7] as 'an essential component of the right to a fair trial and the rule of law'.[8] It is a *sine qua non* principle for a court of law, as also affirmed by the ICJ. In 1970, the Court explained that it was to act

> only on the basis of the law, independently of all outside influence or interventions whatsoever, in the exercise of the judicial function entrusted to it alone by the Charter and by its Statute. A court functioning as a court of law can act in no other way.[9]

In essence, judicial independence demands that a judge should decide freely on a given case, by applying the law to the facts.[10] There are numerous soft-law instruments expanding on the concept of judicial independence, both at the international and domestic level,[11] and a great body of research has been dedicated to it. While the existence and importance of this principle are seldom disputed,[12] one area that continues to be debated concerns the interplay between judicial independence and accountability.

In the case of IOs, generally speaking, accountability is concerned with the extent to which organizations, 'in the fulfilment of their responsibilities, as established in their constituent instruments, are and should be subject to exercising forms of internal and external scrutiny and monitoring'.[13] Accountability is a corollary of power

[7] Statute of the International Court of Justice (signed 26 June 1945, entered into force on 24 October 1945) (ICJ Statute) Art 2 ('The Court shall be composed of a body of independent judges'); Rome Statute of the International Criminal Court (opened for signature 17 July 1998, entered into force 1 July 2002) (ICC Statute), Preamble ('Determined . . . to establish an independent permanent International Criminal Court') and Art 40(1) ('Judges shall be independent in the performance of their functions'); Convention on the Law of the Sea, Annex VI, Statute of the International Tribunal for the Law of the Sea (opened for signature 10 December 1982, entered into force 16 November 1994), 1833 UNTS 397 (ITLOS Statute) Art 2(1) ('The Tribunal shall be composed of a body of 21 independent members').

[8] UN Human Rights Council, Report of the Special Rapporteur on the independence of judges and lawyers, UN Doc A/HRC/38/38, 2 May 2018, para 7.

[9] *Legal Consequences for States of the Continued Presence of South Africa in Namibia (South West Africa) notwithstanding Security Council Resolution 276(1970)*, Advisory Opinion of 21 June 1971, [1971] ICJ Rep 16, para 29.

[10] International Commission of Jurists, 'International Principles on the Independence and Accountability of Judges, Lawyers and Prosecutors, Practitioners Guide No 1 (2007)' <www.refworld.org/pdfid/4a7837af2.pdf> 21.

[11] The Burgh House Principles on the Independence of the International Judiciary, reprinted in Philippe Sands, Campbell McLachlan, and Ruth MacKenzie, 'The Burgh House Principles on the Independence of the International Judiciary' (2005) 4 The Law and Practice of International Courts and Tribunals 247 (The Burgh House Principles); Mount Scopus International Standards of Judicial Independence, Mt. Scopus, Jerusalem, approved by the International Association of Judicial Independence and World Peace on 19 March 2008, consolidated in 2022 <www.jiwp.org/mt-scopus-standards>; Magna Carta of Judges (Fundamental Principles), Consultative Council of European Judges, Strasburg, 19 November 2010; International Principles on the Independence and Accountability of Judges, Lawyers and Prosecutors (n 10); Judicial Group on Strengthening Judicial Integrity, 'The Bangalore Principles of Judicial Conduct' as revised at the Round Table Meeting of Chief Justices held at the Peace Palace (The Hague, 25–26 November 2002).

[12] For example, Posner and Yoo argue that independent inter-state tribunals are 'a danger to international cooperation because they can render decisions that conflict with the interests of state parties', and 'independence *prevents* international tribunals from being effective'. Eric A Posner and John C Yoo, 'Judicial Independence in International Tribunals' (2005) 93 California Law Review 1; cf Laurence Helfer and Anne-Marie R Slaughter, 'Why States Create International Tribunals: A Response to Professors Posner and Yoo' (2005) 93 California Law Review 899.

[13] First Report of the Committee on Accountability of International Organisations, Report of the Sixty-Eighth Conference (1998), Taipei, International Law Association, 599.

and authority—'[p]ower entails accountability, that is the duty to account for its exercise'.[14] In recent decades, the demands for increased transparency and accountability of those in public office have only intensified, both at the domestic and international level.[15] In essence, accountability is a key element of democratic societies, enabling citizens to hold their governments to account for their actions, for example through their voting during elections. State officials must answer for their decisions, including the positions taken on behalf of their country in IOs and in relation to public funds allocated to, or withheld from, a certain organization. Similarly, states must be able to hold IOs accountable for their acts and omissions, in the exercise of mandates entrusted to them by the contracting parties. The existence of appropriate mechanisms to ensure public accountability is essential in a state's decision as to whether to transfer power to an IO or to discontinue such delegation of power. In view of this, statutory frameworks of ICTs entrust certain bodies with an oversight role over the newly created courts, mostly in relation to their financial and administrative management. These structures have been labelled as international judicial governance institutions (*injugovins*).[16]

A common narrative in the debate concerning judicial independence and accountability is that the two concepts cannot simultaneously coexist.[17] Devlin and Dodek note that the two 'ideals' are traditionally seen as opposite extremes of a continuum, 'usually construed as being in tension, if not conflict, and most pragmatists frame their work as an attempt to find the right balance on a continuum between the two'.[18] This debate spans beyond ICTs, and similar arguments have been raised in relation to other types of international bodies carrying out tasks that necessitate a certain level of independence.[19]

Viewing independence and accountability as potentially mutually exclusive has led, in practice, to judicial independence being used as a shield against accountability (Section 21.2.2). In turn, this contributed to instruments of control being used in

[14] Final Report of the Committee on Accountability of International Organisations, Report of the Seventy-First Conference (2004), Berlin, International Law Association, 5.

[15] In relation to accountability of IOs, Blokker points to 'a prevailing general climate ... characterized by increased attention for accountability issues, not only in relation to international organizations but also in relation to states and individuals.' Henry G Schermers and Niels M Blokker, *International Institutional Law: Unity within Diversity* (6th edn, Brill Nijhoff 2018) 1127 para 1683.

[16] See Sergey Vasiliev and Niels Blokker, 'Introduction', Sergey Vasiliev, 'What Is (International) Judicial Governance?', and Niels Blokker, 'International Judicial Governance Institutions', in this volume; in addition: Niels Blokker, 'The Governance of International Courts and Tribunals: Organizing and Guaranteeing Independence and Accountability' in Andreas Føllesdal and Geir Ulfstein (eds), *The Judicialization of International Law: A Mixed Blessing?* (OUP 2018); Sergey Vasiliev, 'Judicial Governance Entities as Power-Holders in International Criminal Justice: A Plea for a Socio-Legal Enquiry' in Morten Bergsmo and others (eds), *Power in International Criminal Justice* (Torkel Opsahl Academic EPublisher 2020).

[17] For example, Scholten refers to the 'classic question' of whether an institution can be both independent and accountable, affirming the contradiction between the terms is 'quite obvious', and setting out to outline why 'independence and accountability can exist only at each other's expense': Miroslava Scholten, 'Independence vs. Accountability: Proving the Negative Correlation' (2014) 21(1) Maastricht Journal of European and Comparative Law 197.

[18] Richard Devlin and Adam Dodek, 'Regulating Judges: Challenges, Controversies and Choices' in Richard Devlin and Adam Dodek (eds), *Regulating Judges: Beyond Independence and Accountability* (Edward Elgar Publishing 2016) 2.

[19] Madalina Busuioc, 'Accountability, Control and Independence: The Case of European Agencies' (2009) 15 European Law Journal 5; Scholten (n 17) (focusing on independent regulatory agencies).

search of accountability that may indeed endanger judicial independence (Section 21.2.3).

21.2.2 Independence as a shield against accountability

ICTs are *sui generis* creations, both as a category of IOs and as individual entities. It is not uncommon to apply domestic practices and standards to them to fill lacunas, to the extent possible under their *leges speciali*. Similarly, the concept of judicial independence has been extrapolated from domestic courts and applied—rightfully so—to protect international judges from inappropriate interferences in judicial decision-making. However, many of the accountability mechanisms that exist in domestic systems while fully respecting judicial independence, have not been replicated in the 'ecosystems' of the various international courts. In turn, certain processes that in domestic systems are subject to oversight by an external authority, are left to international judges themselves to oversee and manage, leading in essence to a self-managed judiciary. That is the case, for instance, of judges' discipline (understood as matters falling outside judicial decision-making). Most commonly, the plenary of judges of an ICT or the Presidency decides on complaints received against an individual judge.[20] A perceived lack of impartiality can lead one to hesitate to come forward with a complaint against a judge if the decision rests with their colleagues. For example, the IER of the ICC found that 'there [was] a general reluctance, if not extreme fear, among many staff to report any alleged act of misconduct or misbehaviour by a Judge .... The perception [was] that they are all immune. A belief [ran] high that Judges are bent on protecting each other'.[21] In contrast, domestic systems often foresee external independent entities entrusted with ensuring professional discipline of judges, be it specialized courts, committees, or judicial councils.[22] The judicial council, or *conseil supérieur de la magistrature*, is a type of entity that can be found across the different systems of law,

[20] ICJ Statute (n 7) Art 18(1); ITLOS Statute (n 7) Art 9; Organization of American States (OAS), Statute of the Inter-American Court of Human Rights, OAS GA Res 448 (IX-O/79) (adopted 31 October 1979, entered into force 1 January 1980) (IACtHR Statute) Art 20(1) (judges 'shall be answerable to the Court for their conduct, as well as for any violation, act of negligence or omission committed in the exercise of their functions') and Art 20(2) ('The OAS General Assembly shall have disciplinary authority over the judges, but may exercise that authority only at the request of the Court itself, composed for their purpose of the remaining judges'); ICC Statute (n 7) Art 40(4) and ICC ASP, Rules of Procedure and Evidence, Official Records of the Assembly of States Parties to the Rome Statute of the International Criminal Court, First Session, New York, 3–10 September 2002 (ICC-ASP/1/3 and Corr.1), part II.A (ICC RPE) Rules 29(1) and 30(1).

[21] IER Report (n 3) para 302.

[22] eg Opinion no 3 of the Consultative Council of European Judges (CCJE) to the attention of the Committee of Ministers of the Council of Europe on the principles and rules governing judges' professional conduct, in particular ethics, incompatible behaviour and impartiality, CCJE (2002) Op No 3, Council of Europe, 19 November 2002, para 71; see further Jan van Zyl Smit, 'The Appointment, Tenure and Removal of Judges under Commonwealth Principles: A Compendium and Analysis of Best Practice', Report of Research Undertaken by Bingham Centre for the Rule of Law, Commonwealth Secretariat 2015, British Institute of International and Comparative Law, xxi–xxii.

often dealing with the discipline of judges and judicial accountability.[23] Over 70 per cent of countries have some form of a judicial council.[24]

The problem that only limited accountability mechanisms are available for the international judiciary is compounded by insufficient delineation of judicial independence in the legal framework of ICTs. Most statutory documents of ICTs affirm that judges shall be independent,[25] but do not clarify what principles other, non-judicial operations of the court fall under or how they should be conducted in view of the obligation to respect judicial independence. The scope of this concept in practice remains subject to interpretation by individual judges or by the Presidency or the plenary of an ICT. Thus, it also depends on the legal culture/system judges come from.

This creates uncertainty as to what falls under the exclusive authority of the judges as judicial independence may be interpreted differently depending on the composition of an international court. For example, the Burgh House Principles recommend that 'the court shall be free to determine the conditions for its internal administration, including staff recruitment policy'.[26] This principle refers to the court and not explicitly to judges or prosecutors. However, at times, the principle has been interpreted as giving authority to such international officials to devise special administrative policies for their staff.[27]

21.2.3 Independence at risk from accountability

The tendency to interpret the principle of judicial independence in a broad manner should be viewed in light of the highly political contexts in which ICTs operate. To a certain degree, this may explain their reluctance to accept external oversight, claiming it would be against the independence of judges, of prosecutors, and of the respective institution in general. Such a position responds to the perceived risk that accountability mechanisms (or the information obtained through them) may be abused by states as a means of interfering in specific cases before the court, whether through threats or rewards to key actors in the judicial process. Considering their role in funding ICTs, one way for states to punish or reward actors in ICTs is through financial decisions.[28]

A now infamous example of this is the 1966 decision of the UNGA's Fifth Committee rejecting a request for additional funds for the ICJ on the explicit basis of the states' disapproval of the Court's judgment in the *South-West Africa* case.[29] Stemming from this power of states is also the fear that they may use their role in the

[23] IER Report (n 3) para 323. On the origins and rationales of the judicial council model: Sergey Vasiliev, 'What Is (International) Judicial Governance?', Section 2.3.2.2, in this volume.

[24] Report of the Special Rapporteur on the independence of judges and lawyers (n 9) para 14.

[25] eg ICJ Statute (n 7) Art 2; ICC Statute (n 7) Art 40; ITLOS Statute (n 7) Art 2.

[26] The Burgh House Principles (n 11) Art 1.3.

[27] IER Report (n 3) paras 48, 82.

[28] Adriana-Maria Manolescu, 'Financial Governance of International Courts and Tribunals', in this volume; Tom Ginsburg, 'Political Constraints on International Courts' in Cesare PR Romano, Karen J Alter, and Yuval Shany (eds), *The Oxford Handbook of International Adjudication* (OUP 2013) 493.

[29] UNGA Official Records, 21st Session, Fifth Committee, 1124th Meeting, 10 October 1966, paras 5–7 and at 25.

financial governance of an ICT to obstruct its work or even paralyse it entirely. In the case of the Inter-American Court of Human Rights (IACtHR), civil society argued that the lack of adequate financing was part of a 'deliberate strategy from States to financially asphyxiate the organs of the inter-American system of human rights, restrict its freedom of action and exercise a major influence on their agendas through specific earmarked funds'.[30] In view of these risks, a perception has developed that once they have appointed or elected the court's judges, states parties should unreservedly trust the judges to manage the court to enable a full respect of their judicial independence.

The aforementioned examples from the ICJ and IACtHR are extraordinary and hardly represent the norm. Therefore, they should not be used as arguments against *any* form of accountability. It should be recalled that states have an interest in that the ICTs they create function independently. An inter-state court perceived as lacking impartiality will not serve its purpose of providing an avenue for the peaceful settlement of disputes. An international criminal tribunal seen as lacking independence will suffer from lack of necessary cooperation and funding enabling it to implement its mandate. At the same time, while states have an interest in enabling ICTs to function independently, 'they also have a clear interest in exercising their functions so as to limit, in so far as possible, the extent and duration of their financial and political commitments to supporting expensive and complex institutions and criminal process'.[31] In response to judicial independence being used as a shield, states parties resort to using whatever instruments of control are available to them in the ICTs' institutional design to effect desired change and ensure that the institutions they create are effective and efficient.

As is the case with judicial independence, accountability mechanisms and practical implementation of the oversight function are often not clearly set out in statutory documents, and develop with practice. For example, Llewellyn explains that oversight of the UN criminal tribunals 'was not a pre-formed and fully developed concept' at the time the ICTY and the ICTR were established; while the need for periodic reporting was explicit, it was not specified what issues should be reported on or what the organs receiving the report could and should do with the received information.[32] The extent and means of exercising oversight, as well as the accountability mechanisms, evolved over time and through practice, and thus understandably also differ from one court to another.

While acknowledging this diversity, a constant element in the oversight arrangements of the great majority—if not all—of ICTs has been states' desire for increased efficiency of the courts, so that proceedings can be carried out at a faster pace and with reduced cost. This is visible firstly in the manner in which the models of international justice mechanisms have developed over time. Hybrid courts are generally seen as having developed as a result of the international community's dissatisfaction with the duration of proceedings and financial (in)efficiency of the ICTY and ICTR (the UN ad hoc tribunals).[33] The management committees for the SCSL, ECCC, and the STL

[30] Sebastián Alejandro Rey (ed), *Los Desafíos Del Sistema Interamericano de Protección de Derechos Humanos En El Siglo XXI. Una Mirada Crítica Para (Re)pensar Su Funcionamiento* (Ediciones de la Universidad Nacional de Lanús 2015) 160.

[31] Huw Llewellyn, *An Institutional Perspective on the United Nations Criminal Tribunals: Governance, Independence and Impartiality* (Brill 2021) 13.

[32] ibid 6.

[33] eg Giorgia Tortora, 'The Financing of the Special Tribunals for Sierra Leone, Cambodia and Lebanon' (2013) 13 International Criminal Law Review 93; Llewellyn (n 31) 8.

emerged out of the same desire to ensure less expensive and more expeditious prosecution of international crimes by enabling states to engage in an almost continuous dialogue with, and scrutiny of, the tribunals.[34] Moreover, it is evidenced by the mandates entrusted to independent experts to review the efficiency of the UN ad hoc tribunals,[35] the SCSL,[36] and the ICC.[37] Further, it is also a concern often shared by states parties in *injugovins*' meetings.[38] Finally, it is also the underlying premise for completion strategies of temporary ICTs. As outlined by the ICTY President in 2000, considering the Tribunal's obligation towards the international community, the productivity and efficiency of the Tribunal had to be questioned, and in view of the very high price of international justice, a timeframe for fulfilling its mission had to be set.[39] While in the ICTY's case the development of the completion strategy was led by the Tribunal itself, it apparently originated from a 'politically charged dialogue among states and UN institutions' and was motivated ultimately by 'the price of international justice'.[40]

Completion strategies may be seen as an attempt by states to reassert control over the institutions they created. However, the instances in which they were applied also demonstrate the difficulty states have in actually enforcing the respective deadlines. For example, despite the initial timeline for the ICTY's completion strategy having been put forward by the Tribunal itself, UN member states struggled to have them respected. The UN Security Council called on the ICTY and the ICTR to take all possible measures to complete work by 2010,[41] but this eventually had to be pushed back until 2015 (for the ICTR)[42] and 2017 (for the ICTY)[43] respectively.[44]

[34] Llewellyn (n 31) 6.

[35] In 1998, the UN Secretary-General appointed an Expert Group to 'prepare an evaluation of the functioning and operation of [the ICTY and ICTR] with the objective of enhancing the efficient use of the resources allocated to the Tribunals' at the UNGA's request. Report of the Expert Group to Conduct Review of the Effective Operation and Functioning of the International Tribunal for the Former Yugoslavia and the International Criminal Tribunal for Rwanda', UN Doc A/54/634, 22 November 1999, paras 2 and 4.

[36] The UN appointed an Independent Expert to review the operation and functioning of the SCSL 'with the objective of ensuring the most efficient use of the Court's resources and the completion of the Court's work in a timely manner'. Report on the Special Court for Sierra Leone, submitted by the Independent Expert Antonio Cassese, 12 December 2006, para 14.

[37] In 2019, the ICC ASP commissioned an Independent Expert Review of the ICC and the Rome Statute system 'with a view to making concrete, achievable and actionable recommendations aimed at enhancing the performance, efficiency and effectiveness of the Court and the Rome Statute system as a whole'. ICC ASP, Resolution ICC-ASP/18/Res.7, 6 December 2019, para 6.

[38] For example, in the 2018 ICC ASP, a state representative affirmed that '[w]e cannot bury our heads in the sand and pretend everything is fine when it isn't. The statistics are sobering. After 20 years, and 1.5 billion euros spent, we have only three core crime convictions. As others have said, and I quote "it is undeniable that the Rome project still falls short of the expectations of the participants at that ground-breaking conference in Rome". The time has come for States to take a fundamental look at how the Court is operating.': Janet Anderson, 'Money Matters at the ICC' (*JusticeInfo.net*, 14 December 2018) <www.justiceinfo.net/en/39771-money-matters-at-the-icc.html>.

[39] As cited in Dominic Raab, 'Evaluating the ICTY and Its Completion Strategy: Efforts to Achieve Accountability for War Crimes and Their Tribunals' (2005) 3 Journal of International Criminal Justice 82, 84.

[40] Bingham (n 2) 701–02.

[41] UNSC Res 1503, UN Doc S/RES/1503, 28 August 2003, para 7, and UNSC Res 1534, UN Doc S/RES/1534, 26 March 2004, paras 3 and 6, reiterating the timeline set out in Resolution 1503 and calling for six-monthly reports on progress made towards implementing the Completion Strategy, in response to indications previously made to the SC 'that it might not be possible to implement the Completion Strategies'.

[42] UNSC Res 2256, UN Doc S/RES/2256, 22 December 2015.

[43] UNSC Press Statement on Closure of International Tribunal for Former Yugoslavia, SC/13151-L/3274, 31 December 2017 <https://press.un.org/en/2017/sc13151.doc.htm>.

[44] Llewellyn (n 31) ch 6.

In the absence of other oversight and accountability tools, states recurrently used their budgetary power in an attempt to reach the desired outcome. Having been informed in 2003 by the ICTY President and Prosecutor of inevitable delays in the completion of the Tribunal's mandate, and in view of the fact that the combined budgets for the ICTY and the ICTR for 2004–2005 exceeded US $500 million, a number of UN member states chose not to pay their contributions to the budget.[45]

In a similar vein, the IER of the ICC heard that

> many States Parties are frustrated with the Court, which they consider does not deliver full value for the funding their taxpayers provide.... Moreover when the ASP does seek to influence the Court to be more efficient and effective, they consider that the latter often resists, citing its independence from state control and its need for confidentiality. In these circumstances, the ASP has wielded what instruments it can to try to direct the Court, notably its power to approve/reject the budget, and broadly its authority to question the Court's administration.[46]

In turn, attempts to exert more control through the budgetary process have triggered an intensified defensiveness from courts in reaction to what they see as evidence of a lack of trust from states, their attempts to micro-manage, or even attempts to 'retaliate' based on disagreements with specific judicial decisions. In the case of the ICC, many in the Court shared with the IER their opinion that states seem more interested in reducing the budget than in adequately resourcing the Court, and that the ASP was 'intent on micro-managing the operation of the Court'.[47] Such perceptions of states misusing their oversight role are not novel in the field. In 1933, in response to calls from a League of Nations member state for reductions in the budget by curtailing activities, staff numbers, salaries levels, and devising a procedure for stricter control over expenditure, the Registrar of the Permanent Court of International Justice suggested that this was part of political pressure to hire representatives of certain governments as Registry staff.[48]

As noted, both ICTs and their states parties share an interest in ensuring that these institutions benefit from judicial independence. Further, states' interest in ensuring the efficient functioning of a court is in essence not dissimilar from the wish of officials and international civil servants working in the ICT to have the court succeed and function well. While these interests align, a fear that a stakeholder would misuse its legitimate attributes to advance one interest over the other, can lead the other party to expand the scope of its own responsibilities as part of a defensive reaction. For example, a fear that states may be using their budgetary role to influence judicial decision-making may lead judges to claim a broader application of judicial independence, as a way of protecting the court's independence. In turn, this approach may be

[45] ibid 272–74.

[46] IER Report (n 3) para 949.

[47] ibid para 948.

[48] Eighth Annual Report of the Permanent Court of International Justice (15 June 1931 to 15 June 1932), Series E—No 8 <www.icj-cij.org/public/files/permanent-court-of-international-justice/serie_E/English/E_08_en.pdf> 329–30.

perceived by states as a way for the court to shield itself from accountability, leading them to intensify their efforts to oversee the court, including through methods perceived to be increasingly intrusive. In essence, this creates a vicious cycle developing through the years, and the entrenchment of antagonistic positions between the stakeholders which may outlast the decisions that triggered the initial reactions.

Such a clash can only be remedied or overcome through increased trust. Institutionally, trust is not—and cannot be merely—about interpersonal relations between the relevant officials. Institutional trust is built through transparency, clarity and dialogue, and (stronger) mechanisms to ensure accountability.

21.3 Towards a Multi-Layered Governance Model

One of the key challenges in designing a theory for ICTs' governance is the need to reconcile independence and accountability. One cannot—and should not—be sacrificed in the name of the other. The proposed solution to this challenge is an innovative model based on a distinction between the types of activities performed by ICTs. It is based on a multiform governance structure (Section 21.3.1), organized according to three layers (Section 21.3.2), each of them corresponding to different accountability modalities and oversight bodies. The model was firstly proposed by the IER for the ICC,[49] but it can be applied to other ICTs as well.

21.3.1 The need for a multiform governance structure

The governance of domestic courts should be the primary source of inspiration for ICT governance, but it is difficult to copy and paste the models that exist at the national level. First, they often rely on the traditional distinction between legislative, executive, and judicial branches. However, this distinction does not exist for IOs, whose structure mainly hinges on the distinction between their board and their secretariat.[50] Second, IOs are not embedded within a domestic judicial system. They are even shielded from domestic courts, partly to avoid being impacted by potential judicial mismanagement. Third, there is no audit body or judicial inspection service[51] or a supreme judicial council[52] at the international level (yet).[53] Therefore, building a theory of ICT governance requires creativity and looking at other governance models.

[49] IER Report (n 3) 12–19. Further Section 21.4.

[50] Blokker (n 15) 301–02 paras 383–85.

[51] European Network of Justice Inspection Services: <www.i-justitia.eu/en/members>.

[52] European Network of Councils for the Judiciary, 'Guide to the European Network of Councils for the Judiciary', 2014 <https://csj.be/admin/storage/hrj/encj-guide-version-june-2014.pdf>.

[53] The IER recommended the establishment of a Judicial Audit Committee that would carry out audits of the administration of justice activities, as well as a form of judicial council with power to render decisions on complaints against elected officials, both ideally, and in the long-term, servicing several ICTs. IER Report (n 3) 18 (R3), 88 (R109), and 104 (R126).

Corporate governance and the accountability mechanisms that exist in company law can be another source of inspiration. Corporate governance is the system of rules, practices, and processes by which a company is directed and controlled. It refers to the way in which companies are governed and for what purpose. It identifies who has power and accountability, and who makes decisions.[54] Of course, the activities of a court are fundamentally different from those of a private company. That said, ICTs and companies both need to balance the interests of multiple stakeholders and need to put in place procedures to ensure a sound management of their budgets, an equal treatment of, and duty of care for, their staff, and the attention to their users and beneficiaries.

Under domestic company law, the board of directors usually performs the main oversight function. However, it is not without limits: some activities can be shielded from the board when they require a certain level of independence, for example, in order to protect creditors. However, the existence of such activities does not preclude the overall accountability of the organization towards the board. Nor does it mean there is no accountability in such areas of operation, even if it is not exercised by the board. The activities of ICTs also require various levels of independence, and their boards cannot be involved in some of their key activities, such as investigations, prosecutions, and judicial work. There is thus a need to adjust the distribution of powers to the types of activities performed by ICTs.

Governance of ICTs usually relies on a board that can take various forms: an assembly of states parties (ICC, ITLOS), an ad hoc management committee representing the major donors (SCSL, STL), or existing IO organs (ICTY, ICTR)—bodies collectively referred to as *injugovins*.[55] They perform an oversight function focused on the adoption of the budget, the completion of regular audits, and the selection of the organization's top management. These *injugovins* are not supposed to be involved in the core business of ICTs, but only in matters related to their organizational structure, processes, and management. The most important challenge in determining ICT governance is to determine the scope of the powers of *injugovins* vis-à-vis the ICTs.

The first step is to identify the different types of activities the ICTs perform. Governance is not monolithic, and each activity does not require the same level of independence or accountability. The governance structure needs to be multi-layered and adapted to each type of activity. The division of powers is not the same whether an ICT is adjudicating a criminal case, trying to improve judicial administration, or ensuring that it respects the budget regulations.

A distinction could be drawn between activities that should be shielded from states parties and others that are more general in nature such that they can be treated as common IO business. The former type of activities should be fully independent from states parties, with accountability mechanisms available through the regular judicial process only. The latter, however, should be subject to accountability mechanisms, with oversight exercised by *injugovins*, as in the case of other IOs. It is also possible to promote accountability through specialized institutions, independent from both the

[54] The Chartered Governance Institute, UK and Ireland, 'What Is Corporate Governance?' <www.cgi.org.uk/about-us/policy/what-is-corporate-governance>.

[55] Sources in n 16.

court and the *injugovins*—ie a form of accountability before peers, such as a form of judicial councils and/or judicial audit committees. In this way, a court can be held accountable in respect of all types of activities by an appropriate oversight body. It is not a matter of choosing between a self-managed judiciary or full oversight by *injugovins* at the cost of judicial independence. There needs to be a combination of several accountability modalities, each with its own oversight body, ensuring a co-existence of both independence and accountability. This is what the Three-Layered Governance Model developed for the ICC aimed to achieve.

21.3.2 The Three-Layered Governance Model in international courts and tribunals

In the context of the review of the ICC, the Independent Experts proposed a theoretical model to distribute powers within the ICC and vis-à-vis the various oversight bodies. This led to what the Experts called a Three-Layered Model of Governance that can similarly be applied to other international criminal courts, as well as international courts in general. This section will introduce the model and outline its applicability to ICTs in general, while Section 21.4 will detail the applicability of the model at the ICC.

The starting point in designing a model of governance for ICTs must be an acknowledgement of the dual nature of ICTs as both international organizations (ICT/IO) and judicial entities (ICT/court). The needs and specific interests related to both aspects must be met and reconciled. As IOs, the states that created and fund the ICT reasonably wish to play a role in guiding and shaping it. At the same time, as judicial entities, the ICTs' judicial and, where relevant, prosecutorial independence must be safeguarded. Understandably, contradictions between the two hypostases of ICTs can arise in practice, leading to tensions between the various authoritative organs, whether internal to ICTs or part of *injugovins* and possibly threatening the effective functioning and governance of the institution. The Three-Layered Governance Model allows distinguishing between these two broad areas of activity of ICTs. For each layer of activity, based on the nature of the operations it covers, and the level of independence required, the authority, oversight entity, and relevant accountability modalities will vary.

ICTs/IO operations (Layer 3) are not judicial but are carried out to indirectly support the judicial activity of the ICT. Such operations include administrative services commonly found in other IOs or 'back office' of national organizations, such as human resources, budget and finance, procurement, facilities management, general services, and public communication. For ICTs, these operations are managed by a registrar as the chief administrative officer, similar to secretaries-general of IOs. By having the registrar as the responsible authority in this layer, the ICTs/IO can (and should) function as a unified organization, with a vertical and hierarchical structure, as is the case for IOs generally. Within this layer of activity, *injugovins* play an active role, for example through the appointment of ICTs/IO officials, approving financial regulations, adopting the budget, and carrying out oversight over the ICTs/IO's financial operations.

The ICTs/court operations refer to the judicial activities of the ICTs (Layer 1), which are their core business. Layer 1 activities include judicial and, where relevant, prosecutorial work, such as judges' deliberations, judges' management of proceedings, judgment-drafting, decisions of the prosecutor as to whether and whom to investigate, the evidence to be presented, and so forth. This category of activities requires absolute independence to enable judges and prosecutors to carry out their mandates free of any interference, and thereby the entities vested with authority in this layer are the Presidency, judges, and, where relevant, the prosecutor. The role *injugovins* play in the ICT/IO should not be used to influence Layer 1 activities, whether through financial oversight or officials' elections/appointments.

A further category of operations intermediate to the above-mentioned functions can be identified. This category can be qualified as administration of justice (Layer 2) and falls between judicial and prosecutorial work, on the one hand, and the administration of the IO, on the other hand. The administration of justice includes activities such as organizing judges' work, determining the availability of the courtrooms, and assigning support staff to judicial panels, among others. Administration of justice supports Layer 1 more directly than Layer 3 does, but the nature of the activities resembles ICTs/IO operations more closely than 'pure' judicial and prosecutorial activities. Due to this difference, administration of justice does not require as high a level of independence as Layer 1 does. This layer falls under the authority of the president and, where applicable, the prosecutor. As this layer is ultimately about management of resources to enable effective and efficient Layer 1 activities, a level of accountability and transparency towards *injugovins* is reasonable, similar to domestic systems, where the administration of justice is subject to audits. Consequently, it is not acceptable for ICTs/courts to invoke confidentiality and independence as shields against accountability in regards to this layer.[56]

The three layers of activities exist in all ICTs, irrespective of differences in name and responsibilities of the relevant stakeholders. The entity providing administrative and judicial support services to the court is called 'Registry' in the context of the ICJ and ITLOS, and 'Secretariat' in the IACtHR and WTO Appellate Body. The ICJ Registry, ITLOS Registry, and IACtHR Secretariat include, for instance, human resources and budget departments, whereas the WTO Appellate Body and its Secretariat rely on such services from equivalent WTO bodies.[57]

Having distinguished the types of activities that an ICT carries out (Layer 1: Judicial and prosecutorial activity; Layer 2: Administration of justice; and Layer 3: Administration of the international organization), the governance of ICTs can be organized by identifying, for each layer, the appropriate authority, oversight entity, and accountability mechanisms.

[56] The IER of the ICC noted that independence (and confidentiality) 'should not be used as a way of deflecting accountability and preventing oversight'; experts were told of an 'instinctive reaction' of the OTP that 'its independence precludes any oversight' by the Court's Independent Oversight Mechanism; further, the Experts considered that independence and confidentiality were often unnecessarily invoked in a manner that was detrimental to the close cooperation between the Chambers, Registry, and the OTP. IER Report (n 3) paras 29, 204, 266, 286, and 308.

[57] WTO, Secretariat chart <www.wto.org/english/thewto_e/whatis_e/tif_e/org4_e.htm>.

Since Layer 1 consists of judicial and, where applicable, prosecutorial activity, which is the *raison d'être* of ICTs, it requires absolute independence. Accountability for this layer is ensured through the judicial remedies foreseen by the court's legal framework. Oversight responsibility is entrusted to the judiciary itself, for example to the appeals chamber or any superior panel, as well as to the prosecutor as far as the activities of the respective office are concerned. Criminal courts, such as ICTY/ICTR, SCSL, and ECCC,[58] had a superior panel or an appeals chamber, while in the case of inter-state courts, judgments are final, but parties may seek their reconsideration or revision. This is the case for the ICJ and ITLOS,[59] while for the IACtHR, decisions issued by the Presidency when the court is not in session, and that are not purely procedural, may be appealed before the complete Court.[60]

Layer 2 comprises the administration of justice, where, like in domestic systems, specific and indirect forms of accountability should be used. Internal and external auditors that are engaged in the great majority (if not all) ICTs usually only audit Layer 3 activities, with Layer 2 often seen as falling under the 'shield' of judicial independence, and thus not open to scrutiny through audits. To protect independence to the extent necessary while enabling accountability, judicial and prosecutorial audits can and should be performed by independent external peers. This would allow for an objective assessment and ensure that no political interference takes place. A judicial audit committee, composed of judges and prosecutors external to the ICT, could perform this function.[61] Administration of justice can notably be audited through performance indicators, which are designed to evaluate efficiency and effectiveness, and through inter-court comparisons. To best facilitate inter-court comparisons, cooperation among ICT officials would be necessary to agree on a set of generally applicable performance indicators. While each ICT has its own characteristics, certain performance indicators would and could be common across ICTs and/or for ICTs in the same category (eg for inter-state, criminal, and human rights ICTs). These common indicators can help build international justice standards and allow a form of benchmarking among ICTs and within each ICT. A further method of accountability within Layer 2 refers to disciplinary matters. Complaints against judges should also be dealt with by a group of independent external peers, for example in the form of a judicial council.

[58] Statute of the International Criminal Tribunal for the Former Yugoslavia, UNSC Res 827, UN Doc S/RES/827, 25 May 1993 (as amended by UNSC Res 1411, UN Doc S/RES/1411, 17 May 2002) Arts 11, 25; Statute of the International Criminal Tribunal for Rwanda, UNSC Res 995, UN Doc S/RES/955, 8 November 1994 (as amended by UNSC Res 1717, UN Doc S/RES/1717, 13 October 2006) Arts 11, 24; Statute of the Special Court for Sierra Leone, UNSC Res 1315, UN Doc S/RES/1315, 14 August 2000, Arts 11, 20; Law on the establishment of the Extraordinary Chambers, Reach Kram No NS/RKM/0801/12, 10 August 2001 (as amended 27 October 2004, NS/RKM/1004/006) Arts 17 and 36.

[59] eg ICJ Statute (n 7) Art 61; ITLOS Statute (n 7) Art 33; ITLOS, Rules of the Tribunal (ITLOS/8), adopted 28 October 1997, amended 25 March 2021, Art 127.

[60] IACtHR Rules of Procedure Art 31(2).

[61] To ensure independence and appropriate expertise of the relevant members, the IER recommended that the Judicial Audit Committee for the ICC (and that could in the long-term service several ICTs) consist of current or former national or international judges and prosecutors with relevant experience, appointed for five or six years for a non-renewable mandate, and ensuring diversity in gender, legal systems, and geographical representation. For the ICC, the members could be appointed as follows: two national judges appointed by the ASP Presidency and one former ICC judge appointed by the Court President. IER Report (n 3) para 34, 18 (R3), 92 (R113).

To further contribute to coherent and generally applicable standards in international justice, as well as to rationalize expenses, states should consider the establishment of a judicial audit committee and a judicial council that would service several ICTs at once.

To illustrate the importance of appropriate accountability mechanisms, examples of audits carried out at the CJEU and ICJ are relevant. In the (perceived) absence of other sufficient accountability mechanisms, the EU Court of Auditors was tasked with evaluating the case management of the CJEU, specifically to assess whether the procedures in place enabled the efficient and timely resolution of cases, and whether accountability mechanisms were in place, even though such matters would fall under the administration of justice, ie Layer 2.[62] Similarly, when the UN General Assembly tasked the Joint Inspection Unit to review the ICJ's management and administration, the Court asserted, though unsuccessfully, its exclusive competency and autonomy.[63] While the scope of the latter example was focused on Layer 3 activities, such audit was still considered to be encroaching on the court's administrative autonomy.

Layer 3, administration of the IO, is in the hands of a registrar, who has a dual role of a secretary-general of an IO and of a registrar of a court. Under their authority, administrative processes and policies, including financial and budgetary, are developed and implemented. In fulfilling this mandate, the Registrar must be accountable to the *injugovins*. This is, for instance, explicitly mentioned in the financial regulations applicable to ITLOS and the ICC.[64] As an example of oversight entities, the UN General Assembly Fifth Committee and the Advisory Committee on Administrative and Budgetary Questions played the role in budgetary matters for the ICTY and ICTY, whereas for the STL, it was the management committee.

The three layers of activities outlined here exist in all ICTs, with certain accountability tools and oversight entities in place, with their mandates or scope of responsibility more or less explicitly stated. Clarifying each stakeholder's role and delineating their individual area of authority and scope of oversight fosters better cooperation between the respective entities and officials, as well as between the ICTs and their *injugovins*. Having clearly outlined accountability methods tailored to the level of independence required for each layer can reassure states that references to judicial independence are not used improperly as a shield, thereby removing the need for *injugovins* to use their governance functions to inappropriately shape or control the ICT.

[62] European Court of Auditors (EU), 'Special Report: Performance review of case management at the Court of Justice of the European Union (pursuant to Article 287(4), second subparagraph, TFEU)', No 14/2017 <www.eca.europa.eu/Lists/ECADocuments/SR17_14/SR_CJEU_EN.pdf> para 11.

[63] UN Joint Inspection Unit, 'Review of Management and Administration in the Registry of the International Court of Justice', JIU/REP/2000/8, 2000 <www.unjiu.org/sites/www.unjiu.org/files/jiu_document_files/products/en/reports-notes/JIU%20Products/JIU_REP_2000_8_English.pdf>; Rosalyn Higgins and others, *Oppenheim's International Law: United Nations. Vol II* (OUP 2017) 1189 paras 29.219–29.228.

[64] ITLOS, Financial Regulations and Rules of the ITLOS (adopted 12 June 2003, entered into force 1 January 2004, as amended 9 December 2020) SPLOS/30/16, Regulation 4.7 ('The Registrar shall be accountable to the Meeting of States Parties for the proper management of the financial resources in accordance with these Regulations and the Financial Rules'); ICC, Financial Regulations and Rules, ICC-ASP/7/5 (adopted 21 November 2008) Regulation 4.9 (The Registrar and the Prosecutor 'shall be accountable to the Assembly of States Parties for the proper management and administration of the financial resources for which they are responsible').

21.4 The Three-Layered Governance Model at the ICC

As noted, the Three-Layered Governance Model can generally be applied to ICTs. To offer a deeper understanding of the model, this section will discuss the implementation of the model at the ICC, for which it was designed.

As part of a wider state-party-driven review process,[65] in 2019 the ASP commissioned an Independent Expert Review, with a view to receiving concrete, achievable and actionable recommendations aimed at enhancing the performance, efficiency and effectiveness of the Court and the Rome Statute system as a whole.[66] This review was carried out between January and September 2020, and concluded with the submission by the Experts of the Final Report.[67] As a further step, the ASP established a Review Mechanism to plan, coordinate, and regularly report to the ASP on the assessment and implementation of IER recommendations.[68] The Mechanism facilitated meetings between state representatives and Court focal points, at times inviting also IER Experts and civil society representatives, to discuss the IER proposed courses of action.

The IER Report itself contains 384 recommendations across three clusters: (i) Governance, (ii) Judiciary, and (iii) Preliminary examinations, investigations and prosecutions. The recommendations were developed based on over 100 written submissions received by the IER and almost 300 interviews and meetings the Experts held with current and former ICC and ASP officials, staff, external defence and victims' representatives, as well as heads of organs, states parties, ASP representatives/bodies, NGOs and academics.[69]

The first recommendation of the IER, referenced at several other points in the Report,[70] is for the Three-Layered Governance Model to be used 'as a tool to ensure effective and efficient governance, clarify reporting lines and improve cooperation among stakeholders'.[71] The essence of the model, and its starting point, is the acknowledgement of the dual nature of the ICC as both a court of law (ICC/Court), and an international organization (ICC/IO), and the tensions that arose over time between the ICC and the ASP in view of this duality.[72]

Figure 21.1 identifies for each of the three layers in the Model the entity/entities who have authority in the respective layer, as well as the bodies that oversee the relevant operations and the tools through which this oversight is achieved. Certain aspects of the model were in place in the Rome Statute system from the outset, whereas others were recommended by the Experts.

65 ICC ASP, Resolution ICC-ASP/18/Res.7, 'Review of the ICC and the Rome Statute System', adopted 6 December 2019, para 4.

66 ibid para 6; Annex 1, 'Terms of Reference for the Independent Expert Review of the ICC', para 5.

67 IER Report (n 3).

68 ICC ASP, Resolution ICC-ASP/19/Res.7, para 4; ICC ASP, 'Review of the ICC and the Rome Statute system—Review Mechanism' <https://asp.icc-cpi.int/Review-Court/Review-Mechanism>. This was in line with the IER's recommendation—IER Report (n 3) para 25.

69 IER Report (n 3) Annex II Consultations in Numbers, para 1.

70 eg IER Report (n 3) 21 (R8), 61 (R76), paras 104, 187, 952, and 978.

71 ibid 17 (R1).

72 ibid para 26.

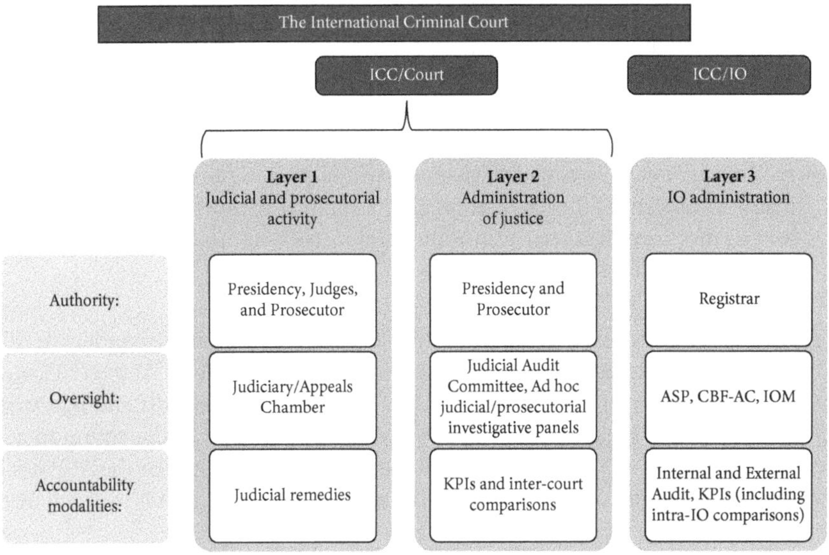

Figure 21.1 The International Criminal Court: Three-Layered Governance Model.
Replicated from Independent Expert Review of the International Criminal Court and the Rome Statute System, Final Report, 30 September 2020, ICC-ASP/19/16, 18, figure 1.

The ICC/IO, or Layer 3, is led by the ICC Registrar as the principal administrative officer who is responsible for 'the non-judicial aspects of the administration and servicing of the Court, without prejudice to the functions of the Prosecutor'.[73] It is in this layer that the ICC 'One Court' principle finds its reflection. By having the Registrar as the authority under Layer 3, a more effective development and uniform application can be guaranteed of administrative processes and procedures, such as those referring to ethical standards and values, staff regulations, and disciplinary processes.

In Layer 3, the ASP is the main oversight body. As the IER noted, states parties play a significant role in Layer 3 also as they elect the judges and the Prosecutor of the Court, finance the Court's expenses, and oversee its functioning.[74] Pursuant to the Rome Statute, the Assembly shall 'provide management oversight to the Presidency, the Prosecutor and the Registrar regarding the administration of the Court'.[75] In line with the Financial Regulations and Rules, the Registrar and the Prosecutor are accountable to the ASP for the 'proper management and administration of the financial resources for which they are responsible'.[76]

To assist the Assembly in its oversight role, the ASP established several subsidiary bodies. Of relevance to the matter at hand are:

[73] ICC Statute (n 7) Art 43(1)-(2).
[74] IER Report (n 3) para 27.
[75] ICC Statute (n 7) Art 112(2)(b).
[76] ICC Financial Regulations and Rules (n 64).

- the Committee on Budget and Finance that advises the Assembly on any matter submitted to the ASP of a financial, budgetary or administrative nature[77] and the Audit Committee;
- the Audit Committee that provides the ASP 'independent advice on the adequacy and effectiveness of the Court's management practices';[78] and
- the Independent Oversight Mechanism, whose purpose is to 'provide comprehensive oversight of the Court through the conduct of independent internal administrative investigations, evaluations, and inspections, in order to enhance its economy and efficiency'.[79]

As Layer 3 covers services common to IO secretariats, activities under the ICC/IO can be audited, which is a standard accountability tool in IOs. At the ICC, audits are performed both internally through the Office of Internal Audit and by external auditors appointed regularly by the ASP.[80] Moreover, in view of the common activities underlying Layer 3, the IER recommended that the ICC and/or the ASP use key performance indicators (KPI) to enable comparisons with other IOs to facilitate efficiency assessments.[81]

Within the ICC/Court, core judicial and prosecutorial activities (Layer 1) require absolute judicial independence. In essence, accountability in this regard is achieved through judicial remedies before the competent panel. In terms of prosecutorial activities, the Prosecutor is the ultimate decision-maker within the Office of the Prosecutor (OTP). In the context of judicial proceedings, the prosecution is a party to the judicial process and thus subject to decisions of the relevant judicial authority.

In Layer 1, accountability can be sought from the competent judicial panel through judicial remedies. Decisions taken by a first instance panel, be that judges in pre-trial or trial stage, can be appealed, either of right or with leave from the first instance panel, before the Appeals Chamber.[82] Additionally, the Rome Statute also entrusts the Presidency, made up of a President and two Vice-Presidents,[83] with certain responsibilities falling under Layer 1, such as decisions related to the enforcement of sentences.[84] The ASP, states parties, or external actors cannot audit core judicial or prosecutorial activities, as they take place in Layer 1. The Experts pointed out an exception in this regard as far as the prosecution is concerned, namely the use of external experts for 'Lessons Learnt' exercises to review and improve OTP practices.[85] Such an exercise is different from an externally-imposed audit, as the decision to carry out the audit comes from the Prosecutor, who receives the report and decides on any follow-up that may be needed.

77 ASP, Resolution ICC-ASP/1/Res.4, 'Establishment of the Committee on Budget and Finance', Annex, para 2.

78 ASP, Audit Committee <https://asp.icc-cpi.int/AuditCommittee>.

79 ASP, Resolution ICC-ASP/19/Res.6, Annex II, 'Operational Mandate of the Independent Oversight Mechanism', 16 December 2020, para 2.

80 IER Report (n 3) para 954.

81 ibid para 46 and section VI. Performance Indicators and Strategic Planning.

82 ICC Statute (n 7) Arts 81–82.

83 ibid Art 38(3).

84 ICC RPE (n 20) Rules 146(5), 215, and 217.

85 IER Report (n 3) para 33 and section XV.

That the ASP is not the ultimate decision-maker in Layer 1 matters is also emphasized in the Rome Statute, where Article 119 foresees that 'any dispute concerning the judicial functions of the Court shall be settled by the decision of the Court'. Any other dispute between two or more states parties related to the interpretation or application of the Rome Statute is to be dealt with by the ASP, similarly to the approach followed in relation to founding treaties of other IOs. Identifying the ultimate decision-maker in a layer does not mean that none of the other governance stakeholder have a role to play. For instance, by virtue of states parties' role in Layer 3, certain decisions such as the elections of judges or the adoption of budget will still influence Layer 1 activities. However, these prerogatives of the ASP should not be used to influence the core judicial and prosecutorial activities, so as to respect judicial independence. As emphasized in the previous sections, in the (perceived) absence of effective oversight, states will use whatever mechanism available to them to try to affect desired change.

Within Layer 2 (Administration of Justice), the Presidency and the Prosecutor, respectively, are the ultimate decision-makers. The Presidency is responsible for the proper administration of the court, with the exception of the OTP.[86] Among other things, the Presidency approves leave and outside activity requests of judges and takes lead in capacity building activities for judges. Under Layer 2, the Presidency can also adopt certain administrative instruments affecting judicial proceedings, as was the case for the Guidelines for the Judiciary concerning the Holding of Court Hearings during the COVID-19 pandemic.[87] As the authority in Layer 2, the IER also emphasized that it is the Presidency that 'is responsible for developing tools and introducing measures required for the efficient management of proceedings'.[88]

The OTP is headed by a Prosecutor who has 'full authority over the management and administration of the Office, including the staff, facilities, and other resources thereof'.[89] The Experts opined that the mandate of the Prosecutor covered both Layer 1 (operations directly related to investigations and prosecution) and issues of organizational administration (Layers 2 and/or 3). In view of duplication of services between the Registry and the OTP, the Experts recommended that the OTP delegates Layer 3 matters to the Registry in view of a more efficient use of resources and a more uniform application of internal regulations.[90]

Most importantly, Layer 2 activities do not require the same high threshold of judicial/prosecutorial independence. Transparency and accountability should be guaranteed and judicial independence should not be used as a shield. Administration of justice is also audited in domestic systems, and the same should be done for the ICC. This is why the IER recommended the establishment of a non-permanent Judicial Audit Committee (JAC), composed of current or former, national or international judges or prosecutors, as oversight entity.[91] The JAC would audit the administration

[86] ICC Statute (n 7) Art 383(a).

[87] ICC, 'Guidelines for the Judiciary Concerning the Holding of Court Hearings during the COVID-19 Pandemic', 23 June 2020 <www.icc-cpi.int/sites/default/files/itemsDocuments/200623-guidelines-for-court-proceedings-covid-19-eng.pdf>.

[88] IER Report (n 3) para 39.

[89] ICC Statute (n 7) Art 42(2).

[90] IER Report (n 3) para 43.

[91] ibid 18 (R3).

of justice activities in Chambers and OTP respectively, with the Presidency and Prosecutor respectively being responsible for assessing the results of the audits and deciding on any needed follow-up measures. The Presidency and the Prosecutor would then inform the ASP on such developments, in line with the ASP's management oversight role towards the Presidency, the Prosecutor, and the Registrar on administrative matters.[92] Such a Committee, working remotely and on a needs-basis, could service several ICTs,[93] making it an even more cost-effective option.[94]

In terms of accountability mechanisms in Layer 2, the Experts recommended the use of KPIs and inter-court comparisons. As emphasized in the Report, 'to accurately measure efficiency, data needs to be compared—in time and with other courts or international organisations'.[95] While every ICT is different, core operations are similar and common KPIs can be identified. Examples could be compliance with timelines for certain decisions or number of days of court hearings. Assessing the evolution of KPIs over time within the ICC, and comparing them with those of other ICTs, enables benchmarking and a determination of what 'normality' in international justice is and thus what expectations are reasonable for an ICT.[96]

At a minimum, the Model can serve as the basis for discussion among stakeholders. Its value is, among other things, in that it maps out the different types of activities carried out within the ICC. It also emphasizes that different activities require different levels of independence, and that regardless of the activity, a form of oversight and accountability mechanisms should be provided.

21.5 Conclusion

Since the first ICT was created in 1907,[97] more and more ICTs have been established to fulfil diverse mandates. With the increased activity of such bodies, attention to their work has intensified. However, this has mostly concerned their output: development of international law through judgments. Significantly less attention has been paid to the governance of such bodies. With increased transparency in the discussions of *injugovins*,[98] challenges and tensions between those defending judicial independence and those advocating for accountability have taken centre stage. The choice has often been seen as either acceptance of a self-managed judiciary or that of a full control by states. Nobody would advocate for absolute judicial independence at the cost of all accountability, or the other way around. But the implementation of the two principles

[92] ICC Statute (n 7) Art 112(2)(b).

[93] IER Report (n 3) 18 (R3) and 92 (R113).

[94] Further recommendations on oversight in Layer 2 were also made as concerns discipline of judges: see ibid, IV.B. Accountability of Judges.

[95] ibid para 365.

[96] ibid paras 365–66.

[97] The first ICT was the Central American Court of Justice (1907–18): Christian Tomuschat, 'International Courts and Tribunals', *Max Planck Encyclopedia of Public International Law* (Oxford Public International Law, OUP, article last updated in April 2019) <https://opil.ouplaw.com/view/10.1093/law:epil/9780199231690/law-9780199231690-e35?rskey=Gcedv1&result=1&prd=MPIL>, paras 8–9.

[98] For example, a great part of ICC's ASP sessions can be followed online, with much of the documentation prepared for the sessions being available to the public through the ASP's website.

has led to frictions between stakeholders who disagree on the proper scope of their powers and the best means by which to ensure effective and efficient governance and the functioning of ICTs.

This chapter proposed the Three-Layered Governance Model as the tool to facilitate such discussion by the stakeholders. Many of the processes and entities that are referred to in the model are already in place. However, those stakeholders' areas of responsibility, powers, and interactions with one another have not been clearly delineated, perhaps due to the fear that such discussions may open a 'Pandora's box'. The two principles are at times seen as irreconcilable, but this is not the case. The Three-Layered Governance Model can assist states which contemplate establishing new ICTs in designing their governance structures considering the different layers of activity, and clarifying, for each layer, the authority, the oversight entity, and the accountability mechanisms. A number of IOs outside the judicial field could also benefit from the same governance approach, both to protect their independence and strengthen their accountability, especially when performing activities that require independence, such as fact-finding, scientific, health, or financial regulation. The Three-Layered Governance Model offers a basis for conversations among stakeholders aimed at achieving both transparency and clarity in relation to the governance processes and roles and responsibilities—the two aspects that are essential components of accountability. It would contribute to more efficient and effective governance, thereby facilitating the functioning of the ICTs and enhancing the international community's trust in international justice and the organizations established to deliver it.

22
Conclusion

Niels Blokker and Sergey Vasiliev

22.1 Introduction

The chapters that make up this volume assemble a wealth of empirical 'raw material' and theoretical insight on the legal frameworks and practical arrangements for the governance of international courts and tribunals—both defunct and extant—across diverse areas of international law, geographical regions, and time periods. The range of experiential, analytical, and normative perspectives on the lived practice and challenges of overseeing international justice institutions is impressive. It far exceeds the expectations editors held when embarking on this exploratory and experimental journey into a field where knowledge gaps had long persisted. By this point in the book, the existence of international judicial governance as a sprawling and rapidly evolving field of international institutional law and practice can no longer be in doubt. Compensating for the decades of obscurity and scholarly neglect, it may be hoped that academic and policy debate on the promises and tribulations of international courts in the years to come will be extended to the judicial governance domain. This would be a justified and desirable, if belated, development. Paying deserving attention to international courts' governing institutions is in many respects the only way to confront in earnest the root causes of operational and legitimacy problems international courts have increasingly been facing.

The central ambition of this book has been to demarcate international judicial governance as a distinct domain of law and practice, as well as a scholarly field — demonstrating that its claim to disciplinary recognition is not only well founded but long overdue. With that objective in mind, the book has proffered a shared vocabulary, laid the conceptual foundations, and presented original material on the governance schemes specific to representative international judicial systems, while also addressing, in a cross-cutting way, some of the main governance functions and common challenges that define this field. Fundamental questions of organizing and performing the oversight of international judiciaries have been addressed, unobtrusively and matter-of-factly, through routine institutional practice for decades. Despite this extensive accumulated experience, the field remains very much under construction. Rather than constituting a definitive treatment of the subject, the book offers an initial contribution to the nascent academic field: one that sets the possible directions for future debates and provides impetus for further research.

In this concluding chapter, we do not attempt to perform the impossible task of recapitulating the arguments developed in each of the preceding contributions; readers are invited to engage with them in their own way. Instead, we draw key insights that are

Niels Blokker and Sergey Vasiliev, *Conclusion* In: *Governance of International Courts and Tribunals*. Edited by: Sergey Vasiliev and Niels Blokker, Oxford University Press. © Niels Blokker and Sergey Vasiliev 2026.
DOI: 10.1093/oso/9780198922131.003.0022

a red thread running through these contributions, in order to highlight the commonalities and tensions between them. Woven together, such takeaways allow us to point out the core problems and questions that are likely to shape the field's future agenda, circling back to the preliminary observations and hypotheses set out in Chapter 1.[1]

22.2 Retrospective Bird's-Eye View

The realm of international judicial governance is marked by irreducible institutional pluralism, attended by a diversity of legal standards and formal (or semi-formal) practices, as well as the overall regulatory and normative complexity. As the totality of the contributions in this book shows, this institutional 'universe' has been populated by a wide array of 'galaxies'—largely unconnected and incommensurable regimes for overseeing international courts, both past and present, each equipped with its own legal scheme, organizational forms, and accumulated practice. As our contributors astutely observe, comparative and intertemporal critical evaluations of judicial governance legacies across institutional regimes *within* distinct specialized domains have been notably scarce.[2] The same observation holds *a fortiori* for the broader field of the governance of international adjudication at large. This diversity and apparent disjointedness certainly pose conceptual and definitional challenges insofar as they may be taken to attest to a deficit of coherence.

The field's claim to a unified disciplinary 'identity' is nonetheless compelling. There is unity within diversity. This is, first, the unity of the field's normative foundations—the fundamental legal principles rooted in the *judicial* nature of the institutions governed—upon which the diverse edifices of distinct institutional regimes are built.[3] Second, there is a unity of core objectives underlying all the international court governance regimes. They have been fashioned, at least in theory, to enable courts' independent, impartial, accountable, and effective functioning, even if they are found to have succeeded therein to varying degrees. This fundamental goal not only permits but indeed necessitates diverse legal-institutional arrangements best suited to promote it in incommensurable contexts. Accordingly, each international court has been run under a scheme of its own—an 'ecosystem' shaped by a distinctive, ever-fluid interplay between the external and internal dimensions of judicial (self-)governance.

The parameters of these divergent and invariably complex schemes have essentially been determined by whether a given regime is embedded within a larger organization (eg the United Nations, African Union, ECOWAS, or the EU), anchored in dedicated treaty-based or self-standing oversight institutions (eg the Meeting of States Parties to the UNCLOS (SPLOS) for the International Tribunal for the Law of the Sea (ITLOS), the ICC's Assembly of States Parties, and UN criminal tribunals' management and

[1] Sergey Vasiliev and Niels Blokker, 'Introduction', in this volume.

[2] On the governance of the UN criminal tribunals: Huw Llewellyn, 'Governance of the United Nations Criminal Tribunals', in this volume.

[3] For an exploration of this perspective: Sergey Vasiliev, 'Governing International Justice: Whence the Uniform Principles?' in Rick Lawson and Ramses A Wessel (eds), *Unity in Diversity: Perspectives on the Law of International Organisations* (Brill Nijhoff 2025) 281–93.

steering committees), or merely coupled to a loose coalition of like-minded states.[4] The variable characteristics of these 'galaxies'—together with their structures, the key players wielding both formal competences and real-world power, and their working modalities—shape the feedback loop between 'the governors' and 'the governed'. They predetermine, within each specific context, how constructive or troubled that relationship will be, and how effective and successful—or otherwise—the respective court is likely to become.

The field's unifying legal-normative dimension has not evolved incrementally and in accordance with a global master design; rather, it has grown in fits and starts following the logic of institutional proliferation. The thickets of legal and regulatory standards and practices were woven separately within each individual 'galaxy', with some interest and attention—but without considerable deference—to the developments, know-hows, and hard-learned lessons from the past or contemporary regimes in the other corners of the 'universe'. Accordingly, from a regulatory perspective, international judicial governance constitutes a sprawling and multi-layered field. It is highly 'juridified' and sophisticated in legal technique, with a cobweb of formal standards and practices permeating and corseting judicial governance relationships within specific regimes. At the same time, it remains piecemeal and underwhelming in terms of normative coordination.

This realm is oversaturated with regime-specific instruments, ranging from treaties that outline governance schemes in broad strokes to rules of procedure, by-laws, and informal ad hoc arrangements designed to oil the minute wheels and cogs of the judicial governance machineries. On the other hand, at the macro-level, it continues to lack a thick *toile de fond* of universal hard norms to cement its homogeneity, beyond abstract and uncontroversial—and therefore ephemeral and inconclusive—general principles. There is little of tangible substance to draw upon when seeking guidance to resolve the tensions and contentions that constantly simmer—and occasionally flare up—between *injugovins* and courts, whether stemming from the overreach of governance powers and the suitability of the modalities chosen to exercise them, or from the resistance those may provoke.[5]

One typically falls back on the recognized legal principles such as judicial independence and impartiality, accountability, transparency, and the rule-of-law 'umbrella'. Additional guidance may be sought in the various iterations of soft 'good governance' standards, adapted and tailored to the domain of governance of judicial systems.[6] As noted, these principles and standards are open-ended and blurry on the edges. They acquire meaningful normative content only through contextualized interpretation, and their regulatory force is lost when transplanted into other institutional settings. The regulatory frameworks leave ample space in their interstices for manoeuvre and improvisation, as *injugovins* translate general principles and regime-specific 'hard standards' into governance practice.

[4] On the typology of *injugovins*: Niels Blokker, 'International Judicial Governance Institutions', in this volume.

[5] On these tensions: Nicolas Guillou and Adriana-Maria Manolescu, 'The Three-Layered Governance Model', in this volume.

[6] For this perspective: eg John Eudes Ruhangisa, 'Governance of Regional Integration Courts', in this volume.

22.3 Common Dimensions and Themes

Considering the still inchoate state of the field, it would be premature and overambitious for this concluding chapter to try and devise a definitive formula for harnessing its complexities and unresolved questions. Likewise, it would seem a fool's errand to devise a single one-size-fits-all model—the ideal blueprint—for the governance of all international courts and tribunals seeking to iron out the field's irreducible institutional diversity in a sterile pursuit of perfect uniformity for its own sake. In synthesizing the takeaways and charting future directions, this section highlights the recurrent themes and interlocking dimensions of judicial governance that have framed our discussions thus far. Without seeking to be exhaustive, this survey contextualizes and engages with the shared insights and motifs which surface across the contributions, and which have structured our authors' analyses or informed their normative positions. We identify seven dyads—conceived as 'and' rather than 'versus'—which will serve as analytical axes onto which such salient issues can be usefully 'strung'.

22.3.1 Independence–accountability

The independence–accountability tandem recurs throughout the book's reflections on the legal frameworks, institutional forms, and practices of judicial governance. This dyad exerts an irresistible gravitational pull, remaining by far the most prevalent lens for highlighting the dynamics and tensions in judicial governance.[7] Indeed, it has served as the main framing for the conceptual and preparatory analyses that formed the stepping stone to this volume.[8] Several contributions engage squarely with the independence–accountability perspective.[9] Moreover, virtually all chapters revert to this dyad's categories as normative goalposts when problematizing judicial governance and assessing how its arrangements correspond to—or deviate from—their underlying demands. Judicial independence—a guiding light in the shaping of judicial governance relationships—runs as a red thread through chapters on individual governance regimes,[10] on the election function of *injugovins*,[11] and on postmortems of

[7] Niels Blokker, 'International Judicial Governance Institutions', Section 3.5, in this volume; discussing the literature on domestic and international judiciaries, Sergey Vasiliev, 'What Is (International) Judicial Governance?', in this volume.

[8] Niels M Blokker, 'The Governance of International Courts and Tribunals: Organizing and Guaranteeing Independence and Accountability' in Andreas Føllesdal and Geir Ulfstein (eds), *The Judicialization of International Law: A Mixed Blessing?* (OUP 2018).

[9] Besides Sergey Vasiliev, 'What Is (International) Judicial Governance?' and Niels Blokker, 'International Judicial Governance Institutions', see Misha Ariana Plagis and Karin Pluberg, 'Paper Lions?', Huw Llewellyn, 'Governance of the United Nations Criminal Tribunals', Evelyn Anoya, 'Governance of the Special Tribunal for Lebanon', Adriana-Maria Manolescu, 'Financial Governance of International Courts and Tribunals', and Nicolas Guillou and Adriana-Maria Manolescu, 'The Three-Layered Governance Model', in this volume.

[10] eg John Eudes Ruhangisa, 'Governance of Regional Integration Courts', Misha Ariana Plagis and Karin Pluberg, 'Paper Lions?', Heikki Kanninen, 'Governance of the Court of Justice of the European Union', and Evelyn Anoya, 'Governance of the Special Tribunal for Lebanon', in this volume.

[11] eg Niels Blokker, 'International Judicial Governance Institutions', Andrew Drzemczewski, 'The Election of Judges onto the European Court of Human Rights', Christiaan Timmermans, 'The Procedure

their failures to uphold this principle.[12] There is consensus that neither element of the independence–accountability pair stands for an absolute value to be enforced without limits and for its own sake. Both principles are instrumental to the overarching aim of ensuring high-quality judicial decision-making, as well as the effectiveness and legitimacy of adjudication.

At the domestic level, the relationship between the principles of judicial independence and accountability is complex and open to divergent interpretations; the same holds for the governance of international courts. These tenets have been variously portrayed as opposing poles on the same continuum; as autonomous sets of interests that may at times clash; or as 'two sides of the same coin'—values that inform and reinforce each other.[13] A judiciary subject to more exacting requirements and stricter accountability measures administered by governing organs—which serve, to a greater or lesser extent, as conduits for executive or legislative control or influence—appears to be institutionally less independent vis-à-vis the other branches. But the distinction between the independence of the judiciary as a system and that of the individual judges operating within that system, is essential to keep in mind, particularly in view of their differing interplay with accountability.[14]

Judiciaries unconstrained by appropriate accountability and endowed with high—or indeed excessive—levels of institutional independence risk becoming corporatist and unresponsive to society, becoming implicated in abuses, corruption, or malpractice, and developing other troublesome symptoms that can ultimately erode the independence of individual judges.[15] This risk—borne out by experience in certain national systems—demonstrates the mutually reinforcing relationship between the two principles and their underlying values.[16] Conversely, a judiciary's perceived or actual accountability helps to bolster its authority and legitimacy, enabling it, when push comes to shove, to leverage the institutional independence it has been afforded to issue rulings that run counter the political branches.

The view of judicial independence and accountability as mutually reinforcing, rather than antithetical, is shared by all authors who address this dyad expressly, even as they acknowledge the tensions inherent in it. Thus, Kanninen states that the purpose of the CJEU's independence is to safeguard its judicial tasks from external influence and not to exclude any relationship with other EU institutions or actors.[17]

for Nominating Members of the EU Courts', and Christian M De Vos and others, 'Electing the Best?', in this volume.

[12] Zsuzsanna Deen-Racsmány, 'Deficient Protection of the Independence of International Judges by International Judicial Governance Institutions', in this volume.

[13] eg Pablo Castillo-Ortiz, *Judicial Governance and Democracy in Europe* (Springer 2023) 19; Stephen B Burbank, 'Judicial Accountability in the Past, Present, and Future: Precedent, Politics, and Power' (2005) 28 University of Arkansas at Little Rock Law Review 19, 25.

[14] eg John Bell, 'Sweden's Contribution to Governance of the Judiciary' (2007) 50 Scandinavian Studies in Law 83, 87.

[15] Castillo-Ortiz (n 13) 19 ('judicial independence is a desirable value, but unaccountable judiciaries can become excessively activist or can incur in bad practices'); Michal Bobek and David Kosař, 'Global Solutions, Local Damages: A Critical Study in Judicial Councils in Central and Eastern Europe' (2014) 15(7) German Law Journal 1257, 1271.

[16] For discussion, Sergey Vasiliev, 'What Is (International) Judicial Governance?', in this volume.

[17] Heikki Kanninen, 'Governance of the Court of Justice of the European Union', Section 9.2, in this volume.

Llewellyn highlights the 'inherent tension' between the broader needs of governing courts—particularly the parent and oversight bodies' interest in keeping the cost and duration of judicial mandates in check—and, on the other hand, the imperatives of judicial independence and impartiality.[18] Starting from the premise that both cornerstone principles must be safeguarded and promoted as integral to the financial governance frameworks of international courts and tribunals, Manolescu stresses the need to foster their harmonious co-existence, notwithstanding the recurrent tensions in institutional practice.[19] Judicial independence is at times wielded as a 'shield against accountability' to counter what are perceived as encroachments on judicial mandates and interference with individual cases. This might turn into a self-fulfilling prophecy, Manolescu warns, as states seek to reassert control and enforce financial accountability, triggering an 'unconstructive and divisive cycle' that can well be deleterious for the court's independence.

These arguments are further developed in Guillou and Manolescu's analysis on the 'Three-Layered Governance Model' (3LGM) devised by the Independent Expert Review for the International Criminal Court, but potentially applicable to other international courts and tribunals as well.[20] The authors show how and why international courts tend to wield judicial independence as a 'shield' against accountability—a tendency rooted in the unique legal order in which they are embedded.[21] Under the 3LGM, however, the demands of judicial independence and judicial accountability can be reconciled in a conceptually and legally coherent manner. This is done by linking up the court's three main types, or layers, of activity—core judicial/prosecutorial work, justice administration, and the functioning of an international organization—to corresponding degrees of independence, each informed by distinct lines of authority, accountability modalities, and competent oversight bodies.[22]

Incontrovertibly, judicial independence is—and must be—at its strongest when protecting the core mandates and decision-making autonomy of judges, to prevent interference in individual cases. In matters of judicial administration—such as case management, composition of chambers, and internal allocation of resources—courts as judicial institutions should admit a degree of peer oversight and accountability, yet they must remain free from political interference or outside pressure.[23] When it comes to the international-organization layer, however, the governance of courts is guided by different rationales and understandably should allow for higher degrees of external oversight and accountability modalities.[24] Notably, the conceptualization of judicial

[18] Huw Llewellyn, 'Governance of the United Nations Criminal Tribunals', Sections 10.1 and 10.7, in this volume.

[19] Adriana-Maria Manolescu, 'Financial Governance of International Courts and Tribunals', Sections 14.2.1–14.2.2, in this volume.

[20] Nicolas Guillou and Adriana-Maria Manolescu, 'The Three-Layered Governance Model', Section 21.2, in this volume.

[21] For discussion, Sergey Vasiliev, 'What Is (International) Judicial Governance?', in this volume.

[22] Nicolas Guillou and Adriana-Maria Manolescu, 'The Three-Layered Governance Model', Section 21.4, in this volume.

[23] Heikki Kanninen, 'Governance of the Court of Justice of the European Union', Sections 9.2 and 9.6, in this volume on the CJEU's judicial operation versus its administrative organization.

[24] Nicolas Guillou and Adriana-Maria Manolescu, 'The Three-Layered Governance Model', Section 21.4, and Huw Llewellyn, 'Governance of the United Nations Criminal Tribunals', Section 10.5.1, in this volume.

independence as a multi-geared safeguard—one that is not only consistent but also interwoven with accountability—is not unique to international courts. It resonates with domestic conceptions as well.[25]

22.3.2 External–internal governance

Coming to the fore in several contributions, the external–internal governance dimension has played a key role in this project. First, it has been indispensable in marking the territory and in defining the object of study with greater precision. In respect of international courts and tribunals, judicial governance was specifically narrowed down to their governance by *external* political or executive organs.[26] Covering decisions 'international courts and tribunals cannot make themselves and for which they need to rely on those who govern them',[27] this notion excludes *internal* judicial (self-) governance processes taking place within the courts themselves.

Second, the ambit of *internal* judicial governance is intrinsically linked to guaranteeing judicial independence. As Kanninen notes, meddling by other entities, especially states, in the internal organization of an international court could compromise its independence.[28] This is echoed by Fernández de Gurmendi on the ASP's governance role for the ICC: the Assembly has no direct management responsibilities at the Court and must duly respect its judicial independence.[29] Self-governance is something that judicial organizations are perfectly capable of doing themselves—and something they have to engage in, both when carrying out core tasks and when facilitating external oversight—such as fulfilling reporting obligations, preparing draft annual budgets for adoption elsewhere, providing information to accountability mechanisms in response to inquiries, and interacting with *injugovins* and state representatives.[30] The line between the *external* and the *internal* judicial governance is drawn differently for international courts than in much of the literature on domestic systems.[31] In the domestic context, judicial self-governance tends to be defined more broadly to encompass the (often problematic) functioning of essentially external entities, such as judicial councils that are positioned between the courts and the political branches and typically include the judicial branch's representatives.

[25] In a similar vein, eg Bell (n 14) 88 ('when it comes to managing the judicial service and setting its budgets, then we are not dealing with potential interference with individual cases, but with the setting of priorities between categories of legal activity, and this involves giving a direction to society, which is an inherently political activity. The suggestion that the judiciary should be given untrammelled authority in this area is seriously problematic').

[26] Sergey Vasiliev, 'What Is (International) Judicial Governance?', Niels Blokker, 'International Judicial Governance Institutions', and John Eudes Ruhangisa, 'Governance of Regional Integration Courts', Section 7.3.1, in this volume.

[27] Niels Blokker, 'International Judicial Governance Institutions', Section 3.2, in this volume.

[28] Heikki Kanninen, 'Governance of the Court of Justice of the European Union', Section 9.3, in this volume.

[29] Silvia Fernández de Gurmendi, 'Challenges to the Governance of the International Criminal Court', Section 18.2, in this volume.

[30] eg Misha Ariana Plagis and Karin Pluberg, 'Paper Lions?', Section 8.3.1, in this volume.

[31] Sergey Vasiliev, 'What Is (International) Judicial Governance?', in this volume.

Third, the dyad of external–internal governance has been central to explaining judicial governance as a real-life phenomenon and to understanding its operationalization in practice. Both conceptually and practically, the distinction is a fine line, not a fault line. Governance implies a form of hierarchical relationship, but it is not, and cannot be, a one-way street or a unilateral, top-down action, particularly when it comes to *judicial* institutions that, as noted, must be (perceived as) independent.[32] Anoya underscored the co-existence of the internal and external oversight processes at the Special Tribunal for Lebanon (STL), as well as the blurred lines and occasional disconnections between them.[33] Llewellyn argues that 'governance' encompasses an array of decisions and measures taken by competent external parent and oversight bodies, at the very least in consultation—or, as he puts it, *in partnership*—with international courts concerned, with the aim of securing the necessary 'legal, political and financial support and cooperation from a broad range of actors that they need in order to function effectively'.[34] Therefore, this is the space shared by both external and internal players, and it is in the relationship and dynamics between these two connected yet autonomous spheres that judicial governance unfolds—succeeding or failing in its key objectives. Given the (ideally) cooperation-based and synergistic nature of judicial governance relationships, players both on the outside and on the inside bear their share of responsibility for preventing and resolving conflicts or disruptions.[35]

Fourth, underscoring said autonomy, the external–internal governance distinction is important for determining competences, apportioning obligations, and allocating responsibilities in governance relationships. Collapsing it could blur different actors' duties, foster 'ungovernance' and 'misgovernance', and create accountability gaps; it is therefore worth maintaining. In this shared domain of judicial governance, powers, and obligations—as well as accountability for their abuse or neglect—must be clearly articulated and made opposable to correct actors—*injugovins* or courts—depending on the issue at hand and the sphere of responsibility in which it falls. As noted in Chapter 1, misattributing faults is damaging to the authority and credibility of courts and can readily be weaponized to mount unjustified politicized attacks against them. It also enables actors who are responsible for preventing and resolving governance crises, yet failing to take meaningful action, to get away with their inaction, facing little scrutiny or repercussions.[36]

[32] Nicolas Guillou and Adriana-Maria Manolescu, 'The Three-Layered Governance Model', in this volume; also Sergey Vasiliev, 'What Is (International) Judicial Governance?', in this volume.

[33] Evelyn Anoya, 'Governance of the Special Tribunal for Lebanon', Section 11.4, in this volume.

[34] Huw Llewellyn, 'Governance of the United Nations Criminal Tribunals', Section 10.2.3, in this volume.

[35] Adriana-Maria Manolescu, 'Financial Governance of International Courts and Tribunals', Section 14.6, in this volume.

[36] Peter Van den Bossche, 'The Demise of the WTO Appellate Body' and Zsuzsanna Deen-Racsmány, 'Deficient Protection of the Independence of International Judges by International Judicial Governance Institutions', in this volume.

22.3.3 Formal–informal governance

International judicial governance remains a largely formal—and formalist—enterprise, operating through a web of legal rules and regulations that allocate competences, prescribe courses of action, and shape practice. This could hardly be otherwise, considering the purposes of governance, actors exercising it (states, international organizations, treaty bodies etc), and the judicial institutions on the receiving end, and the diplomatic or legal-technical expert fora in which it takes place. However comprehensive the effort at formal legal regulation, this realm of institutional activity necessarily combines formality with informal standards, customary practices, and ad hoc and improvised approaches to problem-solving. As these arrangements and interactions form an essential aspect of the lived reality of judicial governance, the formality–informality dimension recurs in various guises throughout the volume.

On the one hand, a degree of informality in (self-)regulation and court governance practice is acceptable and often even necessary: it serves useful purposes in the right contexts and within proper limits. As emphasized in several contributions, the international regulatory framework setting out principles on judicial independence of international courts in their relations with governing institutions remains largely informal or semi-formal soft law.[37] Informal agreements among, and improvisation by, states and other governance actors proved crucial in making governance work in the early instances of international court-construction (eg the Permanent Court of International Justice (PCIJ), the international military tribunals (IMTs), and modern tribunals' management committees),[38] as well as when courts were first established and run by organs of an international organization without meaningful precedent to draw on (eg the UN criminal tribunals).[39] In operational realities, informality can strengthen the bonds of the *injugovins*' partnership with, and ownership of, the judicial bodies they govern. Regular informal interactions between those performing governance functions inside and outside the courts help forge mutual trust, foster collegial working relationships, and sustain goodwill over the long term. Streamlined communication and routine contacts enable governance actors to perform their roles more effectively, prevent misunderstandings, and facilitate smoother governance processes.

On the other hand, formal arrangements and their attendant checks and safeguards are there for a reason. Informality and 'ad-hockery' have their shadow sides, and several contributions highlight the related risks. As Vasiliev notes in his analysis of the Nuremberg Tribunal's governance and the dynamics between the Allied Powers, when informal relations sour and mutual trust vanishes, the very foundations for workable judicial governance can collapse.[40] Without formal procedures or mechanisms

[37] For discussion: Sergey Vasiliev, 'What Is (International) Judicial Governance?', Huw Llewellyn, 'Governance of the United Nations Criminal Tribunals', and Adriana-Maria Manolescu, 'Financial Governance of International Courts and Tribunals', in this volume.

[38] Henri de Waele, 'Managing the Realization of "The Hope of Ages"', Sergey Vasiliev, 'Governance of the International Military Tribunals at Nuremberg and Tokyo', and Evelyn Anoya, 'Governance of the Special Tribunal for Lebanon', in this volume.

[39] Huw Llewellyn, 'Governance of the United Nations Criminal Tribunals', in this volume.

[40] Sergey Vasiliev, 'Governance of the International Military Tribunals at Nuremberg and Tokyo', in this volume.

to salvage them and restore that trust, judicial institutions risk ending up under the rubble. Judicial operations will be abruptly terminated, suspended, or ordered to be wrapped up unceremoniously—as occurred with the Special Tribunal of Lebanon, examined in detail by Anoya.[41]

On a related note, in emphasizing that transparency and inclusiveness are essential aspects of judicial governance, Llewellyn cautions that informal decision-making among a few powerful or active member states—excluding the broader membership, as was characteristic of the UN criminal tribunals' management committees—can undermine transparency and weaken democratic legitimacy and accountability of judicial governance.[42] A move away from governance by (organs of) large international organizations to small committees of major donor states enhances efficiency of decision-making and ownership of the courts and thus has much to recommend it. However, a degree of formality still needs to be maintained in the oversight relationships under this model; for example, express requirements and additional safeguards of judicial independence should offset any risks the informal ways pose and ensure transparency and accountability towards a broader membership. In a related line of thought, Guillou and Manolescu observe that institutional trust in governance relationships cannot hinge on rapport and interpersonal relations; it requires a more solid basis: a transparent and orderly dialogue and robust accountability mechanisms.[43]

The element of transparency—referenced in several contributions—does not fit neatly within the formal–informal spectrum alone and might deserve to be placed in a dyad of its own.[44] It nonetheless merits a brief mention here. In his critique of the governance of African regional courts, Ruhangisa highlights the opacity of judicial appointment processes, which not only leaves room for the arbitrary exercise of power by appointing authorities but also risks producing judicial incompetence and eroding both individual and institutional judicial independence.[45] Timmermans gives this much-vaunted element a slightly different twist in the context of judicial nominations in the EU. His response to critiques of the alleged deficit thereof in the workings of the 255 Panel shows that, alongside transparency, a reasonable measure of confidentiality can also be both desirable and necessary.[46] Without certain guarantees of confidentiality, there is a real risk that the most qualified individuals would refrain from putting forward their candidacies, with negative consequences for the quality of the bench. This corroborates indirectly the earlier point that principles giving expression to generally accepted values and legitimate interests are not absolute and should not be pursued unreflexively to the bitter end. Rather, such principles tend to be open-ended, flexible, and instrumental; they must be operationalized in a reasonable manner that allows them to be balanced against other principles safeguarding countervailing interests while serving the same—or different—legitimate and laudable goals.

[41] Evelyn Anoya, 'Governance of the Special Tribunal for Lebanon', in this volume.
[42] Huw Llewellyn, 'Governance of the United Nations Criminal Tribunals', Section 10.2.3, in this volume.
[43] Nicolas Guillou and Adriana-Maria Manolescu, 'The Three-Layered Governance Model', Section 21.2.3, in this volume.
[44] Transparency is an aspect of accountability (Section 22.3.1), but in the sense used here it refers to the functioning of *injugovins* rather than courts (Section 22.4.2).
[45] John Eudes Ruhangisa, 'Governance of Regional Integration Courts', Section 7.3.3, in this volume.
[46] Christiaan Timmermans, 'The Procedure for Nominating Members of the EU Courts', in this volume.

22.3.4 Continuity–reinvention

The succession of chapters in the book's institution-specific parts (II and III) moves from historic and defunct antecedents, through more recent and well-established schemes, to modern governance regimes. International judicial governance has been a highly diversified and institutionally pluralistic field, with some schemes known better and others entirely shrouded in obscurity.[47] Progress has been neither linear nor guided by a visible logic or experience-driven 'lessons learnt' approach. Thus, the oldest and most well-known experience with international judicial governance was that of the PCIJ.[48] Yet it proved of no use when the Allies established the Nuremberg and Tokyo tribunals.[49] To be sure, the IMTs were ad hoc courts with limited jurisdiction, but they could be expected to encounter governance issues not unlike those faced by the PCIJ's (eg securing financial and logistical bases for their operations, guaranteeing judicial independence and the like). At least some lessons from how such questions were addressed in its rules and practices might have been expected to prove useful—if they had been articulated, learnt, and applied.

While this point deserves to be revisited, a general trend—with some detours and deviations—can certainly be discerned. It is complexification: the development from more direct and fluid forms of governance of international courts by states to thicker institutional veil and more autonomous *injugovins* with the agency of their own. The starting point is characterized by state engagement mediated, if it all, only by basic institutional structures fashioned for that purpose, a high degree of informality giving effect to no more than skeletal formal regulation, and unavoidable improvisation and ad hoc problem-solving that come with it. The governance of the Nuremberg and Tokyo tribunals by Allied Powers, as well as the operation of the management committees of UN-sponsored hybrid tribunals, are notable examples.

Later experiments—particularly the governance schemes of international courts established by and within international organizations (UN ad hoc tribunals and the ICJ, the European Court for Human Rights, and the Court of Justice of the EU) or by states multilaterally (ITLOS and ICC)—are marked by increasingly sprawling organigrams, sophisticated bureaucracies, and elaborate procedures.[50] This is no end point—nor can there be one—in this non-linear evolution and framing it as a straightforward progress narrative would be an oversimplification. The field of international judicial governance represents a repository of rules and practices (and forgotten experiments) that can be refashioned to construct bespoke models. Subsequent institutional forms combine, in varying degrees and configurations, elements drawn from earlier schemes with novel features introduced in response to evolving state preferences and the idiosyncrasies of the institutional context. The asynchronous, multi-directional trajectories of designing and reforming international judicial governance

[47] Revealing some examples: Niels Blokker, 'International Judicial Governance Institutions', Section 3.2, in this volume.

[48] Henri de Waele, 'Managing the Realization of "The Hope of Ages"', in this volume.

[49] Sergey Vasiliev, 'Governance of the International Military Tribunals at Nuremberg and Tokyo', in this volume.

[50] For example, on the organization of the ICC's ASP: Silvia Fernández de Gurmendi, 'Challenges to the Governance of the International Criminal Court', Section 18.3.1, in this volume.

oscillate between continuity with past organizational forms and approaches, on the one hand, and rupture or reinvention, on the other.

Many contributions illuminate this dimension of continuity–reinvention between past and present. The fact that similar features resurface in later institutions, shaped by experiences—lessons well or poorly learnt—and experimentation aimed at meeting changing demands and devising solutions to new challenges can give a fleeting glimpse of possible futures. Opening the book's 'historical' Part II, De Waele discusses how the practice of devising and managing the governance arrangements for the PCIJ provided a formative experiential ground for subsequent endeavours, not only in relation to its direct successor, the International Court of Justice (examined in detail by Forlati), but also later international tribunals.[51] Among impactful innovations re-emerging across a range of institutions, De Waele notes the majoritarian method for electing judges and the requirement of geographical diversity on the bench, the possibility of adding ad hoc judges, and the use of staggered judicial terms.

Vasiliev then details how the governance schemes of the post-Second World War international military tribunals were profoundly shaped by their unique historical and institutional context, forged by their anchorage in military occupation regimes rather than by any direct predecessors. Allied Powers' close—if fragile and fraught—cooperation in running the tribunals through lean multilateral structures, alongside many other often more pressing tasks, produced a hands-on, improvisational 'getting-things-done' approach to judicial governance.[52] The Tokyo IMT's governance scheme was as much the product of continuity as of reinvention, informed by the Americans' determination to break with what they saw as the negative experience at Nuremberg. These antecedents provided no direct governance blueprints or ready-made recipes for criminal tribunal construction efforts that followed nearly five decades later. Nonetheless, elements of their *modus operandi* can be traced in modern managerial *injugovins* composed of representatives of the most interested or major donor states. As analysed comprehensively by Llewellyn, this model offers similar efficiency and ownership benefits, while also carrying the cautionary tales of unchecked proximity and risks to judicial independence familiar since Nuremberg and Tokyo.[53]

Experience shows that governance must be taken more seriously in establishing new international courts and tribunals than has been the case to date. Reflecting critically on the field's directions thus far, contributors have also lamented the tendency to replicate elements of past institutional designs almost mechanically when conceiving new judicial governance regimes. Rightly emphasizing that 'financial governance can make or break a court' and calling for a more extensive, cross-temporal research into the courts' financial governance arrangements, Manolescu points out that 'diffusion by emulation' may be problematic. This is so particularly when it is not underpinned by a clear understanding of why a specific rule or practice emerged, how successfully it has operated, and whether there are sound reasons to follow or depart from

51 Henri de Waele, 'Managing the Realization of "The Hope of Ages"', in this volume.

52 Sergey Vasiliev, 'Governance of the International Military Tribunals at Nuremberg and Tokyo', in this volume.

53 Huw Llewellyn, 'Governance of the United Nations Criminal Tribunals', in this volume.

it in subsequent institution-building endeavours.[54] Likewise, Llewellyn advocated for a more concerted and systematic examination of the standards and practices that should be retained (or discarded) in future judicial governance schemes, as well as the merits and drawbacks of specific models for tribunal governance. This aspect has, regrettably, been a 'black hole' in the 'lessons learnt' from three decades of UN experience of setting up and running criminal tribunals.[55]

The field of international judicial governance will continue to be driven by both continuities and reinventions. Its future trajectories, however, should not be left to mere whim or accident but it should be defined by principled expertise- and experience-based choices and decisions that take into account legal parameters, the needs of judicial bodies and priorities of their mandate-givers, and any constraints imposed by the prevailing circumstances.

22.3.5 Centralized–polycentric governance

The spectrum of centralized–polycentric judicial governance is concerned with the measure of concentration of competences and functions in a single governance body or their distribution among multiple organs. The former approach is exemplified by SPLOS that governs ITLOS and the Assembly of States Parties for the ICC; the latter approach is represented, for instance, by the governance schemes of the UN courts, in which specific functions (or aspects thereof) are performed by different principal organs of the UN.[56]

Although 'decentralization' may seem the more intuitive opposite of 'centralization', 'polycentrism' presents itself as the more suitable counterpart. Judicial governance is—and should be—an ordered system in which power-holders—distinct centers or nodes in the governance 'network'—exercise their allocated roles and competences. They ought to do so without duplicating or encroaching upon one another's functions, as can occur under a completely 'decentralized' arrangement. Judge Abdulqawi Yusuf spoke astutely of 'polycentric governance' in relation to the election of ICJ judges, a process entrusted to the UN General Assembly and the Security Council acting autonomously, with the national groups of the Permanent Court of Arbitration playing a role in nominating candidates.[57] Forlati has also highlighted, in this connection, the formal involvement of academia and civil society in the nomination process and, therewith, the governance of the ICJ, although this does little to dilute the political character of that process.[58] Be that as it may, this turn of phrase—'polycentric governance'—has taken hold and can be used not only to describe and analyse other governance regimes and functions, but also to conceptualize judicial governance as a

[54] Adriana-Maria Manolescu, 'Financial Governance of International Courts and Tribunals', in this volume.
[55] Huw Llewellyn, 'Governance of the United Nations Criminal Tribunals', in this volume.
[56] For an overview: Niels Blokker, 'International Judicial Governance Institutions', Section 3.2, in this volume.
[57] Keynote address by Judge Abdulqawi A Yusuf (Addendum 1). For more on this aspect: Sergey Vasiliev, 'Governance of the International Military Tribunals at Nuremberg and Tokyo', Section 5.2, in this volume.
[58] Serena Forlati, 'Governance of the International Court of Justice', Section 6.2, in this volume.

phenomenon.[59] This perspective has surfaced in several theoretical and comparative analyses,[60] as well as in regime-specific chapters examining the governance models of particular courts.[61] The key question, or set of choices, this axis brings into focus is what approach is preferable under the relevant criteria: safeguarding judicial independence, ensuring the accountable and effective operation of the judiciary, and achieving efficient and responsive governance.

On the one hand, the polycentric approach entails the distribution or sharing of powers among several bodies, thus preventing the concentration of all competences in a single set of hands. This enables the different bodies to counterbalance and keep one another in check, thereby minimizing the risks of politicization and other governance malpractices—or containing their adverse effects when such risks materialize. As Judge Yusuf argued, the interposition of several organs within a polycentric institutional framework offers a more prudent and balanced arrangement, safeguarding judicial independence against undue external interference.[62] This observation is echoed in Llewellyn and Anoya's assessments of the operation of the management committees for the UN criminal tribunals. These were characterized by limited transparency and a monopolization of powers that posed particular risks to judicial independence and integrity—most notably in the case of the STL.[63] Moreover, Anoya reminds us of the STL management committee's failure to secure funding for the completion of its mandate, thereby casting doubt on the much-vaunted effectiveness of this model.[64]

On the other hand, the polycentric governance approach can also make decision-making more dispersed, formalistic, and sluggish, potentially creating problematic governance gaps and ownership deficits. This malaise is less likely to be encountered in courts and tribunals with a single dedicated governance body that consolidates all or some essential governance functions—such as said management committees, the SPLOS, or the ASP. Their exclusive focus on judicial governance—rather than treating this highly complex and specialist task as merely one among many—fosters a more competent expertise- and experience-driven, hands-on, problem-solving approach. This is in addition to shorter lines of communication, informal modalities, and quicker rapport that smaller bodies offer—advantages that may be lost in larger bureaucratized and/or politicized *injugovins* (eg the ASP or the UN organs).[65] For example, Deen-Racsmány demonstrates in detail in her chapter how the General Assembly and the Security Council failed to protect the IRMCT judge Akay from arrest and detention, avoiding a confrontation with Turkey and sacrificing the Tribunal's independence.[66] Would the same have happened if the Residual Mechanism had a

[59] ibid; Sergey Vasiliev, 'What Is (International) Judicial Governance?', in this volume.
[60] Sergey Vasiliev, 'What Is (International) Judicial Governance?' and Niels Blokker, 'International Judicial Governance Institutions', in this volume.
[61] Serena Forlati, 'Governance of the International Court of Justice', Misha Ariana Plagis and Karin Pluberg, 'Paper Lions?', and Huw Llewellyn, 'Governance of the United Nations Criminal Tribunals', in this volume.
[62] Keynote address by Judge Abdulqawi Ahmed Yusuf (Addendum 1).
[63] Huw Llewellyn, 'Governance of the United Nations Criminal Tribunals' and Evelyn Anoya, 'Governance of the Special Tribunal for Lebanon', in this volume.
[64] Evelyn Anoya, 'Governance of the Special Tribunal for Lebanon', Section 11.4.1, in this volume.
[65] Section 22.3.3.
[66] Zsuzsanna Deen-Racsmány, 'Deficient Protection of the Independence of International Judges by International Judicial Governance Institutions', in this volume.

single dedicated *injugovin*? We consider it less likely—provided, of course, that it operated as intended.

The centralized model is not beyond redemption, and unitary arrangements also offer important advantages. Architects of judicial governance frameworks would do well to combine the best of both worlds—taking into account the merits and risks of the centralized and polycentric paradigms—while steering clear of the worst of each: bureaucratic sprawl, indifference, or lack of real ownership, on the one hand, and unaccountable governance diktats coupled with tendencies to over-supervise and micromanage, on the other. The path forward may lie in envisaging dedicated governance institutions with powers and functions distributed or shared among these *injugovins*' autonomous subsidiary organs, each both willing and able to counterbalance the others in vigilantly protecting judicial independence while ensuring accountable and effective governance.

The field offers ample scope for institutional experimentation, capitalizing on the accumulated knowledge and experience. Moreover, it continues to generate demand for creative hybrid approaches that respond to the evolving needs of states and international organizations, as well as to the unique factual and legal-institutional contexts in which new international tribunals are created. The Management Committee for the Special Tribunal for the Crime of Aggression against Ukraine is the latest example of such demand-driven experimentation. The Committee will be established under the auspices of the Council of Europe pursuant to an enlarged partial agreement.[67] Comprising a broader membership, the Committee will be mandated to secure the necessary funding and carry out other 'administrative and managerial'—the better term would have been 'governance'—functions for the Tribunal while being expressly bound to respect the Tribunal's independence and the independence of its principals, staff, offices, and secretariat.[68] The window into (one variant of) the future of international judicial governance is already flung halfway open.

22.3.6 International–domestic

In this book focused on *international* judicial governance, the international–national dimension has proven more present and consequential than might appear at first sight. It has brought into focus the interplay, mutual influence, and occasional divergence between domestic and international concepts and ideas, institutions and arrangements, practices, and principles of judicial governance. In many contributions, this axis has provided inspiration and material for conceptual and definitional observations, and comparative and critical analyses, while also giving rise to normative insights, as well as methodological reflections and points of reference.

[67] Agreement between the Council of Europe and Ukraine on the Establishment of the Special Tribunal for the Crime of Aggression against Ukraine (signed in Strasbourg, 25 June 2025) art 5; Statute of the Management Committee of the Special Tribunal for the Crime of Aggression against Ukraine (appendix to draft Resolution CM/Res(2025)105, Committee of Ministers, 1532nd meeting, 18 June 2025) Art 2.

[68] Agreement between the Council of Europe and Ukraine (n 67) art 5(1); Statute of the Management Committee (n 67) Art 7.

In hindsight, this was unavoidable and will hardly surprise the reader. The dyad is key defining international courts as opposed to domestic courts—a contradistinction defied by some regional courts[69]—and is, by extension, indispensable to demarcating the field of international judicial governance. National systems remain the first natural and intuitive point of reference for lawyers, justice administrators, and legal experts. There is also an ongoing communication between the national and international adjudicative spheres in terms of expertise and professional communities, as domestic judges are appointed to international benches and may at times retain other functions in their home jurisdictions.[70]

One should also bear in mind that the concept of international adjudication is essentially an extrapolation—an adaptation of the ideal of independent and impartial courts from domestic settings to the international level. This is subject to important nuances dictated by the unique characteristics of the international legal order and international organizations' regimes, notably the inapplicability of the classic doctrine of the separation of powers.[71] Nevertheless, the logic of extrapolation applies fully to the related and self-evident notion that international courts, too, must be governed *properly*—that is, provided with appropriate legislative and institutional frameworks, highly qualified judges and staff, adequate financial resources, and other forms of practical and political support—if they are expected to fulfil their mandates. Like their national counterparts, independent courts remain dependent on external actors operating in the political domain for nearly every aspect of their work, apart from the core task of adjudicating individual cases.

Several contributions in this volume draw upon the international–domestic axis to address what it means to govern courts *properly*, highlighting the continuity of the normative ideals and key principles that shape judicial governance relationships across domestic and international legal orders. Blokker and Ruhangisa discuss the guiding principles of judicial independence, accountability, and the rule of law, underscoring their relevance in this context.[72] Llewellyn and Manolescu emphasize that those principles, though originally developed for national courts, are tested—and often proven inconclusive—when confronted with challenges exogenous to domestic systems.[73] There is both room and need to develop further and solidifying the current international (soft-)law framework on judicial independence, tailored specifically to international courts, in particular in their relationships with governing bodies.

Further legal order-based nuances affect the normative content and interpretations of independence and accountability. Unlike national courts, their international

[69] Referring to the CJEU as 'the domestic court of the European Union': Heikki Kanninen, 'Governance of the Court of Justice of the European Union', in this volume.

[70] On part-time international appointments and combination of functions as potentially problematic for judicial independence and accountability: Misha Ariana Plagis and Karin Pluberg, 'Paper Lions?', Section 8.3.3, in this volume.

[71] Heikki Kanninen, 'Governance of the Court of Justice of the European Union', Section 9.3, in this volume. For discussion: Sergey Vasiliev, 'What Is (International) Judicial Governance?', in this volume.

[72] Niels Blokker, 'International Judicial Governance Institutions', Section 3.5 and John Eudes Ruhangisa, 'Governance of Regional Integration Courts', Sections 7.2.3, 7.3.1–7.3.2, and 7.3.7, in this volume.

[73] Huw Llewellyn, 'Governance of the United Nations Criminal Tribunals', Adriana-Maria Manolescu, 'Financial Governance of International Courts and Tribunals', and Nicolas Guillou and Adriana-Maria Manolescu, 'The Three-Layered Governance Model', in this volume.

counterparts are either international organizations or organs thereof—a layer of activity which, as Guillou and Manolescu make clear, requires that they be governed accordingly. They must be equipped with appropriate external and internal oversight and accountability mechanisms—and this should not necessarily give rise to an impression that judicial independence is being sacrificed to (micro-)managerialism or, worse still, to political expedience.[74]

Many chapters contrast international arrangements against the models of judicial governance at the domestic level. Thus, observing that the role of registrars at international courts diverges from their counterparts in national courts, Anoya queries whether international registries indeed ought to operate under the authority of court presidents and, more broadly, what degree of involvement of court presidents in matters of administrative operation and servicing of the tribunals is appropriate.[75] Kanninen notes that the EU judicial system lacks both a ministry of justice and an autonomous governance body of the judicial-council type. This configuration ensures a higher degree of judicial independence for the CJEU, along with its particularly broad autonomy in matters of justice administration, which makes comparisons with national and even (other) international courts difficult.[76] Guillou and Manolescu invoke the domestic judicial-council model to support the notion that judicial organizations must be subject to mechanisms ensuring judicial discipline and accountability.[77]

Readers less familiar with the historical and comparative background of this model could situate these references in the context of the earlier discussion in Part I, highlighting both its associated promises and deliverables, as well as precautions drawn from domestic experience.[78] Guillou and Manolescu note that there is no 'supreme judicial council' at the international level—parenthetically and emphatically—*yet*, while pointing to the IER's recommendation to establish a judicial audit committee to review the administration of justice and a judicial council to decide complaints against elected officials, both envisaged as potentially servicing several tribunals.

International institutional lawyers and judicial governance experts can look for inspiration in domestic experience with developing, reforming, and addressing the challenges of different models of judicial governance. There is much to learn from when it comes to the governance of national courts. Yet, they would be ill-advised to copy-paste solutions or apply 'lessons learnt' directly to 'their' courts: the contexts are incommensurably different. Should an international judicial council ever materialize, it would be imperative that it be designed first and foremost with the unique features and circumstances of international courts in mind. Given the significant idiosyncrasies in their legal-institutional contexts, no domestic prototype—however perfect or promising it may seem—would provide a ready-made fit. This underscores both the

[74] Nicolas Guillou and Adriana-Maria Manolescu, 'The Three-Layered Governance Model', in this volume. For cautionary notes on the African context: John Eudes Ruhangisa, 'Governance of Regional Integration Courts', Section 7.3.1, in this volume.

[75] Evelyn Anoya, 'Governance of the Special Tribunal for Lebanon', Section 11.3.2, in this volume.

[76] Heikki Kanninen, 'Governance of the Court of Justice of the European Union', Sections 9.2 and 9.6, in this volume.

[77] Heikki Kanninen, 'Governance of the Court of Justice of the European Union', Section 9.2.2, in this volume.

[78] Sergey Vasiliev, 'What Is (International) Judicial Governance?', in this volume.

value and the limits of the international–domestic perspective: it offers an analytical spectrum, not a repertory of interchangeable recipes and blueprints.

Finally, this dimension comes to the fore in chapters examining the specific functions of *injugovins*, some of which are performed—at least in part—directly by states. It is here that the international and the domestic intersect most closely, tangibly shaping the reality and directions of international judicial governance. A prime example is the enforcement of judicial decisions and, more generally, the respect states show—or not—for international courts' mandates.[79] Another is the process of judicial nominations and elections. The positions and votes of individual states and state blocs on these matters—like on most others—are informed by their political preferences and interests, their views on the role and authority of those courts, their attitudes towards the international judicial function, and their perception of the need for qualified judges in international courts. In this sense, the 'domestic' proves highly consequential for the 'international'. Procedures and practices for judicial nomination at the state level affect the pool of candidates who stand for, and are ultimately elected to, international judicial office.[80] Securing the high quality of an international bench is impossible unless the procedure compels states—at the risk of embarrassment and electoral defeat—to put forward their very best candidates. Independent expert advisory panels tasked with screening nominees are no silver bullet for the persistent problems with judicial elections to international benches. They do, however, help to narrow the gap in expectations between the international demand and the domestic supply.[81]

22.3.7 Law–politics

The juxtaposition and interplay of law and politics in international judicial governance emerges as the central preoccupation for most contributors to this volume. Adjudication—the main purpose and core activity of international courts and tribunals—is meant, and claims, to be insulated from politics, as the cornerstone principle of judicial independence demands. While the idea of apolitical international justice understandably attracts scepticism, substantial legal, organizational, and discursive efforts continue to be invested in shielding international judging from political pressure and undue external influences.

By contrast, international judicial governance is the realm where political interests and international power politics travel freely and reign (almost) supreme. The alignment of 'political stars' and consolidation of political will give birth to international courts—just as political misalignment and the dissipation of that will bring about their demise. Referring to the 'unexpected and sudden dissolution' of the Civil Service

[79] Dorine Nauleau, 'The Enforcement of International Judicial Decisions' and Hanneke Palm and Roeland Böcker, 'Implementation of Judgments of the European Court of Human Rights', in this volume. On the execution of African regional courts' rulings: John Eudes Ruhangisa, 'Governance of Regional Integration Courts', Section 7.3.6, in this volume.

[80] Christian M De Vos and others, 'Electing the Best?', in this volume.

[81] Andrew Drzemczewski, 'The Election of Judges onto the European Court of Human Rights' and Christiaan Timmermans, 'The Procedure for Nominating Members of the EU Courts', in this volume.

Tribunal, Kanninen highlights the (dis)continuity in the functioning of EU specialized courts, as opposed to the Court of Justice and the General Court, as an illustration of this kind of vulnerability.[82] The STL is another case in point: as discussed by Anoya, it was established when there was sufficient political will to support Lebanon in its fight against impunity for terrorist attacks, but was discontinued once relevant states began to waver and 'no longer wanted to fund it'.[83] In a similar vein, John Eudes Ruhangisa as well as Plagis and Pluberg discuss political oscillations in respect of regional integration and human rights courts on the African continent.[84] Relevant patterns of state behaviour include reluctance to confer human rights jurisdiction on these courts, unwillingness to permit judges to sit on a full-time basis, and the political backlash provoked by unfavourable judgments.

Beyond spectacular acts of creating and terminating courts, the regulatory frameworks, institutional designs, and processes of judicial governance are, to a significant extent, the outgrowth of political agreements and trade-offs. Decision-making (and in some cases indecision) within *injugovins* is informed by relations among states, and between states and the judicial institutions governed. States' political interests and rivalries inevitably impact their agendas and priorities in judicial governance fora, as well as their cooperation with, and demands toward, the courts. As Silvia Fernández de Gurmendi aptly notes, the organs and officials of *injugovins* are required to navigate and, where possible, reconcile the 'various and sometimes opposing interests and goals' of states parties.[85] Every judicial governance function bears the indelible mark of politics, from the adoption of legislation and judicial elections to the approval of court budgets, the enforcement of rulings, and providing courts with political backing.

Taken to the extreme, international judicial governance can be thought of as *the politics* of (and around) international courts. Yet this view does not do justice to the significant role that law and legal expertise play in this field. As the preceding chapters demonstrate, judicial governance is by no means exhausted or wholly absorbed by the political dimension. Politics are here to stay—but so is law. Politicians and lawyers, in governments and in the international civil service alike, will continue to vie for influence and control, bringing their acumen, professional projects, and agendas to bear on the shaping and operationalization of judicial governance institutions, practices, and norms. In this sphere, the boundaries between 'the legal' and 'the political' are constantly shifting, as these dimensions interpenetrate and compete for territory.[86] This dynamic is amply illustrated by the chapters addressing specific governance regimes as well as functions, such as the nomination and election of international judges, financial governance, and enforcement.

To use the former as the example, international judicial nominations and elections represent a sphere where states—and political considerations—traditionally held

[82] Heikki Kanninen, 'Governance of the Court of Justice of the European Union', in this volume.

[83] Evelyn Anoya, 'Governance of the Special Tribunal for Lebanon', in this volume.

[84] John Eudes Ruhangisa, 'Governance of Regional Integration Courts' and Misha Ariana Plagis and Karin Pluberg, 'Paper Lions?', in this volume.

[85] Silvia Fernández de Gurmendi, 'Challenges to the Governance of the International Criminal Court', Section 18.2, in this volume.

[86] On this interplay: Kritika Sharma, 'The Assembly of States Parties to the International Criminal Court: A Good Governance Approach' (PhD thesis, Leiden Law School, April 2025) 3–4.

sway, as De Vos, Pena, and Khudayri discuss in their chapter.[87] From the earliest antecedents, efforts have been made to temper the impact of politics on the composition of international benches by ensuring, as far as possible, the merit-based character of the process. While the second stage—the election of judges within international parliamentary organs or bodies of government representatives—remains largely impervious to depoliticization, the first stage, namely the nomination of candidates for the election as international judges, has been the main focus of endeavours to ensure that the most qualified candidates are selected.

At the PCIJ and subsequently at the ICJ, judicial candidates were/are nominated by the PCA national groups rather than by government representatives, in order to facilitate the election of independent and deserving candidates.[88] In the courts where governments nominate candidates, states are either obliged to present more than one candidate—eg three for the ECtHR and the Andean Court of Justice—or permitted to do so, as at the Inter-American Court of Human Rights and the African Court of Human and Peoples' Rights.[89] Increasingly, the screening of judicial nominees is entrusted to independent expert panels that provide non-binding opinions on their qualifications before election or appointment. A notable example is the Article 255 Panel, which examines the suitability of candidate judges and candidate advocates-general of the Court of Justice and the General Court of the EU on the basis of written materials and hearings, reporting in private to member states.[90] Another is the Advisory Panel of Experts on Candidates for Election as Judge to the European Court of Human Rights, which issues findings prior to formal nomination to assist the Committee on the Election of Judges (AS/Cdh) of the Parliamentary Assembly of the Council of Europe, itself responsible for interviewing nominees and producing recommendations for the Assembly.[91] A third is the Advisory Committee on Nominations of Judges of the ICC, which performs a similar function for the ICC's Assembly of States Parties, in particular interviewing judicial candidates—over and above roundtables with them led by state and civil society representatives.[92]

Neither of these systems—hard-won achievements though they are—is perfect by design or in practice.[93] States still retain room to stall and circumvent them, for example by delaying or refusing to nominate candidates where they are expected to

[87] Christian M De Vos and others, 'Electing the Best?', Section 19.4, in this volume.

[88] Niels Blokker, 'International Judicial Governance Institutions', Section 3.3.1, Henri de Waele, 'Managing the Realization of "The Hope of Ages"', and Serena Forlati, 'Governance of the International Court of Justice', in this volume. Reporting concerns on the operation of this nomination system: Christian M De Vos and others, 'Electing the Best?', in this volume.

[89] Christian M De Vos and others, 'Electing the Best?' and Misha Ariana Plagis and Karin Pluberg, 'Paper Lions?', in this volume.

[90] Heikki Kanninen, 'Governance of the Court of Justice of the European Union', Section 9.4.1 and Christiaan Timmermans, 'The Procedure for Nominating Members of the EU Courts', in this volume.

[91] Andrew Drzemczewski, 'The Election of Judges onto the European Court of Human Rights' and Christian M De Vos and others, 'Electing the Best?', in this volume.

[92] Silvia Fernández de Gurmendi, 'Challenges to the Governance of the International Criminal Court', Section 18.5.1, in this volume and Christian M De Vos and others, 'Electing the Best?', in this volume.

[93] Acknowledging that the ASP 'has been slow in undertaking the appropriate actions to ensure the selection of the best possible candidates' for ICC judges: Silvia Fernández de Gurmendi, 'Challenges to the Governance of the International Criminal Court', Section 18.5.3, in this volume.

do so.[94] Yet these examples demonstrate clearly that the nomination and election of members of (some) international courts are no longer the exclusive province of politics. The work of independent expert panels goes some way towards ensuring that the best qualified persons are nominated and elected. Their procedures have steadily improved, and calls have been made for them to draw lessons from each other's work. Timmermans has suggested that the EU's arrangements should mirror those of the Council of Europe. The Council of Europe's Advisory Panel transmits its assessment of the candidates to the nominating government *before* the final list of candidates is conveyed to the Parliamentary Assembly, which elects the judges. By contrast, the EU's Article 255 Panel forwards its assessments directly to the member state governments. In case of a negative assessment, the EU procedure is more painful both for the candidate and for the government concerned, and it may even deter highly qualified individuals from standing.[95]

Politics cannot—and, some would argue, should not—be fully extricated from the sphere of international judicial governance; indeed, the same is true more generally at the national level. Rather, politics could potentially be corseted by legal requirements and kept in check by procedures and channelled into fora appropriate for political debate and action. In such settings, political engagement can contribute constructively to enabling the independent, accountable, and effective operation of international courts. For example, states, acting individually and collectively as part of *injugovins*, should use political levers to secure enforcement of judicial ruling and to counter non-cooperation by recalcitrant members.[96] Legal procedures thus serve to canalize political dynamics and interests into spaces where they can play out without damaging the integrity and independence of judicial institutions. Accordingly, even when elections are shaped by political voting, and hence notorious practices such as vote-trading,[97] the risk of appointing substandard judges is mitigated if the nomination process is merit-based and the candidate pool consists solely of highly qualified individuals.

22.4 Future Directions

There are many vectors along which future research into international judicial governance could fruitfully be pursued. Such research might take up the threads left by this volume—with its focus on institutions, practices, and norms—and carry them further. As noted at the outset, dozens of lesser-known past and existing courts remain underexplored, along with their governance schemes. Much more 'raw material' still lies to be unearthed and analysed as part of the emerging judicial governance

[94] Discussing this problem in relation to the CJEU: Heikki Kanninen, 'Governance of the Court of Justice of the European Union', Section 9.4.1, in this volume.

[95] Christiaan Timmermans, 'The Procedure for Nominating Members of the EU Courts', in this volume.

[96] On this, Niels Blokker, 'International Judicial Governance Institutions', Section 3.3.3, John Eudes Ruhangisa, 'Governance of Regional Integration Courts', Section 7.3.6, Dorine Nauleau, 'The Enforcement of International Judicial Decisions', and Hanneke Palm and Roeland Böcker, 'Implementation of Judgments of the European Court of Human Rights', in this volume.

[97] Silvia Fernández de Gurmendi, 'Challenges to the Governance of the International Criminal Court', Section 18.5.3, and Christian M De Vos and others, 'Electing the Best?', in this volume.

acquis, including in relation to fledgling courts and those yet to be established. This book has sought to take initial steps in that direction and to move beyond a mere scratching of the surface, albeit within the confines of international institutional law. Prospective historical and comparative work should extend beyond law, engaging interdisciplinary approaches to *injugovins* and their practice. Before wrapping up, it remains to sketch a few lines of inquiry and highlight open questions that merit attention in forthcoming research on international judicial governance.

22.4.1 Objectives

What is international judicial governance for? What objectives does it serve—both in relation to international courts generally and in specialized areas of international law—and are these objectives consistent across the board? Is the governance of international justice merely an adjectival function, in the sense of enabling, servicing, and supporting courts in the exercise of their judicial mandates, and thus subordinate to the courts' primary mission? Or can it also rest on a different logic, one that is directional and strategic, allowing *injugovins* to approach judicial institutions instrumentally on behalf of mandate providers and to steer them in directions deemed desirable from an international (legal) policy perspective? If so, how does this logic vary across different *injugovins* and courts? Where governance is underpinned by multiple, and at times competing, objectives, which of them should take priority, by what principles should they be balanced, and how should conflicts among divergent stakeholder interests be resolved? In particular, in cases where *injugovins* or states exercise their 'sovereign' prerogative to terminate a tribunal—whether on grounds of redundancy of its mandate or due to the unwillingness to continue funding it—how should that decision be weighed against the imperatives of judicial independence, the integrity of judicial mandates, the interests of complainants and victims (in the case of human rights tribunals and criminal courts), and other rationales rooted in the judicial character of the institution? The acts of curtailing judicial mandates and dissolving international courts raise fundamental questions about the constraints applicable to such decisions and, relatedly, accountability of *injugovins* and states for them.[98]

22.4.2 Principles and constraints

The foregoing chapters have demonstrated that the supposed dilemma between judicial independence and judicial accountability is a false one. It must be 'and', not 'versus'; the two principles are interdependent and central to judicial governance. Yet many questions persist across individual governance regimes as to how these principles can be translated into concrete arrangements that achieve an appropriate balance in areas such as financial oversight, judicial elections, and the handling of alleged misconduct by elected officials.

[98] Sections 22.4.2 and 22.4.4.

The obligations and responsibilities of *injugovins*—and of states constituting them—towards the courts and tribunals they govern remain particularly underdeveloped and should become a focus of attention in future research. International courts and their officials can generally be held accountable: existing mechanisms may be imperfect and in need of fine-tuning, but the notion of 'unaccountable' international courts is a myth. By contrast, and paradoxically, international judicial governance itself remains a largely unaccountable affair.[99] Valuable institutional lessons that should become part of the judicial governance *acquis* are rarely recorded, let alone learnt and applied. Institutional mishaps and crises—which may be caused by 'ungovernance'—typically sink into oblivion without feeding into institutional prevention strategies.[100] Worse still, cases of outright 'misgovernance'—glaring, systematic failures or abuses of governance mandates such as those highlighted by Ruhangisa, Deen-Racsmány, and Van den Bossche—remain unaddressed, with relevant actors facing no consequences. There are no clear legal standards or effective institutional mechanisms to deal with them. Accountability vacuums in the operation of judicial governance institutions heighten the risk of compromising judicial independence and eroding compliance with the rule of law.[101] *Quis custodiet ipsos custodes?* The answer to this question given thus far has been horizontal self-regulation; states are expected and implored to constrain themselves and one another.[102] But is this truly the best international institutional lawyers can offer—and can they do better?

With judicial governance powers and prerogatives must also come governance obligations and duties of care towards the relevant courts, as well as responsibilities towards the actors and stakeholders affected by their work. Future research should seek to ascertain and clarify those obligations and responsibilities more precisely, both within existing legal frameworks and as part of normative standards *de lege ferenda*. Equally important is the question of accountability: how can such rules and standards be given teeth and made opposable and enforceable?

Making international judicial governance accountable is a long-term project, one that will require substantial developments in law and in institutional frameworks. Significant progress has been taken at the regional level, for example within the European Union and the Council of Europe. In both systems, the role of governments in nominating and electing judges to the Luxembourg and Strasbourg courts has been curtailed by the involvement of independent expert bodies assessing the suitability of candidates.[103] In the Council of Europe, the Parliamentary Assembly elects the judges of the European Court of Human Rights, meaning that accountability for

[99] Noting that the oversight of regional courts in Africa is performed by the summits of heads of state that 'are not accountable to anybody': John Eudes Ruhangisa, 'Governance of Regional Integration Courts', Section 7.3.7, in this volume.

[100] On this terminology, see Sergey Vasiliev, 'What Is (International) Judicial Governance?', Section 2.4.4, in this volume.

[101] John Eudes Ruhangisa, 'Governance of Regional Integration Courts', Section 7.3.7, in this volume.

[102] Adriana-Maria Manolescu, 'Financial Governance of International Courts and Tribunals', in this volume; Sergey Vasiliev, 'Justitia and Leviathans: The Struggle for the International Rule of Law (inaugural lecture, Open University of the Netherlands, 13 June 2025) <www.ou.nl/documents/40554/10543295/25115_Oratieboekje_Sergey_Vasiliev.pdf#page=21>.

[103] Andrew Drzemczewski, 'The Election of Judges onto the European Court of Human Rights' and Christiaan Timmermans, 'The Procedure for Nominating Members of the EU Courts', in this volume.

judicial governance rests with the Assembly, not only the member states. If the quality of individual judges is later questioned by the member states, these governments can plausibly shift the blame to the Assembly. This is different in the European Union, where judges are appointed by common accord of the governments of the member states, leaving accountability with them. No similar arrangements have been adopted elsewhere.[104] In other regions of the world, and at the global level, judicial governance remains for the most part unaccountable.[105] The 2020 Independent Expert Review of the International Criminal Court provided a welcome exception. Its extensive assessment, containing 384 short- and long-term recommendations addressed not only the functioning of the Court but also that of the Assembly of States Parties, thus extending accountability to the governance level itself.[106] This is exactly what was needed.

22.4.3 Structure and functioning of *injugovins*

A key institutional question is the extent to which *injugovins* are more than the sum of the member states. In earlier chapters, we distinguished three main categories of *injugovins*: (i) governance institutions that are organs of an international organization of which the relevant court is also a part; (ii) treaty organs (eg the ICC's ASP and SPLOS for ITLOS); and (iii) ad hoc gatherings of states.[107] As several authors expressly acknowledge, governance arrangements in practice often combine elements of these models.[108] The question arises in this connection: are the first and second categories better equipped to perform judicial governance functions than the third? In addition, as discussed in connection with the centralized–polycentric dyad: does a dedicated *injugovin* (eg the ICC-ASP) offer stronger guarantees for safeguarding the independent functioning of an international court than *injugovins* such as the UN's General Assembly and Security Council, whose mandates are far broader and more diffuse? Which types of *injugovins* are better placed, and more inclined, to stand up for their courts when these come under political attack—whether through financial sanctions, entry bans on elected officials, or criminal cases against them? What institutional rules and practices have proven more effective in providing robust guarantees of 'good governance'?

This volume records numerous experiences and potential lessons from the still relatively short history of *injugovins*. These lessons concern both institutional 'design flaws' to be avoided when new tribunals are established and 'maintenance conditions' necessary to sustain their effective operation in practice. The fate of the WTO Appellate Body offers a prime example: no single state should be able to paralyze an

[104] On the African Union: Misha Ariana Plagis and Karin Pluberg, 'Paper Lions?', Section 8.2.3, in this volume.

[105] John Eudes Ruhangisa, 'Governance of Regional Integration Courts', in this volume.

[106] Silvia Fernández de Gurmendi, 'Challenges to the Governance of the International Criminal Court', in this volume.

[107] Niels Blokker, 'International Judicial Governance Institutions', in this volume.

[108] Eg on judicial governance within the African Union: Misha Ariana Plagis and Karin Pluberg, 'Paper Lions?', in this volume, Section 8.2.3; also Sergey Vasiliev, 'What Is (International) Judicial Governance?', Section 2.4.3, in this volume.

international court or tribunal by blocking the election of new members.[109] Likewise, reliance on voluntary contributions as the sole source of funding has proven unsustainable.[110] Yet even absent evident design flaws, *injugovins* can only discharge their functions effectively if their members stand firmly behind 'their' courts throughout their lifespan. This entails a range of legal obligations and duties of care: ensuring the appointment of the most qualified judges, providing adequate financing, and fully respecting and implementing judicial decisions. States should not behave as 'bad losers' when outcomes are unfavourable. Rather, they must recognize that with independent and effective international courts, they may well prevail in future disputes, and—more importantly—that faithful compliance with judgments serves the long-term common interest of all states and their citizens.

22.4.4 Underperformance

Some governance functions are characterized by severe underperformance across most institutional regimes. Chief among these are the enforcement of judicial decisions and the protection of international courts from undermining from within and politicized backlash and attacks from without.[111] Particularly in recent years, non-implementation—or delayed and inadequate implementation—of international court judgments has become increasingly common, notwithstanding the binding obligations of states.

In the long run, such non-compliance erodes the effectiveness, authority, and credibility of international adjudication. Why should states create and sustain international courts if their decisions are not taken seriously? If states are genuine about upholding and strengthening the rule of law in the international community—as their creation and funding of numerous international courts in recent decades suggests—they must act consistently: owning the full implications of their own principled decisions, assuming responsibility, and accepting that they can be held accountable if they fail to do so. The genie of international justice is out of the bottle, and states were well aware of the consequences each time they chose to uncork it. However, the persistent subversion of global and regional judicial mandates, coupled with sustained political attacks against some international courts, leaves little doubt that many—including most powerful—states did not truly embrace the idea of strong and independent international justice. This will remain an uphill battle in the years to come.

[109] Peter Van den Bossche, 'The Demise of the WTO Appellate Body', in this volume.

[110] Adriana-Maria Manolescu, 'Financial Governance of International Courts and Tribunals', in this volume.

[111] On enforcement challenges: Niels Blokker, 'International Judicial Governance Institutions', Section 3.4.1 ('rather underdeveloped'; 'an area in which states are reluctant to relinquish control'), Dorine Nauleau, 'The Enforcement of International Judicial Decisions', and John Eudes Ruhangisa, 'Governance of Regional Integration Courts', Section 7.3.6, in this volume. On the backlash against regional courts in Africa: John Eudes Ruhangisa, 'Governance of Regional Integration Courts' and Misha Ariana Plagis and Karin Pluberg, 'Paper Lions?', in this volume. On threats and attacks against the ICC and its officials: Silvia Fernández de Gurmendi, 'Challenges to the Governance of the International Criminal Court', Section 18.5.4, in this volume; Vasiliev (n 102).

A core function of *injugovins* is to contribute to the enforcement of judicial decisions. Over the years, various rules, practices, and procedures have emerged to support this function—for instance, the Committee of Ministers of the Council of Europe plays a supervisory role in overseeing the execution of ECtHR judgments.[112] But overall, the role of *injugovins* in this essential area remains very limited. Future research should therefore examine how governance regimes can be tightened and strengthened to address enforcement challenges more effectively: what legal and institutional reforms are needed, and how could the attitudes and behaviours of states be changed to ensure better compliance?

22.5 Coda

The conversation between the two poets in 'The First Step' by Konstantínos Kaváfis reminds us that the true value of one's journey lies not in reaching a particular destination, but in appreciating the landscapes travelled and the worth of the ground covered:

> Even that first step, even the first,
> is very far removed from the common lot.
> In order for you to proceed upon this stair
> you must claim your right to be
> a citizen of the city of ideas.
> It is difficult, and rare as well,
> to be entered into that city's rolls.
> In its agora you'll find Legislators
> whom no mere adventurer can fool.
> To have got this far is no small thing;
> what you have done is a glorious honor.[113]

The conclusion of this collective endeavour is not an end in itself, but the first step on the path that lies ahead. In this spirit, we hope that the closing of this book will open many new ones.

[112] In detail: Hanneke Palm and Roeland Böcker, 'Implementation of Judgments of the European Court of Human Rights', in this volume.
[113] Excerpt from 'The First Step' (1899) in Constantine P Cavafy, *Poems: Selected with Translation and Notes by Daniel Mendelsohn* (Alfred A Knopf 2014) 141.

PART VII
ADDENDA: KEYNOTE ADDRESSES

ADDENDUM 1

Governance of the International Court of Justice

Keynote address*
Abdulqawi Ahmed Yusuf
President, International Court of Justice

1. It is a great pleasure to address you today at the inaugural conference on the Governance of International Courts and Tribunals: Ensuring Judicial Independence and Accountability. I would like to thank the University of Leiden, and in particular Professor Blokker, for organizing a forum to discuss the important issues of governance of international courts and tribunals.
2. Out of this broad theme, I intend to address a narrower aspect. That is, the governance of the International Court of Justice (to which I will refer as the 'ICJ or 'the Court') and the principle of judicial independence.

I. Introductory Remarks

3. Before I delve into the main theme, I will make some preliminary remarks on governance. What do we mean when we say 'governance of international courts'?
4. In the early 1990s, a Commission on Global Governance was established and produced a report, titled *Our Global Neighbourhood*. This report defined 'governance' as

> the sum of the many ways individuals and institutions, public and private, manage their common affairs. It is a continuing process through which conflicting or diverse interests may be accommodated and cooperative action may be taken. It includes formal institutions and regimes empowered to enforce compliance, as well as informal arrangements that people and institutions either have agreed to or perceive to be in their interest.[1]

5. I must say, I found this definition both too broad and too abstract.

* Keynote address delivered at the inaugural conference 'Governance of International Courts and Tribunals: Ensuring Judicial Independence and Accountability' (Leiden, 20–21 September 2019).

[1] Commission on Global Governance, *Our Global Neighbourhood* (1995) ch 1 at 2.

6. What we most often hear in daily life with regard to governance is a reference either to 'good governance' or 'bad governance', which means that governance is always qualified in terms of its potential outcome. We might therefore start from there. Those of you who may have seen Ambrogio Lorenzetti's *Allegory of Good and Bad Government* in the Palazzo Pubblico of Siena, Italy, will remember that it is flanked by two other paintings, one showing the effects of good governance and the other, the effects of bad governance. In the first, people dance in the streets; there are well-tended fields that yield a plentiful harvest; and merchants exchange goods and make profits. It is a city ruled by Justice. In the second, there is a scene of violence, disease and decay. It is a city ruled by Tyranny.
7. A second example which can also help us bring governance into perspective is the fact that good governance is one of the main indicators of Bhutan's Gross National Happiness. In other words, good governance may contribute to the happiness of the population of a country.
8. So, how does this apply to courts, since I am quite sure that when we say 'governance of international courts', what we have in mind is their 'good governance'? We do not wish 'bad governance' of international tribunals, which have to deliver the Justice that Ambrogio Lorenzetti admired so much in his depictions already in the fourteenth-century city-state of Siena. There is indeed a text on the wall under the frescos, which reads as follows: 'Turn your eyes to behold her, you who are governing, who is portrayed here, Justice, crowned on account of her excellence, who always renders to everyone his due.'
9. The question is: what would 'good governance' imply in the case of judicial institutions? What outcome should be associated with 'good governance' in the case of courts? It is, in my view, first of all, the independence and impartiality of the institution and, secondly, its ability to deliver justice without outside interference or influence.
10. Having this desirable outcome in mind, let me now take you to the nature and structure of the governance of the International Court of Justice as it has evolved over the years, so that we can assess whether it can result in the kind of outcome that we associate with 'good governance' for an international court.

II. The Governance of the PCIJ

11. The ICJ displays some historical and institutional peculiarities in terms of governance, since it is the successor to the Permanent Court of International Justice (the 'PCIJ'). So, we have to start from there.
12. Strictly speaking, the PCIJ was not an organ of the League of Nations in the sense of Article 2 of the Covenant of the League; it was not created by the Covenant.[2] Rather, it had a legal status separate and distinct from that of the

[2] Vera Gowlland-Debbas, 'Article 7 UN Charter' in Andreas Zimmermann and others (eds), *The Statute of the International Court of Justice: A Commentary* (2nd edn, OUP 2012) 93–94.

League.[3] Pursuant to Article 14 of the Covenant,[4] the Council appointed an Advisory Committee of Jurists to prepare a draft Statute, which was then revised and approved by the Council on 28 October 1920.[5] After approval by the Assembly on 13 December 1920, the Statute was attached to a protocol dated 16 December 1920, which was opened for signature.[6]

13. The legal separation between the PCIJ and the League had some legal consequences. First of all, the Members of the League of Nations were not automatically parties to the PCIJ Statute, even though they were expected to contribute to its budget.[7] Secondly, Article 1 of the PCIJ Statute provided that the PCIJ was 'in addition to' the Permanent Court of Arbitration and the special Tribunals of Arbitration to which states are always at liberty to submit their disputes for settlement. The PCIJ was not considered as the 'principal judicial organ' of the League of Nations, but an addition to the existing dispute settlement bodies available to States.

III. The Governance of the ICJ

14. Although the Statute is the same, the governance structure of the ICJ is quite different. Under Article 7 of the Charter, the Court was established as one of the 'principal organs' of the United Nations ('UN'). Under Article 92, the Court's Statute forms an 'integral part' of the Charter. Thus, UN Members are automatically parties to the Court's Statute.

15. The establishment of the Court under the Charter as one of the principal organs of the UN was meant to ensure that it would not be subordinate to any of the political organs of the UN. The drafters of the Charter sought to create a system of governance of the Court based on two pillars: judicial independence and administrative autonomy. While these two notions are closely linked, they serve different purposes. I will therefore address each of them in turn.

A. Judicial independence of the ICJ

16. The Charter and the Statute of the Court seek to ensure the judicial independence of the Court not only from states, but also from other organs of the United Nations. This is done in three main ways.

[3] ibid.

[4] Article 14 of the Covenant of the League of Nations provided that the Council would 'submit to the Members of the League for adoption plans for the establishment of a Permanent Court of International Justice'.

[5] Ole Spiermann, 'Historical Introduction' in Zimmermann and others (n 2) 52.

[6] Protocol of Signature relating to the Statute of the Permanent Court of International Justice provided for by Article 14 of the Covenant of the League of Nations (Geneva, 16 December 1920) League of Nations Treaty Series 1921 Vol 6 ('PCIJ Statute') Art 4.

[7] Spiermann (n 5) 58.

17. First and foremost, as pointed out above, the independence of the Court derives from its nature as the principal judicial organ of the UN. In its Advisory Opinion on the *Competence of the General Assembly for the Admission of a State to the United Nations*, the Court pointed out that the principal organs of the UN are equal amongst themselves.[8]
18. This equality implies that the Court does not and cannot entertain political pressures from any other organ. Thus, in the *Namibia* Advisory Opinion, the Court rejected South Africa's allegations of 'political pressure' applied to it by the Security Council, noting that:

> the very nature of the Court as the principal judicial organ of the United Nations [is] an organ which, in that capacity, acts only on the basis of the law, independently of all outside influence or interventions whatsoever, in the exercise of the judicial function entrusted to it alone by the Charter and its Statute. A court functioning as a court of law can act in no other way.[9]

19. Secondly, an essential component of the governance of the Court meant to ensure its judicial independence is the method for the election of its judges. This method is unique in the UN system. It does not rely on a single organ alone to elect judges. Instead, it spreads the election process among multiple actors at different stages. This is what I will describe as 'polycentric governance'.
20. As you all know, the election of the judges is entrusted under the Statute to two organs of the UN acting independently of each other: the UN General Assembly (UNGA) and the UN Security Council (UNSC). These two organs elect the judges on the basis of a list of persons nominated by the national groups of the Permanent Court of Arbitration (the 'PCA'). Under Articles 8 and 10 of the Statute, successful candidates must obtain an absolute majority in both organs, which 'shall proceed independently of one another to elect the members of the Court'. Moreover, the election procedure requires the General Assembly and the Security Council to take steps to prevent any communications passing between them before the announcement of the official results; this is 'to ensure independence for the voting in the two organs which have to carry out the election of the judges simultaneously'.[10]
21. In order to understand this 'polycentric' arrangement, we must go back to the process of elaboration of the Statute of the PCIJ. It is indeed an arrangement which was the fruit of considerable efforts to ensure the independent function of the PCIJ. At its origin is the 'Root-Phillimore' proposal, intended to vest the

[8] *Competence of the General Assembly for the Admission of a State to the United Nations*, Advisory Opinion of 3 March 1950, ICJ Reports 1950, p 8 ('The General Assembly and the Security Council are both principal organs of the United Nations. The Charter does not place the Security Council in a subordinate position').

[9] *Legal Consequences for States of the Continued Presence of South Africa in Namibia (South West Africa) notwithstanding Security Council Resolution 276 (1970)*, Advisory Opinion of 21 June 1971, ICJ Reports 1971, p 23, para 29.

[10] Resolution on 'The Composition of the International Court of Justice' (1952-II) 44 *Annuaire de l'Institut de Droit International* 474–75, para 2.

power of electing the judges in the Assembly and the Council of the League,[11] to ensure appropriate checks and balances between the small and great Powers of the time, by a simultaneous election. In the words of Mr Root:

> The practical effect of the idea would be to assure to the small Powers the protection of their interests by the Assembly where they are in the majority and to the great Powers the protection of theirs by the activity of the Council where they are predominant.[12]

22. To mitigate the involvement of the political organs in the process, even though they would be acting independently of each other, the Dutch jurist, Bernard Cornelis Johannes Loder, proposed the addition of a third layer to this arrangement: he suggested that the List of Candidates be proposed by the National Groups of the PCA.[13] The interposition of the PCA National Groups was meant to ensure that the candidates would not be *formally* nominated by states.
23. This complex election process provides a system of polycentric governance, with a view to safeguarding the judicial independence and integrity of the Court's membership.
24. Thirdly, the internal governance system of the Court strengthens its judicial independence. It is an expression of its self-governance. Simply put, in the exercise of its judicial function, the Court is the master of itself. Its decisions are taken by the 15 Members, who ensure the orderly dispensation of justice. Under the Statute, the Members of the Court elect their President, their Vice-President, and the Registrar. They also establish the various committees that deal with different aspects of the work of the Court as a judicial organ. No state and no organ of the UN may interfere with the *interna corporis* of the Court, in a manner that would compromise its independence and judicial integrity.

B. Administrative autonomy

25. Let me now turn to my next point: the administrative autonomy of the Court. Although this administrative autonomy is not expressly stated in the Charter, it may be gleaned from the fact that the Court is *not* listed under Article 98 of the Charter, which provides that the UN Secretary-General shall act in the capacity of 'chief administrative officer of the Organization' with regard to a number of organs, including the General Assembly, the Security Council, or ECOSOC.
26. The administrative autonomy of the Court is also confirmed in Article 30(1) of its Statute, which provides that the Court shall frame rules for carrying out its

[11] Advisory Committee of Jurists, *Procès-verbaux* of the Proceedings of the Committee, 16 June to 24 July 1920 <www.icj-cij.org/files/permanent-court-of-international-justice/serie_D/D_proceedings_of_committee_annexes_16june_24july_1920.pdf#page%3D113> 109 (Root). According to Mr Root, '[c]ourts derived their powers from the political power'; the solution could be found 'by articulating the new organisation with the political organisation of the League'.

[12] ibid 108–09 (Root).

[13] ibid 163 (Loder).

functions. To this end, Article 28(4) of the Rules makes clear that the '[t]he staff of the Registry shall be subject to Staff Regulations drawn up by the Registrar', as may be approved by the Court.

27. Nevertheless, even though the Court does not administratively come under the Secretariat of the United Nations, which gives it a certain measure of autonomy, a closer look at the UN Charter and the Court's Statute reveals that the governance of the Court is based on a 'polycentric' structure, which assigns certain administrative functions to various organs with regard to its budget, the salaries of the judges and their pensions.

28. This polycentric structure, in which various actors come into play in different aspects of the administrative and financial needs of the Court, helps safeguard to a large extent the judicial independence of the Court by instituting certain checks and balances amongst them to the advantage of the Court's autonomy. Thus, when certain functions are outsourced to other organs of the UN, in what could be described as 'external governance functions', the process of decision-making is not monopolized by a single organ, but benefits from the intervention of various organs.

(a) With respect to the financing of the Court

29. I will try to illustrate this with a couple of examples. First, with regard to the budget of the Court, Article 33 of the Statute provides that the United Nations shall bear the expenses of the Court in such a manner as shall be decided by the General Assembly. Thus, the Court's budget appears as a chapter of the regular UN budget.

30. Article 33 is couched in mandatory terms, and does not give the UNGA a discretion in the provision of funding. As the former Registrar of the Court Philippe Couvreur has observed, '[t]he UN is thus under an *obligation* to finance the Court'.[14]

31. The budgetary process of the Court is carried out through the interaction of three main actors: the Court itself, the General Assembly, and the Secretary-General of the United Nations.

32. The Court is the main actor in the preparation of its budget. Under regulation 2.14 of the UN Financial Regulations and Rules, it is the Court that prepares its own budgetary requirements in consultation with the Secretary-General. After approval by the Court, the draft budget is forwarded to the UN Secretariat for incorporation into the draft budget of the UN.

33. The second key actor is the General Assembly, and the expert bodies appointed by the Assembly. This includes, in particular, the Advisory Committee on Administrative and Budgetary Questions (ACABQ), which studies the budget proposal, directs questions to the Registrar of the Court, and submits a report to the Fifth Committee. The Fifth Committee examines the budget of

[14] Philippe Couvreur, 'The Registrar of the International Court of Justice: Status and Functions' in Carlos Jiménez Piernas (ed), *The Legal Practice in International Law and European Community Law: A Spanish Perspective* (Martinus Nijhoff 2007) 20 fn 49. Emphasis added.

the Court, which is ultimately adopted by the General Assembly in a plenary meeting.

34. The point I want to make here is that the interposition of the Secretary-General is meant to ensure the orderly administration of the financial governance of the Court. After having received the Court's proposals, the Secretary-General may add observations or recommendations to the Court's estimates. These observations provide valuable insight into the Court's financial needs. However, the Secretary-General cannot make amendments to the budget without the Court's approval.[15] In addition, the helpful role of the Secretary-General is that he can make recommendations on any measures proposed by the General Assembly, which may be found to be incompatible with the Court's Statute, and therefore defend the position and views of the Court on potentially derogatory proposals. Ultimately, this is meant to ensure the administrative autonomy and judicial independence of the Court, free from undue external interference.

(b) With respect to the emoluments of judges

35. This brings me to the second example: the emoluments of judges. The remuneration of judges is very important in so far as the security of tenure is concerned, and in order to ensure the unhindered exercise of the judicial function.
36. Article 32(5) and (7) of the Statute provides that the salaries, allowances, compensation and retirement pensions of judges shall be fixed by the General Assembly.
37. This does not mean, however, that the General Assembly has a *carte blanche* to interfere with the emoluments of judges. In this regard, Article 32 (5) makes clear that these emoluments 'may not be decreased during the term of office'. Furthermore, Article 31(6) of the Statute makes clear that judges ad hoc shall take part in the proceedings 'on terms of complete equality with their colleagues'.
38. In 2007, these provisions operated as an effective legal safeguard to ensure that the Court would not be exposed to influence from the General Assembly. The General Assembly had adopted resolution 61/262, which proposed, for the newly elected Members of the Court, a salary lower than the existing salary level of sitting judges.[16] As the Court explained in a detailed memorandum, this resolution would result in the unequal treatment of judges, including ad hoc judges; as a result, it could amount to a breach of Articles 31(6) and 32(5) of the Court's Statute.[17]

[15] Rosalyn Higgins and others, *Oppenheim's International Law: United Nations* (OUP 2017) para 29.216.

[16] Resolution 61/262 adopted by the General Assembly on 4 April 2007, 'Conditions of service and compensation for officials other than Secretariat officials: members of the International Court of Justice and judges and ad litem judges of the International Tribunal for the Former Yugoslavia and the International Criminal Tribunal for Rwanda' <https://docs.un.org/en/A/RES/61/262%26Lang%3DE>.

[17] cf 'Letter dated 3 April 2007 from the President of the International Court of Justice to the President of the General Assembly', UN doc A/61/837 (2007) <https://documents.un.org/doc/undoc/gen/n07/297/96/pdf/n0729796.pdf?OpenElement>. See also Report of the Secretary-General, 'Conditions of service and compensation for officials other than Secretariat officials: members of the International Court of Justice and judges and ad litem judges of the International Tribunal for the Former Yugoslavia and the International Criminal Tribunal for Rwanda', UN doc A/62/538, Annex II, 'Document transmitted by the

39. The UN Legal Counsel concurred with the Court that Article 32(5) of the Statute and the principle of equality of judges made 'it very difficult to reconcile these principles and requirements, specifically in the context of resolution 61/262, setting out the revised annual salary system'.[18] The UN Secretary-General agreed that the Court's remarks on its 'particular status and administrative independence' were 'justified'.[19] The interposition and role of the Secretary-General and his staff turned out to be decisive, in addition, of course, to that of the President of the Court.
40. Ultimately, the matter was resolved by decision 62/547 of 3 April 2008. This set the annual net base salary of the judges equally, without any reference to resolution 61/262. Thus, the idea that new judges should receive reduced salaries was abandoned, to ensure the equality of the judges and to conform to the provisions of the Statute.

(c) Accountability in respect of administrative and budgetary matters

41. I hope that I have not given the impression in my brief remarks on administrative autonomy that there is no accountability with regard to the Court's administrative and budgetary processes. Quite the opposite, the Court can be held accountable as far as certain administrative and budgetary practices are concerned.
42. For example, the Court's accounts may be audited by the Board of Auditors, the Joint Inspection Unit, and the Office of Internal Oversight Services, following a request from the Court itself.
43. To give you an example, in 2008, the Joint Inspection Unit of the United Nations System published a report regarding the Review of management and administration in the Registry of the International Court of Justice.[20] The Joint Inspection Unit recommended that certain administrative practices of the Court needed to be reviewed, and suggested that certain others be modernized or amended.

President of the International Court of Justice to the Secretary-General on the implications of General Assembly resolution 61/262 in regard to certain provisions of the Statute of the Court' <https://documents.un.org/doc/undoc/gen/n07/589/48/pdf/n0758948.pdf?OpenElement> 26. In her address to the General Assembly of 1 November 2007, the then-President of the Court also referred to the problems raised by resolution A/61/262: Speech of President Rosalyn Higgins to the General Assembly, UN Headquarters, 1 November 2007.

[18] Report of the Secretary-General, 'Conditions of service and compensation for officials other than Secretariat officials: members of the International Court of Justice and judges and ad litem judges of the International Tribunal for the Former Yugoslavia and the International Criminal Tribunal for Rwanda', UN doc A/62/538 <https://documents.un.org/doc/undoc/gen/n07/589/48/pdf/n0758948.pdf?OpenElement> Annex I, 'Memorandum dated 6 June 2007 from the Legal Counsel to the Office of Human Resources Management—Issues raised by the Registrar of the International Court of Justice concerning conditions of service and compensation for members of the Court', at 23 para 13.

[19] ibid paras 10, 67, and 73.

[20] Joint Inspection Unit, 'Report on Review of management and administration in the Registry of the International Court of Justice', UN doc JIU/REP/2000/8 (2000, Geneva) <www.unjiu.org/sites/www.unjiu.org/files/jiu_document_files/products/en/reports-notes/JIU%20Products/JIU_REP_2000_8_English.pdf>.

44. Some of these changes have already been effected. The most recent one took place this year, when the Court decided to bring its staff regulations into full conformity with the UN internal justice system.[21] In addition to the previous acceptance of the jurisdiction of the UN Appeals Tribunal, this will allow the staff members of the Court to benefit from the *entire* justice system of the UN, on an equal footing with all other UN staff members.

IV. Conclusion

45. These remarks allow for some general conclusions: does the ICJ governance structure ensure its independence as a judicial institution? Does the current institutional framework ensure the 'good governance' of the Court?
46. In principle, yes. The Court's Statute follows closely the judicial independence and administrative autonomy of the PCIJ. Even though the composition of the Court is assigned to 'external organs', the relevant rules allow for a 'polycentric governance' which ensures mutual checks and balances. The interposition of different organs is meant to neutralize the political impact of the process.
47. In terms of financial administration, the Court maintains a high degree of administrative autonomy. It is true that the General Assembly maintains some degree of leverage in financial terms. However, the financial governance of the Court is always bound by the provisions of the Statute and the Charter. Any decision on the Court's budget cannot detract from the institutional independence of the Court. It must remain within the limits of the rule of law.
48. In order to ensure the good governance of an international court or tribunal and ensure its judicial independence, it is not prudent, in my view, that its external governance functions be centralized in a single organ. Because that organ might be tempted to interfere with, or correct, the practices of that court or tribunal. When the external governance of a court is placed in the hands of a single organ, this poses a risk for the independence and impartiality of that court or tribunal. It is my view that a polycentric institutional framework fosters a more balanced system for judicial governance as far as the external governance functions are concerned.

[21] Exchange of letters between the President of the International Court of Justice, HE Mr Abdulqawi A Yusuf, and the Secretary-General of the United Nations, HE Mr António Guterres, dated 16 January 2019 and 17 December 2018. See also Speech by HE Mr Abdulqawi A. Yusuf, President of the International Court of Justice, on the occasion of the Seventy-fourth Session of the United Nations General Assembly (30 October 2019) <www.icj-cij.org/files/press-releases/0/000-20191030-STA-01-00-EN.pdf> 8.

ADDENDUM 2

Governance of the International Criminal Court

Keynote address*
O-Gon Kwon
President of the Assembly of States Parties of the International Criminal Court
Your Excellencies,
Distinguished delegates,
Ladies and gentlemen,

It is my great pleasure to be here to speak to you today. I wish to congratulate the organizers for the launch of the International Judicial Governance project, which to my knowledge is the first of its kind. This comprehensive initiative will bring critical reflection and constructive dialogue on the issues of governance and accountability in international judicial bodies.

We live in interesting but very challenging times. Rise of populism and extremism, growing protectionism, and an apparent lack of trust in international institutions are fast becoming the norm, with increasingly complex and violent conflicts in many regions of the world. In a world that is more connected than ever before, our societies are increasingly losing confidence in each other and the international institutions they built. And many of the threats we face today have a global reach that cannot, and should not, be solved in isolation; yet international cooperation is ever more demanding and at times uncertain. Such an environment has the potential to critically undermine the rules-based multilateral order on which international relations are based, at a time when such international cooperation is the only way forward if we are to succeed.

The global fight against impunity is not immune to the challenges I have just described. Both state and non-state actors push the boundaries of humanity with acts of violence conducted with disregard for human dignity and internationally accepted norms. Such violence has a pervasive negative impact on societies; it affects their development and well-being, as well as their ability to work together and thrive. Violence also negatively affects the rule of law. Institutions that do not function according to legitimate laws are prone to arbitrariness and abuse of power, and less capable of delivering their services to people. As a result, lack of access to justice means that conflicts remain unresolved and people cannot obtain protection and redress.

The system of international justice is essential to promote peaceful, just, and inclusive societies. We must avoid losing confidence in our judicial institutions, and

* Keynote address delivered at the inaugural conference 'Governance of International Courts and Tribunals: Ensuring Judicial Independence and Accountability' (Leiden, 20–21 September 2019).

we must continue to work collectively. To quote the UN Secretary-General, Mr Guterres: 'Our future rests on solidarity. We must repair broken trust. We must re-invigorate our multilateral project. And we must uphold dignity for one and for all.'[1]

But how can we rebuild the lost trust and address today's challenges? This is where governance is key. We must ensure that global institutions are credible, inclusive, transparent, and accountable. They must be able to change and adapt to the evolving challenging international environment, while remaining true to their mandate. The International Criminal Court is one of those institutions.

The emergence and operation of international judicial institutions capable of enforcing international commitments, interpreting international treaties, and settling international conflicts have facilitated the growth of international legal norms and co-operative regimes governing important areas of international law and politics. These internationally respected norms represent the collective efforts to create a rules-based international order that is essential to the pursuit of international peace and security, as well as sustainable development. It is within such an international system that a growing number of courts and tribunals with different jurisdictions have evolved. This is a positive development, in my view, as these courts and tribunals complement each other as well as national jurisdictions and strengthen the international rules-based order.

The proliferation of such international judicial bodies, however, also gives rise to a wide range of legal, policy, and governance challenges, from the independence of the judiciary to the relations between domestic and international jurisdictions, as well as the operation of management oversight mechanisms. This is why this conference is highly topical and relevant today, particularly with the growing institutional scepticism in the world today.

Distinguished delegates,

Ladies and gentlemen,

International courts and tribunals are quite unique institutions. They not only differ from other typical international organizations in terms of their mandate, structure, and organization, but also they are quite distinct from each other in terms of jurisdiction; some are permanent, others ad hoc; some are international, others are a hybrid of domestic and international features. For example, the ICC is a permanent autonomous court, whereas the ad hoc tribunals for the former Yugoslavia and Rwanda were established within the framework of the United Nations to deal with specific situations with a limited mandate and jurisdiction. The ICC, which tries individuals, is also different from the International Court of Justice, the principal judicial organ of the United Nations for the settlement of disputes between states.

International courts and tribunals are in some ways also quite different from their domestic counterparts. For instance, in a domestic jurisdiction, the judiciary and prosecutor's office are separate institutions established and administered entirely separately from each other. Also, depending on the state, investigating organs may be entirely independent from the Prosecutor's office. At the ICC, however, while the Judiciary, Registry, and the Office of the Prosecutor are separate from each other, and

[1] Speech to the UN General Assembly, 25 September 2018.

the Judiciary and the Prosecutor's Office fully independent, they are all under one roof in the same institutional structure. This situation generates unique governance challenges. While the Judges and the Prosecutor must maintain a strict separation and independence in matters relating to their judicial and prosecutorial mandates, respectively, the Court's organs must seek mutually agreeable solutions on Court-wide issues such as budget, human resources policies or technical services. This has become known as the 'One Court' principle—a governance tool aimed at developing a united approach on issues of common concern for the Court as a whole. It is a crucial component in the efforts to ensure internal coordination and make the working relations among the Court organs, and also with states parties, as efficient as possible, while respecting their respective separate and independent functions.

Furthermore, when compared to domestic courts, international courts and tribunals have also different management oversight structures. In the case of the ICC's organs, this function is carried out by the Assembly of States Parties (the ASP). The Assembly is further tasked with election (or removal from office) of the Judges, the Prosecutor, and Deputy Prosecutors. ASP decisions are in principle reached by consensus. As you know, these management oversight mechanisms, whether at the UN level or the Assembly of States Parties, consist of sovereign states with at times differing views and positions, and reaching consensus is an arduous and complex endeavour.

This specific governance aspect also has other repercussions. For example, the Assembly of States Parties is the legislative body that adopts the Rules of Procedure and Evidence. This is a sharp contrast to UN Tribunals, where such powers lay with the Tribunals themselves.

As the President of this Assembly, it is my role to oversee the Assembly through its Bureau and through different working groups and facilitations both in The Hague and in New York. However, this geographical dichotomy generates a complex and at times challenging division of labour between The Hague and New York, and can affect how the ASP as a whole concentrates its efforts.

States Parties and the Court have endeavoured regularly to improve the work carried out within their respective mandates. The Court has formalized various best practices to this end, and continues to do so. The Assembly reflected on its own shortcomings and carried out an evaluation of its working methods that resulted in formal Report of the Bureau in 2013 entitled 'Evaluation and rationalization of the working methods of the subsidiary bodies of the Bureau'.[2] We are all aware of the existing challenges, and we are working together to address them.

I will now present to you two examples of how states parties and the Court are currently tackling some of today's governance challenges. The first one is the initiation of a review process aimed at strengthening the ICC, and the second one is the ongoing process for the election of the next Prosecutor.

While the ICC is a relatively recent addition to the emerging trend of international courts and tribunals, it already plays a primary role at the forefront of the global fight against impunity. Nonetheless, the Court navigates in a complex international

[2] ICC-ASP/12/59. See also operative paragraphs 40–43 of the resolution ICC-ASP/12/Res.8.

environment and faces numerous challenges; some external, some internal. Externally, the Court's challenges range from an increasingly negative, and in my view unfair, perception of selective justice and double standards as well as negative attitudes from major powers. The Court also faces negative repercussions from two withdrawals from the Rome Statute, and from the limited, too limited cooperation from states parties and the UN Security Council, without which the Court cannot function properly. Internally, the Court has been criticized for the lack of clarity in the legal standards the Court applies to its criminal proceedings, and the ambiguity of its prosecutorial strategies and policies. The Court has also been criticized for the perceived lack of efficiency of the Court's operations.

It was in recognition of these challenges that the Bureau of the Assembly of States Parties, first considered the idea of a retreat at its meeting in February this year. The concerns raised in the Bureau were echoed by my predecessors, the first four presidents of the ASP, who jointly published an op-ed in April 2019, highlighting the ICC's importance but also some of the concerns surrounding its work, and proposing that an independent assessment of the Court's functioning by a group of international experts should be commissioned. This should not be seen as an attack on the Court or the ASP; on the contrary, honest reflections like this should help create momentum to strengthen and adapt the Court to face new challenges.

The proposal for an expert review of the ICC system resonated with both the Court and the states parties. The Bureau of the Assembly of States Parties then met in June for a retreat which led to the development of a draft non-paper entitled 'Meeting the challenges of today for a stronger Court tomorrow: Matrix over possible areas of strengthening the Court and the Rome Statute', dated 15 July 2019. This document reflects the discussions at the retreat concerning the main areas on which the Court and states parties have to work together to create a stronger, more accountable Court, and to better adapt it to today's challenges. The matrix is a 'living' document in the sense that it can evolve over time to address the different needs. It is meant to be useful as a tracking tool, to enable states to be aware of the progress of the consideration of the respective items identified for discussion. Among the states parties there is broad support for a review process which should be state-driven, inclusive and transparent, in partnership with the Court and civil society, and which strictly respects the independence and the mandate of the Court.

The Matrix was shared with stakeholders, including all states parties, the Court organs and civil society, for constructive feedback in order to decide on and to prioritize the main areas to strengthen the Court. We are currently working on a revised draft in light of the feedback received, and that will be discussed further within the two working groups in The Hague and in New York over the coming months. On the one hand, some of the areas identified in the Matrix will be referred to existing facilitations, or new ones can be created, and all stakeholders will be able to contribute to the process. On the other hand, for a number of more specific legal and technical issues the intention is to involve a group of independent experts. The Bureau entrusted me with commencing preliminary work to identify both the topics on which expert assessment could potentially be sought, and the potential independent experts for the specific topics. The ASP in December this year will be crucial for reaching an agreement on these matters to move the process forward.

However, this process alone will not be enough; all stakeholders must do their part too for this project to succeed. In particular, states parties and the Court need to share a common language for this process. But states parties among themselves also need a common vision for the review process to come to life, and they need to provide the Court with genuine political engagement, and increased diplomatic support. To do this, there must be a genuine reflection on the role and structure of the Assembly of States Parties.

My hope is that carrying out this process in a transparent and inclusive manner will as a result strengthen the trust, resilience, and solidarity among states parties and the Court, and I am doing everything in my power to go in this direction.

This leads me to the second example I wanted to elaborate on: the election of the next Prosecutor of the ICC, which will take place in December 2020. This is one of the most important positions on the Court and crucial for its direction for the upcoming decade. For this reason, the Bureau endeavoured to initiate the preparations for the election process as early as possible. We are making every effort to ensure that the process leading to the election is a transparent and inclusive one.

As you may know, the term of the current Prosecutor, Ms Fatou Bensouda, expires in June 2021. In order to start the election process for her successor, the Bureau of the ASP adopted the Terms of Reference for the Election of the Prosecutor on 3 April this year. This innovative document established a Committee on the election of the Prosecutor, and a panel of experts to assist it in carrying out its mandate. The document provides that the procedures of the Committee will be transparent and with clear reporting lines, while ensuring strict confidentiality throughout the process. The Terms of Reference also foresaw for the first time the publication of a vacancy announcement with the description and requirements to be fulfilled for the position of the Prosecutor.

This process is now ongoing and the Committee is expected to submit its final report to the Bureau and to states parties with a short list of three to six individuals, by the summer of 2020 at the latest; the states parties will then endeavour to ensure to elect the next prosecutor by consensus from that short list of the most suitable and capable candidates.

Distinguished delegates,

Ladies and gentlemen,

I have presented to you some of the unique features of the ICC and its inherent challenges regarding governance and accountability. I also presented to you two examples of how the ASP together with the Court and civil society are taking solid and concrete steps to improve the current governance challenges to strengthen the Court and the Rome Statute System as a whole. While these are state-driven processes, through transparency and inclusiveness, states are nevertheless taking into account the specific views of all stakeholders. Only in this way will we be able to address the current governance challenges and needs faced by the Court, and only in this way will we be able to adapt and tackle the difficulties we encounter head-on. States parties, the Court and civil society must work together in shaping a more transparent, inclusive, accountable and efficient Court that can co-exist in a more coherent and collaborative Rome Statute system.

Let me conclude with a few words on the issue of leadership. Leaders are as important as the organizations themselves. Jean Monnet, one of the father figures of the European Communities, now the European Union, once said: 'nothing is possible without people, but nothing endures without institutions'. For any organization to succeed, leadership is of crucial importance. Good leaders are the gate keepers of the institutions they lead; they are able to recognize their limitations and are ready to learn from others and generate a vision and direction. Good leaders listen to and inspire confidence in the people they lead; and they facilitate cooperation and constructive communication with all stakeholders involved in order to find alternative and innovative solutions to the challenges faced.

As leaders we must do everything in our power to build trust, confidence, resilience, and solidarity in our institutions. In the case of the ICC, this must involve the states parties, the Court, its leadership and its staff, as well as other stakeholders, such as civil society and academia, and also Observer States, who may become states parties one day. And, finally, it is essential to gain the trust of the global public at large in the institution that will make a real difference for the good of humanity. I am confident that the current leadership of the ICC system is ready to face the challenges of today to make a stronger Court tomorrow.

Today more than ever, we must stand firm, and protect and promote the principles and values enshrined in the Rome Statute. But at the same time, we must acknowledge that this Court is far from perfect and we should not be afraid to self-reflect, recognize its limitations, and help it realize its true potential.

I am very hopeful. Just think that twenty-five years ago a system like the one created by the Rome Statute seemed almost illusory. Everybody was wondering at the time how a former Head of State could be tried in a foreign jurisdiction. How could a Head of State be tried at an international criminal tribunal? Nowadays, people think quite the opposite: why has that person not been brought before the ICC? This is an important shift of attitudes and mentality that should not be underestimated. It is our duty to continue shifting that mentality further, through our collaborative efforts and good governance to make the ICC a beacon of light, guiding the fight against impunity and towards true global accountability.

Thank you for your kind attention.

Index

For the benefit of digital users, indexed terms that span two pages (e.g., 52–53) may, on occasion, appear on only one of those pages.